Adirondack Civilian Conservation Corps Camps:
HISTORY, MEMORIES, AND LEGACY OF THE CCC

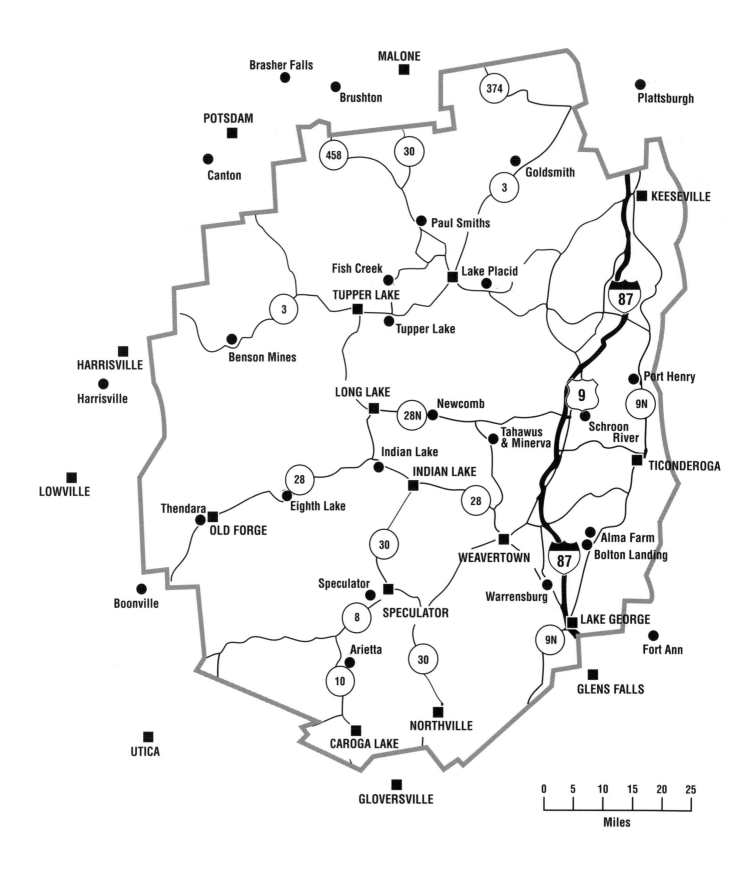

Adirondack Civilian Conservation Corps Camps:
HISTORY, MEMORIES, AND LEGACY OF THE CCC

Martin Podskoch (signature)

Martin Podskoch

Edited by David Hayden

Podskoch Press, LLC
East Hampton, Connecticut

Adirondack Civilian Conservation Corps Camps:
HISTORY, MEMORIES, AND LEGACY OF THE CCC

Published by
Podskoch Press, LLC
43 O'Neill Lane
East Hampton, CT

podskoch@comcast.net
www.cccstories.com
www.adirondackstories.com
www.firetowerstories.com

ISBN 978-0-9794979-4-0

Manufactured in the United States of America

654321
Cover Illustration by Tony Sansevero
Design & Layout by Amanda Beauchemin of Ford Folios
Maps by Paul Hartmann

TABLE OF CONTENTS

FOREWORD

The Civilian Conservation Corps (CCC) was established by President Franklin D. Roosevelt to alleviate the problems caused by The Depression. Millions of people were unemployed and I was one of them. I was a graduate of Syracuse University and had a job working for Western Union in NYC. In 1933 I was laid off and on my way home to the Adirondacks I stopped at Syracuse University and applied for a few jobs. I went to my parents' home in Coreys and decided to go camping for a few days near Cold River.

When I came back I found telegrams for job openings and I decided on working for the Conservation Department in the newly formed CCC. Once the CCC was created in 1933, it wasn't long before the camps began to operate. At the very beginning I was a NYS State Forester on the staff at camp Cross Clearing near Tupper Lake in spring 1933. At the end I closed the last NYS camp at Brushton in 1941. Although at first I had my doubts about the program because there were so many loafers and so few tools, but it turned out that this Federal Program was a great success. Not only did the boys learn to work, they learned pride in a job well done. I learned a lot and have some vivid memories of that time in my life.

The CCC was a hurry up program. Roosevelt wanted these young boys off the street. Some 'enrollees were picked from city streets and dropped in our laps. But over time the situation improved and more competent workers showed up and those first recruits soon learned what needed to be done.

When I first got to "Cross Clearing" camp, Captain John, who was right out of Governor's Island, said to me, " We have to have wood for the stoves to make lunch."

I replied, "Where are the tools?"

"There are none!"

I was just five miles from home so I went and got an ax and a cross cut saw.

When I returned, the captain blew his whistle and 150 men lined up in front of us. He picked out 12 men to work with me. We went into the woods and none of them could tell one tree from another. I was afraid to let them use an axe. Every time they saw a conifer, they called it a "Christmas tree." I had quite a time with the guys looking for dead wood. When I told them to carry wood back to camp they started off in the wrong direction. I was afraid they were going to get lost.

In the spring 1935 we started building the trail to Big Deer Pond. I had a 25-man crew. I had one lumberjack guy who was a local from Tupper Lake. He was a big help to me because he took half of the boys and worked with them. We started out by showing them how to use the tools and by the end of the job those boys knew what they were doing.

A few months later a riot broke out on a weekend. The captain called the State Police for help and the police used tear gas. It turned out the six guys were escaped prisoners and some were wanted for murder. These were the same young guys working with me in the woods. I wouldn't want to repeat that experience!

Most of the boys in the camp were 18-21 years old. We hired local experienced men (LEM's) who were very helpful. They worked with the boys in the woods. One fella said, "Here is where you learn to handle men." I learned what guys were loafers and who was good, someone I could rely on.

I wasn't at the Tupper Lake camp very long before I was promoted to camp superintendent at Brasher Falls in June 1934. The boys at that camp were mostly WWI veterans, who also had a drinking problem. The first payday found all of them lying drunk beside the road to camp. No work got done that day!

I supervised Camp Brushton from 1935-1940. We wanted to train the boys to be truck drivers. There were two types of trucks: stake trucks that carried 25 men and dump trucks. We let the Army have a truck to take guys to the movies in Malone. I liked to cooperate with them.

Each camp had an enrollee who took care of the office records. Ours was from St. Regis Falls and he fit right in. His last name was Wood. His father owned land that had a trout farm. He was a very conscientious guy. One time I loaned him $100 to buy a car.

The camp had sports for the boys. We played baseball against other camps on weekends. We supplied a driver to transport the team. We also held Field Days where other camps competed in ball games and foot races.

There was a big field near the camp. One time I landed my Piper Cub plane in the field and kept it there for a few days. I could only land and fly off in one direction. When I had a weekend off, I'd go to the Malone airport and give flying lessons.

The camp was located on the edge of the Forest Preserve. We did a lot of reforestation work on land that was taken over because the farmers couldn't pay the taxes A bill had passed to buy farm land for not more than three dollars an acre. The state got all that land to plant trees. The soil was often sandy and poor. We planted red and white pine and a few hardwoods. The state nursery had mostly spruce, balsam and red and white pine trees. There were some scotch pine that grew in the sandy places.

The food served in camp was of good quality. The lieutenant selected the boys who were going to work in the kitchen. Sometimes he was lucky to have a boy who had worked in a restaurant.

Each camp had an infirmary with a doctor. He was usually a lieutenant who stayed there. There were about a dozen beds. The injuries were mostly foot cuts from an axe. The injured usually stayed only a few days. If a boy needed dental work, they took him to a dentist in Malone.

Our camp had a room in one of the barracks that was used for education. Most of the boys weren't interested in learning. They only liked movies and money.

There were different grades or rankings for the enrollees. If a guy was good at handling a few men such as in the kitchen, he was made an assistant and paid $36 a month. Leaders were paid $45 and they were put in charge of 10-12 men.

One time in the late spring there was a big freeze and the water pipes froze. A plumber came to thaw them out. He used a torch that heated the surrounding wood. It smoldered unnoticed and at night fire broke out and spread. All the guys got out but fire spread in the partition where the pipes were and the officers barracks burned down.

Once we had some dynamite stolen. We questioned everyone but they all denied it. I called the police in and they took fingerprints but we never did find the dynamite or the culprit. One guy, however, said he took two sticks and blew something up in the woods.

On Saturdays the boys went by truck to Malone. Well, the captain told me that he was concerned with the boys and the women in town. He said, "I've got to keep them away from Little Eva."

I closed the camp Brushton in Dickinson Center in the spring of 1940. The government couldn't sell the left over uniforms. So they burned beautiful trousers and jackets because they had a contract with the manufacturer that stated the government couldn't sell them. What a waste of good wool uniforms.

I was transferred to the Mansville Camp which was south of Watertown. This was an all-Negro camp where I learned quite a bit. I stayed there till 1941.

As the threat of WW II approached I closed the Brushton CCC camp in Dickinson in 1942, the only CCC camp left in the Adirondacks. After the start of the draft all men from 18 to 40 were eligible which meant the end of the CCC. It had been highly successful in helping young men who would never have learned to value of work. It would be a good idea in this day and age to create a similar program to help young people.

Marty Podskoch records the history of this important program in the Adirondacks. His interviews with CCC enrollees and their families brings to life the stories of the young men who worked so hard to improve the forests that had been ravaged by fires and lumbering. We must not forget their accomplishments in the forests and state parks that continue to be enjoyed by millions of people.

Clarence Petty began working at the Tupper Lake CCC camp in 1933
and advanced to camp superintendent at the Brasher Falls camp in 1934.
Christopher Angus

PREFACE

While gathering information in the Adirondacks for my fire tower books during the summer of 2004 I visited Joanne Petty Manning at her home in Saranac Lake. She had a large box on her diningroom table filled with photos that her father, Bill Petty, had gathered while working as the District Forester at the DEC Office in Ray Brook. Joanne handed me a packet of six or more photos that didn't relate to the Adirondack fire towers.

One showed a large group of young men posing for a picture. The men wore dungaree shirts, pants, jackets, and a variety of hats. Some were holding shovels. Other pictures showed a group of guys leveling a dirt road, young guys planting trees, and a group photo of older men posing for a picture. Joanne told me that these were of the Civilian Conservation Corps and I decided to copy them just in case I needed them in the future.

My northern fire tower book came out in the fall of 2005. This was my third book on the men and women who worked on the fire towers of the Catskill and Adirondack mountains. I wondered what I'd do for my next book. I remembered Joanne's photos of the CCC and then I knew what I wanted to work on. I'd write about the young men and veterans who worked in the Civilian Conservation Corps saving and developing our state forests and parks in the Adirondacks during the Great Depression.

As I gave talks throughout 2006 about my new fire tower book, I told my audiences that I was looking for information on the men who had worked in the CCC or for people who had stories and pictures of family members who had been in the CCC.

I also sent news releases and photos to newspapers describing my search for information and photos concerning CCC camps and asked readers to contact me. The response was tremendous. Former CCC enrollees and families contacted me and shared their photos and stories. I visited the former enrollees homes or called them on the phone for interviews.

There were times of frustration when I was told: "Oh, if you were only here a month or a year ago when John was alive. He had great stories." Then there were the times a son or daughter told me: "I only wish that my father told me about his days in the CCC. I don't even know what camp or state he was in."

My book is not a comprehensive history of the Civilian Conservation Corps but the history of the 26 Adirondack CCC camps and the stories of the young men who left their homes to earn $25 a month to help their families survive during the Great Depression. The reader will see how these young men developed a sense of worth. Many had only an eighth grade education and were wandering the countryside and city streets in search of a job. Once in the CCC they felt important, learned how to take orders, developed a love of nature, and learned a trade, all of which gave them a sense of self-worth. They knew they were helping their country and their family.

As you drive through the Adirondack Mountains you pass by the lofty plantations of white pines that were planted by the CCC during the 1930s. You will also pass by and maybe camp at the many state campsites that were established or developed by the young enrollees or veterans.

Now sit back and enjoy a brief history of the Civilian Conservation Corps in the Adirondacks and stories of the CCC boys who worked in the Adirondack forests and some who were sent to Western states and found adventure there.

Marty Podskoch

43 O'Neill Lane
East Hampton, CT 06424
860-267-2442

podskoch@comcast.net
www.cccstories.com
www.adirondackstories.com
www.firetowerstories.com

Marty Podskoch and family at home on Lake Pocotopaug in East Hampton, CT.
Front row: Kira and Lydia Roloff. Second Row: Kristy & Matt Roloff, Matt, Marty,
Lynn, and Ryan Podskoch.

CHAPTER 1
THE HISTORY OF THE CIVILIAN CONSERVATION CORPS

One of the most important events in the history of the United States was the election of Franklin D. Roosevelt (FDR) as President during the Great Depression. With over 13 million unemployed FDR promoted many relief programs that created jobs for the unemployed. The Emergency Conservation Work Act, better known as Civilian Conservation Corps, was the first such program passed by Congress in 1933 during Roosevelt's first "One Hundred Days" and is also considered his most successful program and certainly his most popular. During its nine years three million young men worked conserving our natural resources throughout our country and possessions.

Conservation was important in the Roosevelt family. FDR and his cousin Theodore "Teddy" Roosevelt had a deep love for conserving the land and forests in the United States. Both were governors of New York State (NYS) and presidents of the United States.

While President (1901–1909), Teddy helped preserve approximately 230,000,000 acres in the United States. In this new land the government established five new National Parks, 16 National Monuments, 51 Wildlife Refuges, and huge reserves and National Forests.[1] Gifford Pinchot, a college trained forester, influenced both Teddy and Franklin. Pinchot urged the use of scientific management of the natural resources of the West and worked to prevent developers from destroying the land. Teddy appointed Pinchot to head the new U. S. Forest Service.[2]

When FDR became President in 1933, Pinchot warned him about the depletion of our forests and impressed upon him the importance of purchasing large tracts of privately owned forest lands. When Congress passed the Weeks Act in 1911 it enabled the government to purchase private land. This made it possible for the creation of the national forests east of the Mississippi. Pinchot also urged FDR to purchase the 50 million acres of recently abandoned farmland east of the Mississippi and employ men who were on relief to reforest these lands.[3]

FDR grew up at his family's estate, Springwood, in Hyde Pak, NY where he enjoyed roaming the forest and hills near the Hudson River. Later he went into politics and was elected to the state senate in 1910. Here he became the Chairman of the Committee on Forestry. FDR took over the family estate in 1910 and the following year he hired a forester who developed a management plan for Springwood. In 1912 he had a few thousand seedlings planted, the first of some 550,000 trees planted over the next 40 years.[4]

In 1928 FDR became governor of New York and advocated for government intervention during the Depression. FDR developed relief programs for the unemployed. One program gave 10,000 men jobs working in the state forest and parks. They built park buildings and roads, planted trees, and did erosion control projects.[5]

During his years as governor FDR encouraged the state legislature to pass laws promoting conservation and development of the state forests. In 1931 FDR proclaimed Conservation Week. His press release stated his goals: "...to bring to the attention of the people the great public benefits that are dependent upon the wise use and perpetuation of our forests, the protection of the birds and animals that they shelter, and the safeguarding of our water from alienation and pollution."[6] FDR encouraged the state to purchase substandard farmland and then reforest the land. In 1931 the state legislature approved a $19 million bond issue to purchase submarginal farmland. The Conservation Department supervised this program and purchased farms that had at least 500 acres. In 1932 the state hired 10,000 temporary workers from the relief rolls to plant trees. The land was reforested and helped in preventing soil erosion and provided forests for future timber production.[7]

THE GREAT DEPRESSION

The Great Depression was a traumatic period for millions in the United States. It began when the stock market crashed on October 27, 1929. Many economists thought it was merely a bump in the market but the slow economy dragged on. President Hoover believed that local governments and private charities should provide relief to the unemployed and homeless and not the federal government. Breadlines and Hoovervilles (homeless encampments) sprang up around the United States.[8]

There were nearly two million unemployed men and women who wandered the US on foot and freight trains, lived in caves and shantytowns in search for a job and security. In this group were a quarter million called "the teenage tramps of America" who were in the same search to find security.[9]

In 1932 George Rawick estimated that one in four of the youth between ages 15-24 were unemployed. Of this age group only 29 per cent did part-time work.[10] Jim Johnson of Gansevoort, NY was just one of the millions who quit school to help their families survive the Great Depression. Jim was born in Cohoes in 1924 and there were five other children in his family. He joined the CCC and earned $30 a month of which $25 went straight home to his parents.

"I was just 14 years old but I had to go out and work to help my family. My father, Edward, worked for the Ford Motor Company on Green Island till he fell off a roof at the factory and couldn't work anymore. There was no workmen's compensation and my brother and I gathered coal that had fallen from railroad cars along the tracks to help heat our home. In the summer I worked at nearby farms to earn some money. I quit school and decided to join the CCC just like my older brother Bill. Since you had to be 18 years old, I took my birth certificate, changed my birth date using an old bottle of ink eradicator, and went down to the town hall and signed up. I just had to help my family."

The US was not only facing a financial catastrophe but an environmental crisis as well. States were unable to control the frequent forest fires and the diseases and pests that decimated the forests. Poor farming practices, overgrazing of public lands, and overcutting of forests led to erosion of topsoil. Streams became uninhabitable leading to the decline of fish. Frequent flooding occurred.

During the Great Depression many people were forced to live in shanties. Library of Congress

During the 1932 election the Democratic Party nominated Franklin D. Roosevelt. His slogan in the campaign was a "New Deal" for America. He promised to work to reverse the economic collapse that Hoover failed to achieve. With over 20 of US workers unemployed, FDR pledged to help the "forgotten man at the bottom of the economic pyramid."

Americans were looking for a change in leadership and in November they chose Franklin D. Roosevelt over Hoover by a landslide vote, 22,821,857 to 15,761,845. FDR was sworn into office on March 4, 1933. After FDR was sworn into office he decided to forego the traditional balls and celebrations and sat down with his cabinet and began working on solving the economic crisis.

HUNDRED DAYS & EMERGENCY CONSERVATION WORK ACT

On March 9 he declared a "Bank Holiday" that closed the banks for four days to help stabilize the financial system. Then FDR and Congress passed the Agricultural Adjustment Act, a farm relief law that paid farmers subsidies for not planting part of their land and reduce livestock. Is purpose was to reduce crop surplus and in turn raise their value.

On March 21, 1933 Roosevelt called the 73rd Congress into Emergency Session to hear and authorize his program. He proposed to recruit thousands of unemployed young men, enroll them in a peacetime army, and send them into battle against the destruction and erosion of our natural resources.

"I propose to create a civilian conservation corps to be used in simple work, not interfering with normal employment, and confining itself to forestry, the prevention of soil erosion, flood control and similar projects. I call your attention to the fact that this type of work is of definite, practical value, not only through the prevention of great present financial loss, but also as a means of creating future national wealth."[10]

Organized labor unions were concerned that the CCC would lower wages. They were also worried if the Army was involved in running the program it might lead to regimentation of labor. Others feared the CCC would take jobs from men working in the forests.[11]

On March 27 FDR introduced Senate Bill 5.598,

President Franklin D. Roosevelt signing the Emergency Conservation Work bill. CCC Legacy Archives

the Emergency Conservation Work Act (ECW).

It went through both houses of Congress and on March 31, 1933 FDR signed the ECW Act, more commonly known as the Civilian Conservation Corps. This provided work for 250,000 unemployed young men ages 18-25. FDR brought together two wasted resources, the young men and the land.[12]

By the end of the "Hundred Days" FDR had pushed 15 major bills through Congress, such as the Federal Emergency Relief Administration (FERA), which provided funds for grants to states to establish relief programs, the Tennessee Valley Authority (TVA), which provided hydro-electric power, flood control, and soil conservation to seven southern states, and the National Industrial Recovery Act (NIRA), which stimulated industry and established labor standards.[13]

ORGANIZATION OF THE ECW (CCC)

On April 5, 1933 FDR signed Executive Order 6101 authorizing the ECW (CCC) program and appointed Robert Fechner director. He was a vice-president of the American Federation of Labor. James J. McEntee became his assistant.

FDR established an Advisory Council composed of representatives from the Secretaries of War, Labor, Interior, and Agriculture. These agencies worked together with Fechner in performing miracles in organizing large number of enrollees and camps throughout the 48 states, Alaska, Hawaii, Puerto Rico, and the Virgin Islands.

The Army mobilized the nation's transportation system to move thousands of enrollees from induction centers to working camps. This was the largest peacetime mobilization of men the United States had ever seen. Most of the young enrollees came from the East while the majority of the projects were out West. The Army used its regular and reserve officers, together with regulars of the Coast Guard, Marine Corps and Navy to temporarily command camps and individual companies.

The Departments of Agriculture and Interior planned and organized work projects.

The Department of Labor, with the help of state and local relief offices, selected and enrolled the young men. Each state had a quota for enrollees based on population. Since NYS had the largest population of over 12 million it had the largest number of enrollees. The qualifications for the junior enrollees were: single, male, 18-25 years of age, unemployed, on the relief roll, healthy, and not in school. They signed up for a six-month period. Later enrollees could re-sign three more times for an additional 18 months. They were paid a dollar a day. The enrollee received $5 for spending money and the government sent $25 directly to the parents each month. If the men found employment they could ask for an honorable discharge.[14]

Only 37 days elapsed from Roosevelt's inauguration on March 4, 1933. Henry Rich of Alexandria, Va. was the first enrollee on April 7. Ten days later Camp Roosevelt, the first CCC camp in the US, was established near Luray, Virginia in the George Washington National Forest.[15]

FDR promised to have 250,000 men in camps by July 1. All the agencies and branches of the federal government cooperated in implementing the program. His goal was achieved in July and junior enrollees (ages 18–25)

ECW (CCC) Director Robert Fechner (5th from left with dark coat) visited the Paul Smiths camp in 1933. Workers are busy building camp. NYS Archives

The Army organized and supervised the CCC camps. Captain Brigham (left) and other officers were in charge of the Benson Mines camp. St. Lawrence County Historical Association

were housed in 1,463 CCC camps.

In the July 8, 1933 issue of the weekly CCC newspaper, "Happy Days," FDR welcomed the CCC enrollees:

"I want to congratulate you on the opportunity you have, and to extend to you my appreciation for the hearty cooperation which you have given this movement, so vital a step in the nation's fight for progress, and to wish you a pleasant, wholesome and constructive stay in the CCC.

"I welcome the opportunity to extend a greeting to the men who constitute the Civilian Conservation Corps. It is my belief that what is being accomplished will conserve our national resources, create future national wealth and prove of moral and spiritual value, not only to those of you who are taking part, but to the rest of the country as well.

"You young men who are enrolled in this work are to be congratulated. It is my honest conviction that what you are doing in the way of constructive service will bring you, personally and individually, returns the value of which it is difficult to estimate.

"Physically fit, as demonstrated by the examinations

you took before entering the camps, the clean life and hard work, in which you are engaged, cannot fail to help your physical condition. You should emerge from this experience, strong and rugged and ready for entrance into the ranks of industry, better equipped than before."

Afro-Americans were also accepted into the CCC because the law creating it barred discrimination based on race, creed, or color. The unemployment rate of Negroes was twice that of whites. The CCC administration became frustrated when several southern states like Georgia, Arkansas, and Florida refused to enroll few or no Negroes in 1933. When the federal government threatened to withhold state quotas of CCC camps they gave in.[16] Discrimination, however, led to separate Negro camps with white Army officers in command. Only when there weren't enough Negroes for a company were they integrated with whites. In New York State, however, there were separate "black" or "colored" camps.

In April 1933 there were two modifications to the ECW. On April 14 the program included the enlistment of approximately 14,000 unemployed American Indians.[17] There were only a few such camps and they were on the Indian reservations. Most of these enrollees were married and lived at home. By 1942 over 80,000 Native Americans had worked to reclaim the land.

Another change in the program was the hiring of approximately 25,000 local experienced men (LEM). At first they were called "experienced woodsmen." For every camp with 200 enrollees the camp could hire 16 local experienced men.[18] These men were experienced in carpentry, logging, masonry, etc. They trained the young enrollees in skills that many would use later in life. They also taught the workers proper use of tools, safety skills, discipline, and cooperation. The LEM program benefited the local communities by giving jobs to the unemployed whose salaries pumped money into the local economy.[19]

A third modification of the program occurred when veterans were admitted into the CCC. Their average age was 40. Many were unemployed and filled with despair during the Depression. Many had physical and mental impairments from WWI. They first became a problem to the government during the spring and summer of 1932 when they came to Washington D.C. and demanded a bonus that was promised them when they received Service Certificates in 1924. The government responded by saying they had to wait till 1945 to cash them in but the unemployed veterans

Director Robert Fechner (center) and President Franklin D. Roosevelt are surrounded by CCC enrollees when they visited Shenandoah VA on August 12, 1933. Legacy

wanted to be paid right away. When this "Bonus Army" refused to leave the city, President Hoover had General Douglas MacArthur and the Army drive the veterans, their families, and friends out of the city and burn the protestors' shelters.[20]

The Bonus Army came a second time to Washington D. C. in 1933. FDR's reaction to the Bonus Army's march was different. He didn't send the Army but instead sent his wife, Eleanor. She listened to their concerns and told her husband. On May 11, 1933 FDR issued an executive order authorizing the enrollment of approximately 25,000 veterans of WWI and the Spanish American War. There were no restrictions as to age or marital status and the men were housed in separate camps while working on conservation projects suitable to their age. By the end of the program nearly 250,000 veterans had participated. Veterans received a dollar a-day but three-quarters of their monthly salary went to their dependents. If they didn't have dependents it went into an account that they received when they left the CCC.[21]

EARLY YEARS

During the first five months of 1933 there were 18 forestry camps in New York State and 14 were in the Adirondacks: Alma Farm, Arietta, Benson Mines, Burgess Farm, Eighth Lake, Fish Creek Pond, Goldsmiths, Newcomb, Paul Smiths, Schroon Lake, Speculator, Tahawus, Tupper Lake, and Wanakena.[22] Each camp had about 200 enrollees.

The CCC was popular throughout the US. A poll of Republicans showed that 67 per cent supported it, and 95 per cent of Californians approved. Even the Chicago Tribune, an enemy of FDR, and the Soviet Union praised the program. A Chicago judge thought the CCC was largely responsible for a 55 per cent reduction in crime.

In 1934 the number of camps in NYS increased to 35 while 11 were in the Adirondacks. There were six veterans' camps in the state and one, Brasher Falls, was in the Adirondack region.[23]

By April 1934 the program had almost universal support. The $25 monthly allotment to the enrollees' parents improved the US economy. Families could now provide a better life for their children. During the fiscal year 1935-36 the federal government sent to families throughout the US approximately $123,000,000. At first enrollees were limited to working one 6-month enlistment to allow others a chance to sign up and take advantage of the opportunity to work. Communities near the CCC camps benefited economically, too, because the enrollees pumped into the communities approximately $5,000 a month with their purchases at local businesses.[24]

Word about the camp's positive effects spread throughout the nation. The young men were working hard, eating well, gaining weight and strength, and improving millions of acres of private, state, and federal lands. They built new roads, strung miles of telephone lines, fought fires, cleared forest of dead trees, and planted millions of trees. Newspapers published their accomplishments and many who opposed the program were won over. FDR decided to extend the program for one more year.

By 1935 the CCC program was enjoying one of its best years. The enrollees were no longer living in cold, drafty tents and wearing poor fitting uniforms. Senators and

During the summer and fall of 1933 CCC enrollees lived in Army tents. The wooden building might have been the shower. NYS Archives

congressmen realized the benefits to their constituencies and urged Director Fechner for more camps in their states. By the end of 1935 there were 2,600 camps, some in each of the 48 states. They performed over 100 types of work. There were now 61 forestry camps in NYS with 19 camps were in the Adirondacks. The NYS camps employed 616 men who worked as superintendents, foremen, blacksmiths, tractor operators, and mechanics and their monthly salary totaled some $85,000 a month. Most of the money was spent locally and so benefited the whole area.[25]

The number of enrollees doubled since its beginning in 1933. There were now 505,782 men and more than 100,000 men who were officers, supervisors, foresters, education advisors, and LEMs.

During 1935 New York State celebrated the 50th anniversary of the founding of the Adirondack and Catskill Forest Preserve. In 1885 the state legislature had set aside over 700,00 acres of state land in the Adirondacks and Catskills. Lumbermen had cut over most of this land and abandoned it. Much of the land had reverted to the state because the taxes were unpaid. By 1935 the area had grown to 2,350,000 acres with 95 per cent covered by trees.[26]

A three-day celebration was held in Lake Placid from September 12-14. Forest rangers, game protectors, fire tower observers, and CCC enrollees marched in a parade and President Roosevelt gave a speech.

In 1935 the CCC continued to be popular. Congress voiced their approval and extended the program to increase the enrollment to 600,000. This included enlarging the supervising staff to 6,000 Army, Marine, and Navy Reserve officers. The CCC expanded the age requirements for enrollees from 18-25 to 17-28 in order to fill the larger quota. This made at least 40,000 youths aged

At the Benson Mines camp this group of foremen, foresters, and the superintendent supervised the men on projects outside of camp. St. Lawrence County Historical Association

Enrollees from the Adirondack CCC camps gathered in Lake Placid to celebrate the 50th anniversary of the creation of the Adirondack and Catskill forest preserves. President Franklin D. Roosevelt (right) and NYS Governor Lehman in Lake Placid attended the celebration. Museum Archives

17 eligible.[27] There were many young men who lied about their age or applied using their older brother's name. Now they could apply legally.[28]

The government set a goal of enrolling 600,000 men for 1936 but a new FDR advisor, Harry Hopkins, impeded the attainment of that goal.

In 1935 FDR selected Harry Hopkins, former head of the Federal Emergency Relief Administration, to be the Director of Work Projects Administration (WPA). Hopkins created new rules for the selection of enrollees. These rules were based on relief rolls and ignored the quota systems previously used in the states. Director Fechner did not agree and protested. This caused confusion and delays in the enrolling process. By September 1935 only 500,000 men were enrolled. This number was never reached again during the duration of the CCC. Near the end of 1935 another problem faced Fechner in attaining 600,000 enrollees. FDR secretly told him that since an election year was coming he wanted to balance the budget by a drastic cut in the number of enrollees and camps. This plan eventually caused Roosevelt problems in 1936.[30]

NUMBER OF CAMPS (JUNE 30, 1935)[29]

MIDDLE YEARS

In January 1936 when Roosevelt announced the

elimination of 489 CCC camps nationwide, four were in the Adirondacks: Port Henry, Warrensburg, Minerva, and Thendara.[31] This reduction resulted in a huge outpouring of disapproval that reverberated throughout the nation. The politicians on both sides of the aisle in Congress showed their disapproval. They knew the CCC program was successful in creating jobs and helping their constituents in the communities where the camps were established.

FDR refused to listen to the protests and announced a reduction in enrollment to 300,000 men and 1,400 camps.

California	155	Colorado	31
Pennsylvania	113	South Dakota	31
Michigan	103	Indiana	29
Wisconsin	103	Nebraska	27
Illinois	88	New Jersey	26
Missouri	88	Louisiana	25
Idaho	82	Alabama	24
Oregon	75	Florida	23
Minnesota	74	New Hampshire	23
New York	69	Oklahoma	23
Washington	69	South Carolina	23
Virginia	63	Arizona	22
Massachusetts	58	Connecticut	21
Tennessee	57	Wyoming	20
Texas	55	Maine	19
Arkansas	50	Noth Dakota	19
Iowa	41	Utah	19
Ohio	40	New Mexico	17
Kansas	39	West Virginia	17
North Carolina	38	Martyland	15
Vermont	37	Nevada	14
Kentucky	34	Rhode Island	7
Mississippi	34	Delaware	3
Georgia	33	Dist. Columbia	2
Montana	32		

Citizens responded with an outpouring of letters to FDR. Even Democratic members of Congress protested the reductions. Finally, FDR and his advisors cancelled their proposals and kept the same number of CCC enrollees and existing camps. The CCC program continued to produce successful work during 1936 despite these governmental hassles.

In 1936 the CCC was not only popular with the Republican presidential candidate, Alf Landon, but it had a 67 per cent approval of the registered Republicans.[32]

Although the ECW was originally called the Civilian Conservation Corps it did not become official until June 28, 1937 with an act of Congress.

In 1937 FDR decided to balance the budget by reducing government spending to the states. This resulted in states reducing the number of camps working on park, forestry, and fish and game projects. The number of state camps in New York was reduced to 43. In the fall these Adirondack camps closed: Lake Placid, Benson Mines, and Canton.[33]

Later in 1937 Congress responded by extending the life of the CCC for three years and separated the CCC from the federal relief organization by establishing it as a regular government bureau.[34]

By 1938 there were 31 statewide CCC camps. In the Adirondack region these 11 camps were operating: Paul Smiths, Bolton Landing, Speculator, Harrisville, Brasher Falls, Plattsburgh, Indian Lake, Brushton, Boonville, Newcomb, and Lake Placid.[35]

The enrollees received a present from President Roosevelt in 1938, new uniforms. Since it's beginning in 1933 the enrollees used WWI Army surplus uniforms. On FDR's visit to Warm Springs, GA he was upset to see the CCC men wearing poor quality uniforms. He felt this shoddy clothing weakened the men's morale. FDR had the Department of Navy design a new forest green uniform that became widespread the following year.[36]

Despite the popularity of the CCC, Congress decided not to make it a permanent government agency. For the next two years Congress funded the program as an independently funded agency. Perhaps it was because Congress thought it was a temporary relief program to help with the Depression.

LATER YEARS

In 1939 Fechner was faced with new challenges. The threat of war in Europe and possible German invasions of England and France. Threats of war spurred the economy to produce materials for our allies. Factories needed workers and the number of CCC enrollees began to decrease.

Roosevelt decided to reorganize several agencies. Congress created the Federal Security Agency (FSA) that consolidated several offices and boards under one director. It brought the CCC into this agency. Fechner was furious. He was no longer the director of an independent agency and now had to listen to the directives of the FSA Director. Fechner asked the President to change his plan but FDR refused. To show his indignation Fechner submitted his resignation but later withdrew it. Many think this conflict with Roosevelt led to Fechner's ill health and in December he had a massive heart attack and died on December 31.[37]

The CCC Legacy Foundation states: "Fechner was the CCC. His honest, day-by-day attention to all facets of the program sustained high levels of accomplishment and shaped an impressive public image of the CCC. He was a common man, neither impressed nor intimidated by his contemporaries in Washington. Fechner was considered deficient and lacking vision in some areas but his dedication was second to none. His lengthy and detailed progress reports to FDR were valuable information. He was a good and faithful servant who was spared from witnessing the end of the CCC program."

During 1939 these camps were operating in the Adirondacks: Paul Smiths, Bolton Landing, Speculator, Harrisville, Brasher Falls, Plattsburgh, Indian Lake, Brushton, Boonville, and Newcomb. These Adirondack CCC camps continued to develop these state campsites: Cumberland Bay, Fish Creek Pond, Meacham Lake, Golden Beach (Raquette Lake), Rogers Rock (Lake George), Eighth Lake, Cranberry Lake, Moffett Beach (Sacandaga Lake), Sacandaga, Lewey Lake, Lake Eaton, Poplar Point (Piseco Lake), and Lake Durant.[38]

In 1940 the CCC was now confronted with the loss of their leader and a President and Congress who were more concerned with the conflicts in Europe than the CCC. Congress appointed Fechner's assistant, John J. McEntee, as its director. McEntee was a very knowledgeable person but did not have the patience of Fechner. The new director had conflicts with Harold Ickes, the Secretary of the Interior, who disapproved of McEntee's nomination. McEntee struggled to keep the program going and received little praise for his efforts.[39] He worked until the program ended in 1942.

In 1940 when France fell to Germany public support for the CCC began to waver as the threat of war increased. Emphasis in Congress was now focused on the defense of our country and mobilizing for a future involvement in war. Demands for ending the CCC increased in Congress.

Despite the CCC difficulties, it continued to be a popular program. FDR tried again to reduce the CCC for economic reasons during the election year of 1940 but Congress refused and added $50 million to the 1940-41 appropriations. The number of enrollees continued to be approximately 300,000.[40]

In New York State there were 32 CCC campsites during the beginning of 1941 but with the increase of factory production the number of camps in the US was reduced to 900 camps and 135,000 enrollees. By the end of the year there were only 11 camps in the state and 4 in the Adirondack region: Paul Smiths, Speculator, Brasher Falls, and Plattsburgh.[41]

Towards the end of summer in 1941 the CCC faced new challenges: the decrease in applicants, desertions, and resignations due to better jobs. There were now less than 200,000 enrollees and approximately 900 camps. The citizens and newspapers who had supported the CCC now questioned its continuation. Unemployment was down and the defense of our nation was of the utmost importance.[42]

On December 7, 1941 the Japanese bombing of Pearl Harbor had a traumatic effect on the nation and the life of the CCC. The US had to focus on defeating its enemy and any projects not directly related to the war effort were considered non-essential and many were dropped. Congress appointed a joint committee to study the various federal agencies. The CCC came under close scrutiny towards the end of 1941 and the committee recommended the abolishment of the CCC by July 1, 1942.[43]

In the Adirondacks only three camps continued operating: Paul Smiths, Speculator, and Plattsburgh.

On March 25, 1942, the ninth anniversary of the establishment of the CCC, FDR sent a letter to CCC Director James McEntee to congratulate him for his work:

"There is a real place for the CCC during this emergency and it will be called upon more and more to perform tasks which will strengthen our country, and aid in the successful operation of the war. Many of the young men now in the camps will enter the nation's armed forces. When that time comes, they will be better prepared to serve their country because of the discipline, the training and physical hardihood they gained in the Civilian Conservation Corps."[44]

The CCC plodded on for six months knowing that the end was near. Finally in June the House of Representatives voted 158 to 151 to curtail funding to the CCC. Then the Senate voted on a bill to continue the CCC that twice ended in tie votes. Vice-President Harry Wallace voted to continue funding. Then the Senate-House Committee came up with a decision that authorized $8 million to liquidate the agency. Both the House and Senate confirmed the end of the CCC and it became history.

When the US entered WWII it became apparent that

the CCC program would end. Provisions were made to end work projects. States made provisions to turn over the camp buildings and all operating equipment such as tools, tractors, trucks, etc. to the Army for the war effort.[45] During the war a few of the camps were used as Prisoner of War (POW) camps. In the Adirondacks the Boonville and Harrisville camps housed German prisoners while the Brasher Falls camp was used for Italian POWs. Most of the camp's buildings were taken down and used by the state while some were sold to individuals just to get rid of the buildings.

ACCOMPLISHMENTS IN US & TERRITORIES

The CCC, composed of both young men and veterans, played a significant part in saving and restoring our natural resources. Here are some of its accomplishments throughout the US:

- employed 3,463,766 men
- enrolled 2,876,638 Juniors, Veterans, and Native Americans
- enrolled an estimated 50,000 in territories of Alaska, Hawaii, Puerto Rico, and Virgin Islands
- planted between 2-3 billion trees
- built more than 3,000 fire towers
- constructed 46,854 bridges
- developed 52,000 acres of public campgrounds
- constructed 125,000 mi. of roads
- built 13,100 mi. of foot trails
- built 318,076 check dams for erosion control
- fought fires totaling more than 8 million man-days
- strung 89,000 mi. of telephone wire
- protected 154 million square yards of stream and lake banks
- stocked 972 million fish
- performed mosquito control work on 248,000 acres
- assisted farmer's land by controlling soil erosion and improving 40 million acres of farmland
- provided 814,000 acres of barren & denuded range land with vegetation
- restored 3,980 historic structures
- provided an economic boost to local businesses
- enrollee dependents received $662,895,000 nationwide
- physical health of the enrollees improved through vigorous work and good food

- the education program taught approximately 40,000 illiterate enrollees to read[46]

MAJOR ACCOMPLISHMENTS OF THE CCC PROGRAM IN NEW YORK STATE

- approximately 220,000 enrollees in the program
- Federal government spent $9 million on supervision of enrollees, supplies, materials, etc.
- construted 393 mi. of truck trails
- built 73 truck trail bridges
- constructed 63 dams
- built 145,000 rods of fencing to protect reforested fields
- installed 131, 991 pipe and tile lines
- constructed 80 water supply systems
- built 2,600 table and bench combinations
- made 4,000 signs and markers
- protected 11,000 sq. yards of streams and lake banks
- planted 18,000 acres of trees
- fought fires for a total of 58,151 man-days
- performed tree and plant disease control work on 1,100,000 acres
- performed insect pest control work on 3,700,000 acres
- built 107 fish-rearing ponds
- stocked 346,000 fish
- performed 234 mi. of stream development[47]

FDR's CCC program was his most successful New Deal Program. It had overwhelming support from the enrollees, political parties, families, towns, states, and nation . The CCC had a lasting effect on the lives of the enrollees by giving them a sense of worth because they had a job and were helping their families. Enrollees learned self-discipline, developed a lasting love of nature, learned how to get along with many types of people, and in many cases learned a trade they used when they left the CCC. The enrollees' experiences in the CCC benefited the US when it went to war with Japan and Germany because the Army trained them so that they had discipline and knew how to lead. Many who were leaders in the CCC became sergeants when they joined the army and navy.

THE POST WAR YEARS

There were a few attempts to revive the CCC concept after WWII. The Student Conservation Program

(SCP) proposed by Elizabeth Cushman in her 1955 senior thesis at Vassar College was implemented in 1957 in the Olympic and Grand Teton National Parks. Young people performed jobs such as trail work and collecting entrance fees. In 1964 the Student Conservation Association (SCA) began. Elizabeth Cushman Titus became the president of the organization. It involved high school, college, and graduate students in the 50 states. The volunteers restored habitat, built trails, destroyed invasive species, and did erosion control work. During the summer over 600 youths (15 and older) worked in crews of 6-8 under the supervision of an adult. Work was on federally controlled lands such as national parks, national monuments, national wildernesses, and those under the Bureau of Land Management. The Departments of Agriculture and Interior and some states operated the conservation projects. Volunteers had to provide their own transportation to the projects. They worked from 21-30 days on projects. At the end they had a four to five-day recreation trip.[48]

In 1970 the Youth Conservation Corps (YCC) began. The program employed teens (15-18) for either eight or ten weeks in the summer doing conservation projects on federally managed lands. This federally funded program involved the youth in projects involving repairing and restoring historic structures, removing exotic plants, marking boundaries, restoring campsites, constructing trails, and doing wildlife research. There were 46,000 enrollees in 1978 in the 50 states, Puerto Rico, Virgin Islands, and Guam. The program ended in 1981 due to federal budget cuts.[49]

In 1993 a Community Service Trust Act passed during the Clinton Presidency created AmeriCorps. Each year 75,000 adults covering all ages and backgrounds have the opportunity to work with local and national nonprofit groups doing projects to protect the environment or help individuals. Some of the projects are: helping communities during disasters, fighting illiteracy, cleaning streams and parks, tutoring disadvantaged youths, building homes for the needy, and operating and managing after-school programs.[50]

Cumberland Bay State Park was built by CCC veterans during the 1930s along the sandy shores of Lake Champlain. Podskoch Collection

This is part of Lewey Lake campground that was built by the Speculator CCC camp in the 1930s. It is one of the favorite sites along Indian Lake. Podskoch Collection

CAMP ORGANIZATION

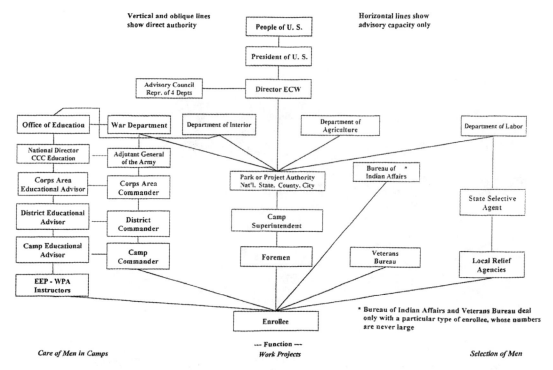

Organization of Civilian Conservation Corps-Lines of Authority. CCC Legacy Archives

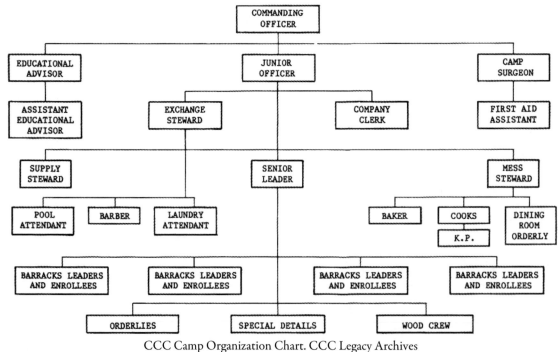

CCC Camp Organization Chart. CCC Legacy Archives

CHAPTER 2
CAMP ORGANIZATION

NINE CCC CORPS AREAS

CCC camps were organized into nine regional Army Corps Areas. New York was in the 2nd Corps Area along with the states of New Jersey and Delaware. An Army general commanded each corps area. The corps area was divided into districts. The general's job was to send messages from the corps area to each district camp, which had an executive officer, an adjutant (an officer who acts as military assistant), a medical officer, and a chaplain.[1]

In 1933 the 2nd Corps Area was divided into

Nine CCC Corps Area map. CCC Legacy Archives

Northern and Southern zones. Each zone was divided into districts. The Adirondack region came under the Plattsburgh Barracks on Lake Champlain.

In June 1935 the districts were rearranged. Two districts covered the Adirondack region. The 1st District was the Plattsburgh District and the 6th District was in Schenectady. The 7th District in Middletown governed the Catskill region. The 8th District was at Fort Totten in Queens. The entire CCC was reorganized again in June 1936. New York State was divided into two large districts: Schenectady and Binghamton. The 1st, 6th, 7th, and 8th districts were consolidated into the Schenectady District. It took in approximately 50 camps in the Adirondacks, Catskills, and Hudson Valley regions. District headquarters and supply offices were at Army Supply Depot in Rotterdam.[2]

The motor unit, composed of an officer, clerk, and three mechanics at the Plattsburgh Barracks, was transferred to the Lake Placid camp. The Schenectady District was divided into sub-districts. Sub-District No. 1 was headquartered at Camp S-71 in Lake Placid. The following 12 camps were in Sub-District 1: Plattsburgh, Lake Placid, Paul Smiths, Newcomb, Indian Lake, Fort Ann, Brushton, Brasher Falls, Benson Mines, Canton, Speculator, and Bolton Landing.[3] Each camp had a company number received when organized at an Army post. Example: Paul Smiths was Company 220. The first number, 2, stood for the 2nd Corps Area and the number 20 stood for the 20th company formed. Each camp also had a state letter and number. An S- was a camp in a State Forest, SP- State Park, P- Private Forest, AF- Army. Example: Paul Smiths camp was S-60. It worked in state forests. The number 60 stood for the 60th camp formed in NYS.

The Army supervised the men while in camp and provided them with food, clothing, equipment, shelter, and medical care. Each camp had a captain who was in charge of administration, discipline, and welfare of the men. He had one or two lieutenants for assistance. Some camps had an Army doctor/surgeon. If they didn't the Army contracted with a local doctor to do physicals and handle emergencies. In order to help with the supervision of the enrollees, the Army selected enrollees with leadership qualities. They helped supervise the barracks and work assignments. Leaders received $45 and assistant leaders $36 a month. Twenty-six leaders were assigned to each camp. Of these 26 men the Army had eight who worked in the camp and the other 18 were assigned to the superintendent.[4]

Cover of the 1937 Schenectady District Yearbook. Podskoch Collection

Bolton Landing CCC group picture of about 200 enrollees in front of the entrance to camp in October 1934. Five barracks, a mess hall, a recreation hall, an infirmary, and offices are in the rear. The garage is on the right. Floyd Pickett

The camp was like a little town. At first during the summer of 1933 men lived in surplus army pyramid tents or wooden tent frames. Later the Army hired local carpenters to build wooden buildings that better protected the men. There were approximately 24 buildings in each camp. There was a kitchen/mess hall, recreation hall, barracks, officers' quarters, school/classroom, infirmary, garages for Army and state trucks, vehicle repair shop, blacksmith shop, officers' headquarters, latrine/shower, water and sewage facilities, streets, and sidewalks. The camp had electricity and telephones. The buildings had large stoves that used coal or wood for fuel.[5]

INFIRMARY

Each camp had an infirmary with four to eight beds. It had a stove and basic First Aid materials and medicines. Each infirmary had one or two assigned enrollees who were there 24/7. They had general knowledge in First Aid. They cleaned cuts and did bandaging and brought the ill food. If an injury was serious the enrollee called the Army surgeon or the contracted local doctor. If the patient needed to go to a hospital an Army ambulance took them to the nearest Army hospital. There was one at the Plattsburgh Barracks. There were accidents and even deaths of enrollees. About half of the deaths were attributed to vehicles. The enrollees drove the trucks and had frequent accidents due to poor road conditions or lack of experience on the part of the young drivers. Other causes of deaths were drowning, pneumonia, falls, fighting fires, and falling objects.[6]

Left - When the camps were established the infirmary was in a tent. This is the Paul Smiths infirmary in the summer of 1933. Later a wooden building was built. Jim Corl. Below - When an enrollee was injured or sick he was taken to the camp infirmary for treatment. If the injury required hospital care the patient was taken by camp ambulance to the nearest Army hospital. Here a patient is taken to the Plattsburgh Barracks Hospital. Jim Corl

CHAPTER 3
ENROLLEE'S LIFE IN CAMP

SIGNING UP

At first young, unmarried, unemployed men between 18-25 whose families were on the relief rolls were eligible to sign up. Candidates applied at the nearest public welfare office. In 1933 there were five applicants for each opening. There were four enrollment periods, January, April, July, and October. The number of spots depended on the town's quota and vacancies available. In 1935 the ages were changed to 17-23 to fill the enlarged quota. In 1933 the enrollees could only sign up for six months to allow others a chance to join. This rule changed so that the men could sign up four times for a total of two years. Once selected the enrollee then had to pass a physical exam and take the oath of enrollment.[1]

COMING TO CAMP

In 1933 the Army transported enrollees to an Army base for one or more weeks of conditioning. They slept in tents. Groups of 200 men formed a company and were sent to establish a camp. After 1933 the men went directly to their assigned camp.

One can just imagine how many enrollees were homesick as they rode in canvas covered Army trucks or on railroads to their new camp. The young men left their homes in the large cities or small towns and traveled to the backwoods of the Adirondacks or way out west to Montana. It was a real culture shock. Many had roamed aimlessly through city streets or rode the rails. Now their life was regimented and they had to follow orders and a schedule. Some men couldn't take this new life and left after just a day or two. The Army didn't chase after them but they received a dishonorable discharge.

Some men went to various camps in their state while some went across the US on Army trains to National Parks and Forests in California, Nevada, Idaho, Montana, Wyoming, etc. while some were sent to the South to Tennessee or South Carolina. The men did not have a choice of camp location but went willingly to get a job and help their families. Then they had to adjust and live with about 200 other young men. Frank Leonbruno, an enrollee at the Bolton Landing camp (1935 to 1941) said:

"In 1935 I quit Whitehall High School after my junior year. The silk mills closed, the railroads laid everybody off. Then I saw a notice in the Whitehall Times about the CCC so I signed up. I told them I was 17.

"On October 17, 1935 I and 16 other young men from Whitehall were officially enrolled in the CCC. They transported us in an Army truck to camp. Fred Letbridge from Clemons was a member of the contingent. He became a carpenter and a good worker who would do KP duty and work weekends for other enrollees who went home. Fred married one of the local girls and settled in Bolton Landing."

The new enlisted men went to the supply office for their clothing and equipment. The clerk gave them work clothes, boots, shoes, underwear, toilet kit, coats, rain gear, and uniforms.

"Our first meal was spaghetti," said Frank. "Then Dr. Joseph Merin, the camp doctor, gave us our physical. Although the local registration offices did an initial screening and eliminated the blatantly handicapped, generally anyone who had a pulse was welcomed by the CCC."

Above, Left - This is the entrance to the Bolton Landing camp which greeted the enrollees in June 1939 as they approached their home for the next six months. Minerva Historical Society.
Above, Right - CCC enrollees lived in Army tents in 1933 while local carpenters built the barracks and other buildings. NYS Archives

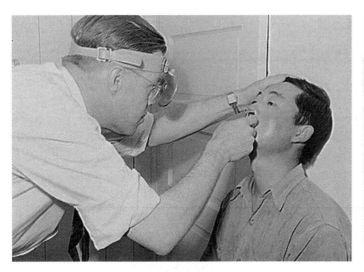

DAILY ROUTINE

Monday - Friday

6 am - reveille (either a bugle call or a whistle)
6:30 am - breakfast
7:00 am - police (clean) the barracks and camp
7:50 am - general assembly, raise the flag, roll call, and work assigned
12 noon - lunch
4 pm - work ends and return to camp
5 pm - retreat ceremony involving the lowering of the flag, announcements, and dinner
6-10 pm - free time to play sports, listen to radio, write letters, play cards, shoot the bull with friends or attend classes
10 pm - lights out[2]

Clockwise from Left - A CCC enrollee getting a physical exam. Library of Congress Enrollees doing exercises at the Paul Smiths camp. NYS Archives. Three enrollees relaxing in their barracks. The young men kept their barracks in an orderly fashion because the Army officers had frequent inspections. Adirondack Museum Archives

Weekends

The enrollees had free time unless they had to make up time due to poor weather or emergencies like fires or flood damage. Some men had a pass to go home. In the evening some went to a nearby town to go to the movies, a restaurant or bar, or maybe dancing or bowling. On Sunday, there were religious services in camp or trucks transported enrollees to local churches.

CAMP ACTIVITIES

Enrollees had opportunities for recreation in the evenings and on weekends. Most camps provided a building for a library or a space in the education building or recreation hall for reading books and newspapers. The rec hall sometimes had a pool and ping pong tables, and tables for card and board games. They also had a beautiful stone fireplace that provided warmth on cold days. Some enrollees brought their guitars and other musical instruments for playing music. Enrollees formed bands that performed for the camp.

In the rec hall was a PX or Canteen where enrollees could purchase, soda, candy, cigarettes, pipe tobacco, and toiletries. A leader or assistant leader supervised the store. Profits from the sales went to purchase items for the camp such as, a pool table, team uniforms, sports equipment, paint, lighting fixtures, etc.

There were opportunities for hunting, fishing, and trapping in the nearby forests, rivers, and lakes. In many

Above - These four Paul Smiths' enrollees just back to their barracks after a swim in nearby Barnum Pond. Lori Lepine. Left - Boxing was popular at the CCC camps and on Field Days. NYS Archives

of the camps baseball, basketball, and football teams were formed. Boxing and wrestling matches were also popular. Some camps built their own ring for matches. The camps had intramural competition with barracks or the team competed against nearby CCC camps or local town teams.

FIELD DAYS

"CCC Field Days" were held almost every year. Each district or sub district chose a town and enrollees from all of the camps came to test their skills in various sports. They participated in a parade and then competed in track and field events, boxing and wrestling matches, and baseball games. The first field day in the Adirondacks was held on Memorial Day weekend in Saranac Lake on May 30, 1934. On Tuesday September 18, 1934 District No. 1, Northern Zone NY held its Second Annual Field Day. Over 500 enrollees from Port Henry, Warrensburg, and Bolton Landing attended the event at the Westport Fair Grounds. Port Henry came in first place.

In 1935 Port Henry again swept the District Field Day competition. The event was held in Lake Placid. The September 20, 1935 Essex County Republican reported the results: Port Henry 57 pts., Fish Creek 32 pts., Paul Smiths 11 pts., Lake Placid 9 pts., and Tupper Lake 8 pts. Conservation Commissioner Osborne presented the first place winners with engraved fobs.

The 4th Annual Field Day was on August 21, 1937 at the Veteran's Hospital Facility in Tupper Lake.

OTHER ACTIVITIES

Sometimes the camp had dances and invited locals to attend. Many romances developed with enrollees and girls they met in the nearby towns. Sometimes they married and settled in the country towns.

Plays and musical performances were held in the rec hall. Enrollees formed bands and performed for the camp. Federal Emergency Relief Act (FERA) sponsored traveling groups of actors who performed plays at the camps.

The Army provided religious service at least once a month in camp. If camp was close to a town the Army provided trucks for transporting the enrollees to religious services on Sundays. There were also Catholic, Protestant, and Jewish Army Reserve chaplains who traveled to camps and held services. There were a few volunteer clergymen who held services in the camp without remuneration, except for board, transportation or lodging.[3]

ENROLLEES' CARS AND CHARACTERS

Frank Leonbruno stated: "Rules prohibited the ownership of automobiles at camp, but our officers at Bolton and at many other camps looked the other way as long as the cars were kept elsewhere. Generally, we hid our cars in the woods near camp. One could purchase a jalopy for $20-60. Thievery with the loss of gasoline or a tire was not uncommon, though the thieves were not always CCC boys."

Frank said he bought his first car, a 1929 Model A Ford, and used it for three years. He estimated 15-20 guys owned cars. Frank Sherman from Warrensburg had a motorcycle. Later, he opened a motorcycle and repair shop in his town.

Frank added, "You always had unusual characters with nicknames like: 'Loan Shark,' 'Gold Bricker,' 'Camp Bully,' 'Camp Comedian,' 'Shorty,' 'Slim,' 'Junior,' 'Muscles,' 'Chow Hound,' 'Stooge,' 'Apple Polisher,' 'Brown Noser,' and 'Stool Pigeon.' "The 'Gold Bricker' was adverse to labor. The 'Loan Shark' was the camp entrepreneur. He would gladly buy a $1 canteen book for 50 or 75 cents and then resell it at face value, $1. He would also lend out money and discount it at 50 or 75 per cent, but would seek his money on payday. Tony Brock was my favorite 'Loan Shark.' He soon amassed enough money to buy a 1936 Chevrolet sedan which he used as a taxi. Loading the Chevy with six of his fellow enrollees, Tony charged 50 cents for a round trip to Whitehall. He made this trip at speeds far exceeding the speed limit. Thank goodness he was a good driver! I rode with him myself more than once and never felt a bit nervous.

"'Junior' was always a small lad with a baby face who, in some cases, actually gave a false statement regarding his age. However, the 'Juniors' were always treated with courtesy and respect.

"Thieves were punished not by Army officers but by the camp's 'kangaroo court,' which doled out punishment unbeknownst to the Army officers. The punishment was severe enough that the thief had second thoughts about stealing from his so-called friends again. Generally, penalties involved some kind of duty performed for members of the court, such as doing their laundry or pressing their shirts and pants-military style of course.

"'Chow Hounds' had no table manners. They would first grab a platter of food and gulp it down and hopefully wait for the cook's call for seconds. We had cafeteria and family style meals. In the latter, the 'Chow Hound' was the first to grab the platters of meat, potatoes, and vegetables. Then load his plate and even his pockets with anything that was portable."

EDUCATION

There was no mention of education in the ECW Act but towards the end of 1933 Fechner appointed Clarence S. Marsh as Director of Education. An education advisor assisted each corps area commander. The Office of Education who administered the program in their area selected him.[4]

In 1934 the education program began operating in June. Criticism was leveled at the methodology used for teaching and even Fechner had doubts that it might impede the work program. His doubts never materialized. The enrollees' skills and education varied from men with little schooling to those who were university graduates. By 1937 the program taught more than 35,000 illiterate enrollees to read and over a thousand received a high school diploma and 39 men received a college diploma.[5]

Each camp had a Camp Education Advisor (CEA) who designed vocational and academic programs, taught classes, and brought in instructors and speakers. An enrollee worked as his assistant. The advisor held voluntary classes in the evenings. Classes covered a wide range of topics: mechanics, photography, forestry, engineering, surveying, high school diploma, carpentry, electrical, woodcarving, and other subjects. There were also correspondence classes from colleges. The education program's success depended on the competency and work of the CEA and cooperation of the camp commander.[6]

Top - The Paul Smiths' mess hall at dinnertime was filled with hungry young men. NYS Archives. Below - These enrollees are leaving the camp and going home. The Army transported them to the nearest railroad station or to towns where they lived. Adirondack Museum Archives

CHAPTER 4
WORK PROJECTS

The CCC earned a nickname of 'Tree Army' because of the millions of trees they planted, but this was only one of the many tasks they performed. Camp projects concentrated on forest improvement and forest protection.

In New York State the CCC camps had seven classifications: reforestation, forest pest control, forest control, recreational development, fish and game, college forest, and Dutch elm tree disease eradication.

The reforestation camps worked only on land that

was abandoned or on depleted farmland purchased by the state. The enrollees planted trees, constructed truck trails and fire lines, made surveys, built fences, reduced fire hazards, did forest stand improvement in woodlots, and constructed fire holes.

Truck trails were dirt roads built into the forests to enable the state to get men and equipment in to fight fires. The roads were 10 ft. wide with 2 ft. shoulders. Roads were built to federal specifications. The subbase was 8-10 in. of broken rock that was covered with 4 in. of fine gravel or shale.[1]

The NYS Conservation Department had the CCC camps build truck trails in the Adirondack and Catskill Forests Preserve.

The Conservation Department (CD) Commissioner, Lithgow Osborne, received complaints from the Association for the Protection of the Adirondacks, which said the CCC was illegally cutting trees for truck roads through the Adirondack Preserve. This violated the "forever wild" clause of the New York State Constitution of 1894.

Commissioner Osborne solicited the NYS Attorney General's opinion on the matter. On April 13, 1935 the Attorney General said the CD "had the authority

Clockwise from Top - Here Paul Smiths enrollees are planting seedlings. This group used mattocks to make holes while the boys with pails of seedlings followed and planted the seedlings into the holes. Jim Corl. Pine seedlings were planted by the CCC on abandoned farmland where the soil was poor. NYS Archives. A CCC crew is clearing the roadside of hazardous material because many fires were started by careless smokers who threw lit cigarettes and cigars from their cars. NYS Archives. CCC enrollees learned to operate heavy machinery. These men are leveling and compacting a road through the Adirondack forest. Adirondack Museum Archives

to construct and use such roads for the purpose of protecting the preserve from the hazards of fire, but the CD did not have the authority to allow the roads to be used for public travel. In fact, the CD should do everything in its power to prevent such public use."[2]

The CD continued building roads but stopped when another organization, the Forest Preserve Association (1934), led by John S. Apperson and Dr. Irving Langmuir, opposed the road construction. Governor Lehman appointed a five-man committee to study the problem. On January 6, 1936 the majority of the committee voted with the Attorney General's opinion. The CD continued building truck trails in 1936. There were now 59.25 mi. of truck trail in the Adirondack Preserve.[3]

The CD responded to the complaints by placing locked gates at the truck trail entrances. During deer hunting season they had local CCC enrollees guard the truck trail entrances from 6 am to 6 pm.

Another CCC work project was forest stand improvement or silviculture. This involved improving the growth of good trees by thinning the ones that were in the way.

In the forest pest control camps, men worked on both state and private lands to protect the forests from blister rust, gypsy moths and other insects, and tree diseases. Blister rust is a fungus that damaged millions of white pine trees. In order for the blister rust to spread it needed a host (ribes bushes such as currants and gooseberries) to complete the cycle. During the spring enrollees scouted state and private forests for ribes plants within 900' of white pine trees. They pulled the plants out and let them dry. Once dead they were no longer a threat to the white pines. The CCC fought the gypsy moths by searching and destroying the egg masses in the fall and winter. They painted the egg masses with creosote.

The forest fire control camps worked not only to fight forest fires but also to prevent them. The young men built truck trails, fire lines, foot trails, bridges, fire towers, fire tower observer's cabins, and telephone lines to the fire towers and cabins.

The fourth camp was for recreational development. The first NYS campsite was developed in 1920 and each year the demand for more camping areas increased. CCC camps worked to improve existing state parks and develop new campsites. They cleared areas for campsites, built bathrooms, installed water lines, constructed ski trails and lean-tos, and improved canoe trails.

The fifth camp classification located in the Adirondacks was college forests camps. Both Cornell and Syracuse universities had CCC camps on their properties. These camps worked to protect and improve the forests. The CCC built truck roads, telephone lines, and administration buildings. The men also did forest stand improvement, tree planting, and experimental projects.

Fish and game camps focused primarily on propagating and conserving fish and game. The enrollees constructed fish and duck ponds and cultivated and planted

Clockwise from Right - This is one of the hundreds of waterholes built by the CCC. These provided a ready source of water for fire fighters. Adirondack Museum Archives. CCC boys fighting a forest fire set up this improvised shelter for resting. Adirondack Museum Archives. This Paul Smiths crew used saws and axes to thin and prune trees in the state forests. Jim Corl.

Above, Left - The Paul Smiths camp replaced the old dam at the outlet of Meacham Lake with this cement dam - this is the beginning of the East Branch of the St. Regis River. It flows under Rt. 30 just north of the Rt. 30 and 458 intersection near McCollums. Lori Lepine. Right - CCC camps worked to improve the habitat of trout. They used logs to prevent erosion. Here logs are used to make pools of cool water and riffles that helped aerate the water. Adirondack Museum Archives.

feeding strips of plants for game birds. Some camps in the Adirondacks did some aspects of the fish and game camps such as stream improvement projects in their area to improve the trout habitat. They removed trees and debris from the water. The CCC built deflectors to increase the speed of the water and V-shaped dams created pools to improve the habitat for the fish. To stop the erosion of stream and riverbanks, enrollees used log cribbing to anchor a log wall or used riprap which is the use of rocks and other materials to protect the banks.[4]

There were two Dutch elm disease eradication camps near the Connecticut border. These camps destroyed infected elm trees and scouted for new areas needing treatment.[5]

"Side" or "spike" camps were established when projects were quite a distance from the main camp. CCC Director Fechner did not want the men to spend half of their workday traveling. The side camp had approximately 10-20 men who lived in tents and were supervised by a forester or foreman. These camps could not have more than 10% of the company's strength. They had a cook tent for preparing meals and enough supplies for a week or more.

CAMP SUPERINTENDENT

The camp superintendent was in charge of the work projects. His salary was $200 a month. Eight to ten foremen assisted him. In NYS once the men left camp to work on projects they were under the superintendent and the CD. The Superintendent drew up projects or received projects formulated by heads of the CD. Projects included order of preference, maps, estimated man-days, and schedules for each project. Copies of the plans were sent for approval to the US Forest Service, the camp superintendent, and the CD Office in Albany. The superintendent assigned work to his foremen and organized the enrollees into small work crews.[6]

The foremen were paid $70 a-month. The camp also hired a blacksmith, a tractor operator, and mechanics. Several enrollees worked in the office doing clerical work. In 1934 the monthly payroll for the 35 state camp's superintendent's employees was $54,269.85. Most of this money went to local men thus boosting the economy of the local towns. All of the financing of the CCC came from the federal government and was distributed by the Army Finance Officer.[7] The superintendent had to send monthly detailed reports to Albany showing work accomplished, man-days spent on the projects, and work that was contemplated. They also showed fuel and oil consumption, tools needing replacement, and the type of work done by heavy equipment and trucks.[8]

ENROLLEES' LEADERS & THEIR JOBS

Frank Leonbruno, a member of the Bolton Landing camp, said: "The Forestry Department was composed of maintenance men, mechanics, equipment operators, truck drivers, and clerical workers. This group never left the camp area to engage in fieldwork. The forestry personnel who were called 'Leaders' supervised them. Leaders were paid $45 a-month and assistant leaders received $36 a-month.

"Truck drivers were important to the company. They had to pass a very strict test administered by an Army officer who traveled from camp to camp just to test these drivers. Drivers also assisted in driving to Glens Falls for supplies for the kitchen. Andrew Borix, famous in camp for his athletic ability, was a camp truck driver who drove me to Glens Falls to purchase food supplies. The drivers also drove to Bolton for ice along with disposing of garbage at the town dump. All trucks were equipped with governors, a mechanical device for automatically controlling the speed at 35 mph. Although ordered to obey all traffic ordinances, Army truck drivers were not subject to arrest by local police. Only a U. S. Marshall could arrest an Army truck driver. I do not recall any arrest being made of any CCC truck driver."

Leonbruno stated there were about 25 men who worked under the commanding officer in managing the Bolton Landing camp. "The first sergeant was the 'top kick' who generally had some prior military service. He also blew the whistle for reveille at 7 am. This man did not win any popularity contests.

"The supply sergeant issued enrollees their long johns, blankets, socks, fatigues, shoes, rubber shoe packs, a woolen olive drab uniform, a jacket, towels, a few toilet articles, a sewing kit, hats, gloves, mess kit, and cup.

"The mess sergeant had the responsibility of ordering food, preparing menus, supervising cooks, and keeping a daily inventory of the amount of food consumed. They assisted the cooks when necessary. I served as a first cook, second cook, and mess sergeant from 1937-1941.

"Another important position was company clerk. He was an aide to the company commander and had to know how to type, keep records of enrollee attendance, and 'leave slips' for weekend passes. He was notified when an enrollee on a weekend pass did not answer roll call on Monday morning. Missing roll call meant the loss of a day's pay for being A.W. O.L.

"Night guards played an important role of checking all stoves in the barracks, mess hall, infirmary, officer headquarters, and other buildings requiring heat. We burned soft coal which needed constant watch. He'd poke a small hole in the stove clear to the bottom of the grate. This gave the stove a draft not only to retain heat but also to safeguard against a buildup of gas fumes which could explode and cause serious injury to enrollees. He also had to get the ranges in the mess hall red hot prior to the arrival of the cooks at 4 am. Night guards often assisted the cooks in breaking eggs and making coffee for breakfast. In fact, some of the guards became cooks.

"The officer's orderly delivered meals to the brass. He was known as 'Dog Robber' because he got the choice leftovers that the dog might otherwise have enjoyed. Since he had frequent contact with the brass, he had the opportunity for promotion to a better line of work."

DISASTERS

The CCC camps also helped communities during natural disasters. During 1937 New York and Vermont experienced devastating floods. Enrollees left their camps to remove debris from roads and make them accessible, distributed pure water, and helped clean flooded homes. The men then worked on cleaning and widening streams.

On September 11, 1938 torrential rains and winds swept through southern New York and New England. Over 50 people died on Long Island. Extensive areas of downed trees littered the forests and road. CCC enrollees were sent to clear the roads and remove downed trees in the forests, which were a fire hazard.

Left - These CCC enrollees from the Speculator camp take a break from digging up rides bushes. These plants were host for blister rust that damaged white pine trees. Adirondack Museum Archives. Below - Each camp had five or more dump trucks that were used to transport gravel, sand, logs or building materials. Enrollees were trained to drive the vehicles and were responsible for their maintenance. Adirondack Museum Archives

CHAPTER 5
ARIETTA

Company #219 established Camp S-64, the first CCC camp in the Adirondacks, in the town of Arietta in the spring of 1933 to work on conservation projects. Before arriving in the Adirondacks, the enrollees gathered at Fort Hancock, NJ on April 13, 1933 for training and conditioning. Many of the enrollees were from New York City.[1]

After a month's stay, the men took a train to a town near Schenectady. The last leg of the trip was made in trucks up Route 10 to the hamlet of Averys Place in the Town of Arietta. They reached Shaker Place on May 19, 1933 and set up their tents in a field. It was in this area in 1810 that the Shaker religious group established a small farming community that became famous the world over for their wood products.[2] Captain W. J. Gilbert, 52nd Coast Artillery, was in charge of the camp. 1st Lt. R. L. Miller, 52 Coast Artillery, and 1st Lt. C. H. Horne, Fifth Field Artillery, assisted the captain.[3]

A June 21, 1933 Associated Press story in The Saratogian reported: "Perhaps to make themselves feel more at home, the boys have set up sign posts reading, 'Broadway,' 'Forty-Second Street,' and 'Bowery,' for the company streets of their camp... It has a 'Bowery barber shop,' where amateurs wield scissors and clippers when they are not too busy with their regular work."

Dave Abrams, of Northville, supervised a dozen camp foremen, local experienced men (LEMs), who supervised and worked with the boys on projects.[4] Hamilton Chequer of Speculator was the camp engineer.

For seven months Company 219 worked on various forestry projects. They worked on the trail to the fire tower on Hamilton Mountain and planted trees in Benson. The October 12, 1933 Au Sable Forks Record-Post reported the Arietta camp planted 340,000 trees that fall. In St. Johnsville they dug up and destroyed gooseberry

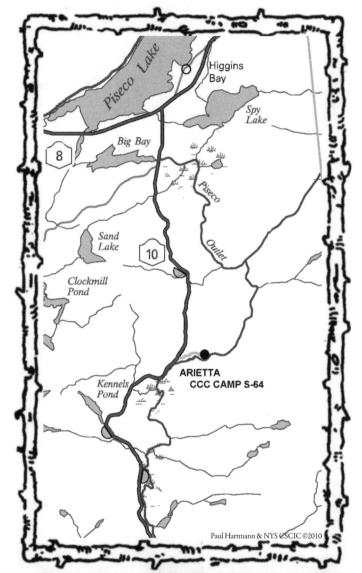

Paul Hartmann & NYS CSCIC ©2010

Left - Company 209 set up Army tents at Shaker Place in the Town of Arietta. The men near the truck may be unloading supplies for the camp. There is a flag pole where the men gathered each morning and afternoon for roll call and assignment of duties. The kitchen and the long mess hall tent are on the lower left and rows of large tents for enrollees are on the right. Robert L. Markovits Collection. Right - An Army officer and two men stand in front of Captain W. J. Gilbert's tent. The seated lady (behind them to the right) might be his wife or a visitor. NYS Archives

219th Co., CCC Arietta, New York   Building Structure for Shower Baths

Army officers supervise enrollees building a structure for showers at the Arietta Camp. One officer (left) is holding a level with water spigots behind him. Robert L. Markovits Collection

a 550-foot concrete dam across the Black River valley.[8]

As motorists drive up Route 10 from Canada Lake to Piseco they pass a state historic marker stating, "CCC Camp, site of first Civilian Conservation Corps Camp in New York, established May 1933 under the Emergency Conservation Work Program."

There are no physical signs of the Arietta CCC camp in the broad field where the tents once stood but as the pictures show in 1933 it was a time when the men of Co. 219 brought enormous energy and purpose to protect the Adirondacks.

and currant bushes because the shrubs hosted the blister rust, a fungus that damages white pine trees

Company 219 also worked on fire prevention projects such as clearing brush along Route 10 and making truck trails in the Arietta area to help fight forest fires. They also fought forest fires in the area. One fire was on Pigeon Mountain (approx. 3 mi. east of Arietta), Stratford, and another at Cathead Mountain.[5]

There was an abundant supply of food for the hard-working men. Every day trucks drove 28 mi. to Gloversville for provisions. It cost 37 cents a day to feed each worker. The cooks served apple butter in place of dairy butter, which was hard to get.[6]

At the end of the six-month enlistment period in October, 60 of the 200 men reenlisted with Company 219 and in November they packed up their tents and moved to Cherry Plain, NY (east of Albany near the Massachusetts border). When they arrived on November 15 they were happy to see that they had wooden frame buildings for the winter. Workers had started constructing the camp on October 1 and completed most of the work in six weeks.[7]

The new camp was located at the Capital District Game Refuge. Here they primarily worked on constructing

219th Co., CCC Arietta, New York

Others Might Be Here, But - no Bathing Suits

219th Co., CCC Arietta, New York   Cutting Firebreak Alongside Country Road

219th Co., CCC Arietta, New York   Chow Factory - Wood Burner Model

Clockwise from Top - After a hard day working in the forest the young enrollees cooled off in the nearby West Branch of the Sacandaga River. Some had bathing suits but many were "skinny dipping." Robert L. Markovits Collection. This postcard shows the young CCC men taking a break from cooking and splitting wood near the mess kitchen. There is also a covered shed for the wood stove where the cooking was done. An Army officer supervising the men is standing with the workers. Podskoch Collection. CCC enrollees are removing logs and dead branches and other fire hazards along a dirt road. The Conservation Department hired local teamsters to move wood. Robert L. Markovits Collection.

CHAPTER 6
BENSON MINES AND WANAKENA

HISTORY

There were two CCC camps established late in the spring of 1933 near the Ranger School in Wanakena approximately 7 mi. SW of Cranberry Lake village.

Camp P-70 was established on June 23, 1933 on Ranger School property. The men lived in tents and worked on forestry projects on the school's 2,800 acres.

The Essex County Republican on December 1, 1933 reported that the Wanakena Camp P-70 located on the Ranger School would be continued through the winter. The plan was to move it to a more convenient place that was better protected but this never happened. Winter set in and the men could not live in the tents and P-70 closed on November 25, 1933.

The other camp was S-84 and first called #20 by the state. It began on June 20, 1933 when Capt. W. C. Brigham, Lt. Robinson, and two non-commissioned officers from Company #229 arrived with an advance cadre from Madison Barracks near Watertown.[1] The District Commander and District Surgeon also arrived that day and looked over the proposed campsite. They rejected it and chose a sloping wooded area near Route 3 for the site of camp S-84. It was about 2 mi. west of Wanakena.[2]

Wayne Allen, historian and professor at the Ranger School, said: "By the weekend a camp of 35 tents and camp streets were cleared out from the hardwood brush just east of the Halfway Creek bridge. The remainder of the unit arrived four days later."

By August the buildings were completed and the men moved in.[3] On the left side of the camp were the Army garages/blacksmith shop/tool room and, the mess hall followed by barracks #5, #4, and #3. In the center were the gas pumps, the headquarters and stock room, and classroom, infirmary, and barracks #1 and #2. Then on the right side were the state garage and repair shop, the canteen and rec hall, and the officer's quarters.

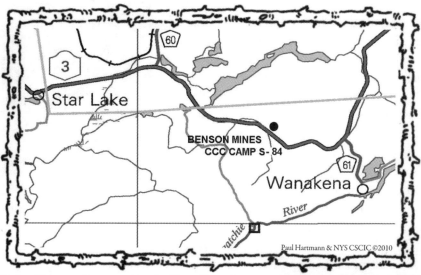

Paul Hartmann & NYS CSCIC ©2010

Right - Two enrollees stand by the Camp Wanakena S-84 camp sign at the entrance to the camp on Route 3 a few miles west of the Ranger School. The camp was also called Benson Mines because the nearest post office was there just 3 mi. away. John Eastlake Collection. Below - The young CCC boys lived in the Army tents during the summer and early fall of 1933 near the Ranger school in Wanakena. Adirondack Museum Archives.

Camp superintendent James D. Vanderveer guided CCC workers in completing projects. Professor Allen, said that the projects were under the jurisdiction of the US Forestry Division and State Conservation Department. The faculty and staff at the Ranger School provided a lot of the technical expertise.

Allen said the first forestry work began on July 5 and consisted of a fire line being cut around the camp with tools lent to the CCC by the Ranger School. The supply of hardware and tool stocks were low due to the demand from other CCC camps. Later that month the boys began constructing a road on the west end of the college forest. In August the camp got some dump trucks, which made road building more efficient.

They constructed seven miles of truck trails through the college forest. This provided access for fighting fires and removing timber from the 2,300-acre forest. The CCC boys did silviculture work. They cleared off stands of second growth trees, removed diseased, damaged or poorly formed trees to give more room for the eventual crop trees. They also cleared areas for tree nursery sites.

About nine miles from the Ranger School CCC enrollees worked at the New York State College of Forestry Pack Experimental Forest Summer Camp on the shores of Cranberry Lake. They improved the forest and continued work the next year.

They also did blister rust control by removing ribes plants near white pine trees.[5]

Local residents were sympathetic to the needs of the camp. Eight residents of Canton donated furniture for the recreation hall. In December 1933 a CCC truck picked up a Morris chair, four straight chairs, one arm chair, two rockers, a 9' x 12' rug, four floor lamps, and magazines and books.[6]

In 1934 they continued building truck trails, planting trees, and doing tree stand improvement. A new camp project was improving streams. They cleaned debris from streams and worked on stream erosion by shoring up banks with riprap.[7]

In 1936 the Conservation Reports stated camp S-84 worked most of the time developing the Cranberry Lake campsite. They constructed latrines and toilets and improved the beach area. The CCC enrollees also protected 370 acres of white pine trees by destroying 6,929 ribes plants

This is an aerial view of Camp S-84 in 1933. The enrollees lived in tents near Rt. 3. One wooden building was under construction in the center, and the seven black spots to the right near the road were trucks. The building on the far left on the hill in the woods was the latrine and shower. St. Lawrence Historical Society Archives

near the white pines.[8]

Camp S-84 also did forest fire control work. They built truck trails; 9 mi. to High Falls and 2 mi. to Dead Creek Flow.[9]

Another job of the CCC boys was fighting fires. During April 1934 the camp fought four forest fires. The next month the whole camp fought a fire on Ranger School land. Two years later during June and July they fought more forest fires in the area.[10]

The young men were frequently involved in search parties. On April 28, 1934 they searched for two lost Ranger School students who were later found drowned. They also searched for and found a lost hunter near their camp, five children who were missing near Newton Falls, and a lost person from Albion. Local residents showed appreciation and respect for the work of the CCC boys.[11]

Here is a view of the left side of camp S-84 from Rt. 3. The first building is the combination garage/ blacksmith shop, and tool shed followed by the large mess hall. Then barracks #5, #4, and #3 came next. St. Lawrence Historical Society Archives

WORK ACCOMPLISHED BY CAMP S-84[*]

PROJECT	1934	1935	1936	1937	TOTAL
Beach improvement - ac.			4.5		4.5
Bridges, foot - number			1		1
Dams - yd^3	221				221
Emergency work - man-days				93	93
Eradication of plants - linear mi.	3				3
Experimental plots - ac.			233		233
Fighting forest fires - man-days	216		16	68	300
Fire breaks - mi.	2	0.5			7
Fire hazard reduction (roadside & trail side) - mi.			2		2
Fireplaces - number			5	39	44
Fire pre-suppression - man-days			232		232
Forest stand improvement - ac.	316	1430	267	521	2534
General clean-up - ac.	140			4	144
Insect pest control - ac.		139	77	261	1199
Landscaping - ac.	7.5	7	1.2		14.7
Latrines - number				4	4
Nurseries - man-days	2754			189	2943
Pipe & tile lines, conduit - linear ft.				900	900
Planting/moving trees & shrubs - ac.		951		22	973
Preparation/transportation of materials - man-days		193	683		876
Public campground development - ac.		1.5	2.5	10.5	14.5
Razing undesirable structures - man-days				32	32
Searching for missing persons - man-days	89				89
Sewage & waste disposal systems - number			1	4	5
Stocking fish - number		20250			20250
Storage facilities - gal.				6000	6000
Stream development/improvement - mi.		20			20
Table & bench combination				75	75
Telephone line - mi.		7	3		10
Timber estimating - ac.		75			75
Trails, foot - mi.		4.5	2	7.5	14
Trails, truck - mi.	602	3	3	3.9	10.8[12]
Tree & plant disease control - ac.	800	404			1204
Water holes - number		4			4

[*]Numerical data from Conservation Reports

Above, Left - Local Experienced Men (LEM) supervise the CCC enrollees building a road through the Ranger School Forest. They used a compressor to power a jackhammer to break up boulders. The men also had a bulldozer. St. Lawrence Historical Society Archives. Above, Right - During the winters of 1936 and 1937 CCC camp S-84 was busy logging.[4] Here, a bulldozer operator is pulling a sled of logs from the forest. St. Lawrence Historical Society Archives

The Army provided sports for the enrollees. Company 229 excelled in athletic competitions winning the District 2 Field Day Championship in September 1934, 1935, and 1936.[13]

The education program was very successful. In 1936 ninety-one boys participated in Syracuse University Home Study courses.[14]

During the fall hunting season of 1936 a tragedy occurred involving two enrollees. Eight CCC boys were returning to camp in a truck after working on the High Falls truck trail. The enrollees were part of a new contingent of 31 boys who recently arrived on October 25 from South Carolina. The truck stopped and offered to give a ride to two hunters: Walter Hughes of Wanakena and removed the cartridges from the feed channel but never checked the chamber. He began climbing onto the truck. Steighter thinking that his 30-40 rifle was empty, accidentally pulled

Benson Mines enrollees began the construction of the Cranberry Lake Ranger cabin. After camp S-84 closed in 1937 the Harrisville camp S-94 completed the construction. Podskoch Collection

the trigger. The gun fired and hit two enrollees Ralph McCall, 24 of Easley, SC and Andrew E. Blanton of Buffalo, SC. Both sat on a bench with their backs against the cab of the truck. The bullet struck Blankton just above his left hip and traveled through his body exiting his right side. The bullet then hit McCall's left forearm because he had his arm around Blankton's shoulder. The bullet caused a deep wound in McCall's arm. They were taken to the Veterans' Sunmount Hospital in Tupper Lake. McCall recovered but Blankton died on the operating table.[14]

Work continued at Cranberry Lake State Campsite in 1937. CCC enrollees began constructing a caretaker's building.[15]

After four years of operation, Camp S-84 closed on October 10, 1937. The Conservation Department stated the camp closed because work at the Wanakena Ranger School was nearly completed and it was "impracticable to keep the camp for another year."[16]

Jean Grimm, Town of Fine historian, stated: "The CCC buildings were moved to Star Lake during the early 1940s when Jones and Laughlin reopened the Benson Mine."

In 1963 the Benson Mines' CCC alumni that regularly met in Massena planned on getting together to celebrate the 30th anniversary of the founding of the camp. The following men planned the event: James Frank, George C. Hoyer, G. R. Widrick, Delon Sharlow, Joseph Szoybel, Lloys Dupree all of Massena, and Harry McCuney of Moira.17 The alumni group held the reunion on May 23, 1964 in Massena and 50 former members and their wives attended. This group had another reunion on May 21, 1966 in Gouverneur and decided to place a historical marker at the former camp site. A plaque was placed on a rock that

Clockwise from Left - On July 28, 1968 CCC alumni gathered with their families and friends at the site of camp S-84 to dedicate a monument and plaque to honor the men who worked in the surrounding forests. The site is now a public picnic area that is maintained by the state. St. Lawrence Historical Society Archives. Most of these 12 enrollees are dressed for dinner after a hard day's work in the forests. Some might be off for a trip to town for a movie, a bar, or restaurant. St. Lawrence Historical Society. Enrollees are taking a coffee break working in the winter on Ranger School land. I'll bet some are saying, "Why the heck did I ever sign up for this job. I wish I were back home in the city with my friends." Wayne Allen

stated: "Original Site Camp S-84 Civilian Conservation Corps 1933-1938." It listed the men who contributed to the cost of the bronze plaque. A dedication ceremony was held on July 28, 1968 and the alumni and their families had a picnic at the site, which is maintained by the Ranger School as a public picnic ground.

MEMORIES

Richard Rummel in his article: "Roosevelt's Tree Army, The Civilian Conservation Corps," described the history of the CCC camp in St. Lawrence County in the April 1990 issue of "The Quarterly" for the St. Lawrence Historical Society. Rummel states the some enrollees, like Leon LaDuke, told him that some of the camp doctors were not liked. He said that the Wanakena doctor, a Mr. Stimentidus, was sadistic in checking for venereal disease and lice and caused more fear in the young men than curing. One of the Benson Mines foreman, former logger Al Snyder from Star Lake, stated the men had no respect for the same camp doctor. "Whenever he would come into camp, the recruits would say 'quack, quack, quack,' which would send the doctor off with a complaint to the captain. The captain told him, 'Doctor, if you can tell me which ones are quacking I'll punish them!' The boys made sure he couldn't."

Another story told by Rummel was that some of the boys went to the town of Benson Mines to Spane's Bar. It was the local watering hole for loggers. The CCC boys said it was noted for "hi-jinks and forbidden behavior." One night the boys said things got wild and they locked the female owner in the kitchen and the boys had a grand old time.

Alex Capiello
"Letters from Camp"

Alex Capiello, a CCC boy from Massena, wrote letters to his hometown newspaper, Massena Observer, and they were published as a column called "Massena Boys at Benson Mines." Here are some excerpts from his letters to get an idea of some of the daily activities and humor of living in a CCC camp. In his first letter published on April 12, 1934 Capiello wrote about his group's first few days:

"We arrived at Benson Mines at 11:30 Thursday morning. We all got examined and all the fellows from Massena passed. The boys all like it here so far. Pat Trimboli and Steve White are going out for basketball. Wilbert Sovie is assistant leader in our barracks. Guy Lashomb is the big eater in camp. He takes three big helpings at every meal. Wally Weaver, Pat Trimboli and Charles Empey went to Benson Mines last week and they woke up the whole barracks when they came in We are all in the same barracks except Joe Garcia, and Edward Opal. Cecil Brothers is running around with girls already. Lloyd Laclair says he is working so hard that he is losing his fat.

"There are five barracks, mess hall, recreation hall, hospital, headquarters, shower, and washroom in our camp. In our recreation hall we have two libraries, a radio, ping-pong table, a place to play handball, two pianos, and a store.

"It rained all day Friday and the place is just a great big mud hole. We worked all day in the rain cleaning up the camp. We all have the afternoon off so I am going to Star Lake with the gang. I'll say so long till next week."

In his May 3, 1934 letter Capiello wrote: "It snowed all day Thursday and part of Friday. Last night it was only 20 degrees above zero and we all used our extra blanket for covering so we would not freeze.

"We are still cutting brush and trees, getting the land ready for planting trees. Some of the boys started digging holes last week. The ranger said that they did about 18,000 holes a day. Last week they started drawing in the trees that we are going to plant. Three truckloads from Syracuse brought 40,000 trees. They were all put in little trenches and covered with dirt. They will stay there until we are ready to plant them.

"Wally Weaver sprained his thumb boxing last night so they let him stay in camp to peel potatoes. Lloyd Laclair goes to bed with the chickens every night and gets up with the roosters. Guy Lashomb is still the champion eater in our barracks. Trimm is the musician of our camp; he is always pounding on the piano. Joe Szybal spends most of his spare time playing cards. Roy Lavine walks around camp as if he owned the place. Joe Garcia and Edward Opal said that if we didn't have spring soon they were going to move down south.

"There is some kind of a sickness going around the camp. None of the fellows from Massena have caught it yet. The infirmary is full and they had to partition off part of our barracks to use for a hospital. Nobody was allowed to go home Saturday because of the throat disease that is spreading around.

"I only have about 10 minutes before the lights go out so I say so long until next week. Alex Capiello."

In his May 10, 1934 letter Capiello wrote that his group just got back from fighting a forest fire. The fire spread quickly because of the dried leaves and grass and high winds from the west. The Ranger School water pump and hose was a big help in extinguishing the fire. The crew put out the blaze in two hours.

"Last week the frogs started singing and the weather has been nice all week. Most of the fellows are sunburned. Lloyd Laclair wants somebody to send him an airplane so he will not have to climb the hills to go to work. Guy Lashomb went home last week and did not come back. Charley Empey is taking his place at the table. He eats three or four plates of everything we have. Last Thursday Steve White worked without his shirt and the sun baked him all over. He did not sleep much that night. We started baseball practice last week. There are four fellows from Massena going out for the camp team. Wally Weaver and Dave Kaner are out for the infield. Harry Bulger and I are going out for the outfield. One of the trucks takes us to the Star Lake baseball diamond. We practice every night except Saturday and

CCC boys are putting out a forest fire by covering the smoldering fire with dirt while the leader on the right supervises the work. St. Lawrence Historical Society

The CCC boys at Benson Mines show off their clean and organized barracks. They had to be ready for inspection each day except on Sundays, a day of rest. St. Lawrence Historical Society Archives

sometimes Sunday.

"This week Captain W. E. McGuire gave an award for the best appearing barracks in the company and our barracks won. We will be awarded a banner to be erected over the front entrance for one week. Also the members of our barracks were treated to ice cream at noon on Saturday.

"Last week most of the fellows were put on planting detail. The ranger that I work for said that we had planted about 120,000 small trees so far and we have about that many more to plant. We have planted white pine, red pine, Scotch pine and spruce. They also have some cedar that we will plant soon.

"Well, I'll have to say so long as the lights go out in ten minutes."

Here is his May 24, 1934 letter: "Hello folks: this is from the Benson Mines, Camp 62, Company 229, New York. The weather is nice up here for the last two weeks. Sometimes when the north wind blows it gets cool enough to snow but it does not blow that often. We are almost through planting trees, only about a week more of planting left. Some of the fellows went to Cranberry Lake to help drag the lake to find Bill North who was drowned about two weeks ago. Later two other fellows that drowned from the Ranger School were pulled up by two fellows from Massena. Harry Bulger found one the first day and Wally Weaver pulled the other one out the next morning.

"Joe Szaybel is still the best card player around camp. Steve White brought up a cake last Sunday and he had it for two minutes and then it was all eaten but the crumbs. The boys who had some of it said it was very good. Charley

Empey went home last Saturday and he said he wasn't going home any more until the Fourth of July because he walked about 20 miles last time. Steve is shoveling dirt on the baseball diamond at the Ranger School and he has raised two blisters. I don't think it was from working but from leaning on the handle too much."

Clyde Anthony Plumadore

Marilyn Hickox of Cortland contacted me and said her father, Clyde Anthony Plumadore, was stationed at six or seven CCC camps: Benson Mines, Newcomb, Lake Placid, Tupper Lake, Speculator, Bolton, and possibly Arietta.

"Dad was born on February 24, 1908 in Malone. He had two brothers and two sisters. His father was a farmer in Moira. My dad had to quit school at about tenth grade to help his father on the farm. His dad had two farmsteads and one tenant farm.

"He got married and had 13 children: Marilyn, Tony, Barbara, Joseph, Daniel, Gary, David, Kathy, Ida, John, Margarite, Diane, and Dean.

"Mom had a rough time with all those kids. Dad would come home once in a while from a CCC camp and he stayed maybe a week. We didn't see much of him. My sisters, brothers, and I picked raspberries and strawberries with my grandmother, Mary Evelyn Plumadore. In the fall we picked green apples to make apple pies and all kinds of berries. Mom was always pregnant. We lived by lamplight on a tenant farm in Moira.

"It was a very hard time for Dad to leave his family. He worked hard for his family.

"At first dad lived in tents at the CCC camp. Then as it got cold they built wooden buildings.

"While at camp Dad had a few jobs. He planted trees, cleared brush, ran equipment, and made fire trails. In the evening Dad and his friends played cards and drank.

"Some weekends he came home. There were guys that he hitched a ride with and sometimes he had to walk the

Clyde Anthony Plumadore worked at six or seven camps as a foreman or LEN, Local Experienced Man. He supervised and trained CCC enrollees. Marilyn Hickox

rest of the way.

"Dad worked with a guy named Henry Saint-Alair. He lived up the road from us and both came home together.

"I remember when I was young there were gypsies who came into our town and other towns in the Adirondacks. They stole things and I even heard rumors that they even stole children to do their chores. The gypsies lived in wagons pulled by horses. Some even had a cow attached to the back of their wagon. They were always looking for things to take.

"Sometimes four to five men and a woman came to a house and asked for food and clothes. Dad would tell them to get out with his gun. If you weren't looking, they'd also steal your garden clean or your cow or pig. If they came at night Grandpa took his Terraplane car (Hudson), turned it around, and shined the lights on the gypsies.

"My dad passed away in 1968 at the age of 60. I wished he had told me more about his work in the CCC.

Emanuel "Manney" Bailey

On August 25, 2006 I drove to Lake Clear to see Emanuel "Manney" R. Bailey at his daughter Lesley Lyon's bed and breakfast called "Sunday Pond." Lesley had written to me about her dad's time in the CCC and invited me to her B & B to meet him. Manney and I sat on the front porch and the 87 year-old told me about his experiences in the CCC.

"I grew up in Clayton, NY. When I was about 15 years old I was interested in visiting my older brother Richard who was in a CCC camp near Benson Mines. During the summer of 1934 my parents, Eugene and Christine, drove me to visit my older brother. The captain let me stay for a week or two and I slept in the barracks with my brother. I remember there was a wood stove in the middle of the large room. In the morning I ate breakfast with the guys in the mess hall. The food was good. The guys gave me clothes to wear. Then the guys went to work at Cranberry Lake. They showed me where the trail to Cat Mountain was and I hiked up there all by myself. I visited the fire tower and talked to the observer. I think he had a horse that he used to get to the tower.

Manny Bailey enjoyed his visits to the Benson Mines where his brother was working and later joined the CCC and worked in Idaho. Cecily Bailey

"I never worked with the CCC guys while visiting my brother. They did reforestation work, and built roads and trails.

"The next year I quit school at 16 because I wanted to join the CCC like my brother. I liked the sound of a dollar a day. That was a lot of money in those days. My uncle was the town clerk in Clayton and I think he fudged my age so that I could get in. You had to be 17 years old.

"In the fall I went to Fishers Landing which is between Alexandria Bay and Clayton on the St. Lawrence River. They had a CCC camp and they were recruiting. They gave me a choice of staying near Clayton or going out west. I wanted to go as far away from Clayton as I could. They had an opening for Coeur d'Alene, Idaho and I chose Idaho.

"I went to the railroad station in Clayton with another fellow who lived on the same road as I did and we got on a troop train. It stopped along the way and picked up other CCC guys. When the train stopped in each state I got off just to say I touched the ground in each state. It took a good week to get to Coeur d'Alene.

"When we arrived they took us by truck to a forest ranger's camp that was way out in the forests just like the Benson Mines camp. They assigned me to be a truck driver. I drove a REO Speed Wagon stake body truck. They couldn't understand how I knew how to drive. I told them I learned just by fooling around with my dad's milk truck. I transported men into the mountains to work. I'd make one or two trips to bring back poles that were used for telephone and electric lines. Then I'd go back to pick up the guys and bring them back to camp.

"To make some extra money I'd carry fire wood into the barracks for the guys who didn't want to do their job. Forest rangers let me use my truck to carry wood back to the camp. They'd give me 10 cents per man and there were 30 guys in each barrack. I carried wood for two different barracks and got $3 for each barracks. With the extra money plus the $20 I earned each month from the CCC, I sent the money home to help my parents. I could also buy some extra ready-made cigarettes instead of rolling them myself.

Camp S-84 is working on the working on Wanakena truck trail. They are improving the side ditch and culvert. NYS Archives

"The canteen sold cigarettes, candy, and gum but we couldn't afford much.

"For entertainment we got 'liberty,' a chance to go to town where we went roller skating and just hung out with the guys.

"The guys liked to play jokes on each other. One time they hauled up my mattress, bedding, and clothes using the rope on the flagpole. When I got to my bunk in the barracks I had an empty bed. So I knew somebody played a trick on me. I went outside and there was a big full moon out. I looked up at it and saw my duffle bag and mattress hanging way up at the top of the pole. I got my stuff down by cutting the rope with an axe.

"The next day the officers couldn't believe the rope was cut down. They wanted to know who cut it but nobody squealed. They had to take the pole down. All the guys were happy because they didn't have reveille or retreat for quite a while.

"Reveille began at 6 am. We cleaned up and went to breakfast. Then we got in a circle around the flagpole and they called out each guy's name. It took about ten minutes. Then we went to work.

"The forest ranger, Johnny Sides, also pulled a trick on me. One day he sent me back to camp with a load of logs. He gave me directions but he didn't tell me about one of the turns and I wound up in Missoula, Montana. I ran out of gas and I was worried about the 40 guys who were waiting in the woods for a ride back to camp. So I talked to the gas station owner into giving me a tank of gas with the promise I'd get the money back come hell or high water. It took me all night to get back to camp.

"I took my keys to the forest ranger and said, 'I presume I lost my job.' He responded, 'I was testing you to see if you could survive on your own which you did. I arranged for another truck to come and pick the men and I up.' He also told me the reason I got the truck-driving job in the first place was because the driver before me went over the side of the road and was killed.

"After six months my time was up and I decided to go home.

"When I got home I got a job on the Great Lakes for three years. I was a coal passer. I brought coal to the firemen in the boiler room. During the winter the lakes froze over so I came home and helped my dad deliver milk. Then I joined the U. S. Merchant Marines. I was on tankers and we hauled high-octane gasoline from Norfolk to South America and Europe during WWII.

"After WWII I met Irene Silva at an attended telephone pay station in New London, CT. This was before pay phones had coin slots and you paid an attendant. We fell in love and got married. We had two daughters: Lesley and Cecily. I ran Arrow Paper and Supply Co. till I retired.

"I moved back to the Adirondacks to be close to my daughter in Saranac Lake.

"The CCC enabled me to help my family during the tough times of the Great Depression."

Erastus Tupper's Life in Benson Mine Camp

Erastus Tupper, a member of the Benson Mines camp, wrote weekly letters to the St. Lawrence Plain Dealer about life in his CCC camp. Here are some excerpts from his letters: January 21, 1936 issue.

"Every morning at 6:25 a whistle is blown by a night guard to awaken us to get dressed. At 6:30 a whistle is blown again and every man in the barracks rushes out to answer his name to the barracks leader's call. He answers 'yo' or 'here' and is marked down. This is done to make sure that no man is missing. If by accident you oversleep and don't hear the whistle and the barracks' leader returns to find you asleep, you might get a hard day's work in the kitchen plus the time when your turn comes to take K. P. or kitchen police. You can rest assured that the next time you will get up when the whistle blows. After this, we go to the washroom, wash and return to the barracks. Breakfast at seven o'clock. Everything is on the table. We stand, eight at a table, and when all are in, a whistle blows and we all sit down to eat.

"Then we all go back to the barracks. Each guy sweeps around his bed and puts the dirt in the middle of the floor and each takes turns every morning and picks up the refuse. Then beds are made, and all are exactly the same. They have to be perfect and bed sheets and comforters are all lined with a string. Fire pails are filled to the brim. Everything is spic and span. At eight o'clock a whistle blows again. This is the work call. Newell MacWilliams, senior foreman, calls every man's name under a certain foreman, calls the number of the truck you go to work in, and we all go on the trucks.

Two enrollees roll a log onto a skidway using peavey or cant hook. Later the logs were loaded onto a led and drawn by horse, bull dozer or tractor to a sawmill. St. Lawrence Historical Society

There are about six or seven different details. One detail, the timber survey, is under Ranger Morrow. I will try and explain this work. He has about six men. He has a given number of acres to survey and divides them into six-acre squares using ropes. Every tree has its height measured by instruments, its diameter, its circumference, and the kind of tree it is. Every individual tree is written down. So from acre to acre and from day to day this goes on. This is done to determine which trees grow the best in certain kind of soil and altitude.

"Another detail under William Sequor goes to Peavine swamp on the Cranberry Lake Road. All timber, brush, and debris is cut to within 100 feet of the main road and then burned. Perhaps the best timber is saved. This is done to prevent forest fires from passing vehicles, etc. Men with saws, axes, and log carriers are constantly busy. This goes on day to day.

"Herbert Mahl has a detail on what is called the Five Hundred acre lot. This reminds us of the old lumbering days. Some boy or man, as you will, is constantly cutting logs. Immediately a crew sets to work lumbering the trees out and cutting it into a 16-foot log. Another crew with a tractor drags three or four logs at a time to a skidway. Here some men are waiting with peavies or cant hooks and it is a matter of seconds and the log is on a skidway. The tractor goes back for more logs, so the men on the skidways have to work or the logs will be a mess to roll up. Another crew is constantly burning brush or limbs and they sure are busy. Still we have a crew that cuts the trees that can't be made into logs into cordwood. The saws are running from morning till night and one man has a sweet time keeping the saws fit. I think that is sufficient for that detail.

"Another detail under 'Pop' Collins was up on the shore of Cranberry Lake. His men were drilling rocks with drill and hammer to clear a part of the shoreline and nearby woods for recreational purposes in the summer. Rocks were broken with a stone hammer and placed along the bank in a slanting wall. How those men did work with stone hammer and drill. I know something about it because I had to drill myself.

"Another crew works on truck trails. These roads are built so that we can get into the forest easier and carry materials with us in case of a forest fire. I think more roads will be built. And building roads through swamps and woods is not any easy job.

"In the past summer a detail called stream improvement was at work. This was for the benefit of our sportsmen. All brush was cut away from small stream banks. They carried logs out and threw even small twigs out of the choked stream. Small log dams with aprons were built. I liked this type of work myself. Also in the summer, thousands upon thousands of trees were planted. Most were evergreen trees.

"There is yet a detail that thins our forests. All poplar, fire cherry, and so called useless wood was cut. As these trees are cut, it gives more light and moisture to the trees we wish to conserve, and it is surprising after a past year of thinning how much the other trees grow as compared to former years.

"At 11:30 am, all details go to the camp and prepare for dinner. On the bulletin board we look at the day's inspection. Each barracks is inspected every day and the one with the least demerits, or highest mark, gets ice cream for dinner on Saturday. That causes competition. We have mess at noon and then rest until one o'clock and go to work. We come in from work at five o'clock. From then until nine o'clock we do as we choose, play cards or go to our recreation hall and practice boxing or anything we like.

"Lights are out at nine o'clock and then all the noise in the barracks must cease. If you must make noise, a place is provided in the recreation hall where lights are on all night.

"We have an infirmary where all medical cases are taken care of.

"Saturday is ours provided we lost no time in the week. If we lose a half a day, we work Saturday afternoon. If we missed all day, we work all day Saturday. If it is more time than we can make up, that's our good luck as we get paid just the same.

"We have a music teacher in camp who will teach you to play any instrument you like. If you have an instrument, he will teach you after working hours."

John "Jack" L. Young

Robert L. Young of Syracuse contacted me and told me his father, John "Jack" L. Young, was in three CCC camps.

"My father went through two years in Potsdam High School and quit to help his family. He was the eldest of three brothers and three sisters. His father, Leonard, had a hard time getting jobs. When he did get a job he worked as a laborer.

"Dad first joined the CCC on April 9, 1937 and went to the Benson Mines camp S-84, Company #229. Every month his mother, Gertrude got $25 sent to her. While there he planted trees and did fire hazard reduction projects. After his six months he left on October 9, 1937. It was also when the Benson Mines camp closed.

"On October 14, 1937 Dad signed up again and he and his Company #229 were shipped by train to camp F-188 Emida, Idaho. The project was F-188. After six months he left on March 31, 1938 and went home.

"Then nine months later Dad enlisted again on January 10, 1939 and went to the Harrisville, NY, camp S-94, Company #1289. After almost a year Dad was discharged on December 23, 1939.

Jack Young of Potsdam joined the CCC to help his family He started in Camp S-84 Benson Mines, then to Emida, Idaho and finally to Harrisville where he is pictured in front of the Education Building where he took evening classes. Each enrollee had a tag at the bottom of his bed. Here is Jack Young's tag. Bob Young

"Dad married Jessie M. MacTurk on August 15, 1941. They had four boys and four girls.

"My father got a job at St. Joseph Lead Co. in Balmat, NY. He worked as a carpenter until his death in 1975."

Daniel Alamond

On June 22, 2010 I met Daniel Alamond at a CCC reunion at the Oneida Historical Society in Utica. He told the audience about his experiences at two CCC camps: North Brookfield and Benson Mines. I called him on June 30 and he gave me more information on his life and experiences in the CCC.

"I was born in 1919 in Syracuse. My father Donald drove teams of horses. Then he moved our family back to Tupper Lake where he lived originally. Dad missed the logging and went back to working in the woods. He worked for the Oval Wood Dish Co. My mother, Margaret Noland, had seven children: Donald, Philip, Marie, Dora, Ernest, myself, and Beatrice.

"My parents separated and she moved the children to Utica when I was five years old. During the Great Depression my family was on welfare. I only had six years of parochial school and then went to public school and quit after seventh grade. They put me to work building trolley tracks in New Hartford and I also worked on WPA. My education came from whatever books I could get my hands on. I took a lot of night school classes, too.

"The CCC was very popular at that time and my brother Ernest went in first in about 1934. He was in Fayetteville.

"When I was only 16 I joined the CCC in the summer of 1935 and was sent to North Brookfield down by Sherburne and Norwich. I guess because we were on the welfare rolls they didn't push the age limits. There were some other guys from the Utica area who joined with me: Jimmy Jenkins, Frank Cizek, Joseph Alberico, Joe Garon, Pat and Mike Cirasuolo. At this camp we mostly cut wood and built roads, fire ponds, and horse trails. We also planted trees. In fact, we planted one million in a year.

"The CCC taught me discipline and how to cut wood. We learned how to get along and work as a team. We had teams of four. Two used a crosscut saw and two did the trimming with axes. We skidded it out to the main road, hauled it to camp, and used a buzz saw to cut firewood.

"While at camp I did have to go to the infirmary

a couple of times because I was constipated a lot. I asked Charley Zabek who worked in the infirmary for castor oil. He gave it to me and then took off. He knew what to expect.

"There were no sports teams at camp. We set up a boxing ring. The guy who ran the PX was a Golden Glover and he was the referee. I had a friend who shot woodchucks for fun.

"They closed the Brookfield camp in 1936 and I was transferred to Benson Mines. When I got there I saw a notice looking for volunteers to go five miles into the woods and work at a side camp. I signed up.

"They took us by truck from the village of Wanakena on a wobbly 2-mile access road to the base of the trail. Our first job was cutting brush along this trail. We got to our camp by foot and had to carry everything, even a heavy cook stove. We set up camp in a clearing where there was an old logging camp. There were even old shoes laying around. Our camp was right below the Cat Mountain fire tower that was on a big rock. One time I went up to visit the observer. He was an old man who had a crutch for his missing leg. Every once and a while we heard the howl of a black panther. We couldn't see it or the tower, only the sharp cliff where the cat came out and sounded off.

"Our group's assignment was to maintain the trails that connected the five ponds. Our camp was on the last pond.

"My buddy and I volunteered to carry food from the beginning of the trail to camp. It was a 6-mile round trip and we made the trip every day. We got fresh provisions from a truck that delivered food and whatever we needed each weekday. We carried supplies in pack baskets. I was young and didn't mind the load. We didn't

Daniel Alamond (left) and a group of CCC enrollees from the Benson Mines camp spent the summer of 1936 maintaining trails from Wanakena to five ponds near Cat Mountain. (this is called Five Pond Wilderness Area today) Daniel is sharpening his scythe at a side camp near Cat Mountain. Daniel Alamond

have to rush. My buddy was taking a health class and picked wild flowers along the way. We saw a lot of deer and a few bear. One time we stopped and a bear got a whiff of us. It stood on its hind legs and then went off.

"The food was good. We didn't pay too much attention to what we ate. We ate a lot of hot dogs and canned goods. We also had a lot of chicken, beef and vegetables. I even liked the S O S. A lot of the food was produced by local farmers. This gave the farmers some assistance and a few dollars in their pockets.

"In the evenings we used to pick up deer trails and follow them. One took a sharp turn and went off to the right and it made the trail shorter when we carried supplies. There were five ponds near there. One was really loaded with bullheads. We also went to a clear pond. You could see to the bottom and there were trout there. I also fished with the forest ranger.

"On the weekends some guys went back to the Benson Mines camp but my buddy from North Brookfield and I just hung around camp. We caught frogs and bullheads and fried the frog legs and fish at camp. One time we got a porcupine. If you ever try to skin one - what a job!

"I left the CCC before my six months were up because I was offered a job. I went home but it didn't work out. I never should have quit. The CCC gave me something to do and I helped my family.

"I finally got a job and worked at Ken-Wel Sporting Goods as a tennis raquett stringer. Then I worked at Julliard Textile Company in NY Mills.

"I was drafted into the Army in 1943 and stationed at Fort Dix, Fort Knox, and Fort Upton. I was in a demonstration outfit and trained others. Then they sent me to radio school and I became an instructor in radio repair and operation.

"After the war I came back to work at Juilliard Textile Company. In 1947 I married Mable Gamache and we had three children: Carolyn, Daniel, and Paula.

"When the Juilliard Mills closed I went to Bendix Corp. Stayed there for 29 years, half of that time as a experimental assembler. I retired in 1982.

"I went up to my old camp in North Brookfield a couple times. It was hard finding the dam we built but finally found it. I also saw the trees we planted.

"I thought the CCC was good. Those were tough times and I was just hanging around doing nothing. In the CCC I had food and pay. It was a good thing. We also got good training and an education."

"A C. C. C.'s Lament"
By Bob Salton and Red Blake

A bunch of C. C. C. were sitting in their camp
It was near October and the weather cold and damp,
Sez one, I'm going home boys, I thought I'd be glad;
But as the time draws near boys, I'm feeling sort of sad.

I'm going home boys as soon as I draw my pay,
I'm going home boys, I'm leaving Saturday.
I left my home last April, it seems so long ago,
I don't know what they'd do with us, I don't know where we'd go.

When I joined this outfit my spirits were real high.
We meant to lick the depression, we swore to do or die.
They sent us to the barracks, to learn some soldier tricks
All of us were greenhorns, most of us were hicks.

They dressed us up in O. D.'s, we learned what G. I. Meant.
They made us march in columns, everywhere we went,
Then they gave us denims, and put us to work,
That's where we learned of K. P. every time we'd shirk.

They sent us to Camp 20, out where the trees are thick,
Some boys couldn't take it, these pansies didn't stick
At first it was no cinch boys, the life was hard and rough
The big boys grew still bigger, the little grew tough.

We learned to swing an ax, boys, and fight old blister rust.
We got to using mattocks and raising lots of dust,
We learned to tell a maple or poplar from birch,
We even stocked the stream boys, with lots of trout and perch.

But now my time is up pals, my last ax I have swung.
I've answered my last whistle, the last chow bell has rung.
I'm going to leave you fellows, whom I have known so well,
And when we meet again boys, not one of us can tell.

And so here is my hand boys, there's a teardrop in my eye.
I'm feeling sort of blue boys, I have to say good-bye,
I'll always remember my days in the C. C. C.
And if we meet again boys, the drinks will be on me.

CHAPTER 7
BOLTON LANDING, ALMA FARM & BURGESS FARM

HISTORY

As one drives along Route 9N seven miles north of Bolton Landing the road is surrounded with majestic white pines. Most are unaware that over 80 years ago this was farm and pasture land of the Alma Farm, one of the best dairy farms in northern New York. Three CCC camps in this area dramatically changed the landscape during the 1930s by planting thousands of trees on the abandoned farmland.

Norman Boas and Barbara Meyer describe the history of the area in Alma Farm: An Adirondack Meeting Place. The farm consisted of 1,000 acres located along Rt. 9N and Padanarum Road. Theodore and Helene Meyer owned the large farm from 1874-1925. Many regarded it as one of the best in New York State because of the quality of its produce and its nationally renowned herd of Jersey cows imported from England. On its 120 acres of tillable land it produced fine oats, hay, buckwheat, and potatoes. Some of the buildings were: a 30-room farmhouse for hired workers, a 40' x 140' cow barn, a 31' x 70' horse barn, an icehouse, tool barn, and pigpens. Its maple orchard produced quality syrup and honey was produced in its apiary. In 1925 the Meyer family sold the farm to the state.

The Conservation Department selected this farmland in the town of Bolton, Warren Co. for the site of three CCC camps during the spring and fall of 1933: The Conservation Reports list Camp S-57 at the Alma Farm, Camp S-66 at the Burgess Farm, and Camp S-82 at Bolton Landing.[1] The camps did reforestation work, fought fires, constructed & expanded state parks on Lake George, fought insects, and built hiking and truck trails.

Since the state had no specific description or maps for the location of the first two camps I spent three years interviewing Ted Caldwell (Bolton town historian), local residents, and CCC alumni and their families to locate these camps.

I learned that the first camp, S-57 Company 205, was established on June 7, 1933 on the Alma Farm about eight miles from the village of Bolton Landing in the hamlet of Wardboro. The Bolton Historical Society gave me a copy of Carl Lamb's "A History of Wardboro." It said that the men in Camp S-57 lived in tents on Padanarum Road near the southwest corner of the "Million Dollar Bridge" that goes over Padanarum Brook. This site was a little past the Alma farmhouse.

I was determined to find the exact location of the camp site. I drove up 9N to Padanarum Road. As I drove on the dirt road a pickup truck slowly approached. I hailed the driver, Jim Grey, a retired state policeman who had a cabin up the road. I asked him if he new anything about the CCC camp site. Jim took me to the "Million Dollar Bridge" and said he had heard that the CCC boys camped below the bridge. I only saw huge white pine trees and no evidence of a camp. Jim's location was the same as the one mentioned in Carl Lamb's book.

The following year historian Ted Caldwell drove me to Padanarum Road to

Bolton Landing camp S-84 in the fall of 1934. The wooden buildings were built in the fall of 1933 on the old Burgess farm that was part of the large Alma Farm. The road on the left led to Route 9N. The mess hall, office, rec hall, infirmary and showers/bathrooms were on the left and the five barracks were on the right. On the hill to the right were the garage and the tall water tower. Joe & Betty Demates

48

Bolton historian Ted Caldwell helped author search for the three Bolton Landing CCC campsites on the old Alma Farm. Podskoch Collection

show me what he thought was the site of Camp S-57. As we drove down the dirt road Ted said, "This was all part of the Alma Farm. The CCC boys planted these trees about 75 years ago."

We drove about a mile and he stopped by a metal pole gate on the right. He showed me the huge cellar hole of the farmhouse. Then we walked a little farther to a flat area below a hill. "This is where the huge barn was. You can see some of the stone foundation." Then he showed me a flat area to the right of the barn. "This is where I think the CCC camp was."

Then I found a picture of the tent camp that Joe DeMatties of Queensbury had from his father-in-law, Howard Barnes. Barnes had been an enrollee at the camp in 1933.

I did not have the exact location of the tent camp site but I was now certain the men did camp on Padanarum Road near the Alma Farmhouse site and they planted thousands of white pine trees on most of the flat land. The Au Sable Record-Post reported on October 12, 1933 that the Bolton camps planted 165,500 trees. They also worked

An Army officer standing near one of the army tents being aired out during the day. This camp was on the old Alma Farm near Bolton Landing. Joe & Betty DeMatties

fighting insects that destroyed trees.

As winter approached in 1933, Camp S-57 closed on November 17, 1933. Most of the enrollees ended their six-month tour and went home. Company 205 transferred to Cherry Plain where they worked with Company 219 constructing a 550-foot concrete dam across the Black River Valley.[2]

The second camp, S-66 Company 204, was established on

Camp S-66 was located on the Burgess farm near Route 9 N. The paths along the tents were lined with whitewashed rocks. The flagpole is at the top of the small hill. Bolton Landing Historical Society

May 27, 1933 on the old Burgess Farm. This farm had been acquired by Alma Farm owner, Theodore Meyer, and had been part of the 1,000 acre Alma Farm. Before coming to the Adirondacks, the CCC enrollees began training and conditioning at Fort Slocum (located on two islands on the western end of the Long Island Sound on April 23, 1933. Captain Joseph B. Hafer and Lieutenant Sweeney left Fort Slocum with 28 men to set up camp. They arrived on May 23, 1933 at the Burgess Farm. Four days later, the remaining 161 recruits arrived at Fort Slocum. They lived in tents during the summer and most of the fall[3] until the site was abandoned November 17, 1933.

Now I had to find the location of S-66. During the summer of 2009, Ted Caldwell helped me again in my search. He thought the camp was just before the quarry and pond on the east side of Rt. 9N at Clay Meadows. We drove to the site and he showed me the old cellar hole of the Henry Burgess farm. Ted said that a hundred years ago the forest was farmland. "All these white pine trees were planted by the CCCs. That pond and quarry on 9N was where construction workers blasted the stone to build the new road over Tongue Mountain that they completed in 1927."

After studying some 1933 camp pictures Ted and I decided Camp S-66 was at another Burgess farm owned by Amariah Burgess. His farm was a little farther up on Rt. 9N past the pond and stone quarry. Ted showed me where old Rt. 9N had traveled over a bridge crossing Northwest Bay Brook. Only the two old stone bridge abutments remained on both sides of the brook. The farm and Camp S-66 were across the old bridge and on the left side of the road.

During the late summer and fall wooden buildings were built near the tents at Camp S-66. By mid November

This October 1934 group photo of Camp S-82 shows the enrollees in front of the camp entrance. The CCC boys built a log entrance and the barracks are on the right and the mess hall and other buildings are on the left. Floyd Pickett

1933 the tent camps S-57 and S-66 on the old Alma Farm were closed due to the approaching winter and the men in S-66 moved to new wooden buildings of Camp-S-82 on the Amariah Burgess farm. The men from S-57 moved to Cherry Plain.

Ted Caldwell took me to see the location of Camp S-82. We drove about a half-mile North on 9N and he showed me a sign on the left, "Site of Civilian Conservation Corps Camp S-82." We parked by the metal gate and walked down a dirt road that was the old Rt. 9N. He pointed out a large flat rock along Northwest Bay Brook and showed me a metal state historical marker:

1830s MORMON ROCK
HERE CONVERTS WERE BAPTISED INTO THE CHURCH OF JESUS CHRIST OF LATTER-DAY SAINTS AFTER HEARING THE GLAD TIDINGS OF THE EVERLASTING GOSPEL.

Ted said, "There were a lot of Mormons in this area during the early 1800s. Then they moved west finally reaching Utah. The CCC boys enjoyed swimming there off Mormon Rock."

We proceeded down the road to a stone abutment. "This was where the old bridge that went over Northwest Bay Brook. All that remain are two quarried stone abutments. This was the way the Army trucks came up 9N from Bolton Landing carrying the CCC boys and supplies to camp."

Then we walked back toward Mormon Rock and turned left up a dirt road. On the left the road was lined with old metal 55-gallon barrels. "This is where Camp S-82 was," said Ted. The main part of the camp was on the left where the land was flat. Ted showed me the indentations in the land on the right where the barracks were. On the left he showed

me some stone foundations, slabs of concrete, and pipes coming out of the ground. This was the site of the mess hall. There was even a cement box used for burning rubbish.

It was at this site over 75 years ago on November 30, 1933 that around 200 enrollees of Camp S-82 celebrated Thanksgiving Day and enjoyed a Thanksgiving dinner in the new mess hall. A few weeks later Capt. John C. Lilienthal assumed command of the camp.[4]

Winfred Codman directed the forestry projects at S-82. Its major work was insect control so it was called a "bug camp." They fought the spread of the gypsy moth, which was moving north from the Hudson River Valley. In 1937 the men spent months scouting for gypsy moth egg masses on trees. The young men cleared more than 125,000 acres in Washington, Warren, and Essex counties. The crews sprayed areas with arsenate of lead to kill the insects.[5]

During the winter of 1938-39 around 50 boys from Bolton Camp spent many winter months along with WPA workers covering 67 miles of road, 22,847 acres of land, and inspected 27,800 trees in Hague in Warren County but their efforts found only one colony and one egg cluster.[6] In 1940 the Bolton Camp received a trophy for "the record for the most acres covered and efficiency each month."[7]

The company also worked to stop the spread of blister rust, which damaged thousands of white pine trees.[8] Foresters learned that the fungi, called blister rust lived on currant and gooseberry bushes (ribes), before it was wafted

These five enrollees were planting white pine trees in 1933 on the old Alma Farm. The young man in the center top row is Joe Morabito. Joann Burgess

up to the white pine trees. LEMs led groups of boys as they searched for ribes that were growing near white pines. In 1933 the men covered 2,240 acres and destroyed 123, 797 ribes near Bolton and Hague.[9] In the spring 1934 they covered 85,000 acres and pulled up bushes within 900' of the white pine trees, thus eliminating the threat.

In 1940 the number of enrollees decreased because there were more available jobs. Thus a small number of men helped fight blister rust in Warren County.[10] The Bolton camp continued to work in the spring of 1941 to control blister rust.

The Ticonderoga Sentinel reported on March 9, 1936 that S-82 worked to eliminate the white pine weevil. They covered approximately 430 acres of white pine plantations during June and July 1935.

In 1933 the Bolton Camp S-82 was also a recreation development camp doing work on and near Lake George. It extended and improved Hearthstone Point campsite about one and one-half miles north of Lake George (village) on Rt. 9N. It also did riprapping on state-owned islands on Lake George to protect them from erosion and improved the campsites there. On Tongue Mountain they constructed and improved trails for hikers and horseback riding.[11]

In 1936 S-82 continued enlarging the campsites at Hearthstone Point and Lake George Battleground.[12] The following year they repaired and enlarged the old Cheney cottage (named after former caretaker William Cheney) and made it into a combination office and residence. Work on the cabin continued in 1938. They

also helped with the clean up of 41 pines destroyed by a windstorm at the Lake George Battlefield.[1]

In 1939 the men began building the caretaker's headquarters at Rogers Rock campsite, approximately three miles north of Hague.[14] The next year they developed Glen Island three miles east of Bolton Landing on Lake George.[15]

On December 14, 1939 the Ticonderoga Sentinel reported that CCC boys continued working at Rogers Rock State Park at the new campsite at Cook's Bay. Here they built a 30,000-gallon circular concrete tank for drinking water that was pumped from the lake and installed an 18,000-gallon tank for the sewage system. The rangers' cabin was now complete and in use. That winter about 75 boys were working on three miles of road and concrete culverts, which was the camp's biggest project in 1940. They also continued work at Hearthstone Point and Lake George Battleground.

In 1940 work crews enjoyed their daily three-mile boat trip from Bolton Landing to Glen Island where they built the ranger's headquarters, which had two living quarters for the ranger and a post office. They also built a workshop, commissary, icehouse, and shed.[16] In 1941 the camp continued working at Rogers Rock campsite.[17]

Camp S-82 also constructed truck trails at campsites. At Rogers Rock they built .7 miles from 1939-1940 and worked during the next year on 1.5 more miles. At Hearthstone Point they constructed 1.2 miles.18 The Ticonderoga Sentinel on March 9, 1936 reported the CCC camp constructed a mile of truck trails near Butler Pond south of Lake George. The forest surrounding the pond was owned by the city of Glens Falls.

Above, Left - The Bolton Landing camp built most of the ranger cabins at the state parks on Lake George. This is the ranger cabin at Rogers Rock State Park. Podskoch Collection. Above, Right - The Bolton Landing CCC camp built this beautiful ranger cabin on Glen Island 2 mi. NE of the village of Bolton Landing. Campers must travel by boat to register at the camp office and select a campsite on the nearby islands. Here canoers in the 40s-50s visiting the island. There is a camp store and post office at Glen Island. DEC Archives.

During the summer and fall of 1935 the CCC boys improved the ski run on Prospect Mountain. The boys worked on the upper trail on state land, while the Lake George Winter Association improved the trail on private land. Skiers accessed the 2.5-mile run by driving up Big Hollow Road.[19]

The Bolton camp did many stream improvement projects. They cleaned brooks, riprapped banks of streams, and made dams that created breeding pools for trout. The company established a side camp at Pharaoh Lake where the boys created a dam to raise the lake to protect the spawning ground of the native trout.

Camp S-82 helped local communities deal with natural disasters. In the spring of 1936 a stream near camp flooded and washed out roads. The CCC boys quickly responded in helping to repair the damaged areas.[20] In the March 26, 1936 issue of The Ticonderoga Sentinel it stated that about 140 men worked on repairing the Brant Lake Dam that was damaged from the 1936 flooding.

In 1940 Camp S-82 replaced old telephone lines for the fire towers on the Black and Prospect mountains on Lake George.[21]

The removal of fire hazards was an important objective of Camp S-82. The Ticonderoga Sentinel in its June 12, 1941 issue reported that the young men cleared approximately 130 acres along the highway on Tongue Mountain. They removed a 100' wide strip of dead & downed trees and inflammable material on both sides of the road. At this time smokers who threw cigarettes and cigars from their vehicles caused many fires.

In the above issue of The Ticonderoga Sentinel it described how the Bolton Landing camp helped fight forest fires. It reported that the spring of 1941 was very dry and a stubborn fire raged on Cook Mountain west of Uncas-on-Lake George. The Bolton camp worked with forest ranger Grover Smith and fire warden John McKee of Hague. The fire destroyed about 15 acres of woods.

The Army provided athletic activities for the enrollees. The Town of Bolton shared its athletic facilities with the CCC camp. The boys used the gym in the winter for basketball and the baseball field in the summer. S-82 also had boxing competitions and some of the men entered Golden Gloves competitions.[22]

The Army held Field Days for the camps to participate with one another. On August 21, 1934 Field Days were held at the Essex County Fairgrounds. Port Henry was the host, and the camps at: Bolton Landing, Warrensburg, Speculator, and Canajoharie took part. The boys competed in baseball games, track & field events, and swimming contests at the Westport beach.[23]

The camp sponsored dances at the Bolton Landing High School. The Ticonderoga Sentinel reported on August 1, 1935 that a dance was to be held on August 8, 1935 at 8:30 pm. "All ladies will be guests of the company but there will be a charge of fifty cents for gentlemen." Music and refreshments were included along with the square dances.

During the boys' free time they played pool and cards in the recreation building, which had a PX/Canteen where the boys bought candy, soda, cigarettes, toothpaste, razors, etc. The camp had its own movie projector and showed weekly movies. Enrollees also raised vegetables and flowers in the camp garden.[24]

The Army provided the camp with education classes. The camp boasted a library with 2,000 books, a mimeograph machine, and a printing press where the boys wrote & published their monthly newspaper called "Kamp Krier." Men converted a garage into an arts and crafts shop for those interested in making projects.[25]

On July 17, 1941 The Ticonderoga Sentinel reported that the Federal government provided money for summer classes in the Warrensburg School for the Bolton camp. The boys learned skills in operating the drill press, planer, lathe, and welding.

Camp S-82 closed on October 31, 1941. The state hired Frank Leonbruno, a former CCC boy, to serve as watchman. Later all the buildings were removed with the lumber going to Conservation Department projects.

On August 12, 1997 nine Bolton CCC alumni joined DEC officials in dedicating Alma Farm Park near the intersection of Rt. 9N and Padanarum Road with a sign commemorating the 1,000-acre Alma Farm homestead. The sign read:

"The Alma Farm Park
Site of the 1,000 acre farm owned by Theodore and Helen Meyer, 1874-1925
Site of the Civilian Conservation Corps Camp S-82 and (white pine) plantations 1933-1941.
In memory of the Alma Farm and those who loved it."

The state built a picnic area with tables and fireplaces. Today the farm is part of the Lake George Wild Forest Management Area.

MEMORIES

Joseph Morabito

Jo Ann Burgess from Bolton Landing contacted me after reading an article about my search for CCC information in Mark Frost's Chronicle newspaper. We met on July 7, 2006 at the McDonald's in Warrensburg and Jo Ann shared pictures and stories of her father, Joseph Morabito, in the CCC.

"My father was a member of Camp 61 in Bolton Landing. Dad was with the first contingent that arrived from Long Island in 1933. He passed away this January at the age of 92. It is a shame that your article did not come sooner as he had so much to tell. Here are some clippings and photos of his stay. Also there are about four men in this area who worked at the camp.

"My father, Guissepe 'Joseph' was one of 13 children of Italian immigrants. Dad was born in 1913 in Blairsville, PA where his father, Rocco, worked in the coal mines.

"Then Dad's family moved to Jamaica Long Island. His father caned chairs and did masonry work.

"One day Dad came home and my grandfather said, 'Pack a bag and be ready to take a bus. You're joining the CCC.' He did not know where he was going.

"The next morning, April 12, 1933 he was officially enrolled and taken to Fort Slocum, NY a 'staging' camp for training and conditioning. He stayed there till June 30 when he was shipped to Bolton Landing. It took two days to get to camp. I think they traveled by train and then by truck.

In 1933 Joe Morabito joined the CCC and left Long Island. He came to the Burgess Farm camp S-61 and lived in a tent. The camp was on Rt. 9 a few miles north of Bolton Landing. Jo Ann Burgess

"The camp was on the old Burgess farm, seven miles from town. Dad worked fighting blister rust on white pine trees. Dad's job was to mark the trail He'd drop pieces of white paper in a straight line into the woods. The guys each spaced out about 12 feet apart and walked parallel to each other along the trail. They pulled out gooseberry and currant bushes with a long handled stick with a metal hook. One time as Dad was walking he heard a rattle in the grass. He called his buddy Charlie Smith who killed the timber rattlesnake. It was over six feet long and had 17 rattles. They brought it to a taxidermist who found two field mice and a chipmunk in its stomach. Dad told me, 'If a rattlesnake was ever beautiful, that one was. There was hardly a day that a snake wasn't brought into camp.'

"Then Dad got a job working in the kitchen and had the title 'Kitchen Foreman.'

"For recreation Dad played on the camp baseball team. On weekends he and the guys went on trucks to Bolton Landing and went to square and round dances. Sometimes the guys walked to town if they didn't have a ride. It was on one visit that he met my mother and the rest is history as they say.

"The boys liked to swim at the Northwest Bay Brook Outlet. Dad said he had to watch out for water moccasins and puffed adders.

Jo Ann handed me a partial newspaper clipping that only had Aug. 14, 1996. It was an interview of her father describing his work in the mess hall. Joe said at first he shared a room with the head chef but as the enrollees increased there were then six cooks. Joe said the meals at first were "terrible" but then food was purchased from the Mohegan Market in Glens Falls and the food got better. I guess the head chef loved the cooking so much he gained 90 ponds while Joe worked in the kitchen. The camp was allowed to spend 33 cents per man and when they started getting Army surplus food, the guys could eat as much as they wanted.

The first winter was very cold, in fact, one day the temperature was 44 degrees below zero. On that day CCC boys were called to help fight a fire at the corner of Main and Horicon Avenue. The water hoses froze and the Sukman block burned down.

"On one of dad's visits to town he met my mother, Doris French. Dad was 23 and mom was 18 when they got married in 1936. They had two children my brother John and I. Ada Rourke rented them a house in Bolton Landing for ten dollars a-month. There were other CCC boys who married local girls.

"Dad's discharge papers say he was discharged from Camp S-61 on June 30, 1934.

"Dad was very proud of his time at the camp and his accomplishments while at the Bolton camp. After the camp he worked for the Town of Bolton Highway Department. When he sanded the roads on Tongue Mountain he had to go up backwards. He went on to become a very active member of the town. He was a fireman for 35 years, town and school board member, assessor for 25 years, and caretaker for three families on the Mankowski estate called 'Tall Woods.' He worked there until he was 86!! Dad also loved to hunt and fish in his free time.

"Several years ago there was a dedication for the living CCC boys. The DEC had crews in to clean up the old camp site and the road leading to it. It was quite wonderful to see it all and imagine the camp as it was. Then we all went back to the Bolton Town Hall for a lunch and the opportunity to visit and tell stories. The four local CCC boys who had been there have passed away and taken much of the history with them.

Howard Barnes

In the fall of 2007 I gave a CCC presentation at the Crandall Library in Glens Falls and met Joe DeMatties of Queensbury. He was a retired DEC senior forester and his father-in-law, Howard Barnes, had been in the Bolton Landing camp. Joe showed me some of his pictures and invited me to his home to meet his wife Betty.

The house was a beehive of activity with Joe & Betty's grandchildren decorating for Halloween. I asked Betty to tell me about her dad in the CCC.

"My dad was from Mechanicsville. He joined the CCC because he couldn't get a job. He told me he got on a train or truck ride to camp and had no idea where he was going. He wound up at the Bolton Landing camp where they lived in tents.

"Dad was an assistant cook. He went on trips with a driver to town to get supplies. Later on he worked with Frank Leonbruno who was the mess sergeant.

"On the weekends he'd go down to Bolton Landing to go to the movies or get something to eat at a restaurant. One day he saw my mother, Verna Dudley, at a restaurant and started flirting. He followed her home and she said, 'If you don't leave I'll call the cops.' My dad was persistent and didn't leave. Then a policeman pulled up to the house in a Marmon car. Dad probably took off fast when he saw that police uniform. The policeman was our grandfather, Earl Dudley.

"Dad walked to town often to see my mom. Gradually, my mother warmed up to Dad. Three months after they met they wanted to get married but Dad's family was Catholic and Mom's was Baptist so they eloped.

Above - Howard Barnes was one of the 200 enrollees who lived in Army tents at the CCC camp S-57 seven miles north of Bolton Landing. The camp was on the Burgess farm during the spring and fall of 1933. The tents had wood stoves to keep the men warm during the fall. Betty & Joe DeMatties. Right - Howard Barnes of Mechanicsville worked as a cook at the Bolton Landing CCC camp from 1933-34. He has his knife and cleaver in the ground in front of him. Betty & Joe DeMatties

They drove to Stillwater and got married on September 26, 1934. They lived in Bolton Landing and Dad worked for my grandfather Earl Dudley, who was involved in many things."

Joe added, "Earl had a huge ice business. He employed 30-40 men to cut ice on Lake George in the winter. They stored it in a three-story icehouse behind their house at the corner of Goodman and Brook Street. Earl also had a garbage business and was a constable in town."

Recently I called Betty's sister, Gertrude Remington of Brant Lake. She said: "My mother's first child, Earl, died after birth. Then I was born. My parents and I moved to Mechanicsville and lived there for a while before moving to Balston Spa. Dad worked for the GE plant in Schenectady. My brother Howard and sister Betty were then born. In 1942 we moved back to Bolton Landing to live with my grandfather. He was alone and was happy to have us live with him. Dad worked again for my grandfather. He was fortunate to get a job at Imperial Paper & Color Corporation in Glens Falls and worked there till he retired. Then both he and my mother worked for a rich family on Lake George doing maintenance and housework. My father died at the age of 88 in 1999."

Joe added, "Howard always said good things about the CCC. He enjoyed getting together with two local CCC guys: Fred Lethridge, who lived next door to him, and Frank Leonbruno. There were two CCC reunions in Bolton Landing and Howard really had a good time seeing his old friends."

Floyd Pickett

On November 16, 2007 I drove to Queensbury to visit Floyd Pickett at his home on Mountain View Road. When I knocked on his front door an elderly, rotund man greeted me. He invited me into his living room and with his walker made his way to his easy chair. Floyd, a very kind and friendly man, proudly showed a picture of him and his wife. Since she had died he was all alone as they didn't have any children.

Floyd pointed out a plaque on his wall, an award he received for driving veterans to the Veterans' Hospital in Albany. He also showed me newspaper clippings about his efforts in helping local veterans. Then I asked him to tell me about his early life and his days in the CCC.

"I was born in Glens Falls on June 11, 1914. My dad, Clifford, was a slate roofer and my mother's name was Maude. I was an only child. I had trouble breathing because of asthma. When I went to school I'd pass out on the floor and I had nosebleeds. The school didn't want me there. I didn't get better till I was about 11 or 12 and then started school. It was hard being in first grade and being so

Floyd Pickett sitting in his Queensbury living room reminiscing about life and experiences in the CCC camp in Bolton Landing in 1934. Podskoch Collection

old. I finally caught up in school.

"Dad was out of work and we didn't have much food. Dad tried to get welfare but couldn't because he owned a house. I told the teacher one day that I didn't want to go home because I didn't have anything for breakfast and I was hungry. I lied just to see what would happen. She went to the principal and told him my story. He talked to me and said you're going to have food for dinner. He ordered something from the cooking class for me to eat. It was two pork chops. I ate one and told the principal I'd keep the other for my mother. The principal said, 'I'm not going to have a boy go to school without food. Don't worry you'll have something for you and your family.'

"The principal called the welfare office and the next day a man came to school and talked to me. He gave me a certificate to get groceries. I got these certificates for about three weeks. When my father got a job we didn't get any more free food.

"When I was in tenth grade the teacher and coach wanted me to play football. I refused and the English teacher said you better join or your grades will go down. I refused to

Approximately 200 CCC boys posing in front of the entrance to Camp S-61 seven miles north of Bolton Landing in the fall of 1934. The last row is composed of LEMs (local experienced men) who served as foremen, Conservation Department supervisors, Army officers, and cooks. They even had a German Shepherd. The mess hall is on the left and the officers' headquarters is on the right. The barracks followed on both sides and way to the right was the garage. Floyd Pickett

join and they were right. I did fail. I was very nervous and I didn't know what was going on in school. I said the hell with them and I quit school.

"It was hard getting a job so in the spring 1934 I went to Glens Falls City Hall and signed up for the CCC. They took 30 other guys and me in a truck to the Bolton Landing camp. I was a little nervous but I made up my mind to get along with everybody.

"I had a few jobs there. I looked for gypsy moth egg clusters. We spread out in a line and marched through the woods looking around and up the trees. We marked the trees with a hooked knife signifying we covered the area. We did this job during the spring, fall, and winter. If the temperature got below 20 degrees below zero, we didn't have to go. We stayed in camp and did odd jobs like cleanup around the camp, mopping floors, cleaning the latrine, or working in the kitchen.

"In the spring we looked for gooseberries and wild currant bushes. We pulled them up with a hooked stick and hung the bushes up to dry. One time when we were working in Chestertown a guy had his whole yard covered with the bushes. We just walked in and ripped them up. The owner was pretty upset but after a while he cooperated with us.

"I also worked in some of the state parks on Lake George. I cut trees at Hearthstone Park and leveled the ground for campsites. We built fireplaces with stones we picked up around the park.

"One day my ax was dull so I sharpened it. Well, the boss saw me do this and said, 'We need someone to sharpen the tools and you're the man.' I worked in the tool shed by the garage toward the front of camp. I did this for a couple of months but I liked getting outside and working with other guys.

"Work ended at 4 pm and we got ready for meals. Sometimes we'd get a pass to go to town. We'd hitchhike or get a ride with someone who had a car parked by the quarry near camp. Nobody seemed to bother them there.

"On weekends I'd hitchhike home. Sometimes it took a couple hours. People didn't mind stopping to give a guy in uniform a ride.

"One night I was walking back to camp on Rt. 9N in the dark. I heard a noise in the woods and got scared. Every time I found a cobblestone I put it in my pocket to use for protection. It sounded like a dog or a wolf. All the way back I kept throwing rocks into the woods. I safely made it to camp. The next day I asked the foreman what he thought it was. I told him I thought it was a wolf. He walked back

down the road and looked in the woods. He said, 'Hell no, it wasn't a wolf but there was something following you. It was a Canadian Lynx.'

"They had an infirmary building and I had to go there a few times. One time while chopping frozen trees the axe bounced off the tree and hit my shin. I still have the scar."

I asked Floyd if anything funny happened to him. "Well, one time the foreman said to me, 'You are pretty good on the mountains. Take these four guys on Tongue Mountain and clear this trail'

"We were driven up in a truck and began trimming out branches knocked down from a storm. As we got up a ways we found the most beautiful blueberry patch you ever saw. The berries were huge. So we began eating as if they were going out of style. The foreman said we had to be back by four so when we noticed it was getting close to that time we had to work like hell to hurry and finish work.

"After working for around two years at the CCC camp I left in the spring of 1936. The day I left the water tower in camp burned down because the stovepipe in the pump house at the base of the tower fell down and the tower caught fire.

"I got a job working for the WPA. I worked in Glens Falls on South Street. We were replacing a collapsed sewer line to the Empire Movie Theater. I had the job as a First Aid person. I just walked around and if someone got hurt, I bandaged him.

In WW II I was drafted in 1943. I was trained to be a military policeman in New London, CT and then transferred to the infantry. I stayed in the US and was discharged in 1945.

"After the war I worked for Imperial Color Works in Glens Falls making paints and dyes.

"When I look back at those days in the CCC it was a good place to be. We were well fed and I learned to get along with different people. If I had a chance to do it again, I would. I met some darn nice people there."

As I was leaving Floyd handed me a rolled up picture. It was a huge panoramic view of the enrollees, Army officers, Conservation Department men, and LEM's at the entrance to the camp. Floyd said, "Take this map for your book. I don't have any family to give it to and I'm sure you will appreciate it."

Tony Satiroff

In 2007 Richard Cipperly, a retired state forester, gave me a list of CCC boys who had attended a reunion 1997. In the fall of 2007 I tried to visit as many as I could. On November 15. I drove to Mechanicville and interviewed Tony Satiroff. His younger brother Paul greeted me and introduced me to Tony.

We sat in the living room and I asked him where he grew up. Tony replied, "I was born on March 15, 1919 in the town of Stillwater. My parents, Olga and John, had seven children. I was the second eldest. My father worked on a farm and in the nearby paper mill. Jobs were hard to find then. I only went to eighth grade and quit school because I wanted to join the CCC. I was only 15 years old and you had to be 18 but I signed up anyway in the summer of 1933. They drove a group of us boys from Mechanicville by bus to camp in Bolton Landing. When I got to camp the doctor examined me. He pointed to my chin and said, 'What is that?'

"I said, 'Cat whiskers.' He laughed and passed me.

"Our camp was on the Alma Farm about two miles north of the Burgess Farm where they were putting up the new wooden buildings. A private company was hired to do the work. Near the construction there was another tent camp.

"We slept in tents for a short time. Our tents were in an open field. They were on both sides of the stream by a white bridge and near the barns and farm house. Living in tents was rough. We had Army mess kits to get our food at the kitchen. When we moved to the new camp we had chinaware.

"I had many jobs. I worked in a lot of the state parks on Lake George. I took care of the picnic areas in Hearthstone and Eagle Lake parks. At Rogers Rock I did cleanup work, built fireplaces and picnic tables. We built cabins on Glen Island and built dams on Northwest Bay Brook to improve the habitat of the speckled trout.

"We planted pine trees in all of the surrounding open farm fields.

"In the winter I worked searching for egg clusters of the gypsy moths. We painted them with creosote. They even had us out working when it was 20 degrees below zero and sometimes we were 20 miles from camp. They drove us to work in state trucks. About 24 guys sat on four benches in the back. It was freezing cold with just a canvas to protect us. In the summer we sprayed the infected trees with arsenic. Then when it rained the poison was washed into the brooks and wound up in Lake George.

"Another job was building trails on Tongue Mountain. There were a lot of timber rattlesnakes up there. We only killed one. I was really scared of them. Remember I was just a kid of 15.

Tony Satiroff of Mechanicville gestures how he held a hooked stick to pull up gooseberry and currant bushes to fight blister rust that infected white pine trees near the CCC camp in Bolton Landing in 1934. Podskoch Collection

"During the spring and summer I looked for gooseberries and currants. I was made an assistant leader and had five guys in my crew. We spread out about five feet apart. We took a hooked stick and moved the bushes away searching for the currant bushes. Sometimes we went on private land. We told the owners that we had to remove the bushes. There was one owner who refused to let us because he was cultivating them as a crop. I felt sorry for him but we had to call the state police who read him the law

"After work I fished in the nearby Northwest Bay Brook where there were a lot of trout. In the winter I brought my new Savage 30-30 rifle and kept it in my barracks. I went deer hunting but didn't shoot any. Some of the guys went trapping. In the spring a bunch of guys tapped maple trees. We collected the sap in gallon cans and boiled it but we didn't get much syrup."

I asked him what he did on the weekends. "On Saturday night they drove us to Glens Falls. There were a lot of girls there. Their mothers got mad at us. As soon as they heard the CCC trucks were in town they told their daughters to get into the house. We went to movies, beer joints, and shopping. Some guys brought back booze and hid it in their barracks.

"You won't believe this but the government hired actor Tom Ewell who later was in the movie 'The Seven Year Itch' with Marilyn Monroe. Ewell was out of a job and the government had him do shows in our camp. He helped get actors from the city to do shows with him. They performed plays. Ewell and his actors lived right with us.

"I was able to stay for three years in the CCC because I was an assistant leader. The other guys could only stay for one or two years. In the summer of 1937 I left the CCC. I got a job working at the West Virginia Pulp & Paper Mill in Stillwater.

"Then I was in the Army for five years during W W II. One day when I was in training at Fort Benning, Georgia, I was in a line with about 1,000 men. The major came over and picked me out. Me and everyone else were wondering why I was picked. He assigned me to an infantry school and I was made a staff sergeant. My job was to help pass out and collect papers for the teachers. I worked for two famous Boston Red Sox baseball players, Johnny Pesky and Hank Gowdy who were instructors. I had the best job in the world for five years. I probably got this easy job because I had been a leader in the CCC.

"I really enjoyed my days in the CCC. I made out good. I met a lot of friends and it helped me in the Army."

Leonard Streeter

Leonard Streeter was another name that I received from Richard Cipperly. I visited Leonard on November 16, 2007 at his home in Queensbury. The first thing he told me was about an experience he had at the Bolton Landing camp. "Normally a rainy day was considered 'a day in the hay' where we didn't have to work. Well, the captain said we had to make up the day on Saturday. I'll never forget it because the captain decided that the coal pile at the end of the camp street by the flagpole was unsightly. So he had us move it. He assigned two dump trucks for the job and I was one of the drivers. We backed up the trucks and seven guys were assigned to load. One truck had five guys and I only had two brothers. You never saw two boys shovel so fast as those two Russian boys from Fort Edward. Their last name was Komsa. We moved the pile in one day."

I asked about his early life and what led him to join the CCC.

"I was born in St. Johnsbury, Vermont on December 20, 1918. My father, Chester, died when I was two. He used to work at the Fairbanks Scale Company. My mother, Catherine, had four boys and I was the youngest. She couldn't raise us by herself and the state stepped in. My oldest brother George went to live with my grandfather. The third brother, Bernard, went to a foster family in Fairhaven, Vermont. But nobody wanted my second brother, Arnie, and I. The state took us away and we both wound up in the same foster home nearby in Danville. The Bowman family were wonderful people. They had a dairy farm and we were there for around four years.

"My mom remarried and her husband worked in paper mills. They moved to Hudson Falls where she worked as a waitress. They bought a house and got us released from Vermont and we lived with them. When I got older my stepfather began complaining about supporting us.

My older brother, Bernard, came home one day from his Army base in Plattsburg. I told him that I wanted to join the CCC but I wasn't old enough. Bernard took my birth certificate and had the company clerk doctor it up to make me two years older. So I was able to get in. My brother Arnie and I signed up in Hudson Falls in January 1935 when I was 16 years old. We were both in barracks #2 which was the second building on the right.

"I lived right across from the infirmary and I wound up running it for a time. Everyone knew where I lived in case they needed help. I stayed one night each week and slept in the infirmary. Other guys rotated with me at nights. If I needed help I got Dr. Merin in Bolton Landing. His wife was also a doctor.

"One night some people driving on 9N had a small car accident. Someone brought a girl into the infirmary. She had a small cut above her knee. I was ready to help her. Then her boy friend came in to see what I was doing. He stayed right there with me. He wasn't going to leave her alone with me. Her injury wasn't that bad. I stopped the bleeding and bandaged it. Then they left.

"I never had any training for the job. I was really interested in it though and studied all the bones in the body. There weren't many injuries in the camp. I just cleaned the room and made the seven beds.

"One day Jim Mitchell, a big handsome guy, was working in the woods cutting a downed tree. As he cut the trunk a big branch came up and hit him right in the crotch. One testicle swelled up as big as a football. It was unbelievable. They called Dr. Merin to help. We kept him in the infirmary for a while and it went down.

"I worked on gypsy moth control and pulled up gooseberries to prevent blister rust.

"I was also a truck driver. That was fun. My bunk buddy, Lee Corlew, was a terrific guy. He was a mechanic in the garage. When they ordered new Reo dump trucks, Lee got me and two other guys to drive down in a suburban, to get the new trucks at the Army Depot in Rotterdam. I wound up driving one of the big yard and a half trucks. The camp needed gravel so on the way home I drove down to South Glens Falls for a load. We also drove to Ticonderoga to a railroad siding for bags of cement for a concrete job.

"I also drove a pickup truck and worked for a surveyor, Orville Hunt. We laid out roads at Rogers Rock campsite. He taught me how to set up a transit and a lot of other stuff. One time I set up the transit on grass and sighted across the bay. I saw a tent set up. Then a guy came out and he was naked. He walked down to the rocks and stretched out. I looked again and there was a naked lady walking out of the tent towards him. I told Orville, 'Take a look at this.' He looked and exclaimed, 'Oh my lord!' She had a good build and was good looking but we went back to working.

"On weekends I drove home. I had a used Model A Ford coupe. My brother, who was in the service, bought it for me. I didn't even have a license. I parked my car across 9N where the bridge went over the stream. It needed new tires so I bought four tires in Glens Falls and paid a dollar a week. They gave me a contract that listed the tire serial numbers.

"One day I went over to my car and every tire was bald. I went back to camp and told my friend Lee in the garage what happened. He said, 'Come with me. I think I know the guy who has a car just like yours.'

"I gave my friend the serial numbers of my tires and we drove to where the guy hid his car. He checked the car and it had my tires. So Lee went back to camp and told the guy to come with him. He was reluctant but finally came. Lee said, 'Either change the tires or I'll beat the sh__ out of you. If these don't work, I'll call the police.'

"We followed the guy back into the woods and watched him swap the tires. It was a really hot day and hard work. We just sat and enjoyed watching him sweat. Lee was quite a guy.

"I got five dollars a month pay. You could buy coupons on credit if you didn't have money. You could buy three coupon books at one dollar each. Then at the end of the month when it was time to get paid they looked at your sheet to see how much you borrowed.

"In the spring of 1937 I left the CCC because I got a job at Imperial Color Works where my stepfather worked. He drove up to camp and went to the administration office. He explained to the Army officer that I got a job and wanted to be discharged. They sent me to Dr. Merin to fill out a physical form for a discharge. Then I came home. I started my job at the factory on Monday. I worked there for only seven months but was laid off.

"I contacted Frank Wren in the Hudson Falls welfare office and he got me into the CCC again. I went back to Bolton Landing in September 1937. I enjoyed going back. I had a lot of good friends there. The staff was great, too.

Leonard Streeter of Queensbury worked at the CCC camp in Bolton Landing for two years where he drove truck, worked in the infirmary and did blister rust control. He said he loved his days in the CCC because it was a great experience where he made a lot of friends. Podskoch Collection

"My jobs were the same, driving truck and blister rust control. I never found an egg cluster but I did find some phony ones that the foremen put on trees to test us.

"In the spring of 1938 I got discharged because I got my job back at the factory. I worked for a while but hated the job because it was so filthy.

"In 1941 I volunteered to join the Army. I was assigned to the artillery and then transferred to the Army Air Corps. I was stationed in Italy.

"I got out in October 1945 and worked for GE. Then I went to Fort Worth, Texas. I worked for Ben Hogan with his golf club business. A guy from GE worked there and called me to straighten out their manufacturing production.

"In 1945 I got married but got divorced in 1965. I remarried in 1970 to a widow with two children. My second wife died and I now live alone here in Queensbury.

"I loved my days in the CCC because it was a great experience. I learned how to make friends at an early age and met some of the greatest people like Lee Corlew. He was my guardian angel."

Frank Leonbruno

Frank Leonbruno, worked at the Bolton CCC camp for six years, from 1935 to 1941. He wrote about his experiences in the Bolton Landing camp in an unpublished story entitled "The Saga of the CCC." Parts of his description of camp life are in Chapter 3 of this book. Frank and a group of his Whitehall friends joined the CCC in October 1935 and were taken to the Bolton Landing camp. They had their first meal of spaghetti and the camp doctor, Joseph Merin, gave the boys physical exams. Then they got their supplies and clothing and were shown their barracks.

"Next we were told what our details would be and were assigned a crew. During our first year I did pest control. During the first couple of years they had us search for artificial egg cluster. Heaven help the guy who missed the egg cluster. About two years later, actual gypsy moths appeared. Tony Satiroff was a first class gypsy moth scout."

Frank mentions other work projects like the search for gooseberries that caused blister rust and the development of state campsites. He states all of the projects were accomplished by the excellent supervision of the state and federal foresters. Winfield Codman was the camp superintendent who had about a dozen foremen and LEMs, local experienced men. Some of the foremen who the enrollees liked were: Milton Brickner (Bolton Landing), Bernard Ramsey (Lake George), Dan Hewitt (Warrensburg), Larry Sheehan (Glens Falls), Mike Buckley (North Creek), and George Stewart (Glens Falls).

"Foreman Brickner attended RPI and had experience in plumbing, electricity, carpentry, and blueprint reading. He loved music. His favorite song was 'Everyday is Lady's Day with Me.' He loved to entertain the boys with a lunchtime song or two and he also sang in local musical dramas.

"Bernard Ramsey was a good carpenter and an excellent stone mason. He instilled his knowledge in the minds of the enrollees working under him so successfully that some found their careers and earned their livelihoods as carpenters and masons. Bernard later became DEC Park Superintendent for all the campsites in the Lake George area. Rogers Rock was his favorite. He was involved in it from start to finish.

"Larry Sheehan was the foreman with unmatched carpentry skills. He was involved in the construction and carpentry work at Glen Island which eventually became my headquarters when I was in charge of campsites on the state islands on Lake George.

"George Stewart was an assistant to Superintendent Win Codman and was involved with work in planning in the field. He later became a Forest Ranger and then promoted to District Forest Ranger in Ray Brook.

"The winter of 1938 was merciless with Mother Nature's cruelty giving us subzero weather for many days.

The enrollees spent a lot of time hunting up warm clothing. This was the same year that a small group of enrollees from Georgia was assigned to our camp. Unaccustomed to the extreme cold, this group suffered terribly, and we northerners could offer them nothing but moral support. Many went 'Over the Hill.'

"This severe winter caused other problems in camp. Our water supply to camp froze. What a terrible misfortune! No water to shower, shave, scrub, and share with others. An old timer showed us how to solve the problem. We built a small trench-type form around the pipeline and placed pack horse manure from Artie Bradley's Riding Stable in Bolton Landing around the pipe. Horse manure maintains heat for a considerable length of time, even in the winter. The pipes eventually thawed and the men had water.

"During my tenure at Bolton, Capt. Lilienthal, Capt. Francis Rednor, Lt. Wilbur Strickland, Lt. Edward Carlson, Lt. James Watts, and Lt. Horace Freeman were the officers in charge. Lilienthal, Carlson, and Rednor were my favorites. Carlson was my mess officer while I was cook and later mess sergeant. He supported my request for better utensils and other equipment that enhanced our mess hall for the enrollees. Lt. Carlson and his wife gave my wife Betty & I baby clothing and a crib when our first daughter, Gail, was born. Capt. Rednor praised my cooking after I created some special Italian dishes for him. These men were more like fathers to me.

"Officers in some CCC camps required enrollees to salute, and bed checks by the commanding officers was common. Our officers never required our enrollees to perform in such military fashion. However, they expected 'Yes sir!' or 'No sir!' all of which was good discipline."

"The CCC was a

Frank Leonbruno worked at the Bolton Landing CCC camp from 1935-41. When he left the camp he worked for the Conservation Department and became a forest ranger. He is pictured wearing his forest ranger uniform. Gail Street

godsend for me. It taught me discipline which I needed. It gave me education from my mentors, a more mature group of men with wisdom and common sense that I respected and tried to emulate. My experience with my mentors taught me that they were obedient, patriotic, resilient, and grateful for the opportunity to serve in the CCC. In my opinion, the CCC is just as good idea today as it was from 1933 to 1942."

When the Bolton camp closed in October 1941 the US Department of Agriculture hired Frank as custodian of the Bolton Landing camp. He had to watch the buildings and remaining equipment. Some of the buildings were burned or dismantled. Frank said:

"Those were lonesome days when one yearned to have time turned backward.

"My wife Betty and my one year-old daughter, Gail, spent October to April 1942 living in what had been the infirmary. We had no neighbors except 'Forestry,' a gentle old mongrel dog who adopted the camp while I was there. Forest Putney took my place in 1942. His family adopted 'Forestry' who later died. and put to rest in the camp's wooded area."

In 1941 Frank started working for the NYS Conservation Department. He retired from the DEC in 1983, having been supervisor of Lake George operations since 1973. He also served his community and the Town of Bolton as president of the Bolton Central School Board, town councilman & supervisor, and county supervisor. Frank was also a member of the Bolton Volunteer Fire Company and past director of the Lake George Association. In 1998 Purple Mountain Press published his book, Lake George Reflections: Island History and Lore. He described his 42 years as a state ranger supervising the state campgrounds on the islands on Lake George. It is filled with his experiences with locals and campers and tells the historical background of the area.

Frank and some his CCC friends often visited the old CCC camp site.

"We reminisced about the activities that took place there and we all agree that our experiences were not only days of joy, and days of continual education and recreation, but also days of lifelong friendships developed. Some of us compared the camp to a 'college of hard knocks' which majored in common sense. The closing of the camp was a day of sorrow for us at that time. Perhaps at some time in the future, the CCC will be resurrected and our men and also women may perform and repeat the same program and

reap the same rewards that were ours."

Russell Gordon

On a rainy May 15, 2007 I traveled to New York State and interviewed five CCC boys who had worked at the Bolton Landing camp. My first stop was in Mechanicville. I had a twelve o'clock appointment to meet Russell Gordon but no one was home. I hoped this wasn't a bad omen to start the day but after a 15-minute wait a car drove up and it was Russell. We sat in his living room and he told me he joined the CCC in 1935 when he was 17. "I joined the CCC in Whitehall because I just couldn't find a job and I had to help my family. There were nine children in our family and I was the eldest. When my mother Ruth died in 1935, I had to help Dad even more.

"My dad, William, ran a tavern in Whitehall during the Depression after getting laid off from the silk mill in town. I helped my family by fishing and trapping small game to put on the dinner table."

"What jobs did you do in camp?" I asked.

"I had a few. My first job was doing bug control work. We searched for gypsy months.

"My second job was canteen steward. I waited on guys who wanted soda, ice cream, candy, and cigarettes. A carton of cigarettes cost $1.50. We didn't sell any beer. I worked there from 4 pm until 9:30 at night. The guys played pool and ping-pong there. I also worked there on weekends.

"The guys gave me the nickname 'Goose.' I enjoyed the camaraderie of the camps.

"Another job was night watchman for the two truck garages. There were two stoves in each garage that I had to keep loaded with soft coal at night. There was another watchman, Waite, who took care of the stoves in the five barracks.

"My next job was supply sergeant. In 1936 the Army sent two of us to Fort Dix, NJ for a month's training. We had to set up bunks and mattresses for a bunch of guys coming back from the west coast. They needed to be checked out before they went home. This was an OK job. When we got back to our camp we handed out WW I clothes to the guys. It was good stuff.

"I also did carpenter work at state parks. My carpentry crew worked like bulls, and I loved it. We put up the buildings on Glenn Island. A flat-bottomed scow with a blunt bow took materials and us to the island. One

Abover Left - Russell Gordon of Mechanicville reminisces about his four years at the Bolton Landing CCC camp from 1935-39. He spent most of his time doing carpentry work on Glenn Island in Lake George. Podskoch Collection. Above, Right - Russell Gordon and his friend "Red" Smith in front of Barracks No. 5 at their Bolton Landing camp. Russell Gordon

building housed the ranger's quarters and post office. We also built a machine shop to the left of the main building and icehouse. In 1938 we finished the work.

"Then I went to Rogers Rock and built the ranger's quarters. It was finished in 1939. Then I went back to camp and repaired the broken boards on the barracks."

"On weekends my buddies and I regularly packed into the bed of a pickup truck and traveled to the movies at the Rialto in Glens Falls. We pooled our change to buy eight gallons of gasoline for $1. I got a ride from guys who hid their cars in the woods. I didn't know how to dance but I did raise hell. On Sunday a minister came to camp for church service.

"We had a lot of fun up there. We played softball a lot. There was a camp baseball team that played games at the high school field.

"There were education classes in camp. The teachers were Mr. Sharp and Mr. McCovey. They had classes like leather craft. I liked that class.

"There was one guy from Cohoes who slept by me in the barracks. He didn't like to take a shower. He was a big guy and smelled. One day a bunch of us took him to the shower and scrubbed him up with Octagon soap. From that day on we didn't have any problems with his odor."

I asked Russell to describe a typical day.

"During the week there was reveille at 6 am. We went to breakfast and the food was great. At 8 am we went off to work. If it was below zero we didn't have to work. At noon we had lunch. Sometimes towards the end of the month they ran out of food. We'd be surprised when we got lunch. It might be a slice of canned pineapple between two slices of bread. Suppertime was the best. We had as much as we wanted and we had a good time in the mess hall."

Then I asked if he ever got injured at camp.

"One morning after reveille I was working in the kitchen with Frank Leonbruno. When I was flipping eggs, grease spattered all over my hands. They took me to the infirmary where they bandaged my hands. Dr. Merin from Bolton Landing came up every day to check my wounds.

"I worked for four years in the CCC. I went right to the limit in working in camp. I wished I could have stayed longer. I got out in April 1939 and lived with my aunt.

"Then I got a job in the National Youth Administration. I worked in Whitehall making ball peen hammers. This lasted till the end of the summer and then I washed houses for 25 cents an hour. It took me about a week to finish a house.

"In 1940 I moved here to Mechanicville to be by my girlfriend, Lola Duchesne. Her aunt got me a job driving a delivery truck for a laundry. I got paid 35 dollars a week. The next year Lola and I got married and we had four children

"Working in the CCC was a great experience. I loved working outside. I'd join again if they had a program like this."

Leonard Corlew

After my talk at the Darrin Fresh Water Institute in Bolton Landing on August 24, 2009, Mary Lou Doulin came up to me and said her good friend, Leonard Corlew, was in the CCC. She asked me if I'd like to see his CCC memorabilia. I asked if I could visit her the next day and she agreed.

I traveled to the beautiful quaint town of Hague on the northwestern shore of Lake George and went to Mary

Lou Doulin's cottage. It was located on a hill overlooking the lake. Mary Lou said:

"I lived next door to Leonard Corlew. Four months after I moved to Hague, Leonard's wife, Lulu, died. We were good neighbors for three years. Then in 1990 the house I was renting was sold and Leonard and I agreed that I would help him out with his landscaping in exchange for temporary housing. I was going to search for another house when the summer season ended.

"He was 75 years old and in good health. We got along well. I began taking over the house chores and living together was mutually beneficial. What started as a friendship grew to be a profound platonic relationship. He was the best friend I ever had.

"As Leonard got older he developed health issues such as two heart attacks and a knee and a hip replacements. I stayed and gradually over the next 15 years he shared his life stories."

I asked her to share some of those stories.

"Leonard was a wonderful guy. He knew so much about the land and the animals of the Adirondacks. It was probably due to his experiences growing up in Wevertown where he was born in 1915. His parents were Merten and Jean Parker. She was half Seneca Indian and that influenced his world view. He was able to read the signs of nature. There were nine children in Leonard's family and he was the third youngest.

"He only finished eighth grade and drove a meat truck throughout the Adirondacks. He also worked for a hotel and did many jobs that were required. In 1933 when he was 18 he joined the Army and traveled to Hawaii and China. When he was discharged in 1937 he had difficulty getting a job. His older brother Lee may have influenced Leonard in joining the CCC because Lee was a leader in the Bolton Landing camp S-82.

"Leonard joined and was assigned to the Bolton Landing camp. He became the "Top Kick" or first sergeant of the camp because he had experience in the Army. He helped maintain order and discipline for the camp. Leonard always worked hand in hand with the captain, who always backed Leonard 100 per cent.

"He was highly respected by the enrollees even though he was tough and thorough. Leonard went by the book and was not really close to the men. If a guy didn't get up in the morning, he went into the barracks and flipped the mattress or poured cold water on their faces. Then they got up. After that he didn't have any trouble getting them

Brothers Lee & Leonard Corlew were members of the Bolton Landing Camp. Leonard was the "Top Kick" or first sergeant who helped keep order in the camp. Mary Lou Doulin

up. Even though he knew the guys from the local area he wouldn't grant them leave just because he knew them. They respected him even though he was strict.

"Leonard made sure the camp ran efficiently and everyone was doing their job. He went on the jobs and supervised their work such as searching for gooseberries. While checking for gooseberries at the world famous sculptor David Smith's property in Bolton Landing, Leonard often sat and visited with David and his wife Dorothy Dehner. Smith had numerous sculptures in the open fields surrounding their home.

"When the doctor visited the camp for physicals, Leonard worked with the doctor in recording the information.

"There was one humorous story that Leonard told me. There were reports of sightings of a mountain lion around the camp. The captain was determined to get it. The captain put a raw piece of meat on the tree in front of the officers' quarters. The captain sat for hours by the window at a table with his gun pointed at the raw meat.

"After hours of sitting at the table he asked Leonard to get him a sandwich. Leonard went out and brought him a sandwich. The captain turned his head to take one quick bite and then glanced back. The meat was gone. The captain was so furious and wanted Leonard to take him into the woods to hunt the lion. Leonard told him they'd have no chance because the mountain lion was long gone and headed for his cave.

"Leonard was part Seneca Indian and he knew all the characteristics of all of the wild animals in the Adirondacks. He was an avid hunter and loved venison. He could identify my friend's tire tracks as well as the tracks of wild animals. He could also forecast the weather by looking at the colors of the mountains.

"On the weekends and evenings the guys had a rec room where they listened to music on the radio, played cards and pool. Leonard who was in his 20s and close to the ages of the guys he was in charge of often went to Bolton Landing with his brother and his friends. They dated the local girls many of whom worked at the Sagamore Hotel. They heard all the stories from the girls who cleaned the rooms of the rich and famous. Leonard and his brother boxed at the camp for amusement.

"His older brother Lee palled around with a group of guys and one day they decided to play a trick on Leonard. Leonard always had a vehicle but he had to hide it away from the camp like the other enrollees because cars weren't allowed.

"One day his bother and friends took Leonard's tires off his car. When Leonard went to his car and saw they were gone he became angry. He finally found out who pulled the prank. So after that experience he decided not to pal around with those guys.

"In 1939 he married Lulu May and lived with her parents in West Hague. In 1941 they bought their own home in Hague. He loved living on the lake. Then the Japanese attacked the US on December 7, 1941 and Leonard was called back to the Army

"After the war Leonard was contemplating on being a state trooper because he was a military policeman in WW II. He also applied for a job at International Paper and started working the day after he returned from the war. He worked there for approximately 28 years and retired in 1973 but he never stopped working. He enjoyed planting and maintaining his big vegetable and rose garden.

I asked Mary Lou what effect did the CCC have on Leonard.

"The CCC was an enjoyable job for him. He liked it just like he enjoyed being in the Army. Leonard liked the military structure and was comfortable with it. He maintained his distance from his men but had respect for them. Working in the CCC cemented his love of the Lake George Area. Leonard died in 2005. We were very fortunate to have found each other."

Clement "Bo" Rounds

Muriel Lapointe from Wevertown wrote me a letter in June 2006 stating that her brother, Clement "Bo" Rounds, was in the CCC and would be interested in telling about his experiences in Bolton Landing and California.

I contacted Bo and I visited him on August 17, 2006 at his home in Athol. We sat in his living room and he told me about his family.

"I was born in February 1919 the fourth in a family of six kids. My dad worked in the woods logging and he raised animals on our land. We had a horse, cattle, and sheep.

"I only finished eighth grade. I did odd jobs or helped out at home till I was 18. There wasn't much going on in town. My folks were on welfare, and I couldn't get a job.

"Then Arthur Curran, the minister in Thurman, spoke to me about the CCC. He took Milford Baker and me to the county welfare office in Warrensburg. Not long after that Curran took Milford and me to Bolton Landing. We had a physical examination and got three shots. They took us to the supply room and gave us clothes. Then they took us to our barracks.

"We were happy to get new clothes. When we tried them on if they were too big or too small we exchanged them with other guys. I was lucky and got the right sizes.

"I knew some of the guys: Billy Bills, Leonard and Gordon Cameron from Thurman, George Bunker and Fred Stewart from Baker's Mills, and Clint Brown. There were quite a few guys from Whitehall, New York City, Ti, and Mineville.

"I was made a truck driver. Dan Hewitt was my boss. I drove men to where they were working and then worked with them.

"They needed an Army truck driver to pick up movies in Schenectady and I got the job. I drove the movies to Blue Mountain camp and ate my lunch there. Then I drove to Paul Smiths and back to Bolton Landing. I also drove guys to Hearthstone Park where we worked on the roads.

"The guys liked to play jokes on the new guys in camp. Some city guys took them to Tongue Mountain for a snipe hunt. They dropped them off in the woods and left them there holding a bag. They told the guys they were going to drive this animal towards them and they were to catch it in the bag. After a few hours the guys walked back to camp with an empty bag.

"I came home on some weekends and sometimes we had KP duty. We weren't supposed to have a car but I had one, a 1929 DeSoto roadster. I hid it across the road in the woods. One time the captain said there was an inspector and that I'd better get it out.

Clement "Bo" Rounds outside his home in Athol wearing the CCC hat he wore during the 1930s at the Bolton Landing camp. Podskoch Collection

"In spring they found gypsy moths in Hague. We went and sprayed the trees. Another job was checking for blister rust. We pulled up gooseberry bushes and left them to dry.

"If the weather got below zero, we didn't go to work.

"After working in Bolton Landing for a year I signed up to go to a CCC camp in Idaho. Before I left I snuck out of camp to go home. I missed morning roll call and the captain fined me two dollars out of my pay. I was an assistant leader and was getting eight dollars extra per month. I thought they forgot about it but when I got to California they took the two dollars out of my pay.

"One time a guy from Brandt Lake, Stanley Wilcox, took a day off or was late for roll call after a weekend. The captain asked Stanley, 'Was it worth losing two dollars?' He replied, 'Yes sir. I had so much fun it was worth two dollars.' The captain replied, 'Well, we'll take out five dollars then.'

"The Army took us to Schenectady by truck on a Sunday to go out west. We got on a train and wound up in Reno on Wednesday. We stayed overnight in Reno and went to a gambling place. On Thursday we went on a bus and traveled about 200 miles to Camp G-15 Co # 6407 in Juniper Flats. It was seven miles east of Likely in the Modoc National Forest in the northeast corner of California.

"It wasn't the camp I signed up for in Idaho but it was a good camp. I was there for just six months. I drove truck. We did roadwork, cut juniper trees for fence posts, strung barbed wire, and built drift fences so the cattle didn't stray."

Bo then proudly showed me his "CCC Driver's Record" book. It showed that he passed his physical and written test on September 9, 1937. It described what vehicles he drove and the conditions of the road. He took this book with him to California and it helped him to get the same job.

"I'd fix sandwiches for the guys or drive back to camp to get food for lunch.

"They liked to pay jokes on the rookies at this camp, too. They'd took them up on the hill and told them to sit and watch for the air mail. Ha, those guys were really gullible.

"On weekends we went to the small town of Alturas. We walked around some and then went to the movies.

"People out there weren't friendly to us. Some guys were from the city and they gave us a bad name.

"They wanted me to be a supervisor and sign up again but I didn't. I came home and worked in the woods.

"In 1941 I married Edith Bills and we had two girls and three boys. Then I drove a truck for the town and county and worked in a sawmill and at Emerson Lumber in Warrensburg. Later I moved on to driving a gas and oil truck and then I worked at a paper mill, the Warrensburg Board and Paper Company. After that I was a caretaker at a summer place.

"I liked working in the CCC. I got a lot of experience driving that helped me in most of my future jobs."

Rayburn Persons

When I visited my good friends, Vernis and Beverly Knickerbocker, at their home in Potterville in 2006, I asked them if they knew anyone who was in the CCC. Beverly said: "Yes, Marty, my father Rayburn Persons was in the CCC."

Bo Rounds and his friend John from Whitehall in Army shirt and ties. Bo Rounds

Beverly had been a major source of information for my book on the fire towers of the Adirondacks because her grandfather, Byron Monroe, was an observer on Swede Mountain. She then called her brother Brandt to come over with some information.

Brant handed me his dad's CCC discharge papers and a photo of his camp.

"My dad enrolled in the CCC on April 24, 1935 at the Warrensburg camp S-101. Then Dad went to Camp S-82 in Bolton Landing where he was a laborer and showed 'satisfactory work' till he was discharged on March 31, 1936."

Then there was a pause. "Uh, oh. Here's something I didn't know. Dad was AWOL on February 10, 1936."

I said, "This doesn't necessarily mean he did something really bad." I had heard stories from CCC boys who said it happened to them but that it was nothing serious.

Brandt added, "I remember Dad telling me that he hitchhike home on weekends and went to my grandfather's house in Graphite. He said sometimes the weather was bad and he had a hard time getting back in time. I later checked this date on an Internet calendar and the date he was AWOL was a Monday.

I asked Brant to tell me about his dad's early life.

"Dad was born in Horicon in 1914. His father Joseph Leroy worked doing lumbering, guiding, and building boats. His mother, Lillian Eunice Haskins, had four children. Dad went to ninth or tenth grade and quit school and joined the CCC to help his family. He loved the outdoors and loved being in the CCC.

"I do remember Dad saying he did blister rust control by removing gooseberry bushes. He also planted white pine trees on Tongue Mountain to control flooding on Padanarum Road.

"One scary thing happened to him. One day while working in the woods he got chased by a bear.

"After being discharged from Bolton Landing, Dad signed up again in 1936. He went to Boston Corners along with Les Jenkins of Corinth. He stayed there for only six months and rushed home to marry his girlfriend, Gertrude Mae Monroe. They eventually had nine children.

"Dad worked on a big estate on Brandt Lake. He also worked on a farm raising Black Angus cattle. He then worked for the town clearing the road around the back side of Brandt Lake. He died in 1955.

Leroy Van Patten

While doing research in the Crandall Public Library in Glens Falls in the fall of 2006, Bruce Cole, the research librarian and avid Adirondack hiker, showed me a collection of 11 newspaper articles published from 1975-76 written by Leroy Van Patten a former enrollee of the Bolton Landing CCC camp. Here are some excerpts from his stories.

Rayburn Persons came home to visit his family in Warrensburg and proudly saluted his family in his CCC uniform. He served at the Bolton Landing camp from 1935-36. Beverly Knickerbocker & Brant Persons

"My part in the Bolton camp began late in 1937. Already a 'veteran' of three hitches (18 months) of C's camps in Alabama, Florida, Nevada, and Western New York, I returned home in December 1936 to Ballston Spa to discover that nothing had changed. Jobs were still non-existent for a high school drop-out (or nearly anyone else)."

He hitchhiked to Amityville, LI, Brooklyn, and Newark, NJ but only finding part time jobs. He returned to Ballston Spa in October 1937 and signed up again for the CCC.

"It was pretty cold and snow was on the ground, the day the green Forest Service trucks pulled in front of the Court House on High Street in Ballston Spa to load about half-dozen of us on. Already on board those 'covered wagons' were guys from Schenectady and Mechanicville, and we filled the trucks en route in Saratoga and Schuylerville—perhaps fifty in all on the two trucks.

"The trucks had drop-down benches mounted along both sides and a couple extra down the middle, all of which responded to gravity and motion as we traversed the bumpy roads north.

"The combination of cold and bumpy ride began to rudely infuse our bladders ... Soon we were all in major discomfort. A few loud raps on the back of the cab communicated our needs to the knowing driver and soon, along a wooded area north of Schuylerville, he pulled off the road and boomed, 'Piss-call!' The spoor remaining on the snow undoubtedly left a curious site to a subsequent passerby."

The trip was quite slow because the trucks were limited to 35 mph. The driver stopped in Bolton Landing to pick up a mail bag and proceeded up 9N.

"From there on we were somehow expecting every bend in the road to be 'camp,' our impatience mounted with our discomfort. Over that last seven miles, about one house per mile seemed visible. We were overdue for another 'nature call' when the truck lurched forward, crossed a bridge, and ground up the grade to the camp entrance. We boiled off the trucks like conquering troops and I noticed that, like myself, most of us carried our possessions in our pockets."

The men rushed to the latrine and were taken to the supply room for clothing and supplies. They brought them to their barracks where they were introduced to their leaders. The final step was their physicals. Van Patten recalled his first physical three years before in the D & H Building on State Street in Albany.

"It had really been in two stages of mortifying indignity. About fifty at a time, we were told to strip to the buff and as we worried about our meager possessions piled on the floor of the room behind us, traversed a prescribed route between half-dozen or so examiners. The examination was cursory; it appeared that they needed to determine only that we indeed had two of each ears, eyes, arms, legs, a sufficient amount of teeth, and were provided with the proper equipment to function as male humans."

The last part of the physical was the dreaded "hook." There were two pairs of men: one group rubbing alcohol on each arm followed by two administering the shot. Van Patten remembered getting shots at Fort Dix and one in thirty passed out while everyone else looked on in horror.

"I remember being twice surprised as one arm at a time was cleansed with alcohol. We were focusing our eyes on each other with anticipation. I was alarmed watching the wrong arm when the other was quickly

Leroy Van Patten worked in several CCC camps in the West and South before coming to Bolton Landing. He worked as a truck driver, carpenter, and electrician. Later he became a music teacher in the Queensbury School system. David Van Patten

jabbed; then while I was commiserating with that one—WHAM!—they got the other one! I did, however, catch the last vaccination which disappointed me because it didn't hurt."

The next stop was a visit to the infirmary where he met Dr. Merin of Bolton Landing.

"I gained a respect and love for the sympathetic, gentle human being who conducted the necessary examination in a manner much more considerate of our feelings. Somehow the shot seemed to hurt less."

It was now about 4 pm and the guys were coming back to camp from work. They joked with the rookies trying to scare them with wild stories of the rigors of camp life. A few rookies had some money and went to the PX/Canteen to buy some goodies like soda or candy. Others met some of their hometown friends while others went to their barracks and bunk to nurse their loneliness.

"A loud whistle got us all, rookies and old timers, out to line up for chow. I was pleased to learn that the Bolton camp had graduated to dishes, instead of the mess kits I had used in other camps. I wish I could remember what we had to eat that first meal but I do remember that it was always sufficient and good.

"That night we settled down in our 'sacks' after lights out. There was some low conversation but we were mostly alone together favoring a tender arm with this kind of arthritic kind of hurt caused by the shots."

The typical day began, except on Sundays, with a loud whistle at 6 am. The guys jumped out of their sacks and streaked to the latrine and washroom. Some guys huddled before the potbellied stoves in their barracks to warm up till the bathrooms were available.

"The facilities were functional: typically one long metal urinal down one wall and a long metal sink with a couple dozen faucets down the other. Along the center, back-to-back, were long, handcrafted outhouse style board seats, perhaps a dozen or so. Off to one end was the gang shower room. Usually, with chow due in about a half hour, little time was wasted with morning ablutions. For chow we trooped into the mess hall by long serving tables centered in front of the three ranges. We were served cafeteria style and then split off to either end of the hall to the large picnic style tables to eat.

"During my earlier hitch in the CCC, after chow we filed by a couple rows of three each, 30-gallon 'G I' (Government Issue) cans filled with boiling water, the first of which was deep in soap suds (shaved yellow 'G I' soap) and the other two with rinse water. Attached to the soapy cans by ropes were a couple of scrub brushes with which we cleaned the mess kits and cups. The cans were meticulously cleaned and carefully inspected by the cooks and mess sergeant."

The guys went back to the barracks to clean up and get ready for the daily inspection. Anyone who didn't do their job they got KP or coal duty or worse if they had to clean out the latrine or garbage cans.

At 7:30 am the guys got ready to line up for work. The first job was to 'police the area.'

"We combed the entire camp area and retrieved 'everything that doesn't grow there' off the ground, in about two minutes. Any announcements of the day were then made (and at supper line up), then 'sick call' took place. The hurt and lame lined up under the gimlet-eyed watch of the Top Kick at the infirmary for treatment of real or imaginary ills. Sometimes the number was dependent upon the anticipated work assignments by some 'gold brickers.' Few remained, however, to wait for 'Doc' Merin, who was not too sympathetic toward any except those who really needed him. Pills and patches were generally sufficient with perhaps a few temperatures taken by the infirmary men. We were usually disgustingly healthy.'

There were various jobs, reforestation, blister rust and gypsy moth eradication, trails, stream reclamation, and the development of campsites at Eagle Point on Schroon Lake, Rogers Rock, Hearthstone, Fort George, and Glen Island.

"We either took our mess kits along to work or picked up a bagged lunch depending on where we were to be at noon. If we were reasonably available, we could get a hot lunch delivered in huge thermos cans, passed out from the tailgate of the chow truck. In the deep woods (gypsy moth scouting), we ate a bagged lunch, if we had not already consumed it by noon. There was usually plenty: two or three sandwiches, some fruit and another goodie of some kind. I acquired detestation for the frequent peanut butter and jelly sandwiches.

"About 3:30 pm the cry went through the woods, 'Let's go back!' and more swiftly than they began the day, the gangs piled into the trucks and headed back to camp. For supper we generally expected to be in full dress uniforms, since a somewhat formal 'Retreat Formation' (flag lowering) was the order of the day.

"After supper hour many converged on the rec' hall and PX for ping pong, pool or other games, or bull sessions.

The well supplied PX had all the necessary and unnecessary items the guys wanted including beer (3.2%) for those over 18." The profits of the PX went to purchase sports or camp equipment.

"Some boys went instead to the Library or Education Building. We had a really good library with many traveling volumes out of the Schenectady District Library. The Sub-District Education Advisor, W. A. 'Bill' McConvey, was a popular man and apparently Bolton was his favorite camp. In frequent residence at the camp he guided many of us in pursuit of further education. There were dozens of available extension courses, at no charge, from the Universities of New York and California. I guess I covered about a half-dozen of them in my spare time."

Other guys who enjoyed music gathered together to play their harmonicas or guitars. Country music was popular in those days. The lights were shut out at 10 pm. Guys were allowed to stay in the rec hall or library till eleven.

The guys were happy when it rained in the morning because it meant no work and "a day in the hay." If rain began while working in the woods a joyous shout rang out, "Send it down David!" "In mock prayerful attitude, on bended knees we praised 'David' with exaggerated prostrate 'Salaams' (deep bow with the right palm on the forehead). There'd be at least one card game in each barracks and if the rain continued all day, at least one fight, rarely monumental in dimension."

Van Patten was happy to get another job as truck driver. He passed the test and had a shiny Army truck.

"I thus joined what we called the BTOs (Big Time Operators) and didn't have to eat peanut butter and jelly sandwiches any more. There was another driver named

These enrollees are lined up near the garage as the Army sergeant calls the roll and gives them their work assignments for the day. Wayne Allen

'Wimpy' (C. H. Winfield from Schenectady) and he became my best buddy. Our responsibilities generally prevented us from socializing away from camp and when one of us was free, the other had to remain on duty. Wimpy courted and married a vivacious waitress, Peggy, who worked in Casey's Bar located on the hilltop just south of where Animal Land was located."

There were other guys who married local girls. Frank Leonbruno married Betty Weller and Tom Ody from Ballston Spa married Mary Nichols.

"We usually made a daily trip, except Sundays, for mail and to the dump that was a couple miles down a dirt road off the top of Federal Hill."

Railway Express and freight deliveries occasionally arrived at the Bolton dock via the Lake George 'steamers,' but more frequently we picked it up at the freight terminals at Lake George or Fort Edward. The freight yard at Lake George used to be where Gaslight Village now stands.

"The people of Bolton Landing were warm and friendly toward us and we tried very hard to keep that friendship. One or two evenings a week, we had a 'rec' trip into Bolton for ball games, movies, stores, homes, or local bars."

Usually once a week Van Patton and the mess sergeant drove to Glens Falls to pick up supplies for the kitchen, office, or PX. Most of the staples or canned goods came from the Schenectady District Army Depot in Rotterdam while the bread, eggs, fresh meat, milk, and some PX supplies were bought at local businesses.

"For the mess hall we generally patronized the Mohican Market on Warren Street in Glens Falls, a fascinating market with warm friendly people in charge. I remember the cheese counter in the center as one entered. There was always a generous slice of cheese handed out with a big grin by its manager, Reggie Miner. On the right side of the store was the pastry counter. The first order of business there was, at the gentle urging of the produce manager, Mr. McCann, a trip through the rear doors and loading area to the back door of Fitzgerald's Bar on Glen Street, where he bought us a large mug of cold beer. This was tacitly allowed by the C. O. as a small breach of rules—no drinking and driving. Then back to the store to assemble the crates and boxes of food."

Van Patten states that the two Army truck drivers and ambulance driver, Roy Ralston, were meticulous in maintaining their trucks. Each week they changed the oil every 300-500 miles and washed and polished the truck

Here is one of the type of trucks that Leroy drove at the camp. This one is of Howard Barnes in 1934. Betty & Joe DeMatties

including the motor and undercarriage for the weekly 'white glove' inspection. Each month they won the award for excellence and the prize was a carton of cigarettes.

The drivers made a monthly trip to the Schenectady Army Depot to pick up supplies and a truck check-up.

"About a half dozen mechanics serviced and adjusted separate mechanical components of the truck in about an hour. At 40,000 miles, they pulled the motor and replaced it with a reconditioned motor with a shiny new paint job. This operation rarely took longer than three hours.

"The Schenectady District Headquarters, at the end of Broadway in South Schenectady, was an immense plant, about six rows of warehouses, each about 1,000' long and perhaps 15 in each row. We drove right through many of them to load the necessary supplies which appeared limitless. The supply management there was amazingly efficient. From a central office we were quickly dispatched to the appropriate warehouses for our various needs—from new Army ranges to toothpicks and from blankets to canned pears. They quickly gathered material, loaded us to the tailgate, and we were en route back shortly after lunch at their first-rate mess hall."

Leroy Van Patten had a lot of experience fighting fires in his western CCC camps.

"One cannot describe the grueling, hysterical pace of suffocating work entailed in beating back a forest fire with picks, shovels, axes, saws, hoes, rakes, water packs, and equipment like bull-dozers, shovels, and loaders. With only sandwiches and coffee to sustain us, we toiled—often with hysterical panic—until after dark before it was considered controlled. We were as black as the burned acreage when we finally dragged ourselves back to the cars and trucks. Luckily at Bolton, we were called out only four or five times but as a driver I was spared the 'line' work of one of the toughest grinds one may experience."

In the middle of the summer of 1938 Van Patten was appointed camp carpenter and a month later camp electrician. He still had his driving job, too. Van Patten felt comfortable doing carpentry but he had to learn electrical work on the job. He helped build a new PX in back of the rec hall. It had knotty pine walls and suspended ceiling. He learned how to wire the new PX and then went on to wire the whole camp by replacing the two wire and knob system. Then he rewired the library, education building and a photo dark room.

During the summer of 1938 Van Patten and 'Wimpy' drove down with six volunteers to the closed Fort Ann camp and each brought back eight 5' slate sidewalks. They used them for the company street. Then volunteers hauled in wheelbarrow loads of topsoil for a flower garden around the flagpole and planted annual flowers. They circled it with stones.

"At Bolton our foremen in the field, the Forest Service men, and the LEMs were most generally respected because they were willing to pitch in and do what they told us to do as well as show us how. They created a strong plus for the work force. We jokingly called ourselves the 'Boogaloo Army,' but with some considerable pride. At Bolton we became proud men because we were treated like men and we were quite convinced that we were the best Damned Outfit' in the C's.

"About once a week we had a traveling movie outdoors (indoors in bad weather) brought to us from Schenectady District Headquarters. Each camp had the responsibility of delivering the operator, his equipment, and the film to the next camp. Wimpy and I enjoyed this duty because we managed to visit several other camps: Fort Ann, Indian Lake, Newcomb, Speculator, Brushton, and others."

Another job that Van Patten acquired was manager of the PX. He got paid an extra 15 dollars a month and bought a $20 clunker. It used a crankcase full of oil while driving to his home in Balston Spa. He bragged, "I instantly solved the disposal problem of our truck crank case oil drainings. I left obnoxious blue clouds en route through Warren County."

On Saturday mornings the boys belonged to the Army. "Bedding was aired out on long lines in the rear of the barracks and buildings were industriously scrubbed down. The woodwork attained a bleached white from the strong G I soap. Then all was returned. Bunks were made up with drum-tight blankets and a precise length of sheet folded down. Wall and foot lockers were 'neatened up,' and all stood by, usually in full dress uniform, for the weekly inspection by the Top Kick and an officer.

"Sundays gave us an extra hour of sack time. Then breakfast was most usually well attended. We had the luxury of fried eggs, right off the griddle either up or over, and toast. We ate at our leisure. About 10:00 am we had a church trip in to Bolton in a couple of trucks which were rarely crowded. Occasionally the priest from Bolton or the District Chaplin, Lt. E. C. Sensor, visited camp and held services for a considerably larger group."

After serving six years at the Bolton camp and meeting hundreds of enrollees, Frank Leonbruno, mess sergeant, said his favorite was Leroy Van Patten. "He was a jack of all trades but he seemed to be master of most of them. During his tenure as enrollee he had been a mechanic, utility man carpenter, generator and compressor operator, crew pusher, truck driver and First Aid infirmary man. He knew how to play all the standard bugle calls which was one of his talents he kept a deliberate secret throughout his entire career in the CCC.

"Pat was a veteran of WW II, serving in the US Army in Europe. He married Catherine and had one son, David.

"In later years Pat pursued a college education, graduating with a Bachelor's degree from New England Conservatory of Music. He sang in several churches and was a member of the Glens Falls Operetta Club. He taught music at Brant Lake schools for 10 years and retired after 15 years with the Queensbury School District. He later studied electronics and was employed at the Fort William Henry Corporation.

"Pat

CCC Camp S-82 was located just off Rt. 9N seven miles north of Bolton Landing from 1933-1941. Here 200 young men aged 18-25 lived in five wooden barracks. Each morning and evening they lined up by the flagpole in the center of the road. Bo Rounds was an excellent organizer, as evidenced when he assumed the responsibility for a reunion of former CCC enrollees, Army officers, and other 'Big Wheels.' The reunion was at the Bolton Conservation Club House on June 28, 1975. That day was one that none of us now living will ever forget. In attendance were Ed Carlson, ex Company Commander; Doctor Joseph Merin, our camp doctor; foremen Milton Brickner & Larry Sheehan, and Ken Morehouse, Conservation employee. It also included these former enrollees: Mike Marzinsky, Leonard Corlew, Russell Gordon, Tony Satiroff, and Leroy Cameron.

"On December 29, 1983 Leroy Van Patten died at the age of 67."

Van Patten described his experiences in the CCC "as priceless preparation for my subsequent jobs. I worked at construction jobs before and after the war and summers while attending college. I spent five summers as maintenance man in a Boy Scout camp and five recent summers working with crews of boys developing the Gurney Lane recreation area in Queensbury."

Clarence J. Hilton Jr.

The Schenectady Historical Society had just finished a CCC reunion of about 12 alumni and their families on Friday, June 25, 2010 when someone rushed to me and said there is someone who needed help getting into the building. I quickly walked to the stairs and there was this man breathing heavily and laboring to climb the stairs. A crowd gathered and we gave him a seat to rest. He gasped for air a few times and then spoke. "I have to see someone to tell them about my brother who died at the Bolton Landing CCC camp. My name is Herm Hilton and my brother was Clarence Hilton. He was just 19 when he died of pneumonia. I wasn't even born yet. I just wish I knew more about him." He handed me a tattered picture of his brother and said he might have a better picture at home.

I told Herman and his wife how to apply for his brother's records and told him to contact me when he got the information. He thanked me and in a few months I received a thick envelope containing 23 pages of Clarence Hilton's records.

Clarence was born on April 19, 1920 and lived in Schenectady. His father Clarence Sr. was a conductor on a trolley car and his mother Mary was a homemaker. They had 10 children: Leo, Raymond, James, Richard, Robert, Charles, Ethel, Leslie and Herman.

He dropped out of high school after ninth grade in January 1936 and didn't have a steady job.

Clarence signed up for the CCC on April 19, 1937. He went to Camp S-78, Company 219, in Cherry Plain, NY. He worked there as a laborer till May 7, 1937 then he was assigned to Camp S-82, Company 204, at Bolton Landing, where he did forestry work. He fell seriously ill and was sent to the Army Hospital at the Plattsburg Barracks on September 26, 1937. Clarence was treated for lobar pneumonia of the left lobe. He was a patient till December 11, 1937 when he was discharged and taken back by ambulance to S-82.

He recovered enough to work as an assistant (orderly) for a foreman and received a satisfactory rating. He worked for 22 months. On February 13, 1939 while working in the kitchen he reported being sick with a cold and was taken to the infirmary for treatment.

Dr. Joseph Merin, a doctor from Bolton Landing who was hired by the Army to be the camp doctor wrote a report concerning Clarence. He stated Clarence "applied for treatment at the Camp Infirmary the morning of February 8, 1939" complaining of a cough. Clarence said he wasn't that sick. His temperature was 99.2 and "there was evidence of diffuse bilateral bronchitis."

Clarence was placed in bed and they encouraged him to drink fluids and gave him quinine and aspirin every four hours and two terpin hydrate compound tablets every two hours.

The report stated Clarence continued coughing and his temperature increased but he said he didn't feel bad.

They gave Clarence "Occasional doses of codine sulfate (half-grain) and barbital (five grains) were given to aid in sleep or control severe coughing."

His condition deteriorated on February 12, 1939. "He appeared toxic and his temperature had risen to 102.6. There were no signs of consolidation in the chest.

"That after being irrational during the night, there was definite evidence of consolidation in the right lower lobe the morning of February 13, 1939, at which time he was transferred to the Glens Falls Hospital, N.Y. under the care of Dr. James S. Shields. Signed Joseph H. Merin, M. D."

A Board of Army Officers from the Schenectady District Office met on February 18, 1939 at the Bolton Landing camp to investigate Clarence's death.

After studying the evidence from Dr. Merin and the Glens Falls Hospital reports, the Board concluded

Clarence Hilton was just 17 years old when he joined the CCC. Herman Hilton

that Clarence Hilton died on February 15, 1939 from lobar pneumonia, Type 22. There was no serum for Type 22 pneumonia and the Army gave Clarence all possible medical attention. There was no evidence of a traumatic injury, alcohol, or narcotics. Also, death was not due to a work injury or by exposure to inclement weather.

After reading these reports one wonders how Clarence Hilton would have fared if the doctors during the 1930s had modern medicines to treat pneumonia. When Clarence died it left a void in the Hilton family.

When Herm Hilton received Clarence's records he said, "I felt there was something more that could have been done. My mother said she heard at the hospital they gave Clarence an ice bath in a tub to get his temperature down. We thought that was the cause of his death. Now at least I know the cause of his death and the efforts of the Army and hospital. I also know where he died and I feel a lot better about that."

Thomas Judkins

On November 16, 2007 I visited Thomas Judkins at his home in South Glens Falls. When I knocked on the door a voice from inside called me in. I found Tom seated in his living room He told me he had trouble walking and had to use a walker. This was difficult because he had a vigorous life working in the CCC, Navy, and State Police. He also lost his wife and lived alone. He was eager to tell me about his experiences in the CCC.

"I was just 14 when my father John died. He had worked for the D & H railroad. I was the eldest in my family and my mother, Edna Hardwell, needed help. We lived in Troy. My grandparents tried to help her so I stayed with them for a while. To earn money I worked for Western Union as a delivery boy. When I was 15 I quit school and I signed up for the CCC in the winter of 1938.

"It was January or February that a bus took several of us up to the Bolton Landing camp. The camp checked us in. Since it was a day off from work due to the severe

cold the guys were in camp and made us feel welcome. I felt accepted even before I got off the bus.

"They took me to my assigned barracks and it was cold outside. There was one potbellied stove but by morning it was cold inside. The night watchman didn't do a good job of stoking the stove. Even though it was cold we were warm because we had blankets and warm Army clothes.

"We basically worked in the woods. I rebuilt fireplaces in Hearthstone State Campground and on the state islands in Lake George. Another job was cutting dead trees in the state forests. We brought some of the wood back to camp or just hauled it out of the park.

When the cook asked for someone reliable they moved me to the mess hall since I was a pretty good worker. So I served food and did the dishes. The mess sergeant was Frank Leonbruno and I knew him before I got the job.

"I do remember one weird thing. There were two brothers in camp who had an unusual way of washing their hands. They used their own urine. I don't know if that was why they had soft hands.

"There was another funny story. We had some cannon balls from the Revolutionary War at the entrance to the barracks. One night someone came in and rolled them down the middle of the barracks. It woke everybody up.

"We worked hard and slept hard. At the end of the day we were exhausted from hard work in the outdoors. We didn't have any trouble falling asleep when the lights went out.

"On the weekends we hung around camp, played sports or cards. I was quite conservative and watched my money. No gambling for me. If we went anyplace we had to wear our uniforms. It was an order. People knew who you were and you couldn't get away with anything. When I went to town I walked around, went to the movies or did whatever was free. Once or twice I went home to be with my brother.

"During the week there were education classes in the mess hall from eight to ten. Mr. McConvey was the teacher. Some of the classes were for a high school diploma.

"On August 5, 1939 I left after serving six months. I enlisted in the Navy and traveled all over the world. I married Judith Ann Beaver in 1942. I stayed in the Navy for 20 years. When I got out I joined the NY State Police in 1959 and was stationed at Troop G in the Town of Moreau. I retired in 1979.

"When I look back at my days in the CCC I think it was a great organization. It helped a lot of young me to

Thomas Judkins, a retired state trooper, was an enrollee at the Bolton Landing camp. He did a lot of forestry work and worked at many of the state parks on Lake George. Podskoch Collection

grow up and it would do the same thing today. It made me more of a man and I never had any trouble in the Navy because of my CCC experience."

On February 22, 2011 Thomas Judkins passed away.

Paul Campagnone

My interview with Paul Campagnone was the closest to my home in Connecticut. I was fortunate that Paul was visiting his daughter, Michelle Donahue, in Portland only 12 miles away. I visited him and his daughter's family on November 23, 2008.

"I was 15 years old in the summer of 1938 when I signed up for the CCC. I quit school because I wanted to help my parents. My father Artillio and mother Philomena had 14 children. A lot of the babies died. I was the fourth child and was born in Glens Falls on October 31, 1923.

"The Army picked us up from city hall on Ridge Street. We rode in an old Army truck. When we arrived at the Bolton Landing camp they took us to see the officers who told us what we were to do. We went to the barracks which were nice inside. There were two wood stoves and single beds.

"My jobs were fighting blister rust and searching for gypsy moth egg clusters. We searched the trees but never found any.

"Every week I had KP duty. I didn't like it but I did it. I put the dirty dishes in a tub and then in a steam washer. The best part of this job was that we got to eat better than the other guys.

"In the evening we went to the PX or watched movies. On the weekends we went to Glens Falls to the movies or beer joints.

"We used to hitchhike from camp to Glens Falls. One time the sheriff stopped me for hitchhiking in the Lake George city limits and I was told to walk till I reached the outside of the city.

"Sometimes we'd miss the truckride back to camp from Glens Falls and we'd have to walk or hitchhike back.

"If someone didn't give us a ride as we were hitchhiking we'd wait at a spot on the hill going towards camp. When a truck slowed to shift we'd jump on the back and get a ride up the long hill to camp. When we got to camp we jumped off.

"In 1939 they asked if someone was interested in transferring to the Army Depot in Schenectady and I volunteered. We took ammunition boxes and stenciled them where they were going. Then we loaded them on boxcars. They had barracks for us to sleep in.

"Then I heard they were hiring guys for the Army Depot. So I quit the CCC and stayed in Rotterdam where the depot was. My job was shipping clothing. I stayed there till I was drafted in the Army in 1942.

"I came home in 1945 and I worked for 47 years at Leigh Cement in Glens Falls as a repairman. I got married in 1948 to Charlotte Lapoint and we had four children: Albert, Paula, Danny, and Michelle.

"I loved the CCC. It took a lot off your mind and you learned a lot. I would join again."

Andrew Borix

My fourth interview on May 15, 2007 was in Fort Edward with Andy Borix's. As I entered his home I noticed a lot of handcrafted wooden furniture and complimented him. His wife Beverly proudly stated Andy had made them and that he also made the house.

"I joined the CCC in 1938 and worked there for two years. I was a carpenter and built the manager's building at Rogers Rock. Then I moved down to the Lake George Battleground State Campground and built the manager's house. They had just come out with ceramic tiles and I used them.

Paul Campagnone told his experiences working at the Bolton Landing CCC camp to his children and grandchildren at his daughter's home in Portland, CT. Podskoch Collection

"Another job I worked at was building the fireplaces at the Hearthstone State Park. I learned the masonry skills from our foreman.

"On the weekends I played basketball. I had been the captain of the Fort Edward High School basketball team. We were in a league with other CCC camps like Port Henry.

"For entertainment they took us to Glens Falls to the Rialto, State, Paramount or Empire movie theaters. Sometimes we walked down to Bolton Landing to go to the movies. As we walked the seven miles back to camp, deer and bear came out of the woods by the Northwest Bay Brook. We had fun chasing them back in the woods.

"On Sundays a priest came to the canteen and said mass.

"We had a little excitement one day. A few bears came into camp and we grabbed some clubs and chased them back into the woods."

"Tell me about your family and why you joined the CCC?," I asked.

"My parents Michael and Helen lived in Fort Edward. I was the third of four children. Dad was a farmer and then worked at International Paper. After I graduated from high school I just couldn't get a job. Then I read in the newspaper that they were enrolling men for the CCC. I went to Granville and signed up. They sent me to Bolton Landing.

"During my last six weeks in the CCC, I did carpentry at our camp. I helped put an addition on the kitchen and canteen center. The food and drinks in the canteen were cheap. We paid 5 cents for a piece of pie or a bottle of Coke.

"After I left the CCC in 1940, I worked at International Paper Co. in Fort Edward. Then I joined the Army and spent 39 months in Europe.

"In 1945 I did carpentry and mill work and kept at it for over 30 years. I married Beverly Doyle in 1948 and we had two children, Edward and Andrea.

"I liked the CCCs. It gave me a job and I developed my carpentry skills there. We worked hard and we had fun playing sports. I still keep busy building making things of wood."

Frank "Red" Sherman

When I visited Frank "Red" Sherman at his home in Warrensburg on November 11, 2007 he told me, "In the fall of 1938 I didn't see how I'd have any work in the winter besides shoveling snow so I decided to join the CCC. It was about October 3, 1938 when I hitchhiked to Bolton Landing to see if I could get in. I talked with the officers and looked the camp over. They explained all the details and I signed up. I was 18 years old. There were some delinquent city boys who were forced to join the CCC or go to jail.

"My first job was using a pick and shovel in building a new road that went north from camp to Tongue Mountain. We moved sand to fill in places for the road.

Andy Borix described how he learned his carpentry skills while working at the Bolton Landing CCC camp from 1938-40. After WW II he built his home in Fort Edward and worked as a carpenter for over 30 years. Podskoch Collection

"My next job was at Rogers State Park. We built the sub base for a road. I broke rocks the size of basketballs with a sledge hammer.

"During the winter I worked on the bug crew. We walked through the mountains searching for gypsy moth egg clusters. There was a line of six guys side by side. The supervisors planted a few artificial clusters but we hardly found any real ones. They penalized us if we missed a planted egg cluster. Sometimes the brush was so thick we had to walk around it. We marked the trees that we had looked at. It was a terrible job!

"We wore WW I clothes. The boots had buckle overshoes and we wore long underwear. They never gave us snowshoes. The snow was high and sometimes over our knees and covered with ice. It was exhausting work. Sometimes our leader gave us breaks. They'd start a fire and melt snow for coffee. Our shins were bloody each night.

"The winter cold was unrelenting. In our barracks they used soft coal for the stoves. At night we'd bank the fire to make it last longer. There was a fire pail by the stove but it was frozen in the morning. If there was a fire you'd never be able to put it out. The wooden floor was three-quarters of an inch pine and there were spaces that you could see the ground. The walls were six-inch wide boards covered with tar paper. If there was a knot in the board, hell, you were looking right outside. The building was on 8" square posts dug into the ground. When we went outside the smoke was so thick you could almost reach out and grab it. We'd start coughing and spitting out black phlegm. At times we had some portable kerosene heaters but sometimes they were out of fuel. We'd give a guy a dollar to drive to town and get a gallon of kerosene.

"The kitchen had a coal stove in the winter but they cooked using gas that came in canisters. When we went to the camp for the reunion in 1997 I saw old tank canisters scattered all over the valley.

"The coal was dumped in a pile and covered with a heavy oil canvas tarp. Some were probably from WW I.

"They brought in some gas bottles to heat the office. It was a complicated affair.

"They had a generator that made electricity for the camp. There was one fat telephone cable that went all the way down to Bolton. Sometimes the line was damaged from downed trees or limbs. The phone operators were in Bolton Landing.

"One building had a coal boiler that made steam heat for the officer's building. The steam line also ran under ground to the combination canteen/library and to the kitchen. The kitchen also had a water wheel at the back that generated electricity. It had a transformer and a big wet cell battery.

"Our drinking water came from the brook. They pumped it up the hill to a water tower by the truck garage. The whole hillside around camp was full of springs.

"The camp had one big tractor that started when it wanted to. The dump trucks had canvas tops to cover the back when transporting guys in bad weather. It was cold when you rode in the back. There was also some kind of machine that crushed

Frank "Red" Sherman in his home in Warrensburg describes the hard times he had searching for gypsy moth egg clusters during the cold winter of 1938-39. Podskoch Collection

rocks. It had a steam engine.

"The toilets were next to the library/canteen. There were wooden pallets that we walked on from building to building when it was muddy. You tried to keep a can or bottle by your bed at night to piss in. You didn't want to walk outside to get to the latrine in the cold. A lot of times it was below freezing in the barracks.

"Once I strained a muscle in my chest. They taped me up. I had to live with that for 3-4 weeks and I still had to work. The doctor came once a week. If you wanted to go to the infirmary and not go to work it was held against you by your squad leader. You only went to the infirmary if you were half dead.

"If you wanted to go to Bolton Landing you could get a pass. We'd go for a beer or something. One time I walked the whole seven miles to town. There wasn't much traffic on 9N in those days. Maybe you could ask the bread truck driver for a ride. Nobody lived up near the camp. The closest residences were down the hill where there was a big estate that was owned by John Wood. The road was just dirt.

"One day the steel bridge over West Bay Brook collapsed as a truck drove over. We went down to drag the people out of the water. It was a wonder nobody got killed. Then they put a cable and walkway across the brook. It was a suspended catwalk. You could also cross the brook if you walked up the road were they built the new bridge.

"In the spring of 1939 they had me doing carpentry work. I built railings along the buildings. This was hard work because when you dug down for the wood posts, you hit slate. Another hard job was making a square hole in the posts to join the railing to the posts.

"That summer the weather was getting hot and the bugs were so thick. The mosquitoes were big, too. In May 1939 I decided to leave. You could get out of camp if you were guaranteed a job. I got a job painting a house in Warrensburg. I had already signed up for another six months but I was happy to get out.

"I went to California and studied at the National School for Diesel Mechanics and studied gas power plant operation. I was there from June till December 1940. I had to pay for it all by myself. I stood in lines from 5 am looking for a job but couldn't find one.

"So I came back to Warrensburg. My father was ill and my mother had an operation. I still couldn't find a job. Then I heard that an aviation school opened in Glens Falls and they were training workers. I was in the first class. By

March I had a job in a Buffalo factory that was crying for workers. I worked there till December 1943 when I joined the US Army Air Force.

"Being in the CCC was a test of courage. The conditions were very primitive. There was never enough food or kerosene. Sometimes we got low on coal. We had to stretch out what we had to burn in the stoves. We used old crates by the garage and cut them up for fuel. It was cold in the latrine, too. The showers were damn cold, too. I learned what a man could withstand. Even if I was young again I don't think I'd go again."

Peter Zacek

When I visited the Westernville Library north of Rome, NY, I met Peter Zacek. He told me about the two CCC camps he worked at.

"I worked in the Boonville camp from August 1938 until August 1939. I went home searched for four months for a job around by farm in Hinckley but work was very scarce. So I joined again in 1940 with my friends Ken and Bud Barrett, and Julian Poczatek. We took a train from Utica to Troy. They sent them to Middleburg in the Catskills and I went to the Bolton Landing camp near Lake George.

"When I got there the captain found out that I had experience driving at the Boonville camp. He said, 'I have this city boy driving and he keeps getting in accidents. You're going to take his place and also you'll be our movie operator. The next day he sent my partner and I to get supplies at the Middleburg CCC camp and to the District Office in Schenectady. We drove a ton and half canvas-covered Army truck.

"Each week we took two portable 35 mm projectors and showed a movie at a new camp each day. They were all recent movies, too. During the days we spliced film, played ping-pong, or we just hung around the camp we were visiting.

"On Monday we were at our camp in Bolton Landing. On Tuesday we drove to Speculator and stayed there overnight. The next day we'd drive down Rt. 8 and stop at my parents in Hinckley. Sometimes we'd set up a movie in the afternoon for the old people in town. Then we'd drive up Rt. 28 to Blue Mountain Lake and show movies to the young fellows at Indian Lake camp. One time we were almost late and the captain said, 'I want you to be there on time or else.'

"On Thursday we were at Paul Smiths camp where there were WW I veterans. Our last day, Friday, was at Newcomb and then we drove back that night to our home camp in Bolton Landing.

"I had to teach my partner, Joe Smith from NYC, how to drive and operate the equipment. He did OK driving around the base, but once on the way from Bolton to Speculator he was all over the road because it was icy. I was scared to death. I said, 'Pull this thing over and I'll drive!'

"All the roads were paved but between Speculator and Indian Lake it was dirt and not open in the winter.

"One time when I was at the Paul Smiths camp I drove a sergeant back to my Bolton camp. All the trucks had a governor that limited the truck's speed to 35 mph. Well, soon after we drove through Lake Placid the sergeant said, 'Stop this slow truck! I'll fix the governor so we could go faster.' He opened the hood and in a few minutes closed it and he said, 'Let's go.' I started driving but it went even slower than before. He said to stop and he tried to fix it again. This time the truck went faster. Both of us were happy.

"The next morning the captain called me into his office and said, 'Do you know who broke the seal on the governor?' I said I didn't know. Luckily nothing happened to either of us.

"After six months of working in the CCC, I got an offer for a job from Niagara Mohawk but I failed a test because of the loss of my fingers due to an accident with dynamite caps when I was young. I then got a job at the Savage Arms Co. in Utica. I ran a profile machine cutting metal to make machine guns. Then I worked for Kelsey Hayes in Whitesboro for 34 years treating metals for jet engines.

"In August of 1942 I got married Delma Baker. We had five boys.

Peter Zacek's job at the Bolton Landing camp was driving a truck and showing movies at five different camp each week. Here he is stopping at his home in Hinckley on his way to Blue Mountain. Peter Zacek

"It was a good experience for me. I learned a lot while working in the CCC, especially how to drive large vehicles. I continued to use this skill throughout my life."

Robert Hewitt

Robert Hewitt of South Glens Falls told me about his experiences in the CCC in the fall of 2007. "In June of 1939 I quit high school and joined the CCC. I was 18 years old, the third oldest in my family of eight. I wanted to help buy clothes and help my family financially. My parents, Robert, a conductor on the D & H Rail Road, and my mother Johanna, had a hard time feeding and clothing my family during the Depression.

"When I went to camp I was lonesome for home but I got used to it. My oldest brother Donald was there, too. He was a leader in another barracks. I also knew some other guys from my town like Frank Leonbruno and Russell Louson. I was originally from Plattsburg but my family moved to Whitehall when I was five.

"During that summer I worked at Rogers Rock building a water tower across the street from the park. I worked hard wheeling cement."

I asked Robert if he remembered any funny incidents? "One morning while riding in the back of the truck a guy began yawning. Pretty soon another guy started yawning. It was so catchy the whole truck was yawning. We all couldn't stop laughing and yawning.

"After working on the concrete water tower I was assigned to the project of pulling out gooseberries. I enjoyed this because I loved working in the woods.

"For recreation I played on the camp baseball team. I played one game in Crandall Park in Glens Falls. Sometimes I went home on the weekends. There was a boy who had a car. He'd take 7-8 guys back to Whitehall. We paid him 25 cents each way.

"At the end of the summer I left camp in order to finish my senior year in high school. When I graduated in 1940 I signed up again in Whitehall for the CCC. I continued working at Rogers Rock where I built bathrooms. I dug sewer lines, built latrines, and a room for showers.

"After work I played softball and went to the canteen to play pool, ping pong, and listened to the radio.

"When winter came I quit again because I had a job setting pins at the YMCA bowling alley. Then I got a job as a brakeman for the D & H. In February 1941 the Army drafted me and was discharged in 1945.

"I did a lot of hard work in the CCC but there wasn't someone standing over you like they had a whip. If I had a chance to do it again, I'd definitely do it again."

Charles Smith

While driving on Old Military Road that bypasses Lake Placid I drove past the site of the CCC camp. Only one building is left, the old mess hall. Lake Placid Rod and Gun Club now own it. Every time I passed by, the gate was locked and there were no cars. So I decided to stop and ask at one of the neighboring homes to see if anyone had any information on the camp.

The first home I visited I hit the jackpot. Charles Smith answered the door and he said he had been a member of the camp. I asked if I could ask him some questions but he said, "I'm sorry but could you come back again. I'm watching a big NASCAR race and I don't want to miss it." I told him that I lived in Connecticut and asked if I could call him and do a telephone interview. He agreed and I continued on my trip.

On August 28, 2009 I called Charles. He said he spent some time at the Lake Placid camp but most of his time was spent at the Bolton Landing camp. I asked him to tell me about his life and family.

"I was born 86 years ago right here in Lake Placid on September 4, 1921. My father, Merrill Smith, drove truck for the Lake Placid Club. He died at age 47 from black lung disease because he hauled coal every day from the railroad station to the club. The buildings were heated with steam from the coal boilers. I had one brother, Merrill, and a sister Maude. My mother Ruth Pratt Smith worked as a nurse's aid and she also died early at the age of 48.

Robert Hewitt of South Glens Falls helped build Rogers Rock State Park while in the CCC camp in Bolton Landing. Podskoch Collection

"It was tough raising a family during the Depression. My father was often sick and died of pneumonia caused by black lung disease. I earned money by caddying at the golf course. I made more money than my father. With the money I helped my family and I bought my first car, a 1931 Model A Ford Roadster that was missing two tires and a fender.

I joined the CCC on October 19, 1939 to help my family. I didn't have to go far, just right across the street where that baseball field is. I was there for only two weeks then they shipped me to Bolton Landing

"Having a driver's license probably helped me in getting my first job, driving trucks for the camp. I drove dump and transport trucks. The driver was responsible for taking care of the truck. I made sure the mechanic greased and serviced the truck. Another job was changing tires if needed. There was an old man who supervised the garage and I hung around there a lot. All the trucks were parked in the garage every night.

"When I was assigned to a dump truck I had to help load it. The trucks held 2.5-3 yds. We hauled gravel or picnic tables that needed repair. Truck drivers had to take a First Aid class to help injured workers.

"One group that I drove was the gypsy moth crew. I drove them to a job and I just hung around or I read books. The guys wore leather leggings for walking through brush and protection against rattlesnakes. They called their job 'bugging and rattling.' There were some guys who caught the rattlesnakes and brought them back to camp in white bags. I never saw any guys with snakes on my truck. Luckily I never heard of anyone getting bitten. There were a lot of guys who were scared to walk in the woods.

"When guys found trees with gypsy moth nests they either sprayed them or cut off the branches. Then they put them in bags and placed them in the truck. I don't remember what they did with them.

"Other crews that I drove for cleaned up the wood at campsites. I hauled the wood back to camp. Some were for loggers who picked them up and sawed them for lumber. We kept the hardwoods for firewood.

"Our work day began at 8 am and we were given our assignment. At lunchtime we had a bag with a sandwich, fruit and milk. Then we left work at 3:30 and got back to camp at 4 pm.

Left - Charles Smith at his home on Old Military Road in Lake Placid. Podskoch Collection. Below - Charles Smith polishing his car at his home in Lake Placid. He didn't have far to go to his first CCC camp. It was right across the street. Then he was transferred to Bolton Landing. Joe Smith

"Dinner was between 4:30-5 pm, after which we just fooled around. We played horseshoes, basketball, or listened to a radio. We'd go to the canteen and buy stuff like cigarettes or soda. When we first came to camp they gave us coupons. At the end of the month when we got paid they took out any money we borrowed. We had to be careful how we spent money because we only got paid five dollars a month.

"The bathrooms had a large water tank. There were about five shower stalls with three showerheads in each. Guys had to wait in line outside for their turn. There was no heat in the bathroom so the water was always kept dripping so it didn't freeze. There were two buildings that had five toilets. Underneath the toilets were 55 gallon barrels on railroad ties. Every once in a while they were taken out and cleaned.

On weekends we just hung around camp. On Saturday and Sunday nights guys could sign up and go to the local towns. I volunteered to drive the ambulance. My job was to drive to the police stations in Glens Falls, South Glens Falls, and Lake George and pick up the sick and drunk guys. They gave me a helper to handle the drunks who sometimes didn't want to come. I drove two trips each night. The first was at 4:30 pm. I made the loop from town to town. My last trip I left at eight and was back by midnight. Sometimes the ambulance was a mess so I had the guys clean it up the next day. I didn't get any extra pay but I did it because I got to see a lot of the towns.

"There were education classes but I didn't take any. They probably would have helped me since I only had nine and one-half years of school.

"The first time I went home was three months after I arrived. My friend Ecky Borden and I hitchhiked. We got a ride to Elizabethtown. We tried to get a ride but we were forced to walk up the steep mountain to Keene. It was winter. I sat on the porch of a bar just to get warm. There were no rides so we walked 14 miles all night to Lake Placid. I got home at 7:30 am and stayed in bed for two days.

"I decided to take my car back and parked it about a mile north of camp where there were about seven other cars. I only came home one other time.

"After I had my car at camp for three to four months I was discharged. I think they kicked me out of camp because I had a car near the camp.

"On May 15, 1940 I left the camp. I got a job working at the Harmony Iron Mine in Mineville. After two years they transferred me to the Joker Mine where I would be working under Lake Champlain. The boss took me underground and I saw this six-inch pipe pumping water out. He said, 'If you work here you won't be drafted.' I told him I'd rather be drafted than work in this terrible dangerous job.

"The boss was right. I got drafted in October 1942. They stationed me in Panama and I had guard duty. It was hot, about 110 degrees, but I got used to it.

"After the war I got married and drove heavy equipment. My experiences driving in the CCC helped me in my last profession."

Fred Floyd Stewart

Fred Floyd Stewart was born the fourth of seven children to Mott Floyd Stewart and Alta (Hitchcock) on April 13, 1917. He often reminded folks that he was born on Friday the 13th, but no one who ever knew this kind and gentle man would ever believe that it was an unlucky event. He grew up during the hard times of the depression era, but his hard work ethic kept him in a variety of jobs starting at age 17 in the CCC camps.

Dr. Dan Way of North Creek interviewed Fred Stewart of Bakers Mills and shared this information: "Fred was a crew leader of 40 men, many of whom were twice his age. He was only 16 when he joined the CCC in 1933. His crew built dams throughout the Adirondacks and at one point had to fight a major gypsy moth infestation. They sprayed a concoction that included lead, arsenic and fish oil on the larval nests! For some reason they also sprayed it on the surface of ponds. I suppose the fish oil initially kept most of the heavy metal poison on the surface of the water, but it must have eventually dissolved into the water or sediment to the bottom. I wonder if there is any documentation of this method of pest control anywhere else?"

Fred Stewart's daughter, Linda Hutchins of Malone said, "Dad was the unofficial barber of the camp. When we were cleaning out my dad's home we found all of his shaving brushes, straight razors, and barber scissors.

"After Dad left the CCC he married Lareta Ann Dunkley of Baker's Mills on May 8, 1937. They moved to Bolton Landing and Dad commuted to work on the construction of Route 28 from Wevertown to Warrensburg.

"So many of his CCC crew were from New York City and a lot of them were of Polish decent. One of the CCC guys lived with my parents in Bolton Landing. He was one of dad's crew and they were great friends."

He also worked in a variety of lumber camps. After a brief stint working for the mine at Tahawus, Fred got a job working for Barton Mines. He became foreman of the maintenance department and worked there until his retirement in 1987. Those who remember him there still miss his leadership and expertise.

Fred and his wife had three children, Fred, Jr., Linda, and Janice.

On Sunday, April 30, 2006 Fred passed away at Glens Falls Hospital.

A young Fred Stewart, dressed-up
in a suit and tie. Linda Hutchins

A June 6, 1939 photo of the leaders and assistant leaders of camp
S-82, Co. 204 in Bolton Landing. From the left, comma the 6thper-
son is W. S. Cadman Project Superintendent; the 7th, Lt. Edward
Carlson, USNR Commander; and the 8th, William A. McConvey,
Education Advisor. Bolton Historical Museum

CHAPTER 8
BOONVILLE

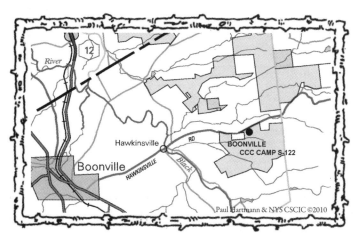

Paul Hartmann & NYS CSCIC ©2010

The Boonville CCC camp, S-122, established on August 9, 1935, was set up 7 mi. west of Boonville village on Hawkinsville Road. During its six years the camp did reforestation work, fought insects and tree diseases, built truck and foot trails, did stream improvement, stocked fish, did survey work, built parks, fought fires, and did fire prevention work such as building fire breaks and a fire tower.

One of the camp's projects was fighting blister rust, a fungus that damaged white pines. The crews destroyed the gooseberry and currant plants (ribes so called from the genus ribes) that were the host of the fungus. In 1941 Camp S-122 searched 1,170 acres in Boonville and destroyed 1,779 ribes. The enrollees also searched for caterpillar egg clusters on trees and applied creosote to them.[1]

The camp built the seven-mile truck trail from Thendara to Big Otter Lake to help in fire suppression.[2] They also completed the two-mile truck trail east of the Hamlet of Otter Lake.[3] They reforested 1,700 acres in Lyonsdale.[4] In 1941 the young men planted seedlings on 824 acres.[5]

The camp did silviculture work which is the art, science, and practice of establishing, tending, and reproducing forest stands of desired characteristics. They thinned forest by taking out undesirable species and fostered the growth of valuable species. The boys also removed crooked or damaged trees. In 1941 the CCC boys did silviculture work on 313 acres.[6]

CCC boys stocked the streams, ponds, and rivers with rainbow and brook trout. In 1941 they stocked 22,000.[7]

One of the projects of the CCC was the building of Pixley Falls State Park located 6 mi. south of Boonville village on Route 46. In 1940 enrollees set up a side camp with tents for sleeping and cooking. They made clearings for campsites and created a wading pool with a stone masonry dam on the stream.[8] The next summer the boys built a 25-ft. reinforced concrete bridge and the park project was completed.[9]

Clockwise from Right - CCC enrollees leaving their barracks and off to work on projects in the Boonville area. Joe Gaetano. The Boonville CCC camp built Pixley Falls State Park on Rt. 46. They built the fireplaces, picnic tables and pavilion. Podskoch Collection. This is the 1938 group picture of the Boonville CCC camp on the Hawkinsville Road. There are 135 enrollees, foremen, Conservation Department foresters and Army officers pictured in this beach photo. The camp was operating from 1935-1941. Joe Gaetano.

81

WORK ACCOMPLISHED BY CAMP S-122*

PROJECT	1935	1936	1937	1938	1939	1940	1941	TOTAL
Boundary marking - mi.				6.2		6.3	12.1	24.6
Bridges, vehicle - number		1					1	2
Buildings, misc. - number				1				1
Emergency work - man-days			500			94	117	711
Experimental plots - ac.				3	2			5
Fences - rods		678	451	492	822	1035	803	4281
Field planting trees - ac.	114	3183	1511	1137	437	1260	824	8466
Fire breaks - mi.		11.8	14	13				38.8
Fire fighting - man-days		133			12.5	46	39	230.5
Fire hazard reduction - ac.			227	141.1	185	190.1	111	854.2
Fire pre-suppression - man-days		120			188	455	255	1018
Fire towers - number							1	1
Fireplaces - number					10			10
Forest stand improvement - ac.		65	115	155	173	208.5	313	1029.5
General clean-up - ac.		1.5		21	25	17	23	87.5
Insect pest control - ac.			20			5	5	30
Latrines - number							2	2
Loading platforms - number		3						3
Observer's cabins - number							1	1
Other structural improvements - number			3	21			1	25
Parking areas - yd²				2667	1200	14529	5653	24049
Pipe & tile lines, conduit - linear ft.							170	170
Planting/moving trees & shrubs - man-days				100	30	95		225
Preparation/transportation of materials - man-days		303		329	865	188		1685
Razing undesirable structures - man-days			260		614	29	41	944
Riprap or paving - yd²					230			230
Searching for missing persons - man-days		134						134
Seed collection - bushels	20	3	3.5	7	6	32	15	86.5
Seeding & sodding - ac.							0.1	0.1
Sewage & waste disposal systems - number					1		1	2
Signs - number					96	26	35	157
Stocking fish - number							22000	22000
Stream development - mi.				4.7	4.3	0.9	0.3	10.2
Surveys - linear mi.		31						31
Surveys - man-days			368	488	511	388		1755
Table-bench combination - number							25	25
Timber estimating - ac.						224		224
Trails, foot - mi.		7.5				1.6	0.4	9.5
Trails, truck - mi.		0.3	2.3	3.1	0.5	0.3	0.6	7.1
Tree & plant disease control - ac.		2162	1543	1279	618	800	548	6950
Tree planting in gullies - yd²				950	1100	21660		23710
Water holes - number		9	6		5	4	1	25
Water lines - linear ft.							2400	2400
Wind erosion control - ac.		2085	3585	67	20.7	32.3	6	5796

*Numerical data from Conservation Reports

Above, Left - The fire tower on Gomer Hill was built by CCC Camp S-122 in 1941. It is no longer used for fire protection but for communications equipment. Paul Hartmann. Abobe, Right - Winter Lodge at Camp Russell Boy Scout camp on White Lake was a building at CCC Camp S-122. Podskoch Collection

On the first day of deer season in November 1940, seventy-five men searched for three hunters in Oneida and Herkimer counties. The next day all were reported safe. Later that month superintendent Edward Hamlin sent 25 of his CCC boys to search for lost hunters in the area between McKeever and Okara Lakes.[10]

The Boonville camp built a 67.5-ft. fire tower in 1940 on Gomer Hill 4 mi. west of Turin. They also built an observer's wooden cabin and erected a telephone line.[11] The tower was first staffed in 1941 and reported two fires and 161 visitors.

The Boonville CCC camp closed on October 31, 1941.

During WW II the abandoned Boonville CCC camp became a prisoner of war camp in 1944. More than 100 German prisoners cut wood for the Johnson Pulp Corporation in Boonville.[12]

When the POW camp was closed in 1946 most of the buildings were removed. In 1946 one of them went to Camp Russell, a Boy Scout camp on White Lake, south of Old Forge. The building is still used today and is called Winter Lodge.

The Conservation Department saved one of the CCC camp buildings and uses it as a workshop and for equipment storage.

MEMORIES

Jim Prime

In 2006 I was surprised to get a letter from Janice Prime in Glenville, NC. She wrote, "I'm Janice Musser Prime and I grew up in Boonville. Clayton Musser was my dad and Gladys Willard Musser was my mother. My grandfather, Garry Willard was owner and head of the Boonville Herald and Willard Press. I still get the Boonville Herald here in North Carolina. There was a story in the paper about you writing a book on the CCC. Well, my husband, Jim Prime, was an Army officer at the Boonville CCC camp. I just thought you'd like a letter from me for your project. I'm 93 years old and living with my son in North Carolina.

"My husband was born in 1910 in Bergenfield, NJ. He joined the Army and received a commission. In 1935 Jim came from Fort Hunt, Alexandria, VA to the Boonville S-122 Camp as a Second Lieutenant. The camp was on the Woodgate Road out of Boonville.

"I dated a lot of fellahs but when I met Jim, I knew he was the one. We got married in 1936.

"Jim spent weekdays at the camp and he came home when he wasn't on duty. We lived at my family's home on Schyler St. in Boonville. Then I got pregnant and had Clayton about 10 months later. It was a lot of fun having my husband working at the camp. They had a lot of dances that we went to at night.

"In 1937 Jim was made camp commander.

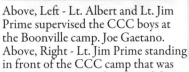

Above, Left - Lt. Albert and Lt. Jim Prime supervised the CCC boys at the Boonville camp. Joe Gaetano. Above, Right - Lt. Jim Prime standing in front of the CCC camp that was located on the Woodgate Road during the 1930s. He married a Boonville girl, Janice Musser. Janice Prime

"He was at the camp until 1938 when he took 200 young men from New York City by train to Priest Lake, Idaho. The boys had never been out of N. Y. City. Priest Lake was just 10 miles or so from Canada. I took my first son Clayton to Priest Lake when he was one year old. We lived in a camp on the Lake not far from the CCC camp where my husband was stationed. Jim was the commander of the camp. My nearest neighbor was an Indian woman. I lived at a camp in the woods on the lake not far from the CCC camp. I took Clayton in a stroller to the store. I had to pump water from the well and we used an outhouse.

"Jim and I stayed there until the camp closed. I left by train with Clayton and lived with my parents in Boonville.

"My husband then was in World War II from 1942 until 1947. He was a Lieutenant Colonel when the war was over.

"After the war Jim and I lived in Boonville with our three sons: Clayton, James, and Stephen. Jim worked at Willard Press."

Joe Gaetano

One Sunday af-

Joe Gaetano of Dolgeville developed a life-long friendship with Joe Composto (left). Another enrollee, Sunny Marsh, is on the right. Joe Gaetano

ternoon I got a call from Joe Gaetano of Dolgeville, NY. He told me that he had seen an article in the Little Falls newspaper about me writing a book on the CCC.

He said, "I was in the Boonville CCC camp and I have a lot of stories and some great pictures that I'd like to show you. Those were the best years of my life. I met great people. This one guy, Joe Composto, came in 1933. We became fast friends. He was from Brooklyn and married a girl from Boonville. I used to visit him through the years. He bought a house and had two kids. One time I went there and nobody was home, so I got a room at the Hulbert House in town.

"The next day I went to Mass and breakfast and then to Joe's. When I told him I had stopped by the night before, Joe handed me a key and said: 'You are always welcome.'"

"Other times when I went to see Joe Composto in Bloomville, I loaded my suitcase with butter, meat, and pastries from camp. Joe had two young girls. I'd stay there for the weekend and if I met a girl I'd be with her. Then on Sunday if I didn't have a ride, I'd have to walk back seven miles. Sometimes in the winter the temperature was −20 degrees. I'd be swearing to myself that I'd never do it again. As soon as I got back to camp the heat from the stoves warmed me up and I felt good. I'd go over to the kitchen and the cook would give me a hot cup of coffee and a piece of pie.

"If a man has one good friend in life, it is so great. I was always welcome in his house and he showed me love."

On August 13, 2006 I drove to Dolgeville to visit Joe. It was a double block home. Joe's wife Helen greeted me at the door and sent me to the kitchen where Joe was frying some red peppers and garlic in olive oil. It was two o'clock in the afternoon but Joe had the dining room table set for only one person, me. He sat me down and brought out a dish of pasta with broccoli and garlic, and a slice of Italian bread. Then he dished out the red peppers plate. I felt so

welcome. After I ate Joe went down cellar and brought out fresh canoles from his nephew's bakery in Utica. Then he began to talk.

"I was born in Utica in 1918 and had a large family. There were eleven children: Tony, John, Sylvester, Elvira, Nittie, Angie, and me. My mother's name was Gertrude and my dad was Joe. He worked in a textile factory in Utica. Dad died before I was born and Mom married a widower, Tom Marrotta, with two boys, Frank and Carmen. My mother then had two more children named Walter and Albert.

"I quit school at age 17 and was a barber for a time. I needed a job and in the winter of 1937 I signed up for the CCC in Utica. I heard about it from a lady at the welfare department. It was either go to work or go on welfare. I was the only one who joined from my family.

"There were four barracks with about 30 men in each. We had a potbellied stove that burned soft coal. One time the fireman didn't open the vents and carbon monoxide started spreading inside. Luckily, somebody came in late and smelled something funny. He woke everybody up and saved our lives. There was a lot of gas in the soft coal. From that day on we always slept with every other window open about 3". Sometimes we'd get up in the morning and there would be 3" of snow at the foot of my bed.

"The food was good. We had a Polish cook who didn't speak English too well but could he bake pies and cakes. The main cook Joe Egan was excellent, too.

"One guy asked me for a haircut and when the other guys heard about it I cut theirs, too, for 25 cents a person. It was a good way to make money.

"We had a lot of different jobs. We planted trees, fought fires, built trails and fought insects and disease. We sometimes walked up to two hours to get to a fire. We carried Indian tanks and dug trenches. Sometimes the fire went deep into the ground and we had to dig down to get to it. We also worked on blister rust, which killed white pine

trees. We had to dig up roots of gooseberries and hang them up to dry. Once they were dead the blister rust did not have its host to live off.

"Some of the area around camp was very sandy but we had to plant trees there. We had contests to see who could plant the most trees. One fellow said, 'We planted 20,000 more trees than you.' So I asked a guy to keep an eye on him. He secretly followed him and saw him throw a bunch of seedlings down a woodchuck hole. Now we knew how they won.

"We worked as a team planting trees. One guy had a mattock and the other guy carried the seedlings in a bucket. The guy with the mattock drove the sharp end in and pulled it back to make the small opening for the seedling. The other guy put a seedling in the hole. Then the mattock guy stepped on the hole. We worked fast so you had to be careful that they didn't step on your fingers.

"In summertime we picked up the dead trees and brush and burned them in the winter.

"One of the camp foremen I worked for was Mike Gentile. He was Italian just like me. Mike was a good-looking guy and one of the nicest guys in camp.

"When we came back to camp sweaty we wanted to get a shower. We sometimes left money on the bed but didn't worry about someone stealing it because if they did, they'd suffer the consequences.

"The clothes they gave us had a certain smell. It was a nice smell. I can still smell it today.

"Our Army camp leader was Lieutenant Prime. His family lived in Boonville. We used to bum rides from him when he was on his way home. He'd stop and pick us up. Boy, was he a fast driver.

"On weekends we used to go different places and bum around. One time Lew Carrra from Lyons Falls and I went to a beer joint in Woodgate. We had a few drinks and later decided to go to Boonville. As we were leaving, Don

Left - Five CCC boys have just set the mess hall tables for a special dinner. They even decorated the ceiling beams with branches.
Right - A work crew taking a break in the woods during the winter. There was always a pot of coffee on the fire for lunch and breaks. The boys were happy to have new leather & rubber boots provided by the Army because many had joined with holes or cardboard in their shoes.
Joe Gaetano (Both)

Covey was outside. He said come in for a drink. We said, 'No, but we'll wait outside for you.' Then the camp Chaplin, Mr. Tusk, saw us and asked what we were doing? We said we were waiting for Covey for a ride. The Chaplin asked us to come in and have a drink and then we could get a ride with him. We didn't see Covey inside, so the Chaplin, Lew, and I had a beer. Then the Chaplin told us he'd take us to Boonville, so we left with him. It was raining as we drove on the winding Hog's Back Road. We saw troopers on the roadside and asked them what happened. 'A car hit a tree and the three people were killed. The car was split in half. It was Covey's car. We realized that we could have been in that car, too. The bodies were lying on the ground covered with blankets. It was horrible."

"One of the activities at camp was boxing. My friend, Joe Composto, was a boxer, but I never wanted to fight.

"We used to play tricks on the guys in camp. At night we'd nail a guy's shoes to the floor near his bed and in the morning he'd have a hell of a time getting his shoes off the floor. Another trick was short sheeting a bed. Guys would fold the sheets so the person couldn't get their feet all the way down. One poor guy was out late and we hung his bed from the ceiling with ropes. When he walked in it was dark and he couldn't see the bed so he slept on the floor.

"Some guys went home on weekends but I mostly went home only for holidays. I was having too much fun with the girls. They showed movies at the camp. One day my girlfriend came to the movies at camp. She told a friend to tell me in the movies that she was there and that she had a girlfriend who was looking for a boyfriend. So everybody begged me, 'Hey, Barb (barber), can I please go with you?'

"Sometimes we'd take a ride to a friend's camp at Black River to have fun. We had to be back for roll call about 7 am Monday.

"There were some days I'd be so tired after work that I didn't feel like going out, but after I took a shower

Forty young men lived in this barracks. Three pot-bellied stoves burned coal to keep them warm. The beds had to be made and all clothes in lockers for inspections by the Army Captain. Joe Gaetano

and ate I'd be ready to go.

"One time we were doing blister rust work. We were taking a break so I decided to sleep for a while cause I was out late at night. I put some paper under my head and fell asleep. When I woke up there was nobody around. So I panicked and ran off to where the truck was. The guys were just loading up and were ready to leave. I said to the foreman, 'Hey, why didn't you wake me up?' He replied, 'I just wanted to teach you a lesson for staying out so late. I hoped when you woke up we'd be gone, then you'd have to walk back to camp'

Joe Gaetano making me a fried red peppers and garlic sandwich. Podskoch Collection

"After they changed the law allowing us to stay more than two years I was able to stay through 1940. During that time I was the camp barber. I'd take two trunks for the guy to sit on. I had a regular barber cloth. After the haircut they signed a paper and I'd be waiting for them when they were getting paid. That's how I got my quarter for the hair cut. When I got some money saved up I went to Utica and bought a barber's chair. They even shipped it to camp in a truck.

"While I was cutting hair, another friend of mine, Tommy Ferraro from Rome, was running a craps game. He'd give me a percentage of the game.

"Sometimes when I was in town I'd see the guys hanging around a restaurant waiting for the truck to take them back to camp. They'd be broke and I'd treat them to a coffee and a doughnut. I was loaded from cutting their hair.

"I married a girl from Boonville, Ellen Crandall. She was a beautiful girl. I saw her at a dance but I figured I never had a chance with her. I'd dance with others but not her.

"One day I went to the movies alone. Someone came over and tapped me on the shoulder. It was her uncle. He said, 'Do you want to sit with us?' I said, 'Sure.' I went and sat with her and her aunt and uncle. My heart was pounding and I thought it would bust. That was the beginning of our romance. When I got out of the CCC we got married in Boonville in 1941.

"I was going to open a barbershop but my brother, Sal, said to come to Dolgeville where there was a job for both of us in Eastern Footwear. I had two boys, Drake and David.

"I joined the Navy in 1944 and I came out in 1946. Then I opened a barbershop. I'm 87 years old and I'm still cutting hair. Let's take a ride now and I'll show you my camp pictures."

We drove down Main Street to a one-story brick building. Inside was a vintage 1950 barbershop with three barber chairs. Joe walked over to a bulletin board and proudly showed me his CCC pictures. He carefully took them off and said, "Here Marty, take these. I don't have anyone in my family to give them to. I know you are really interested in them and you can use them in your book." He also gave me his large camp photo with all of the guys in camp.

We drove back to Joe's and he said, "I have something else for you. You're going to be hungry driving to your talk tonight." He went to the kitchen and sliced his fresh Italian bread. Then he took the pan of roasted red peppers and made me two sandwiches, wrapped them in aluminum foil and said, "I hope you enjoy them. Thanks for writing about my CCC camp and please stop by again."

Whenever I'm near Dolgeville, I stop to see Joe. I drop off a bottle of burgundy that he loves and he always has some Italian treats for me.

Marion Francis Shean

In May 2007 Peg Masters, Town of Webb historian, told me to contact a former CCC boy who had called her about getting information on fire towers for his book about his experiences at the Boonville CCC camp.

I called Marion Francis Shean at his home in Watertown. The first thing he told me was: "Marty, if it wasn't for the CCC who knows what might have happened to me. I was just wandering and searching what to do with my life. I kept getting into trouble.

"I self-published a book about my life and experiences in the Boonville CCC camp and want to send you a copy. I'll also send you some pictures of the camp and you can use my stories and pictures in your book."

Here are some excerpts from Marion's book, "My Life in the Civilian Conservation Corps."

"I grew up in Harrisville and quit school in the spring of 1937. I ended up going to Gouverneur to work as a cook in an all night restaurant. I soon tired of this. So in September I came back to stay with my Dad in Harrisville. I went back to school. I tried to buckle down and study, but the wanderlust had got to me. In the last part of October while sitting in school I felt that I had to do something, therefore at noon I went outside just to clear my head. While thinking things over I spotted one of my grandfathers trucks coming up the hill loaded with logs and headed out for Lowville. I knew then what I wanted to do, so I ran out and hailed the driver for a ride. I rode along with him talking about what I should do and he agreed that what I planned was probably the best for me. Soon we got into Lowville and I had the driver let me off in front of the county building. I then went in to see about the Civilian Conservation Corps where I signed an application to join. The truck driver picked me up on his way back and I rode home telling him to say nothing to anybody about my trip. I was very much aware of what the C's were all about for the CCC boys had been coming to town on weekends since the insertion of the camp over on the road to Croghan, about five miles from us. Moreover, one of the boys from camp was courting my sister Myrtle.

"School was now only a stopgap for me while I was waiting for news about the Civilian Conservation Corp.

"I was always doing something that the consequence got me into bad trouble. It all started out at a dance at the school on a Saturday night. I had teamed up with this boy and we went to a local grocery store, that wasn't open, after the dance. Well, we took what we wanted, some small change, some candy, and then climbed back out the side window we had used to get into the building in the first place. This all happened about one o'clock in the morning. I think my sister Myrtle heard me sneaking into the house, for later she told me that she knew that I was in on this deal. Well, on Monday at school the state police came and picked up the other boy. They knew he was one of the guilty participants, but he said that he did it alone and had broken into the place at ten o'clock. As I was at the school dance till midnight I was never connected to this affair. I was really lucky, for this boy could have blabbed but he didn't. This was just one of the many instances that brought me to my senses and helped get me on the right path of reality.

"I had no guidance back then or anyone to help me in my planning for the future, no one to talk to about what I should do, just the truck driver who was merely a friend

87

Boonville Camp S-122 was located in Hawkinsville about 6 mi. east of Boonville. It was the home of 200 poor boys aged 18-25. The camp roads and paths were bordered with whitewashed stones. Each morning the boys lined up by the flagpole for roll call and raising of the flag. Across from the camp is a white farmhouse of the neighboring farmer. Marion Frances Shean

of the family. I suppose that this all came about because I always had been so set in my ways and now I would have to pay for it the hard way. I don't know what I would have done without baseball, basketball and the band. All this helped to keep me from going nuts. I was becoming more and more restless as time went on.

"It was a little before the Christmas holidays of 1937, that Dad and I had gone to my grandparent's house for supper. While everyone was seated, my grandmother brought out this letter that had come in the mail at her house addressed to me. The letter was to inform me that I had been accepted into the Civilian Conservation Corps. I was to report on January 19, 1938. While I was reading it to myself, Dad asked me what the letter was about. I hadn't told him that I had been to Lowville earlier in the fall to sign up for the CCCs. Well, when I showed it to him he just said, "You might just as well go, for you won't amount to much around here anyway." I remembered this for a long time as it truly hurt me.

"He did take me to Lowville on the appointed day since I needed him to sign the necessary papers for my enlistment. In filling out the part about my monthly pay of thirty dollars a month, I signed over to my dad twenty five dollars to help him and my sisters with the bills at home. After the necessary paperwork was signed, we said our good byes. I observed by his expression that maybe he did care about me after all.

"With about six other boys I was taken to the Boonville Camp S-122, Company 1241 the camp was about six miles from Boonville, just past Hawkinsville on the road to Woodgate, where we given a physical, some army clothes that were the vintage of World War I. We didn't get dress goods just clothes for working and then we were indoctrinated with the awe-inspiring ways of camp life.

"For the new recruits this was culture shock. For many it was their first time away from home, and now they were holding their first steady jobs. Many of the boys who participated in the CCC were from the city or other urban areas,

"Our way of life was strictly controlled. There was a daily routine, including everything from working and leisure hours and bathing. The barracks had to be kept clean, beds had to be made before breakfast with no wrinkles in the covers. We also had to clean the campsite and more.

"Our day started with the sound of a bugle from the P.A. system, blasting out reveille at 6 am. We had just enough time to get dressed, then hurry to the mess hall for our breakfast, and be at the parade ground ready for roll call by seven o'clock. At this time we would be turned over to the state and they would assign us to work crews for the day. If the temperature was lower than twenty below zero, we did not have to go out to work and we could now lounge around, or maybe catch up on our laundry work and do whatever we wished.

"On the nights that the movie house in Boonville was open we might go to town and see a show. The first few weeks that I was in the CCC was a very lonesome time for me. Homesick? Yes, I suppose I was, but after a few weeks of working and making a few new friends I soon became adjusted to being away from home.

"For a couple of weeks I worked out in the woods trimming trees and the building of fire trails but I soon tired of this. At the canteen I kept expressing my desire to my buddies about working in the garage repairing the trucks and to become a mechanic. I guess the boys at the canteen had enough of this so one of them suggested that I get a couple of cigars and take them up to the personnel officer and give him the gift while telling him what I wanted. Well, I got two cigars right then at the canteen and I went up to the Personnel Office where I asked for the transfer to the garage, but I did not give him the cigars.

"After being on the waiting list a week or two I was assigned to the garage as a mechanic's helper. I never did tell my buddies at the canteen that I did not do the bribe. On my first day of work on my new job I found that a helper was just that. I soon found out that it was my duty to keep the place clean and picked up by sweeping out the garage

Marion Francis Shean is starting the Army truck with a crank with two unidentified friends. Marion Frances Shean

and bringing in coal for the stove. I washed and waxed trucks, but not in the winter for the garage was extremely cold.

"I do remember one time when I took a can of Simonize with the intention of giving it to my grandfather. The boss found out and I was ordered to report to the camp counselor. I was told in no uncertain terms that this was not sanctioned and that I could be kicked out of the C's if I did anything like this again.

"While working around the garage, I could move the trucks in and out but that was all because I didn't have a license yet. I was issued an army permit so I could drive the Army vehicles. Later in the spring the camp personnel officer took me to Lowville where I took a road test for my state license. It was not long after this, that I was transferred to driving a state vehicle to transport a crew to job sites.

"A significant advantage now was that I did not have to report for roll calls any more for it was my duty to have my truck ready to take a crew to the work site. The eighteen boys in the crew rode in the back of the truck, which had a canvas top. The trucks did not have heaters back then. Earlier when I had been at the mess hall for breakfast, I had picked up some coffee, sugar, and a bag lunch for each boy that rode in my truck. When we got to the work site and the boys were all out working in the woods dragging brush, I would start a fire so the boys could get warm and dry off.

"At noon time they all came to sit around the fire for lunch and coffee. I made the coffee over the fire using two water pails. When the coffee was hot and steamy, I always cracked an egg and dropped one in each pail. The coffee grounds got cooked with the egg making a cleaner brew. O yes, I had acquired the eggs at the mess hall when I picked up the lunches. If I got cold while waiting for lunchtime, I would pitch in and help the boys drag out some of the brush. Dragging brush was not a bad chore because when we were passing each other on the return trip someone was sure to start wrestling with a buddy. We did have some liberty in working, just as long as we showed up out at

the burning pile now and then.

"Some time in later part of March my duties were changed and I had to go up to the side camp at a place called Highmarket on Tug Hill. This temporary camp was built so as to be closer to the work area. It was about fifteen miles away from our main camp. The living quarters for the boys consisted of three tents for sleeping and one for our meals. The tents had wooden floors and a small stove so it was not awfully cold sleeping, even when the temperature got below zero.

"I recall another trip I took with a load of timbers up to the boys to use in the construction of some cribbing they were building along a creek. It was late in the day when we had all the timbers unloaded, so the other truck moved out in a hurry, taking all the other boys. It had been raining most of the day and the field I had to drive across had thawed considerably and the truck broke through the rutted road. By the time I got to the end of the road I found that I was not able to get out of the ruts and onto hard ground. I backed up the truck a few yards for a good running start, but no use. I just could not get enough momentum to get out. After spending an hour or so of this, my next move was to walk about three miles in the rain to a farmhouse that had a phone. I called the main camp for them to send out the bulldozer to pull me out. Since the duty man did not want to send out the dozer so late at night, I had to do some explaining to convince him that if the truck was left over night, it would be frozen in solid by morning. Well, it was 11:30 before I got back to camp that night and I was soaking wet and half frozen.

"A little later in the spring I was trucking some logs back to camp, and as I started down the hill into Hawkinsville, the load shifted and a chain broke. It wrapped itself around the axel of the truck thereby breaking the brake line. Down at the bottom of the hill was a sharp left-hand turn. There was no way that I was going to make it. But I must have said some awfully good prayers for the

Ludwick Osiko, camp blacksmith and crew leader, standing on the cribbing built by the CCC to protect the stream and riverbanks from erosion. Marion Francis Shean

next thing that occurred was the chains tangled with the other wheel thereby locking it tight and this brought me to a standstill. It was amazing that young boys could do the things that they were called on to do.

"When we had to haul gravel for stream erosion we would back our trucks up to a gravel bank to get it loaded. We did not have any bucket loaders or any power shovels, just eight or nine strong backed boys with shovels. They would get the truck loaded in about twenty-five minutes. At first, being new on this kind of a truck I had a devil of a time getting out of the pit. I had to depend on our crew leader for the first few loads to drive up the bank and then I took over from there. We had 1937 Reo speed wagons for dump trucks, and the shift pattern was crazy and it took awhile for me to get used to shifting on a hill. This was my first introduction to double clutching.

"On the weekends we sometimes went to the movie theater in Boonville. There was an embarrassing episode that happened in the theater. There were a couple of CCC boys and I watching the show. Then all of a sudden we got a whiff of a horrible odor. Couldn't figure it out, but after the show when we were all standing around outside talking, another boy from the camp come out of the building and joined us. We knew then what the smell was. We then went back to camp in the Army truck. I was not in on the G.I. bath that was given to this smelly guy but I know that from then on he took a bath at least once a week A GI bath is when a bunch of boys give a scrub down to a boy that is too lazy to take a shower regularly.

"Weekends were a boring time at camp for the ones that got stuck with no place to go but one thing in our favor was we could go dancing. Understand, we were in farming country and it was predominantly Polish. They were great people. They worked hard and

All of us waved to the farmer's daughter when we saw her on the road going to or coming home from school. She would wave back with only her hand moving and not her arm, so someone nicknamed her 'Short Wave.' Marion Frances Shean

played hard and dancing was a big thing for them. They had picnic groves set up all around the area and one thing they all had was a plank-floor for dancing. Well the CCC boys were always there having fun at these affairs but we soon learned not to mess with the girls when off the dance floor or you could get into big trouble.

"How about this, some boys had gone into Boonville to see a show. Well anyway on the way back to camp they came by a cemetery and picked up a gravestone that was about two inch thick and flat. When they got to the barracks, they put it under the bed covers of another member. A little while later the victim to be came in and just jumped on the cot and what a surprise he had. The cot collapsed and everyone made believe they were asleep. He had no one to help straighten it up again. Of course, the barracks leader made the jokers return the stone the next day. Another joke that was played on other members was to fold the legs of a cot, just a little, and then a rope was tied to the legs in such a manner that with one good tug on the rope the bed would collapse, this was done after everybody was sound asleep.

"Stream erosion was also a major concern for the state. So when called upon for their services the crews would go out and install log barriers along streams to keep the banks from eroding. This work was not limited to just state land; it could be done for farmers that had trouble with a creek overflowing their land. All they had to do was put in a request for work to be done on streams running across their property. The crew consisted of a state forester and a crew leader and of course about eight or ten boys to do the work. By the time the weekend came around the boys were ready to go back down to the main camp. If they didn't have KP duty or any other weekend duty, they could draw a pass and go home.

"Since I was a truck driver I was also a 'gofer.' So when the cook or boys needed fresh water it was up to me to go and get some. Our fresh water for the side camp was picked up at a farm down the road and at various times I went alone. This filling of 20 or 30 milk cans at a hand pump was quite a job for one boy. That was hard enough but the cans had to be swung up onto the truck after they were full. When I had help, it was easy, but being alone was tough and it took awhile before I got the hang of swinging the cans up onto the truck.

"There were boys in our camp from all over our country even some from Puerto-Rico. It was a lot of fun trying to understand the ones from Puerto-Rico for they spoke Spanish. The ones from New York City were the best of all, for they spoke English with a different accent. This was no big deal we just had a lot of laughter now and then.

"Week-end passes were hard to get during a summer dry spell since we might get called up for fire duty to go fight a fire. I always had to be available for driving a crew out to wherever the fire might be. I never did any fire fighting myself but I did take a crew to a fire up in the Schroon Lake section. Fire fighters back then did not have the equipment like today. All they had were shovels and pick-axes to work with. Although they did have an Indian water tank on their back with a pump-gun for wetting down hot spots. To control fires a lot of work was put into building fire trails in the woods so that fire fighters could get to the fire much quicker and easier. These trails were also a very good firebreak for any fire that got started because of someone throwing a cigarette from a vehicle."

I asked Marion why he left the CCC. "Well, I had been writing back and forth to my mother who was living down in Hartford, CT. I had just signed up for another term in the C's and I had some leave time coming. She had already sent me her address so in September of '38 I caught a ride with a vegetable truck driver to Albany. Then after a few problems I found my mother's house.

"With a lot of rain and the 1938 hurricane hitting the east coast I become trapped in Hartford. I worked on flood control for a few days along the river, and then with no money in my pocket I thought it best for me to get a job. I found one at a sheet metal shop. I liked the work so decided to get out of the Cs. As my two week pass was about over I called the camp and was able to get a leave of absence on the stipulation that I would return within 30 days to be discharged and I was instructed to bring at least two pay stubs for verification of employment. I lived with my mother for a while. Then she left and went to Vermont to live.

"At the age of 18 I was again on my own and ready to start a new life in Hartford, CT. It was there that I met a nice girl, Florence Beaulieu. After courting her for about a year we got married on August 2, 1940.

"After leaving the C's I realized how much it had done for me. I was a changed person. I had more confidence in myself and it instilled in me a more honest way of life."

Peter Zacek

I met Stan Slusarczyk of Prospect at the Westernville Library north of Rome, NY, in October 2007 and he introduced me to his friend Peter Zacek, who had been in the CCC. We sat at a library table and Peter told me his life story.

"My dad worked in the nearby pulp mill in Hinckley. Then they started building the Hinckley Dam and the mill closed because it went bankrupt. My family moved to Erie, PA and dad worked in a mill there. I was born there on February 23, 1921. There were eight children. In 1921 when I was six months old my family moved back to Hinckley. My parents then had a small dairy farm. When I was just six years old I blew off some fingers. It happened in March of 1927. There was a boarder who had lived in our house and left some blasting caps. One evening my brothers, sisters, and I watched my older brother, Charles, take one of the blasting caps and loosen up some of the powder using a long match stick He dropped the powder on the red, hot, wood stove. It acted like a sparkler on the Fourth of July. We all thought it was great.

"Early the next morning my parents went to the barn to do chores. I could hardly wait to hear the door close so I could get one of the dynamite caps. I took a cap and tried to do what my brother did the night before. When I couldn't get the powder out of the cap, I held the cap on the hot stove. It exploded and blew my hand all to pieces. Blood and parts of my fingers were all over the kitchen.

"My younger sister ran to get my mother in the barn. I ran out on the porch and shoved my hand in the snow. My mother rushed home and diluted some iodine in a pan of lukewarm water. My father took me two miles on a horse and sleigh to Doctor Kline in Prospect. When he looked at my hand he said, 'It's so bad, I'll have to take his hand off.' My dad said no way. Please try and save it.

"Dr. Kline called Dr. Lewis in Holland Patent to see if he could help. Dr. Lewis came and both of them worked on my hand. They did the best they could in those days. The result of the explosion was the loss of my thumb, the next finger and up to one joint of the middle finger.

"Dad had to take me back to the doctor in Prospect every day for a couple weeks because I got an infection. Blood poisoning set in and the doctor had to draw the fluid out with a needle.

"This loss of fingers did not stop me from working on the farm. I learned to drive a tractor and truck. This would be a big plus when I joined the CCC.

"When I was 17 I joined the CCC in 1938 and was enrolled at the Boonville camp. The jobs that I had were planting trees, clearing dead trees, and being a night guard. I

Pete Zacek standing near one of the dump trucks he drove at the Boonville CCC camp from 1938-39. Peter Zacek

had to go to each building every hour to check the fires. I stoked the fires with coal. I was a night watchman for the camp buildings and my friend, Julian Poczatek, was the night watchman for the lower part of camp where the gas pumps and garages were. He watched so no one stole gas or bothered the trucks.

"I had to punch a clock at each building every hour. I didn't like this job and became a truck driver. This is where my farming experience paid off. A lot of the guys in camp were from the cities and didn't have that experience. I worked with a crew building Pixley Falls State Park. Each day I drove 40 boys in a big rack truck from camp to the work site. The foreman sat in front with me. I didn't have much to do, just drive. It was too easy. We stopped work at noon for lunch and someone made coffee on a campfire. We left the site to get back to camp around four o'clock.

"I worked in the Boonville camp till late 1939 when I left the CCC. Work was very scarce so I joined again and was sent to the Bolton Landing camp near Lake George."

Peter Zacek's experiences are continued in the Bolton Landing camp chapter.

Newell Wagoner

On June 7, 2006 I talked with Newell Wagoner, a long-time Boonville native and insurance agent. I asked him about his childhood memories of the Boonville CCC camp.

"I was just a teenager when the camp was in operation. Captain Jim Prime was in charge of the camp in Hawkinsville just east of Boonville. He married Janis Musser of Boonville. Janis' family started the Boonville Herald. After he finished working at the CCC camps he came back to this town with his wife and settled here.

"The town used to hold dances for the CCC boys.

The boys met girls and some married and became members of our community.

"Another CCC guy who lived here was Joe Composto. Most of his family is gone. One thing that stands out in my mind is that he didn't drive yet he worked in a mill in Rome. Joe always got to work because he bummed a ride from someone. He never missed a day of work.

"Neil Short, another CCC boy, married Dorothy Joslin from town. He stayed in Boonville. Another girl, Marion Dye, married Roy Gerrish who was in the CCC.

"The CCC boys had their own softball team. Our Boonville team used to go out there and play them. The field they used was very bushy in the outfield. One time I was playing in the outfield and somebody hit a home run into the woods. We searched and searched but we couldn't find the ball. We had to end the game because the camp could only afford one ball. They were all very nice guys at the camp and we had fun playing them.

"The camp was located in a desolate, sandy plain. They planted and trimmed trees and helped prevent the buildup of sand dunes. They saved a lot of land that is productive today."

Roman Charney

On June 27, 2007 while speaking at the Erwin Library in Boonville, someone told me Bridget Charney's husband, Roman, was in the CCC and she lived a few blocks from the library. The librarian, Donna Ripp, called Bridget and asked if I could interview her and she agreed to a visit.

I drove to Charney's home and she shared her husband's CCC album. It had a collection of photos and news clippings of his CCC days. It also had information about his CCC Alumni group. They had monthly meetings during the 1980s in Rome. Most of the pictures were about his days in a CCC camp down South. Mrs. Charney let me take the album to the library where I copied a few of the pages.

Then my interest in Roman Charney revived when I received an email on July 16, 2009.

"I just read with interest your article in the Boonville Herald about the Boonville CCC camp. My name is Theresa Phelps and my father was Roman Charney. We are originally from Boonville. My father passed away in 2004. Dad couldn't get into the Army because he had been shot in a milk strike in 1939 so he joined the CCC. He was in the Boonville camp where he worked and also learned to box. He won the Golden Gloves in New York City.

"Dad was first in the CCC in Washington DC. At some point in his stay he was the chauffeur for Eleanor Roosevelt. I didn't learn about Dad driving Mrs. Roosevelt until before he had his stroke in 1993. He never talked about his 'life' before my brother and I were born."

On August 25, 2009 Theresa came to my talk on the CCC at the Old Forge Library. She shared her dad's photo album. She also had a picture of a CCC reunion at Pixley Falls.

From all of the information Theresa and her mother gave me I learned that Roman Charney first went to Fort Dix for conditioning on March 26, 1934. He received a satisfactory rating and was sent to Fort Hunt, Virginia on May 11, 1934. Charney told Utica Daily Press reporter R. Patrick Corbett in a June 20, 1983 article, "Remember the CCC Camps?" about when he went for his physical exam. "We were divided alphabetically by last name and the A-F group was sent to work for the National Park Service in Virginia and Washington. We maintained many of the Washington-area parks and built a riding path that was a favorite with President Roosevelt's family. That job earned us a handshake from a grateful president."

Roman's father, Nicholas Charney, of Westernville received a monthly allotment of $25. This was a big help for his father and mother, Maryanne, who had three more children, Michael, Emil, and Peter, to feed.

On March 31, 1935 Roman was discharged from NP-6 at Fort Hunt, Virginia. The Army furnished his transportation by train from Washington, DC to Utica, NY.

Charney left the CCC to return home to Boonville to buy a farm. The plan never materialized and he didn't have a job. He was fortunate to find out that his former CCC company in Virginia was being transferred to Boonville. He re-signed with the CCC and worked there for 11 months.

He said the food in the CCC was plentiful and good. The young men weren't used to this kind of food during the Great Depression. "The most I ever weighed in my life was when I got out. But the hard work kept my 217 pounds hard," said Charney.

A Boonville Herald dated March 4, 1937 stated that heavyweight boxer Roman Charney left for New York City to participate in the NY Daily News Golden Gloves semi-finals. He used his weight, strength, and physical training to win the New York State Golden Gloves heavyweight championship in 1937.

In 1939 dairy farmers in New York State were protesting the low price they were receiving for their milk. They held a strike and refused to deliver milk to creameries. Some farmers refused to abide by the strike and continued to deliver their milk to plants. This led to picketing, which prevented farmers from delivering their milk to processing plants.

Roman Charney was involved in the strike by promoting the milk boycott. On August 29, 1939 The Lowville Journal and Republican reported Roman Charney and three other men were shot in Oneida County when dairy farmers clashed with pickets who were trying to maintain a milk blockade. Charney from Boonville and Russell Ossont from Lyons Falls were in a group of about 50 pickets who rushed a milk truck as it entered the milk plant. Rocks were thrown and fights broke out. Some pickets began dumping the milk. Gerald Blowers was one of the 12 men on the truck protecting the milk. Blowers allegedly shot the two men. The skirmish took place at the Dairymen's League Cooperative Association plant in Camden. Charney was shot in the abdomen and reported to be in serious condition. Charney eventually recovered from the shooting but when WWII broke out he failed the physical.

In 1941 he married Bridget Lastowski and they had two children, Theresa and Bernard.

James Sherman and
The New York State Civilian
Conservation Corps Veterans
Chapter # 1

James Sherman from Rome joined the CCC and

Roman Charney worked at the Boonville camp and participated in boxing matches. He even won the NYS Golden Gloves match in NYC. Here are the Boonville camp boxers: Roman, "Slim Dolan, "Pop" O'Connell, Tuffy" Casanoola, Joe Compasto, and Don Atken. Theresa Phelps

Roman Charney on the porch of the camp office. Theresa Phelps

traveled a short distance of 35 miles to camp S-122 in Boonville for his CCC tour.

During his six-month stint he worked building Pixley Falls State Park in the Boonville Gorge five miles south of Boonville on Rote 46. He also cut trees behind his Boonville camp. Sherman said, "Then we took them over to West Leyden and they cut them up into lumber for the pavilion and other buildings that we built at Pixley Falls State Park. We also cleared the trees at the park and built the roads to and into the park.

"Our Boonville camp planted thousands of trees throughout the Boonville Gorge area along Route 46. As you drive up Buck Hill you can see the beautiful reforested area that came from the seeds of our hard work. We planted red pine, white pine, jack pine, Japanese larch, Norwegian pine, and silver spruce.

"The soil was quite sandy. I never thought we'd be able to grow trees there. We planted willow trees in the sandy soil to prevent erosion. Then we cut branches off the willows at an angle and stuck them into the ground to take root and grow.

"Along the Lansing Kill and Black River the guys placed brush in the stream and cut back the banks to provide fish places to spawn and hide.

"I also benefited from the CCC because that's how I got my driver's license. I had to learn how to drive the CCC trucks.

"The CCC helped a lot of young men learn how to live together and get along. They respected each other's rights. This came in handy when they joined the military during WW II.

"While out West I saw what they did with rowdy guys. They shipped them to camps that were in the wilderness like Billings Montana. Some of the camps were up to 150 miles from the nearest town."

Sherman signed up for another six-month tour in Boonville but after 13 days he was fortunate to find a job with General Cable Corporation in Rome.

On June 9, 1982 Sherman founded and organized the New York State Civilian Conservation Corps Veterans Chapter # 1 in Rome, NY. At first the group had 16 members and was part of the National Association of Civilian Conservation Corps Alumni (NACCA). Sherman told reporter Francis L. Lamb: "Its not only a fraternal group, but an attempt to get the CCC going again for the younger generation."

The group gathered each month on the third Thursday at Smith Post American Legion or at Colonial Towers Apartments.

One of the group's primary efforts was to urge the federal government to organize a modern-day civilian conservation corps that would occupy the nation's unemployed youth.

By 1983 the group had 39 men who lived in the Mohawk Valley area. Here are some of its members: August Oldfield, Donald Woodruff, John Wolf, Carl Franky, Kenneth Leach, Herbert Thorpe, Theodore Gomelski, John Halupka, Francis Kenneally, John Scalise, Joseph Griffo, Jim Walsh, Stanley Rebizs, Virgil Reid (Rome), Norman Nelson (Verona), Roman Charney, Joseph Composto, Peter Kolodziej (Boonville), Ray Jollie (Sherill), Robert Sticles, Earl Simmons (Holland Patent), David Lemon (Ava), William Lusk (Fort Plain), Lewis Willy Pelton, (Westernville), Edgar Lalonde Blossvale, and Albert Connors (New York Mills).

One of its' members, Jim Walsh of Rome, told reporter Francis L. Crumb: "There were no jobs. I left South Ozone Park, Long Island on a troop train from Grand Central Station to Boise, Idaho. There were 1,000 CCC boys from all over the country. The train stopped and dropped off enrollees along the way. Its final destination was Spokane Washington.

"I was a teamster, driving horses for a spike camp that made drinking troughs for wild animals in the mountains. The CCC gave you a terrific idea of what life was all about. You learned to live with other people. I think it helped me out an awful lot in later years."

Another CCC Alumni, John Halupka of Rome, joined the CCC and went to a camp in Reno, Nevada. He worked on government lands and occasionally he was loaned out to help private landowners. Halupka also worked at the Sherburne camp near Norwich, NY where he built roads and did reforestation work.

After three enlistments, a total of 18 months in the CCC, Halupka left and joined the Navy in 1940.

The public relations officer of the club was Joseph Composto of Boonville. He spent over four years in the CCC. Joe worked in Alabama, Mississippi, Idaho, and nearby in Boonville.

Composto said, "I have always said it was the nicest four and one-half years of my life. The fellows I met and worked with were all compatible and in the same boat. We needed a job. It took us off the street. It was a blessing. I look back and wonder how many of us could have turned out to be criminals.

"When I was at the Boonville camp from 1937-1939 I was the Assistant Educational officer. There were courses in First Aid, typing, auto mechanics, and arts and crafts.

"Today's society needs a program such as the Civilian Conservation Corps, a program that knew what brotherhood was all about."

Information came from two undated Utica Daily Press articles: R. Patrick Corbett's "20 from Rome Area Get Together Again" and Francis L. Lamb's "CCC Alumni Hope to See 1930s Program Revived."

Truman Guinup

Millie Guinup of Little Falls called me and told me her father-in-law, Truman Guinup, was in the CCC camp in Boonville and invited me to her home to see his photo and discharge papers. On June 27, 2007 I drove to the Guinup's home on Shells Bush Road. Millie and her husband Ray welcomed me into their home and told me about Truman.

Ray said, "My brother Truman joined the CCC on October 6, 1938. He was 17 years old. There were 12 children in our family and he had to help my parents who were very poor."

Millie handed me a January 12, 1938 issue of the Little Falls Evening Times. "This story describes how the Guinup family was trying to survive on a farm 2 mi. outside of the village of Poland. The father, Truman, was a logger and his leg was damaged due to frostbite and he could barely walk and provide for his family.

The newspaper stated that the boy walked a long distance through ice and snow to the Poland grocery store and told the owner, Mr. Norton, his family's plight.

Truman said, "Mister, I want to join the Sons of the Legion because my daddy is a veteran. He's Mr. Truman Guinup and we live on the old Seifert farm north of town."

Mr. Norton, a member of the American Legion, said he didn't know that Mr. Guinup was a veteran and told Truman that he would try to get more information so that the boy could become a junior member of the American Legion.

Later Norton found the elder Truman Guinup limping along the street in town. Truman told Norton that he was a lumberjack and had been in WWI. He froze his feet in the woods and wasn't able to work much due to the injury. He said he knew he should go to a doctor but didn't have the money to pay.

Norton realized he had to help his fellow veteran and took Guinup to Dr. Fred C. Sabin's office in Little Falls. Dr. Sabin saw that Guinup needed quick medical help and called the nearest Veterans' Hospital. They said Truman should come as soon as possible.

That night Norton transported Guinup to Utica and put him on a train to the Veterans' Hospital.

Norton later learned that doctors had to amputate Truman's left foot but they felt he would recover.

All was not well at the Guinup farmhouse because Truman's wife was very sick and unable to help her family. The eldest son Truman knew his mother needed medical help so again the 16 year-old ran two miles over icy roads to Norton's grocery store. He told Norton his mother was very sick and needed help.

Norton again came to his aid. He knew he couldn't drive the treacherous roads so he called the doctor and told him the symptoms. The doctor gave Norton medicine who in turn handed it to young Truman to take to his mother.

When Norton found that Mrs. Julia Guinup was not getting better he called the local Herkimer Welfare Office for help. They told him to bring her to the Herkimer Memorial Hospital.

Even though the roads to the Guinup's were in terrible shape due to the snow and ice, Norton was determined to help. After quite a while he made it up the mountain. The young Truman helped him get his mother into the car and Norton took Mrs. Guinup to the hospital.

On the way home from the hospital young Truman told Mr. Norton that he figured he could act as cook, housekeeper, nurse, mother, and father to his brothers and

Truman Guinup helped his poor family survive by joining the CCC in October 1938 and worked at the Boonville Camp till March 1939. Millie and Ray Guinup

sisters who ranged in age from 1-15 years old. He said, "Believe me Mr. Norton the first thing I will do with the first three dollars I earn, I'm going to buy my father a membership in the Legion. Next, I'm going to join the Sons of the Legion. Mother'll want to get in the Auxiliary, too."

Later that year Truman earned money for himself and his family when he joined the CCC in October. He did reforestation work at the Boonville camp.

Ray Guinup said, "All they did was live in tents and they planted a lot of trees. They also cleaned out a lot of brush along the roads. He was discharged on March 31, 1939 and came home.

"Truman then joined the Marines. When they found out that he was in the CCC they placed him in charge of an advanced unit. The CCC was a big help to our family. My brother earned $25 a month that the government sent to our home to help our family survive the Great Depression."

Henry Plummer

Henry Plummer was the Superintendent of the Boonville and Camden CCC camps from 1934-1942. He was born in South Paris Maine in 1909. He received a BS in 1930 from the University of Maine. From 1930-1934 he worked as a forester for Finch, Pruyn & Co in Glens Falls and Newcomb.

In 1935 Plummer became the Superintendent of the Boonville CCC Camp. The Boonville Herald reported in the February 6, 1936 issue that Plummer supervised forestry projects such as making firebreaks, thinning trees, and forest stand improvement work.

In 1936 he married Sara Frances Jones of Boonville.

The Boonville Herald reported in the March 3, 1938 issue that Plummer was transferred to be superintendent of the Camden camp. He had been cited many times for the excellence of his fieldwork.
He worked with the US Civil Service Commission in NYC

from 1942-1945. He moved back to Maine in 1946 and was an instructor and later professor at the University of Maine.

When he earned a MF from Yale in 1950 he became an assistant professor at the University of Maine.

CHAPTER 9
BRASHER FALLS

HISTORY

Captain George H. Seitz and one hundred war veterans from Company 2216, arrived by train in Brasher Falls on Friday, May 11, 1934 to establish Camp S-95 on Vice Road. The veterans pitched their tents on a 25-acre parcel of flat sandy terrain and began organizing the camp. Three days earlier five Army officers from the Plattsburgh Barracks had come to prepare the area for the veterans, who had been working during the previous year on a dam project in Montpellier, Vermont.[1]

The 25-acre parcel was leased by the NYS Conservation Department for one year from James McNulty of Brasher Falls. According to a 1934 contract in the Potsdam DEC office, the state had the option to renew the lease after a year for an additional six-month period at ten dollars a month or the option of purchasing the land at four dollars per acre.

Clarence Petty was the first camp superintendent. The camp's chief purpose was the reforestation of land in northern St. Lawrence County. The state purchased tracts of non-productive forests that had been either cleared of timber and never replanted, destroyed by fires, insects, and diseases, or poorly managed.

During the fall of 1934 Camp S-95 planted 22,000 trees and continued planting till the ground was frozen below two inches.[2]

By April 1, 1935 camp S-95 had planted over one million trees.

In September 1935 there was a change as C. E. Mason replaced Petty as camp superintendent. That same month Lt. Frambach took over for Captain Seitz.

In 1935 the camp was no longer under the Madison Barracks. It was under the supervision of the Plattsburgh Barracks and renamed S-95.

In March 1936 Horace J. Harris became the Superintendent. The following men assisted Harris: Harry V. Beresford and George A. Cook, foremen; Herman J. Coughlin, Wallace G. Liberty, and John H. Moran, junior foremen; James H. Ruff, junior forester; Alfred N. Baxter,

Above - On October 5, 1934 the wooden buildings were completed and the men moved into their new facilities. In the upper left is the garage and to the right is the mechanic's garage. The next long building to the right is the mess hall. Then to the right are the five barracks. Carl Goodric. Below - An aerial view of the Brasher Falls camp S-95 in 1934. In the center are the five barracks under construction. In the upper right are the Army tents in a square where the Veterans first lived. NYS Archives

mechanic; Horace Millmore, blacksmith; and Kenneth W. McCarthy, tractor operator.[3]

The camp newspaper, "The Daily Bull," printed a list of foremen and the number of trees planted by each man. For example on May 12, 1936 the men planted a total of 58,096 trees. Each man in foreman Moran's group planted 808 trees. During the spring of 1936, S-95 planted 1,469,585 trees on 1,000 acres.

FOREMAN (GROUP)	TREES PLANTED PER MAN IN GROUP
Moran	808
Bedresford	803
Liberty	718
Cook	536
Coughlin	308

By 1938 the state had acquired 20,000 acres near Brasher Falls in St. Lawrence County. The men planted thousands of trees during four weeks in the spring and a six-week period in the fall. In the spring of 1938 they expected to plant 1,250,000 trees that were mostly evergreen trees: balsam, cedar, hemlock, spruce, and red, white, scotch, and jack pines.

In the spring of 1939 the camp was allotted 1,222,850 trees ranging in age from 3-5 years. They were shipped from the Lowville and Saratoga state nurseries.[4]

The Veterans also constructed fire lanes, plowed strips (14 ft. wide) truck trails, water holes, and removed brush. They also worked to eliminate diseases such as blister rust and insect pests. Once they had planted trees they pro-

tected them from grazing animals by building fences. Near sand dunes the men planted trees and used fences and mats to prevent soil erosion.

Another camp project was the construction of a 345' x 16' high earth dam on Redwater Brook 2 mi. north of North Lawrence. Construction began in summer of 1935. The men first removed trees and other vegetation on the 22-acre pond site. By the end of 1937 the dam was at the 50 per cent stage.[5] It was completed in 1938. The pond provided recreation for people and habitat for fish and migratory birds.[6]

On July 2, 1936 the original Company 2216 V assigned to camp S-95 was disbanded and Junior Company 3259 composed of young enrollees was established in Brasher Falls. After less than a year Co. 3259 disbanded on April 2, 1937. Eighty-four young enrollees left for their homes in Tupper Lake, Massena, Plattsburgh, Malone Cohoes, and 26 from New York City. The men left in good physical health having gained an average of 14 pounds. Two of the men had attended college, 42% graduated from high school, and the remaining men graduated from eighth grade. Two days later Co. 2217V under the command of Lt. Maurice arrived at S-95 from Wawayanda, NY.[7]

In 1937 camp S-95 built a toboggan slide and ski slope in Potsdam on the State Normal School campus. At first water had to be transported by hand the length of the chute. The next year they laid a water pipe from the city water line for the chute.[8]

In September of 1937 the Brasher Falls Veterans had another project with the Potsdam State Normal School. They were to build a toboggan run and a short ski slope on land along the Raquette River. The project involved removing a few trees on the slope, and relocating the toboggan slide.[9]

In order to complete projects the camp had a fleet of trucks and equipment. Here is a list found in the DEC Potsdam Archives: 1935 Chevy stake-body trucks (6); 1935 Chevy pickup trucks (2); 1935 1.5 ton Reo dump truck (3); 1935 2-ton Reo dump truck (1); T 40 International tractor (1); SA Rome grader (1); McCormick Deering breaker plow (1); McCormick Deering disc harrow (1); Ingersoll-Rand garage compressor (1); and Baker snow plow (1).

Above, Left - The veterans planted millions of trees on poor farm lands the state purchased during the Great Depression in St. Lawrence County. This September 17, 1937 Conservation Department photo shows red pines growing in the sandy soil. NYS Archives. Above, Right - This is one of the 100 fire holes the Veterans of Brasher Falls S-95 constructed in St. Lawrence County. They provided a ready source of water to fight forest fires in the reforested lands. Two rangers are testing a pump using water from the stone-lined water hole. The average depth of the hole was six feet. NYS Archives

Above - This photo was a mystery because no one could figure out what the structure had to do with the CCC. When a photo in the Potsdam Public Museum showed a different angle we saw it was a toboggan slide. The Brasher Falls CCC enrollees are building a shed near the toboggan slide by the Raquette River on Potsdam State Normal School property. St. Lawrence Historical Society Archives. Left - The toboggan slide provided a lot of entertainment to the students and residents of Potsdam. Mimi Van Deusen Potsdam Public Museum Archives

There were frequent changes in command of the camp. On July 7, 1936 Captain Charles F. Arny replaced Captain Spitz. Also, Lt. W. C. Braun, Inf. Res. took Lt. R. P. Maurice's command in April 1938. Then Captain Harry Myers became commander on June 16, 1938. A year later Captain Allen G. Spitz succeeded Myers. After only four months in command, Spitz retired. He had spent the past five years commanding CCC camps in Tupper Lake and the Plattsburgh Barracks. Then Francis B. Redner took command in September 1939. At this time C. J. Yops was superintendent.

In 1940 the US was preparing for war. During the summer the Army held maneuvers in northern St. Lawrence County. Approximately 100,000 soldiers, thousands of cars, trucks, and trailers, and several thousand cavalry horses were involved. A huge influx of tourists and friends of soldiers flocked to the area to watch. The state assigned three patrolmen and 36 veterans from camp S-95 to patrol the reforested areas and prevent damage to the new trees and prevent forest fires. The Army provided 2,000 yellow signs for the reforested lands stating "Entry on Foot Only."

The veterans and patrolmen were successful in preventing the Army soldiers, horses and vehicles from damaging the fledgling forest.[10]

Camp S-95 continued its seventh year of controlling the spread of blister rust in 1940. They protected 1,065 acres of reforested area in the town of Brasher by destroying 58,235 ribes plants.[11] In 1941 S-95 continued to eradicate blister rust. They covered 720 acres and destroyed 49,049 ribes.[12]

During the summer and fall of 1941 the state was plagued by very dry weather resulting in large forest fires. Camp S-95 contributed many days of hard work fighting forest fires in surrounding towns.[13]

In the evenings an education advisor provided classes for the men. They included leather craft, metal craft, and rustic furniture building.

With two colleges, Clarkson and Potsdam Normal School, nearby the education advisor arranged for speakers and classes for veterans. In February 1936 veterans began taking a diesel engine class. College professors came to the camp and gave lectures. Some topics presented were: "Tree Planting in the Northeast," "Sound Care & Treatment of Feet," and the "Three M's: Men, Materials and Machines."

Here is a list of classes offered in February 1936: Monday: Reading and Writing, Leather Craft, Journalism, and Diesel Engines, Tuesday: Journalism (Advertising), Letter Writing, Arithmetic, Leather Craft, Journalism (Production Mechanics), Wednesday: English and Spelling, Forestry, Leather Craft, Leadership, Thursday: Commercial Law, Journalism, Leather Craft, Diesel Engines, Friday: First Aid, Citizenship, and Courtesy.

The education advisor also supervised the bimonthly camp newspaper called the "Sixty-Niner." During the first years a staff of 10 produced it. There was also an advertising staff that solicited ads at a rate $2 a month for one-sixth of a page or $2.50 for an ad with an illustration. Those selling ads received 10 per cent of their sales. The enrollees used a 30-dollar junior mimeograph machine to produce the newspaper. A staff of artists did the illustrations and cartoons. The circulation department mailed out 100 newspapers each week to other camps and corps area and district officers. A copy was also sent to the University of Illinois, which collected camp newspapers from the US.[14] When the camp's number changed from S-65 to S-95 around May 1935 the paper retained its old name for a while. Frequently "The Sixty-Niner" received a rating of four out of five stars from the Office of Education at Governors Island, NY.

The March 31, 1935 cover of The Sixty-Niner Brasher Falls camp newspaper. Podskoch Collection

On April 1, 1936 the men began producing a daily two-page newspaper called "The Daily Bull." It contained sporting events, work assignments, jokes, weather, lists of new enrollees, safety rules, men in the hospital, deaths, and national and international news. It also produced a monthly newspaper called "The North Woodsman." A popular section was an advice column called "Heart Throbs by Mme Lotta La Treen."

One humorous story in the May 8, 1936 issue was an article by the Captain cautioning the men about keeping a "receptacle" under their bed for urinating in the night. "That is not good at any time particularly in the summer time... otherwise the aroma of the barracks is going to smell like anything but lilac."

"The Sixty-Niner" had a section called "Sick, Lame & Lazy." It describes the men who were legitimately and illegitimately nursing their wounds. There were a lot of funny stories of 'goldbrickers' faking in order to get out of work.

The camp had an infirmary for sick and injured enrollees. In 1935 the camp had an Army surgeon, Bruno Jastremski. The camp also contracted with a local physician, Doctor Fingar. During the first few years the seriously injured were transported to the Madison Barracks Hospital near Watertown. When the camp came under the jurisdiction of the Plattsburgh Barracks, the camp ambulance transported men to the Plattsburgh Barracks Hospital.

The Army provided trucks to transport the men to various types of entertainment. During the week trucks left the camp at 6 pm for Shines Movie Theater in Massena on Monday, Wednesday, and Friday nights. The trucks left Massena at 9:45 or 10 pm depending on the length of the movies.

Sporting activities were very popular. The camp had a baseball team that played local CCC camps and town teams. Inter-camp baseball games were played along with softball, volleyball, swimming, and horseshoes. There was even a golf class taught by the education advisor. He taught them how to use the various clubs and used the nearby field for practice. Each year a District Field Day was held. Brasher Falls camp competed against another veteran's camp from Plattsburgh in baseball, hundred-yard dash, sack race, 220-yd. dash, three-legged race, mile run, 440-yd. relay, mile relay, shot put, broad jump, high jump, and tug of war.[15]

Another popular camp event was "Smokers." This featured boxing matches with opponents from neighboring CCC camps and cigarettes were passed out to the audience. Sometimes wrestling matches and musical entertainment by the men were held.[15]

The Emergency Relief Bureau provided traveling plays and shows for the CCC camps. "The Fall Guy" was a play presented at the Brushton camp in June 1935.

The recreation hall had a large selection of reading materials such as 44 magazines: Life, Adventure, Field & Stream, Short Stories, True Detective, etc. and six daily newspapers: New York Times, New York Sun, New York Journal, Brooklyn Daily Eagle, Rochester Democrat and

Brasher Falls S-95 Activities. This collage of photos is from the 1937 Schenectady District Civilian Conservation Corps Area Yearbook.

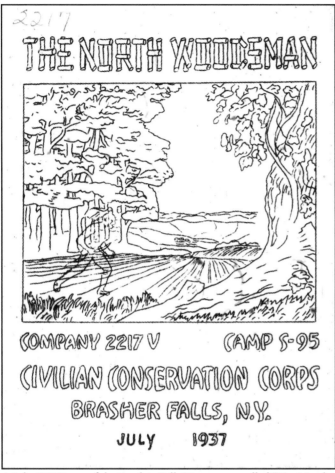

A July 1937 issue of the Brasher Falls Newspaper called "The North Woodsman." During 1936 the camp produced a daily two-page newspaper called "The Daily Bull." Podskoch Collection

Chronicle, and New York American.

The camp also had a Reading Room containing books where the men could come relax and read. There was also a traveling library of 100 books that went from camp to camp. The men had three days to return a signed out book.[17]

On the weekends men got passes to leave camp. One camp rule was that there had to be at least 40 per cent of the camp present on the weekends for basic duties and ready to help out in case of emergencies such as forest fires. Some men hitchhiked home to see their wives and families while some went to neighboring towns for drink and entertainment.

The men were given spiritual aid by the local church ministers, priests, and traveling Army Chaplins. Army trucks transported the men to Sunday services at local churches.

Since many of the veterans were 40 years or older, the education advisor worked to develop their work skills and improve their confidence in searching for jobs. The camp provided Home Study Courses from Syracuse University. These courses were offered: Aeronautics, Arithmetic, Auto Mechanics, Blue Print Reading, Bookkeeping, Diesel Engines, English, Forestry, Geometry, Journalism, Business Law, Photography, and Psychology. The men paid 25 cents for a 12-lesson course. They then took tests for each lesson and the education advisor sent the answers to Syracuse. If the student received a grade of 75 per cent or more, they received a certificate.[18]

Here is a partial list of the education advisors: Forest G. Read (1934-35), William A. Bode (1935-36), Richard G. Smith (1936-37) Philip Napoli (1938), L. A. Labounty (1939), and Gerald Gorman (1940).

The St. Lawrence Historical Society Library had an undated article by Geraldine Dulles, Brasher Town Historian, entitled "CCC Camp- Brasher Falls, New York." She described how local businesses and families benefited from the Brasher camp. The camp purchased equipment from Kannehana Foundry and materials such as nails and rope from Murphy's Hardware. The Springbrook Dairy, operated by Walter Locke and his sons Don and Stan, supplied the Brasher Falls and Brushton camps with dairy products. Many local residents rented either rooms or homes to camp employees such as surveyors or supervisors.

The camp made a positive impression on the local community because of their work in rebuilding and protecting the forests. In December 1935 the enrollees fought a fire on the nearby Babbit farm and received praise from the town. Citizens attended many of the camp dances and enrollees' baseball games. Some of the local professional men spoke at the camp.[19] The veterans were also invited to join the local veterans organizations.

The veterans showed pride in their camp by volunteering to maintain the lawns, flowerbeds, and shrubs planted around each building.

WORK ACCOMPLISHED BY CAMP S-95[*]

PROJECT	1934	1935	1936	1937	1938	1939	1940	1941	TOTAL
Boundary marking - mi.			35	22.7	23.2	49.5	19.8	2.6	1528
Bridges, vehicle - number						1			1
Dams - number						1			1
Emergency work - man-days				112			328		440
Eradication of plants - linear mi.	14								14
Experimental plots - ac.					6	10			16
Fences - rods	9.5	5416		2955	4221	3444	1275	3041	20361.5
Fire breaks - mi.	26.4	2	20.5	0.9	1.3	0.3			51.4
Fire fighting - man-days	141	82	28	53	141	39		2406	2890
Fire hazard reduction (other than roads) - ac.		223	467	581	577	818.7	451.6		3118.3
Fireplaces - number							5		5
Fire pre-suppression - man-days						247	1218	315	1780
Forest stand improvement - ac.		302	302	754	497	823.4	1013.3	1369	5060.7
General clean-up - ac.				1.8					1.8
Horse trails - mi.							1.7	0.5	2.2
Insect pest control - ac.				1.3	981	3218	4225.4	2494	10919.7
Lake, pond & reservoir site cleaning - ac.			22		5	7			34
Levees & dikes - yd³								38	38
Maps & models - man-days				29	39	40			108
Nurseries - man-days		21	78	280	321	146	293	126	1265
Other structural improvements - number					2				2
Pipe & tile lines, conduit - linear ft.					596				596
Planting/moving trees & shrubs - man-days							67		67
Preparation/transportation of materials - man-days				333	1303	1533	744	595	4508
Public campground development - ac.				1		1			2
Razing undesirable structures - man-days			8	115	286	186	90	45	730
Reconnaissance & investigation - man-days							3	10	13
Seed collection, conifers - bushels			17		5	6	25	51	104
Seed collection, hard woods - lbs.			200	101	597	3364	174	354	4790
Shelters - number					1				1
Surveys - linear mi.		82.7	32.8						115.5
Surveys - man-days				189	439	462	400	54	1544
Surveys, type - ac.			803						803
Telephone line - mi.	0.6								0.6
Trails, foot - mi.				12		3.8	2		17.8
Trails, truck - mi.	2.9	1.1		1	0.2	0.9	7.3	1	14.4
Tree & plant disease control - ac.	3442	3875	628	757	2444	2371	159.7	235	13911.7
Water holes - number	11	3	1	38	23	9	9	6	100
Wind erosion control - ac.				5	12.1	77.7	8.4	9.9	113.1

[*]Numerical data from Conservation Reports

When Camp S-95 closed in 1942 it was transferred to the Army, which used it for a Prisoners of War (POW) camp. WWII Italian prisoners were housed there.

The camp was dismantled in 1945 and the buildings donated to the 4-H clubs of St. Lawrence County. The buildings were taken to the 4-H site on the Raquette River in Hannawa Falls.[20]

The DEC Maintenance Center in Brasher Falls is on the site of the old CCC camp and only one CCC building remains.

LEGACY

Millions of trees now flourish and tower over the land once deemed useless during the 1930s. Most of the approximately 100 water holes built to protect the forests have been filled in by the state for safety reasons.

The Redwater Brook Dam pond and forest area is named the Walter Pratt Memorial Forest and Pond but locals call it "CCC Dam." In 1995 the CCC Dam Association was formed to execute projects and improve the recreation value of the area. Camping in the area is open to the public and is free of charge. The CCC Dam Association, the DEC, and State Police patrol the area.

"Planting is Over"
by D. Kinnard

Red Pine, White Pine, Cedar and Spruce,
We planted them to beat the deuce;
One hundred cents was the daily wage,
The mosquitoes were on a mad rampage.
With work and torture rolled into one
We more than once wished we were done.
But CC spirit and CC guts,
The job is done-hail the day
Let's all go in and hit the hay![21]

This is one of the campsites on Redwater Brook Dam Pond. The CCC built the dam that created the pond. Locals call it the "CCC Dam." Campsites and picnic areas are open from mid-May to October. DEC

Clarence Petty at the Brasher Falls veterans' camp in 1934. He was in his late 20s and as camp superintendent supervised forestry projects. Most of the Army veterans were older than he was and some had difficulty following orders from a young man. Chris Angus

MEMORIES

Clarence Petty

During the summer of 2007 I visited Clarence Petty at his home in Coreys a few miles east of Tupper Lake in the home where he and his two brothers grew up. His mother was the postmistress and the post office was in their home. I asked him to tell me about his CCC days.

"After I was at the Tupper Lake CCC camp just south of here at "Cross Clearing" where Rts 30 and 3 intersect, Ernest Sterling recommended me to be the superintendent of the new Brasher Falls camp.

"When I got to the camp in May 1934 the enrollees were WWI Vets. I heard that for the first month they all went down to town and got drunk.

"On Monday morning I went outside to give the work assignments and found most of the guys on the ground drunk. I didn't know what to do. I was the superintendent and there was work to be done. I asked Captain Spitz, who was tall and weighed about 230 pounds: 'How am I supposed to get them to work?' He replied, 'You won't be able to do anything with them today.'

"I was just 28 years old and had to tell these guys who were in their 40s and 50s what to do. I didn't get them to work for two days. There were other vets who were pretty good workers but they were all drinkers. They had a lot of potential but were alcoholics. There were quite a few who were complaining all the time.

"I had seven foresters, a blacksmith and two surveyors that I used as foremen. Everyday I had 178 men to assign duties. I divided them up into crews of 20-25 which could be transported in trucks. For equipment I had six stake-body trucks, four dump trucks, and one 1932 or 1933 Chevy pickup for myself.

"For housing I stayed at the Sullivan's farm and had room and board. They had two teachers who stayed there, too. When we started the camp we only thought it would last till the fall but they decided to stay the winter and so they built barracks. Then the men moved from the tents to the permanent wooden buildings.

"Bill Foss of the Conservation Department (CD) was my boss. He was in charge of all the CCC camps. Bill was a real fine guy. He came from Maine and got a job as a forester for the CD.

"I finally got them working and tried to use and develop the skills that they had. The Army set up night classes to teach them reading and writing. I also had my mechanic who helped them get driver's licenses to drive the trucks.

The Army was in charge of disciplining the men and running the camp. I often had arguments with them because they wanted to keep a lot of men doing jobs in camp.

Finally I got the captain to keep only 20 men so that I'd have the remaining 180 men to work on forestry projects. We had a lot to do and I'd get upset when I'd see some guys just hanging around the camp.

Carl Goodrich

Brasher Falls Historian, Carl Goodrich, shared his memories of Camp S-95 when I visited him in July of 2007.

"I used to deliver milk to the CCC camp with my cousin, Martin Andrew. I was only nine years old. My great-uncle, Walter Locke, owned a bottling company and had a dairy farm. We put the cases of bottled milk in a big walk-in icebox. The camp had its own ice, which the men cut in the winter. They had electricity and I can still remember the string of clear light bulbs hanging from the ceiling.

"When we went to the camp the guys would give us food. They had their own theater in camp where they watched movies. Sometimes I went with Martin Andrew. My uncle also sold milk to the Brushton CCC camp."

Then I showed Carl a picture of the boys in the camp and he pointed out the Brasher Falls area men: "Raymond Andrews, Martin's father, who was a foreman, Milton Bombard from Bangor, Harry Froberg, Clifford Sharlow,

and Mose Villeneau.

"One of the jobs Raymond Andrew had his workers do was gather pinecones, take the seeds out of the cones, and plant them at the camp nursery. When it came time to transplant the seedlings they planted them on farmland that the poor farmers sold to the state during the Depression.

"When they closed the camp, Jerry Hammel, a local carpenter, tore the camp buildings down and sold the materials. I think there is only one original building left at the camp site."

James "Ray" Raymond

Carl Goodrich told me to contact Joy Normile's father, James "Ray" Raymond, who was a foreman in the CCC camp. I called her and visited her camp on Lake Ozonia near St. Regis Falls. The lake is a hidden treasure in the northwestern corner of the Adirondacks. We sat at her dinning room table.

"The CCC boys were always kind to the children in town," said Joy. "Dad worked at the camp and I remember him coming home each night. He wore a Mackinaw coat. It was always filled with goodies from camp like the little boxes of cereal, fruit, bananas and oranges, and Mounds candy bars that the workers gave to my dad from their daily rations. They knew he had seven children.

"My dad got paid 40 dollars a month. We charged food at Durham's Grocery Store. Gladys, my mom, paid the bill at the end of the month. The grocer man used to give Mom a bag of Oxhart candy when she paid the bill.

"Dad was a salty guy. He could swear for five minutes without repeating himself.

"CCC boys used to come to our house, which was about a mile from their camp. They got a taste of family life and they'd bring us candy bars. A lot of them were drinkers. I think they were drunk when

James "Ray" Raymond was a foreman at the Brushton CCC camp. Joy Normile

they came over but they were respectful.

"We didn't have a car so Dad walked to work each day. I remember a few of the men he worked with. Harry Beresford was a good friend of Dad's. Wally Liberty was a tech person. His sons, John and Tommy, run Tri-Town Meat Packing.

"In the morning some of the kids and their families in town waited along the road for the CCC trucks to go by to see the boys on their way to work in the forest. When the CCC men passed they threw out boxes of cereal and fruit to children.

"We went a few times to the CCC camp but most of the times the girls stayed home.

"Dad was a foreman at the camp and rode in one of the trucks with a crew of CCC men. They planted trees and constructed truck trails and fire lines. Dad was a woodsman and he was great at this job. He was born around 1899 in Vermont and moved to Clintonville, NY. He met my mother in Loon Lake where she worked at the hotel. Dad was a chauffeur for rich city people. Mom was from Brasher Falls. They got married in 1927 or 1928 and moved to Brasher Falls. They had seven children. I was born in 1932.

"Dad was a rough and tumble guy. He taught us our prayers and how to sing. I remember him rocking us and watching over us. If we ever got hurt we ran to him.

"Mom died in 1944 when she was just 36 and Dad had to care for a 6-month old to a 14 year-old. My grandparents helped out. It was like the expression 'It takes a village to raise a child.' If I did something, they told Dad. Everyone had an input on our growth. My Aunt Libby also helped. I went to live with her for a while.

"After the CCC job Dad began working at the Alcoa factory in 1938. He died at age 63.

"The CCC camp was important to our family. It gave Dad a job and helped support our family during the Depression."

CHAPTER 10
BRUSHTON

HISTORY

On August 9, 1935 Camp Brushton S-120 was established by Company 1260 in East Dickinson four miles south of Brushton, NY in the foothills of the Adirondacks. The camp was named after the town where the mail was delivered and Brushton had the nearest post office. It was 11 mi. SW of Malone near the intersection of Rt. 7 and 11B.[1]

Lt. William D. Meurlin established camp on a large open area called "The Heath." Forty-three men from Camp S-120 in Port Henry joined the men because their camp had just closed. Captain L. A Jacobs took command of the camp assisted by Lt. Norman P. Barnett.[2]

Clarence Petty was the camp superintendent. In an article in the April 10, 1936 issue of The Chateaugay Record he described the camp's accomplishments. In late August 1935 the camp with less than 100 men planted 1,060,000 trees on 650 acres and constructed approximately one mile of fence to protect the new seedlings from cattle. They removed slash on seven acres and surveyed approximately 30 miles of boundary lines on newly acquired state land. The young men also improved over 200 acres of hardwood forests.

Petty stated all of the work was done on State Reforestation land that it acquired from abandoned farms that were unprofitable due to poor soil. The goal of the camp was to develop a productive forestry crop that would not only be profitable but prevent erosion and provide a refuge for wild life. The camp then proceeded to eradicate ribes bushes to avoid blister rust. They also constructed truck trails, water holes, and fire lines and removed slash to prevent forest fires.

During the winter Petty said the two main projects were surveying land that was about to be acquired and doing

Above - Joe Kozma of Westport took this picture of his Brushton CCC camp S-120 from a nearby hill. Conservation Road ran in front of the camp along the fence line and intersected Rt. 11 B to the right. There were five barracks in the center rear and a garage on the far right and along the front along the road. Joe Kozma.

Far Left - These enrollees are taking a break after planting trees. The two boys in the front are holding mattocks, an adze-like tool for digging a hole for planting trees. Joseph Kozma. Left - These CCC enrollees from Brushton are planting trees on the abandoned farmland the state purchased. Small trees have been cut and are lying on the ground. NYS Archives.

silviculture work in the hardwood forests. They removed trees that had no commercial value such as gray birch, aspen, and pin cherry and planted softwood trees.

The Brushton camp did many forestry projects: constructed truck trails, built water holes, and did forest stand improvement such as removing dead trees. Each year the camp had a tree planting contest and the winners received a turkey dinner.[3]

The Chateaugay Record (5/15/36) reported amazing tree planting statistics for the Brushton camp. They planted 805,600 trees in 12 days. This averaged 67,100 trees per day.

The young men enjoyed baseball, basketball, softball, and skiing on the nearby hills during their free time. In 1936 the softball team boasted of a near perfect record with only one loss. The basketball team traveled to Malone where it practiced twice a week. The camp also competed in a basketball league with teams from Bombay, North Lawrence, Fort Covington, and Winthrop.[4] Boxing was also popular and the boys traveled to nearby camps and fought in "smokers."[5] The boys had other activities. They watched a weekly movie and had their own 16-mm projector. On weekends they also had dances at the camp and locals were invited. The young men also went 17 miles to Malone to relieve boredom.[6]

On January 15, 1936 an additional 53 men arrived. Forty-four men came from Applegate in Medford, Oregon and nine from a "spike" or side camp in Rogue River, Oregon.[8]

William A. Bode, the education director, started many programs. Enrollees went to Malone and took classes in auto mechanics and woodworking. At Current Events Night speakers presented interesting topics. The boys published a monthly newspaper called "The Ice Box."[9]

Captain Jacobs remained in command of the camp till December 23, 1936 when Capt. George W. Stewart took command.[10]

I n

Clockwise from Top - A quiet time in the rec hall. Joseph Kozma. This is the only remaining building at the Brushton CCC camp. The DEC uses it for storage. Podskoch Collection. The enrollees built V-dams on Trout Brook in 1937. These dams provided pools for fish to hide, rest, and feed. They also create waterfalls that add oxygen to the water. NYS Archives.

A collage of activities at the Brushton camp S-122.[7]

1937 S-120 completed one-mile of stream development work on Deep River in Franklin County.[11] The next year the CCC camp continued working on two miles of Deep River and the Little Salmon River.[12]

Another project of the Brushton camp was blister rust control work. In 1939 the young men removed ribes plants on 110 acres near white pine forests. They also built a 53' I-beam bridge.[13]

During 1940 men in camp S-120 continued work in blister rust eradication. They also constructed 1.7 miles of truck trails and maintained 3.5 miles of truck trails.[14]

In 1941 enrollment at CCC camps declined and resulted in a reduction in work projects. Even with a limited number of men the Brushton camp continued blister rust eradication. In the town of Dickinson they covered 240 acres and destroyed 92,771 ribes plants.[15] They constructed 1.7 miles of truck trails and maintained a total of 6.9 miles.[16]

The camp participated in the CCC Field Day in Tupper Lake on August 21, 1937 and competed against eight other CCC camps.[17]

The Fort Covington Sun reported in June 1941 that the Brushton camp participated in a softball league playing Hogansburg, Bombay, and the St. Regis Indians teams.

Camp S-120 closed on August 15, 1941.[18]

When St. Augustine Catholic Church in New Bangor burned on December 23, 1943 the parishioners began building a new church. State Representative Clarence E Kilburn secured permission for the parish to use materials from the Brushton CCC camp buildings.[19]

MEMORIES

Clarence Petty

I was fortunate to interview Clarence Petty on September 12, 2008 and he told me about his CCC experiences.

"After working at the Tupper Lake CCC camp I worked at Brasher Falls for a year and was transferred to the Brushton Camp in August 1935. It was actually located in East Dickinson. The camps were usually named after the town where the mail was delivered and Brushon was the nearest post office.

This is the Brushton barracks # 2 in tight military order, except for an object on the floor, with heavy blankets and large stoves that had to be tended through the cold winter nights. Joe Kozma. Kenny Cox, Janet Noreault Dana, and Tim Lonkey in front of the only remaining building of the Brushton camp in Dickinson Center. Podskoch Collection

"The men at the CCC camps were often called out to fight forest fires. In the summer of 1941 there was an uncontrolled forest fire south of Massawepie Lake. It was labeled 'The Boot Tree Pond" fire. The fire began during the very dry summer when sparks from a train. High winds fanned and spread the fire. Bill Foss, head of the CCC camps, called me to help District Ranger Moses La Fountain of Cranberry Lake. When I got to Cranberry Lake I found that La Fountain had serious heart problems and couldn't control the situation. He hadn't any idea where the hell the fire was, where the margin was or anything. It was a going fire and running fast, so I said I'd go out to look it over. Well, that fire was all over the woods and at least several thousand acres were burning. The smoke was so thick you could hardly see anything. I knew that if we were going to do any good, we were going to have to cut the point of it off, where it was blowing.

"I quickly called everyone I knew to help. The next day I had one hundred and eight CCC boys who were divided in groups of twenty-five men. I eventually had a force of eleven hundred men composed of two CCC camps and local men.

"After three to four days the fire crews were able to control the Boot Tree Pond fire. My CCC boys continued to fight small brush fires for three more weeks and then returned back to the East Dickinson camp. It continued to smolder underground till winter set in.

"A little after the Boot Tree Pond fire the Brushton camp was closed in August 1941. I was transferred to the Mannsville camp 20 miles south of Watertown where I was the camp superintendent for approximately six months. It was a segregated camp composed of African Americans. This camp was closed in November 1941. Then I was sent back to close up the Brushton, Brasher Falls, and Mannsville camps. It was a big job because I didn't have a lot of help. All the camp records and tools had to be shipped to headquarters in Albany. It was also sad to have the guys burn the left over CCC clothing. The government had a contract with the manufacturer of the clothing that said they couldn't be used or sold.

"After nine years working in the CCC I learned how to organize and lead large groups of men and how to provide all sorts of backwoods services, from fire fighting to road building, from blister rust control to reforestation. These years provided a job for me to support my wife and son Donald who was born in 1939."

Raymond Noreault

On Thursday, October 4, 2007 I went to the Town of Moira Historical Association Museum in Moira to meet Janet Dana, the President of the Historical Association. She invited me to check their archives and go for a tour of the Brushton CCC campsite. Janet found one CCC item, a picture of a group of CCC boys at Fort Dix, New Jersey who were going to Idaho. Janet introduced me to local historian Tim Lonkey who wanted to join us on our exploration of the campsite.

We drove to Dickinson and picked up another local resident, Kenny Cox. Kenny said his brother was in the Brushton camp and often brought fiends back to their farm on the weekends.

When we got to the camp we found the old CCC entrance gate, but only one long building remained. We thought it

Raymond Noreault started as an enrollee in the CCC and later took classes and became subaltern, a junior officer, who helped the captain run the camp. Janet Dana

might have been the mess hall. As we walked around the open area we found an earthen ramp with stone walls for support. It looked like a loading platform for heavy equipment.

As we walked, Janet told me her father, Raymond Noreault, was a member of the camp. She said she would check with her mother, Jean, for more information.

A few months later she emailed me a picture of her dad. Her mother told her that Raymond had been in three camps, Brushton, Altamont near Albany, and Paul Smiths. Janet said: " My mother informed me that Dad was a clerk in some office and earned $40 a month. When the camps were closing, he had the opportunity to go to school somewhere near New York City to become an officer. She wasn't sure about the site. Dad was assigned to the Altamont camp where he was in charge but had a difficult time since he was sent many troubled kids from New York City.

"My mother said she and her young baby lived with a couple in town, while Ray lived at the camp. When they closed that camp, she thought he was sent to Paul Smiths. This camp was filled with veterans who were not too fond of taking orders from some young guy."

I suggested that Janet could find more information about her dad by contacting the National Archives and Records Administration in St. Louis.

In July 2010, Janet sent me 11 pages of CCC records of her father. They stated he was born on April 28, 1916 in Malone. Raymond graduated from St. Joseph's Academy High School in 1935 where he took a year of commercial work. He was unemployed for a year before he signed up for the CCC on October 15, 1936. He was recommended for clerical work and sent to the Brushton camp.

His fist job was running the PX (canteen). Then he worked for a year as the education assistant. In January 1939 he became the company clerk and earned the rank of Leader on May 4, 1939. This brought his salary up to $45 a month.

During his three years at Brushton he took advantage of the classes offered in the evenings, such as First Aid, Safety, Typewriting, Leader Training, Journal Writing, Company Clerk Class, and Subaltern School. Most of the classes he got excellent ratings.

Raymond got married on November 24, 1939.

On February 17, 1941 the Army sent him to a Subaltern School. A subaltern was a junior officer or other subordinate who helped the captain run the camp. At this time the Army was calling the Reserves to active duty because of the threat of war. Many had to leave their positions in the CCC camps. Civilians were then called on to be subalterns and help run the CCC camps.

Raymond stayed at the subaltern school for a month and received a performance rating of 'Excellent.' He returned to the Brushton camp on March 17, 1941 where he did office work until he was discharged from the Brushton camp on May 10, 1941. The Army sent him to the Altamont camp where he was the subaltern with a salary of $1,800 a year.

Janet told me, "Dad never told us about his CCC years. I was hoping to find out more information from his CCC records about his work at the Altamont camp near Albany and his last camp that my mother thought was the Paul Smiths."

These records helped Janet discover more about her father's role in the CCC. Moving from enrollee in 1936 to subaltern in 1941 and supervising a camp was quite an accomplishment for a young man from Malone.

Janet said she wished her father had been more willing to discuss with his children those years in the CCC and his time overseas in WWII that followed.

"After the war we moved to Winooski, Vermont where Dad spent the rest of his life. Dad worked for Federal Tea Company and Metropolitan Life. What I remember most about Dad was his integrity, intelligence, love of reading, and respect for his government. Dad died on May 25, 1995.

Leander "Lee" Gebo & Brothers
Edward & Hector

At my talk at the Plattsburgh Historical Society someone told me they knew Lee Gebo who was in the CCC. I called him in June 2006 and asked him to tell me about his life and experiences in the CCC.

"I was born on January 2, 1922 in Plattsburgh. My family had 11 children. My father was disabled when he busted his back in a stone quarry in about 1919. I lived in Cumberland Hedge on the east side of Plattsburgh. We worked hard and lived in the country. There weren't any school buses in those days. I was used to walking six miles to school.

"When I was 16 in September 1937, I quit school because my family needed a lot of help. My parents and I went to the Government Building in Plattsburgh to sign up for the CCC. They signed for me because I was young. They shipped us out in an International bus to Brushton. It took about one and one-half hours to get there.

"The camp was just off Rt 11 B. In the barracks we had three coal stoves and everyone took turns feeding the fire. There was one in the middle and one at each end. Our barracks had about 60 guys. There were two other barracks that had about 20-25 in each.

"We worked eight hours a day building roads and leveling brand new roads, cutting trees, and trucking in gravel. I was a laborer.

"Mr. Barnaby, our foreman, lived in a separate building with the other foremen. He was a nice man. One day he saw that I wasn't removing the trees like the other guys. I told him I had been operated on for appendicitis about six months before I joined the CCC. He said that I was doing a good job and not to worry. We had a job to do and we did it. We worked hard.

"Every other week we came home because a good friend of mine, Bob Lucia, had a model A Ford at camp. When we drove back to camp and went up the steep mountain by Dannemora, we had to go up backwards because the gas was gravity fed. There was no fuel pump and the gas tank was in front of the windshield. We paid him two dollars every week to take us home. We left camp on Friday night and came back on Sunday afternoon.

"On the weekends that we stayed at camp, we used to go down to the Brushton Fire Hall. They had activities and games like ping pong and sold sodas and doughnuts.

"We got canteen tickets worth $8 a-month and $22 went home to my family.

"They didn't give us uniforms. We wore knickers and wool socks that came over the knickers. In the winter we got a pea coat, gloves, and big winter boots.

"Clarence Petty was a fast worker. He was our supervisor and was a nice guy.

"I stayed at the camp till 1939 when they gave us wooden

rifles to practice with. Then I knew it was time to go.

"When I left I got a job working in a stone quarry. I got 65 cents an hour.

"In 1939 I met my wife, Kathleen Frederick, at her cousin's birthday party. We got married on June 7, 1941. We had two children: Gary and Carole.

"I enlisted in the Army in 1942 and was sent to Fort Dix. Then I went to St. Augustine, Florida for police training. After military police training, I took a train to Alaska. It took seven days and nights to reach Dawson Creek. Then we went to White Horse, Canada. I patrolled the Alaska Highway and the cities of Fairbanks, Juneau, and Skagway.

"After the war I drove a cab for my father-in-law and took up auto mechanics under the GI Bill. Then I worked in the Chevrolet dealership in Plattsburgh. After two years, I worked in a service station. I transferred to an International dealer and finally worked as a heavy equipment mechanic at the Air Force Base. I retired in 1983.

"My brother Hector, the eldest in our family, joined the CCC after me in 1937. He was at the Plattsburgh camp. It was located at the entrance to the 82nd Infantry Division. He took care of the mules for the infantry. They didn't have many vehicles then. He also worked at Macomb State Park in Skyler Falls about 6 miles west of Plattsburgh where he built tables, fireplaces, and roads.

"I think he was in for about 10 months. He then worked in the stone quarry where my father worked.

"My other brother, Edward, joined the CCC about six months after Hector. He went up to Paul Smiths Camp. It was about 10 miles south of Meacham Lake. He worked at Tupper Lake and Meacham Lake building campsites. There are private camps there now. Hector died about six years ago.

"The CCC experience made my brothers and I grow up fast."

Leonard Abare

My good fire tower friends in Dannemora, Larry and Colleen Seney, told me that Larry's uncle, Leonard Abare, was in the CCC and he lived in Newcomb. In January 2010 I called Leonard at his home and he shared his stories about his life and experiences in the CCC.

"I was born on November 12, 1917 in Chazy, NY. My parents were Napoleon and Nettie (Dumah). They had 11 children: Lulla, Howard, Henry, Herbert, Martin, Bertha, Lottie, Katherine, Francis, Hiram, and myself. I was the youngest.

"We couldn't afford to go to school and buy books so I quit school after seventh grade. I got a job working in Plattsburgh at a chamois factory. Then I worked for National Recovery Act cleaning graveyards.

"When I was 18 years old I joined the CCC in 1935. They told me I wouldn't be in New York and sent me out West on a train to Lovelock, Nevada. I was excited about traveling and I felt good about leaving home.

"When I got there we lived in barracks. I had a couple jobs while there. Each morning after revile Sergeant Bill, the 'Top Kick,' told me where I was supposed to go and what to do. I'd stand by the road and someone picked me up and took me to my assignment.

"My first job was cutting wood for the camp. I had a buddy and we used a crosscut saw. Then I ran the company laundry. The guys brought their clothes in. The clothes were all labeled with each boy's name. I had two boys working for me. They did the washing. The Army furnished an electric washer. I think we had a dryer because there wasn't a clothesline. On payday I sat with the paymaster. It was compulsory for everyone to pay 50 cents a month for getting their clothes washed.

"My third job was painting the insides of buildings.

"Our camp leader was Captain Smith. He and former President Herbert Hoover owned a nearby gold mine. My next job was working in the gold mine. I handled little bags of gold ore down a chute.

"In the evening and on weekends I got together with some friends and played music. One guy, Ted Solomon, played the guitar and I played a harmonica. We even got to play at an amateur show in town. They all thought we should have gotten first place but we came in second. We often played for the boys in our camp.

"We used to go to Limerick Valley near Oreana and watch the wild horses run across the road. An old man prospector took me there. I threw stones at the horses to scare them away.

"I also took a photography class. We learned how to develop pictures. Our Education Advisor, Mr. Hastings, told me one day, 'Leonard, I have some negatives. Would you print them for me?'

"I did it with my photo paper and he was pleased. After that he said, 'Well no one else can do it. You will now be in charge of the dark room.

"In camp we had a CCC boy, Kehoe, who thought

Leonard Abare worked at three CCC camps and loved playing his harmonica. Joanne & Andy Stengrevics and Paul Hai

he was a prospector. One weekend he told me: 'I have some beans. Let's go prospecting. We went out into the mountains and I made chuck wagon beans for food. But we didn't find any gold.

"The food in camp was good. We had a lot of vegetables and meat.

"Sometimes the leaders and guys played jokes on each other. One time I sent a guy on a wild goose chase. I sent him to different buildings and told him to ask for a clipboard stretcher. The guys in the other buildings knew the joke. They sent the rookie to another office. He kept asking for a clipboard stretcher. Then he was sent to the Department of Grazing. Finally, someone said there was no such thing. We loved to play jokes on guys.

"I stayed for six months in Nevada and came back to New York and went to Gilbert Lake near Laurens and Oneonta. We were building a state park. I helped build the cabins. I worked with a foreman named Starr.

"Then I was placed in charge of company laundry.

"On some weekends I had friends from Buffalo, Walter Bowman and his sister Erma. They'd come to visit me. Some weekends we went to Oneonta to dances. I stayed at the camp for quite a while.

"They transferred me to the Brushton camp near Paul Smiths. I liked it there and worked doing reforestation work. We planted a lot of trees. "One time while painting the inside of a building someone noticed spots on me. I went to the infirmary and I found out I had the measles. I stayed there till I got better and I didn't have to work.

"I had a lot of good times there. We drank a little beer.

"Sometimes on weekends I got a ride home from a friend in Champlain. I paid him 50 cents for gas. While home I sawed wood for Bill Burl. He made me work hard.

"One time I came home and my mother died.

"Then in 1941 I was drafted into the Army. One day after being there for three months while I was in our mess hall they announced that the US was declaring war. I trained at Camp Maxey in Texas.

"I was in Army for four years and nine months. I was in five major campaigns in Africa, Italy, France, Germany, and Austria. I was with the Army engineers. We built pontoon bridges over the Rhine and Danube rivers.

"I met my wife Agnes Seney when my brother Francis took me in a restaurant. I introduced myself to this young lady. We fell in love. When I was on Army leave we got married in 1943 in Lyon Mountain. We had one son Leonard who died a year ago.

"I got out of the Army in 1945. My brother-in-law, Albert Bruce, got me a job in Newcomb. I worked at National Lead mines in Tahawus. I was a vulcanizer fixing the rubber conveyor belts. I had my own shop. I worked with anything that was made of rubber.

"In my spare time I enjoyed playing the harmonica and was a member a small band called the 'Sanford Lane Irregulars.'

"The CCC prepared me for the Army. We had barracks and learned to take orders. I also learned a lot about photography. I had a dark room and printed my photographs."

Leonard died at the age of 92 on May 24, 2010 before I could meet him in person.

CHAPTER 11
CANTON

HISTORY

The Canton CCC camp S-134, which began in the summer of 1935, was classified as a reforestation camp. Although S-134 was called the Canton camp. It was 7 mi. southeast of that village Canton in the town of Pierrepont in St. Lawrence County. It was named Canton because the village had a railroad station and post office. The Canton area was chosen for a CCC reforestation camp because it had large tracts of land purchased by the government for reforestation. Reforestation Area No. 3 contained three large tracts: Taylor, Hewitt, and Erskine Van Brocklin, totaling 1,200 acres. The area was essential for Canton's water supply.[1]

After a search for a camp site the government chose to lease 13 acres from Bower E. Powers, a dairy farmer on Powers Road just off State Route 68 approximately a mile NW of Pierrepont Center.

Captain Charles M. Cormack was in charge of constructing the frame buildings for camp S-134 and hired 40 local workers. The cost of materials and labor was approximately $20,000. They used around 240,000 board feet for the 18 buildings.[2] To aid Captain Cormack, 1st Lt. William K. Brame brought a cadre of twelve men in two Army trucks from the Tupper Lake Camp S-63. When they arrived the camp was far from being completed. Captain Cormack pushed construction and the buildings were completed on schedule.[3]

On August 9, 1935 camp superintendent Horace G. Harris brought several truckloads of equipment and tools for the camp projects. The next day 178 enrollees arrived from Fort Dix, NJ.[4] Fifty-seven were from the Ogdensburg area and the rest from New York City and large cities in New Jersey.[5] The 12 experienced men from Tupper Lake worked around the camp to help the new men get used to camp routine.

Four days later the Army sent the enrollees over to Superintendent Harris' forestry workers. Martin A. Burnstein, George Mayo, Anthony J. LaBanca, Leo Dissotelle, Floyd E. Strader, Emmet Hall, Lindsay L. Pond, Gregory H. Lawton, George H. Miles, and Michael Scully assisted

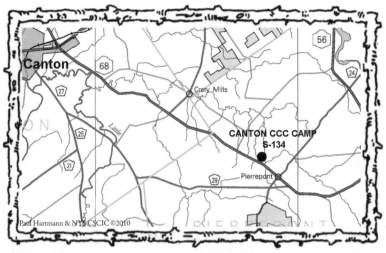

Left - These CCC boys are planting seedlings. A few are using shovels to dig holes for the boys who are following them carrying pails of seedlings. NYS Archives

Harris. They supervised the workers in their first projects: building camp roads, an approach from the main road, and walkways.[6]

Then Harris led a convoy of six stake-body trucks to the reforestation areas. On one tract in Pierrepont they worked on improving a three-mile trail through the reforestation area. A group of approximately 50 men scouted for gooseberry and currant bushes and removed them because they helped in the spread of blister rust. By mid-September around 150 enrollees began planting 3-4 year-old white pine and white spruce trees for the next two months. They constructed about three miles of fire lines around the trees. By the end of 1935 they had planted over 1,250,000 trees.[7]

The camp had a change in command in August 1935. Captain James Miller replaced Captain Cormack. First Lt. John F. Maroni was his assistant.[8]

The August 6, 1935 Canton St. Lawrence Plaindealer described how local businesses could bid on food supplies for the Canton CCC camp. The mess sergeant ordered supplies for the kitchen a month in advance. Here is the list of supplies the camp publicized for bidding: 5,000 lbs. of beef; 200 lbs. of bacon; 1,500 dozen eggs; 1,800 lbs. of pork; 200 lbs of cheese; 3,000 loaves of 1 lb. of bread; 400 lbs. of chicken and fowl; 1,200 lbs. of butter; 300 lbs. of onions; 400 gallons of pasteurized milk; 7,500 lbs. potatoes; 48 lbs. of lard and 500 lbs. of lard substitutes.

Canton citizens had mixed reactions to the new camp. Rev. C. H. MacVey took an interest in the welfare of the young men. He felt the Army was lax in not having a curfew to keep the men from roaming the town at night and the Army did not provide an adequate number of chairs and reading materials for the enrollees. MacVey asked residents for donations of materials for the camp.

On the other hand Canton Mayor Hamilton praised the CCC men for their behavior and stated he hadn't received one complaint. He felt there was no need for a curfew but agreed the camp needed more chairs and reading materials. The Army officers stated they were looking forward to a friendly atmosphere with the residents of Canton. The newspaper reported the camp would have a positive effect on the merchants because the enrollees would spend thousands of dollars for food and entertainment.[9]

Superintendent Harris had many projects for his Canton camp: blister rust control, reforestation, truck trails, forest fire control work, waterhole construction, and forest stand improvement. The camp was involved in the state's purchase of reforested land that contained at least 500 acres. First enrollees surveyed new parcels to be purchased and made maps. Then when the parcel was purchased, they cleared the slash and debris. In the early spring and fall they planted the seedlings. During the summer they fenced the area to prevent damage from grazing cattle and constructed 14' wide fire breaks using a tractor and plow. The men constructed waterholes near springs to provide a ready supply of water to fight fires. Finally, they built truck and foot trails for administration and for suppression of fires in the interior of the parcel. Enrollees worked to prevent blister rust that killed white pine trees by removing gooseberry and currant bushes. In the winter they did forest stand improvement by clearing dead trees and removing undesirable trees.[10]

During 1935 and 1936 camp S-134 did blister rust control in surrounding communities such as Pierrepont, Hopkinton, and Stockholm.[11] To entertain the men the Army held a dance in the Recreation Building on October 31, 1935. Forestry trucks went out to nearby towns to pick up those interested in attending. A local orchestra played to an enthusiastic crowd that had a great time dancing.[12]

The reforestation area increased to over 4,800 acres by the end of 1935. Parcels were in the towns of South Colton, Pierrepont, Parishville, Russell, and Hopkinton. George E. Mayo supervised the survey work.[13]

An education program began when Dell J. Sharp arrived on November 11, 1935. He offered these classes to interested students: reading, arithmetic, spelling, and algebra. Another teacher, Lincoln Grieb, came and taught arts & crafts. When 1st Lt. G. B. Ashcraft came to camp he started a class in auto-mechanics that was popular with the boys.[14]

The boys had the opportunity to participate in athletic activities. Dell Sharp organized a basketball team with the help of forester Alvin Brown. They practiced and played games at the Canton Grammar School gym. In the recreation hall the boys played ping-pong on camp-constructed tables. They also held tournaments to see who was the champion of the camp. Some boys played baseball but softball was the camp's favorite. The camp formed a team in the summer and competed in the Canton Industrial League. At the end of the season, they came in second place.[16]

Towards the end of 1935 the camp received

Above, Left - In June 1936 Foreman Jack Clawson supervised his crew of enrollees from S-134 in digging a hole that they later lined with rocks. They located waterholes near springs providing water in fighting fires in the newly reforested lands. NYS Archives. Above, Right - Two CCC enrollees from the Canton camp by a recently constructed waterhole. They fenced the hole to keep out farm animals. They made an overflow ditch that kept the holes approximately 6 ft. deep. NYS Archives

Clockwise from Above, Left - The Canton Canteen/PX sold cigarettes along with camp matches with the camp logo. Podskoch Collection. Canton camp S-134 activity collage.[15] The Canton CCC camp built this waterhole near Parishville. NYS Archives

word that it would move to the Pacific Coast. The enrollees began preparing to move. At this time, Captain Brame, who had replaced Captain Miller, left with a cadre of men to form a company in Montana. On January 20, 1936 Capt. Edward F. Redmond became the new camp commander and Lt. Delos Calkins replaced Lt. Maroni.[17]

In March Col. Raymond W. Briggs, commander of the Madison Barracks near Watertown, announced the Canton camp would close on April 1, 1936. The men were to transfer to the Pacific Coast and the Canton camp would reopen the next winter. The Madison Barracks sent four officials to burn the enrollees' supplies: clothing, boots, etc. because they didn't need to be shipped to the new western camp. Residents were upset to see this destruction of materials because there were many needy families who could use the clothing. Local businesses were also upset with the administration of the camp because food had been supplied by out of town companies.[18]

Just as the camp was to close, the government

changed its mind and notified the Canton camp that it postponed plans to move the camp. S-134 continued with its reforestation projects. One possible reason for retaining the camp was the tremendous amount of trees planted by the Canton camp.

District Forester Walter F. Pratt sent a letter to A. S. Hopkins, the Assistant Director of Lands and Forest in Albany. He stated the Pierrepont camp planted 131,674 trees during the week of April 11, 1936. In another letter Walter Pratt stated S-134 was to receive their last spring shipment of 268,500 trees for lot #11.

WORK ACCOMPLISHED BY CAMP S-134*

PROJECT	1935	1936	1937	1940	TOTAL
Boundary marking		10	19.1		29.1
Fences - rods	221	2800	1844	874	5518
Field planting trees - ac.	52	2113	1004	480	3644
Fighting forest fires - man-days		48			48
Fire breaks - ac.			3.6		3.6
Fire hazard reduction (roadside & trail side) - man-days	10	234	570	2	816
Fire pre-suppression - man-days				242	242
Forest stand improvement - ac.		168	259	358	785
Preparation/transportation of materials - man-days		701		61	762
Razing undesirable structures - man-days			195		195
Searching for missing persons - man-days	15				15
Seed collection, conifer - bushels	18	60	5		83
Surveys - linear mi.		32.5	285	11	328.5
Trails, truck - mi.	1	1	1.1		3.1
Tree & plant disease control (blister rust) - ac.	545	1261	135		1941
Water holes - number		1	20		21
Wind erosion control - ac.				12.5	12.5

*Numerical data from Conservation Reports

By 1937 camp S-134 continued working a total of six reforestation areas totaling around 5,000 acres. The Conservation Department's new camp superintendent was C. E. Mason. He was assisted by these men: J. D. Clawson, junior forester; Anthony J. LaBanca, cultural foreman; Leo J. Disotelle, Emmet Hall, Lindsay Pond, Floyd Strader, junior foremen of construction and maintenance; Herbert J. Foley, mechanic; George H. Miles, blacksmith; Michael D. Scully, tractor operator.[19]

By the spring of 1937 Captain E. Redmond received notification that the camp would close because the Emergency Conservation Work programs had been reduced. This time the Canton camp did close on June 30, 1937.[20]

On July 21, 1937 C. F. Burnham, state CCC inspector, sent a memorandum to District Forester Walter F. Pratt describing his visit to the camp on that day. He stated custodian G. H. Miles was on duty. The other custodian, Herbert Foley, had the day off. "The buildings are in very good shape and properly cleaned out. Grass scythes are needed to keep the grass and weeds mowed around the buildings." He also reported there wasn't any heavy equipment stored there but these items might be needed for other camps: 1 new fire break plow, 3-15' culvert collars, 8-sacks of blister rust paper, 1 Chevy stake-body tarpaulin frame, and several drums of oil. All the buildings were open because Miles said he was instructed to keep them open on hot days otherwise he was to lock and nail them up.[21]

During the summer of 1940 Army Company K, 28th Infantry, from Fort Ontario in Oswego set up a tent city in the vacant camp S-134. They were part of a huge Army maneuver held in August in northern St. Lawrence County in which over 100,000 troops participated.[22]

On October 14, 1940 members of the Paul Smiths camp occupied the Canton camp.[23]

On May 15, 1941 Camp S-134 officially closed and the enrollees moved to the CCC camp in Lake Placid where they worked at the Olympic Bobsled Run.[24] This company then moved in October to the Plattsburg camp AF-1.[25]

The buildings at the Canton camp were removed

and the only CCC building remaining on the Power farm is a small well house. Bower Power, Jr. built a ranch style home in the field where camp S-134 stood.

MEMORIES

Bower Powers Jr.

For two years I searched for the location of the Canton CCC camp. In 2007 I visited the St. Lawrence County Historical Society (SLHS) to give a talk on the CCC. Canton residents told me they had never heard of a camp in their town. In the SLHS Archives I did find mention of the camp in the Town of Pierrepont but no specific site was mentioned. A visit to the Potsdam Historical Society yielded mention of a request from the Potsdam Normal School asking for CCC work on a toboggan slide and a picture of the slide.

"Then in the fall of 2007 when I was driving on County Route 29 to visit my friends Carolyn and Gene Kaczka in Hannawa Falls I spotted the Pierrepont Highway Department building and decided to stop to see if someone might know the location of the Canton CCC camp. I met the highway superintendent, Shawn D. Spellacy, He noticed my Connecticut license plates and asked me where I lived. I told him Colchester and he said he was from the next town of Lebanon. He had come up here hunting, fell in love with the area, and moved up to Pierrepont 20 years ago.

"The camp was located a short distance north on Rt. 68 on the Powers' farm," said Shawn. "Go approximately three-quarters of a mile and turn right on Powers Road. The camp was on the right."

I drove up Powers Road and found a blue ranch style home on the right in a wide space that had been a farm field. There weren't any CCC buildings in sight. I knocked on the door. Bower Powers answered the door and I got right to the point. I said: "I'm looking for the site of the Canton CCC camp."

He replied, "My father, Bower Powers leased about 15 acres to the government in 1935 for a CCC camp. I was just four years old. My parents, Bower and Anna, came here in the fall of 1909 from DeKalb and bought this 200-acre farm. The only CCC building left is that pump house over there. There was a water tower on stilts next to it by the road. Our farmhouse was across the street but it burned in 1954. Only the barn remains."

I asked Bower if he would draw a map of the camp buildings. "Two camp roads went down the center forming a square with a flag pole in the center. There were five barracks in a row on the right. Behind them was the latrine. The roads led to the rec hall in the back. To the right of it was the coal shed. On the left starting at the town road were these buildings: supply, offices, infirmary, and kitchen. There was another road behind these buildings. The water tower was by the town road followed by garages and workshop.

"The camp's main project was planting trees on state land. One of the sites reforested was Taylor State Park (10 miles SE of Canton near County Road 27) in Pierrepont.

The Army officers kept the CCC boys in control but one time the boys raised hell at Mr. Butterfield's sugarhouse. They were destructive to his equipment.

"I was between four and eight years old at this time and my brothers and I didn't go across the road. After the camp closed my father worked as a caretaker for the camp.

"The Army came in the summer of 1940 and occupied the CCC camp. They were having maneuvers before WWII. The soldiers pitched their tents in the field behind the barracks buildings.

"I remember Jimmy Spencer was the assistant of Major Shum. George Moss drove an Army truck in the camp. He transported soldiers to different places during the maneuvers.

"Then the buildings were torn down and some went to the 4-H Camp. Dad got the office buildings and shop. We took them down. They were on posts. Dad used one building for his sawmill and the other he used for machinery and storage.

"The only picture that I have is a postcard of the camp taken in 1940. I had another panoramic photo but it was destroyed when our farmhouse burned.

"My dad and I farmed the land for 30 years. I stopped farming in the 1980s. Now I just raise horses.

"I remember a guy named Sweeney from New York City who visited our farm. He had been at the camp and he was surprised to see the area. He said nothing looked like it did when he was there."

Army Camps, St. Lawrence County War Maneuvers, 1940.
(Sykview D. P. Church, Canton, N. Y.)

The Canton CCC camp on Bower Powers farm in Pierrepont. Photo was taken in 1940 when the Army was conducting maneuvers in St. Lawrence County. They pitched tents near the vacant CCC buildings. The five barracks were on the left and on the right were the supply building, offices, infirmary, and kitchen. Behind the latter and across the road was the Powers farmhouse and barn. Bower Powers Jr.

Bower Powers owns the land where Canton CCC camp was during the 1930s. Powers is standing next the last remaining CCC building. Podskoch Collection

CHAPTER 12
EIGHTH LAKE

HISTORY

The Eighth Lake CCC Camp S-58 or Camp No. 10 was established on June 20, 1933.[1] The site was in a field near the carry between Seventh Lake and Eighth Lake just off Route 28, five miles west of the hamlet of Raquette Lake in Hamilton Co. The site of the CCC camp was on land purchased from William Webb in 1899.

Thirty men arrived at the Thendara railroad station in June 1933 on their way to Eighth Lake. Army Captain O. F. Morstan was in charge. The men bivouacked in the clearing while they built a wooden mess hall with a large stone fireplace and began the work of developing roads, campsites, and trails.[2]

The Niagara Falls Gazette sang the praises of the Eighth Lake camp in a June 26, 1933 story "Conservation Corps Is Doing Good Work in New York State."

"In four days one camp of 200 youth at Eighth Lake, in the Adirondacks tore out five acres of undergrowth leaving fine trees and a healthy uncluttered forest bed to grow in. Before the four days were over one-half miles of roadway was also under construction, a bridge had been thrown across the inlet of Raquette Lake, and the entire camp had been put up."

A 1933 untitled newspaper clipping from the Town of Webb Historical Association Archives stated: "Work is progressing rapidly on projects by the boys in the CCC camp at Eighth Lake. In the past few days the boys have started cleaning the shore in many places along the Fulton Chain, greatly improving the line, taking out dead timber, and flood wood,

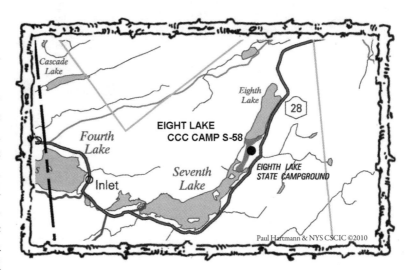

Right - An aerial view of a CCC side camp on the shore of Pigeon Lake (10 miles NW of their camp at Eighth Lake) in the Brown Tract where boys from Eighth Lake camp stayed while building trails. Al Blue

which in many cases is a menace to navigation. At present a crew is working along the shore of the channel between Fifth and Fourth Lakes. With high hip boots the men are working the edge of the stream, hauling out great piles of driftwood and burning it on the wet, marshy ground."

In another 1933 newspaper article, "Golden Beach Camp Popular: Better Facilities Are Provided by the C. C. C., states: "... the boys from Camp S-58 cleared the underbrush along the road that led to the campsite. They enlarged the number of campsites to accommodate 300 campers. At first the campsite had only one pump and the CCC boys worked to improve the water system by piping water to the campsite from the new well they dug.[3]

The boys were involved in sporting activities in their free time. The Army furnished baseball equipment for a camp team that played the Thendara CCC camp.

Ephram H. Courser was the oldest member of Camp S-58 at Eighth Lake. The former Vermont native and resident of Long Lake joined the CCC in the summer of 1933 when he was pushing 80. Courser was interviewed in an undated newspaper story in the Town of Webb Historical Association files, "Active Tree Soldier Tho 79". The writer said: "During the first two weeks of camp the city-bred youths in the C. C. C. found the going rather tough when it came to breaking stone, but Courser carried on, setting a good example, when his younger fellow workers fell by the wayside.

"Courser likes the C.C.C. life so well that he signed

119

Chauncey Hatorn settled on Golden Beach on Raquette Lake in 1891 and took in sportsmen at his lodge. His dock and lean-to are on the right. Today this is a swimming area at the Golden Beach State Park. Jim Kammer. The Eighth Lake CCC boys built the fireplace and picnic tables at the Golden Beach campsite on Raquette Lake. Jim Kammer

for re-enlistment for another six-month period and will go with the rest of the boys when the camp moves to Gibsonville in the Catskills.

"The 79 year-old man hasn't missed a day of work. He has been regular at his formations, does his share along with the other boys, and asks no favors."

Raquette Lake historian Jim Kammer told me the Eighth Lake CCC began developing the Golden Beach campsite in 1933. He referred me to Harold K. Hochschild's book: Township 34: A History with Digressions of an Adirondack Township in Hamilton County in the State of New York.

Kammer told me: "Chauncey Hatorn was one of the earliest settlers where the Golden Beach campsite is located. Chauncey came in 1877 and Dr. T. C. Durant and later his son, William, owned the land. He built a lodge and housed guests till he died on November 10, 1891.

"There were a few people who settled in Chauncey's buildings at Golden Beach. Then in 1897 W. W. Durant sold most of Township 6 that included Golden Beach to the state. Freeland Jones took over Golden Beach in 1903 and stayed till 1909. Joseph Murphy lived there during the summers from 1910 and stayed there a few years before the state claimed it and took it over. In 1929 the Conservation Department began developing a campground at Golden Beach and in 1931 they opened it to the public. Then in 1933 the CCC continued the development of the state camp site. The CCC boys also began developing a campground on the site of their camp on Eighth Lake."

Camp S-54 closed on November 8, 1933 due to cold weather and inadequate housing for the winter.[4] The 94 men who were left took a special train from Thendara

to Rochester, where they transferred to the Pennsylvania Railroad for the trip to the Mount Morris CCC camp near Oneonta for the winter.

The Conservation Department continued working on the Eighth Lake campsite in 1934 and opened it to the public in 1935. Over the next years the state removed the CCC mess hall and left the fireplace and chimney.

In 1939 the Indian Lake CCC camp came to Eighth Lake State Campground and continued to improve the site. They improved the water supply and added 34 campsites with tables and fireplaces. They also expanded the campsites at Golden Beach State Park to 30 more sites.[5]

LEGACY

There have been many improvements to the Eighth Lake since the CCC began improving the campsite. In 1970 the water system was improved and flush toilets were added. In 1975 the state constructed a showerhouse. There are now 126 tent and trailer sites.

Many canoers and kayakers traveling the Fulton Chain canoe route stop at the Eighth Lake beach for a refreshing swim or camp for the evening.

CCC camp S-58 extended Golden Beach campground and the state opened it to the public in 1935. There are now 205 tent and trailer sites, flush toilets, showers, a dump station, and picnic areas.

Larry Brenton with ladies in front of the large fireplace built by the CCC. It was part of the mess hall for around 200 hungry men. Larry Brenton. This historical marker states the CCC were the first to do stream development work to improve the trout habitat of Trout Brook between Raquette and Long lakes in 1933. This was one of the projects of the Eighth Lake CCC Camp. Podskoch Collection. These campers are enjoying the golden sandy beach at Golden Beach State Park. Jim Kammer. This is the picnic and beach area at Eighth Lake State Park that the CCC improved during the 1930s.

MEMORIES

Larry Brenton

In the fall of 2009 I visited the Eighth Lake Campground and talked to the manager, Chris Mueller. He told me that an old camper, Larry Brenton, had pictures of the camp during the 1940s. I called Larry at his home near Buffalo and he said, "I have been camping at Eighth Lake campsite with my family since I was four years old in 1940. When I was young camping with my parents and grandfather at Eighth Lake, I had the job of loading a large stone fireplace with wood. Grandpa worked for the railroad and he used railroad flares to start the fire. Campers gathered around the fire at night and I remember people saying that the large fireplace and two story chimney was built by the CCC. It might have been the District Forest Ranger Ernest Blue from Old Forge or the regional ranger, Mose Leonard, who told me that story."

David H. Beetle in his book Up Old Forge Way (1948) substantiated Brenton's CCC fireplace story. He said, "They built a lot of stone fireplaces. One big one looks as if they had a lot of rocks left over and they decided to shoot the works. Actually this was their 'mess hall fireplace' and it stands statue-like as a stone remnant of their camp." The state opened the Eighth Lake campsite to the public in 1935.

Jack Sherman of Raquette Lake told me he had vaca-

tioned in the area since his youth in the 1940s and knew some of the history. Jack said that before the camp was closed the CCC boys dug cesspools for the outhouses, built the men's and women's bathhouses, and dug a well for drinking water at the Eighth Lake campsite. He said that the fireplace in the mess hall was two stories high and stood by itself for a long time. He wasn't sure when the wooden structure was removed. Later the state took the fireplace and chimney down and moved the rubble to near the old Uncas Road trail.

Doug Jones

While traveling past Lake Durant campground in Blue Mountain in 2007, I stopped by the campground and talked to the manager Doug Jones. I told him about doing research on the work of the CCC at Golden Beach and Doug said: My great-great grandfather, Melancton (or Malanckton) Jones started Golden Beach prior to 1880. He's listed there along with his wife, children, and several laborers in the 1880 census. Just after 1900, the family left Golden Beach. It may have been traded, or it may have been a case of a lease expiring. I do know that they received land on North Point in Raquette Lake in exchange, and later sold that to move to Blue Mountain Lake.

CHAPTER 13
FISH CREEK

HISTORY

The Fish Creek CCC camp was set up in 1933 at Fish Creek Pond, one of the most popular campsites in the Adirondacks on Rt. 3 in Santa Clara, Franklin Co. In 1920 the Conservation Commission opened the campsite with lean-tos and fire rings. Six years later the state established 20 designated campsites with sanitary facilities. In 1928 the campground doubled to approximately 40 sites. The following year, 1929, the Fish Creek Pond sites doubled again to 80. In 1931 there were 264 campsites with 45,750 campers.[1] During the 1930s the campsite was also called "The Birches."

Fish Creek Pond Camp Site expanded dramatically when Company 261 commanded by Captain John S. Miller established CCC camp S-56 (No. 8) at the state campsite on June 3, 1933. The CCC camp was also called Lake Clear Junction because this was the nearest railroad station and post office. The CCC camp complex was located to the right of the road driving up from Square Pond to Rollins Pond, behind the present-day soccer field. There were 200 young men who were ready to expand and improve the campground. They constructed and maintained trails and canoe portages in that area. In the winter they planned on doing silviculture on state plantations.[2]

The October 5, 1933 article, "More Than a Million Trees Planted by Local Foresters," of The Adirondack Daily reported the accomplishments of camp S-56 during its first four months of work: cleaned and improved 24-acres of state campsite, built 2.5 miles of roads, cleared 1 mile shore line, and planted 372,000 trees.

Camp S-56 also did work away from the state campground. An undated newspaper clipping in the Sara-

Clockwise from Top, Left - This 1922 picture shows one of the lean-tos built by the Conservation Department at the Fish Creek campsite. NYS Archives. An aerial view of Camp S-56 at the Fish Creek State Park, which was located between Square Pond on the right and Rollins Pond on the left. The long building at the top is the garage, the only remaining building. Below it in a row are the five barracks and other unidentified structures. NYS Archives. An Army officer is showing Robert Fechner the building plans for camp S-58. NYS Archives. In 1933 CCC Director Robert Fechner (2nd from left) came to inspect the Fish Creek camp along with two Army officers and two aides. NYS Archives

nac Library files entitled, "Urge Caution in Woods Because of CCC Workers," stated the boys from Fish Creek were building ski trails near Glenwood estates and Lake Kiawassa, constructing a road into the fish hatchery located near Saranac Inn, and working at the Lake Clear tree nursery.

The Conservation Report of 1934 stated S-56's primary work was developing the recreation facilities of the campsite. It described the expanded projects: forest fire suppression, blister rust control, forest stand improvement, reduction of fire hazards, construction of truck trails, and forest stand improvement & thinning the forest plantations. George Hugh Collins of Saranac Lake was the camp superintendent. Collins had previously worked in the lumber and contacting business. Collins was assisted by these men: Edward Ryan, Ernest White, Floyd Nokes, Gerald Yousey, Fred La Mora, and Burt Blade.[3]

William A. McConvey ran the camp's education program

122

Clockwise from Top - A May 1935 group photo of the Fish Creek CCC camp. The four cooks dressed in white are on the top right followed by the foremen and foresters. One enrollee in the front row is holding the camp dog. MaryEllen Salls. After a busy day building roads or campsites or thinning the forest the enrollees were happy to sit and enjoy their dinner. This picture was in 1933 when the boys lived in tents while the barracks were being built. The mess kitchen was screened in. JoAnne Petty Manning. Fish Creek CCC enrollees built this 125-seat outdoor ampitheater with a stage and two fire pits for campfires. Campers arranged evening entertainment, such as movies and slide shows. Dave McGrath. Three men are taking a break outside the administration building. NYS Archives

that developed reading, writing, and vocational skills to help the boys get jobs when they left the CCC. In the fall of 1934 he organized an automotive class. Twenty boys attended weekly classes at the J. A. Gallaway Garage in Saranac Lake. At the end of the course those who passed a test received a certificate.[4]

McConvey also arranged for speakers who came to camp and gave guidance on securing employment. One of the speakers was Harry K. Dewitt, manager of Saranac Lake New York Telephone Company. In November 1934 Dewitt talked to the boys about the opportunities at his company. He explained what qualifications they were looking for and how the boys could apply.[5]

The Army strove to provide tasty and nutritious meals. Mess officer 2nd Lt. J. J. O'Donovan did a great job of providing a delicious Thanksgiving dinner in 1934. Here is the menu: fruit cocktail, pickles and celery, turkey, dressing, giblet gravy, cranberry sauce, mashed potatoes, pineapple salad, creamed carrots, mince pie, cheese, ice cream, cigarettes, cigars, coffee, and mixed nuts.[6]

The Army under Captain Albert E. Garvin super-

vised year-round sporting activities for the enrollees. A Tupper Lake Free Press article, "Basketball and Bowling Teams at CCC Camp 8 Ready to Take on All Comers—Line-Up Strong," on November 29, 1934 reported: "One night recently two trucks loaded with men left Camp 8, CCC, at Fish Creek Pond. One truck carried a basketball squad of twenty men to Saranac Lake and the other carried a bowling team with its rooters to Tupper Lake." The bowling team members were: William Babbitt, Sam Coullier, George Guyette, Neil Crook, and Sam Perrier.

In 1933 the camp basketball team was district champion and came in second the next year in the subdistrict championship that composed these camps: Tupper Lake, Paul Smiths, and Lake Placid.

The basketball team also played non-CCC teams such as the National Guard in Malone, Saranac Lake High School, 26th Infantry in Plattsburgh, Plattsburgh High School, Holy Ghost Academy in Tupper Lake, and Plattsburgh YMCA. The team practiced at the Oval Wood Dish Hall in Tupper Lake and the Saranac Lake Armory. Some of the players were: Clifford Lemieux, Grant Plumadore, and Walter Hartigan.[7]

In 1935 a Conservation Department work plan

listed two projects to instruct the tourists. The first project was to construct 10 miles of nature trails and make 200 trail signs. Another project was to build two tent platforms. One was for a museum of nature specimens and the other for the man in charge of the nature museum.

A "June 19, 1935 Inspection Report" found in the Saranac DEC Office stated there were 193 enrollees. Twenty-four worked in the CCC camp with the Army while the other 169 worked under the supervision of 10 foremen in the Conservation Department. One four-man crew worked on blister rust, three crews constructed truck trails, one crew did campsite maintenance, another crew did beach improvement, and a crew constructed foot trails.

An October 23, 1935 "Summary of Work Projects" stated the enrollees built a stage, guardrails, 125 seats, and a rostrum for the outdoor theater. They completed the following truck trails: one-half mile at Lake Clear Plantation, one mile at the fish hatchery, and five miles at the Fish Creek Pond campsite. They completed 23.5 miles of fire hazard reduction on Rt. 3 and two miles on Forest Home Road.

Camp S-56 closed on October 26, 1935. The company led by Captain Briant went to a new camp at Camden, 40 miles northwest of Utica.

Captain Spitz and enrollees from his Tupper Lake camp took over the unfinished work of the Fish Creek CCC camp.[8] In a little over a month Conservation Department workmen began taking the Fish Creek CCC camp buildings down.[9] By the first week of January 1936 Camp S-56 was completely razed and all the supplies and equipment were removed.[10]

LEGACY

During the two years of operation the Fish Creek camp improved the size of the state campsite and its facilities. Today it is one of the most popular campsites in the Adirondacks. There are 355 campsites, a picnic area, a beach, and a playground. The CCC enrollees also built many miles of hiking trails to explore the

WORK ACCOMPLISHED BY CAMP S-56*

PROJECT	1934	1935	TOTAL
Beach improvement - ac.		6	6
Bridges - number		1	1
Buildings, misc. - number		7	7
Concrete masonry - yd³		75	75
Cribbing - yd³		1355	1355
Erosion control, bank protection - yd²	4000		4000
Fences	1	3.4	4.4
Field planting trees - ac.	259	124	383
Fine grading - yd²		2500	2500
Fire breaks - mi.	4	1	5
Fire fighting - man-days	1869	448	2317
Fire hazard reduction (roadside & trailside) - ac.	3	7	10
Fire hazard reduction (other) - ac.		226.8	226.8
Fire prevention, roadside clearing/cleaning - mi.	3	2.7	5.7
Fireplaces - number		20	20
Forest stand improvement - ac.	15		15
General clean-up - ac.		63	63
Guard rails - rods		177	177
Insect pest control - ac.		213	213
Lake, pond or beach development - ac.	11.3	2	13.3
Landscaping - ac.	9		9
Parking areas - yd²			24049
Pipe & tile lines, conduit - linear ft.			170
Planting/moving trees & shrubs - man-days			225
Power lines - mi.		0.1	0.1
Preparation/transportation of materials - man-days	303		1685
Public campground buildings & facilities - number	332		332
Public campground clearing - ac.	26		26
Seats - number		125	125
Sewage & waste disposal systems - man-days		43	43
Signs - number		175	175
Stream development - mi.	0.3	1.1	1.4
Structures, misc. - number		4	4
Surveys - man-days		29.2	29.2
Telephone line - mi.		4.5	4.5
Tool houses & boxes - number	1		1
Trails, foot - mi.	7		7
Trails, horse - mi.	4.5	11.2	15.7
Trails, truck - mi.		4.5	4.5
Water holes, wells - number	11		11
Water supply systems - man-days		20	20

*Numerical data from Conservation Reports

Clockwise - The last CCC building at the Fish Creek State Park is the garage. The state continues to use it to store equipment and vehicles. Podskoch Collection. A 2007 photo of tents and campers at Fish Creek State Park and people enjoying a boat ride on Square Pond. Dave McGrath. A postcard of the Fish Creek camp site from the 1940-50s. Dave McGrath

nearby lakes and forests.

MEMORIES

Harold Barcomb

In June 2006 Alton "Red" Barcomb of Altona called me and said: "I read in a newspaper article that you are looking for guys who were in the CCC. Well, my father, Francis, was in the CCC. The article had pictures showing a group of young guys fighting a fire and another with boys eating in a mess tent. I think my father was in the mess tent photo.

"My dad gave me CCC pictures with him in the barracks and standing by a fire tower. I'd like to share them with you.

"I don't remember much of what he did in the CCC but I do remember Dad saying that one time he worked on Angelville Road in Chazy. My father died but you should call my Uncle Harold in Chazy. He might know more about Dad in the CCC."

In the fall of 2006 I called Harold and asked if he knew where his brother Francis had been in the CCC.

"My brother Francis was with me. We were both at Fish Creek/Lake Clear and worked there for six months. We joined in November 1933 and boy was it cold. They kept the ambulance and mail truck running day & night. I was about 18 when I joined and Francis was 19. We all knew about the CCC and we were poor so we joined. We had a large family with seven children. Our father, James, worked at whatever job he could find. He often worked at

the large Miner Farm in Chazy. This was about the only job Dad could find.

"My brother and I took the CCC job because we got $30 a month and $25 went home to our family. We got $5 spending money but we really didn't have to buy anything. We got our food, clothing, and a place to stay.

"It was the coldest winter I ever saw. It was 60 degrees below zero. They had two and possibly three potbelly stoves in each barracks to keep us warm. We stayed inside for pretty near a month in the barracks. It was too cold to work outside.

"There were at least four barracks, a bath house, a building with a library for reading, and a mess hall. The Army officers had their own barracks. They were good guys.

"We had a lot of guys from the Buffalo area. Everyone got along pretty well. The officers kept good order in the camp. There was one time when one guy was caught stealing a blanket or something. So we had a kangaroo court. This guy was found guilty and he had to suffer the consequences. The guys laid him down on his bed and pulled his pants down. Everyone took off his belt and swatted his rear end. He never stole again. The men were a good bunch of guys.

"Most of the time I did outside work. We did manual jobs with a pick and shovel. St. John was a big husky guy I worked with. We drove a crow bar 4-5' in the ground at the edge of a gravel pit. There was an older man who put dynamite in the hole to blast the dirt down. Then the guys loaded the truck with shovels and used the gravel for the camp roads.

"The food was good. One time, however, it got pretty bad. We had a strike because they didn't give us enough food. So we said that we weren't going back to work. Then they straightened things out and we got more food.

"The officers assigned guys to check on the fires all night. We took turns filling the barracks' stoves with coal. We also filled the pot belly stoves in the mess hall. We couldn't touch any of the food or we'd get into trouble.

"We had Saturdays and Sundays off. Once in a while we went to Tupper Lake for movies. Sometimes we hiked or thumbed it home. It wasn't easy in those days.

"There was one guy, Clayton McBride, who had a car. His folks lived on my road. I rode home with him quite a few times. He had a Model A Ford with a rumble

Harold Barcomb working at the Fish Creek camp in 1934. He did a lot of pick and shovel work building roads. Larry Barcomb

seat. When you sat back there you had to have blankets to keep warm. We all chipped in to help with gas money. He was a good guy.

"One of our jobs was fighting fires. One time we fought a fire at the Rockefeller Estate. It was quite a large fire. They had at least two CCC camps fighting it. We slept right on the ground without blankets. It wasn't too bad because it was warm out.

"After six months I signed up again but I was sent to the Brushton Camp. Clarence Petty was the superintendent. We worked building roads. I drove a truck and a bulldozer.

"Then I transferred to the Plattsburgh CCC camp and worked on the state beach campsite. We cleaned up the brush and did general maintenance work at the beach. At night we stayed in tents at the Plattsburgh Barracks camp south of Plattsburgh.

"In the fall I quit and got a job working on a small dairy farm in Mooers. Then I worked in the Plattsburgh Mill. I also worked for farmers.

"I married Winnie Gokey in 1940. We had three children: Owen, Larry, and Sheila.

"During WW II, I worked in Mineville at the Fisher Iron Ore Mine. I was there for three and one-half years. We worked underground.

"Later, I bought a dairy farm from my father-in-law on McBride Road. I milked 50-60 Holstein cows.

"Working in the CCC was quite an experience. People don't really know how tough it was during the Depression."

William A. McConvey

In the fall of 2007 I visited Bill McConvey at his home in Wilmington near Whiteface Mountain. He told me that he and his parents always lived in Wilmington for the summer. Bill said my grandfather bought land in Wilm-

ington in 1920 and built a house. He also rented out cabins on the property. Two of the cabins were engineer shacks that were used during the building of the Whiteface Memorial Highway in 1935.

He took me to a cabin nearby and showed me a leather bound book with this inscription: "The Log Book Company 2205 CCC." I looked inside and it was the daily log of Kenneth Reed who was the assistant to the education advisor for Company 2205 at Quaker Bridge. There were over 200 pages detailing the history of the company from the Plattsburgh Barracks in 1933 to Vermont and then to Quaker Bridge, near Croton-on-Hudson. I asked Bill if I could copy the book and he let me borrow it.

We went back to his house and I asked him to tell me about his father's life. "My dad was born in 1900. He went to Canisius College in Buffalo and graduated in 1928. Then he went to McGill University in Montreal.

"After he graduated he taught chemistry at Canisius High School.

"It was during the Depression that he worked in the Civilian Conservation Corps as a teacher and then became the Education Advisor for the Schenectady District. He traveled from camp to camp checking on the teachers and their programs. He initiated programs to help the young men improve their education and develop skills to get a job when they left the CCC.

Dad even had his own car and a driver to chauffeur him from camp to camp. One slippery night they were coming down a steep hill. My father was in the back seat and calmly told the young driver to put his feet up on the passenger seat. When they hit the engine was pushed through the firewall and would have seriously injured the young man.

"I think Dad lived a lot in Tupper Lake and in Schenectady where the main CCC office was. Dad got married in 1941 to Helen Regan. I was their only child.

"My dad told me that when they got a new recruit in camp they would

William A. McConvey was the Educational Advisor for all the camps in Sub-District 1 of the Schenectady District in New York. He supervised all the teachers and their programs and made frequent visits to the 12 camps. Bill McConvey

play a joke on him. The guys had the recruit go to the mess hall for dinner. The men would always have one particular man who was a blacksmith pass a hot platter of potatoes to a newbie. They would immediately drop the platter as they were not accustomed to handling hot items with no protection. It was an initiation of sorts.

"After the CCC position Dad worked in the Office of Price Stabilization. Then he worked for Bell AirCraft Co.

"When I was in sixth grade in 1954 we moved to Rome, NY. Dad worked at Griffiss Air Base in the procurement office for research and development. He retired in 1965 and passed away on June 21, 1986."

George Fountain

MaryEllen Salls, Brighton Town Historian, told me her uncle George Fountain was in the Fish Creek CCC camp. She said: My uncle was born in Chasam Falls on November 15, 1912. He was the third son of Edmond and Carrie Boyea who had five boys and four girls. The family was quite poor and he couldn't afford to go to high school in Malone. In those days you would have to pay a family to board you while going to high school. So after eighth grade he got jobs to help his family.

"When Uncle George was 19 he joined the CCC and worked at the Fish Creek camp.

"After the CCC he worked on the family farm. He got married to Dora Helms. They had had five boys: Rouse, George Jr. John, Richard, and Patrick

"George was a lineman for Paul Smiths Electric Co. Then he went into the logging business and worked for Benjamin Muncil in Paul Smiths. Later he went to work as caretaker at Meacham Lake state campground

"Before he retired he took his team of horses and pulled stumps to make roads and to draw logs for the state

at Mountain Pond.

"In 1995 both George and his wife won awards at the Woodsman Field Day in Tupper Lake. George was named Grand Marshall and she was awarded Woodswoman of the Year.

"Uncle George was a licensed Adirondack guide and terrific hunter. I wish you were able to meet him.

Right - George Fountain (left) with his friend Julio Tanzena at the Fish Creek CCC camp MaryEllen Salls. Below - This is a group picture of CCC camps education advisors. Bill McConvey

CHAPTER 14
FORT ANN

HISTORY

Company 205 left its camp in Cherry Plain, NY where they had constructed a 550-foot concrete dam across the Black River valley in Cherry Plain and established Camp P-121 in Fort Ann in Washington County. The camp was just north of the village along the right side of Route 4 just past Halfway Brook. At the rear of the camp were D & H Railroad tracks and the Champlain Canal. The camp opened on October 25, 1935.

During the first winter the boys had their "baptism by water" when the Halfway Creek, which flowed next to the camp, flooded because of an ice jam. Water reached halfway up the barracks walls.[1]

After two weeks of cleaning up the buildings and campsite the boys began their primary project, fighting the spread of gypsy moths and blister rust. The foresters conducted training in surveying areas and destroying the insects. They traveled to many nearby towns such as Whitehall, Granville, Hampton, and Dresden destroying gypsy moth egg clusters. In the spring and summer of 1936 the enrollees destroyed ribes (gooseberry and currant) plants that were host to the blister rust.[2] Since equipment for spraying trees to kill the gypsy moths was limited in 1936, some crews had to work 12-hour days and even on the weekends.[3]

The January 3, 1936 issue of the Essex County Republican reported that when the Port Henry CCC camp closed, the camp equipment was shipped to the Fort Ann camp, which made their work more efficient.

The education building had two classrooms where advisors taught reading and writing. Another class offered radio and telegraph communication. The telegraph instructor had experience in the Navy and Harvard University.[4]

The boys played sports such as baseball and basket-

Paul Hartmann & NYS CSCIC ©2010

Clockwise from Top - These barracks of the Fort Ann CCC camp housed 200 young men from 1939 to 1937. Halfway Brook is in the foreground along the back of the barracks. Telegraph lines and the D & H tracks are behind the camp. Carol Smith. These enrollees from Fort Ann camp spent the winter searching trees for gypsy moth egg masses. When they found them they destroyed them by painting them with creosote. Carol Smith. The cooks and assistants have set up picnic tables and shortly the building will be bustling with hungry boys after a busy day in the woods searching for pests that destroy the forest. Carol Smith.

ball. The basketball team usually practiced at the National Guard Armory in Whitehall. One winter the basketball team played in the Outing Club Basketball League in Glens Falls.[5]

In the spring of 1937 Fort Ann enrollees traveled 36 miles to Greenfield, west of Saratoga Springs, and did an experimental planting in the No. 1 Reforestation Area in that town. They planted a total of 12,859 trees that included 10 species of hardwoods and 14 species of confers.[6]

During the camps' two-year duration these Army captains supervised the camp: Capt. Hugh Parker; Capt. W. H. O'Mohundro; Capt. Jacobs; Capt. Marion; Capt. George C. Traver; and Capt. Robert Millis.[7]

The Fort Ann camp closed on October 1, 1937. All of the buildings were taken down except the mess hall that is still used as an indoor shooting range.

WORK ACCOMPLISHED BY CAMP P-121[*]

PROJECT	1935	1936	1937	TOTAL
Field planting trees - ac.			12	12
Insect pest control - ac.		51246	47741	98987
Maps & models - man-days			508	508
Telephone line - mi.		2		2
Tree & plant disease control - ac.		24304	16533	40837

*Numerical data from Conservation Reports

Above - Fort Ann Camp P-121 activity photos from Schenectady District Civilian Conservation Corps Area Yearbook, 1937. Three boys relaxing and reading in the library that was part of the education building. Carol Smith. Right - Five Conservation Department workers playing poker in their building at Fort Ann CCC camp. Carol Smith

MEMORIES

Lillian Bradway Allen

After speaking at the Hudson Falls Library on October 22, 2007 I traveled north to gather information on the Fort Ann CCC camp. My first interview was Lillian Bradway Allen. She told me she taught at the Knapp Estate at Shelving Rock on Lake George from 1931-33. It was a very large tract of land. Mr. Knapp hired a lot of help to maintain it. He had a school for the workers where I taught. Then she married Robert Allen of Fort Ann who was a funeral director for 40 years.

Left - Fort Ann CCC camp was located just north of the village of Fort Ann on Rt. 4. It was behind Paige's gas station. Podskoch Collection. Right - A stone fireplace that was part of one of the Fort Ann CCC camp buildings is on the former Eva Georgi's property. The present residents still use the fireplace. Podskoch Collection

Lillian said: "I remember the CCC camp in town. The boys worked in the area forests fighting blister rust. On the weekends they came to our town hall to watch movies."

I handed her a copy of the 1937 New York State CCC Yearbook and asked her if she recognized any of the boys in the Fort Ann group picture. "That's Clark Manning in the front row. His mother was a widow and his work at the CCC camp was a big help to her. He moved to Pennsylvania and managed a Borden plant.

"George Sherwood lived on Rt. 4 in the Flat Rock section. As you go out of the village it is to the right of the Mobile gas station. He has a few grandchildren.

"On the top row is Kenneth Campp. I know that one of his children is alive in Limerick, Maine.

"You're probably wondering how I know all this information but this is a small town and my husband was the undertaker so we knew everyone and their families.

"Lloyd Manning on the top row worked as a fireman running boilers in the state prison in Utica.

"Then there is George Paige listed as a foreman. He was Jim Paige's uncle. George had TB and died. He never got married. He had one brother Ralph and a sister Agnes."

I asked Lillian who owned the land where the camp was. "Luke Sheldon owned the gas station in front of the camp. I think the gas station was there when they built the camp. I'm not sure if he owned all of the land where the camp was. Luke lived in the house next to it. He built a motel behind it when the camp closed. Luke died but his daughter-in-law lives in South Glens Falls."

After talking with Lillian I drove to the old camp site. I stopped at Paige' gas station in front of the old CCC camp site and asked if they knew anything about the camp but they had no information. To the left of the gas station was a dirt road that I presumed was the entrance to the camp. As I walked I found two old stone base foundations on each side of the road. The road led to a long wooden building covered with red asphalt brick siding. The door was locked but when I looked through the windows it appeared to be the mess hall. Locals told me this was being used as a rifle range for a hunting club.

The road continued to the rear of the camp. Amidst trees and brush was a fireplace with a chimney about 14' high located near the 8' high railroad track bed.

I walked towards the stream and found a few metal pails and other rusted remnants of the camp but no buildings. As I walked back towards Rt. 4 I found another stone fireplace and chimney to the right of a pink house. It was used for burning trash. I wondered if this was the infirmary, officers' headquarters or the rec hall. Lillian said this was the Gullo's home. I knocked on the door but no one was home.

Eva Gullo

When I got back home in Connecticut, I called Eva Gullo. She said: "Luke Sheldon built a gas station in the late 30s. Then Glens Falls Distributing built a new gas station in 1959. They sold heating oil. Ed Monahan rented the station from 1951-1962. In 1962 Jim Paige took it over. Our house was a garage for the CCC camp. We bought our home from Peter and Eva Georgi. Peter came as a child from Germany after WW II. We traded our campground in Lake Luzerne with the Georgi's. Eva Georgi had a ceramic shop.

130

Left - CCC enrollees walking through snow to Army trucks after spending the day searching for gypsy moth egg masses. Carol Smith. Right - These foresters and forest rangers standing in front of the Fort Ann mess hall supervised the enrollees in destroying gypsy moths egg masses and destroying currant berry bushes that were hosts for blister rust. Carol Smith

Carol Smith

On October 23, 2007 I visited Carol Smith at her home in Fort Ann. I showed her a group picture of Fort Ann foremen on page 28 in the 1937 NY CCC yearbook. Carol pointed to one of the men. "My father-in-law, Roy Smith, is on the far right of the back row. He didn't stay at the camp but came home each night. They lived by the Stone Library."

Then Carol showed me a group of pictures that her father-in-law had. Four pictures showed the CCC boys and foremen walking through fields and woods in the winter. I couldn't figure out what was going on but later learned that the boys were looking for gypsy moth egg masses.

The next two pictures showed the interior of the Fort Ann camp buildings. One was the mess hall and the other the recreation room. The next showed five barracks buildings along Half Brook. The last showed 12 men in uniforms. Carol said they were probably the Conservation Department foresters who supervised the work projects.

"My father-in-law was born in 1910 in Saratoga and grew up Schushen (near Salem and Cambridge). His father worked on farms. Later he married Edna Wittemore and had five children: Della, Donald, Mary Lou, Dorothy, and Martha. Roy became a forest ranger in 1947 in Whitehall. In 1958 he was transferred to Fort Ann. Then he became paralyzed and stopped working as a ranger.

"My husband Donald also worked for Conservation Department. He was in charge of the campsites on Lake George."

Carol told me to call Leroy's daughter Della Smith.

Della told me: "My father Leroy Smith was there as a foreman, and my father's youngest brother, Whitney, was an enrollee at the camp. After the CCC camp Uncle Whiney joined the service during WWII. After the war did a little bit of everything. He remained a bachelor.

Kenneth Campp

Lillian Allen told me that Kenneth Campp was in the CCCs and his son Steve lived in Limerick, Maine. In a telephone interview in February 2010 Steve told me:

"Both my father and uncle, George Paige, worked at the CCC camp. Uncle George was a foreman who worked with the boys searching for gypsy moth egg clusters. He used to tack fake clusters, like hard baked clay, on trees to see if the boys were really checking. They made a grid of the area to be surveyed and placed small pieces of papers on the trees. This was a guide for the boys to know what area needed to be surveyed.

"After the camp closed. He worked for the Conservation Department as a foreman. Uncle George contracted TB in about 1947-48. He went to Saranac Lake sanitariums for the cure but died.

"Luke Sheldon owned the land where the CCC camp was. When it closed he used several buildings as cabins back there and rented them to the tourists. Luke sold TVs and gas all things such as soda etc.

"I'm not sure if they were old CCC buildings. When the Fort Ann Catholic Church bazaars ended. Then the Fireman took it over and they moved their bazaars to Luke's property. They held them in August. Everyone looked forward to it.

Luke Sheldon was the sheriff of Washington Co. and after WWII. He hired schoolboys in the summer to do blister rust eradication right.

"Then Luke Sheldon and a few other guys like Harry Wrie, Bob Herrick and others were involved in the shooting club. They used the old CCC mess hall."

The old Fort Ann CCC mess hall is used as a shooting range by a local gun club. It is the last CCC building of the camp. Podskoch Collection

CHAPTER 15
GOLDSMITH

HISTORY

The Conservation Department chose the deserted village of Goldsmith for the site of Camp S-61 (originally camp No.13). Goldsmith got its name from Thomas Goldsmith who purchased 14,000 acres near Loon Lake in Franklin County from the abolitionist, Gerrit Smith, in July 1846. He began to remove the timber but had difficulty transporting it to Plattsburgh so he gradually sold off parcels. Mills were established in Goldsmith near the North Branch of the Saranac River and by the 1870s there were about 25 homes, a school, and a post office. Thomas Goldsmith built the North Branch House and died in 1871. Hugh P. Collins purchased and remodeled the North Branch House and made it into a hotel with a ballroom.[1]

E. C. Baker described Goldsmith's lumber industry in "Lumbering in Saranac Lake." They sawed the trees in Goldsmith's mill and floated the lumber down the North Branch of the Saranac River. They removed the lumber before it reached the high falls and teams of horses drew the lumber over treacherous roads to Plattsburgh 35 miles away.[2]

The village of Goldsmith began declining around 1910 and when the CCC enrollees arrived on June 22, 1933 and set up their tents most of the town's buildings had deteriorated or been removed.

Before coming to Goldsmith, Company #257 trained at the Plattsburg Army barracks for a month under Capt. W. S. Tuttle. Then they moved to the "ghost" village of Goldsmith, four miles east of Loon Lake and approximately 18 miles north of Saranac Lake in Franklin County. In July, Capt. W. H. Waugh took command.[4]

Superintendent John F. Paul's main task was to improve forest fire protection. The CCC enrollees constructed fire lines along highways, built foot trails and truck trails, and removed flammable material along highways.[5]

In July 18, 1933 the Essex County Republican reported the Goldsmith camp constructed 2.5 miles of fire lines and worked 320 man-days removing gooseberry and currant bushes to prevent blister rust.

Paul Hartmann & NYS CSCIC ©2010

John Paul also supervised his men planting trees. The Essex County Republican reported on September 8, 1933 that the enrollees were going to plant approximately 1,000 acres north of Bloomingdale to Alder Creek and Morrisville. There was another 170-acre parcel near Owls Head for planting.

By October 5 the Adirondack Daily Enterprise reported in the article, "More Than a Million Trees Planted by Local Foresters," that the Goldsmith camp planted 410,000 trees, scouted and removed gooseberry and currant bushes on 17,000 acres, and cleared seven miles of fire lines.

Another camp project was stream improvement. The Ausable Forks Record-Post' article, "Dams to Save Trout Will Be Built by CCC," in May 10, 1934 stated that the Goldsmith camp built and maintained numerous small dams near the camp in 1933. The pools that were created provided shelter for fingerling trout during the summer drought. This program was so successful that it was adopted by the Conservation Department during the following years.

A small group of men went to Plattsburgh and began developing the Cumberland Head state campsite just north of the city. Forester Ralph Unger and 20 enrollees began clearing and cleaning the state beach at Cumberland Head. There were 43 acres of land and a half-mile of sandy beach.[6] By October the CCC had cleared one mile of the beach.[7]

As winter approached, Camp S-61 moved to the White Face Inn near Lake Placid on November 13, 1933.[8]

LEGACY

Any signs of Goldsmith and the CCC camp S-61 have vanished and the area is mostly composed of seasonal hunting camps. The CCC left their mark on the area with the stately white pine forests.

CHAPTER 16
HARRISVILLE

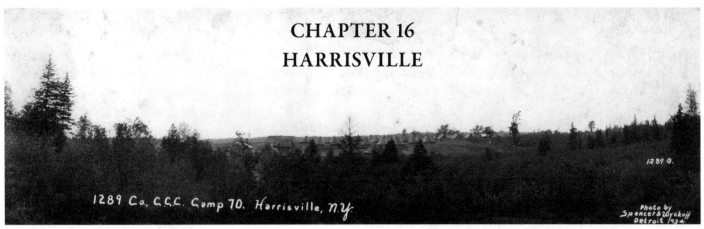

1289 Co, C.C.C. Camp 70. Harrisville, N.Y.

Photo by Spencer & Wyckoff Detroit 1934

HISTORY

Harrisville CCC Camp S-94 (originally called No. 4) Army Co. 1289, was located approximately eight miles SW of Harrisville on Rt. 812 in the town of Diana. On May 11, 1934 Captain Harvey R. Cook brought 43 enrollees from Sand Park CCC Camp in Milton, Vermont to Harrisville. More men arrived on June 4 from the Madison Barracks, in Sackets Harbor, NY. Enrollees lived in tents while 1st Lt. Clark W. Pennington, Reserve Engineer, supervised construction of the buildings.

A reporter for the Black River Democrat visited the Harrisville camp at dinnertime and interviewed Captain Harry Cook who was supervising the construction of the camp. "'We are on daylight saving time since it gives the boys more time for baseball and recreation.' He was sitting on the sandy ground with his back against one of the uprights of the water supply system, balancing a plate of fried fish and potatoes on his knee and with a fork in one hand and a cup of lemonade in the other. The sand blowing across, into and onto his supper only helped season it and seemed not to bother the army officer at all. A short distance away, also sitting on the ground and similarly engaged, was Lt. Pennington, of the Engineers, the camp construction officer. His home was Kansas and a little blow sand wouldn't bother him."[1]

The enrollees erected 25 army tents that housed six men. Two long tents were the mess hall. There was one wooden structure that was the kitchen. The men were constructing a building for the showers. Most of the enrollees left their camp in Vermont and were mostly city boys from Brooklyn and Long Island.[2]

A driven well supplied the camp with water for drinking, washing, and cooking. A large Lister or "water skin" bag with spigots was hanging from a tripod and pro-

Top - In late spring of 1934 200 men (18-25) lived in tents near Rt. 812 a few miles SW of Harrisville. They worked under Conservation Department supervision doing forestry and stream improvement projects. Stan Slyzarcik. Middle - This 1934 photo shows the wooden barracks at the Harrisville CCC camp. The Army tents where the men first lived are to the right of the buildings. Route 812 is to the upper left. Peter Gydesen

A group picture of the Harrisville CCC camp taken in 1936-37 was found in Sattler's Barber shop by Mary Gydesen. Her husband Peter identified these enrollees: bottom row L to R; #1 Jeff Allone, #2 Bob Snyder, #5 Ken Newton, #12 "Two Gun" Keenen, second row L to R: # 2 ----Riville, #10 Bob Murtaugh, third row L to R; #20 ---Dano, #24 ---Lampi, #26 Stanley Bovee, #29 Ike Stalliker, Fourth row L to R; #18 Peter Gydesen, #19---Demitchovich, #21 Ray Leaf, #25---Johnrow, #33---Hayes, #34 Harold Hayes (last one in row), and top row L to R; #2---Yauger, #10 Glenn Johndrow, #11 ---Hubbard.

vided drinking water that was chlorinated.[3]

By May 3 workers completed the lavatory and mess hall and by August 17 enrollees moved into the barracks.

The NY State Conservation Department supervised the work projects of the CCC boys. S. M. Farmer of Little Falls was the superintendent. These five forestry foremen assisted Farmer: George Clemens (Osceola), Frank Jadwin (Belmont), Harold Sperry (Forestport), Leon Segovis (Carthage), and Carlton Scofield (Peekskill). All of these men graduated from Wanakena Ranger School and they supervised the boys thinning out the state forests, planting trees, and eliminating blister rust.[4]

The Harrisville camp did many forestry and stream improvement projects in NE Lewis and S St. Lawrence counties for seven years.

Peter Gydesen, a former CCC boy from Glenfield, shared a newspaper article in Bonnie Colton's column "Roundabout" in which she reported on a May 1936 "dinner program", a term that described the year's completed work. The Harrisville CCC camp was celebrating its third anniversary. They had built 26 miles of fire lines, 13.3 miles of truck trails and 1,020 rods of fences. They reduced fire hazards on 660 acres, devoted 2,500 man-days fighting forest fires, improved 1,200 acres of forests, constructed 15 water holes, planted 6,000,000 trees, checked 12,235 acres for blister rust on pine trees, made boundary surveys covering 110 miles, stocked 16,350 fish in local waters, and devoted 200 man-days searching for missing persons.

One project entailed 25 miles of stream improvement on the West Branch of the Oswegatchie River that was to be dedicated by landowners for public fishing. They constructed six V-shaped stone wall dams that funneled the water to the center of the stream to control bank erosion. The CCCs built 900' of bank piers that confined the stream to its original channel. This prevented scouring new channels and created attractive areas for trout. The men built three miles of rock pools where trout could winter. They cleaned three miles of tributaries and four miles of the river of debris such as wood, old cars, and garbage carried by floods. To accommodate fishermen the CCC built three parking areas, nine-foot bridges, and 23 miles of trails along inaccessible parts of the stream.[5]

In 1939 The CCC boys traveled to Cranberry Lake where they worked on the state campground. The campsite opened to the public that same year.[6] They nearly completed the nine-mile truck trail from Cranberry Lake to High Falls.[7] They also built the two-mile Dead Creek Flow trail near Cranberry Lake.[8] The boys did blister rust control work in the towns of Oswegatchie, Rossie, and Pitcarin.[9] They did 2.6 more miles of stream improvement work on the Oswegatchie River.[10] The High Falls truck trail was also

Top - The sign in front of the headquarters at the Harrisville CCC camp states: "Sand Bar Camp" because of the sandy soil. Town of Diana Historical Society. Middle - CCC boys standing by the numerous stacks of firewood. A fleet of some 15 trucks was housed in the truck garage in the rear. The boys muscled two-man saws to cut the trees down and buck them up. Stan Slyzarcik. Bottom - The Harrisville camp built many V-shaped dams that funneled water to the middle of the stream to prevent erosion. NYS Archives

WORK ACCOMPLISHED BY CAMP S-94[*]

PROJECT	1934	1935	1936	1937	1938	1939	1940	1941	TOTAL
Bathhouses - number						2			2
Beach improvement - ac.					2.3	2			4.3
Boundary marking - mi.				21.5		16.6	10.5		48.6
Bridges, foot - number			9						9
Bridges, vehicle - number						1			1
Buildings, misc. - number		8				1			9
Dwellings - number						1			1
Emergency work - man-days				483				121	604
Experimental plots - ac.						5			5
Fences - rods	0.2		7457		691		190	188	8526.2
Field planting trees - ac.	256.6	3012.9	4141	1363	1342	1513	1742.3	1230	26600.8
Fire breaks - mi.	11		22.7	0.5	7		5.5	5	51.7
Fire fighting - man-days	3260	25	316	73		402	264	150	4490
Fire hazard reduction - ac.		8.1	362.8	1011	715	962	806.9	60	3015.8
Fire pre-suppression - man-days		300				270	464	345	1379
Forest stand improvement - ac.		965	279	36	308	973	793.9	689	4043.9
General clean-up - ac.			4	13	10	17	10		54
Guard rails - rods		1036		516					1552
Insect pest control - ac.							563.4	609	1172.4
Latrines - number							1	1	2
Loading platforms - number			3						3
Parking areas - yd^2			1155	900			889	400	5399
Pipe & tile lines, conduit - linear ft.						2000			2000
Preparation/transportation of materials - man-days			675			912	1255		2842
Public campground development - ac.							2		2
Razing undesirable structures - man-days								133	133
Reconaissance & investigation - man-days						159		86	245
Searching for missing persons - man-days			127						127
Seed collection, conifers - bushels							3		3
Sewage & waste disposal systems - number							1		1
Signs - number						200		16	216
Stocking fish - number		6600	50550	57000		18900	17200	26200	582350
Stream development/improvement - mi.		1.6	2.5			2.6	0.3	27.9	34.9
Surveys - linear mi.	31.1	79.7	16.9						127.7
Surveys - man-days				616		997	422	335	2370
Surveys, type - ac.		5540							5540
Telephone line - mi.		8	3						11
Timber estimating - ac.	1426	665							2091
Trails, foot - mi.			24.6	8.3	14.9				47.8
Trails, truck - mi.	6.5	5.8	1.3		1.5	2.5	0.1	12.3	19.6
Tree & plant disease control - ac.	6695	5540		1221	1917	708	516.6	445	17042.6
Water holes - number	8	5	11	15	4	1	1		45
Wildlife activities - man-days							1134	912	2046
Wind erosion control - ac.			2085	3585	67	20.7	32.3	6	5796

[*]Numerical data from Conservation Reports

Above, Left - Young CCC boys taking a break. They wore woolen WWI Army clothes while they looked for gypsy moth egg masses or cleared deadwood in the forests of Lewis County. Stan Slyzarcik. Above, Right - Camp S-94 had baseball and basketball teams that played CCC camps and local teams. This undated newspaper picture shows the 1934 undefeated Harrisville CCC camp basketball team: Richard Wright (Beaver River), Kermit Van Brocklin, Francis Broccloltta, Francis Devine, Stephen Alteri (all from Watertown), and Thomas Huttemann (Sacketts Harbor). They played their games at the NYS Armory on Arsenal Street in Watertown. Jefferson County Historical Society Archives

completed this year.[11]

In 1940 Camp S-94 in Harrisville continued to work on the Cranberry Lake campground by building a latrine and a waste disposal system that was 190 rods in length. Some of the other projects were: forest stand improvement on 1,742.2 acres in forests and 793.9 acres in nurseries, collecting three bushels of conifer seeds extracted from pine cones, did insect control on 516.6 acres of forests, and stocked 17,200 fish.[12] They did blister rust control work in the town of Croghan where they destroyed 2,808 ribes bushes on 1,140 acres and in the town of Lewis where 5,134 ribes were destroyed on 470 acres.[13]

After seven years the Harrisville CCC camp came to an end on November 31, 1941.

In early 1944, the camp was reopened to house German POWs. The Army built fencing and guard towers around the camp. In May, 160 German POWs arrived. Military Police supervised the prisoners and the US Forestry Service supervised the prisoners' work. They cut pulpwood for the St. Regis Paper Co. in Deferiet. Almost every day a bus took prisoners to work in the woods near Long Pond in the town of Croghan.

A relaxed atmosphere existed between the prisoners and the guards. When MP George M. Van Wyck married a Harrisville girl, a German cook made the wedding cake. Gladys Van Wyck, the bride, said the cake had a soft peanut brittle icing. "It was a total surprise to us. It was delicious."

There were very few escape attempts. One prisoner escaped and broke into homes in Natural Bridge and Carthage. He even took a bath, shaved, and stole clothes in one of the homes. He was captured in the Strand movie theater in Carthage. Town of Diana historian, Ross Young, told me there were few escapes because of the tight supervision and remoteness of the area. He said, "Once they did escape, there was nowhere to go."

After the POW camp was closed the buildings were demolished except for the camp garage and tool shed on the other side of Rt. 812. A reporter saw them in 2001 but they have since been removed. Croghan historian Jack Sweeney said, "D. C. LeFerve bought a lot of the lumber from the camp. It was piled in the Beaver Falls schoolyard for most of a summer. A lot of the lumber was used to rebuild the Methodist Church in town and on other LeFerve projects. There were several cannonball stoves left over from the camp. I still have an axe that has CCC stamped on the head and handle."

In the fall of 2007 I visited the CCC campsite with Ross Young. We located the entrance to the camp and the circular driveway. There were huge white pines throughout the area planted by the CCC enrollees. Only a crumbled chimney near the location of the officer's building on the right side of the circular drive remained. "The barracks area in the rear had been leveled out when construction workers buried a natural gas pipeline through the camp," Ross said.

LEGACY

Today the Harrisville campsite is part of the 20,000-acre Frank E. Jadwin State Forest. Jadwin was a state forester and worked in the Har-

Far Left - Four German POWs stand in front of the bus that brought them into the forest near Harrisville where they did logging. They wore POW armbands and were housed in the old CCC camp. Lonnie Herzig. Left - These German prisoners of war were captured in Africa and brought to the old Harrisville CCC camp where they cut pulpwood for the St. Regis Paper Co. Lonnie Herzig

Clockwise from Left - Ross Young, Town of Diana historian, took me to the Harrisville CCC camp site. Tall white pines and a circular road are the only remnants of the camp. Podskoch Collection. Education director Mike Frohlich at the beginning of the circular driveway near Rt. 812 where Ross young was standing in the previous picture of the Harrisville camp in 2007. Bob Moran. CCC Camp S-94 traveled to Cranberry Lake in 1938 and 1939. They developed campsites, a swimming area, and beach and hiking trails at the Cranberry Lake State Park. Podskoch Collection. CCC enrollees built the ranger cabin at Cranberry Lake. The inside has a beautiful stone fireplace and knotty pine walls. Podskoch Collection

risville CCC camp. He supervised the CCC enrollees who planted thousands of trees in the Harrisville area.

MEMORIES

Peter Gydesen

In the fall of 2007 I met Peter Gydesen in an unusual way. I had stopped to purchase a flower at Colwells Gardening Shop in Glenfield to give to the Arnold family in Watson where I was staying for the night. I asked the saleslady, Mary Gydesen, if she knew anyone who was in the CCCs.

"Yes, my husband, he's 92 years old and he has quite a few pictures."

I called Peter the next day and visited him at his home on River Road in Lyons Falls. He showed me his kayak in the back yard and told me how he and his wife enjoyed hiking and kayaking.

Left - Peter Gydesen on his motorcycle that he rode home on weekends. He hid it in a nearby barn owned by foreman Chet Rice. Above - Peter Gydesen (holding axe) and his survey crew by their tripod and transit. Mary Gydesen

We went inside and he told me about his life. "I was born on April 5, 1914 in Lyonsdale. My parents, Gyde and Eva had 12 children. I went to school until the eighth grade but then went to work to help my family. I worked on farms and helped my dad who worked with horses in the woods dragging out logs for the mills.

"I heard about the CCCs through gossip in town. I signed up on July 9, 1934 and went to the Harrisville camp. They were still putting up the wooden buildings so I lived in a 16' x 16' tent for the first couple months with three other guys. During my first stay I did general work such as making trails and planting trees.

"After six months I signed up again. I was a woodsman and knew how to use a saw and an axe. That helped get me a job as a leader and I got six dollars more each month. I also had the job in our barracks of getting everyone to sleep at 9 pm and turning off the lights. But I had a car that I hid away from the camp and I was down in Carthage at night. "I went to town a lot with a friend. It was only 15 miles away. We met girls at dances and bars. When I got found out I lost that job.

"Later I had a motorcycle and hid it in Chet Rice's barn which was below camp towards Harrisville. Chet was a foreman at our camp.

"In the winter we cleared land and in the spring we planted trees near present-day Lewisburg. The next summer in 1935 we fought a forest fire in the same place we planted trees the year before near Lewisburg. "I became a surveyor. I chopped down trees and I used a chain and a tape for measuring. I liked this job very much."

Peter handed me a small box with pictures of his days in the Harrisville camp. In one the guys were standing

Cloclwise from Top Left - These young CCC enrollees are waiting their turn to get into the Mess Hall for supper. Peter was always first in line because of his long legs. - The personnel office was located near Rt. 812. - The Harrisville CCC Camp won the 1934 District 2 Baseball Championship. Here are some of the players with their championship banner. - This 1934 photo shows Peter (2nd row, 2nd on rt.) with the crew of young men that he supervised in the woods. He was chosen because of his forestry experience. All courtesy of Peter Gydesen.

in line by the mess hall. "I had long legs and when they rang the bell for chow, I was always first in line. The food was good and you could have all you wanted."

He showed me a picture of the camp, which was located on Rt. 812 between Harrisville and Croghan. The tents were standing in the back of a field and the wooden buildings lined up in the front. "There were five barracks in a row and each had about 40 guys. We were placed in the barracks by alphabet and once we were assigned, we couldn't change it. Across the road was a work area with a garage and a tool shed. The camp road circled back to Rt. 812. You first passed the officers' and foresters' building, then the water tower, dispensary, rec hall, latrine, five barracks, and the office."

"There were inspections every day except Sunday. You can see in this picture the beds weren't made in the barracks. It must have been a Sunday."

Another picture showed Peter with his crew in the woods. "See that guy lying down in the back? He was okay. I never had any trouble with him. My crew was thinning out trees in the winter. We also girdled trees, which killed them.

"There were quite a few activities. We had boxing

on Saturday nights and our baseball team played Watertown. There was no place for swimming to cool off. In the rec hall guys could buy candy, soda and even a beer for ten cents.

"Sometimes we had KP duty. I was lucky and only had it once. Everybody got a turn. On the weekend trucks took the guys to the movies in Carthage and Harrisville.

"I remember a few guys. Bill Lucas stayed in the camp all the time. He was a clerk in the office. There were two brothers, Harold and Marty Hayes, who worked in the dispensary.

"There was one mean guy in camp named Peter Hopsicker who chewed tobacco. One day there was this mini earthquake that scared the heck out of him. He turned to religion and became a minister. He married a Harrisville girl and moved to Rochester.

"We also had six Indians in camp. They were awfully good guys and hard workers.

"I was in the CCCs for two years. I liked it better than working in the barn on farms.

"In June of 1937 I left the CCCs and got a job in Henderson Harbor working for General Electric. I also delivered ice and soda on Lake Ontario near Watertown. In the fall I came back home and ran the grinders at the Gould Paper Mill. Then I drove a log truck to Tug Hill. After that I did carpenter work for the Gould Co.

Left - Peter is with his friend Richard (right) while they were cutting wood. Peter Gydesen. Above - The Army provided transportation to and from the camp. The truck in the background brought these 11 enrollees from the Harrisville camp to the nearby train station for a trip home. Peter Gydesen

"In 1938 I married Maude Rhone and we had five children. Then my wife died and I married my present wife, Mary.

"The CCCs was a good experience for me. I was able to help my parents and I learned how to get along with other people."

Julian Slusarczyk

On June 6, 2006 Stan Slusarczyk met me at the Westernville Library and told me his brother Julian was in the Harrisville CCC camp. He also brought a number of photos that his brother had taken while at camp in the 1930s. I asked Stan to tell me about his brother, family, and CCC experiences:

"My father John emigrated from Poland in the late 1890s. He and his brother Louis worked for six months in a coal mine in Hazelton, Pennsylvania. Then Dad went to work a new coal mine in Oklahoma. My dad worked there for about 20 years. While there he met my mom and they got married about 1906. They lived in Alderson, Oklahoma in Indian Territory. My brother Julian was born on March 10, 1916. We had three other brothers: John, Frank, and Joe, and two sisters: Annie and Ellen.

In 1920 Dad and his brother Louis, who had a farm in Prospect, NY went to their brother's wedding in Detroit. Louis told my father: 'You should leave the mines and come east and work on a farm. You don't want your sons to be stuck working in the mines. They could live on a beautiful farm in New York like my family and me.

"In 1921 Dad decided to follow Uncle Louis' advice and got some information about farms for sale in Prospect, NY. He saw an advertisement for a farm and he bought it before he even saw it.

"When my family arrived on July 1, 1921 the owner had a hot lunch on the table. My parents liked it and bought the farm. The owners packed their clothes and left. They left everything. The farm cost $9,500. It included 250 acres, barns, house, cows, kitchen utensils, and cats and dogs.

"That's where I and my sister Nellie were born. We all went to Remsen schools. Life was tough during the Depression.

"My brother tried to join the Army in the 1930s but they didn't take him right away. So he joined the CCC to help my family. He went to the Harrisville CCC camp. I think it was 1934 because his pictures show the tents they lived in when the camp was established in 1934. He was 18 years old.

"You can tell by looking at the pictures the boys were working in the woods the winter of 1934-35 cutting trees for logs and making firewood. That winter the guys moved from the tents to the wooden barracks.

"After about a year he came back home and worked on our farm for a while. Then in 1939 he joined the Army.

"On December 7, 1941 Julian was stationed in Pearl Harbor, Hawaii and survived the Japanese attack on Schofield Barracks. He was awarded the Silver Star and Oak Leaf Cluster for Gallantry in action in the Solomon Islands.

Stan Slusarczyk showed me his brother Julian's picture of his fellow enrollees at the Harrisville camp using a Cletrac crawler to pull a sled of split logs from the forest. He said the tall guy standing on the tongue of the sled was Julian. Stan Slusarczyk

Julian retired in 1963 with the rank of colonel.

"He came home and bought his brother Frank's farm and raised livestock.

"He married Margaret and had four children: Sharon, Merri, Colleen, and Steven.

"Julian died in 1980 at the age of 64. He was hunting in the town of Remsen.

"The CCC had a good effect on my brother in that he was able to make money to help my family and the Army officers had a positive effect on him. Julian learned discipline and how to work hard. He then chose the Army for his life work."

Chester Rice

In June 2006 I received a letter from Clara Bowe of Fulton, NY who had read about me in the Boonville newspaper.

"My dad, Chester Rice, was part of a CCC camp in Oswagatchie in the early 1930s. I have one picture of him and have the hat that was issued to him as part of his uniform. He wore it throughout his life whether he was working outdoors or just relaxing. Dad said it was good for any weather: sun, rain, or hail, He had painted it different colors through the years. I remember green, yellow, brown and finally white.

"He used to tell us stories of the times in the camp, mostly funny stories of the things the men did. It seemed they had a good relationship with each other. I believe my dad formed lasting friendships from those early experiences.

"In later years Dad said that not too many men wanted to talk about that time because they would be admitting to poverty. Dad died in December 2000 at the age of 91."

When I called Clara, she told me: "Dad was born 1909 in Peru, NY. My grandfather was a Presbyterian minister and moved around to different churches. His mother was Nora Slye and had one child. I believe Dad graduated from a technical high school where he studied electrical engineering. In 1932 Dad married Priscilla Edick from Martinsburg.

"Bonnie Colton of the Lowville Journal and Republican interviewed Dad about his WPA job: 'I worked for the WPA putting water pipes in Martinsburg. It was cold work. Some of those ditch diggers had never done that work before. They were just glad to find a job. They came

Left - Chester Rice wore a Conservation Department uniform with its baggy jodhpur pants while working as foreman at the Harrisville CCC camp during the 1930s. Clara Bowe. Below - These boys are having fun making a pyramid in their barracks. Peter Gydesen

in long dress coats and thin hats and pretty near froze to death.'

"Next he moved to Harrisville and worked for the CCC camp. He was designated a LEM, (local experienced man) and made $45 a month. He supervised the enrollees. My parents rented a farmhouse down the road from camp for $5 a month. Mom often did washing and mending for the men. Dad would say with a twinkle in his eyes, 'We had running water. She ran after it.' There were no pumps. Water was drawn by rope and pail from the well. Dad carried water from the spring in two five-gallon wooden pails using a neck yoke.

"He worked on reforestation projects at Harrisville, Pine Camp (Fort Drum), Croghan, Star Lake, and Belfort. They also built telephone lines, did survey work and built a power plant for the whole camp. Mom baked a lot to give to the boys. Dad used to bring friends from the camp for dinner.

"He told funny stories. One was about 'snipe hunting.' They would wake new recruits in the middle of the night, give them a bag and a flashlight, and tell them to stay in the woods all night to catch a snipe.

"When Dad left the CCCs my parents moved back to Martinsburg for a while. Then they moved to Boonville in 1943. There were 10 children in our family: Ester, Gladys, Alice, James, Edwin, Clara, David, Elaine, Richard, and

Roger.

"Dad worked all over Lewis and Oneida counties He worked for the hardware store in Boonville and they sent him out to wire houses and farms.

"In 1999 my sister Alice and I took dad to see if we could find the farm house where they lived while working at the CCC camp. We found his 'vine covered shanty' still standing but when we searched for the CCC camp there was nothing left. Just the tall white pines that the boys probably planted."

Julius Lehosky

On June 23, 2010 I traveled to Lowville for a CCC reunion at the Lewis County Historical Society. There were three CCC alumni and one of them was Julius Lehosky. He shared these stories about his life and his days at the Harrisville camp:

"I grew up on a farm at Chase's Lake in Sperryville near Watson. My dad, Julius, had worked in Pennsylvania coal mines but hurt his leg in a mining accident and moved to this area and farmed. He was sickly and had a stiff leg from his mining accident. He tried to make some money and food for the family by hunting and trapping in the winter and fishing during the other seasons.

"I had to help my family so after seventh grade I quit school and helped out on the farm. I was the eldest in my family. There were five other kids: Maria, John, Elizabeth, Joe, and Helen.

"In the spring of 1937 my family saw an article in the paper about the CCC and my mother, Mary, suggested I go because our income was low. I was 17 and I joined with a few guys from Lowville, Castorland, and Harrisville. I loved every minute especially KP because you could eat any time you wanted."

Someone in the audience asked Julius what jobs he had at the camp.

"My first was planting trees. Our foreman taught us how to plant them and work in teams of two. One guy dug a hole with a mattock and another placed it in the opening and stepped on

Julius Lehosky joined the CCC in the spring of 1937. He loved KP duty because he could eat anytime he wanted. Patricia Bullington

the earth. We planted balsam and white pine on some big lots near our camp in Croghan and Harrisville.

"Then I worked in the gravel pit shoveling gravel onto trucks. There were about 4-5 guys loading. We didn't have equipment for loading like we do today. They used the gravel for roads.

"Another job was doing stream improvement on the Oswagatchie River. We moved debris out of the streams. Then we put logs along the bank to stop erosion.

"When we worked in Wanakena we stayed in tents. We fought blister rust by pulling up currant bushes near white pine trees.

"But the biggest thing we did was fight a fire near Star Lake. It got into the moss and duff and that is hard to get at. Then at night we came back to camp. It was an awful fire that I'll never forget. A lot of the guys got smoke inhalation. I think it was near the old CCC camp on Rt. 3.

"In the evenings we gathered around and shot the breeze in our barracks or listened to the radio in the rec hall. I had two good friends, Francis Luther and Martin Konkol. If I stayed at camp on the weekend I did a little boxing in the camp ring on Saturday afternoon. There would be a few guys watching us box and they'd be hooting and hollering.

"We liked to play jokes on each other. One popular trick was short-sheeting the guy's bed. We also fixed the folding bed so that it fell down when they went to sleep. Two other tricks were with shoes. They tied the shoes together or drove a nail into a guy's shoes. It happened to me. When I tried to stand up I couldn't go.

"On weekends we sometimes hitchhiked home. Sometimes we had to walk a lot before we got a ride. We hitchhiked on the road to Carthage. Then it was easier to get a ride to Lowville because there was more traffic.

"Sometimes I got a ride from Martin Konkol on his motorcycle to his house near Glenfield. Then I'd bum a ride or walk home at night. There were times when I got home at 3 am. If I was tired, I'd sleep in the pasture. At home I helped out with chores. Then on Sunday Dad took me to Martin's home in Glenfield or Otter Creek where Francis Smith lived. He had an old car and I'd get a ride from him.

"After two years in the CCC I came home and got a job with the town of Watson loading trucks by hand. Then I got a job logging on the Independence River for the Frank Murphy Co. We were cutting four-foot logs. I put the logs on a conveyor belt and loaded the trucks.

"In 1942 I worked at Lyons Falls Paper Mill. The next year I was drafted in the Army and sent to Camp Up-

143

Peter Gydesen & Frank Bush on the Harrisville camp boxing ring.
Peter Gydesen

ton, Long Island.

"After the war in 1945 I got married to Doris Brown and had two daughters, Judy and Pat.

"Working in the CCC was good for me. I learned to get along with people. You learned discipline from the Army officers. I just liked it. I met a lot of guys."

Martin Konkol

Retired District Forest Ranger Randy Kerr of Gregg told me that his friend, Martin Konkol, was in the CCC. I visited Konkol at his home in Turin on June 28, 2007.

"Things were tough in the Depression. My father, John, was a farmer with about 20 cows. He and my mother, Frances, had a hard time providing for their four children: Joseph, Stanley, Mary and myself. I was born in 1919. We all helped out working on our farm.

"I was 17 and I think it was 1936 or 1937 when I signed up for the CCC. They sent me to Benson Mines camp. I worked on building roads. After a brief time the camp closed. Then they shipped me to St. Maries, in northern Idaho. It was called Camp Avery Company #1204. I spent six moths there building roads along the mountains. They had bulldozers but I was a laborer. It was in the northern part of the state but there wasn't much snow.

"After six months I came back home and worked on our family farm for a year.

"In the spring of 1939 I joined the CCC again in Harrisville. I worked there for about a year and a half. I liked it there. During that summer I lived in a side camp

in Benson Mines. We lived in tents. They had me driving a bulldozer and a truck. I drove guys about 10 miles to Cranberry Lake each day where we were building the new state park. I didn't have to do much.

"During the winter I stayed at the main camp in Harrisville. We shoveled snow and on the weekends I drove a truck and took guys to the movies in Carthage. I remember one of the foremen, Chester Price. The foremen had their own barracks and were paid $100 a month.

"I only had one problem with a foreman named Farmer. One time he gave me the devil because two guys were supposed to be with me but weren't.

"One of the funny things that happened was when one of the NYC guys got drunk and peed in his own shoes. When he woke up in the morning and put his shoes on, boy, did he start cursing.

"While in camp I had a Harley. I parked it at a beer joint in Benson Mines that was about a half-mile from camp. Then when I was in the Harrisville camp I hid my bike too.

"In November 1940 I joined the Army. I was stationed in Staten Island. I got out of the Army in 1945.

"After the war I worked at our family farm. Then I got a job at the paper mill in Lyons Falls.

"I liked being in the CCC because I loved working in the woods."

David J. Alberico

In June 2010 David J Alberico and his son David came to a CCC reunion at the Oneida Historical Society. He told me he was in two CCC camps: Mannsville near Watertown and Harrisville. Here is what David told me about his life and time in the CCC:

"Jobs were hard to find and I wanted to help my mother, Paulma (Dolcenome). She had seven children to clothe and feed: Dominick, Joseph, Nicho-

Martin Konkol of Turin worked at three Civilian Conservation Corps camps: Benson Mines; St. Maries, in northern Idaho, and Harrisville. He worked as a laborer, truck driver, and heavy equipment operator. He is pictured in his Army uniform during WW II. Martin Konkol

las, Carl, Mary, Ermalinda, and Lucia. In those days the kids in poor families only went to eighth grade. That's what I did.

"I joined the CCC on April 7, 1939. I felt good about going away from home because I now had a job and could help support my family. The CCC was good for me and the other guys in camp. Times were hard back then. At the CCC we all had a place to live and three meals a day.

"We did work that needed to be done. At first I worked with the mechanics. My next job was planting trees. After that we did projects such as cleaning streams of debris, making V-dams, placing logs along the riverbanks, and building roads.

"After work we had dinner. Then we played cards and ping-pong, and once a week we had a movie. On the weekends we went to town and went to church, did some shopping, or went out to eat.

"Some guys played sports in their spare time. I liked to swim.

"Everybody in camp worked together. We were all friends. Later on in life I continued writing to Clayton Christenson.

"My two brothers Dominick and Joseph were also in the CCC.

"On September 13, 1941 I was discharged. They were getting ready to close the camp because they saw war was coming. So I came home. I went to work in Buffalo at the Chevrolet factory and built US bomber engines. I wasn't drafted into the army because my health restricted participation in the war.

"In 1946 I married Alice Shufran. We had five children.

"After the war I continued working for Chevrolet. Then I worked for Dupont and Dunlop.

"I felt the CCC was good for me because I now was earning money. They made me an assistant leader and I made an extra $6 a month. I saved enough money to buy my mother her first refrigerator. I learned how to work in a team and learned the importance of doing a good job."

Steve Dzimitrowicz

"I was born in Herkimer, NY in 1922. My parents Peter and Helen had a large family and it was difficult feeding their 12 children: John, Josephine, Helen, Walter, Anthony, Stanley, Connie (boy), Edith, Steve, Irene, Leo, and Hank.

"My brother Tony and I decided to join the CCC because when we were going to high school we couldn't afford to buy books because we had no money. I think I was 17 when I joined. It might have been (1939).

"The first camp I was in was in Galupville, NY. During my six months there, I trimmed trees and shoveled snow for the farmers so they could get through with their milk. The camp was okie dokie.

"My second six months were in the summer time in Fallon, Nevada which is 63 miles east of Reno. I built irrigation ditches and culverts along the highway. There was a group of 40 or 50 Cubans in my camp. They didn't associate with us but stayed with themselves. We didn't understand them.

"My last six months in the CCC were in Harrisville, NY. We worked on trees again.

"One day an officer asked if I wanted to work in the latrine. So I said, 'OK.' I had to go there twice a day to clean it. I just cleaned up after they were done for work in the morning about 8 am. At night I went in about 7 pm. I went in with rubber boots and wore long rubber gloves. I sprayed the toilet seats with a hose and then scrubbed them with a long handled brush. It wasn't a bad job. The showers were in another section of the building. They made me a corporal and I got paid $6 more a month.

"After six weeks the same officer asked me to work in the canteen. I had to be there every evening and on Saturday and Sunday afternoons. I was made sergeant and got paid $45 a month. My job there was to run the store where I sold candy, soda, toothpaste, and cigarettes. The guys played cards, pool, and ping-pong.

"Then after six months I was discharged. I worked in Standard Desk Co. in Herkimer till I was drafted into Army. I was first sent to Paris, Tennessee for basic training. Then I went to Casablanca and Oran, Africa. Then I was in four invasions: Sicily, Anzio, Salerno, and Southern France.

"After the war I worked in the power plant of the Remington Arms Co. factory in Ilion, NY. I was married in 1948 and we had one son, Steven Paul, who lives in Bloomfield, Indiana.

"After working 31 years at Remington Arms I retired to Clearwater, Florida where I live today."

Bob Moran

Bob Moran Jr. from New Hartford, NY sent me an

email in June 2010 stating: "My Dad watched your recent television appearance on the 'Joe Kelly Show' regarding CCC camps in New York. My Dad was a member of the CCC in 1941 in Harrisville, NY. He even has certificates stating he completed Forestry I and Forestry II classes. He'd be happy to share his stories."

I called Bob Sr. the next month: "It was tough during the Depression. My father, Clinton, sold insurance but when he lost that job he worked for the Town of Whitesboro. He was making about 13 dollars a week and it was hard providing for his wife Yvonne and three other children: Richard, Douglas, and Dolores.

"My older brother Richard was in the Boonville camp in about 1940. He had a lot of good times with the girls and he sent money home to help my family. When I was 17 and in tenth grade, I quit school and joined the CCC. On July 9, 1941 my friend Bob Freson and I signed up in Utica. They sent us up to the Boonville camp in an Army truck.

"When we got there we met Captain William Shakespeare, the company commander. I wasn't nervous but there were some guys from NYC who were tough dudes. Cities made them join the CCC to get them off the streets. The Army separated them from the good guys. They'd tip your bed at night and do other tricks.

"My first job in camp was a job laborer. They took us by truck to a plot and we planted trees. I did this for a short while and became a second cook. I scooped out food at meals.

"I was a good friend of the company clerk, Joe Isgro, and then became his assistant. I worked where the supplies were and did paper work. That was a good job and I didn't have to go out in the field and plant those damn trees.

"In the evenings I took classes. I got certificates in Forestry I, and Forestry II. Francis McHarris was in charge of the classes. I also took classes from Harold L. Dunn who taught Shop Practice.

"We had very little recreation. There was only indoor stuff like ping-pong and cards. Sometimes guys would challenge each other to a boxing match. There was a ring way down past the barracks.

"On two weekends my friends and I hitchhiked home. We first went to Copenhagen and then home. This was a busy road and it was easy to get a ride on Rts. 26 & 12 to Utica. Sometimes a friend of mine and I hitchhiked and made a loop. We went to Benson Mines and Cranberry Lake and came back to camp. One time we didn't make it all the way back and we slept on a store porch in Carthage.

"After six months I left because they were closing

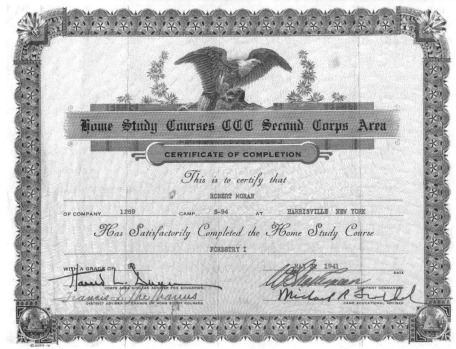

Clockwise from Top, Left - Bob Moran (left) worked with the education advisor, Mike Frohlich. Bob was the teacher's assistant and helped him with paper work. - Joe Isgro, the company clerk, posing with some flamingo lawn ornaments in front of the barracks. CCC enrollees could take evening classes at their camp. - The certificate Bob Moran earned after taking a Forestry I course. All courtesy Bob Moran

the camp and I could go back to school. They discharged me on September 30, 1941.

"My brother Richard and I joined the Navy in August 1942 and were sent to boot camp at Great Lakes, Il. While home on leave in September, I married Rose Mary Magee. We had six children: Barry, Stephen, Michael, Patricia, Robert Jr., and Thomas.

In December 1942 I graduated from Aviation Ordnance School in and in February 1943 I graduated from the Naval Mine Warfare School in, Yorktown, VA. Then I joined VP-92, a PBY (patrol bomber) squadron that participated in anti-submarine warfare that operated out of North Africa, South America, and the Caribbean area.

"In October 1945 I was discharged and worked at Griffiss Air Base in Rome.

"I learned a lot of forestry and clerical skills in the CCC. I went to Syracuse College in Utica and took courses in geography and geology. In 1953 I received a BS degree in accounting. Then I went to work with GE in Utica and retired in 1987.

"The CCC was good for me and other young men. We learned how to get along with people, even the tough guys. It was almost like high school. You had your friends and enemies. It gave us something to do and helped our families out."

Bob Bailey

Bob Bailey, a retired District Forest Ranger from Lowville, helped me with my books on the fire towers where he had worked. I stopped by his home in June 2007 and he talked about the projects the Harrisville CCC camp did and the men who worked there:

"Frank Wisner of Croghan took crews out on projects. He was a quiet kind of guy. They did stream improvement and a lot of reforestation off the Jorden Falls Road that runs east of Rt. 812. The CCC worked about 15 miles east of their camp as far as Pitcairn.

"The state bought a lot of land for $4 an acre during the 1930s because people were hard up for money during the Depression. The CCC helped construct access roads on the state land. They reforested the land with seedlings that were grown at the Dadville (northeast of Lowville) Nursery.

"Milo Boliver was the camp blacksmith. He lived in Indian River. He has some children that live in Croghan.

"Oscar 'Doc' Cleary was a CCC enrollee who lived on the South Shore Road.

"There were quite a few guys in the CCC camp who married a local girl. Mert Cochran met a woman and wound up marrying her and lived here. Another guy Bill Bradish married Ursula Laplatney. Even my sister, Roberta Hale from Massena, married a CCC guy.

"There was a prisoner of war camp at Montague on Tug Hill. Part of the camp is still up there. There is a concrete building with steel bars. Some prisoners came to the DEC building in Dadville. It was a 20' x 40' T-shaped building where they worked. They brought 12 guys there at a time. They even had a cook. There were German and Italian prisoners.

"There was also a POW camp at the old Harrisville CCC camp. It closed after the war in 1945. When I came to this area in 1968 there were two buildings on the left side of Rt. 812. On the right side of the road was only part of the cook shack. There was an old cook stove inside. It was a monster in size that weighed 1,100-1,200 pounds. It had 12 griddles and a hot water reserve. I heard there were four towers around the camp that

Retired District Forest Ranger from Lowville Bob Bailey shared his stories of the Harrisville CCC camp. Nancy Bailey

was fenced in. They had a generator for the big floodlights. When you drove by it looked like a city.

"When I came here Frank Wisner was a general foreman for the Conservation Department. When he worked for the CCC he supervised the crew. He supervised the guys doing timber stand improvement, constructing truck trails, digging ditches, and placing culverts under roads. The boys did log cribbing along the stream banks to prevent erosion. Later he became the work general foreman for the DEC. He used to store the dynamite in the empty cook stove at the old camp.

"When I became a ranger in the 1950s in the western part of the state, I went into the tool room and I couldn't believe my eyes. There were rows of shovels and six-pound mauls used to split wood. There were tons of tools. There were scythes still in bundles.

"The CCC boys used the stones from nearby farm walls in building roads. They used six-pound mauls to bust up the stones to make gravel for the roads. They didn't have machines like we have today. It was labor-intensive work. There were no stone crushers.

"As you drive around here you will see these old plantations of white pines. The CCC planted them all. The CCC had a tremendous impact on this area."

CHAPTER 17
INDIAN LAKE/BLUE MOUNTAIN

Paul Hartmann & NYS CSCIC ©2010

Clockwise from Top, Left - Mrs. William West Durant speaks at the dedication of a stone and marker naming Lake Durant after her late husband. Richard Stewart. - The close-up view of the Lake Durant dam. Forest Ranger Greg George is standing on the old Rt. 28/30 bridge. The road was closed and built away from the lake because of the problems with drifting snow. The new road went right through the Indian Lake CCC camp site. Podskoch Collection. - Indian Lake camp in winter with barracks (left), mess hall (right), and Blue Mountain in the background. Every morning and evening the enrollees gathered for the raising and lowering of the flag. Ted Roy. - In 1935 Camp S-115 enrollees are pouring concrete into wooden forms to build a dam near the Rt. 28/30 bridge. The dam created three-mile long Lake Durant.[4]

HISTORY

Indian Lake Camp, S-115, Company 3215, was located near present-day Lake Durant State Park on Rt. 28/30 in Blue Mountain. It began on May 26, 1935 when 1st Lt. Charles F. Crone directed the construction of the camp. On September 10, 1st Lt. Austin W. Smith from Company 221 in Port Byron, NY arrived with a group of enrollees. The remaining men came on September 14 from Fort Dix, NJ. Two days later Capt. Harvey L. Meade Jr. assumed command.[1]

On September 14, 1935 George Hutchins of Indian Lake became the camp superintendent. His staff had nine men with 2-3 foresters.[2]

The men worked on many state park projects. They created Lake Durant at the 34th Flow near Rt. 28/30 in Blue Mountain Lake. Preliminary work began at the site from February 19 to March 31, 1934 when 30 men worked two days a week clearing brush from the land that would be flooded for the future lake.[3] In 1935 Camp S-115 constructed a concrete dam near their camp that created Lake Durant.

Some of their other projects were: constructing campsites, building fireplaces, and constructing ranger's

cabins and toilets at Lake Durant, Lake Eaton (near Long Lake), Eighth Lake, and Golden Beach SP.[5]

They also constructed a 40' log cribstone-filled dam that replaced a decaying dam on Cedar Lake in 1936.[6]

At first the camp was called Blue Mountain because it had a Blue Mountain P.O. address. A few years later the P.O. address was changed to Indian Lake and the camp was then called Indian Lake.[7]

The camp provided many activities for the young men during their free time. On January 11, 1936 F. Clarke Woodruff left the Newcomb CCC camp and became the camp's education advisor. Boys were able to choose from a variety of classes: business law, English, First Aid, journalism, auto mechanics, and business.

A Drama Club was begun and the young men gave performances at high schools, banquets, American Legions, and churches. They also performed on radio station WMFF in Plattsburg.[8]

Camp S-115 closed on October 13, 1939 and its men were transferred to Camp Upton S-87 on Long Island. They worked during the winter cleaning up flammable material from the blowdown of the devastating 1938 Hurricane.[9]

The Indian Lake camp was reoccupied on May 10, 1940[10] and continued to work on developing Golden Beach, Lake Eaton, Eighth Lake, and Lake Durant campsites.[11] In 1941 they began construction of the caretaker's cabin at Lake Durant. Work was halted when the camp closed on June 30, 1941 because the number of camps in NY was being reduced.[12] The Newcomb camp S-129 completed the cabin by the end of 1941.[13]

Above, Top - Camp S-115 activities from the 1937 Schenectady District Civilian Conservation Corps Area Yearbook. Indian Lake camp in winter with barracks (left), mess hall (right), and Blue Mountain in the background. Every morning and evening the enrollees gathered for the raising and lowering of the flag. Ted Roy. Above - After dinner and on weekends the enrollees played baseball near the garage along Rt. 28/30. Ted Roy

Clockwise from Top, Left - Camp S-115 stored their trucks and equipment in this 12-bay garage along Rt. 28/30 and Lake Durant. - R. W. Roshon and Ted Roy by a large pile of wood their crew cut and split in the state forest. - Ted Roy of Little Falls drove this Dodge dump truck. - These boys are standing near the dinner bell that the cooks rang. It was a round flange from a railroad wheel. - These enrollees are loading rocks at a stone quarry on the road between Blue Mountain and Indian Lake. The rocks were used to build fireplaces and walls at nearby state parks. They also crushed the rocks to make gravel for roads. All courtesy of Ted Roy

LEGACY

Left - A camper walks along the shore of Eighth Lake. Camp S-115 continued developing the state campsite that was begun in 1933. Indian Lake CCC boys built the ranger cabin, campsites, and latrines. Ted Roy. Middle - CCC camp S-115 built Lake Durant State Park along the shores of the lake they created in 1935 after they dammed 34th Flow of the Rock River. The area was just a swampy area. Today thousands of people camp and picnic at this state park. Podskoch Collection. Right - The Indian Lake CCC built campsites, bathhouses, picnic areas, and developed the beach at Lake Eaton State Park that is north of Long Lake. Podskoch Collection

Clockwise from Top, Left - These two barracks were behind the garage that was located on Rt. 28/30. - These four enrollees, Oralick, Otropech, Maksinski, and Roshon pose in front of their barracks at the Indian Lake CCC camp. - Indian Lake CCC enrollees: Barlow, Ludrieguss, and Rodregus were cutting and removing dead trees along the state road that could be fire hazards later in the year. - Ted Roy moving coal in a wheelbarrow to his barracks. Each barracks had two or three stoves that burned coal. All courtesy of Ted Roy

MEMORIES

Ted Roy

On June 27, 2006 Ted Roy called me from his home in Little Falls because he heard that I was writing a book on the CCCs.

"I joined the CCCs in 1940 because my buddy, Mike Martinovic said he was going to do it if I did. I was 17. We went up to city hall, signed up, and grabbed a train to Utica. Then we got another train to Thendara. A guy with a truck was at the station to pick us up and drive us to the camp in Blue Mountain.

"When we arrived at camp early in January it was pretty cold. They took us to a building and gave us warm woolen clothes.

I asked Ted to draw me a map of the camp. "The kitchen and infirmary were next to the creek. Along Rt. 28/30 were the rec hall, office, truck garage, and truck repair building. Behind that was the tool shed. There were five barracks behind the truck garage. The library was between the kitchen and the last barracks. The showers and

outhouse were set back towards the hill. The coal pile was located towards the outhouse. Set behind the showers was a water storage tank which was a wooden silo on stilts. Near the tower was the foremen's building.

"We built new campsites and did what we could to finish campsites that had already been started. At first I was on a maintenance crew and then moved to a truck driver position.

"Did you ever get into trouble? I asked.

"One Sunday evening my buddies and I snuck into the kitchen. We saw these three delicious apple pies for the next meal. We snuck off with the pies and ate them in the woods so nobody would see us. Boy, were we stuffed after that.

"The next day we went to work as usual and before supper when we were lined up for the lowering of the flag the captain looked very sternly at us and said, 'I want to know who stole the three pies from the kitchen last night. That was a terrible thing to do and when I find the culprits, they will be dishonorably discharged from the camp.' The three of us didn't dare raise our hands.

"'Well,' the captain decided, 'if nobody is going to

Ted Roy of Little Falls shared funny stories and pictures of his CCC days at the Indian Lake camp in 1940. Podskoch Collection

be honest and confess, there will be no dessert for the entire company for a week!'

"After supper all the guys were talking and complaining. We had some rough guys from New York City who said if they caught the culprits, 'We'll kill them!'

"Steve Otrutcat and Mike Martinavec from Little Falls and I knew we could never let on to anyone that we had caused the loss of desserts for a week.

"The foremen in camp were older guys who had crews of 20-25 men. On weekends the foremen alternated staying in camp to keep an eye on the guys. In my barracks there were 50 of us. One Friday night most of the boys had gone home. About 15 others and I were lying around talking or resting when the door burst open and about 15 guys from another barracks came in with their pillows. A huge pillow fight began and feathers were flying all over. One of the camp leaders heard the commotion, came in and saw all the feathers, and turned our names in to the subaltern commander.

"The next morning he said, 'You guys aren't going into town tonight because of your behavior. He assigned us to a work detail and marched us over to the tool shed. He made us each grab a shovel. Then he marched us over to the pile of coal that we used to heat the buildings. We had to move two carloads of coal, about 40 tons, from one spot to another. He said if we finished the job, we'd be able to go to Tupper Lake. We all wanted to go because there was a bowling alley, theater, and girls.

"We worked like hell to move it. When we finished the leader said, 'You guys aren't done yet.'

"We said, 'You told us to move it to this spot and we did.'

"He replied, 'It doesn't belong there, it belongs here where it was.'

"By the time we got done, everybody was too tired to go, so we missed out on town and the girls were probably sad.

"In the spring of 1940 there was a lot of talk around camp of war so a lot of guys left to join the Army. Since there weren't enough men to keep our Blue Mountain camp open they closed it in July. I reenlisted for another six months and was sent to the Speculator camp where I continued to drive an Army truck. When I was there for about four months I had a lot of furlough time because I was taking tools from the closed CCC camp in Blue Mountain to a warehouse in Delmar. I was allotted some vacation time and went home. I was lucky to find a job working at Snyder's Bicycle Shop.

"After my vacation I went back and told the subaltern commander that I had a job. He said he wanted to know where I was going to work. He checked to see if I really had a job. I was honorably discharged.

"I worked at the shop and later got a job in Scotia at the Navy Depot. In 1943 I was drafted into the Army.

"I loved being in the CCCs and if I had a chance I'd go back today. Everybody did their work."

George Bowles

On Tuesday June 6, 2006 I visited George Bowles at his apartment in Watervliet, NY.

"I joined the Civilian Conservation Corps in 1939 when I was just 16 years old. It was the first week in January when I went to the Watervliet City Hall. I walked there from my home and wore an old pair of shoes that had cardboard in them because they had holes in the soles because our family was so poor. I was supposed to be up there at eight o'clock but the truck didn't come till 10 or 10:30. It

George Bowles standing on a bridge near his old Indian Lake CCC camp with Rock River in the background. The CCC built a dam on the Rock River that formed present-day Lake Durant. George Bowles Jr.

An Indian Lake camp wood crew warming up by a campfire. They got out their sandwiches and toasted them on the fire. They also had a pot of coffee brewing. Ted Roy

was a very cold day.

"Then a canvas-covered Army truck pulled up and 12 to 14 of us guys got in the back. It seemed like we were driving forever when we finally stopped at a diner in Glens Falls in the afternoon. We were freezing. All of us went in and we all got a cup of coffee and then went back out to the truck.

"Our next stop was in Blue Mountain. It was dark by then. We went inside the mess hall and had dinner. They had a big pot of chipped beef that they poured on toast. We had hot coffee. This was heaven!

"They took us to the barracks where 20 to 24 people lived. There were two coal stoves at each end of the big room. Beds were on each side and the middle was open. At night a fireman came around to each barracks every hour to check on the fire.

"The next morning they took about 40 of us new recruits to the infirmary. The medic had us strip down and gave us physical exams.

"Then they brought us to the supply barracks. They gave us new clothes: two sets of socks, a pair of shoes, long johns, two pair of pants, two shirts, one light and one heavy coat, and a pair of rubber overshoes with buckles. In other words I had more clothes than I ever had.

"Another truck brought in more guys. They took us over to the rec hall and talked to us. There were about 100 guys. An Army Chaplain told us when and where there would be religious services. He told us that maybe somebody might not be there because of an accident or whatever. He just told us what living and working together would be like and what the camp procedures were.

"Every morning a bugle called us to reveille at 6 am.

We made our bunk, washed up, and went to the latrine. It was at the end of the barracks. It was like a big out house. There was a row of sinks but no flush toilets. In the winter you had to walk up there in your long johns.

"At seven we went for breakfast. The food was good. We had pancakes, chipped beef on toast, eggs, toast, coffee, and milk.

"After breakfast we walked to a lot where trucks were parked. We boarded and there were about 14-15 in a truck.

"If it was 20 below we stayed in the barracks. We were happy if we didn't have to work.

"At that time we were cutting trees just above Long Lake and below Tupper Lake. This was going to be a new road. We did this all winter.

"Our routine for working in the woods was the same. When we first got there we gathered wood and started a fire. Then we made a big pot of coffee.

"At noon we ate sandwiches and put them on sticks and roasted them on the fire. I lost a lot of sandwiches that way. Every Friday the cooks made us tuna fish sandwiches. At least half of the guys in camp complained but they kept giving us tuna fish. The guys finally revolted. One day as we drove through Long Lake on the way to work we all threw the tuna fish sandwiches on the road. Word got back to camp and when we got back the captain gave all of us hell. But after that we never had tuna fish on Fridays again.

"I loved the CCCs. We took a half-hour to eat lunch and the next half-hour we played 'King of the Hill.' It was a lot of fun in the winter when there was snow.

"An older guy who was the foreman drew a line in the snow to show us what trees had to be cut. When we were cutting trees we used a two-man saw. My job was trimming the trees with an axe when they fell the trees. Then we dragged the logs to a pile. Later the wood was taken to campsites.

"The older guys made a game of dropping trees. Someone would draw a line in the snow and we'd see who could hit the target. I never saw anybody get hurt.

"In the spring they took us to Lake Eaton just north of Long Lake. Our crew creosoted all the bathhouses and cleaned them up. We went to the campsites and piled wood that we got from the road job.

"After the spring we were building an outdoor theater. I had to use a jackhammer and I was only 116 pounds. We worked most of the summer keeping up the park.

"Another job we did was building fire trails around

the camp. We cleared trees in a 6-12' wide path. Forest rangers were with us working every time when we did roadwork at Lake Eaton.

"Every night we played pool or cards in the rec hall. Food and drink were available in the canteen. Items were cheap and most were only a nickel. We got up to $2.50 script paper money from the office to buy things like ice cream, cigarettes, candy, beer, or soda in the canteen.

"There were two old men in our barracks who worked around camp. They were brothers and in their 70s. They lived someplace in the north. I'll never forget, every night these old guys knelt down by their cot to pray.

"Once or twice a week we'd go into Indian Lake to see the movies. We paid five or ten cents for the movie.

"In the winter time we went into the school for classes: spelling and reading for about 45 minutes. This was helpful because I dropped out of school after eighth grade. Then after classes we'd stay in the gym and play basketball.

"If somebody screwed up in camp, the whole barracks got a detail like creosoting buildings, cutting grass, painting rocks white that were on the side of the paths and roads. Most of us didn't think it was work but fun.

"Sometimes you got KP duty. You worked in the kitchen all day from 5 am. to about 8 pm. It was a long day. You peeled potatoes and washed pots and pans.

"Around the end of May we played baseball at the camp.

"On Sundays we sometimes hiked up Blue Mountain for something to do. There was a trail with a telephone line to the fire tower. When my brother Charles was there in 1938, he helped string a new telephone line up. When I went up there I saw a big rock off the trail with his name painted on.

"A few Saturday nights a truck took us to Tupper Lake. I can remember the first time I drank beer. The loggers were in the tavern having a good time. I never had to buy a beer. They always treated us.

"On Memorial Day they brought the whole outfit to Tupper Lake. We dressed up in our uniforms and wore Army hats. We marched in the parade.

"In the afternoon they took us to Long Lake for another parade. They gave us a big lunch.

"There was another time when I went to Tupper Lake. They dropped me off at the hospital

to get a filling for my tooth. I stayed there all day till they picked me up.

"In June they had our barracks out after dinner doing 'close order' marching drills using broomsticks. I guess they were getting us ready for war.

"I came home three times while in camp. The first time I hitchhiked. It was late Friday afternoon. I got ride with the forest ranger from the camp to Glens Falls. Then I got a ride to Albany from a guy who supplied movies to theaters. Then on Sunday I started hitchhiking back to camp. The last ride that day was from North Creek to Indian Lake.

"The second time I went I had two other guys: Raymond

Clockwise from Top - George Bowles revisited the Indian Lake movie theater in the summer of 2005. This is where he and his fellow enrollees enjoyed movies on Saturday nights. George Bowles. - George Bowles having a drink of water by the pump at the Indian Lake camp. George Bowles Jr. - Ted Roy and John Gudjella taking a break from painting the rocks that lined the paths at camp. Ted Roy

Reel from Troy and another guy, I can't remember his name, was from Albany. We got a few rides to Saratoga. It began snowing like mad and it was very cold. There was hardly any traffic and nobody stopped to pick us up. It was now 3 am as we trudged through the snow. Then we saw a farmhouse with a light. We knocked on the door. A farmer came to the door and we asked if we could sleep in his barn. The first thing he asked was, 'Do you smoke?' We replied, 'Yes.'

"The farmer said he couldn't let us because he feared a fire but he made us coffee and gave us some buns. We stayed there for an hour and warmed up.

"We walked the rest of the night. Raymond was too tired to walk and he wanted to lie down in the snow. We had a hard time trying to keep him going. Finally we got to Latham and stopped in a diner. We all called someone to see if they'd pick us up. My parents didn't have a car but asked a neighbor who picked us up and drove us home.

"On Sunday morning I went down to Albany and took the 'Ski Train' to North Creek. Then I began hitchhiking. Luckily there were more people out and I got back to camp at about 7 pm.

"The third time I got dribs and drabs of rides. It took a long time to get home. I was so tired of walking; I waited till Monday morning to go back. I missed the morning roll call and I was AWOL (Away Without Official Leave) I was fined $1 and it came out of my $5 pay.

"My father worked for the D & H Railroad during The Depression but he only worked one or two days a week. He was too proud to take food from the government. In the spring and summer he worked on a farm. Every day he brought home a bag of food. He was also a handyman doing jobs and gardening for a rich person outside of Troy. So the $25 a month that my family got from my work was very helpful. We had a big family: seven boys and three girls.

"One time when I hitchhiked home my father looked at me and said, 'What the hell are you coming home for?'

"In July 1940 I got my discharge. They took a truckload of us to North Creek. Most of the guys were from New York City. We got on the train and I got off at Watervliet. I was going to sign up and go to Idaho but because I had one bad mark on my record, AWOL, I couldn't go.

"When I hitchhiked home after being discharged my father looked at me and said, 'What the hell are you coming home for?'

"I got a job with my brother at Roy's Mills. I thought it was great making $12.50 a week working 40 hours.

"In 1942 I enlisted in the Army. Then in 1944 I was walking down the street in Worms, Germany and who should I meet but my brother who was also in the Army and assigned to a tank outfit. In 1944 I got married and my wife and I had three children.

"I learned a lot in the CCCs. It really helped me when I went into the Army. I was used to making my bed and Army procedures. Nobody pushed you while you were working. It was like a vacation. I think we should have it today. The young people would learn how to work and get along with each other."

Jesse Merrill

Carol Finke phoned me and said her partner's father, Jesse Merrill, was in the CCCs and I should contact him. I visited Jesse at his home in Argyle, NY.

On May 3, 2007 I drove to Merrill's home and was warmly greeted by Jesse's wife Peg. Jesse joined us in the kitchen and we enjoyed crumb coffee cake and coffee. Jesse said he thought he was going to be working in a CCC camp in the Adirondacks but wound up in Long Island. I asked him why he joined.

"There weren't many jobs and there were four kids in my family. My father, Jesse, worked part time as a fireman in the boiler room of paper mills in Ty and Fort Edward. I just turned 16 in August and I quit school and joined the CCCs in Saratoga.

"They bused several of us to Blue Mountain Lake. We stayed in a building across from the present site of the Adirondack Museum. We were in a big room with cots for about a week. We cut wood to keep the potbelly stoves going. I remember one of the guy's was named Washburn. There were young and older guys. Some of them were right out of the woods and others were city boys. Ten of us were from the Saratoga area.

"When they assembled 200 boys, we were

Jesse Merrill of Argyle joined the CCC in 1938. He started at the Indian Lake camp in Blue Mountain but was sent to Long Island to help clean up fallen trees caused by the hurricane of 1938. Podskoch Collection

taken down to North Creek and put on a D & H train. We didn't know where we were going.

"Then we got to Patchogue, Long Island. They drove us in trucks to an old Army base called Camp Upton. It was here after WW I they deloused soldiers before they sent them home. A hurricane had gone through there and we were there to clear the large elm trees.

"The old buildings were all dried out. They had us creosote all the buildings. We didn't have rubber gloves so they gave us glycerin to coat our skin because if the creosote touched our skin it burned. They gave us tobacco and gum to chew because the fumes were so strong. I don't know if it worked but we'd keep spitting tobacco juice to get rid of the fumes. They had 200 guys painting a single coat to all the buildings.

"We worked clearing trees as far east as Montauk Point. We worked there for six months. I was with an ax crew and we cut off the limbs. Another group were the two-man saw crew. I was used to doing this from the time I was 12 years old. My brother and I had the responsibility of bringing in wood to keep the family warm

"We had to wash our own clothes. They had something that looked like a toilet plunger and scrub boards. There were no washing machines.

"For recreation they took us to Patchogue for roller skating and shopping. We couldn't go into bars. We stayed pretty much together. If it rained we stayed in the barracks and played cards.

"On weekends we even worked on Saturdays. There wasn't a church but ministers came to camp.

"One day while I was cutting up a downed tree, a branch snapped up like a spring. I ran away and tripped on brush and fell on my leg. I couldn't walk on it. They took me in an old ambulance to Fort Upton Hospital. I had a broken leg and they set it. There were quite a few boys there who had injuries from cutting wood, too. Every morning all the patients had to take care of their own bed. One guy spilled water on the floor while washing his bed and threw paper on the water to absorb it. As I was walking by his bed one of my crutches slipped on the wet paper and I came down hard on the heel of my cast, which knocked the broken bone out of position.

"My mother and sister came to visit me in the hospital. This helped a little with my homesickness. After three months the doctor took off my cast and saw that my leg was crooked. He wanted to rebreak it but I said no. I didn't want to stay for another three months. I had been away

from home for nine months and I wasn't going to stay any longer.

"I left the hospital in June 1939 and came home by train. I worked at Van Rallte & Co. I was a batcher preparing bundles of cloth in baskets. Then the bundles were taken to a dye house.

"In 1942 the Army drafted me. I wasn't sent to war because of my leg but went to Fort Miles in Delaware. We planted three rows of mines across the Delaware River from Lewes, Delaware to Cape May, NJ. The persons on duty tracked the ships from towers along the beach. As a boat came up the river they had to identify themselves. If they didn't the men in the casemate (control room) could push a button and blow them up.

After the war I did home construction till 1973. Then I got a job working on bank vaults. I went around to banks and changed their combinations every year. I also repaired bank vaults and safety deposit boxes. I did this till I was 81.

"I enjoyed it all in the CCCs, especially chopping wood."

Martin Bezon

In August of 2006 I traveled to Port Henry to speak at the Sherman Public Library. That afternoon I visited Martin Bezon on Tobey Street to learn about his experiences at the Indian Lake camp. We sat on the porch of Walter Wojewodzic and enjoyed the beautiful view of Lake Champlain and the Green Mountains of Vermont in the distance.

"I was 18 years old when I signed up in the old jailhouse here in Port Henry in 1940. I joined because my good friend, Johnny Grover, said, 'Let's join.' His mother was signing him up and he was underage. We joined in June right after my eleventh year of high school. The day before I left we were playing baseball. We only had a first baseman's glove and a catcher's mitt. I was playing outfield and when I caught a ball my two fingers split apart and made about an inch cavity. My mother washed it off and said, 'The CCC will take care of it.'

"The next day after injuring my hand Johnny and I went directly to the Blue Mountain CCC camp in an open truck. We stood up all the way just like a herd of cattle. There were about 20 of us.

"The first thing was a physical. The doctor looked at my hand and said, 'Wait till the end and I'll take care of it. I sat there a while but the room was filled with the smell of ether and I almost passed out so I went outside to clear my head. I went back in and the doctor cleaned it out with alcohol and taped it up.

"It was now dark and it was strange standing in front of my new home, Barracks #3. I thought to myself, 'If I could find the way home to Port Henry, I would leave now.' I walked in and the lights were out. Then I heard Frank Wojewodzic and Frank Mydlarz calling me. They guided me to my bed. They had it all made up and I was so thankful. I was lucky because about 80 per cent of my barracks was from the Town of Moriah.

"The next morning I was all right. They put us on a truck to clean brush. At 11:30 two guys were delegated to start a fire. They made a big pot of coffee. Around 12 we sat down and relaxed and talked with the other city guys. We each had a brown bag filled with three sandwiches: cold cuts and peanut butter and jelly.

"After lunch the foreman asked Johnny Grover and me if we knew how to cut trees. We said, 'Yes.' He took out to a big cedar. Someone had already marked the trees to be cut because they were going to be used to build a latrine for a state park on Long Lake. We would haul the logs across the lake with a rowboat.

"At the end of the day the foreman asked us how we did. We told him that we cut 13 trees but only three fell down. The rest got hung up. He showed us how to notch a tree to get it to fall a certain way.

"After we dropped the trees we used the logs to make a latrine with rolled roof on top.
"The foremen warned us not to go swimming with the young girls but Johnny had a plan. He fell in first and said, 'I lost my footing.' Then we both were in the water. The foreman came over and said, 'What's going on?' He was a good guy and said just don't mess with the girls.

"Another job was digging water lines around the camp. The ditches weren't that deep. One time we came to a stump with ground hornets. The city guys were scared of them. I said, 'I'll run over it if you give me something.' Johnny also made the bet. We both got 13, mostly jelly sandwiches. We ran right through the nest. I was stung three times. It hurt like hell, but we had 13 sandwiches.

"After work and on weekends we loved to play baseball. There was a camp team made up of officers and noncommissioned men. We asked if we could be on their team but they refused. We put together a team of Mineville and Port Henry guys and challenged the camp team. Their team came up first and had one scratch hit and then three outs. Then we came up to bat. The first seven men hit home runs and the camp team quit. We still couldn't get on the camp team.

"One Sunday morning we decided to hike up to a pond on a nearby hill to go swimming. When we got there we went swimming naked. Then we heard the chow bell. We jumped out, put our clothes on, and ran like hell. We got there just in time. They had fat, juicy hot dogs with sauerkraut for dinner. You could have as much as you wanted. I ate 19 and Frank Wojewodzic 21. You could always take as much as you wanted at meals but you couldn't throw food away.

"One day they kept me and three other guys in camp for four days. All we had to do was burn clothes, socks, hats,

Clockwise from Top - Frank Wojewodzic was one of the enrollees in Martin Bezon's barracks who made Martin feel at home when he first came to the Indian Lake camp in 1940. Martin Bezon. - Martin Bezon and his friend Walter "Jigger" Catonzerita, the company clerk, in front of their barracks #3. Martina Bezon Lavigne. - Dembroski, Martin Bezon, Grover, Brown, and LaBounty taking a break from chopping trees and cleaning brush at Eaton Lake. Martin Bezon

t-shirts, and shoes. I kept taking clothes up into the woods and hiding them because they were good.

"Once in a while I hitched a ride with Tony Urban. He used to come up on Fridays from Port Henry. We gave him two bucks each and he brought us back on Sunday.

"Towards the end of August Johnny and I asked the captain for an honorable discharge. They wanted me to stay and were even going to promote me but I wanted to go home. They discharged us because we wanted to go back to school. That fall we went out for football and were in great shape after cutting trees and digging ditches. Our team's record was 7-0 and we scored 190 points.

"Johnny quit school and joined the Marines in January 1942. He was killed at Guadalcanal.

"After high school I worked for Republic Steel and worked on the trestle unloading rail cars. Then in 1942 I joined the Air Force. In November 1945 I got back to the US. I went back to Republic Steel and retired in 1971. I got married in 1948 to Elizabeth Zydik and we had Rosalie, Martina, and Martin. My wife died and I remarried Anna White.

"I loved the CCC. It was one of the best things I ever did."

Joe Veneto

In 2007 while doing research in Port Henry I learned that Joe Veneto, a retired local ironworker, had been in the CCC. I called Joe and was invited to his home. His wife Wilma invited me into their living room. I asked Joe to tell me about his life in the CCC.

"I had to quit school after ninth grade. I wanted to help my parents, Dominic and Angeline, because there were nine kids in my family. Dad didn't do anything because he had heart trouble. I was the fourth eldest in the family. The older kids had to help but there was nothing to do. There weren't any jobs. I knew about the CCC because my two older brothers, Philip and Bruno, had already been in the Port Henry CCC camp in 1933. There was a lot of information in the paper about the CCC and where you could join. So when I was 17 in the fall of 1938 I joined. I signed up in Port Henry. I was able to join because my family was on welfare. It was better than being a bum.

"You didn't have a choice of where to go. They sent me to Blue Mountain. When we got there they issued us clothing and assigned us to a barracks. It didn't bother me being away from home.

"My job was to clean up the dead wood in the forest and burn it. If a tree was half way down we cut it and made it flat to the ground. We cleaned up a couple of hundred feet along the roads.

"We also made tent campsites, a ranger cabin, roads at Golden Beach State Park.

"On the weekends I just hung around the camp. There wasn't much to do in Blue Mountain. I did my laundry by hand and used yellow Army soap. There weren't any washing machines. Sometimes a truck took us to Tupper Lake on Saturday night. We went to movies, bar rooms, or dance halls.

"We liked to play tricks on the city guys. We short-sheeted their beds. Another trick was we took the bed-springs off their beds and tied strings enough to hold their mattress on. Then when they laid down they and the mattress fell to the floor.

"When we had new recruits we told them they were on fire guard. We gave them a broom and told them to climb on the roof in the winter and sweep off the sparks. When they climbed up we threw paper inside the stoves and poked the hell out of the paper to make sparks fly up the chimney. The recruit would be up there swatting away at the sparks.

"Another trick was we tied buckets of water above the door and when they pushed the door open the bucket tipped and they got soaked.

"Then there was the 'snipe hunt.' We gave the guys burlap bags. Then we took them into the woods and told them to hold the bags on the ground and wait while we went into the woods to drive the snipes towards them. We snuck back to the barracks and left them 'holding the bag.'

"After six months I really wanted to go out West. In October I signed up to go out West. They took me to Saratoga and I caught a train to Fort Dix, NJ. Then I got another train to Idaho. It took about five days. They had sleeper cars and the train stopped occasionally so we got to walk around. I went to Priests River, Idaho. It was a small town like you see in the western movies. It had a post office, store, and hotel.

"I stayed again in barracks. There were five barracks with 40 men each.

"My major job was doing park maintenance. I fought two bad fires: one on Mt. Gleason and the other on Mt. Baldy. We had fire rakes and made fire lines. We removed all the flammable materials. At night we went back to camp to sleep.

159

"I also worked in the shop repairing heavy equipment like bulldozers, etc. I was the blacksmith's helper.

"In the winter I was a laborer at the park sawmill. The winters were tough, a lot of snow.

"On weekends we either went hunting or went to Priests River to one of the bars.

After a year in Idaho I had to quit because you were only allowed to stay in the CCC for 18 months. I got a job at Republic Steel where my two brothers also worked after they got out of the CCC. I loaded ore cars and ran an overhead crane. When the wind blew it got scary up there.

"In August 1942 I got drafted into the Army. After the war I got my job back at Republic Steel.

"In 1955 I got married and my wife, Wilma, and I had three children: Donald, Donna, and Tammy.

"The CCC was a big help to my family. They got $25 a month and that helped them during the Depression."

Evelyn Thompson

I stopped by Evelyn Thompson's home in Blue Mountain on August 14, 2006 and asked her if she knew anyone who worked at the Indian Lake CCC camp:

"My brother Ernest Blanchard worked at the camp. He joined the CCC because he had to help our large family that had nine children. My father Ernest was the fire tower observer on Blue Mountain fire tower. He worked there for about seven months. Then he worked as a guide and trapped, hunted and fished to keep his family going. My brother was 17. It must have been around 1937 because he was born in 1920. He was there for at least a year and stayed till it closed. When they took the buildings down they took the lumber and built the building where the Grill Restaurant is. The building next to it used to be the Lumber Jack Restaurant. Another building that used CCC lumber was where they stored the school bus.

"Ernest was a paratrooper in WW II. When he came back from the war he was a plumber for the local water company. Then he was the caretaker for the Tioga Point Camp on the backside of Raquette Lake.

"Then I showed Evelyn a group picture of the Indian Lake camp in a 1937 CCC yearbook. "That's Ernest LaPrarie, my first husband. I never knew he was in the CCC. There is Don Gauvin. He worked at the Lake Durant State Park. His brother Gordon lives in Raquette Lake."

John Stewart

Richard Stewart of North Creek contacted me in June 2006 and told me his father, John, was in the CCC camp in Indian Lake. He invited me to his home and shared these stories about his father:

"I'll start out with my dad's family. Dad's father, Floyd, ran the family farm here in Peaceful Valley. He was a blacksmith and worked on building the Sacandaga reservoir. He cut brush and then sharpened drill bits for building the dam. He worked as a foreman for the WPA on projects like building roads, a reservoir for the village of North Creek, and the North Creek Ski Hut. It was a place for skiers to warm up and buy food. My grandfather was also a guide and a fox hunter.

"Floyd married Alta (Hitchcock) and they had seven children: Rosamond, Mary, John, Fred, Mildred, George, and Earl. My father was born in 1915.

"In 1936 Dad joined the CCC. I believe my father and his brother Fred both joined because there was no work in the area. Fred was only 17 when he went to the Bolton Landing camp. Uncle Fred said working in the CCC was the hardest job he ever had but it was enjoyable because he was young and tough. Everything he did was on the run just like being in basic training. One job he had was looking for gypsy moth egg masses.

"Several years ago, I found a book in my father's CCC footlocker. It showed all the CCC camps and named all of the employees. The book is on display at the

John Stewart was the bookkeeper at the Indian Lake CCC camp in 1936. Richard Stewart

Indian Lake town museum in Indian Lake, NY. The camps were organized like military units and the workers became valuable members of the armed forces.

"Dad said camp was the melting pot of the scum of New York City and Buffalo.

"One time somebody was getting into Dad's locker.

Another fellow asked Dad's friend for his lock. He took the lock, hid it behind his back, turned the dial, and opened it. That's how safe his lock was with guys who knew how to steal. A lock was worthless.

"My dad was the bookkeeper at camp. He took Enoch Squire's place when he left. Later Enoch was a reporter for radio station WGY. Dad mainly kept the records and did stenography in the company office. He didn't leave camp to work in the woods like the other guys.

"He liked the food. Every day for lunch he got three sandwiches: one peanut butter, one baloney, and the other was apple butter which he hated.

"My father fell in love with my mother Catherine. She left New York City to live with her older sister in Bakers Mills near here. Her mother was a widow and had no money. Mom's sister married Nate Moore who owned land up here in the Adirondacks. They moved up here and learned how to live off the land. They used wood for fuel and used the land for farming and got meat from hunting. It was in this area that my parents met and began dating.

"Dad told me on the weekends they took the guys to the movie theater in North Creek. One winter's night, a group of men from the Indian Lake CCC camp came to North Creek to see a movie. My father used this opportunity to visit his family. My father walked three miles to visit his parents in Peaceful Valley. After a short visit, he walked another three miles to Bakers Mills to visit his bride to be. Later that evening, he walked six miles back to North Creek.

"It was snowing hard that night and my father wasn't aware that the group had decided to leave North Creek early. The canvas-topped army truck was pulling away from the theater as my father approached. He didn't have a flashlight to signal the truck and his voice couldn't be heard above the roar of the old army truck.

"Rather than face disciplinary charges, my father decided to walk the 30-plus miles to Lake Durant. The snow was over a foot deep and my father wore felt shoes and overshoes. These shoes were designed for warmth and not long-distance walking.

"My father arrived at camp in time for roll call. He was exhausted from walking over 40-miles through deep snow, but he was relieved that he was able to get to camp on time.

"Luckily, the camp commander decided to curtail the construction project until the weather cleared. My father resigned himself to his bunk for a major part of the day.

It was his award for being on time.

"When Dad left the CCC he joined the Forest Service in Owego. He was a timber cruiser there. He moved back to this area and he delivered propane and worked on appliances for 32 years. He passed away in 1994.

"The CCC is where he learned stenography and bookkeeping from correspondence courses. He wanted to have these skills as a backup in case he wasn't able to find a job."

Donald Gauvin

Mary Wilson Gauvin of Saratoga talked to me by phone and told me her husband, Donald, worked at the Indian Lake CCC camp:

"My husband came from a large poor family. Donald's father died in 1933 at the age of 49. Donald was 13. There were six children in the family: twin boys Albert and Alfred, 23, Virginia, 18, Donald, 13, Gordon, 8, and Nelson, 6.

"Donald joined the CCC to help support his family. He was only 15 but he was desperate to get a job. Doc Carroll in Indian Lake told Don that he would see if he could pull some strings. He did and Don got in even though he was two years younger than the required age of 17. When Don got older he went to apply for social security but they had the older age because he had lied when he enrolled in the CCC. He and Ernie Blanchard from Indian Lake joined together.

"While at the CCC camp Donald learned how to run heavy equipment from foreman Ernest Hutchins.

"Don enjoyed working at the camp and he eventually was moved up to become a leader.

"Donald was in the camp for about two years. He left CCC at the end of 1937 or beginning of 1938. He went to Glens Falls to help build the airport and then to Imperial Wallpaper. They also made paper used to make money.

"In 1942 he joined the Army and became a paratrooper medic.

"After the war he tried lumbering in Indian Lake for a few months but lumbering was dying out. He moved to Newark, NJ where he worked at Otis Elevator as a general contractor. Later he went in the Army reserves in the early 1950s. From 1951-1954 he worked at American Locomotive in Schenectady as a foreman in the tank division. Then he moved to Schenectady and did painting and carpentry.

"His younger brother and he went into a gas station business in Scotia and then Donald was a mechanic at Wedekinds Motors. We retired to Indian Lake and worked for the DEC as Supervisor of the Lake Durant campsite. He started at Lake Durant and ended there."

Leroy Spring

On August 30, 2007 I drove to the Village of Indian Lake and interviewed Leroy Spring. On this warm summer day we sat on the front porch of his trailer. He said that he regretted he couldn't drive anymore because he had macular degeneration. Leroy was born in 1915 and his parents were Clyde and Lena Burgey Spring. They had five children: Margaret, Bernice, Buster, Leroy, and Ted.

"My dad was a laborer," said Leroy, "who worked in the woods. It was hard raising a family during the Depression. When I was 18 years old I joined the CCC in June 1933 because there weren't any jobs. I was sent to Speculator where we lived in tents. Our job was working on Moffitt Beach and Sacandaga campsites. We cleared up the timber to make places for the tenters.

"In November I was transferred to Lake Durant where I lived in barracks. My job was mostly driving trucks carrying men and logs. We also dug a well by the brook. We cleared the land of brush and timber. Then we burned the piles of brush. We also built a concrete dam that flooded the land and created Lake Durant.

"We also worked at the Lake Eaton campsite cutting trees and building more sites for campers.

"At camp I had some friends, including Donald Demarch and Lee Locke. My brother Buster was there, too. He was a mechanic.

"I stayed there for two years and left in 1935. For the next few years I worked in the logging industry.

"I liked working for the CCC. It gave me experience living with other people and we had good Army officers who ran the camp."

Stephen Dennis

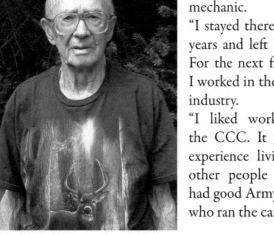

Leroy Spring, at his home in Indian Lake in 2007. Podskoch Collection

After giving a talk at the Mechanicville Public Library on May 8, 2006 I asked an elderly man who was reading a newspaper in the library if he knew anyone who was in the CCC. He responded, "Yes. I was in the CCC at the Indian Lake camp. I joined the CCC to help my mother because my dad couldn't find a job. I was only 16. My brother Andrew dropped out of school at Ithaca College because my parents couldn't pay for his schooling.

"I was a good student in school. I skipped two grades. So I was 16 and just had to finish four more months of school to graduate high school. But in March I quit school to help my family. I just hung around town and looked for jobs but they wouldn't hire me because I was too young.

"Then my older brother Frank joined the CCC and he went to Medford, Oregon. I really liked it so I decided to give it a try.

"I signed up for the CCC in September or October. A bus took a group of us boys to Blue Mountain. One of the jobs I had was completing the cement dam on Rock River that created Lake Durant.

"Then the camp closed in the fall of 1939 and the remaining men and I went to an old army base called Yaphank. We took over the old barracks and our job was to help clean up the destroyed trees that were felled by the 1938 hurricane. We drove along the coast and cut up trees. Everywhere we went were duck farms. The only thing we did was work hard all day and at night we played cards, pool, or darts. We did get one big treat and that was a visit to the 1939 World's Fair in Flushing Meadows, NY.

"After my six months were up in the spring of 1940. I came home and was a caddy at the local golf course. I met the personnel manager of the West Virginia Pulp and Paper Mill Co. He gave me a job and I was an electrician's helper.

"After the bombing of Pearl Harbor I joined the Navy on December 12, 1941. I was on the 'Atlanta.' We were in the battles in the Coral Sea and Guadalcanal.

"The CCC was important for my family and me because it gave me a job and money for my family."

Greg George

During the summer of 2007 I visited Forest Ranger Greg George at his home near Lake Durant. I asked him if he knew where the CCC camp was located. He said that the state forest ranger home that he now lived in was on land where the Indian Lake CCC camp was located. When the

Stephen Dennis, a former CCC enrollee at the Indian Lake camp, at the Mechanicville Public Library. Podskoch collection

state had snow drifting on Rt. 28/30 as it went along Lake Durant they moved the road to the east. The road went right over the old CCC camp site.

He took me across Rt. 28/30 and showed me the location of the cement foundations of the latrine and shower house. We also found a hole that was the sump for the shower and bathroom. We could see an old terra-cotta pipe along the wall of the hole. This was the cesspool. Richard Stewart of North Creek told me his father told him how they constructed the cesspool: "They dug a large hole and laid planks over it. Then they laid tarpaper over the planks and added another layer of planks. The tar paper kept the dirt from falling in."

Then we walked back towards his home and behind it he showed me the old Rt. 28/30. Right near the old bridge that went over Rock River he showed me where the kitchen and well was. One can just imagine what a busy place this was during the late 30s when there were 200 young men living here.

On the east side of Rt. 28/30 and across from the Forest Ranger home in Blue Mountain is the foundation of the camp latrine and shower. Podskoch Collection

WORK ACCOMPLISHED BY CAMP S-115*

PROJECT	1935	1936	1937	1938	1939	1940	1941	TOTAL
Bathhouses - number					2			2
Beach improvement - mi.				0.5	1.5		1.5	3.5
Bridges, foot - number		4						4
Dams - number		1						1
Ditches - yd^3		920						920
Dwellings - number					2			2
Emergency work - man-days			98		32			130
Field planting trees - ac.		10						10
Fire breaks - mi.						1.3		1.3
Fire fighting - man-days		471	30		953	507	133	2094
Fire hazard reduction (roadside & trailside) - mi.		1	6.3	3	1	279.7	0.5	291.5
Fire pre-suppression - man-days					200	442	251	893
Fireplaces - number		7	47		100		14	168
Forest stand improvement - ac.		183	43					226
General clean-up - ac.	5	128	30	25	110			298
Guard rails - rods					15			15
Insect pest control - ac.				600				600
Lake, pond & reservoir site cleaning - ac.	2	240	125					367
Landscaping - ac.		25						25
Latrines - number					4		14	18
Parking areas - yd^2						5500	3000	8500
Pipe & tile lines, conduit - linear ft.		4900			3000		1200	8790
Planting/moving trees & shrubs - man-days						85	225	825
Preparation/transportation of materials - man-days		656	2026	3976	626		802	8086
Public campground development - ac.		41	27	30	15	2	10	125
Razing undesirable structures - man-days			336	853			131	1320
Reconnaissance & investigation - man-days					675			675
Shelters - number			1		6		1	8
Seedling collection - number						12488		12488
Sewage & waste disposal systems - number		4	1		1			6
Signs - number		1			110			111
Stream & lake improvement - yd^2		1900	200					2100
Surveys - man-days			9		365			374
Table-bench combination - number			60		8		50	118
Telephone line - mi.		3	29.5					32.5
Trails, foot - mi.		8.5						8.5
Trails, truck - mi.	0.5	0.7			1.9	1.4		4.5
Tree & plant disease control - ac.			1485	10	4			1499
Wells & pumphouses - number				1				

*Numerical data from Conservation Reports

CHAPTER 18

LAKE PLACID

This Associated Press photo dated December 29 1933, shows Lake Placid CCC enrollees with their shovels and picks at the Whiteface Inn listening for their orders of the day with the bugler poised to give the "charge" to go to battle in the cold weather. Podskoch Collection

HISTORY

On November 13, 1933 Company 257 established Camp S-71 at Whiteface Inn on Lake Placid. This company was originally stationed during the summer in tents in Goldsmith Camp 63 near Loon Lake. As winter approached Company 257 moved to warmer quarters at the Whiteface Inn near Lake Placid.[1] The Conservation Department signed a lease to use the hotel buildings for $1 and promised to install a costly heating system that would remain when the CCC left in the spring. The 184 CCC enrollees lived in three areas of the inn which served as barracks. One was over the large garage, the second was over the mess hall, and the third was the area over the recreation hall that was used as the laundry room. Army officers and the camp superintendent lived in luxury in cottages used by summer guests who paid $1,800 for the season.[2]

The December 14, 1933 article "Officials Inspect Whiteface Camp" in the Au Sable, Record-Post reported that Gen. Charles D. Roberts of Oswego, the commander of the Northern New York CCC, inspected the Lake Placid camp. He gave a favorable report on the living conditions at the Whiteface Inn. Five other Army officers accompanied him on the inspection.

Camp Superintendent John F. Paul supervised the projects of Company 257. The Conservation Department classified S-71 as a Forest Fire Control camp. It constructed fire lines, truck and foot trails, footbridges, and telephone lines. The men fought fires, eliminated fire hazards, and built and maintained state parks.

In November 1933 foreman W. Kibbe and 20 enrollees began thinning and pruning the nine acres of red pine along Rt. 86 four miles west of Lake Placid near the Meadow Brook Golf Course. This was part of the Pettis Memorial Forest. In January the work force increased to 120 men. Foreman C. E. Mason supervised the work that continued on the 90-acre forest till the spring. The men then moved to Chubb Hill Road and removed hardwoods from the pines. They removed approximately 300 cords of wood and moved it to their camp and a nearby campsite.[3]

In January 1934 Captain Francis B. Redner took command of the camp from Captain W. H. Waugh.[4] Captain Redner stated: "Naturally I like our quarters but just the same I am anxious to have the camp moved. The present quarters for the men offer a constant fire hazard."[5]

Plans to move out of Whiteface Inn and build a

permanent camp site for Camp S-71 began to take shape in March 1934 when Captain F. R. Bowman arrived at Whiteface Inn from the Paul Smiths camp. He was to help with the construction of the permanent camp at Call's Corner when ground conditions permitted. The Lake Placid Club owned this property. A March 9, 1934 article, "To Build Permanently for C. C. C. Camp 63" in the Au Sable Record-Post, reported the camp would move to the new site by May 1.

The April 4, 1934 Record-Post article, "Period Opens at CCC Camp 63," reported a new group of enrollees arrived at Camp 63. The 50 new young men from Essex County brought the camp total to 206 men. Some of the new recruits were: Clifford Allen, Rewell Bickford, Clinton Bamford, Paul Crowningshield, Leo Durgan, Clarence Gregory, Rupert Jewtraw, George Lelonde, Edward Patterson, Francis and Ralph Southmayd, Theodore Cayen, Edward Connor, Donald Dunn, William Dwyer, Fred Hough, George Whitney (Lake Placid). Kenneth Babcock, Gilbert Dudley, Albert and Leander Lawrence, Paul Sorell (Wilmington), Milton Baker, (no first name) Durett, (Saranac Lake) Bernard Barton (Bloomingdale), Paul Blando, Leward Pelkey, Ernest Stevens, Lee Tucker, (Ray Brook), Robert Blanchard, Noble Dickinson, John Lacey, Ernest Molette, Norman Rathbun, Augustus Rivers (Willsboro), Emerson Ducharm, Walter Proctor (Keene Valley), Howard Rueyone (Malone), Marcell Call, Francis Landry, Warren Erwin, and Edward Wilkins (Ausable Forks). Captain William F. Campbell was now in command. Camp surgeon, Dr. George C. Owens examined the recruits and the enlistees were issued equipment and assigned to quarters.

Camp S-71 fought one of the largest fires in the Adirondacks in May of 1934 at Bay Pond approximately 8 miles west Paul Smiths. They along with four other CCC camps, rangers, and local residents fought the fire for many days. Camp S-71 set up a side camp and spent 1,800 man-days working to put out the fire.[6] During the summer 1934 Camp S-71 was busy constructing a telephone line from Lake Placid to the fire tower on Whiteface Mountain. A reporter visited the enrollees and wrote an article, "Find Life in Whiteface Camp to Their Liking," in the July 27, 1934 issue of the Lake Placid News.

"A small settlement of army tents perched high in a cranny over a mile up the side of Whiteface Mountain spells home this summer to 40 members of Company 257, CCC Camp S-71, engaged in erecting a telephone line to the fire tower on the summit."

The reporter describes the end of the workday when the shovels, picks and axes are lined up and the workers ready for supper. "Cooked under a canvas fly on army field ranges by Irving Talbot who has spent many years in the woods and knows how to cook for hearty men working in the Adirondack air, the food soon becomes a thing of the past. Then the boxing gloves appear, a whistle blows and would-be Max Baers keep themselves in a trim circle by interested onlookers, admiring or jeering as the case might be.

"Horseshoe pitching is a popular sport with the youths, although it is difficult to find a level spot on the grade to plant the pegs . . . Added to the spirited gibes of the contestants and audience is the constant accompaniment of ambitious musicians, a flutist, harmonica player, and accordion enthusiast. This continues until the patience of the helpless listeners wears thin when the players are told to take their instruments for a walk in the woods so that concentration on the sports may become keener.

"Many of the youths prefer the life at the mountain camp to that in the main camp in the village. Except for one trip a week, deprived of the attractions of the movies and the other amusements, they seem content with what life offers in the solitude to be found in the woods."

By the end of the summer, The Au Sable Record Post reported in a September 27, 1934 article, "Telephone on Whiteface Is Nearly Ready" that work on the telephone line was almost completed. The CCCers were busy drilling holes in the bare rocks and installing steel poles to hold the telephone line because there were no trees. Before the men reached the treeless summit they used wooden telephone poles for the telephone wire. The steel telephone poles carried approximately 7,000' of wire to the summit fire tower and down the other side to the observer's cabin. The young men also laid an underwater telephone cable from Cone's camp across Lake Placid to the base of Whiteface Mountain.

Another Camp S-71 project was rebuilding Marcy Dam on Marcy Brook, which created Marcy Pond. The pond was a natural habitat for trout. Enrollees also improved the road to Marcy Dam and constructed two miles of fire line that served as a hiking and horse trail. A similar project was constructing the dam at South Meadows. The men cleared the land for a distance of a mile before building the dam.[7]

There were other camp projects. The young men scouted over 1,500 acres and removed ribes bushes. They also continued working on the Lake Placid-Saranac Lake trail that they had begun working on in the fall of 1933.[8]

In the spring 1934 Conservation Commissioner Lithgow Osborne visited Wilmington Notch and approved the creation of an artificial lake next to the Connery campsite. The CCC boys from Camp S-71 began removing underbrush and stumps from the 15-acre swamp. They also removed a beaver dam and began constructing a 160-foot dam. The lake would be stocked with trout.[9]

Tourists and local residents praised the work and behavior of the Lake Placid CCC camp. Captain William E. Campbell received these letters that were printed in the August 3, 1934 Lake Placid News.

Rev. Benjamin Louis Ramsey, rector of St. Peter's church in Mountain Lakes, N. J. wrote: "During the latter part of June while hiking with my wife and children I was coming down Mt. Marcy on the Adirondack Lodge trail. Our daughter was ill and we were with great difficulty trying to make Indian Falls camp for the night. Within a mile of the camp we encountered a squad of CCC boys from your command. They informed me that they had taken possession of the camp and had completed their preparations for the night's stay. This would have of course prevented us from occupying the camp which was too small to accommodate another party. But upon learning of our plight they very graciously offered to pack up and move on up the steep trail to another cabin.

"Needless to say we were very grateful for this generous and kindly act and I wish to convey to the men concerned our sincere thanks and appreciation. There have been so many criticisms leveled against the CCC boys that I am glad to be able to offer this testimony."

Milton L. Bernstein, owner of the Red Gables cabin on Lake Placid wrote: "I wish to take the opportunity of informing you of the admirable work performed by Company 257, Camp S-71 stationed in Lake Placid. A fire occurred on the Pulitzer property here around midnight of July 11. I had first hand information of their work as I was the person giving the alarm to the Lake Placid fire department and also to the Shore Owners Association fire-boat and the CCC camp. Within 20 minutes after I had notified the camp, a detachment was on the way to the fire, and 200 men were loaded on trucks, fully equipped for fire fighting and held in readiness until notified by the fire warden's assistant that the fire was under control and that their services were not needed. I am sure that you will be very pleased to learn of the splendid work done by this camp."

Near the end of August 1934 the entire Camp S-71

was called out to fight another fire on Thompson Mountain near Peasleeville, between Au Sable Forks and Dannemora. The fire burned 700-800 acres before it was brought under control.[10]

The October 12, 1934 issue of The Lake Placid News reported these 14 local men were added to the 40 other replacements at Camp S-71: Donald E. Lamica, Herman Lincoln, Ira Herbert Potter, Cleon Taylor (Lake Placid), Francis Betters (Au Sable), Willard Blaise, Frank Lamere (Keeseville), Francis DeFay, Luther Monica, Irwin Kilburn (Elizabethtown), Edward A. Donaldson, Roland J. Hier (Schroon Lake), William Trombley (Saranac Lake), and Qufice D. Mitchell (Wallonsburg).

The Lake Placid News reported on October 12, 1934 that Company 257 moved into the permanent barracks. Men began moving stoves into the kitchen and meals were going to be served on Saturday. The whole camp had 14 buildings over three-quarters completed: recreation hall, infirmary, mess hall, garages, foresters' and officers' quarters.

On Thanksgiving Day most of the boys who lived near the camp went home but those who stayed were treated to a delicious dinner in their new mess hall. The following items were on the menu: stuffed celery, half grapefruit, radishes, pickles, cream of mushroom soup, roast turkey, oyster dressing, cranberry sauce, mashed potatoes, creamed corn, lettuce salad, Russian dressing, assorted rolls, pumpkin and mince pie, cheese, coffee, cigars, and assorted nuts.[11]

The Lake Placid News reported on March 22, 1935 in "Origins and Progress of New York's New Stream Improvement Program" that the Lake Placid camp par-

An aerial view of Lake Placid Camp S-71 located near the Old Military Road. NYS Archives

In 1935 Camp S-71 constructed this stone monument at Wilmington Notch on Rt. 86. Conservation Governor Lehman (left) and Conservation Commissioner Lithgo Osborne (right) unveiled the monument. The inscription is: "This tablet commemorates the fiftieth anniversary of conservation in New York State. On May 15, 1885 Governor David B. Hill signed the law establishing the forest preserve. The surrounding mountains, streams and woodlands have been acquired for the free use of all the people of the state and are maintained as wild forests for the enjoyment of future generations." NYS Archives

ticipated in a new Conservation Department program of doing stream improvement projects. Camp S-71 worked on South Notch Brook and Whiteface Brook creating pools for the trout during the dry summer.

In July 1935 Captain Edward McGall became the new commander.[12] During the summer and fall of 1935 the Lake Placid camp built and maintained ski trails in that area. They maintained the five Heart Lake and Sentinel Range loops. They also constructed the new loop trail over Mount Pisgah near Saranac Lake.[13]

In the fall of 1935 District Forester James H. Hopkins warned hunters to watch out for CCC workers. He said that Camp S-71 was busy working on projects at these locations: Hurricane Mt. in Elizabethtown, Connery Pond campsite in Wilmington Notch, Marcy Dam and Marcy Road, John Brown's farm and Avalanche Pass.[14]

Chester J. Yops became the new superintendent in February 1936. Under his direction men worked on building and maintaining Connery Pond, Wilmington Notch, and Meadow Brook campsites. They completed a 60' X 9' masonry dam below the Whiteface Mountain Memorial Road Toll Gate.[15]

Superintendent Yops' wrote the article "Accomplishments and Record Lake Placid CCC Camp" published in the Au Sable Record-Post on April 2, 1936. He stated the camp improved the state lands and historical sites in the area. They also constructed two dams: Marcy and Little Cherry Patch in North Elba.

At the 50th Conservation Anniversary in Lake Placid in 1935 Yops added that the enrollees had constructed the stands for President Roosevelt at the Olympic Arena and Wilmington Notch Memorial and landscaped both areas. They also built log lean-tos at the arena and high school.

Camp S-71 installed the stone monument at Wilmington Notch on Rt. 86 that celebrated the 50th anniversary conservation in New York State.. They also spent many days and nights decorating the Olympic Arena and rifle range in Lake Placid for the celebrations. The men also constructed two cabins.[16]

Yops also cited other accomplishments. He stated the men built and improved horse, truck, and foot trails. The truck trails were important in transporting men and equipment to fight fires. Three important truck trails were from Connery Pond to Whiteface Mountain, the trail up Hurricane Mountain, and the one to Marcy Dam. They also constructed the horse trail from Lake Placid to Saranac.

Camp S-71 worked to improve the famous abolitionist John Brown's homestead in North Elba. They landscaped a circular plot and in the center poured a two-ton cement foundation for the bronze John Brown Memorial Monument. Enrollees installed cedar rail fence around the memorial grounds and laid four flagstone walks that led to the center.[17] Then they graded and seeded the grounds, built a two-mile fence around the farm, and painted the buildings.[18]

In the fall of 1936 the CCC built the Mt. Marcy and Mt. Van Hoevenberg ski trails.[19] These trails were very popular during the winter of 1936-37.

By the end of 1936 the Lake Placid camp completed over 12 miles of truck trails: Marcy Dam (2 mi.). Plantation Road (1.25 mi.), Saranac Lake to Lake Placid (5.5 mi.), Connery Pond (3.2mi.), and Hurricane Mt. (5 mi.).

The Army arranged for plays by visiting actors as part of the Federal Theater Project that provided work for unemployed actors. The Buffalo Historical Marionette Unit performed at Camp S-71 in August 1936. The enrollees enjoyed the program in the recreation hall and after the program the performers showed the men how they manipulated the marionettes.

During the boys' free time a few from Camp S-71 competed in bobsled races at the nearby Mt. Van Hovenberg Olympic Bobsled Run. It was the only CCC camp to boast of two and four-man bobsled teams.

In January 1936 the Lake Placid CCC two-man bobsled team came in second place competing from the half-mile mark. Mike Kalinsack drove the sled with the time of 1:27.33. The guys might have been embarrassed when the Sno Birds team driven by Katharin Dewey beat them and came in first place.[20]

The next month The Lake Placid News reported

Above, Left - These Lake Placid camp CCC enrollees are loading gravel into one of the Conservation Department trucks to be used for the building of truck trails and campsite roads. DEC Archives. Above, Right - Camp S-71 in Lake Placid was the only CCC camp in the US that had a four-man bobsled team. The team at the Mt. Van Hovenberg Olympic Bobsled Run is: Paul Baker, driver, 2nd, Whitey Kamm, 3rd, "Eggs" Lundy, and 4th, brakeman "Babyface" Bruce. Bunk Griffin

on February 18, 1936 the results of the North American Championships. The CCC team piloted by Mike Kalinsack came in second place with a time of 7:46.34.

The next week the Adirondack Association held its championship race. Paul Baker was the driver of the CCC four-man sled that came in second place. Another novice, Mike Kalinsack, won the two-man race. He teamed up with Paul Baker as brakeman.[21]

The Lake Placid News interviewed a few of the CCC boys on racing in the February 23, 1936 paper. CCC member Frank Case said: "'Babyface' Bruce, brakeman and second cook at the camp, goes down with Mike Kalinsack to cool off after facing the cook stoves all day. The four–man team is piloted by none other than the mess sergeant, P. O. Baker. He quiets his nerves on the bob run after a busy day figuring out calories and vitamins. In his team are Whitey Kamm, the singing bobsledder, who thinks no more of his fast ride than in getting up in front of the boys and singing a love song. Right behind him comes the man known as 'Eggs' Lundy, the canteen steward, who goes down the bob run and eats egg sandwiches all day. He has been known to eat seven for lunch. A few rides down the run puts him in great shape for the grueling hours he spends opening beer bottles. Whitey and Chief Kennedy spend a hard day in the field just getting ready for the bob rides."

Boxing was very popular in Lake Placid. The Lake Placid News reported on July 28, 1933 that the Lake Placid Athletic Club was holding their annual boxing show at the Olympic Arena and CCC enrollees from seven surrounding camps were participating in the bouts. They were also holding wrestling matches. Some of the CCCers entered in the events were: Joe Sansome, Pete Kowalski, Bill Prendergast, Jerry Cicarell, Norm Aiken, and A. L. Kolaz (Goldsmith).

These Army officers were judges: Captain Waugh, Goldsmith; Captain John, Tupper Lake; Captain Miller, Fish Creek; and Lt. Brady, Paul Smiths.

In July 1934 another boxing tournament was held at the Lake Placid arena featuring boxers from six CCC camps and local towns. They competed for the Adirondacks Golden Gloves Championship. Some of the contestants were: Steve Archimbault (Lake Placid), Red Gilbert, Larry Griffin, Red Plumadore, Tony Angelo, Joe Bush, Jimmy Gardiner, and Jack Buehler Jr.[23]

Lake Placid was the site of many events celebrating the 50th anniversary of Conservation in New York. Camp S-71 competed against seven other CCC camps in a Field Day held at the Olympic Stadium that began on Thursday, September 12, 1935. Field events included 100-yard dash, shot put, sack race, 220-yard race, high jump, mile relay and tug of war. Swimming events were held at the Municipal Beach. In the afternoon baseball games were held at the Horse Show Grounds. On Friday the CCC members attended a dinner in the evening and provided entertainment for the guests. The next day President Roosevelt reviewed the groups of CCC enrollees, Game Protectors, fire tower observers, and Forest Rangers, dedicated the Whiteface Memorial Highway, and helped present awards.[24]

Education was an important part of the company program. Many enrollees took Syracuse College of Forestry correspondence classes. There was also a weekly course that taught the boys surveying and they applied these skills in their fieldwork.[25]

In 1937 the enrollees built the caretaker's headquarters in the Wilmington Notch state campsite. They also continued constructing and maintaining the following truck trails: McMaster Road (1 mi.), Plantation Roads (1.25 mi.), Saranac Lake to Placid (5.5 mi.), Connery Pond (3.2 mi.), Hurricane Mt. (.5 mi.), and Marcy (2.7 mi.).[26]

That same year the camp constructed dams used for recreation. The boys worked with Paul Smiths camp and constructed a concrete dam at South Meadows. They completed 60% of a log dam at Duck Hole. They also began work on an earth dam at Duck Hole Dike.[27]

In the summer of 1937 Captain Edward McGall permitted the Lake Placid Fish and Game Club to have

Lake Placid Camp activities.[22]

their supper and meeting at the camp. The Conservation Department personnel addressed the club and discussed their CCC work. This group would later build their clubhouse on the abandoned camp site.[28]

In September 1937 Captain Edward McGall received word that his camp was one of 22 camps in New York that were to close in October. Local officials tried to save the camp but were unsuccessful. Camp S-71 closed on October 10, 1937.

The Lake Placid News reported on May 6, 1938 in the article, "104 at Annual Meeting of the Fish & Game Club," that the Lake Placid Fish and Game Club asked the town board if they could take over one of the buildings and use it as a clubhouse. In June the Lake Placid News reported the club was almost done constructing a new 21' X 48' clubhouse and they were going to add a kitchen and living room for a caretaker's quarters. The July 15, 1938 Lake Placid News reported the club was raising money to pay for the construction of a building at the former CCC camp site and were also building an area for skeet shooting.

On May 18, 1940 Camp S-102 at Plattsburgh's Cumberland Bay State Park closed and the veterans of Company 2207-V moved to the Lake Placid Camp S-138. They spent the summer completing Marcy Dam, constructing a telephone line up Whiteface Mountain, and continuing work on the bobsled run.[29] On October 15 Company

2207-V was transferred to Paul Smiths.[30]

Camp S-138 rebuilt the telephone line from Lake Placid to the fire tower on Whiteface Mountain.[31] They also worked at the Olympic bobsled run.[32]

The log crib Marcy Dam that Paul Smiths camp began rebuilding in 1939, was completed in 1940 by S-138 of Lake Placid.[33] The camp also completed 50% of a 20' reinforced concrete bridge.

The men of S-138 worked till October 15, 1940 when the Lake Placid camp closed. The company moved to the Plattsburgh Barracks camp AF-1.

After the camp closed the buildings were removed. The only building on the camp site is the Lake Placid Fish and Game Clubhouse. The part where the CCC buildings stood is now a little league baseball field.

A camper is about to sign in at the caretaker's cabin at Wilmington Notch state campsite. The Lake Placid CCC enrollees constructed it in 1937. It has a stone masonry foundation and fireplace. Podskoch Collection

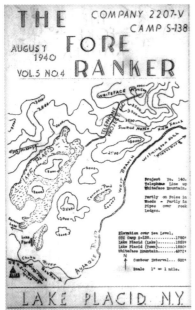

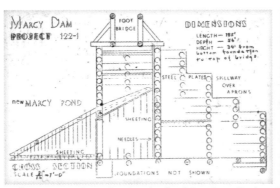

Left - Veterans from the Cumberland Bay State Park in Plattsburgh moved to the Lake Placid Camp. This June 1940 cover of their camp newspaper the Fore Ranker is a map showing the construction of the telephone line up Whiteface Mountain. Middle - Plans for the building of the Marcy Dam were in the June 1940 issue of the Lake Placid camp newspaper, The Fore Ranker. Right - This is the completed Marcy Dam the CCC enrollees constructed during the 1930s. DEC Archives

LEGACY

The CCC enrollees of the Lake Placid CCC camp built many of the nearby campsites that are used each year by thousands of campers.

Another campsite developed by the CCC is Meadow Brook State Park. It began in 1933 and the CCC expanded the park. The campsite is just four miles from downtown Lake Placid and offers 58 campsites with hot showers, flush toilets, picnic pavilions, and hiking trails. A camper is surrounded by huge white pines planted by the CCC over 75 years ago.

Marcy Pond is a popular camping area. It was created when the CCC built Marcy Dam in the 1930s. DEC Archives.

Left - The mess kitchen of the Lake Placid CCC Camp on the Old Military Road is the only remaining building. It is used as the clubhouse for the Lake Placid Fish & Game Club. Middle - One of the 58 campsites at Meadow Brook State Park on Route 86 in Raybrook, NY. Right - One of the original stone fireplaces built by the CCC during the 1930s at the Wilmington Notch State Park campsite. All courtesy of Podskoch Collection.

WORK ACCOMPLISHED BY CAMP S-71 & S-138*

PROJECT	1934	1935	1936	1937	1940	1941 S-138	TOTAL
Bridges, foot - number						1	1
Bridges, vehicle - number	12		1	1		1	15
Buildings, barns - number		1					1
Buildings, cabins - number		2	3				5
Buildings, garages - number		1					1
Cribbing (includes filling) - yd^3		1000				15	1015
Dams, earth-filled - yd^3		300					300
Dams, rock-filled - yd^3		750					750
Dams, excavations - yd^3		750					750
Dams, impounding & large diversions - number		2					2
Dams, recreational - number	1			2			3
Dwellings - number			1		1		2
Emergency work - man-days				87			87
Fences - rods			650		2		652
Field planting trees - ac.			20				20
Fine grading - yd^2		2135	800				2935
Fire breaks - mi.	0.5	1					1.5
Fire fighting - man-days	1937	240	95	18		624	2914
Fire hazard reduction (roadside & trailside) - mi.		1	6.3	3	1	279.7	291.5
Fire pre-suppression - man-days					200	442	893
Fireplaces - number		7	47		100		168
Forest stand improvement - ac.	136	110.8	225	234			705.8
General clean-up - ac.				15.5			15.5
Guard rails - rods		30			2		32
Improvements, misc. - number			5				5
Insect pest control - ac.		30	69	111			210
Lake, pond & reservoir site cleaning - ac.		25	2				27
Landscaping - ac.		1		3			4
Obliteration of dumps - man-days			105				105
Portals - number			1				1
Planting/moving trees & shrubs - man-days			35	17			52
Preparation/transportation of materials - man-days		574		4224			4798
Public campground development - ac.		2		4			6
Razing undesirable structures - man-days				4			4
Searching for missing persons - man-days			4				4
Seed collection, conifers - bushels		80					80
Seeding & sodding - ac.		3	0.2	0.5			3.7
Sewage & waste disposal systems - number		1			5	2	8
Sewage line - linear ft.		40					40
Shelters - number			5	1	10		16
Signs - number		1		34	86		121
Stream & lake improvement - yd^2	0.5						0.5
Structures, improvements - number	5	8			9	1	23
Structures, water-control - number					1		1
Surveys - man-days				843			843

*Numerical data from Conservation Reports

The Lake Placid Camp S-71 taken May 1935. The five barracks are in the background. In the front row is the camp bugler and there are three camp dogs. In the back row are the cooks in white followed by foresters, foremen, army officers, officials, and enrollees. Joan Reandeau and Glenda at Swiss Kitchen Restaurant in Tupper Lake

MEMORIES

Ralph Denno

While traveling through Tupper Lake on August 28, 2007, I stayed at Clarence and Francis Reandeau's home. I met them while writing about the Adirondack fire towers. Clarence worked as an observer on the Ampersand Mt. fire tower in 1956. The Reandeaus always invited me to stay with them when I needed a place to stay.

The next morning their son Dale and I went for breakfast at his cousins' Swiss Kitchen Restaurant in Tupper Lake. As we walked past the booths and counter I couldn't help but stop to look at the numerous historic photos on the wall. One of them caught my eye and I had to take a closer look. It was a large group photo of a CCC camp. On closer scrutiny it said: "C. C. C. Co. No. 257, Camp S-71, Lake Placid, N. Y. May 1935 Capt. Wm. E. Campbell." I wondered who had given the picture to the restaurant.

Then Dale introduced me to his cousins, Glenda and Julie who own and run the restaurant along with their brother Mike. I asked Glenda where she got the CCC photo.

"That was my grandfather's camp photo. His name was Ralph Denno Jr. If you'd like more information you could ask my mother, Joan. She is sitting in the last booth with some friends."

Dale and I walked over to the booth and he introduced me to Joan. I asked if her father told her anything about his CCC days.

"Dad didn't tell me much but he did say that he worked cutting brush and it was in Lake Placid that he met my mother, Betty Grady. She was a waitress at the Lake Placid Club.

"Dad also said he did some cooking in camp and when he got married he showed my mom how to cook."

I asked Joan to tell me about his early life.

"He was born in 1914 in Tupper Lake. His father, Ralph Sr., came from Ticonderoga to work at the Sunmount Veteran's Hospital. He married Leona Lalonde and they had five children, Ralph, Marian, Louis, Daisy, and Edith.

"My grandfather died young and my grandmother went to live with her parents. Dad's younger brothers and sisters were placed in foster homes. My dad had to quit school and work at farms to help his mother.

"I'm not sure how he found out about the CCC but it must have been in 1935 that he joined because I have his 1935 group picture."

I asked Joan if I could borrow the picture to copy it and she agreed.

"Dad had a good friend in camp, Gus Dandro. He was even Dad's best man in his wedding. I also have a picture of Mom and Dad at John Brown's Farm in Lake Placid. If I can find it you can use it, too.

"I don't think my dad came home on weekends because he spent his time in Lake Placid as he didn't have a real home."

Betty, Joan, and Ralph Denno at their home. Joan and Julie Reandeau

173

Why did your dad leave the CCC?

"He got married in June 1936 and they moved to Tupper Lake. Dad got a job at Benson Mines where he stayed during the week and came home on weekends. Later they bought a house on Dugal Road. I was their only child.

"After Benson Mines Dad worked for the Village of Tupper Lake. Then he collected scrap iron and antiques and had two buildings. Dad died in 1992.

"Dad's participation in the CCC had to help him. It gave him discipline and he was able to help his mother financially.

Francis Seymour & Walter A. Sprague

The September 1, 1977 Lake Placid News article, "CCC Left a Lasting Monument Here," includes interviews of former CCC men. It begins with William "Bill" Petty's comment on the northern Adirondacks where he was the regional DEC director in Ray Brook. Bill said, "The Civilian Conservation Corps left a lasting and valuable monument here and it was in campsites, dams, and trails."

Francis Seymour, a former CCC enrollee from Saranac Lake, said: "There were no jobs around at all—no work of any kind in the Saranac Lake area. My parents thought it would be the best thing for me. I was able to send something home each month to help them out. It was automatically taken out of my pay. I was happy to be off the streets and productive."

Seymour said he went to the North Elba Town Hall in 1936 and his group prepared to go to Idaho and spent a few weeks of indoctrination at the Lake Placid camp. He didn't want to leave the Adirondacks and was permitted to stay at the Lake Placid camp.

"I worked on the Scotch Pine program establishing plantations, built and maintained trails on Whiteface, helped build Marcy Dam, and fought blister rust and forest fires."

Like most CCC alumni Francis Seymour was in favor of reviving the CCC. "There are few changes that I would suggest since it was eminently successful then and it would be the same today."

Walter A. Sprague was another young man from Saranac Lake who joined the CCC. "I was 20 years old and had been working on road and power line clearing, driving truck, and as a carpenter at Camp Drum. Any work was hit or miss from one month to the next.

"I decided to sign up for the CCC with a friend, Graham Brown, since we both wanted to see the western part of the country. We had heard that many CCC camps were set up in Oregon, Washington, and California.

"I registered at the Harrietstown Town Hall late in September of 1937 and reported to the Lake Placid Camp. We both signed up for six months, which was the minimum period required. That was about the last time we saw each other. Once we were outfitted and equipped, we were loaded on separate trains and away we went to where we were needed.

"I ended up at Seaside, Oregon and my friend ended up farther north on the west coast working on a museum. It was beautiful country. The boys from the city, without a future or a hope and who had never seen the grandeur of the forests, rivers, and mountains, were suddenly our best men. They learned how valuable just sharing an experience could be. They had become part of something to be proud of and not just street drifters and derelicts banded together for survival.

"Our work was healthy outdoor construction. We built the Ecola and Saddle Mountain Parks both of which have survived to this day as points of interest in Oregon. We built the trails, roads, picnic grounds, fireplaces and when necessary, we fought forest fires. I was a truck driver since I had previous experience. Driving was considered an enviable job.

"The CCC trained men in a healthy, though Spartan atmosphere, and many of our best fighting men in World War II served in the CCC. I very much favor its revival."

CHAPTER 19
MINERVA

HISTORY

In the spring of 1935 Army officers inspected and approved the site for a CCC camp in Minerva in Essex County. They selected a spot a mile and a half N of Aden Lair on Rt. 28N where the Vanderwhacker River crosses the highway at the foot of Kay's Hill. It was approximately 10 mi. SE of Newcomb.

The April 25, 1935 Ausable Record-Post stated that the CCC camp would " . . . mean work for carpenters and woodsmen in nearby towns and then later lasting benefits to the state forest of their vicinity."

Camp S-107 Company 1267 was established as a forest fire control camp on June 31, 1935 in the town of Minerva in Essex Co.[1]

The camp newspaper, "The Kay's Hill Tower," listed the following camp administrators: Captain George H. Seitz, Jr., commanding officer, 1st Lt. A. Frambach, and 1st Lt. J. Hochstim. Second Lt. L. Bellavia was in charge of the Post Exchange.

The project superintendent was Chester J. Yops who was assisted by these men: A. Chenier, L. Sheehan, A. Talbot, R. Haskins, F. Gallagher, H. Gallagher, E. McNally, and J. Clifford.

Yops described in the camp newspaper what had been accomplished and what he hoped to do during the winter:

"Up to date we have partially completed several projects, namely a telephone line from Tahawus to Blue Ridge, a truck trail two miles long, several miles of fire breaks and some trailside and roadside fire hazard reduction, a forestry garage road and three foot trails: from Elk Lake up Dix Mountain, Lake Sanford to Bradley Pond, and Newcomb up Vanderwhacker Mountain.

"When the weather becomes severe that we are compelled to discontinue work on the projects, we will work on forest stand improvement, some further roadside forest fire reduction, and also general cleanup."

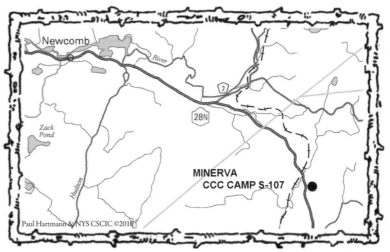

Paul Hartmann & NYS CSCIC ©2010

Cover of Minerva camp newspaper: "The Kay's Hill Tower." It got its name because it was at the foot of Kay's Hill. Vanderwhacker Mountain fire tower was nearby. Podskoch Collection

WORK ACCOMPLISHED BY CAMP S-107[2*]

PROJECT - 1935	TOTAL
Fire hazard reduction (roadside) - mi.	8.5
Fire hazard reduction (trailside) - mi.	9
Forest stand improvement - ac.	0.5
Surveys, linear - mi.	3.5
Surveys, other - man-days	36
Telephone line - mi.	10
Trails, foot - mi.	10.1
Trails, truck - mi.	2.75

*Numerical data from Conservation Reports

The largest accomplishment of Camp S-107 was the construction of a 2.7-mile truck trail through the Roosevelt Forest. The trail extended from the Minerva CCC camp on Rt. 28N to the Blue Ridge Road, also called Boreas Road (Co. Highway 26).

George J. Kelley was the Education Advisor. One of his jobs was the supervision of the camp newspaper called "The Kays Hill Tower." In the paper's first and only issue dated December 10, 1935, he stated his main duty was to develop a suitable education program as well as advising the enrollees as to what subjects they should take to help them get a job when they left the CCC. Kelley added he was also ready to help any enrollee in solving any of their problems.

Another news item in the camp newspaper stated Barracks Five was converted into a schoolhouse. Typing class was the most popular and many enrollees came in at all hours of the day to practice. Lt. Hochetin taught the Bookkeeping class. Another popular class was Photography which was taught by J. P. Britton, a camp enrollee.

There were other instructors appointed by Temporary Emergency Relief Administration (TERA), a program started in New York State in 1931. TERA provided projects for white-collar workers. They taught athletics, drama, music, etc.

The camp newspaper stated that on Sunday evenings an "Amateur Nite" was held. One Sunday featured a comedian and singers. The camp awarded prizes to the winning contestants.

The big news in the mess hall was the enrollees did not have to use mess kits for meals because the kitchen now had dishes. One man stated: "It makes the meal seem more like home."

The paper also listed the names of the 140 enroll-ees including their leaders and assistant leaders.

In December 1935 the Federal government lowered the number of CCC camp enrollees nationwide to 300,000 for the coming year. New York closed 12 camps, including Minerva.

Late in December 1935 Minerva Town Supervisor Francis Donnelly secured a unanimous resolution from the Essex County Board of Supervisors calling for the saving of the Minerva CCC camp. It stated the Minerva camp did valuable work in Minerva in the local forests. The camp helped the town economically because it employed 22 forestry workers in addition to the men who were enrollees. The resolution was sent to the War Department in Washington, DC.

Despite the pleas of town and county officials Camp S-107 was shut down on January 9, 1936.[3] The boys were then transferred to the nearby Newcomb and Indian Lake CCC camps.

It was sad for residents to see this 6-month-old camp with brand new buildings be abandoned. Many families and businesses depended on the camp for jobs and income. The state hired a watchman for the facility. Shortly after the closing men from the Newcomb CCC camp removed the buildings. Today there are no signs of the camp.

MEMORIES

Gerry Galusha

During my research I tried several times to locate the Minerva campsite. Martha Galusha of the Minerva Historical Society looked in their records without success. Then her husband Gerry said he thought he knew the location and offered to show me. In the summer of 2008 we drove up 28 N towards Newcomb to search for the site.

Gerry said: "I remember when I was a boy traveling with my dad delivering groceries on Route 28 N. I saw a bunch of guys on the left-hand side of the road waiting for the trucks to take them to work."

We drove towards Newcomb and searched the woods on the left side of Rt. 28 N near Kays Hill but found nothing to show that there was a camp there. Gerry mentioned that it might be on the right side instead because the roadway had been changed and the new road might have gone through the camp site.

We drove a little farther north and turned right on

The Minerva CCC camp was on the right side of old Rt. 28N. There was an old cellar hole that was part of the Old Kays' farm. Farther on the left was the dirt road the CCC enrollees improved that went two miles to the Blue Ridge Rd. Podskoch Collection

the old paved section of 28N by Kays Hill. The road came to an abrupt stop at a stream. On the left was the gate marking the start of the truck trail that Camp S-107 worked on in 1935. After searching all around we only found a cellar hole across from the trail entrance but no signs of a camp.

Charlie Kays

Then in the summer of 2009 I visited 93 year-old Charlie Kays at the North Creek Nursing Home. Charlie had shared a lot of stories about his years as fire tower observer (1960-62) on Vanderwhacker Mountain that I used in my fire tower book. I asked him if he knew where the CCC camp was: "It was built on state land by my grandfather's old farm on Kays Hill. Grandpa had horses, cows, and sheep on his 50-acre farm. Then the state took over his land when the lease ran out.

Charlie Kays in 2003 standing by his woodshed. He worked as an observer at the Vanderwhacker Mountain fire tower. He used his pack basket to carry supplies to the observer's cabin. The Minerva CCC camp was located on Charlie's grandparent's farm. Bill Brannon

"There was an old truck trail there and the CCC boys widened it and built culverts. At first residents used the old road as a short cut to the Boreas/Blue Ridge Road. Only horse and wagons used it.

"I remember some of the local guys who worked at the CCC camp. John and Frank Gallager from Boreas Road were LEMs (local experienced men). Fred Bruno also worked there. John Clifford from Olmsteadville was a foreman and Fred Bruneau was the mechanic. Arthur Lynn, James O'Connor, John Sheehan, and Bill Barnes were laborers.

"When they closed the camp in 1936 my uncle Bill Kays who lived in my grandmother's house near the camp was hired as caretaker for the empty CCC buildings. I was around 18 years old and I helped him on his day off by watching the camp. I just sat around or cleaned the buildings. In the winter I shoveled snow from the roofs. One time my uncle fell off the roof and broke his wrist.

"My grandparents' farmhouse is gone. Grandma moved across the road to the old schoolhouse building on the hill. It's still up there. The CCC camp was built on the left side of the road across the street from my grandmother's home. It was near the old farmhouse cellar hole that you and Gerry saw. There were around 15 buildings on the left side going north on the old Rt. 28 N. I remember the barracks and a kitchen/mess hall were across the road (old 28N) from my grandmother's house.

The CCC garage was on the right side along with my grandmother's house. Vanderwhacker Brook flowed by on the southern part of the camp. They pumped water out of the brook for showers.

"The buildings were up for about 3-4 years. Then one day a group of CCC boys from Newcomb came in the morning and began tearing the buildings down. They didn't sleep there but brought their lunch down every day. The buildings were built on posts in the ground."

This explained why I couldn't find any traces of buildings. There were no concrete foundations and the posts rotted.

Jack Sheehan

Helen Wagar, a newspaper writer from Queensbury, wrote the story, "CCC Camps Leave No Clues," in an August 28, 1997 issue of the North Creek Enterprise describing a trip she took with 86-year-old native Jack Sheehan to find the Minerva CCC camp.

"After jockeying up and down Route 28N, we pulled off on a side road to find the old white farmhouse that was the Kays' homestead in the 1930s. Using that as our compass point, Jack knew that we should travel south on 28N. Around a bend, he exclaimed, 'Here it is!'"

They came upon giant balsams that were about 60 years old. Helen and Jack got out of the car. "While Jack waited for me at the edge of the forest, I entered onto soft, thick, spongy moss that would put any modern carpet to shame.

"It is a unique spot, balsams as far as the eye can see, all about the same size; no underbrush and absolutely no vegetation.(except moss). Hushed and still, it was keeping its secrets...for there were no other clues to the past...only great balsams competing for space, reaching for the sky to prove that once, long ago, the hand of man had been here to plant them.

"Jack Sheehan was never a recruit in the CCC, but as a twenty-three year old in 1934, he worked at this camp as a laborer while it was being built, along with a group of other local boys.

"Many Minerva boys were hired to help build the camp. Jim Strohmeyer worked at the camp during his summer vacation in 1934 and performed such tasks as digging ditches for water and sewer lines, helping roofers and assisting a 'drill team.' These were the men who hand drilled rocks for blasting. He was paid 12 to 15 dollars a week.

"Being older, Jack Sheehan was paid 50 cents an hour for the grueling job of carrying 6-foot Balsam logs on his shoulders with a partner from the woods to the camp. 'It hurt at first, but then we became accustomed to it,' Jack said. The logs were used for foundations and corner posts. (Which explains why there are no foundation ruins at the site today.)

"'Everyone worked very hard,' continued Jack. 'There was no fooling around, nor were we allowed to speak to other boys or even our partners. We really looked forward to lunchtime when the constraints were off and the atmosphere became more light-hearted.'

"'Every job was performed by MAN power since there were few machines in those days. Men dug postholes and if they ran upon large rocks, they were hand drilled and dynamited. Then the fragments were also dug out by hand. The work day was from 8-5, one hour for lunch and you gave your best effort every minute of the day.' Jack said.

"He remembers there were 10-12 barracks stretching back from the road sloping down a gentle incline. There were other buildings but by the time they were built, Jack was gone from the job. When the young men of the CCC came to the camp they sometimes came to the Mt. View Hotel in Minerva for a night of dancing and Jack remembers talking to a few but the conversations are lost in time.

"The structure of the CCC was based loosely on the army. It was a civilian operation based on military ideology and some of the commanding officers were actually military personnel as was Edward Murphy, husband of Eloise Cronin, who was the officer in charge of the Minerva camp.

"Jack Sheehan passed away on July 15, 1997 just three days short of his 88th birthday."

Jim Strohmeyer

I was unsuccessful in finding any living member of the Minerva Camp but Shirley D. McNally, the Minerva Town Historian, sent me letters from the Minerva Historical Association files that described the Minerva CCC camp.

Jim Strohmeyer wrote a letter dated 9-14-1993 to the Minerva historian: "I worked on the construction of the CCC Camp in Minerva. The camp was located at the Kays Place between Minerva and Newcomb on the left side of the road (Rt.28N) going north. I worked there during summer vacation from high school. Here is a list of the jobs I had while I worked there: dug ditches for sewer lines, worked with roofers on the buildings, worked with the drill team hand drilling rocks for blasting. I think the pay was $12 or $15 a week for forty hours of work.

"Here is a list of some of the people from town who worked there: Arthur Lynn, John Sheehan, & William Butler from Minerva, James O'Connor from North Creek, and Bill Barnes from Olmsteadville. Army Captain Murphy was in charge of construction."

Chester Kowalski of Perth Amboy, NJ wrote in a letter dated September 3, 1987: "I was a member of Co. 1267 S-107 Minerva in 1935. I served from September 2, 1935 to December 1935. When the camp was disbanded half of us were sent to the camp at Newcomb and I went with the other half to the camp near Blue Mountain."

CHAPTER 20
NEWCOMB

HISTORY

Two CCC camps were established at the Huntington Wildlife Forest (HWF) in Newcomb, Essex Co. Camp P-69 existed from late June to mid-November in 1933, and Camp S-129 began in May, 1935 and closed at the end of December, 1941.

The forest is named after Archer and his wife Anna Huntington. Archer (1870-1955), a philanthropist, art patron, scholar, and poet. received his wealth from his stepfather Collis Huntington, founder of the Southern Pacific Railway. (Archer, born Archer Worsham, took his stepfather's name.)

In 1932 Archer and Anna Huntington, passionate lovers of wildlife, donated their 15,000-acre estate to the New York State College of Forestry (NYSCF), Syracuse (now called State University of New York/Environmental Science and Forestry, or ESF). The Huntingtons requested it be used "for investigation, experiment and research in relation to the habits, life histories, methods of propagation, and management of fish, birds, game, food, and fur-bearing animals and as a forest of wild life."

The forest, approximately seven miles long and 3-4 miles wide, is located in the towns of Newcomb and Long Lake. HWF, a private facility, contains several low mountains and lakes as well as the publicly accessible Goodnow Mountain (2,685').

Camp P-69 Company 270 was established on June 28, 1933.[1] Ray Masters in his book, The Huntington Wildlife Forest, states the boys, "... were housed in tents in the field behind Chase beach (Director's Residence area) The tents were on wooden platforms and included a cookhouse and several administration tents. This was a full-sized camp of about 200 men." In 1933 NYSCF used the CCC enrollees to improve Huntington Wildlife Forest.

Oscar Oja of NYSCF, who gave a talk to the Tupper Lake Rotary Club in the fall of 1940, stated the 1933 CCC camp developed roads through difficult terrain in

Paul Hartmann & NYS CSCIC ©2010

Above - A supervisor watches two enrollees digging and jack hammering for a truck trail through the rugged Huntington Forest in Newcomb. ESF Archives.
Left - Army tents housing around 200 young men near the shore of Rich Lake in the Huntington Wildlife Forest in 1933. The administrative tents, mess tent, and flagpole are at the left rear. ESF Archives

179

This was Newcomb camp S-129 in 1935. The sawmill on the left is operating and the wooden buildings are being completed with stacks of lumber on the side. ESF Archives. Camp S-129 is almost complete in the fall 1935 with its five barracks on the left side. Planks serve as a sidewalk to the mess hall on right. Rich Lake is across Rt. 28N. ESF Archives

the forest, and built telephone lines and a small dam creating a shallow body of water.

The camp closed on November 11, 1933 because of inadequate housing for the winter. Company 270 was moved to the newly-constructed Camp S-72 in Delmar.

Masters states: "In the summer of 1934, there was a side camp of 50 men (at Huntington) from Camp S-101 at Pack Forest in Warrensburg. They continued doing the same work as the 1933 camp: construction and maintenance work on roads and trails in the Huntington Wildlife Forest.

In the spring of 1935 Newcomb was again selected to have a CCC camp at Huntington. Captain W. A. Tooth began work on Camp S-129 on May 23, 1935.[2]

The Essex County Republican reported on July 12, 1935: "Newcomb has been enthused since June 1, over building the new CCC camp located there. Every available carpenter, electrician, plumber, and laborer in that vicinity is actually engaged in building CCC Camp S-129... about 75 per cent of the labor is recruited in Newcomb and vicinity. Many 'old timers' feel natural again to see the old hands as well as the youngsters enthused over building sixteen modern camp buildings."

On July 18, Captain Harold C. Holtz replaced Captain Tooth. Lt. Edmund C. Murphy arrived on August 5 with 12 men from Lake Placid Camp S-71 to prepare the camp site and pitch tents near Rich Lake since the wooden barracks were still under

construction. The tent camp was completed on August 9, 1935 and 178 men arrived. Captain Chester A. Lee took command on August 12.[3]

The Conservation Commission hired a superintendent, six foremen, a mechanic, and a blacksmith to supervise the work of the young men in the forest. Marilyn Cross in her book *Growing Up Strong* wrote that in November 1935 the men went on strike because they didn't like the food. The army discharged 35 men and sent them home. The remaining boys were willing to comply with the leaders and eat the food.

Newcomb Camp Superintendent W. J. Macaulay, a 1917 College of Forestry graduate and superintendent from 1935-38, wrote an article in the April 10, 1936 issue of *The Lake Placid News* stating that the camp's purpose was "to develop the Huntington Forest as a wild life sanctuary, to protect it from fire and other enemies of game."

The CCC constructed Arbutus road at the Huntington Wildlife Forest. ESF Archives. CCC boys are measuring the depth of one of the lakes in the Huntington Forest. One is lowering a rope through the ice while another uses a transit to measure the exact location on the lake. ESF Archives

Newcomb CCC Camp S-129 Activities from Schenectady District Civilian Conservation Corps Area Yearbook, 1937

Macaulay also said the main camp project was to build an 11-ft. wide truck trail to be used for fire protection and supervision. It began on Rt. 28N (two miles west of Newcomb in the town of Long Lake) and traveled five miles north to Catlin Lake. An earlier Newcomb CCC camp, P-69, had built 2.5 miles but parts had to be reconstructed by the new camp.

Camp S-129 also built a seven-mile telephone line that connected the ranger's quarters at Catlin Lake with the new ranger headquarters at Chase Point on Rich Lake. Another telephone project was a 2.5-mile line connecting the ranger headquarters with the commercial line on Rt. 28N.

The enrollees removed dead and fallen trees in a 100' strip two miles long along both sides of Rt. 28N that traveled through Huntington Forest. This improved the beauty of the forest and helped to prevent fires. They also removed fire hazards along the new truck trail by burning on site or cutting it into firewood for the camp.

Other projects done by the CCCs at the new rang-er headquarters were: a new icehouse and woodshed, stone walls, grading of the land, driveway and walkways, reconstructing and surfacing 0.25 mile of roadway, and thinning and pruning trees in the 20-acre headquarters parcel.

The boys took down abandoned fireplaces and chimneys from buildings that had fallen down along the trail to Catlin Lake Ranger Station, and did four miles of stream improvement along Vanderwacker Brook. The men surveyed three-miles of boundary lines, did three miles of maintenance on the Roosevelt Truck Trail, and constructed 28 miles of foot trails.

Macaulay then outlined the projects for 1936. He planned on having the men do forest stand improvement on 500 acres south of Rich Lake and north and south of Rt. 28N. They were to remove the alders, wolf trees (a large wide crown tree that prevents the growth of small trees), aspen (unless near water for beavers) and some hardwoods that suppressed the growth of conifers. They were also to began mapping Catlin Lake and Wolf Pond.

Capt. Ray N. Cooley took command of the camp on January 12, 1936. He was assisted by 1st Lt. E. W. Wooters.

Oja and his family lived in the new ranger home. During one cold January he wrote in his journal: "Postponed work on ice on account of difficulty of ice freezing as fast as cut was made . . . Three C. C. C. boys fell in lake on ice cutting job. Hole had drifted over (with snow) during the night. Boys were warmed up and taken to barracks none the worse for wetting."[4]

Camp-129 razed the buildings of the Minerva CCC Camp S-107 in 1938 that had been closed in January 1936.[5]

William Furlong directed the camp's education department. Students took forestry, First Aid, reading, writing, arithmetic, civics, and Early American history courses. They also took correspondence courses in: psychology, algebra, auto and diesel mechanics, English grammar, journalism, public speaking, bookkeeping, and business English.[6]

Furlong held weekly educational programs for the enrollees. He secured lecturers and entertainers from the community. The Essex County Republican dated May 22, 1936 stated that 150 men listened to Professor H. L. Salbitano, from Long Lake High School, give an entertaining talk about his trip to France and Italy.

The boys participated in the following activities during their free time: cards, billiards, ping-pong, basketball, baseball, softball, and recreation trips.[7]

The camp celebrated winning the CCC Field Day competition with a duck dinner that included pie and ice cream. The winning teams were served at a special table. After dinner the camp gathered in the recreation hall to listen to the camp orchestra to be serenaded by seven boys, who sang two camp songs. W. A. McConvey, District Education Advisor, presented a banner "Civilian Conservation Corps, District No. 1 Northern Zone, NY., Athletic Champions, 1935." Harvey Napier, senior foreman, accepted the banner for the camp. Captain Cooley then came to the platform and congratulated the boys. The boys then enjoyed watching three movies.[8]

The boys had a good relationship with the citizens of Newcomb. They attended local churches and the high school let the boys use their gym for basketball twice a week.[9]

In 1937 the young men built ski trails in Newcomb and near North Creek.[10]

During the hunting season The Lake Placid News reported in the November 26, 1937 issue that the Newcomb CCC camp helped the state police search for two lost hunters. The hunters got lost when their compass didn't work properly because of the abundance of iron ore in the ground. They pitched their pup tent near Goodnow Flow and waited there with the hope of being rescued. They fired shots over a four-day period to attract attention but to no avail. The night they used their last bullet a CCC boy heard it and found them in their tent. The rescuers carried the cold, exhausted, and hungry men on improvised stretchers back to town.

In the fall of 1938 the Essex County Republican reported in its September 12th issue that after three years of young men in Newcomb a company of WW I veterans arrived. The youths of Company 1297 led by Captain Cooley left for California. Captain Harry Myers assumed command of the camp and Macaulay continued as superintendent in charge of forestry projects. His staff included: foremen Hugh Bickford, T. R. Phillips, and Fred Burneau; junior forester H.D. Clark; junior civil engineer E. W. Jones; junior construction foremen Edward Dillon and S. R. Harran; semi-skilled worker Caleb Chase, and forestry clerk Leslie Smith.

The August 4, 1938 issue of The Ticonderoga Sentinel described some of the camp's accomplishments. They constructed a 14-mile telephone line from Long Lake to Shattuck Clearing and a branch line to the Kempshall fire tower, 25 miles of three-foot wide boundary trails, 25 miles of interior trails in the Huntington Forest, log boathouses with beach improvement. They also did forest stand improvement by pruning and thinning the white pine plantations.

Camp S-129 continued working in the Huntington Forest and "the Finch-Pryn Experimental Forest of the U. S. Forest Service doing truck trail construction work and forest stand improvement.[11] In addition the men performed a large amount of work on projects in recreational development and forest fire control. Two new ranger cabins were constructed—one at Shattuck Clearing and one near Minerva. They also built a suspension bridge over Moose Creek at Shattuck Clearing.

The Ticonderoga Sentinnel dated October 20, 1938 reported Camp S-129 also traveled outside the area to fight a fire near Brant Lake when 80 men from the Newcomb camp fought a fire that destroyed 16-acres.

By 1940 Camp S-129 had completed construction of four bridges. The longest was 53' using steel I-beams. The

Above - Workers built scaffolds and partitions for construction of the concrete dam on Military Lake. Pumps are also being used. ESF Archives. Left - The CCC Camp S-129 site is now just an empty field along Rt. 28 N. There is a sawmill built by ESF in the back. Podskoch Collection

others used log stringer construction: one measured 25' and the other two were 13.'[12]

A side camp built the observer's cabin on Owl's Head Mountain in 1941. Another group of men finished building the caretaker's cabin and other facilities at Lake Durant.[13]

Camp S-129 closed on December 31, 1941. Ray Masters states that the boys from the Paul Smith CCC camp completed the unfinished projects. "The abandoned camp was maintained for a few years for some possible war-time use. Late in the summer of 1941, for example, ESF granted the Army use of the open fields in the forest for overnight encampments in connection with training maneuvers. Some of the buildings became ESF property, but most were torn down. One building was used as a shop and maintenance center for a few years until the Huntington's Stone Garage, an old building in the Huntington Forest, was remodeled. Then the garage in the CCC building was removed."[14]

MEMORIES

Walter J. Macaulay

Barbara M. Jennings, daughter of Walter K. Macau-

ley who had been the superintendent of the Newcomb CCC camp, collected her father's life stories and published them in "Recollections" and "All That I Remember." He wrote these before he moved to Long Lake with Barbara's stepmother, Alice, in 1984. Then in 1987 both moved to the Masonic Home in Utica.

The following are summaries and excerpts from Walter Macauley's memoirs:

Walter was born in 1894. He grew up and was educated in Lansingburgh, a section of Troy, NY. He was an industrious boy. At age 11 he worked on many of the farms picking vegetables and doing chores at a dairy farm. During the winters he delivered newspapers and even helped deliver milk. He'd meet the milkman at 5 am and help with deliveries. "In those days people would leave a container on their steps. I would pick the container up, take it to the wagon where the milkman, using a dipper, took milk from a large can and I would return the filled container to the house." Then the milkman dropped him off at school. Sometimes he was late for school and got into trouble with the principal.

After Walter's junior year in high school, he quit and got a job at the Universal Brush Co. where he was paid for piecework. His job was filling the holes with bristles that came from hogs raised in China. He worked from 7 am to 5 pm during the week and on Saturdays from 7 am to noon. His pay ranged from 12-15 dollars a week.

The next year he returned for his senior year. Walter said he did well in school. He also took on a job working at a cigar factory where he stripped leaves of tobacco from the stems.

He graduated high school in 1913 and was accepted to the New York State College of Forestry in Syracuse.

"During my junior year at Syracuse, the superintendent of Timber Preservation Division C.

Walter K. Macauley, former Superintendent of Newcomb CCC camp (1935-36), at a CCC reunion in Lake Placid. Chris Blumberg

WORK ACCOMPLISHED BY CAMP S-129*

PROJECT	1935	1936	1937	1938	1939	1940	1941	TOTAL
Bathhouses - number			1			2		3
Beach improvement - mi.		2						2
Bridges, foot & horse - number		22		1	5	1		29
Bridges, vehicle - number		1	1		2	4	2	10
Buildings, other - number		6		1	11	1	1	20
Dams - number							1	1
Dwellings - number				1		1	1	3
Emergency work - man-days			221				161	382
Experimental plots - number					2	90		92
Fences - rods						182		182
Field planting trees - ac.			20					20
Fire breaks - mi.		3.2	3					6.2
Fire fighting - man-days		10		194	291	73	580	1148
Fire hazard reduction (roadside & trailside) - mi.		5				12.8		17.8
Fire hazard reduction (roadside) - ac.					10		2.3	12.3
Fire hazard reduction, other - ac.			14	137	18	121	75	365
Fire pre-supression - man-days					255	472	370	1097
Food & cover planting - ac.						12	1	13
Forest stand improvement - ac.		105	215	217	157	106	88	888
Improvements, misc. - number			5					5
Insect pest control - ac.			220	350	710			1280
Landscaping - ac.		5	1.5	15		1	1	23.5
Latrines & toilets - number			1			2		3
Marking boundaries - mi.		7.5	21					28.5
Mosquito control - ac.					3			3
Museums - number						1		1
Overnight cabins - number			3					3
Parking areas - yd²							2500	2500
Pipe or tile line - linear ft.			320					320
Portals - number		1						1
Power line - mi.						1		1
Razing undesirable structures - man-days		3	1904	853		725	2379	5864
Reconaissance & investigation - man-days			27	163		393	269	852
Reservoirs - number							2	2
Sewage & waste disposal systems - number					2	1		3
Shelters - number					2	1		3
Signs & markers - number						181	17	198
Stone walls - rods		1						1
Stream development - mi.		4.4						4.4
Surveys - man-days		123	277	923			99	1422
Table-bench combination - number						100		100
Telephone line - mi.		22.5		2	3		3	30.5
Trails, maintained Roosevelt Forest Trail - mi.					2.75			2.75
Trails, truck - mi.	1.5	4.2	2	1 (6.6 total corrected)	2.2	1.7	0.2	10.7
Tree & plant disease control - ac.		200	275	835				1310
Walks - linear ft.						60		60
Water supply systems - number				2	1	2	1	6
Wildlife activities, other - man-days					666	722		1388

*Numerical data from Conservation Reports

B. & Q. Railroad spoke at the college. He offered me a job during the summer at the plant. Later he sent me a railroad pass to go to Galesburg, Illinois. My job was checking ties and timbers as they were being loaded, before going to the pressurized tank for treatment."

This was one of the many jobs he had that helped pay for his college. During his last two years he played in a semi-pro basketball league in and around Central NY. He received $15 a game.

After graduation in 1917 he enlisted in the Army and entered WWI in an engineer regiment. After the war in 1919 he went back to work with C. B. & Q. Railroad for six months.

In September 1923 he worked as superintendent constructing the American Legion Camp at Tupper Lake. He said, "I went up there and found that I had to walk in five miles from Horseshoe Railroad Station to the camp over a tote road. We built a dam for a water supply, a convalescent hospital, and several other buildings. During the winter all the construction material had to be carried from Rock Island Bay."

Walter then worked near Sherill doing concrete road construction work for the Corbett Co. In the fall of 1926 he supervised the construction of abutments for a bridge over the Indian River. He also hauled steel from North Creek to the bridge site.

During the fall and winter of 1927 and 1928 he supervised the clearing of land near New Milford, CT for Candlewood Lake. He also supervised the construction of several retaining dams.

He came back to the Adirondacks and during the fall of 1928 and spring 1929 he and a friend had a contract to remove and burn about 5,000 trees and stumps. From 1930 to 1934 he did construction work in Munnsville, Verona, Lafayette, and Sherrill.

"In the fall of 1934 I went to Albany and interviewed the Director of Lands and Forests, NYS Conservation Department for a job with the C. C. C. program. At that time I was a Republican but did not advertise it as I did not think it mattered. I was not given much encouragement as to the appointment.

"Later I approached Albert Egan, the local postmaster for any leads. Politics at no time was mentioned. I made an appointment with Charles Donnelly, the Utica postmaster, and also Oneida County Democratic Chairman. We went down to see him and he called the office of the Conservation Commission in Albany. He told them he wanted Macauley to be given an appointment in the C. C. C. organization."

When nothing happened Walter again visited Donnelly who called Albany and told the Conservation Department that he wanted me appointed at once. About two days later Walter received word to report to the District Forester in Norwich. Walter was assigned to the DeRyters CCC camp on January 1, 1935.

"In June I was transferred to Newcomb, NY to take charge of the new camp being built in the Huntington Forest. At that time Captain Hill from Binghamton had charge of the inventory part, dorms, non-working days, feeding, recreation, etc."

As superintendent he was in charge of the foremen who supervised the work. "The work hours for five days a week were 8 to 4. Each camp had a work program prepared by the Albany Office, CCC, and Conservation Department. The Newcomb camp had some programs furnished by the NYS College of Forestry in Syracuse.

"One of the first jobs assigned to the camp was a telephone line from Long Lake to Shattuck Clearing. It followed the Long Lake Placid Trail. Poles were brought near Cherry Valley and rafted along Long Lake. When landed, horses towed the poles along and also rolls of wire. A scow was rented from Harry Bridges for moving material down the lake. The camp had a 75 hp engine.

"We built roads in the (Huntington) Forest area, trails to Mt. Marcy and Elk Mt., cabins, and work on several state camps. A side camp was established at Shattuck Clearing providing a ranger cabin and two suspension bridges. Material for Shattuck Clearing was moved by scow from Long Lake to Harper's Landing then hauled by team to Shattuck. Two bridges were built in the area for Huntington on the Northeast Forest program.

"Rangers' cabins were built near the Roosevelt Memorial Stone, Kempshall Mt., and Owls Head. The house occupied by Oja, the caretaker, was built by the CCC as one of the first jobs.

"A survey of the Huntington Forest was made in 1935 and 1936 by a foreman who was a graduate Civil Engineer from Syracuse University. I do not know what became of the survey.

"The work organizations had two stake-body trucks, three dump trucks, and one pick-up.

"One thing that helped the Newcomb Town and the State was the discovery of an immense hill of almost pure sand in the NE Tract. A recent look at the area showed that thousands of tons of sand had been discovered.

"During 1935-36, the enrollees worked under State supervision on the blister rust program in the area close to Minerva.

"Water for the camp was pumped from Rich Lake. At first the camp used coal-burning stoves for heat, but after 1936, it was turned to wood-burning.

"Sometime after 1935, I registered as a Democrat, for without knowing just what my politics were, people in that party went out of their way to help me. In 1938 I was appointed the supervising inspector of CCC Camps operated by the Conservation Department in recognition of my work at Newcomb.

"I remained in that position until the closing of all CCC Camps on July 1, 1942, and received several letters of commendation."

"While working for the CCC from 1935-1942 politics was not mentioned. I was later told that if I changed my politics, I could be appointed to a District Ranger job when the CCC closed. I said, 'No.' The Democratic Party had been good to me."

In 1943 Walter took a position at Griffiss Air Force Base in Rome where he worked as Ground Safety Director till he retired in 1962.

Barbara Jennings wrote that her family stayed many summers in Newcomb where her father was stationed. "We made many friends and I feel great attachment to the beautiful area. The CCC program was unique and beneficial, not only to the young men who participated, but also to the areas they served."

In 1985 she and her father attended a CCC reunion in Lake Placid. Barbara stated: "The enthusiasm at the (CCC) reunion was heartwarming and one of the men said: 'It made a man out of me.'"

Marvin Bissell

Marvin Bissell, owner of Bissell's General Store in Newcomb, is a wealth of information on the people and history of Newcomb. He sent me these newspaper clippings on the CCC camp in Newcomb.

"The first white settler in Newcomb was John Chandler. By an odd coincidence the CCC tent camp was established on the very land Chandler first cleared, the so-called Old Chase Farm.

"One of the foremen at the CCC camp was Caleb Chase, the grandson of Caleb Chase who was one of the early settlers of Newcomb. Caleb and his brother Daniel originally came from New Hampshire. Caleb was a boat-builder. Daniel had a son Washington who owned the drug store and post office.

"William H. Furlong was the education advisor. He organized a job training program and did counseling for the veterans. He also organized recreation activities, lectures by guest speakers, and local entertainment. Furlong was praised for his cooperation with the local church and school.

"In a Ticonderoga Sentinel article dated August 4, 1938 it stated that the CCC camp was composed of war veterans but '...for the past three years youth of the CCC have been developing a magnificent wildlife sanctuary on land owned in part by Syracuse University. The veterans will take over the work of protecting beautiful Huntington Forest from fire, and will construct truck and foot trails, bridges and other facilities. In their daily life of physical work and simple living, the veterans will resemble the pioneers who many years ago settled this mountain town and put the mark of civilization upon its hills.

"The Junior Co. 1297, scores of members of which are well known in this town and its environs, has been transferred to California for forestry work out there. Company had been at work in the woods here since November 1935. During most of this period the company was commanded by Capt. Ray Cooley. The veteran company will be commanded by Capt. Harry Myers, Coast Artillery Reserve...

"A telephone line has been constructed from Long Lake to Shattuck Clearing. A branch of this line goes to the fire watchtower on Kempshall Mountain. The line is 14 miles long. Twenty-five miles of boundary line and twenty-five miles of interior trails have been constructed in the Huntington Forest. Those trails are three feet wide, and where they pass over water are provided with footbridges. Log boathouses have been built and beaches improved. Rich Lake is 400 feet away from the CCC camp site. Forest stand improvement, consisting of pruning, thinning of white pine plantations, removal of all alders wolf trees, where such removal would aid the growth of softwoods, has been accomplished on a great expanse of forest.

"W. J. Macauley is work superintendent of the project. His foremen are: T. R. Phillips, Hugh Bickford, Joseph Dogherty, and Fred Bruneau. The technical staff includes H. D. Clark, junior forester; E. W. Jones, junior civil engineer; Edward Dillon, junior construction foreman; S. F. Harran, junior construction foreman; Caleb Chase, semi-skilled worker, and Leslie Smith, forestry clerk.

"The project for the coming year includes two suspension steel foot bridges, four long bridges, two steel bridges for vehicles, one new garage on the Havaeran tract in the forest, two ranger cabins, six miles of telephone lines, three waterholes for fire protection in Roosevelt Forest, two truck trails, maintenance of three truck trails, construction of 35 miles of foot trails, twelve miles of ski trails, 225 acres of forest stand improvement, fire hazard reduction on fourteen miles of roadside, and on 50 acres in the forest; blister rust eradication work on 500 acres of landscaping, three miles of stream development, 500 man-days on wild game protection, and 350 man-days on game investigation."

Marvin also told me: "The CCC men were good most of the time but one time I think it was two or three that vandalized the cemetery. They were arrested and probably kicked out of the CCC.

"George Shaughnessy said that when he was fire observer on Goodnow Mt., he went to get a haircut in Newcomb. There were some CCC men waiting when he went in. When the barber saw him he said: "There is the man who will keep an eye on you fellows from the fire tower.'

"When George came down off the mountain that night he found his tires slashed. He figured it was the CCC boys who thought he was spying on them from the tower and getting them in trouble."

George Fennessey

On August 23, 2007 I visited George Fennessey at the Newcomb Town Hall and he told me about growing up in Newcomb and his experiences at the Newcomb CCC camp:

"I was born here in Newcomb on November 12, 1926. When I got older I worked as a guide at the Tahawus Club. Then I worked at National Lead as an operating engineer. I drove dozers and loaders.

"When I was seven years old in 1933 I remember seeing Army tents in the fields near the beach on Lake Harris. It was Camp P-69 that was a temporary CCC camp that closed when winter came. Then the field was empty for two years. On August 9, 1935 the CCC camp was back and the men lived in tents. Then they built the wooden buildings about a quarter of a mile up Rt. 28N and across the road. I went there and sold the men the newspaper "Grit." The paper sold for five cents and I got two cents profit. With the profits I bought my first balloon tire bike for $7.50 from Montgomery Ward catalog.

"I got to know the guys and they invited me to come on Saturday nights and have dinner and watch movies with them in the rec hall. Sometimes I was the only town person but sometimes a few people from town came, too. They had pool tables in the rec hall.

"They built a lot of roads and trails through Huntington Forest. I don't remember seeing any bulldozers. They had a lot of Army trucks. They pulled out the gooseberry bushes with grub hooks.

"The camp hired some local men who worked as foremen supervising the workers. Edward Dillon was a foreman. He had a store and also worked at the camp. He helped build roads and trails. They built the trail to Catlin Lake and the trails where the Interpretive Center is. They also built the road to Goodnow Pond.

"The CCC built the steel bridge that goes into Archer Huntington's place.

"The CCC guys cut a lot of wood to keep warm. The camp buildings didn't have any insulation.

"Another foreman was Floyd O'Donnell. Each day he took men out and fixed trails. Later he worked for National Lead Co. He had four kids. Then Floyd moved to New Jersey.

"Clarence J. Chase was a guide and an Adirondack boatbuilder. He was a great fishing guide for the Lake Harris House. The hotel was always full during the summer and fall for hunting. Chase was an assistant leader at the CCC camp.

George Fennessey at the Newcomb Town Hall holding a picture of the Newcomb CCC enrollees in 1937. He reminisced about selling the national newspaper "Grit," to the men and attending camp movies. Podskoch   Collection

"One of the local boys, Noah LaCasse, was a member of the Newcomb camp. Later he worked at the Tahawus Club and for the town.

"For recreation the boys came to the old school and played basketball. When the weather got better they played baseball on the town field that was four miles from camp.

"The CCC camp closed in 1941. The buildings were vacant for a long time. Then the college took them over. Later the college built a sawmill on the camp site.

"I really enjoyed visiting the camp when I was young. The CCC guys were very nice."

Gordon Taylor

On July 4, 2009 I visited Gordon Taylor of Cranberry Lake. His wife, Nina , helped me with the history of the fire towers because her father, "Mose" La Fountain, had been the District Forest Ranger in Cranberry Lake. I asked Gordon if he knew anything about the CCC. He responded:

"I think it was 1947 or 48 that Professor Delavon from ESF (College of Environmental Science and Forestry) wanted workers to go to the Huntington Forest in Newcomb and tear down the old CCC buildings. He wanted us to bring the lumber to the Cranberry Lake Biological Station by Sucker Brook where he taught. We drove down from Cranberry Lake and began tearing the CCC buildings down. We stayed at the Santanoni Lodge in and Professor Delavon cooked for us. We loaded the lumber in trucks and drove to Cranberry Lake.

"When we got to the lake we put the lumber on a barge and took it to the Biological Station. The professor hired a couple carpenters to construct a building. The school had a beautiful boat and it carried myself and the other laborers: Bob McKenny, Fred Smith, and Ed McChesney to the work site. We used a lot of the CCC lumber to build a long building. It had a room for teachers and a meeting room with a nice stone fireplace that was built by a local mason. We stayed there for a week and slept in a cottage.

"Al Snyder was in the Benson Mines CCC camp. He was a brute of a man and was a good boxer in camp. Later he worked for Professor Delavon at the biological station. He was his righthand man."

Ted Phillips

While Ray Masters was working on his book about Huntington Forest, Ted Phillips, a former employee at Huntington Forest sent Ray a letter with information about the Newcomb CCC camp:

"The first CCC camp, 1933, was in the field back from Chase Beach. Platforms were built for the tents. The Administration tents were along the road leading to where the log cabin is, and above Chase spring. The kitchen was along the edge of the woods, to the east of the road. This was a full strength camp (200 or more enrollees). The Army camp commander was Captain Lonnie Field, of the Field Artillery.

"Road construction ended near the Huntington Reservation's north line and had come to the Arbutus Lake-Long Pond trail.

"Some (horse) teams were used that first summer and they were stabled a short distance up the stream from the start of the road. Billie Cosgrove was the hostler and he had a room just west of the stable. The CCC supplied the food and he did his own cooking.

"The next summer, 1934, there was a side camp of 50 men from the full strength camp on the Pack Forest in Warrensburg. They used some of the tent platforms that were built in 1933.Grant Beswick was foreman, with one other foreman. Grant had worked for Cliff Foster on the Pack Forest I believe he built the sawmill that was mounted on a long bed truck. The progress on the truck trail took it to near Long Pond Landing.

"The home near the stone garage was torn down by the CCC, and the new house was built by them in 1940."

CHAPTER 21
PAUL SMITHS

Above, Left - Army officers and civilians pose in front of workers constructing the wooden buildings for the Paul Smiths camp in the fall of 1933. NYS Archives. Above, Right - An enrollee at Paul Smiths is painting the street sign 42nd Street and Broadway to make the young men feel more at home in the Adirondack wilderness. NYS Archives

HISTORY

On April 14, 1933 Company 220 was established at Fort Hancock, NJ under Capt. Willard W. Scott's command. An advanced cadre of 30 men led by First Lieutenant Jasper E. Brady Jr. left Fort Hancock on May 28 and arrived by train at Lake Clear Junction on Sunday, May 29. They helped set up camp S-60 (No. 12) at Paul Smiths by erecting tents and did temporary construction work of the camp.[1]

The camp was called" Barnum Pond" because the pond was just north of the camp. S-60 was located approximately two miles north of Paul Smith's College on the east side of Rt. 30. Phelps Smith, the son of hotel owner Paul Smith, owned the land where the camp was established. The men were proud of the 20-ft. well they dug and lined with rocks and cement.[2]

On June 5 the remaining 169 men arrived with their commander, Captain William M. Carter assisted by 1st Lts. J. E. Brady and C. E. Woodruff of the 26th Infantry. On July 15 thirty-three Franklin County young men arrived and were enrolled.[3]

On June 8 Conservation Commissioner Osborne and other state officials inspected the camp. Approximately

200 enrollees lived in large hospital tents that had wood flooring. Each tent housed 16 men who slept on cots. The camp had electric lights, showers with hot and cold water with a cement floor and a screened infirmary. The men ate in a wooden screened mess hall and the kitchen was unique in that it had a refrigerator from Phelps Smith. Osborne had lunch with the workers. Then he emphasized the importance of their work in reforestation and preserving the natural resources.[4]

The enrollees came from many walks of life. The Barnum Pond camp had a young unemployed barber who became a hero because he was the only one who could give a decent haircut. He set up his barber chair at the corner of Broadway and 42nd Street. The men placed improvised street signs on the roads in the tent colony. Many of the men came from the cities and used familiar street names to make them feel at home. There was a licensed pharmacist, aviator, and Cornell graduate of civil engineering.[5]

The 1933 Conservation Report stated the camp S-60s main task was to improve the forest fire protection in that area. Superintendent C. A. Mattison and his foremen directed the enrollees in constructing fire lines along highways, building trails, reconditioning 'fire' roads, removing slash and flammable material along highways, reconstructing telephone lines, and most important, the suppression of forest fires.

The boys got their baptism of fire a few days after arriving in camp. They were called out to fight a fire about 10 miles away. Since the camp had a limited supply of trucks

Clockwise - Jack Corl on his way to the lavatory at Paul Smiths CCC camp during the 1933-34 winter. Camp S-60 enrollees clearing the forest of dead trees in the winter 1933-34. Paul Smiths enrollees having fun after work tossing another enrollee using an Army blanket. CCC enrollees joined local residents and vacationers swimming in nearby Barnum Pond. All courtesy Jim Corl

the boys who didn't have a ride showed their enthusiasm by walking and running to fight the fire.[6]

New York Sun reporter, Malcomb Johnson, traveled to Barnum Pond in July 1933 and described camp life. "It is 6 am, the beginning of the work day... Three sharp blasts from the whistle, and the camp springs to life. The recruits roll out of their army cots, rub the sleep from their eyes and snap into the routine for the day. Dressing quickly, they pile out of their tents—16 boys from each tent—into the gray, misty light of early morning in the mountains.

"They dash for the water pumps and plunge their faces into the clear cold water. Freshened and on the alert now they return to their tents and begin 'policing up,' making their beds, rolling up the tent flaps to give their quarters the benefit of the crisp mountain air. They do their work thoroughly, leaving the quarters neat and clean. The army officers must find nothing amiss when they make their inspection during the day.

"Besides, there is a keen rivalry among the groups occupying the various tents. The occupants keeping the neatest and cleanest tent over a period of a week are rewarded. They get a few extra privileges. Delinquents get demerits and enough black marks against them means privileges revoked.

"Seven am, another blast of the army officer's whistle. The men line up for roll call. All present and accounted for. Then sick call. Anyone reporting sick today? No, not one.

"At 7:15 there is a brief period of setting up exercises, just to limber the boys up for the day's work in the woods and in camp.

"At 7:30 they fall in for breakfast, and a whopping breakfast it is: a heaping plate of scrambled eggs, just off the fire, crisp bacon, fried potatoes, cereal with fresh milk, and plenty of piping hot coffee, good and strong.

"By eight o'clock the men have shouldered their picks and shovels and other forestry tools and tramped off to the woods for the day's work, accompanied by the foremen of the State Conservation Department, under whose direction they work. Those detailed to camp duty get busy cleaning the streets, chopping firewood and miscellaneous duties.

"With a rest period of 10 minutes each working an hour in the woods the men work until noon, when they return to camp for lunch. They go back to the forest at 1 pm and work until 5.

"Returning to camp, their time being their own now, some of the boys make a bee line for their bathing suits and plunge into the cool waters of Barnum Pond, nearby. Others get busy with their washing, using the old fashioned rubbing board for cleaning their clothes. Still others just rest and swap yarns.

"After supper, at six o'clock, they go in for an evening's diversion. The boxing gloves are produced and two lads square off for several rounds in an improvised ring, surrounded by a rooting audience.

"Some of the recruits have radios in their tents. They bought them with money pooled from the $5 each of the them receive from his pay each month. It seems a little strange, here in the heart of the Adirondacks, in wild country, to hear the crooning voice of a Broadway nightclub entertainer and the popular music of a swanky New York hotel orchestra.

"The lights go out at 10 pm, the recruits retiring

Clockwise from Top, Left - The Army hired local men to build the barracks and other wooden buildings. Workers are framing the structures. NYS Archives. These enrollees were happy to move from tents into warmer barracks. Lori Lepine. A partial map of the Paul Smiths Hotel property and the location of the CCC camp S-60. Saranac Lake Library Adirondack Research Center Archives. Snow came to the Adirondacks in October 1933 and enrollees continued to live in Army tents while barracks were being built. Jim Corl. These are the new wooden buildings at the Paul Smiths CCC camp during the winter 1933-34. The flagpole is in front where the enrollees gathered in the morning and evening for the raising and lowering of the flag. Jim Corl

for a good night sleep in preparation for the next day's work. Thus ends a typical day in one of the conservation camps in the Adirondacks."[7]

On June 9 one hundred-fifty enrollees went out to fight six fires: four at Fern Lake north of Ausable Forks, a fire between Keene Valley and Keene, and one three miles north of Barnum Pond.[8]

In Saranac Lake a committee was formed in July, 1933 to develop entertainment for the six northern district CCC camps. Since funds were lacking for programs heads of churches and civic organizations were to seek loans or donations of items such as pianos, radios, books, magazines, and athletic equipment. The committee hoped to plan concerts, baseball games, boxing matches, lectures, movies, and religious services. They decided to start programs at Barnum Pond and then expand to the other camps.[9]

In August 1933 Superintendent C. W. Mattison found Mountain Pond strewn with white and spruce pine logs from windfalls and early logging operations. He decided to clean up the pond and convert the wasted logs into useful boards for state use. His New York City boys enjoyed being Adirondack lumberjacks. They used a boom to hold the logs together and towed the logs to the chute they built on the shore. The city boys got quite adept wearing calked lumberjack shoes and rode the logs. These young loggers

didn't mind occasionally falling into the refreshing water on the hot summer days. They also took some logs to build a bridge on the nearby truck trail.[10]

As winter approached administrators of S-60 were proud of the enrollees accomplishments. They planted 310,000 trees, constructed 4.5 miles of truck roads, cleared five miles of fire lines, and removed 515 logs from a pond.[11]

In early October CCC National Director, Robert Fechner, visited Barnum Pond and the other northern Adirondack CCC camps. He was pleased with their progress in building winter quarters for the men.[12]

On October 15 the camp battled its worst fire on Jenkins Mountain. It started on the first day of hunting season and it took the boys several days to get it under control. Even though it snowed several underground fires were reported in December.[13]

Snow came to the Adirondacks in late October forcing Captain Carter to move some of the enrollees from their reforestation work and help the carpenters finish the buildings. On October 26 some men moved from their tents to a completed barracks. These men were happy to be in warmer quarters.[14]

In the spring 1934 the enrollees were busy beginning the development of a state campsite at Meacham Lake,

191

Counter-clockwise from Right - During the winter 1933-34 Camp S-60 had a dog sled team for recreation and help transporting materials. Captain Herman Eckart and an unidentified officer on the left in front of the camp circa 1933-34. Both courtesy Jim Corl. Paul Smiths CCC camp group picture in October 1934. Paul Benoit & Judy Hitchcock. A panoramic view of the Paul Smiths camp S-60 in October 1934. Walter Stahl. Paul Smiths CCC camp firefighting crew taking a break for a photo at the Bay Pond fire in 1934. Joanne Petty Manning

C.C.C. CO. NO. 220-CAMP 12-N.Y. OCT. 1934, PAUL SMITH'S, N.Y., CAPT. *Charles P Eckart*, COM'D'G.

C.C.C. CO. NO. 220-CAMP 12-N.Y. OCT. 1934, PAUL SMITH'S, N.Y., CAPT. *Charles P Eckart* COM'D'G.

Courtesy of Walter Stahl

approximately six miles north of Paul Smiths on Rt. 30. A. R. Fuller of Malone first opened a modest building on Meacham Lake for sportsmen. The Meacham Hotel Company purchased the building and added more land. Then Rockefellers purchased it. They catered to the well to do families and some built cottages along the lake. It was a favorite destination and hundreds of tourists from the eastern US and was noted for its excellent trout fishing and hunting. Gradually the trout population decreased and the hotel lost customers. Rockefellers sold the land to Johnston and Gould in 1929, who formed the Lake Meacham Lumber and began logging the property. In 1930 they sold the 7,000-acre tract to the state. The enrollees began dismantling the remaining 25 hotel structures. The young men began clearing the underbrush for the new campsite began along the northwest shore of the lake.[15]

In April they set up a sub camp at the foot of Loon Lake Mountain. Forty enrollees improved the trail and installed a new telephone line to the observer's cabin and fire tower.[16]

Since the winter weather was so severe the young men were unable to improve the camp site. In May, 1934 the men leveled the ground, blasted & removed stumps and rocks, stained the buildings, erected a flag pole, made paths, and planted flower beds.[17]

The spring season was very dry and forest fires began to spread through the Adirondacks. About June 1 a force of nearly 1,000 composed of 200 CCC enrollees (from Lake Placid, Paul Smiths, Fish Creek Pond, and Benson Mines), rangers, woodsmen, and local residents were summoned to fight a huge fire at Bay Pond approximately nine miles west of the S-60. Captain Charles Eckart of Barnum Pond and commanders from nearby Fish Creek and Tupper Lake camps called back 150 men who were on leave for the Memorial Weekend to help fight the blaze. The new truck trail built near Bay Pond by the CCC was very important

Paul Smiths CCC Camp-S-60 Activities from Schenectady District Civilian Conservation Corps Area Yearbook, 1937

in reaching the fire. For 14 days three shifts of men fought eight hours a day. The fire destroyed 27,000 acres. Governor Lehman praised the men for their valiant work in saving lives and property.[18]

The good works of the CCC boys were damaged in June when Barnum Pond enrollee Thomas Frederick Showers of Syracuse was arrested for assaulting and killing 14-year old Cleo Tellistone of Bloomingdale. Cleo left her home on June 23 to mail a letter but never returned home. Her body was found the next day by her brother in the nearby woods. State police learned that a CCC truck passed the Tellistone home shortly after she left home. They also found a cigarette near her battered body. Police learned that Showers had driven by the Tellistone home. After intense questioning, Showers admitted that he killed her but said it was only an accident. In November the jury found Showers guilty of murder and sentenced him to 20 years in prison.[19]

On the morning of November 6 another tragedy occurred to a member of camp S-60. Byron Beebe, a 56-year old former prohibition agent and native of Malone, accidentally shot himself. He was in an adjoining room to the tool shed which he managed. Beebe picked up his 25-caliber revolver from his desk that he thought was unloaded but it discharged shooting him in his chest. Dean Smith, the forestry superintendent, discovered Beebe lying on his bed. Smith summoned Dr, T. L. Piazza, camp physician, who then traveled with Beebe in an army truck to the Saranac Lake Hospital. Doctors thought he'd recover but Beebe died a few weeks later.[20]

During 1934 Camp S-60's mission was to continue building foot and truck trails, do forest stand improvement, develop campsite at Barnum Pond, and reduce fire hazards along the highways and forests.[21]

Commissioner Osborne announced in 1934 that a CCC camp would be awarded the Governor Lehman trophy for the best camp in New York. They'd be judged on their work, care of equipment, reports & record keeping, and morale. In January 1935 Osborne announced the winner, Paul Smiths. In February Osborne came to the Tupper Lake Town Hall and presented the trophy and gold buttons to each member of the camp.[22]

On January 1, 1935 the education director began eight classes. They ran for 15 weeks and met twice a week.

The camp staff taught the following classes: carpentry, radio, forestry, journalism, mechanics, hygiene, applied psychology, and bookkeeping and merchandising. Mr. Turner showed how to build and repair radios and Mr.

Bunch taught carpentry. Mr. Smith and Turner gave instruction in forestry. Dr. Piazza, camp physician, instructed the men in the function of the body and importance of hygiene. Lt. Brame taught accounting a merchandising and had the men gained experience by working in the camp canteen.[23]

One barracks was converted into an education building that had a library, reading room, and an industrial arts shop. A shop teacher guided the young boys in building projects. They used these tools: lathe, circular saw, drill press, and band saw. They displayed their projects at the National Sportsmen Exhibition in New York City.[24]

On April 1 camp S-60 began an experimental project improving the nearby streams to increase trout population. The enrollees worked till October 1 working on Winnebago Brook (near Meacham Lake), Duane Stream (near Mountain View), Hatch Brook (near Loon Lake), Big Alder Brook (near Sugar Bush), and Barnes Brook (near Bellmont).[25] They built barrier dams to prevent perch from going up trout streams, built diversion dams to create pools, and cleared debris to make the water cool and clear.[26]

Besides fighting forest fires Paul Smiths camp was called to help in residential fires. In May 1935 the camp received a call for help at Paul Smith's Hotel. The Guide House was on fire and 45 male workers and fortunately they escaped without injury. Sixty-five boys from camp helped local fire departments battle the blaze.[27]

The enrollees continued work in 1935 at Meacham Lake. They cleared the debris along the road to the lake, constructed a 3,000-ft. water system that supplied spring water to stand pipes throughout the campsite.[28]

Camp Superintendent Vedene Smith listed the camps forestry accomplishments in The Tupper Lake Free Press. They planted about 1,500, 000 trees and collected spruce and cedar cones used at the state nurseries. They expanded the Lake Clear nursery by collecting muck from drained swampland and they did grading and filling work.[29]

Verdene said his men did pest control work. They eradicated ribes from nearly 3,000 acres of white pine plantations preventing the spread of blister rust. Throughout the winter the boys pruned and thinned about 2,000 acres of plantations in Lake Clear.[30]

During 1936 the enrollees were involved in quite a few projects. They built the fire tower observer's cabin on DeBar Mountain and worked with the Bureau of Fish Hatcheries enlarging and remodeling Saranac Inn Hatchery.[31]

The men constructed three truck trails: DeBar Game Refuge (1.5 mi.), Fish Pond (2.5 mi.), Slush Pond (2 mi.), Hayes Brook (5.5 mi.), and Grass and Moose Road (1.5 mi.).[32]

At Meacham Lake the young men built 100 fireplaces, 100 table & bench combinations, diving float, garbage pits, parking & camping areas, two toilets, and a bathhouse.[33]

The CCC boys were always ready to help state police in the search of lost people. At the end of April 1936 around 125 woodsmen and Paul Smith CCC boys searched for Charles A. Nash who was reported lost near Fish Pond by his wife. The searches successfully found the dazed man about thee miles from where he entered the woods.[34]

One search didn't have a happy ending. In September Mrs. Matthew E. Davis reported her 73-year old aunt, Cora Johnson, missing. Residents, police and CCC boys from camp S-60 searched the dense forest and found her body in Lower Saranac Lake.[35]

In 1937 S-60 was the last Adirondack CCC camp classified as a forest fire control camp. It continued to do silviculture work on state plantations.[36] They also did extensive work developing the Lake Clear Fish Hatchery.[37]

Camp S-60 built and lowered a wooden stave pipe that went across the frozen Little Clear Pond. The thousand-foot line was lowered 65 feet through the ice. The pipe carried cold water to the fish hatchery at Saranac Inn. This helped control the water temperatures for the fish to survive as they developed.[38]

The enrollees also did recreation projects. They completed building the concrete dam at Meacham Lake. Another project was working with Camp S-71 constructing the dam near South Meadows (near Heart Lake).[39]

By the end of 1937 The Civilian Conservation Corps Schenectady District Yearbook 1937 listed these completed projects: built 45 miles of truck trails, eradicated 3,000 acres of ribes, pruned and thinned 3,000 acres of forests, planted 2 million trees, reduced fire hazards on 2,000 acres, salvaged logs from ponds and lakes worth thousands of dollars, milled timber from the Wawbeek highway right-of-way, and constructed free public campgrounds that included fireplaces, bathhouses and campsites.[40]

Camp S-60 achieved awards in athletic competition. In the Sub-District championships they won the 1934 Track & Field championship and were co-champions in the 1935 baseball championships. In the 1936 Sub-District Field Days they came in third place.[41]

During 1938 S-60 continued developing recreation areas at Meacham Lake and Fish Creek Pond. At the latter they installed a water supply system and constructed a hard surfaced road. Enrollees expanded the Meacham Lake campsite to accommodate 300 campers.[42] They also completed log dams at Duck Hole and Duck Hole Dyke.[43]

Another tragic death occurred at camp S-60 on Friday July 25, 1938. William Nye, the mess sergeant from Malone, was accidentally electrocuted when he apparently tried to shut off the camp's refrigeration system. Authorities believed an electric storm caused a short circuit to the system. Another member of the camp, William Revell, had previously tried to pull the switch and was burned. When Revell heard that Nye had gone to pull the main switch, Revell went to warn him but it was too late. He found Nye on the ground. Lt. F. A. Formicia and fellow workers attempted to resuscitate Nye but failed. Dr. Mariano declared Nye dead at 12:15 am Saturday.[44]

In 1939 camp S-60 continued work at Fish Creek Pond and Meacham Lake state parks. They also maintained the Slush Pond and Hayes Brook truck trails.[45]

A big project in 1939 was the construction of Marcy Dam, two miles south of Heart Lake in the High Peaks region. This log

Left - Paul Smiths camp enrollees lowering a 1,000-ft. wooden stave pipe across Little Clear Pond. Lori Lepine. Right - Senior DEC Forester Sean Reynolds suggests this unidentified Paul Smiths CCC side or "spike" camp may have been at DeBar Meadows where the enrollees lived while working on fire truck trails at Debar Mountain Game Refuge and Hayes Brook (ca. 1936). NYS Archives

crib dam was 25 per cent complete by the end of the year.[46]

During 1940 enrollees completed the 3.9-mile truck trail to Fish Pond. This was an important project because the area was a fire hazard section. The men also maintained the following trails: Slush Pond, Hayes Brook, DeBar, Rollins Pond, Bone Pond, and Little Clear Pond.[47]

Bridge construction was important for the truck and campsite roads. In 1940 they began constructing bridges that were more permanent than was done in the past. By the end of the year, S-60 constructed four bridges: a 15-ft. log stringer, a 13-ft. multi-plate arch, and two 11-ft. and 13-ft. multi-plate arch bridges.[48]

That same year the young men continued to improve the campsites at Meacham Lake and Fish Creek Pond. At the latter they improved the water system.[49]

During the fall Company 220 in S-60 was transferred to Camp S-134 in Canton. The Plattsburgh veterans Co. 2207 which moved to the Lake Placid camp in the summer to complete Marcy Dam were transferred in the fall to Paul Smiths.[50]

The 1941 firefighting season used a lot of manpower that limited Barnum Pond's work on projects but Camp S-60 did complete some work. They constructed a new telephone line from the base of DeBar Mountain to the fire tower on the summit. They also built a boathouse and ranger's cabin on Lower Saranac Lake. At Saranac Inn they constructed a storehouse for the Conservation Department.[51]

The enrollees continued their work at Meacham Lake and Fish Creek Pond campsites. They installed a new water system at Meacham Lake.[52]

After nine years of work Paul Smiths camp S-60 closed on July 22, 1942. In the March 3, 1943 issue of Au Sable Forks Record-Post reported the government gave the camp buildings to Paul Smiths College.

The army officers, Conservation Department foresters and foremen had a positive effect on the men who worked and lived at the camp. This November 6, 1934 Syracuse Herald newspaper clipping, "North Woods C.C.C. Sends Its Despondent Rookies" Home Fit and Confident" found in the Saranac Lake Library research files illustrates this point.

One group of 52 was boarding a train while a Conservation Department camp superintendent, army sergeant and captain watched.

"Blow your whistle Sarg," begged one of the youths on the coach.

The Sergeant grinned as he obliged.

"We won't get up!" came the chorus from the coach.

Then a youth swung from the coach and approached the captain with outstretched hand.

Captain William Carter, of the 26th Infantry, commanding officer of Barnum Pond, smiled.

"Thanks Hymie. You fellows don't realize it—it took us some time to see it—but you have done a lot for the army. You pulled us out of a rut. Good luck to you all."

The youth turned to C. W. Mattison, camp superintendent.

"Good-bye, Mr. Mattison. You worked us hard, but you were fair. We haven't any kick."

Mattison chuckled. "You were a tough guy, Hymie, when you first came up here. But you couldn't take it in the woods."

He studied the husky youth. "You can take it now."

Hymie dropped his voice.

"I am not so tough now. I have learned some things."

A whistle sounded, and the youth swung aboard the train as it pulled away. A cheer went up from the 52 boys returning to the city. Some of them had jobs. Others did not.

Upon the running board of a truck sat a youth who wore the uniform of the forest army. He jerked a brown thumb at the departing train.

"Fifty-two darned fools," was his forcible verdict.

Regardless of that verdict, fair or otherwise, the 52 and the other youths who left the CCC have left their mark upon Northern New York. Some dry figures serve to tell a partial story.

"...When these 52 men arrived in the Adirondacks and when they departed for their homes at the end of the six months. They came to the Adirondacks licked, youths for whom the industrial scheme had no place. They returned to that outside world hardened physically, disciplined, confident, and unafraid."

On August 20, 1995, over 50 years after the closing of camp S-60, Brighton Architectural Heritage Committee honored the CCC by dedicating a plaque at the site of the former camp.

The monument states, "The site of Camp S-60 Barnum Pond Town of Brighton 1933-1942 U S Civilian Conservation Corps Company 220 Paul Smiths, NY ... fought fires, helped build campsites, planted trees, built trails, and

WORK ACCOMPLISHED BY CAMP S-60[*]

PROJECT	1934	1935	1936	1937	1938	1939	1940	1941	TOTAL
Bathhouses - number					2				2
Beach improvement - mi.	178	4	2				2		186
Bridges, foot & horse - number			1			1			2
Bridges, vehicle - number	5	1	1	1			4		12
Buildings, equipment & supply storage - number			1						1
Buildings, other - number						1	2	1	4
Cribbing - yd³			1130						1130
Dams - number					1				1
Dwellings - number				1	1		1	1	4
Fences - rods					225				225
Field planting trees - ac.		120							120
Fire breaks - mi.	1.9		2						3.9
Fire fighting - man-days	2563	544	286		18	642	111	1275	5439
Fire hazard reduction (roadside) - mi.	56	15	3					2	76
Fire hazard reduction (trailside) - mi.		3	1						4
Fire hazard reduction, other - ac.		362	48	12					422
Fire pre-supression - man-days			352		151	131	571	700	1905
Fireplaces - number			78				30		108
Fish rearing ponds - mi.				4					4
Forest stand improvement - ac.	464	377	338	180			50		1409
Garages - number					1				1
General clean-up - ac.		5	1				98	90	194
Guard rails - rods			150					6	156
Insect pest control - ac.			250						250
Landscaping - ac.				0.3	10	67			77.3
Latrines & toilets - number			2	2			16		20
Nurseries - man-days			1547	151		141	86		1925
Parking areas & overlooks - yd²				500					500
Pipe or tile line - linear ft.		4000	2000		29275			4775	40050
Planting/moving trees & shrubs - number	796								796
Power line - mi.					0.4				0.4
Preparation/transportation of materials - man-days				7957	485	1144	2878	950	13414
Public ground development - ac.	29	7	15			8	8		67
Razing undesirable structures - man-days					1579		894		2473
Reconaissance & investigation - man-days								152	152
Reservoirs, small - number					1				1
Searching for missing persons - man-days	15								15
Seats, benches, chairs - number					1				1
Seed collection (cones) - bushels	22.5	105						13	140.5
Seeding or sodding - ac.		1							1
Sewage & waste disposal systems - number			10		4	8	8	9	39
Shelters (trailside) - number		1		1		2			4
Signs, markers, monuments - number								28	28
Storage facilities - gal. (M)					6		1		7
Stream & lake bank protection - mi.		6.3		0.5	1				7.8
Stream improvement - mi.	1.8								1.8
Structural improvements, misc. - mi.		102	9	55	1			18	185
Surveys, timber estimating - man-days	1580			48					1628

[*]Numerical data from Conservation Reports

Left - Retired Paul Smith's College professor Gould Smith standing by an abandoned CCC camp S-60 fireplace and chimney. Right - Sandy Hildreth, a Saranac Lake artist and fire tower preservationist, standing by the Paul Smiths CCC monument on Rt. 30 by the camp site that was dedicated in 1995 honoring the men for their work in the area. Both courtesy Podskoch Collection

dams and improved forest stands."

The ceremony began with Ruth Hoyt, a member of the Brighton Architectural Heritage Committee, read a letter from Joseph Brownell, son of the camp superintendent Roland Brownell (1937-1942). Then former members of Paul Smiths camp spoke: Paul Benoit, Leroy Smith, and Chuck Komeraski. Other CCC members present were: Clayton Winters, Elmer Charleston, and camp forester William Lytle. Jim Helms, Brighton Highway Superintendent, donated the rock and Glenn Perrino, a member of the highway crew, prepared the plaque for the rock. Ruth Hoyt and Benoit spearheaded the drive for the plaque. CCC members, their families, Brighton seniors, Boy Scouts, Asplin Tree Farm, and others contributed money for the plaque.[53]

MEMORIES

John "Jack" Corl

Reverend James Corl of Manlius, NY contacted me in January 2008 and told me his father, Jack Corl, served in the CCC at Paul Smiths camp. He sent me a CD containing 65 photos of his father from a family album. He also sent his biography.

"My father was born April 29, 1916 in Yonkers, NY. He lived most of his early life in and around Homer, NY.

"Dad joined the Civilian Conservation Corps when he was 17 years old. His discharge papers state he served

from October 3, 1933 to October 1, 1934 at a camp near Paul Smiths. He told me that to be eligible one had to be 18 and on welfare. Dad was 17 and not on welfare. He went to the recruiter in Syracuse and attempted to sign up. When the recruiter asked Dad his age, Dad replied that he was 17. The recruiter then told him the rule and said he was ineligible. Dad told him he was without a job and had no income. The recruiter repeated the rule and told him to go. As he moved toward the door, Dad told the man that he would be back in about an hour. The recruiter asked him what he meant by that. Dad said, 'I am going to sign up for welfare and then come back.' The man gestured him to come back and said, 'Today you are 18.' Dad signed on and entered the corps."

James went to visit his mother, Marie, and asked about his dad's early life and his days in the CCC.

"Your dad's parents were Merton John and Mary Obridge Loch Corl. Your grandfather, Merton, did a lot of odd jobs. He worked for the WPA and once worked at the Franklin automobile plant in Syracuse. There were eight children in the family: Emily, Eugene, John, George, Lucille, Russell, Ida, and Janice.

"I'm not sure I know how he found out about the CCC. Dad had a bad home life so he was happy to leave. He loved the CCC, his experience there, and being in that environment.'

"Jack said his camp was rustic. They built it from the ground up. He was in the first group that went to Paul Smiths which was also called Osgood Pond or Barnum Pond. The boys lived in tents. Their first task was to build the barracks and other buildings. They did a lot of physical labor.

"They built the CCC camp buildings, did reforestation, cut fire trails, and built trails to the fire towers. They worked in groups. When they planted trees one used a mattock to cut a hole in the ground. The second placed a seedling in the hole, and the third stepped on the dirt around the seedling."

"Did Dad tell you if any funny things happened in camp?"

"One time a group ganged up on a practical joker, tied him to his bed, and tied the bed up on the rafters.

"Jack said he and the other guys just sat around the camp or read in the evenings and on the weekends. He came

Above - When Paul Smiths CCC camp was established the young enrollees lived in tents. Here is an Army tent that Jack Corl and seven other enrollees lived in for the first five months. NYS Archives. Right - Jack Corl (right) of Homer, NY and Briggs Kean on a pile of wood that was later used to build the barracks at the Paul Smiths camp in the fall of 1933. Reverend James A Corl

home a couple times on the train for a weekend visit.

"He said the food was good. It was a healthy place to be. It was cold, especially in the winter. Jack put on weight and a lot of muscle."

"Why did Dad leave the CCC?"

"His father got sick and Jack went home to take his father's job in Syracuse to support the family. He supervised work crews building stone walls along Onondaga Creek in the city.

"Jack told many stories about his time in the CCC. Here are three I remember:

"There were quite a few guys from New York City in Jack's camp. He and some of the others had the duty of training them to use tools, one of which was a double edged axe. He said several were quite dangerous with them until they got the hang of it. One of them made his axe so sharp he could shave his leg with it.

"During the winter several men came to camp from the South. They had never encountered such cold or snow. One of them cried because he was so cold. Jack told him to keep moving and do some work and he would not be so cold.

"The last story was that work crews would sometimes meet bear on the trails. This caused quite a stir!

"Jack often looked back at his days in the CCC and said he had a great sense of accomplishment. He learned teamwork and how to manage work crews."

Jack died in August of 2004.

C. W. Mattison

In the winter of 1934 Malcolm Johnson, a reporter for the New York Sun, visited the Barnum Pond camp. His story "CCC Boys Get Frisky As Colts As 18 Below Zero Seems Balmy" came out in the March 17, 1934 issue. Here are a few excerpts about the enrollees and C. W. Mattison, camp superintendent, and his wife.

"The temperature in this neck of the woods, in the heart of the Adirondacks, was 18 degrees below zero a day or so ago, and the members of the Civilian Conservation Corps at camp 12 at Barnum Pond kicked up their heels like frisky colts and pronounced it a nice spring day.

"To prove they really believed it, they shed some of their heavy outer garments and pranced around the camp grounds without helmets or gloves, although the snow drifts were waist deep in the forest.

"'But it is like spring to us.' The boys insisted. 'You should have been with us when it was 58 below—that's what it has been here this winter.'

"'How did you stand it?' the reporter asked.

"'Swell,' the boys chorused. But you shouldn't ask us that—ask Mr. Mattison. He and Mrs. Mattison have been living in a tent all winter.'

The reporter went to see Mattison who said, "'I guess we are known as the 'damn fools of the Adirondacks. Sure we have been living in a tent, all right—the missus and I. We like it; we haven't suffered.'

"'Did you have to do that?'

"'Oh, no, we did it from choice. There are quarters here at the camp for us if we want them. So far we haven't wanted them. We have been in a tent all winter—even during the 58-below period."

Mattison invited the reporter to his tent.

"The tent was there all right—a mile or so away from the keep and within a stone's throw of Barnum Pond. Mrs. Mattison, an attractive, blonde young woman, was kneading dough when the sightseers barged in.

"'Shut the door,' she ordered. 'I don't want a cold draft on this dough.' Mr. Mattison obeyed.

"'Certainly, I like it.' Mrs. Mattison announced. 'We haven't been cold, really. 'See, we have a really good stove. No, maybe I wouldn't want to live in a tent every winter, but this winter, at least, it has been fun.'

Above - Paul Smiths' camp Superintendent C. W. Mattison & wife lived in a tent during the winter of 1933-34. Adirondack Museum Library Archives. Right - Lu and Richard Bourcier standing outside their home in Malone. Richard shared stories about his experience as a store clerk, night watchman, cook, and mess sergeant at the Paul Smiths CCC camp during the 1930s. Lu told me about her brother Gerald Patnode who worked at the Plattsburgh Barracks camp. Podskoch Collection

Above - These workers at the Paul Smiths CCC camp take a break for a group picture. Richard Bourcier is crouching on the left. Next is Wood Bachnaw, unknown, and ___Venne. In the back row left is Harold Lepine 2nd, Leo Perry 4th(holding unknown object), Lynwood Koop stooping in front of unknown work foreman wearing hat, and Fred Tyler, shirtless, 2nd far right. Lu Bourcier

"The tent is a regulation Army size and is boarded on the inside. A view of the lake is obscured by a dozen or so cords of wood, stacked there as protection from the icy wind blowing off the water.

"'We have lost not a single day of work on account of the storms.' Mr. Mattison said on the way back to the camp. 'And we lost only days because of extreme cold.'"

Richard Bourcier

While speaking at the Wead Library in Malone on July 1, 2007, a woman named Margaret told me to call her friend Lu Bourcier's husband Richard who was in the CCC.

I called Richard and he told me about his early life. "I was born on June 23, 1916. My dad Oliver was a farmer in Chasm Falls (south of Malone). Later on he got a job working for the county highway as a grader operator. My mother Bernice Thayer had two children, my sister Regina and I.

"After I graduated from eighth grade I dropped out of school and worked on my parents' farm. My dad found out about the CCC for me. He knew somebody in politics and I got in even though I was only 16 years old. I signed up in the spring of 1934 and they sent me to the Paul Smiths camp.

What jobs did you have?

"When I first joined I was the tool clerk. My job was to take care of all the hand tools. My shop was in a separate building. I had some help. There was a guy in my shop who painted all the signs for directions because we were building a lot of truck trails. The camp took care of trails going up St. Regis, DeBar, and Loon Lake mountains. We made rock steps up the mountain. I didn't get any increase in salary or rank.

"My next job was night watchman. I took care of all the stoves in the barracks, outbuildings, and garages. I also had to walk one-quarter of a mile through the woods to Osgood Pond to get to the pump house because it had a small stove. I had to keep the small stove going so the water wouldn't freeze up. If the fire went out there wouldn't be water to the latrine, shower, canteen, rec room, infirmary, and officer's quarters.

200

"I was going steady almost all night long although I took breaks to eat. Sometimes there was a note to wake somebody like a cook or a truck driver. I made about three to four trips throughout the night to the pump house. It had a small stove that was very temperamental and the fire sometimes took off.

"Most of the stoves used soft coal. The Conservation officers' building, barracks, and mess hall all used soft coal. I had to watch it closely so it didn't burn too fast or too slow. There was also a danger of carbon monoxide. Some guys got cold in the night and got up and opened the bottom damper which caused it to burn too fast. If the pipe damper wasn't fully opened, carbon monoxide gas would come into the room and could kill the men. I could tell by a certain smell as I walked into the building if something was wrong. I'd open the pipe damper and close the lower stove damper. If I made too much noise filling the stove a guy might throw a shoe at me.

"Then I got a job working in the kitchen as assistant cook. I was sent to Fort Dix for two months for training. There were 1,500 men there. They were being discharged. Imagine cooking for all those cooks. I had one of the best cooks for an instructor. He was a cook in WWI and worked at McAlpin Hotel in New York City. He taught me a lot in two months. He was an excellent cook but one fault was that he was an alcoholic.

Did anything unusual happen in the kitchen?

"The weekend I came back to Paul Smiths there was a thunderstorm and the mess sergeant, Bill Nye, went out to start the fan for the refrigerator. When he stuck a stick in the fan he was electrocuted. I was there on duty. They brought him to the infirmary. The doctor was unable to resuscitate him. The doctor wanted two people to give artificial resuscitation. I had training in this so I volunteered. There were only 15 men in camp so the doctor called the Boy Scout camp nearby. Their leader came and both of us worked on him for four hours. Then we knew he was dead because rigamortis was setting into his arms. Then the officer asked me if I would take his job as mess sergeant and I did.

"Now I was the boss of about six cooks and a pastry cook. I also had assistants to the officers called 'pratt boys.' They dressed in white and served the superintendent, army officers, and Conservation Department officials. The officers had a separate mess room attached to the large mess hall. The 'pratt boys' served the officers and also cleaned up. Once in a while they had to help us in the kitchen.

"Everyday there were six or more enrollees who had KP duty. They did all the cleaning of potatoes and other hard work for the cooks. If some guys did something wrong they were given KP. On weekends some guys had to do extra KP for punishment for something they did wrong. They stayed the whole day and might get some time off for a swim or go to the rec room.

"As mess sergeant I had to take care of all purchases and contracts for meat, bread etc. We made a lot of food using our own recipies. I had to check on cooks and plan the menus a month ahead of time. I got food from Malone, Saranac Lake, and Tupper Lake. All the items had to be bid on and had to meet certain standards. Beef was about 16 cents a-pound.

"We had a walk-in freezer run by ammonia gas. It was very touchy. You had to watch out that it didn't spring a leak. It was very large and adjacent to the kitchen. It was very nice and took care of an ungodly amount of food. You had to keep an eye on its temperature. The delivery truck guys had to carry the meat into the freezer and they didn't like that extra work. If we had extra help we'd help them.

"The Army had a commissary in Plattsburgh where we could pick up special foods (spices, salt, etc.). It was very cheap.

"I made a big boo boo once and ordered 12 cases of pepper thinking it was 12 boxes. One case had 144 boxes. When I got it I couldn't believe it. The Army wouldn't take it back. I called other camps and was able to trade off a good portion of it.

"In the middle of my term as mess sergeant they built a pantry section onto the building. Here we stored ar-

It's dinner time at the Paul Smiths mess hall. Richard Bourcier worked as a cook and then became the mess sergeant. He planned, ordered, and supervised the six cooks and a pastry chef. NYS Archives

ticles for a month just in case there was an emergency. We had 30 cubicles. Each one had a full day's supply containing anything that didn't need refrigeration.

"We had a total of six cooks and two were on each day. One cook was a pastry cook. If he could get his things out then he'd be free the rest of the day. He went to the town of Saranac Lake where they baked bread and pastry and they offered to train him. The other two cooks alternated.

"They started cooking about 5 am and served breakfast about 7.

"We prepared lunches the night before. There were usually three sandwiches: a meat sandwich or egg salad made in the morning. We had a lot of canned meat like liverwurst and ham. We also made peanut butter sandwiches or peanut butter and jelly. When we used butter they had to be done fast so we melted the butter and used a pastry brush for speed. You put in two buttered pieces of bread, a can of sardines, and a piece of fruit (banana or apple). About one-third of the men didn't like sardines. So they traded off with others. We wrapped the sandwiches in butcher waxed paper. If we had cookies or a piece of cake we put that in for lunch. Sometimes we put in a hot dog. They'd put them on a stick and roast them on a fire.

"On the job one guy made coffee. He put a pail over the fire and added coffee to the boiling water. It was a powerful drink.

"The crew also had a water boy. He'd bring them water when they hollered 'water boy.' If it was hot, he was kept busy all day. Sometimes he'd drop a frog in the water for a joke. The logging crew liked to get even. Sometimes they'd call him. As he came they tried to drop a medium sized tree they were cutting on top of him. He never got hurt but they just wanted to give him a little scare.

Another trick they played on the water boy was when they were working on a pond in the winter, they cut a hole near the edge in the ice and covered it with snow. Then they'd call him and he'd fall in the water. Anything to spice up the day.

"We had side camps that were 30 or more miles away from camp. The guys set up tents and worked on dams, truck roads etc. They needed a cook and crew of two or three guys. It was usually an apprentice cook. I went in at least once a week to check on him. A guy drove me and we took supplies into the camp. Some of the men stayed there over the weekend. One camp was at Loon Lake and another near Cold River. I have a picture I took of the her-

mit Noah Rondeau who lived there. We built a beautiful dam up there. One guy hewed out logs. There were about 20 men there.

"Another camp was on surveyor Lem Merril's property. He came up there after working with Verplanck Colvin who surveyed the Adirondacks. It was here that we had a side camp on Merril's property. We could fish on his property, too. He had some little camps he rented out to sportsmen.

"We mainly built roads. One was to the top of Loon Lake Mountain where there was a gold mine. There were still some of the old tools laying around the mine. We also built a road up Debar Park. It was fenced in and had deer. One deer called Mickey was quite tame.

"Supper started at 5 pm. All the men sat for one seating in the mess hall. They were always hungry. The ones who did the most complaining were the ones who didn't have much at home.

"KP guys and cooks did the cleaning up. We had a dishwasher that took a rackful on a conveyor belt through hot water. By 6 pm we were out of there.

"I had an aversion to bugs. We had an infestation of cockroaches. They came out when it got dark and devoured all night. As you walked you heard the crunching sound. They hid behind the range and the celotex walls. There was an officer in charge of the mess hall but he didn't know how to do anything. I told the officer we had to get the celotex out to get rid of the cockroaches. I didn't want to poison them because we had open food. They were all over everything. Then we finally tried poison but they were too abundant. They came in almost constantly on the delivery trucks on any kind of food. We finally stopped them by making the walls tight so they couldn't hide behind the stove.

"Often on weekends we had fish. We'd make a shrimp salad for a small crowd. One time one of my cooks made it and was mixing it on the table. It was a large metal bowl. It accidentally fell off. He picked it up off the floor and put it on a cooking sheet. I said no. It's unsanitary. He replied, 'Oh, they won't know the difference. What the eyes don't see the belly don't feel.' I was mad and made sure he didn't serve it.

"We often heard of boys in Vermont who had E. coli or trichinosis in pork. I didn't want anyone to get sick from my food.

"Guys had ways of protesting about food they didn't like. Once a month we had mutton stew that had a strong smell. If we had it, the guys started bleating like a lamb. We served it because it was cheap. They guys wouldn't eat it so I cut down on serving it.

"The boys loved roast beef and mashed potatoes and gravy. We didn't have baked potatoes. It was hard to bake them in the oven.

"There was a detail that nobody liked, cleaning the grease pit. We gave this job to guys who had extra KP. First they opened the cap, took the grease out with scoops, placed it in containers, and hauled it away from camp. It smelled something awful. You did it every 3-4 months. Their clothes were ruined and smelled terrible after doing this job.

"One of my cooks carried his boning knife in his back pocket. I told him a hundred times not to. So one day when it was sleeting, he slipped and the knife went an inch or better into his butt. He went up to the infirmary to get stitches. Most of the time a doctor was there every morning with a First Aid man. If the doctor wasn't there the First Aid guy did almost everything the doctor did except stitching. They were there day and night. You could wake them up if you needed help.

"In camp we had a big Indian, Kenneth George, who was a college graduate. He'd get drunk in Saranac Lake. When he came back to camp he'd wake a guy up in the barracks and slug him and knock him out. He did this several times until we caught him and he was dishonorably discharged.

"One time we saw about 30 guys from Cohoes came to camp. They were given a choice of going to jail or joining the CCC. The captain asked if I'd take over supervision of their barracks. I said sure. I saw I had some tough guys. I told this big guy, 'You're in charge of all these guys.' and he said, 'OK.' I never had any problems with them."

Did anything funny happen in camp?

"The minute new guys got in, the others tried to play jokes on them. I heard the guys from the other barracks were going to play a trick on my barracks. I told the new guys to be prepared for the jokesters and they were. They met them and chased them.

"Guys couldn't stay in camp for more than two years but since I was the mess sergeant I stayed longer. I still lived in a barracks.

Why did you leave the CCC?

"I heard they were going to close down the camp so I left in about 1939. I worked for the state with the Bureau of Plant Entomology and Plant Quarantine on blister rust crews. I had a gang in the woods pulling up the ribes plants.

"Then Colonel Waugh (ret.) came up to Chasm Falls. He had made an expedition up the Yukon River and did big game hunting throughout the world. He hired me to get a crew to work on his 127-acre farm. We had to plant trees on the whole property.

"I was drafted in the Army in January 1942. While I was training my father died. I got a deferment because I was the only son and had to run the family farm. I came home but didn't like the farm so I joined the Navy. I became a corpsman at the San Diego Army Receiving Hospital and worked in the psychiatric ward.

"When I got out I worked at Alcoa for a few years then I went into the antique business and that is where I excelled.

"I have two children, Tamara and Bradley from my first marriage and I married Lu in 1986.

"The CCC was good for me because I got a lot of training and learned how to live with guys and supervise groups of men. I also learned how to be a good cook."

Paul Benoit

While visiting Winfred "Win" Benoit in Tupper Lake he told me his brother Paul was in the CCC in Paul Smiths. Win told me that Paul died and his daughter, Judy Hitchcock, had some of her dad's pictures and information but she lived in Wisconsin.

"But you are fortunate," Win said, "in that she is visiting her daughter in Old Forge."

He called her and I talked to Judy about my research on the CCC. She said she'd send me his CCC memorabilia when she got back to Wisconsin.

After a few months I received a box containing Paul's 1937 New York State CCC Yearbook, personal papers, and many newspaper articles.

Paul Benoit was born on August 13, 1915 in Owl's Head. His father, Harrison, was a game protector and his mother, Alice Benware, had nine children. His father instilled in him a love for the outdoors and the Adirondack Mountains. Paul went to Franklin Academy in Malone where he played baseball. He earned the nickname "Smokey" because of his blazing fastball. Paul graduated high school in 1933.

"I had trouble getting accepted as a CCC worker because my father had a job. There were nine children in my family and my family needed help."

In 1934 Paul succeeded in joining the CCC and

203

worked at Paul Smiths camp.

"The CCC helped develop us morally and physically. Our camp was run by the Army which ran it in semi-military fashion. We were well disciplined.

"The work was hard and we weren't given the easy way out. We worked on reforestation, construction work, trails, roads, and bridges. We made a trail up Loon Lake Mountain fire tower. It had a great view.

"We weren't allowed to use much dynamite so moved huge boulders with a big pole as a pry and 20 men.

"When I left the CCC I went from one job to another. I did railroad work then spent three summers at Loon Lake House and then went back to the railroad."

Paul married Evelyn Campbell in 1938. They had two daughters, Judy and Jane and a son, Jonathan.

"In 1941 my father retired as conservation officer and I got his job in the Owl's Head and Loon Lake area. I loved working outdoors. My job was interrupted when I was in the Navy from 1945-46."

Benoit continued work as a conservation officer in Franklin, St. Lawrence, and Jefferson counties. While working he earned a forestry degree at Paul Smith's College in 1961. In 1965 Benoit was transferred to Albany and became assistant superintendent of the Bureau of Law Enforcement in Albany and in 1972 the state's chief Conservation Officer. In 1976 he ended his 39-year career working for the Conservation Department.

Five years later he left the town of Malta and returned to his hometown of Owl's Head. He continued his love of nature by hunting, fishing, gardening and growing Christmas trees. He also advocated a return of this program for today's youth. It was one of the best programs this country ever had."

"I owe my successful career in the Conservation Department to my three-year CCC experience at Paul Smiths. I was there from 1934 to 1937 and 20 days. They really got me off to the right start. I'll never forget it."

Paul Benoit died at age 87 on October 18, 2002 in his beloved Adirondack Mountains.

Paul Benoit (left) with three other CCC enrollees at camp S-71 Paul Smiths camp. They are standing by one of the canvas-covered Army trucks that carried both men and supplies. Judy Benoit Hitchcock

Edgar Lamphear

The contacts I made writing my two books on the Adirondacks fire towers helped in finding many CCC guys. Doris Lamphear of Raquette Lake and her husband Frank had a lot of stories on the fire tower on West Mountain. She called me and said her brother-in-law, Edgar, was in the CCC. She arranged to meet me at his house on August 2, 2009 when she planned on giving Edgar's wife Anne a perm.

Edgar and I sat in his living room and he told me about growing up on Raquette Lake. "I'm 96 years old and sometimes I have a little trouble remembering what happened to me but I do know that I was born in April 1914 on my mother's farm on Cedar River Road. My father Orrin built our house on Poplar Point and worked as a carpenter. My mother, Hazel McKane, came from Cedar River. She had two children.

"When I graduated from Raquette Lake High School I got jobs raking yards and trimming trees. I worked for a lot of people.

Why did you join the CCC?

"I joined the CCC because my folks were poor and needed money. Someone came to my house and drove a bunch us to the CCC camp in Paul Smiths.

"When I first got there I lived in a tent. When it got cold we had wood stoves in the tents.

"For dinner we stood in line with our mess kits and the cooks filled them up. We sat outside to eat at tables. It was hard keeping the mess kits clean. They turned black and needed steel wool to clean them.

"One of my jobs was cutting and trimming trees. The forester marked trees 8' to 10' high that had to be removed. Then we burned the limbs and brush. Another job was planting trees. I planted thousands of white pine trees. We had some city boys at the camp. You couldn't let them use a sharp axe because they'd hurt themselves.

"There was one time when the temperature was 40 degrees below zero and a big shot came along and raised hell that we were out in such cold weather so we came in and just sat around the fire to keep warm.

"In the fall local men and CCC boys worked together to build barracks and they put them up real fast. When the barracks were completed we were happy to move in. There were wood stoves to keep us warm. Someone stayed up all night and went from building to building

Edgar Lamphear of Raquette Lake reminisces about his days in the CCC in 1933-34 at the Paul Smiths camp. Podskoch Collection

stoking the fires.

"All the guys in camp got along pretty good but sometimes local guys ganged up and had fights with the city guys.

"On weekends we just sat around and visited or walked to town. Sometimes I went to Saranac Lake and went to the movies. They also had dances at our camp. A few times I'd hitchhike home to Raquette Lake but there was more going on at camp than at home.

"I worked in the CCC for six months because that is all you were allowed to stay. I came back to Raquette Lake and got a job with the state working at Golden Beach State Park. We built campsites and fireplaces.

"During WW II the Army drafted me. Then after the war I worked as a caretaker at camps on Raquette Lake. In 1946 I got married to Anne and worked for the state at Golden Beach and Eighth Lake as assistant caretaker. I retired when I was 70 years old.

"When I look back on my days in the CCC it got me a job outdoors and when I left I continued working for the state in the local parks."

Howard "Pete" Mosher

In 2007 Beth Mosher contacted me and said her father, Howard "Pete" James Mosher, worked at Paul Smiths CCC camp and while he was there he worked building Meacham Lake State Park. The camp was near his home in Brushton.

"My father joined the CCC because his father, Albert, had a difficult time raising his four sons, Ralph, Varick, Stanley, and Howard, nicknamed Pete, after his wife, Hazel Vail, died in 1918 in the Spanish flu epidemic.

"Dad said that his father lost his farm in Dickinson Center during the Depression, not due to incompetence on his part, but because he was too generous of a heart. Many people were having hard times prior to the Depression. My grandfather had many loans out to other farmers. The crash happened and the bank came to my grandfather wanting their money. Grandpa asked for his loans to be returned, but of course at that point no one had any money. So the bank foreclosed on the farm. I know Dad went hungry as well.

"After he finished eighth grade he went to work at several different area farms. He was a hard worker and had a gift for working with horses. At one time, he was helping drive a team of horses that was pulling a plow to clear the Dickinson roads of snow. Dad always rated the farms based on how good the cooking was. He would speak of a Nevada Snell and how good her biscuits and pancakes were. When Dad was 16, he went to live with a Dr. Kingston and his wife in Moira. Dad helped with odd jobs there. Dad had great affection and respect for this couple.

"He joined the CCC on July 2, 1934 when he was 18 years old and went to the Paul Smiths camp. I think my father would have been looking forward to camp since he was young and looking for adventure.

"There was lots of hard work and he enjoyed the camaraderie with the other enrollees. They cut trees, cleared brush, created trails, and built trails to fire towers.

"Dad said he liked the food for the most part and I know they had all they could eat.

"I know there were 'bare knuckle' fights and Dad traveled to other camps to face competitors. The men watching would throw coins into a container and the winner would take it home. Dad said that he won many of his fights, but he didn't have a number for me.

"Our father told us that once he fought a 'Golden Glove' boxer from downstate in a bout. Dad said that although he did manage to land some punches, the other guy pretty much hit at will, and when he connected, Dad said he saw stars. He did go three rounds, however.

"Dad left Paul Smiths camp on December 16, 1935 because he got a job. Later he met my mother Katherine Laura Richards and they got married on July 11, 1943. They had three children: Kenneth, John, and myself.

"That same year he joined the navy and trained at the Navy base in Chicago. He was assigned to Quonset Point, RI. Then Dad saw action in the South Pacific (Saipan and the Marianas). He was a gunner on a PBY (patrol bomber) plane. He was discharged in 1945, with the rank of aviation machinist's mate, first class.

"After the war Dad and a friend bought a milk route and ran that for four years. He then sold the route

Howard "Pete" Mosher waiting for the steam shovel to finish loading gravel into his dump truck. Beth Mosher

and went to work on the St. Lawrence Seaway project in Massena.

"My brother reminded me of something Dad said while working on the Seaway. Like many area people, Dad went to seek employment at this project. He was hired immediately and was given two 5-gallon pails. He had to use these to haul rocks that were being used to build the cofferdams. After two days of this labor, Dad walked into the supervisor's office and threw the pails on the floor. He said, 'Maybe you can stop the St. Lawrence River with five-gallon pails, but I sure as hell can't.' (Believe me, that statement was so Dad!) The boss then told Dad that he was waiting to see how long he could last. He stated that now he would give Dad a good job. He initially drove truck and at the end of his stint, was handling a bulldozer.

"At the same time he worked on the Seaway, he and my mom bought a dairy farm and were beginning to build that up. In 1957, he went to work for Brushton-Moira Central School as a bus driver. He did this mainly to avail himself and his family of the insurance benefits.

"My Dad was very proud of the trails that he worked on while he was in the CCC. He would always look over to St. Regis Mountain and mention his time there. When we would picnic at Meacham Lake he would talk about the campgrounds that they had cleared and made."

Elbert Hanchett

Elbert Hanchett and his family came to my talk at the Ticonderoga Heritage Museum on October 24, 2007. He had been a member of the CCC at Port Henry and Paul Smiths camp. I visited him the next day at the Heritage Commons Residential Health Care in Ticonderoga.

"My father William was a carpenter and my mother, Lillian, had four children: My older brother Leon, my younger sister Ada and a sister who died before she was one.

It was very hard for my family and I needed a job that could help.

"I joined the CCC right after I graduated from Moriah High School in 1934. I think I went down to the camp and signed up there. It was all right but quite different from living at home.

"One of my first jobs at camp was fighting the spread of gypsy moths. We walked through the woods and spread out in a line. We were about ten feet apart. Our foreman went ahead and stuck fake cocoons on some trees. If you went by that tree and didn't see it, they showed you. This was a training period. This was to help us find real cocoons.

"Then I went to the Paul Smiths camp. My job there was truck driver. I think all of the trucks were Chevys. They had stake bodies and there were seats on three sides for the guys when I took them to work. The foreman rode in the cab with me. I didn't have anything specific to do because my main job was driving. Sometimes I helped the guys burn brush that they gathered in the woods.

"Each week I went into the garage to service my truck. I greased it and changed the oil.

"Driving during the winter was sometimes tough in the snow. You'd sometimes get off track and slide off the road. The guys would get out and help push me out. I don't remember any starting problems.

"On weekends I sometimes hitchhiked home. There was a guy from Crown Point who had a car and sometimes I got a ride home with him.

"On Saturday night I drove guys to Saranac Lake to the armory to play basketball or go to the movies. When the movie was out about 9:30 to 10 I took them back to camp.

"After a year in the CCC I got out in 1935. The iron mines were running and my brother, Leon, worked there. Later on I got a job as a laborer. I carried both wood and steel I-beams and dynamite.

"I met a girl I was in high school with, Gertrude Holden, whose father and brother had a grain

Elbert Hanchett of Ticonderoga was a laborer at Port Henry CCC camp and a truck driver at Paul Smiths CCC camp from 1934-35. Podskoch Collection

store in Ticonderoga. Then her brother left and her father needed someone so I got the job. Then Gertrude and I got married and we lived in Ticonderoga. We had five children: David, Bill, Alvin, Sylvia, and Donald.

"I worked at the grain store for several years. After we took on the John Deere dealership I assembled machinery.

"During the war I got a deferment because I had children.

"After the war I had a few other jobs. I worked above ground at the mine, at the paper mill, and as a mechanic at a few car garages. I retired at age 62 and did a lot of volunteer work till 2006. Then I came here to Heritage Commons.

"When I look back at those days during the Depression the CCC was the only job you could get. It helped me and my family."

Walter Stahl

The June 3, 1985 issue of the Adirondack Daily Enterprise had a story written by Matthew Russell entitled, "Paul Smiths CCC Men: Stewards of the Land." Russell interviewed Walter Stahl of Saranac Lake who spent two years at Paul Smiths CCC camp.

"It was good to be working. Times were hard! You can't imagine what it was like . . . back then. You couldn't even buy a job. The men I lived with were in good spirits and the work was rewarding. The pay was fabulous—a dollar a day! They gave us clothes and they fed us."

Walter said he didn't mind being disciplined. "It was no problem. You did as you were told. There was kitchen duty; you had to keep the place neat, and you had to have a pass to go to town."

Stahl said he was 20 years old when he joined. He said one of the biggest challenges he and others had was fighting the large Bay Pond fire in 1934. It consumed 27,000 acres of timber.

"We fought it for months. The fire kept burning underground."

Walter Stahl said the men fought the fire in shifts. He said he had one close call. The fire surrounded his crew and he was forced to abandon his truck. He said, "It was a new truck, too. They weren't too happy about that."

He remembered the boys having boxing and wrestling matches and they went to Saranac Lake for "socializing." After serving in WWII Stahl returned to Saranac Lake because he liked the area.

Stahl added, "the skills and experience I got at the camp helped me in later life. During the war, I was a combat engineer, serving in the Pacific theater.

"We were just starting out in life, and needed to get our feet on the ground. We learned how to use saws and tools...a lot of guys were lumberjacks. The CCC gave me a chance to learn something."

After the war Stahl worked for 30 years as a meat distributor for Swift and Company. On December 22, 1998 he died at the age of 83.

Earl Barcomb

Sharon Noreault from Mountain View helped me when I was writing my book on the fire towers. Her father and husband were both fire tower observers on Loon and St. Regis mountains. I asked her if she knew anyone who worked in the CCC she told me her uncle Earl Barcomb was at Paul Smiths camp. I called Earl in June 2006 and he told me about his family and his days in the CCC.

"My father Thomas was a lumberman who had a crew that cut pulp wood. Then jobs were scarce so he took his family to East Hampton, Massachusetts. I was just a kid when we moved. We stayed there till I was seven and then returned to the Adirondacks. It was tough times. We were lucky to have food but we all worked. My older brother Harry drove Dad's team of horses when he was 14. One day he got stuck. Dad went over and calmed the horses. He got on the load and said to the horses, 'Come on Sam, etc.' and they got right out.

"I joined the CCC in the spring of 1936. I did this because work was scarce in those days. I was just 16 and had no problem joining even though you had to be 17. Politics was probably involved. Dad talked to the right people and that's how I got in.

"I just went to the camp by myself. The commander took my name and assigned me to a barracks. They were a good size with rows of bunks on both sides. There were five barracks and each were about 100' long. There were two to three round-bellied stoves in each that burned coal. A night watchmen came and filled the stoves.

"I made friends with a lot of the boys. There were guys from all over. Some were from New York City and others from southern states. They were very nice fellows. The only one that was still alive a few years ago was Paul "Smoky" Benoit. He lived in Owl's Head.

"My parents kept the money that I earned. They

didn't take the $25 from my pay like other parents did. I was quite a hot shot, free as a bird with the 30 dollars a month. There were some pretty hard up people in the camp. My family was very fortunate. We weren't destitute as other families were. We made out OK.

"On weekends we used to hitch hike home. Then I bought a 1929 Model A for $25. The guys with cars had a parking spot in the woods and the officers didn't bother us even though we weren't allowed to have a car in camp.

"Then someone began stealing gas from the cars. The first sergeant found out who it was. He had everyone with a car come to his office for a meeting. He talked about gas being stolen. Then he pointed his finger right at me and said, 'You're the one who's been stealing it.' I was stunned but it wasn't really me he was pointing at but the guy behind me. All the guys were going to lynch the bastard but the first sergeant had great command of the men. He calmed everyone down and said, 'This guy is going to retire tonight and leave.' and that was it."

"Sometimes I went hunting, sometimes to the movies in Malone. We also went to dances at the school in Owl's Head.

"On weekends they trucked the guys into Saranac Lake. Some went to the movies or hung out. Some had girl friends in town. They stayed till about twelve and a truck picked them up.

"The camp had a canteen that showed movies and it was also a place to buy candy bars and cigarettes. We bought coupons and used them as money in the canteen.

"KP duty was the only part of camp that nobody liked. The worst job was cleaning the grease pit. It was a hole covered by boards and once uncovered the smell was bad. Every weekend someone had to clean the grease trap. It was a sloppy job. We took the grease out and put it into barrels and carried it to the dump.

"The latrine was a good-sized building that always had hot water that was heated by a coal fire. It had sinks and flush toilets.

"I had a few jobs. I worked for an engineer building a bypass bridge. After that I worked at the fish hatchery at Saranac Inn where we made dams and kept the water clean. Then I became a truck driver. I drove a Reo dump truck and drew gravel. Most of the loading was done by hand. They had a few dozers in camp. One time a guy drove a tractor from Chasm Falls to our camp.

"Sometimes they sent you to a side camp where you set up tents for three months. We did work such as building a dam. My job was hauling gravel for a slit trench for an outhouse. It with just a furrow in the ground. We had tents for cooking and eating. We also had a side camp at Cold River. I believe we were repairing a dam. There was no netting for the tents so we used citronella smudges to keep out the bugs.

Did anything funny happen to you?

"Well, I had this buddy, Jake Lapine from Malone. He had worked for Agway and retired. Then he got a job at our camp assigning guys to jobs. I heard we were going to have a side camp by a river. I said to Jake, 'Please don't assign me to that side camp.' Then when the guys were assigned I was the first name called. What a friend.

"Another funny incident happened when we fought the big Bay Pond fire. Boy were we dirty. One time we got back to camp really late at 4 am. The old mess sergeant got up and made us a meal. He looked at us and said, 'I don't think you guys fought a fire. You just rubbed ashes on your face.'

"One winter I worked in the dining room. I didn't like that and went back to driving. Our average day was six hours. One foreman, Pop Van, always brought a couple of eggs. A guy cooked him three-minute eggs. They looked so good on toast. He was quite a character. He was an old timer from the old school.

"The foremen were good at showing us how to

Earl Barcomb at his home in Mountain View. He worked at Paul Smiths CCC camp in 1936. Sharon Noreault. Three friends of Earl Barcomb in camp in 1938. Earl Barcomb

work. One foreman saw this guy using a pick the wrong way. He told him, 'You won't last a day working like that. Just lift it up shoulder high and not all the way to your back. You won't get tired out so fast.'

"Each day the cooks packed us a lunch. They gave us three sandwiches and some cookies.

"The camp had sports teams. I enjoyed watching my buddy play baseball. He was a good catcher. They also had boxing. One time I went three rounds in a boxing match. Paul Benoit persuaded me. I was training with this guy who was 6' tall and arms around 7' long. He kept popping me in the nose. My match was the longest three rounds in the world.

In 1938 I left camp because work began to pick up. I got a job paying 50 cents an hour for a Connecticut construction company building a farm. Then I went to Massachusetts and worked in Chicopee Falls at the Savage Arms Co. I was the set up man on drill presses. In January 1943 I was drafted in the Army. I was in the European Theater from Scotland to Berlin. I was a radio operator and never fired a shot. We were far back enough from the shots except for some shrapnel.

"After the war I went into sales. I got married and had two children: Earl and Nancy. I had a night job but it was too hard. So I got a job working for a building contractor. Then I left him and went on my own.

"Now that I'm retired I enjoy working 3-4 hours a day splitting wood just like I did in the CCC."

Floyd Dumas

After interviewing four men on November 23, 2007 who were at the Bolton Landing camp I traveled to Queensbury and visited Floyd Dumas. Floyd said he quit high school in the fall of 1936 because his father, George, lost his job working for the NY Central Railroad where he was a boilermaker.

"I was 16 years old and signed up in Malone. There were around 10-20 guys from Malone who signed up. They took us not too far from home to Paul Smiths camp.

"My first job was digging up pine trees and transplanting them near the beach on Lake Meacham. It took two of us a day to dig a tree out of the frozen ground and it was cold, around 30 degrees below zero. But we weren't that cold because we were moving. There was one time when I was working and I froze my ears. I had to go to the infirmary to be treated.

"In the summer I cleaned the floor of the forest and raked the debris in Meacham Lake Park.

"Another job was we built a dam north of our camp along the right side of Rt. 30. We collected rock from the brook and built a cement dam. The water was so clear we filled our canteen and drank it.

"The food at camp was just wonderful and the guys got along well. There weren't any fights. After dinner we played cards, shot dice for cigarettes, and read a lot.

"One weekend I went to visit my sister, Grace, in Saranac Lake. Someone had a car and drove me there. She had three children and I sat around and played with them. She worked in a restaurant. I stayed till Sunday night.

In the spring I left the camp after working there for six months because they were going to work at a side camp that was filled with mosquitoes. I remember when I came home my mother said, 'What are you doing home!' My mother Margaret had six children and she needed the $25 that she received each month from my CCC work.

"I got different jobs: waiting on tables and caddying at the golf course. I had other odd jobs one of which was cooking for 12 hours a night in a restaurant in Malone. In 1942 I went to Alexandria Bay and cooked and tended bar.

"Then the Army drafted me. I was in the 45th Infantry Division and sent to Europe. In 1944 Germans captured my regiment and we were prisoners of war in Italy."

Floyd proudly handed me a 10-page story about his days as a POW and how he escaped from the Germans. When I called Floyd in 2010 he said someone made a movie of his and his friends' escape from the Germans and they showed the movie in Saratoga in May. "There were 150 people there and they gave me a large applause when he was introduced."

"When I came back home in 1945 I got married to Vivian Lapage from Fort Covington. Then I saw an ad for a job at Stein's Store in Malone. I got the job and the manager taught me all about tailoring. In six months I became the manager. Then the owner sent me to Danbury, Connecticut to manage their other store. In 1949 they transferred me to be the manager of their Glens Falls store.

"I'm very proud of my days in the CCC. Those were happy days because I was able to help my parents. The CCC gave us something to do and made men out of us."

Roland Brownell

After reading an article about my search for CCC

Floyd Dumas spent the fall and winter of 1936 at the Paul Smiths CCC camp. After WW II he became a tailor. At 90 he continues sewing in the basement of his home in Queensbury. Podskoch Collection

information written by Dick Chase in the Syracuse newspaper, Joseph Brownell contacted me in 2007. He told me his father, Roland, had worked as a superintendent in CCC camps in the Adirondacks. Joe wrote an unpublished book about his life, "Almost Charlie, Growing up in the Twentieth Century," and he sent part of it to me for this article.

Roland Brownell was the superintendent of the Thendara CCC camp (1935-36), Howland Island near Port Byron, and then in May 1937 he got word from Albany that he was being transferred to Paul Smiths. In the fall Joe's family moved to Gabriels four miles SE of the CCC camp.

Joe recalled: "There was something wrong with our well and for most of the year I was sent across the road to bring back pails of drinking water from a neighbor's house. Next door one of Dad's foremen lived with his new wife. My friends thought she was all right."

Joe enjoyed listening to radio station WGY from Schenectady which broadcast "Little Orphan Annie," "Captain Midnight," "Jack Armstrong," "Tom Mix," and the "Lone Ranger."

The following year the Brownells moved to Saranac Lake in the fall because the schools were better and it also had a five and ten cents store, a movie theater, and sidewalks and streetlights. The drive was longer but his dad drove home each night as before. The little green pickup truck was the same but the uniform had become more dressy. The breeches and puttees had given way to straight trousers and the 'mountie' hat was gone in favor of a felt fedora. His father's salary at the camp was $2,600 a year.

"I remember accompanying my dad to the Fish Creek campsite to look around to see how the work had been done. Another time he took me to a side camp in Lake Placid. The cook asked me if I wanted a fried egg. I had never had one before so I said sure. He took out a large frying pan and made me one. I felt like a grown up and ate it. Boy, was it good.

"In 1940 my friends in junior high school were slow to notice it but times were changing. Selective Service had been instituted and men were being drafted. War orders from Britain, and even our own armed forces, began to pare away at the unemployment rate. Several of the young CCC companies were disbanded, and at S-60 a unit of World War I veterans replaced the company of young men. One of the stories that went around the table was the old guys went steady all day.

"A year later in December my family were at our home in Oswegatchie one Sunday when, after lunch "Mamp's" (Grandpa) static ridden radio sputtered something about a Japanese raid on a naval base. We decided to go back to Saranac Lake immediately and on reaching Drutz's store on Broadway stopped for a newspaper and bread. The Drutz family was listening to a radio and their faces were very serious. It was December 7, 1941 and we were at war.

"Our own life style was turned around in the middle of winter. Men flocked to the colors and it became difficult to keep younger foremen on the CCC rosters. No one was surprised then, when my father came home with word that the camps were all being closed down and he was to be laid off. We left Saranac Lake on March 17, 1942 more than half way through my sophomore year.

"We were quickly back in Oswegatchie in late spring in a house that had not been for year round occupation. Insulation was not completely installed and newspapers covered studs in some rooms where the walls had not been finished. The only central heat came from a hot air furnace brought down from a house in Cranberry Lake. It consumed great quantities of chunk wood in the basement.

"My father had to go to Massena to work for the Alcoa Company; it was the only job he could find in a hurry. Help was on the way, however, for the old iron mines at Ben-

Joe Brownell in 1938. Joe Brownell

son Mines reopened as a defense plant corporation under the direction of the Jones & Laughlin Steel Corporation. By summer Dad came home and commuted to J & L."

Joe Veneto

In 2007 while doing research in Port Henry I learned that Joe Veneto, a retired local ironworker, had been in the CCC. I called Joe and was invited to his home. His wife Wilma invited me into their living room. I asked Joe to tell me about his life in the CCC.

"My two older brothers, Philip and Bruno, were already in the Port Henry CCC camp. They joined in 1933. My brothers told me they did blister rust control which was the removal of currant and gooseberry bushes. Another job was spraying trees to kill gypsy moths in spring and summer. In the fall and winter they searched for their egg masses."

I told Joe that I did some research and found that his brother, Philip, was on the staff of the camp newspaper and that the two of them won a field day competition: "...in the three-legged race, the Venetos, Phillip and Bruno, won over a field of prone athletes from neighboring camps."

"Bruno was a very good athlete. He played baseball at the camp. But I'm sorry to tell you that both my brothers died and I'm the last of the five brothers. There were eleven children in my family. My father Dominic couldn't work because he had heart troubles. My mother Angelene and all the kids helped out.

"I had to quit school after ninth grade. There was nothing to do. There weren't any jobs. In the fall of 1938 I joined the CCC. It was better than being a bum. They sent me to Blue Mountain. We cleaned up the dead wood in the forest and burned it.

"On the weekends I just hung around the camp. There wasn't much to do in Blue Mountain. I did my laundry by hand and used yellow Army soap. There weren't any washing machines.

"After six months I signed up to go out West. We traveled by train. It took about five days. They had sleeper cars and the train stopped occasionally so we got to walk around. I went to Priests River, Idaho and spent a year out there. My major job was doing park maintenance and in the winter I was a laborer at the park sawmill. The winters were tough, a lot of snow. This town was just like Blue Mountain. It only had a post office and a few stores.

"When I came back to Port Henry I got a job work-ing at Republic Steel. My two brothers also worked there when they got out of the CCC.

"In 1955 I got married and my wife, Wilma, and I had three children: Donald, Donna, and Tammy.

"The CCC was a big help to my family. They got $25 a month and that helped them during the Depression."

Leroy Smith

I met Leroy Smith at a CCC reunion at the Franklin County Historical Society in Malone in June 2010. Here is what he told the audience and later to me in a telephone interview about his experiences in the CCC:

"When I was almost 17 years old some of my friends and I joined the CCC in Malone. One of them was my best friend Robert Hastings. I didn't mind leaving home because Robert and I were best friends.

"In those days most kids only went to eighth grade. I was forced to quit to help my family. I'll never forget my dad had 29 boils and was in terrible shape. My teacher begged me to come back but I couldn't leave him. I had to help with the farm chores.

"My father George and my mother Nettie Lawrence raised seven children: Arlington, Mildred, Freda, Wilford, me, Emma, and Gaynell. I was born in Constable on December 28, 1920.

"Robert and I were sent the Paul Smiths camp. I did a lot of different jobs. One of them was building the outdoor theater at Fish Creek State Park. It was on a hill and all made of logs. There were logs on the ground for people to sit on. It was like steps and was in a semi circle. Other projects at Fish Creek were the building of bathhouses and fireplaces.

"Another project we worked on was building the cement dam at Meacham Lake. There was an old log dam and we took it out. That was interesting. We had an old cement mixer and we wheeled the cement to the dam. We also finished the road around part of the lake.

"We also worked at the fish hatchery near Lake Clear. The guys and I mixed cement and built troughs for the different-sized fish.

"Then we went down towards Tupper Lake and we planted a lot of trees.

"In camp I had another job. I worked in the kitchen and served the officers in their dining room.

"I enjoyed working with all the guys and foremen.

Rowland Brownell was one of the guys I liked and foreman Pop Knapp was a great guy. There was one enrollee that had web fingers like a bat. Oh boy, could he play the guitar. He was from Paul Smiths on Easy Street.

"There was one scary thing that happened to me in my barracks. Someone drove through a small town with a CCC truck and killed a young girl. I'll never forget the state police came to camp and had us walk in dirt. They took each guy's footprint because they had the murderer's footprints. The murderer was in my barracks. I thought he was a nice decent fellow, but he certainly didn't prove it.

"I also had some funny experiences. One night someone said I'll give anyone five dollars if they run naked in the falling snow, jump into Barnum Pond, and run back to camp. Robert Hastings and I took the bet. We took off our clothes and streaked all the way in the snow to Barnum Pond. It was cold. When we got halfway back we saw a car coming and Robert said:

'What are we going to do?'

I replied: 'We're just going to keep on running.'

"Yes, we got back and we both got our five dollars. I'll never forget when I told Harold Lepine about streaking to make five dollars.

"He said, 'That's nothing, I did it once before and made money.'

"The lunches were great at camp. I know one thing, I liked the P & J, peanut butter and jelly, sandwiches. The rest of the meals were good, too. I wasn't too crazy about KP duty. I had to clean the grease pit but I wasn't alone. Luckily I only had to do it once. I think it was made out of logs with boards on top and was about 10'x 10'.

"In the evenings we usually played cards or shot craps.

"On most of the weekends I came home. Just above the camp there was a road and we'd wait for this beer truck to go by. He'd give us a ride to Malone. Then I'd call somebody from my town for a ride home.

"For recreation I remember being in a three-legged race. Robert was my partner and we could run very fast because we were used to each other. I also was good running by myself in the bag race.

"After working there for two years I left in 1939. I started working for the county but was laid off. Then I got a job at Lyon Mountain in the iron mine. I liked it the best because if you worked hard you made more money. I was there for four years.

"In 1942 I got married to Eileen Sullivan from Chasm Falls. We had two children: Mildred and Robert. Then I went into the Army and went overseas to France and Germany. I was a tank driver and we liberated Pilsen, Czechoslovakia.

"I came back home in March 1946. I bought my father's farm in Burke. Then we had five more children: Helen, Donald, Madonna, Leland, and Anne. I ran the farm for 33 years. Then I drove truck for the Franklin County Highway Department.

After working at the Paul Smiths CCC camp, Leroy Smith served in the Army during WWII. Madonna Smith Damour

"On August 29, 1995 there was a CCC reunion and dedication of a monument at the CCC camp site. Oh yes, I was there when they dedicated it. Oh my God, the camp doesn't look the same. Trees and brush have grown in. We had a ball field across the road towards Osgood Pond.

"I always thought the CCC helped improve me. I took all the classes they had. What we did was very interesting to me."

CHAPTER 22
PLATTSBURGH-CUMBERLAND BAY SP & PLATTSBURGH BARRACKS

HISTORY

The Plattsburgh area had two CCC camp sites established in January 1935. The first site was Camp S-102 on Rt. 9 at the old entrance to the Plattsburgh Municipal Beach on Lake Champlain in the Town of Plattsburgh and the other, A-4, was at the Plattsburgh Barracks in the city of Plattsburgh on New York Road where the Air Force Hospital was.

On January 5, 1935 a special train from Vermont brought 200 WW I veterans of Company 2207-V to Plattsburgh in Clinton Co. and then trucked them two miles north to the newly erected Camp S-102 that was on the municipal beach. It adjoined the new state park.[1]

Capt. Donald L. Marsh commanded Camp S-102 and Lt. Leon Kasprack assisted him. Carl Getman was the camp superintendent and Robert H. Ewell the education advisor.[2]

Their major projects were to clear brush along the shore of Lake Champlain and build the Cumberland Bay State Park next to Plattsburgh's Municipal Beach. They transformed 160-acres of swamps and sand dunes and 2,800' of Lake Champlain shoreline into a beautiful state campground.[3]

While developing the campsite at Cumberland Bay, veterans found Algonquin Indian artifacts as they leveled the sand dunes. They found clay pottery, spearheads, hammer stones, scrapers and other relics. Camp Superintendent, Carl B. Getman, displayed the artifacts in a glass case in the forestry office for all to see.[4]

When the state acquired the land in 1932, 1936 and 1937 it was occupied mostly my French Canadians who had settled under the first growth white pines in the late 1800s along the lakeshore. They lived in shacks that locals called "Stovepipe Village." The settlers fished in Cumberland Bay using seines and did ice fishing in the winter and in winter did ice fishing.[5]

In the early 1930s the state purchased land that was part of the "Stovepipe Village" (also called Stovepipe Alley) with the purpose of building a state park. It adjoined the Municipal Beach that began in 1928.

The preliminary work on this state park had begun

When a CCC enrollee was seriously ill an Army ambulance took them to the Plattsburgh Army Barracks Hospital. Here is an ambulance crew from Paul Smiths camp posing by a cannon near the hospital. Jim Corl

in the summer of 1933 when Ralph G. Unger, a forester at the Goldsmith CCC camp S-61, was transferred to the Plattsburgh Army Barracks with 20 CCC boys who cleared and cleaned the state beach near Cumberland Ferry. Plans were to make the 43 acres with a half-mile of beach into a campground.[6]

214

Left - CCC veterans of Camp S-102 built this stone entrance gate to the Cumberland Bay State Park during the 1930s. Podskoch Collection.
Right - The veterans at the Plattsburgh CCC camp built this V-dam on Steep Bank Brook in 1935.[11]

Besides working at the new Cumberland State Park, the veterans did maintenance and new construction work in Clinton Co. in an area 80 x 40 sq. mi. They often lived in side camps to complete projects that included fire protection, building truck trails, fire tower observer cabins and telephone lines, lean-tos, latrines, fences, water control dams, and dams for swimming and the improvement of fishing.[7]

The 1936 Conservation Report stated CCC veterans traveled 23 miles to Poke-O-Moonshine Mountain and built the fire tower observer's cabin. At the foot of this mountain they also did maintenance work at the Poke-O-Moonshine State Park campsite. The following year they began construction of the park caretaker's headquarters.[8] In 1939 they dug 200' of diversion ditches, built two toilet buildings, and constructed 1.5 miles of telephone line.

Robinson Franklin, the Poke-O-Moonshine park manager in 2008, said: "The CCC built a children's playground during the 1930s but only a foundation remains. We also found camp signs in a storage area that had about 15 names of the CCC guys who worked there. They also built the camp fireplaces and a lean-to on the mountain."

After two years of developing the Cumberland Bay State Park, it was formally opened on July 1, 1937.The Ausable Forks Record-Post reported the CCC Veterans camp cut down the sand dunes and filled in the swampy area. The park had 22 campsites for trailers and 75 tent sites. The CCC built fieldstone fireplaces and installed running water that was within 200' of each campsite.

During the 1930s the Cumberland Bay State Park did not provide parking for picnickers or bathers. They had to use the Plattsburgh Municipal Beach next to the state park.

In 1938 Camp S-102 worked on blister rust eradication in Clinton Co. It covered 5,607 acres in Schuyler and Plattsburgh towns and destroyed 82,140 ribes plants.[9] This work continued in 1939. From May 15 to September 30 veterans worked in the towns of Peru, Schuyler Falls and Plattsburgh. They destroyed 91,000 gooseberry and currant bushes. From October 1 to November 10 they destroyed 69,000 currant and gooseberry bushes on 600 areas in the Town of Chazy.[10]

That same year CCC veterans partially completed a stream improvement project on .3 mile of the Boquet River that had been dedicated for public fishing. They deepened pools to provide cool water and cover for the fish, removed debris, and built log structures to prevent bank erosion.[12]

On April 3, 1938 Camp S-102 held an open house to celebrate the fifth anniversary of the CCC. Plattsburgh residents were invited to visit the camp and inspect the camp projects.[13]

The Ausable Forks Record-Post dated June 2, 1938 stated that the new Cumberland Bay State Campsite was to reopen after the CCC veterans did some grading and cleaning.

Superintendent Carl Getman described some of the camp's projects in 1938 in the February 2, 1939 issue of The Plattsburgh Daily Press. Veterans traveled to Lake Placid and developed a 22-acre public campground at the bobsled run. At the Cumberland Bay State Park they constructed: three toilet buildings; three and one-half miles of truck trails; 41 fireplaces; 1,400' ft. of rip rap to protect the shore; two life guard chairs; and 123 combination tables and benches. They installed a sewage disposal system, plant-

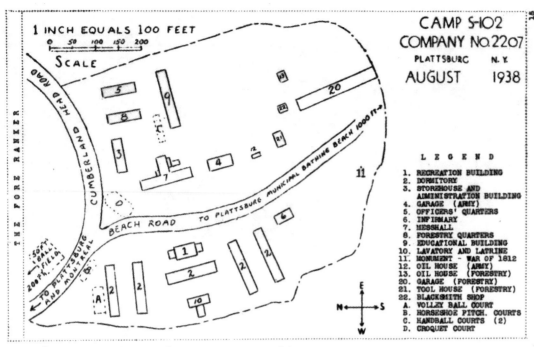

CAMP S-102
COMPANY No. 2207
PLATTSBURG   N.Y.
AUGUST   1938

L E G E N D
1. RECREATION BUILDING
2. DORMITORY
3. STOREHOUSE AND
   ADMINISTRATION BUILDING
4. GARAGE (ARMY)
5. OFFICERS' QUARTERS
6. INFIRMARY
7. MESSHALL
8. FORESTRY QUARTERS
9. EDUCATIONAL BUILDING
10. LAVATORY AND LATRINE
11. MONUMENT - WAR OF 1812
12. OIL HOUSE (ARMY)
13. OIL HOUSE (FORESTRY)
20. GARAGE (FORESTRY)
21. TOOL HOUSE (FORESTRY)
22. BLACKSMITH SHOP
A. VOLLEY BALL COURT
B. HORSESHOE PITCH. COURTS
C. HANDBALL COURTS (2)
D. CROQUET COURT

A map of veterans camp S-102 in the August 1938 issue of the camp newspaper, The Fore Ranker. Center for Research Library

ed 1,100 ac. of trees, and seeded and sodded seven acres.

In 1939 the CCC made further camp improvements. The veterans built 35 more campsites and resurfaced the dusty main camp road into the park with macadam.[14]

Camp S-102 had an advisor who supervised the education department. He tailored the program to the needs of the veterans whose average age was more than 44. These classes were offered: English grammar, American history, journalism, typing, trigonometry, blacksmithing, cooking, carpentry, masonry, leather craft, radio building, diesel engines, truck driving, firemen, mechanics, mess steward, orderlies, and electrician.

The men produced a newspaper called "The Fore Ranker" that came out twice a month. The Army District conducted a CCC camp newspaper contest. "The Fore Ranker" received the highest rating from the National, Army Corps, and CCC Sub-District judges.[15]

The Conservation Department's Supervising Forester, William Foss, stated: " I consider S-102 one of the most outstanding camps in New York State." Major J. L. Ballard, Executive Officer of the District, said: "Whatever assignment may be given Company 2207, their work will be outstanding because it would be unlike them to perform their duties otherwise."[16]

Camp life was not all work and no play. The Army organized sports activities. Once a week veterans went to the Plattsburgh Barracks' bowling alley and three times a week trucks took them to the Barracks' movie theater. There was also a handball and volleyball court for use in the summer. Horseshoe pitching was also very popular with the veterans. Every month men went to the Plattsburgh Barracks for boxing and wrestling matches.[17] The veterans also played in the Plattsburgh softball league.

The camp recreation hall had table tennis, cards, and a library with 700 books. There was a stage for plays and musical entertainment.

On weekends some men got passes to go home. Others went to nearby Plattsburgh for entertainment. They frequently walked or hitchhiked. On Sunday evening the 25th of September, 1938 a tragedy occurred to one of the CCC veterans as he was walking back to camp. Harry Pambrio of Plattsburgh was driving at 10 pm on the Plattsburgh-Chazy highway (Rt. 9) when he struck and killed George Brooks. Pambrio said he was blinded by lights from an oncoming car and hit Brooks who was walking in the middle of the road.[18]

The April 18, 1940 issue of The Plattsburgh Daily Press wrote an editorial singing the praises of Camp S-102's work ethic and accomplishments:

"Camp S-102 is composed entirely of men who have followed the flag across the sea and who are deserving of the best their country can give…"

"Many of these men have had more than their share of personal knowledge of the seamy side of life, but it is not in their spirit. They have taken what they have found to do and have done it with a thoroughness that has made an amazing change for the better of a section of Plattsburgh which for years had been dismissed as a worthless series of sand dunes and a cluster of shacks known as 'Stovepipe Village.'

"They have made what might be called a garden spot out of acres of sand at the edge of Cumberland Bay…have built an auto camp which is second to none in the State…it

Above, Left - This cartoon of two Company 2207 CCC veterans reading newspapers at their tent camp near the bobsled run near Lake Placid. It was in the February issue of "The Fore Ranker" camp newspaper. Center for Research Library Archives. Above, Right - Members of CCC Company 211 standing in their dress uniforms in front of the camp headquarters at the Plattsburgh Army Barracks Camp A-4. Joe Weaver. Right - The veterans from camp S-102 in Plattsburgh completed the Marcy Dam. DEC Archives

was largely a breeding place for mosquitoes. Now we know it for one of the most attractive spots to visit. When the history of Camp S-102 is written it will prove these men have been no less effective in peacetime pursuits than they were when they were called upon to come to the aid of a threatened democracy."

On May 18, 1940 Camp S-102 closed and Company 2207 composed of veterans was transferred to Lake Placid Camp S-138. It spent the summer completing Marcy Dam, constructing a telephone line up Whiteface Mountain, and continuing work on the bobsled run.[19]

Some of the projects at the Marcy Dam included: building a small footbridge, a multiple-arch bridge on Marcy Dam Road, a crib dam at Marcy Creek, and the maintenance of 2.7 miles of Marcy Dam truck trails.[20]

The dam was constructed to provide a pond that would be stocked with trout and also a place for hikers and fishermen to clean up. Mr. Brownell, Paul Smiths camp superintendent, and his enrollees did the preliminary surveying. Then superintendent Carl Getman from the Plattsburgh camp S-102 was in charge of the work. Foreman Martel was in charge of a 20-man veteran crew. There was a blacksmith and an assistant on the job plus a truck driver and tractor operator.

"The crib and rock foundation went six feet un-

der the dam proper. The men worked in water to build this foundation—a flume carrying most of the water overhead, and two pumps being used to take care of the scopage. The dam will be 185' wide with a foot bridge across the top."[21]

During that year the veterans worked at other sites doing projects. At South Meadows there was a project planting 40,000 trees. At Meadow Brook campsite they worked on constructing a cesspool and excavating a garbage pit. The projects at the Olympic bobsled run were: constructing a bridge at the entrance, making alterations and repairs to the caretaker's house, a ticket booth and two telephone and timing booths.[22]

In the winter Company 2207-V was transferred to Paul Smiths.[23]

While camp S-102 at Cumberland Bay State Park was vacant a unit from the Cornell ROTC occupied the camp getting infantry training.

This was not the end of the CCC in Camp S-102 because five months later 180 junior enrollees in Co. 211 arrived by train from Sag Harbor, Long Island on October 21, 1940. Philip E. Pons was in command.[24] These men continued working on gypsy moth control projects and developing Cumberland Bay Park.[25]

Many of the CCC camps held an "Open House" to acquaint local citizens to what was going on in their neighborhood. On Sunday April 6, 1941 Camp S-102 celebrated the 8th anniversary of the founding of the CCC in the US. The camp was open from 3-6 PM for people to see how the enrollees lived.[26]

The Conservation Department often called the CCC camps to help fight forest fires. During the spring

Army officers in front of Camp A-4 Company 211 headquarters building. Joe Weaver

1941 a devastating forest fire swept over 10,000 acres near Clintonville and Chesterfield. More than 1,000 workers helped to bring the fire under control. The Ticonderoga Sentinel dated May 1, 1941 stated 300 CCC enrollees from both Plattsburgh CCC camps helped.

The enrollees were fortunate to have a sandy beach and swimming area right next to their camp. After work the young men swam at the Municipal Beach. One evening an unidentified CCC boy got a cramp in 8' of water. Luckily lifeguard Benton Barry, a St. Lawrence athlete, was on duty and rescued the drowning swimmer.[27]

During 1941 Camp S-102 continued working on the development of Cumberland Bay State Park where they built two bathhouses. They also did blister rust control work but were hampered due to a decrease in the number of enrollees. The men covered these towns: Altona, Beekmantown, Plattsburgh, and Schuyler Falls.[28]

On October 21, 1941 Co. 211 under the command of Lt. Nat Bender was transferred to Grafton, 15 miles east of Troy. Company 220 left Lake Placid's camp and occupied the Cumberland Bay camp S-102. They continued doing pest control work.[29]

On September 26, 1941 the Plattsburgh S-102 camp was redesignated AF-1. The A meant that it was at an Army reservation. The enrollees were not at the Cumberland Bay State Park but at the Plattsburgh Army Barracks. (It is unknown what the F represents. Neither the NYS Conservation Department or CCC Legacy records has information to explain the AF designation)

The 1941 Conservation Report states, camp AF-1 was: "...assigned to activities correlated to the national defense program with plans initiated for the development of the Macomb Reservation at Schuyler Falls and rifle range at the Plattsburgh Barracks." The Macomb Reservation, approximately 8 miles SW of Plattsburgh and west of Schuyler Falls, was a 7,000-acre parcel on the Salmon River that provided additional space for training soldiers from the Plattsburgh Army Barracks.

On July 23, 1942 Plattsburgh Camp S-102 at Cumberland Bay closed.[30] The Plattsburgh Daily Press stated in the June 24, 1942 issue that the Army was to take over the camp and house a battalion of military police from the Plattsburgh Barracks. The federal government was to pay the city $1 yearly rent.

In the summer of 1945 the City of Plattsburgh moved a few buildings from Camp S-102 to the new municipal airport.[31]

In the June 7, 1946 issue of The Plattsburgh Daily Press reported the city converted the former CCC camp located at the entrance to the Municipal Bathing Beach into apartments for 19 families at a cost of $4,000. "Sunshine City" as it was called was home to 62 children who had the nearby beach and state park to enjoy.

By November 1946 the new village of "Sunshine City" was not deemed a pleasant place to live. The Plattsburgh City Council voted to evict 171 residents of "Sunshine City." The Health Department stated the buildings lacked proper sanitation and insulation and rats were present. When the residents vacated the buildings, they were dismantled.[32]

Camp A-4 was the second CCC camp, in the Plattsburgh area. It was a composed of veterans in Company 2204. It was located south of the city of Plattsburgh at the Plattsburgh Army Barracks and established on January 15, 1935.

In the spring 1935 the Plattsburgh Army Barracks acquired a ferryboat from the Green-Mountain Ferry Company. They used it to transport CCC enrollees to beautify nearby Crab Island.[33]

In the evenings the camp provided classes that education advisor George Sime organized and supervised. The courses were similar to the classes at Cumberland Bay's S-102 CCC camp.

The Army provided professional entertainment for the enrollees in the two Plattsburgh area CCC camps. In November 1935 CCC enrollees enjoyed two plays. The drama, "Friendly Enemies" was performed. This was part of the federally funded Temporary Emergency Relief Administration (TERA) that hired unemployed actors.[34]

WORK ACCOMPLISHED BY CAMP S-102*

PROJECT	1935	1936	1937	1938	1939	1940	1941	TOTAL
Bathhouses - number							2	2
Beach improvement - ac.		35	3	2				40
Buildings, other - number			1					1
Ditches, diversion - number				200				200
Dwellings - number		1	1	1		1		4
Eradication of poisonous weeds - ac.		15	25	34	130			204
Experimental plots - number				1	4			5
Fences - rods		71		100	50	2		223
Fine grading - yd^2	1575	17401						18976
Fire fighting - man-days					157		388	545
Fire hazard reduction (roadside & trailside) - mi.	5							5
Fire pre-supression - man-days					146		78	224
Fireplaces - number		44	101	41	34	95		315
Garages - number		1						1
General clean-up - ac.	40			40				80
Guard rails - rods			450		16	2		468
Insect pest control - ac.							31412	31412
Incinerators - number			1					1
Landscaping - ac.				1.5				1.5
Latrines & toilets - number		3	4	4	3	10		24
Maps & models - man-days							108	108
Mosquito control - ac.		150	5	34	30			219
Parking areas & overlooks - yd^2	13000	12132	25000	2800	15000			67932
Picnic ground development - ac.		2.5						2.5
Pipe or tile line - linear ft.	4790	450	900	2500				8640
Planting trees - ac.		1350			16000			17350
Planting/moving trees & shrubs - number	600		4100	600			600	5900
Power line - mi.			0.1				0.1	0.2
Preparation/transportation of materials - man-days	133		186	122	579		1090	2110
Public campground development - ac.	5	3.8	8.9		37		16	70.7
Razing undesirable structures - man-days		10	179					189
Retaining walls - yd^2							1093	1093
Riprap or paving (rocks & cement) - yd^2				800	320			1120
Seats, benches, chairs - number				2				2
Seed collection - lbs.					25			25
Seeding or sodding - ac.	8	7		4	7			26
Sewage & waste disposal systems - number				2		5		7
Sheet erosion planting - ac.			12					12
Shelters - number	3		1	4				8
Signs, markers, monuments - number			25	192	113	86		416
Soil preparation - ac.		8.5	1.5	1	11		6	28
Stream & lake bank protection - yd^2				600				600
Stream development - mi.	3	0.3		0.3				3.6
Structures, misc. - number	2	23						25
Surveys - man-days			200		16			216
Table-bench combinations - number	150	20	30	123	150	2	150	625
Telephone line - mi.	1	5	0.1			2.1		8.2
Trails, foot - mi.	3	1						4

*Numerical data from Conservation Reports

Plattsburgh Barracks Camp A-4 Company 208 group picture taken August 1936. Lu Patnode Bourcier

In the November 23, 1935 issue of the Plattsburgh Daily Press reported another drama, "Turn to the Right" that was also performed at both camps.

During the 1935 Christmas season a group of singers from Plattsburgh and CCC veterans from A-4 at the Army Barracks sang at a Christmas Eve midnight service at the Plattsburgh Barracks. CCC members and guests listened and participated in the singing.[35]

In the December 17, 1935 issue of The Plattsburgh Press stated Camp A-4 would hold its first dance in the recreation hall on January 12, 1936. A party and dance were going to celebrate the 1st anniversary of the camp. It included free refreshments, dancing and entertainment.

Camp A-4 veterans enjoyed many sports activities. During the winter the basketball team competed against Plattsburgh city teams, Army teams, and nearby CCC camps in leagues and tournaments. In the spring and summer the young men played in the Plattsburgh softball league. In 1937 the CCC boys competed in the annual Northern NY Sub-district field day on August 21 in Tupper Lake.[36]

In January 1936 Company 2204 V disbanded. Most of the veterans were transferred to Camp S-102 and Company 2207 at Cumberland Bay.[37]

Although Company 2204 V was disbanded in 1936 Camp A-4 continued with a new company 208. They competed on August 21, 1937 in the Field Day competition in Tupper Lake.[38]

In September 1937 Camp A-4 had a farewell dinner for 25 men. Camp commander Capt. George H. Seitz, Jr. praised his 126 men and said it might be the last gathering at the post because Company 208 was expected to leave for Wyoming. The camp was to be converted into housing for non-commissioned officers and their families. These officers were at the dinner: Lt. Burton Koffler, Lt. F. L. Mohr, R. H. Ewell (education advisor), Capt. Donald March, and Lt. Arthur Frambach of Company 2207. These men were the camps' technical staff: Frank Fitzpatrick, John Light, Frank McKeefe, and Percy Raymo.[39]

The Plattsburgh Press dated July 12, 1941 reported Camp A-4 was playing in the Plattsburgh City Softball League.

Camp A-4 CCC buildings were removed. In the 1954 the Air Force took over the Army Barracks. In 1959 the Air Force built a hospital on the site of Camp A-4. In 2008 the hospital was demolished.

MEMORIES

Gerald Patnode

When I interviewed Richard Bourcier on October 5, 2007 in Malone he told me about his work at the CCC camp in Paul Smiths. Then his wife, Louva (Lou), told me her brother, Gerald Patnode, was also in the CCC. She said he was in a nursing home in Malone and gave me his phone number. Lou also gave me a three and one-half-foot long panoramic picture of his camp. I was unable to visit him but I called him on February 24, 2008.

"I was in three CCC camps: Plattsburgh; Grand Coulee Dam in Washington; and Brushton near St. Regis Falls. I joined the CCC because I couldn't get a job and I had to help my parents. My mother, Rose, had eight children. I was born in Churubusco on October 17, 1917, the third eldest in my family. My father, Maxim, had a farm for a while but lost it due to the Depression. He worked for the town of Churubusco. In those days many of the boys my age quit school in eighth grade. I did the same and worked for different farmers and an uncle doing haying and odd jobs.

"I still couldn't find a regular job. Then a lady in charge of the welfare department made arrangements for my cousin, Rubin Rober, and I to get in the CCC. Dad drove us down to the Plattsburgh CCC camp. We had no idea what to expect. We felt it was quite a strange place but if we wanted to eat we had to do something. Rubin and I got accustomed to the guys who turned out to be nice fellows.

"Most of the jobs I did were landscaping. My first

Gerald Patnode from Churubusco at his CCC Camp A-4 Company 220 at the Plattsburgh Barracks. Lu Patnode Bourcier

job was building roads in camp. It was a short distance from the Army base. Our camp was on Rt. 9 across the road from the Army base and there was a cemetery nearby. Another job I did was fixing the cemetery headstones.

"In the winter we hauled ice from Chazy Lake. Then we built something like bunker silos and filled them with ice. There were four of us who worked in a team. We handled the Army mules because we were farm boys. The mules pulled ropes that skidded the ice onto the pile. We started about 6' below ground and we built up a stack 6-8' above ground. Some blocks were 2' x 4' and from 18" to 2' thick. The size of the blocks depended on the winter. When we finished skidding the ice to the top, other people covered it with sawdust and straw. The ice was used by the Army base and for our camp.

"We also worked in the woods behind the camp. We trimmed the low limbs of the tall pine trees that were up to 30' high. The rifle range was right behind our camp. We were south of the 26th Infantry Base in Plattsburgh. Today this area is now in the city and built up.

"Did you ever get sick or injured?"

"Yes. I was in the Army hospital with the mumps for a couple of weeks. The hospital was three stories high.

"What did you do in camp in the evenings and on weekends?"

"The guys hung out in the recreation hall. They were all a hell of a good bunch of kids. Some boys hung out at the PX for a few beers. Sometimes they had a few too many and got into trouble. I used to read newspapers and hunting magazines in my free time.

"In the evenings we could sign up for classes. I took a mechanic course and that is where I learned to work on trucks and cars. Classes were taught in the headquarter's building. It was mostly book learning. Then we went to the garage.

"At 9 pm we had to cut out the noise and the lights went out. We had leaders in our barracks that made sure we listened.

"When Friday afternoon came along, they said we were free for the weekend. On our first weekend Rubin and I hiked all the way home, 34 miles! We were pretty well played out. Our feet were swollen. Eventually we got to know some guys from Malone who had cars at camp. They'd give us a ride to Chateaugay and we'd walk from there. I usually went home at least once a month.

"I stayed in this camp for 18 months. When they were ready to close the camp, I signed up to go out West to Grand Coulee Dam. In September 1937 the Army shipped about 400 guys out by train. It stopped along the way and dropped off guys at different camps. It took about five days to get there.

"They made me an assistant leader. I worked with another leader and we were trying to control city kids while they worked building an outdoor swimming pool and skating rink for a school. We had some trouble with the CCC boys. Finally, I got another sergeant to help me. Luckily they transferred the bad kids out of camp. It got to the point where I couldn't stand supervising guys any more and I asked the foreman if I could be transferred and be a truck driver. I got the job and hauled stone and dirt to fill around a school that they were building. Then in April 1938 we were discharged.

"I came home to Churubusco. I worked through the summer in the local cemetery. There was a terrible hurricane in Keene, New Hampshire. A bunch of guys from the area went to Keene to cut up the downed trees. It was hard to make money to pay for room and board because a lot of the days it was too windy to work in the woods. Finally, two guys from Burke and our town of Churubusco got in an argument as to how they were cutting the trees. The foreman fired all of us.

"We came home and the welfare lady in our town was able to get us into the Brushton CCC camp around January of 1939.

"Clarence Petty was the supervisor. He had his plane across the road in the field.

"The Brushton camp was pretty similar to all the camps, five barracks with 30-40 men in each. The boys had some schooling but didn't know how to work. The majority didn't know how to behave either. We had to train them. There was one guy, Art Vann, from Riverview (Saranac) who was all man. He showed them how to listen.

"I drove truck and then worked in the garage as a mechanic. I became a leader and got $45 a month.

"Sometimes I'd transport machinery to the Schenectady Depot and return that night. On the way back if they needed to return a compressor to the Veterans camp in Lake Placid, I delivered it. They said to stay there for the night but I said I had to get back. I'd drive home and get back after midnight. Sometimes it was about 2 am. I'd just park the truck outside and go to sleep. Petty, our superintendent, never questioned when I came back.

"I worked in the garage with Eddie Baker, the head mechanic. He was from Moira. Eddie and his brother-in-law also ran a bar there.

"One day the Ford dealer in Malone came to camp and asked Eddie to work for them. When Eddie said no, I took the job. I worked there till July 1941 when I was drafted. They sent me to Fort Belfore, Virginia and later to March Field, California where I was a mechanic.

"I got out of Army in 1945 and opened my own garage in Churubusco.

"In 1950 I got married to Theresa Gervais from Montreal. We didn't have any children. In 1979 I had a heart operation and had to retire. Then we moved to Malone.

"The CCC helped me a lot. I learned mechanics, traveled, and learned how to educate young men who didn't know how to work. I had learned how to work from my father. He showed his children the importance of work and didn't have to tell us what to do. We did it."

Hector Gebo

On June 10, 2006 I had a telephone interview with Leander "Lee" Gebo of Plattsburgh. Lee told me he was in the Brushton CCC Camp in 1937.

"There were 11 children in my family. My father was disabled when he busted his back in a stone quarry in about 1919. In 1937 when I was 16, I quit school because my family needed a lot of help and I signed up for the CCC.

"I had two other brothers who joined the CCC. My brother Edward was at Paul Smiths camp and my eldest brother, Hector after me in 1937. He was at the Plattsburgh camp. It was located at the entrance to the 82nd Infantry Division. Hector took care of the mules for the infantry at the stables on Rt. 9. They didn't have many vehicles then. He also worked at Macomb State Park in Schuyler Falls about

6 mi. W of Plattsburg. There he built tables, fireplaces, and roads.

"He took up boxing at the camp and did fairly well. He boxed against the Army guys. He broke his nose a few times He had a big nose for a target.

"I think he was in for about 10 months. He then worked in the stone quarry where my father worked. After that he worked at the Georgia Pacific Paper Mill. He married Ann Mae Parant and they had three girls and one boy. Hector died approximately 1998.

"My brother said he enjoyed being in the CCC because he liked supporting his family."

Joe Weaver

In the summer of 2007 I met John and Diane Jazeboski of Scotia at a talk in Speculator. They told me their neighbor, Joe Weaver, was in the CCC and I should contact him. That fall I visited Joe and he told me he was in the Plattsburgh camp for six months in 1940. I asked Joe why he joined?

"I just graduated from Amsterdam high school and I studied to be a machinist under a government training program. I took classes at the junior high school building in the summertime. They had a machine shop there. I earned a certificate and got a job at Mohawk Carpet Mills in Amsterdam where my dad, Andrew, was a head loom fixer.

"Around October I was laid off. I was 18 years old and living with my sister. Since I didn't have a job I owed her money for rent. I needed a job badly.

"How many were in your family?"

"There were seven of us. I was the fourth child and the oldest son. My parents needed some financial help, too. Then I heard about the CCC on the radio. It was in November when I went to the Court House in Amsterdam and signed up.

"They took us on a bus to Plattsburgh. It didn't bother me leaving home because I loved to travel and I knew I'd be working in the woods so I

Joe Weaver at his home in Scotia telling stories about his experiences in the CCC at the Plattsburgh Army Barracks in 1940. Podskoch Collection

Left - Joe Weaver wore a white jacket while serving dinner to the Army officers and Conservation Department foresters at the Plattsburgh CCC camp. Joe Weaver. Above - Joe Weaver took this picture of his three friends, Pete Moran, J. Rodgozinski, and Walter Blahert at the Plattsburgh Barracks CCC camp. Joe Weaver

looked forward to it because I loved to hunt and fish."

"What jobs did you have?"

"The first job was in the motor pool doing maintenance on the trucks. There were three garages. I got the job because I had the mechanics' certificate and I did chores and drove tractors and equipment at a friend's farm.

"They also made me a chauffeur. I drove Conservation officers to town and to meetings. I had a buddy named Ernie Fonda who worked with me in the garage and as driver.

"Another job I had in the evenings was as an orderly in the officers' building. I served the officers and foresters their meals.

"Around 85 per cent of guys were from New York City. I got along good with them. The officers made me an assistant leader because I had training when I got there. I was an outdoors' man and I could teach the boys how to work in the woods and how to work safely. I grew up on my friend, Joseph Knapp's farm in Hagaman. After school and on weekends I went to his farm and helped out.

"Part of my job in the motor pool was to transport the workers to their jobs. When I drove, my friend Ernie Fonda sat in the cab with me. I was also made assistant leader and I supervised the boys in the woods. All we did was wander around looking for gypsy moths in the trees. We marked them with a flag. I had guys put white flags at the top of the trees around the whole perimeter of infested areas. After the area was surveyed airplanes flew over the flagged area and sprayed it."

"Did anyone ever get hurt?"

"A few times guys fell off the trees. They were up there pretty high and when they hit the ground there was a loud 'THUMP.' No one was ever seriously hurt.

"When we got back to camp we had dinner. The food was very good. After dinner we listened to radio, played cards, or went to the movies in town.

"On the weekend we took trips to visit surrounding towns. Sometimes we took the bus to town. A couple times I signed a vehicle out of the motor pool because I worked there and took a bunch of guys. We would also hitchhike or even walk.

"Did you do any funny things?"

"Oh yes. We put pinecones in the guys' beds. Another joke was we tied the guy's shoes together and when they got up in the morning we would laugh as they struggled and cussed to untie them."

"Why did you leave the CCC?"

"After six months I left camp in April 1941 because I got my old job back at Mohawk Carpet and I heard they were going to disband the camp. I worked for a while and was laid off again. They were going to draft me so I enlisted in the Army in April 1942.

"In January 1946 I got out of the service. I took it easy for a while and went back to Mohawk Carpet.

"I got married to Genevieve Maryzak on September 20, 1947. We had one son, Paul.

"Then I got a job at General Electric. I had a lot of jobs there: swept floors, drove a lift truck, and worked on Army and Air force engines as a machinist. I made pistons and valves. Then I worked in the foundry. I retired on April 1, 1984."

"Did you ever go back to your camp?"

"I went up once or twice in the 1940s. I saw people living in my old camp buildings that had been converted into apartments by the town in 1946.

"The CCC was a good experience for me because I learned how to live with a bunch guys. I also learned how to be a leader and get guys to work and get along."

Joan Roach Amell

On July 19, 1910 I met Joan Roach Amell at the CCC Reunion at the Schenectady Historical Society. She told me:

"As a kid we lived on Sally Avenue in Plattsburgh. I remember a group of CCC guys walking by and asking for formation to go back to camp. Perhaps they were coming back from a parade. I was in fourth grade. I was born in 1933 so it was about 1941.

"There was a building near the city beach that the Girl Scouts used during WWII. We made crafts like wooden bookends and other little crafts. It was one big room with tables with electricity. The outside was stained dark brown.

"Route 9 turned right on Beach Road and the CCC building was on the right."

An August 1936 panoramic view of CCC Camp A-4 Company 208 located at the Plattsburgh Army Base. Lu Patnode Bourcier. The interior of one of the barracks at Camp A-4 at the Army Barracks south of the city of Plattsburgh. This camp was staffed by junior enrollees aged 18-25. Joy Prue Long

CHAPTER 23
PORT HENRY

Top - An October 1934 photo of Port Henry P-74 showing the garage area (far left back) and the rear of the mess hall (right). Joan Daby & Iron Center Museum Archives. Bottom - An October 1934 group photo of CCC Camp P-74 in Port Henry. Notice the boys in the front row with three camp dogs. Joan Daby & Iron Center Museum Archives.

HISTORY

On November 15, 1933 Port Henry Camp P-74 Company 203 began operating on County Route 4 in the town of Moriah in Essex County. It was composed of men from the recently closed Schroon River camp and new enrollees. The camp was built on the James Farm and was approximately 1.5 miles from downtown Port Henry.

When the enrollees arrived on November 15 only the main buildings--barracks, mess hall, and kitchen-- were completed. Workers continued building the recreation hall, latrine, and state and federal garages.

The men were happy to be out of the Schroon River camp where they drank stream water and ate out of mess kits. The new camp had dishes and a dishwasher in the kitchen.

In 1934 Camp P-74's principal work was forest pest control: scouting for gypsy moths and eradicating blister rust.[1]

"CCC Camp at Port Henry Declared a Model Camp" was the headline of a story in the Essex County Republican dated December 15, 1933. It described enrollee Royce Pusey's letter to the CCC headquarters in Washington describing his Port Henry camp. "All the comforts of a modern hotel are provided in "Cold Springs" camp for the Civilian Conservation Corps Company No. 203 at Port Henry. Large buildings with plenty of windows, smooth floors with tightly fitted boards, Celotex (fibrous board used for insulation) lined interiors, two big coal burners in each building, and an unlimited supply of pure spring water."

Pusey said the men were happy to be out of the old tent camp at Schroon River. "There would be no more huddling around small stoves feeding them wood and no more sleepless nights during snow storms and winds. The bathhouse boasts plenty of wash basins and mirrors. There is a nicely planned infirmary and a supply room with all necessary bins and compartments."

Above, Left - A group picture of one of the five barracks at camp P-74 in 1935. Martin Bezon. Above, Right - Camp P-74 constructed a stone and masonry dam that created Gero Pond along County Highway 4 west of Port Henry. Podskoch Collection

The March 22, 1935 Lake Placid News reported the Port Henry camp was one of four Adirondack CCC camps that did stream improvement. Camp P-74 worked on the following streams from April to October 1934: Lindsy Brook, West Mill Brook, South & North Forks of Boquet, and Niagara Brook.

On October 12, 1934 The Essex County Republican described the makeup of Camp P-74 and its effect on the community after a year. In October there were 201 enrollees. Many were local boys: 14 from Granville, Whitehall 10, Fort Edward 5, Mineville 5, Hudson Falls 4, Salem 2, and one each from: Greenwich, Colton, Fort Ann, Glens Falls, Rouses Point, Cambridge, and Crown Point.

Enrollees had a wide range of education. Two finished fourth grade while two had college degrees. The rest of the men were between these two extremes.

The camp had weekly meetings on Thursday evenings. The reporter described an October session in which the camp doctor, Lt. Oscar Palatucci, spoke about personal hygiene. The education advisor, John C. Evans, spoke on how to make adjustments in life and then he read an article on "Discretion."

The meeting was cut short so that some men could attend and even participate in an amateur play presented by the Catholic Daughters of America in Port Henry. Twenty-two enrollees were in the chorus and dance scene. The men practiced for three nights and were in three of the performances.

The Sherman Public Library Board let the enrollees sign out books provided they made a deposit of $1 that was refunded when they left the camp.

The education advisor had speakers came to the camp for the weekly meetings. The Essex County Republican reported on September 14, 1934 that W. H. Burger, state YMCA Director from Westport, spoke about the geology and history of the area. The boys then watched three reels of movies and enjoyed cake and ice cream.

The CCC camps had a monthly newspaper that described work projects, staff, and activities. Port Henry's camp newspaper was The Adirondack Range. I had the December 1935 issue. It described four weekly meetings from the past month of November. Frank Gibson, physical education director of the state YMCA spoke on the history of modern sports competition. Another evening Victor Moore, president of the Au Sable Bank, talked about the "Pioneer Values" and his grandfather's experiences building the D & H Railroad. One night there was even an inter-barracks spelling match. Almost all the meetings had one or more movies. Some of the meetings had enrollees singing and playing musical instruments. One week Richard Carpenter played the piano while Dave Burns made music with bones. James Blanchard played guitar. Another week Eric Davis played violin while Dave Bevins shook himself and the bones. One night they had three boxing matches. Refreshments of ice cream and cake followed.

Camp P-74 also built dams to improve fishing and camping. In 1934 the camp established a side-camp on Putts Road in the Paradox Lake Region.[2] The October 26, 1934 Essex County Republican reported more details. Work began in mid-September with 25 enrollees. They worked for about eight weeks rebuilding a dam across Putnam Creek that had been built in the 1890s. It was used to power a sawmill. When the lumbering ended in the area, the dam deteriorated. In the 1930s sportsmen and politicians advocated rebuilding the dam to increase the height of Putt's Pond by two and one-half feet. This would flood the marshy land between Putts and North ponds creating one large body of water.

Isaac Boudrage was transferred from the Tupper Lake CCC camp and supervised the dam construction. He

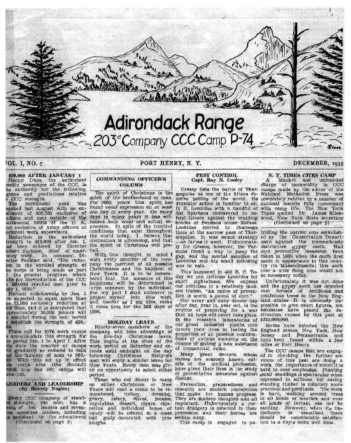

The front page of the December 1935 issue of The Adirondack Range Port Henry camp newspaper. Peg Porter

and his men used mostly material in the area. The dam was 200' long, 8' high, 12' wide at the base, and 8' at the top. The core contained planks and gravel and had a concrete spillway.

The two ponds became one and renamed Putnam Lake and later the state built a campsite that today has 72 campsites.

Camp P-74 built other dams in the area. One was in North Hudson creating Gero Pond. This beautiful dam is one-half mile east of Rt. 9 on County Highway 4 going toward Port Henry. I visited this site in 2007 after Jim Williford of Schroon Lake told me the CCCs built it. I was amazed at the cut stone masonry dam but I had no research to prove it was a CCC project.

Then while reading a December 1935 issue of Adirondack Range, there was an article by Philip Venito and Stanley Walkanoski entitled "Pine Ridge Dam." It described what I thought was the Gero Pond Dam. Then I saw a picture I took of the nearby cemetery. It was called Pine Ridge. Then I knew it was a CCC project. I also learned that there was a guesthouse in that area during the late 1890s called Pine Ridge Cottage. The Adirondack Range story

stated that State Engineer John V. Dolan supervised the construction of a stone and masonry dam on Black Brook. Work began in the spring with the clearing 75 acres of land along Black Brook. Then CCC boys built a cofferdam of sand bags to divert water from the construction site. There were two other cofferdams built during different stages of construction. "A large hand-operated derrick was built at the camp to drop the large boulders in place. Face stones were drilled, cut, and dressed on the job. The walls of the well housing and outlet valves were built in concrete forms and iron steps were imbedded in the concrete."

The dam was completed on Friday, November 15, 1935. Its dimensions were: 106' long, 9' thick at the base, and 4' at the top.

The reporters stated building tools and derrick were transported by truck the following Monday, November 18 to Berrymills where workers began clearing a site for a new dam. This pond is south of Putnam Lake in the Pharaoh Mountain Wilderness.

Bernie DeZalia, a former CCC enrollee at Port Henry, said his father was the foreman who supervised the building of many of these dams. His dad also had a crew rebuild the Penfield Pond Dam on County Rt. 2 six miles SW of Crown Point in the old town of Ironville.

Another project the camp worked on was fighting the spread of gypsy moths. Captain Ray N. Cooley in another December 1935 Adirondack Range article stated his men were patrolling the area for the gypsy moths. He described the history and destructive effects of the insects and said recently they had been found in the woods near Port Henry.

Education advisor John Evans who was also the newspaper advisor, was a talented writer and had a positive effect on the enrollees. He wrote a book, Mrs. Astor's Horse, which described early American life and the Prohibition era.

In September 1935 The Adirondack Range was rated second best of 48 camp newspapers.

In the December 1935 issue it listed the editorial staff: Nelson Beebee, Joseph Emru, Frank LaMere, Harvey Napier, William Phillips, Philip Veneto, William Morrison, and Stanley Walkanowski.

The paper also listed the camp administration: Commanding Officer, Captain FA-Res., Ray N. Cooley, 1st Lt. Thomas D. Heath, 2nd Lt. George Wetzel, surgeon Dr. Thomas Cummings, and recreation director Arthur Vanderhoff.

The technical staff were: A. W. Goodger, camp superintendent; W.E. Maimberg, first foreman; John V. Dolan, Engineer; H. R. Burlingame, Milton Gelbert, John Lantinen, B. F. Muzzy, division foremen; Walter Kuder, Mechanic; George Fanning, York Hazelton, Harry Hickok, Charles Kolodzey, John Leonard, Harold Passino, and Raymond Pepper, sub-foremen.

The Captain and Superintendent appointed leader and assistant leaders to help with camp supervision. A leader received $15 extra per month. The following were leaders: Kenneth Dudley, Lester S. Joiner, Joseph Kozma, Harry Rivers, Leslie Smith, George Fanning, Charles Kolodzey, Walter Kuder, and John E. Leonard. The assistant leaders received and extra $6: Frank Blahut, Augustus Fish, Robert Harper, Bernard Heustis, Freeman Jordon, Joseph Junco, Thomas H. Murphy, Zeb M. Robare, Thomas Rosselli, Louis Rollier, David Tefoe, Douglas Witherbee, Andy Daniels, and Harold Passino.

Sports were an important part of the camp's program. Members competed in track, boxing, basketball, and baseball.

Field Days involving several CCC camps were held each year. On Tuesday September 18, 1934 District No. 1, Northern Zone NY held its Second Annual Field Day. Over 500 enrollees from Port Henry, Warrensburg, and Bolton Landing attended the event at the Westport Fair Grounds. Two hundred men competed in track & field, swimming, and baseball. The swimming events were held at Clark Brothers Boat Landing on Lake Champlain in Westport. Port Henry won the championship with 61 pts. compared to Bolton Landing's 38 and Warrensburg's 24. The first place winners were awarded a watch fob. The August 24, 1934 issue of the Essex County Republican reported all the events and winners.

In 1935 Port Henry again swept the District Field Day competition. The event was held in Lake Placid and the Essex County Republican dated September 20, 1935 reported the results: Port Henry 57 pts., Fish Creek 32 pts., Paul Smiths 11 pts., Lake Placid 9 pts., and Tupper Lake 8 pts. Conservation Commissioner Osborne presented the first place winners with engraved fobs.

The reporter stated, "Port Henry's Captain Cooley's team opened the day by winning two novelty events that were not scored. Clarence Ferguson hopped to an easy first in the sack race. In the three-legged race, Venetos, Phillip, and Bruno won a field that was contested only by prone athletes from neighboring camps."

That same day Camp P-74 also won the championship in baseball by defeating Paul Smiths 10-4. Kalna and Dukett were the winning pitcher and catcher.

There were also nine boxing matches at the Lake Placid Arena. Port Henry's John Hickey from Whitehall won the 125 lb. event.

During the winter the camp's basketball team competed with both CCC camps and local town teams. Many of the games were played in the local high school gyms.

Joan Daby of the Town of Moriah Historical Society shared camp pictures and a menu from the 1935 Thanksgiving dinner. The young men enjoyed roast turkey, oyster dressing, cranberry sauce, candied sweet potatoes, snow flake potatoes, baked squash, fruit salad, pumpkin pie with whipped cream, coffee, salted nuts, and cigarettes.

During the Christmas holiday of 1935 ninety-seven enrollees received five day passes to go home. Those who remained were feted in the decorated mess hall with the following Christmas dinner meal: turkey, dressing, gravy, celery, olives pickles, vegetables, dessert, cigarettes, cigars, and individual boxes of candy. The remaining 66 members had passes to go home for the New Year holiday.

At the end of 1935 CCC National Director Robert Fechner in Washington ordered a reduction in the number of enrollees in 1936. New York State reacted by closing camps and Port Henry was one of them.

Captain Ray N. Cooley announced the closing of Camp P-74 in January 9, 1936. That same day The Ticonderoga Sentinel stated the camp enrollees whose time hadn't expired would be transferred to camps at Indian Lake, Lake Placid, Paul Smiths, or Brushton. Cooley was transferred to the Newcomb camp and Lts. Heath and Wetzel were reassigned to other camps. All of the state equipment was transferred to the Fort Ann camp. The buildings were not going to be salvaged and William H. Martin, was hired to look after the property.

WORK ACCOMPLISHED BY CAMP P-74*

PROJECT	1934	1935	1936	TOTAL
Concrete - yd^2		10.5		10.5
Dams - number			1	1
Excavation, earth - yd^3		90		90
Fighting forest fires - man-days	112	22		134
Fill, earth - yd^3		20		20
Fire hazard reduction, other - ac.		31		31
General clean-up - ac.		14		14
Impounding & large diversions - number		1		1
Insect pest control - ac.	51830	58389	26710	136929
Lake or pond site clearing - ac.		13		13
Masonry - yd^3		64		64
Planting trees - ac.	151			151
Steel - lbs.		50		50
Stream development - mi.	13	16.7	2.9	32.6
Tree & plant disease control - ac.	25063	31429	286	56778

*Numerical data from Conservation Reports

In February 1936 The Lake George News reported the American Legion of Essex County asked the state and federal government if the Allied Child Welfare Committee could take over Camp P-74 and use it as a children's summer camp. The Federal Government rejected the proposal.

The Ticonderoga Sentinel reported on October 7, 1937 that the Newcomb CCC camp members tore the buildings down and be used in rebuilding projects.

The Moriah Central School is at the site of the Port Henry CCC camp.

MEMORIES

Bernie DeZalia

Fran DeZalia Provoncha contacted me in September 2006 and said a friend of hers, Cathy Moses, had seen one of my presentations in Schroon Lake. Cathy told Fran that I was writing a book on the CCCs. Fran said that her father was a foreman in the CCC camp on the Johnson Pond Road in Schroon River and her brother Bernie was in the Port Henry camp. She sent me his phone number and I called him. He said he'd be happy to have me stop at his home in Schenectady for an interview.

On October 14, 2007, Bernie and his wife Anna warmly greeted me and we sat down and Bernie told me his CCC stories:

"I entered the CCCs in November 1933 to help my family. My parents had 10 children so they were happy to get the $25 a month that I earned. Our home was on Johnson Pond Road. My father James worked in the woods for the Conservation Department doing blister rust control and planting trees. He worked as a foreman at the CCC camp right down the road from our home. When this camp moved to Port Henry, I signed up for the CCCs and was assigned to that camp.

"When I got to camp there were brand new buildings. It was better than the tent camp on John-

Bernie DeZalia of Schenectady draws a map showing the location of the buildings of the Port Henry CCC camp where he lived and worked from 1933-34. Podskoch Collection

A 1935 group photo of Port Henry Camp P-74. Joan Daby & Iron Center Museum Archives

son Pond Road. I worked in the woods looking for gypsy moths. I also built little dams on streams using timbers cut on site. We built V dams with the logs and used stones behind them. We created pools on the side of the stream. These were very helpful to provide fish a place to live in the summer when the water was low.

"Dad worked at the Port Henry camp, too, as foreman. He helped rebuild the Penfield Dam and the Putts Dam in Ticonderoga.

"They picked me to be a second cook. I started at 5:30 am. I cooked ground meat for gravy and fried bacon and eggs. It took a lot of eggs. The cooks also made the workers sandwiches for their lunch. They were mostly peanut butter and jelly. Another sandwich was 'corn willy' (corned beef). It came in big blocks in a can. It had something that looked like mold on it. We just scraped it off. It didn't kill anyone. Your stomach was strong.

"For breakfast we served eggs, toast, coffee, pancakes, and corn meal that was like oatmeal.

"After breakfast we had a little rest. Then we went back to the kitchen to make lunch for the Army officers and their staff. We prepared regular meals, not just sandwiches. After lunch we scrubbed the floor and did dishes. Then we had a little free time in afternoon to rest.

"Usually about 3 or 4 pm the process of preparing food began. About 4:30 they beat a triangle to signal dinnertime. For some meals the guys used their mess kits. They washed their gear themselves. We then cleaned up the pots and floor and we left the kitchen a little after 8 pm. We had a long busy day.

"In the evening we went to the rec room for entertainment or bought a snack at the canteen. We ate a lot of ice cream. It cost 15 cents a pint.

"The lights went out at 10 and we had quiet time. Sometimes the guys played jokes where they took the bottom sheet and pulled it up to the top. It was called short sheeting.

"There were some tough boys from the city but we didn't have any problems. We had one problem with one guy who stole sheets and sent them home. He was a very quiet guy. Finally, they sent him home. When they inspected his belongings they found sheets and a pistol in his locker.

"Another unusual thing was when a guy who worked around Essex killed a timber rattler. He brought it back and hung it on an outside bulletin board by the headquarters and supply house.

"I stayed there for one year and then I got a job working in the Mineville mines the summer of 1934. The work was mostly shoveling and taking care of the mining tools.

"One day while riding my Excelsior Super X motorcycle, I had an accident and I shattered my leg. I was laid up for a year. When I got better I went to Schenectady and did odd jobs. Then I got a job at American Locomotive Co. and was the head of the automotive maintenance repair crew.

"In 1941 the Army drafted me. I went to Fort Dix and then Sackets Harbor. I went to different parts of the US but never left. On August 10, 1944 I got out and went back to American Locomotive. About 1952 I worked repairing toll equipment for the NY Thruway System and went into business on my own in 1956 repairing tollbooth equipment on the Thruway.

"In 1944 I married Anna Harper and we had six children: Pamela, Tamara, Phillip, Bernadette, Scott, and Camille.

"The CCC was a great experience for me. I was able to work and help my family."

Joseph Kozma

On September 7, 2006 I received a letter from Joseph Kozma of Westport, who had seen a story in the Ticonderoga newspaper about my search for CCC information telling me that he had been in the Port Henry camp. "I graduated from Moriah High School in 1934 at the age of 19. There were no jobs for young men and there were many jobless fathers so the CCC was a blessing. My brother went to a camp in Paul Smiths.

"I want to send you some material that after my death will no doubt go into disregard. At age 91 plus six months I desire to give you a camp newspaper, an 8 x 10 photo of enrollees, and a 1935 Thanksgiving program. I do not want the CCC story to be forgotten."

I called him back, thanked him for writing, and said I'd be interested in his CCC material.

Joseph sent me his materials but they remained in a folder for over three years until I finally got to write the Port Henry chapter. I realized I hadn't interviewed Joe to get the details of his life and his experiences in camp.

On February 15 I nervously dialed Joe's phone number, wondering if he was still alive. Finally after five rings a frail voice answered and it was Joe. I told him I was so happy to know he was still alive and asked if he would tell me about his life. Brushton CCC camps from 1934-38.

"Well, I'll start from the beginning. I was born on March 14, 1915 in Witherbee. My father Raymond and mother Mary Nagy had eight children. The first two died from the flu during WW I. Dad worked at odd jobs doing carpentry. He worked as a foreman in the Harmony Mine doing maintenance and carpentry.

"I was the eldest in my family and after I graduated from high school in 1934 there weren't any jobs, but there was a CCC camp in town so I applied with Mr. St. Clare in Mineville. He was in charge of Memorial Hall. I was happy when notified that I was accepted.

"In August 1934 I walked six miles to the camp. At first I was nervous but I got used to it and it felt like home.

"The buildings were symmetrically arranged: The nearest building was the headquarters. Next in line were the five barracks. At the end was the recreation building. Directly across an expanse of lawn was the kitchen and dinning room. Next in the same line was the infirmary and beyond that a separate building for toilets and showers.

"My first job was blister eradication. We pulled up gooseberry bushes. Sometimes we had a special tool to pry the plants. We traveled all over Essex County.

"The second job was planting seedlings. We used a grub hoe to dig up the soil and plant the tree and then step on the soil.

"After about a year I became an assistant leader. My job was to maintain sanitary conditions, clean up the barracks and supervise the workers on the job. They were all well-behaved.

"Then I was made leader. I kept $20 and my parents got $25. When they needed a new stove or refrigerator my brother Steve who was a cook in Paul Smiths and I would chip in to help them.

"After work and dinner I either visited with other people or read books and newspapers. When it was warm they took us to Ensign Pond on Rt. 4 near North Hudson. We like to fish and swim there."

I asked Joe how the food was in camp?

"As far as I was concerned it was good. There were a few who ruffled their feathers but most of us took it in stride.

"On almost every weekend I went home because it was only six miles away. The weekends I stayed at camp I sometimes walked to the movies in Port Henry.

"When they closed the Port Henry camp in January 1936 I was transferred to the Brushton CCC camp where I had the same jobs and was a leader again.

"When I left the CCCs in the fall 1938 I got a job in Mineville working in the Harmony Mine. I didn't like it and I saved my money to further my education. I went to Milwaukee, Wisconsin to the School of Engineering. I stayed for about a year. I studied blueprint reading and mechanical drawing. They taught me how to recondition acetylene torches and regulators.

"I had an apartment and paid a modest rental. To make some extra money I worked at Mader Restaurant as a busboy.

"When I graduated I got a job in a machine shop in Mineville laying out designs on blueprints. I did the metal cutting and the welders made the assembly.

"In 1943 I married Ethel Lobdell. We had two children Jerry and Jo Anne. I worked till 1971 when Republic Steel closed and my company didn't have work. In retirement I did volunteer work in a nursing home and in other community work with the elderly.

"My days in the CCCs were very good from the standpoint of getting along with guys and not fighting. I learned how to behave and be a gentleman. I learned how to be a leader."

Vincent "Pete" Stanger

In 1999 while writing my book on the Catskill fire towers I visited the beautiful hamlet of Cragsmoor on the Shawangunk Mountains near Ellenville and I met John Stanger. He in-

Joseph Kozma worked at the Port Henry and Brushton CCC camps from 1934-38. Joseph Kozma

troduced me to his father, Pete, and mother, Marie. They told me about the history of the local fire tower on High Point. John, an ironworker, helped restore many of the towers by replacing damaged steel supports.

Eleven years later, on June 14, 2010, I spoke at the Cragsmoor Historical Society on the history of the CCC and their work in the Catskills. It was then that John surprised me by saying his father was in the CCC in the Adirondacks, the camp at Port Henry. The sad part was Pete had died on January 4, 2010 and most of his experiences were gone.

Vincent "Pete" Stanger was in the Port Henry CC camp in 1934. John Stanger

"Dad never talked much about his days in the CCC. It was just a few years ago that he placed his CCC camp picture on the wall of our porch. I just wished I had asked him more about his CCC days."

A few months later I called John and spoke with him and his mother, Marie. She said: "Pete's real name was Vincent Stanger. It's a long story about how he got the name Pete but I won't get into it all. At first he was not a country boy but was born in Brooklyn in 1913. His parents, Herman and Catherine, had four children and Pete was the eldest.

"When Pete was only nine years old, he fell off a stonewall and broke his elbow. His father took him to the wrong doctors and they did a poor job of fixing it. His left hand didn't heal properly. His whole hand contracted and his muscles got smaller and weaker. The medical term is atrophy. Pete could use his arm but not his hand very well.

"This injury did not stop Pete. He played baseball in high school and college. He used his right hand to catch and took his glove off to throw the ball.

"I called Pete the 'Everything man.' He did carpentry and painting. There wasn't anything he couldn't do. He even played golf and had two holes in one.

"After his accident the family moved to Keesville where Pete's father worked as a prison guard at the Clinton Prison in Dannemora. Then his father was transferred to the Great Meadows Prison in Comstock. The family lived in nearby Fort Ann where he went to school. Pete graduated from high school in 1931. For the next three years he did odd jobs to help his family but wasn't able to get a good job because of the Depression.

John added, "I followed your advice and secured Dad's CCC records from the National Archives Records Administration in St. Louis.

"The records state Dad joined the CCC on July 25, 1934 and was sent to Camp S-74 Company 203 in Port Henry. This was a 'bug camp' and Dad worked with the other enrollees trying to stop the spread of gypsy moths. He and his fellow workers searched for and destroyed the insects' egg clusters. He also helped build a dam. Dad mentioned this to me when I told him that I was building a dam near New York City."

Marie said, "On some weekends he hitchhiked home. It was about a 50-mile trip."

"After serving five months in the CCC," John added, "Dad was discharged on December 1934. He went to Plattsburgh Normal School and majored in education. He became a teacher and taught in Monticello, NY. He met Mom (Marie Cantrell) while teaching. In 1943 they got married and had five children. While teaching he studied in Albany for his masters in Administration and he became an elementary principal in Ellenville in 1955. He retired in 1971. I'm sure his work in the CCC was a big help to his parents. Each month they received $25, which was most of his salary."

Joe Veneto

Joe Veneto, a retired local ironworker and enrollee at the Indian Lake CCC camp, told me:

"My two older brothers, Philip and Bruno, were already in the Port Henry CCC camp. They joined in 1933. My brothers told me they did blister rust control which was the removal of currant and gooseberry bushes. Another job was spraying trees to kill gypsy moths in spring and summer. In the fall and winter they searched for their egg masses."

I told Joe that I did some research and found that his brother, Philip, was on the staff of the camp newspaper and that the two of them won a field day competition: "…in the three-legged race, the Venetos, Phillip and Bruno, won over a field of prone athletes from neighboring camps."

"Bruno was a very good athlete. He played baseball at the camp. But I'm sorry to tell you that both my brothers died and I'm the last of the five brothers. There were 11 children in my family. My father Dominic couldn't work because he had heart troubles. My mother Angelene and all the kids helped out.

"The CCC was a big help to my family. They got

$25 a month and that helped them during the Depression."

Elbert Hanchett

Elbert Hanchett and his family came to my talk at the Ticonderoga Heritage Museum in October 24, 2007. He told me that he was a member of the CCC at Port Henry and Paul Smiths camp. I visited him the next day at the Heritage Commons Residential Health Care in Ticonderoga.

"My father William was a carpenter and my mother, Lillian, had four children: My older brother Leon, my younger sister Ada and a sister who died before she was one. It was very hard for my family and I needed a job that could help.

"I joined the CCC right after I graduated from Moriah High School in 1934. I think I went down to the camp and signed up there. It was all right but quite different from living at home.

"One of my first jobs at camp was fighting the spread of gypsy moths. We walked through the woods and spread out in a line. We were about ten feet apart. Our foreman went ahead and stuck fake cocoons on some trees. If you went by that tree and didn't see it, they showed you. This was a training period. This was to help us find real cocoons.

"Then I went to the Paul Smiths camp. My job there was truck driver. I think all of the trucks were Chevys. They had stake bodies and there were seats on three sides for the guys when I took them to work. The foreman rode in the cab with me. I didn't have anything specific to do because my main job was driving. Sometimes I helped the guys burn brush that they gathered in the woods.

"Each week I went into the garage to service my truck. I greased it and changed the oil.

"Driving during the winter was sometimes tough in the snow. You'd sometimes get off track and slide off the road. The guys would get out and help push me out. I don't remember any starting problems.

"On weekends I sometimes hitchhiked home. There was a guy from Crown Point who had a car and sometimes I got a ride home with him.

"On Saturday night I drove guys to Saranac Lake to the armory to play basketball or go to the movies. When the movie was out about 9:30 to 10 I took them back to camp.

"After a year in the CCC I got out in 1935. The iron mines were running and my brother, Leon, worked there. Later on I got a job as a laborer. I carried both wood and steel I-beams and dynamite.

"I met a girl I was in high school with, Gertrude Holden, whose father and brother had a grain store Ticonderoga. Then her brother left and her father needed someone so I got the job. Then Gertrude and I got married and we lived in Ticonderoga. We had five children: David, Bill, Alvin, Sylvia, and Donald.

"I worked at the grain store for several years. Then it took on the John Deere dealership and I assembled machinery.

"During the war I got a deferment because I had children.

"After the war I had a few other jobs. I worked above ground at the mine, at the paper mill, and as a mechanic at a few car garages. I retired at age 62 and did a lot of volunteer work till 2006. Then I came here to Heritage Commons.

"When I look back at those days during the Depression the CCC was the only job you could get. It helped me and my family."

Charlie and Peggy Porter

While driving near Crown Point I took a side trip to visit the Penfield Homestead Museum in Ironville. I was surprised to find a beautiful restored hamlet that had been very active in the iron mining industry in the 1800s.

As I entered the homestead, a guide, Charlie Porter, welcomed me and then gave me a tour. He told me Allen Penfield bought land with rich deposits of iron ore in 1827. He and his partners formed the Crown Point Iron Co., set up a mining operation, and built workers housing. In 1830 Penfield purchased an electromagnet that separated iron

Marty Podskoch interviewing Elbert Hanchett at the Heritage Commons Residential Health Care in Ticonderoga. Elbert was a laborer at Port Henry CCC camp and a truck driver at Paul Smiths CCC camp from 1934-35. Podskoch Collection

particles from the ore. It was the first time electricity was used in industry.

I told Charlie that I was looking for information on the CCC camp in Port Henry. He replied: "You'll have to come to our home across the street and talk with my wife, Peggy, who has a picture of it and information on the camp."

We sat in their living room and Peggy said: "I'm an avid lover of the area's history. The Port Henry CCC camp site that you are writing about was first owned by the wealthy Witherbee family who owned the local iron company. They used the farm for their guests. The farmhouse even had a ballroom and a bowling alley. The Hendrix family owned it next. Then Emerson James picked it up at a tax sale. In 1958 we purchased the site of the CCC camp."

Peggy handed me an aerial photo of the camp and a copy of the camp newspaper, The Adirondack Ranger, and said: "Take these and use them for your research."

I asked Charlie what was in the buildings. He sketched a diagram of the camp: "As you drove down the camp road from County Rt. 4 there were seven buildings on the left. The first one held the recreation room and the PX. Then there were five barracks buildings. The last building was the storehouse/Army office.

"On the right side were four more buildings: showers, latrines, infirmary, and kitchen/mess hall.

"Behind these four buildings and next to the tree line was the motor pool area with three garages. To the right was the water tower."

Peggy continued: "The James family leased their farm to the New York State Field and Stream Improvement Board. The farm had a large grouping of springs with springhouses. Water was piped to northerly parts of the village. We bought the farm and continued to furnish water to units on Upper Broad Street, We had planned to have a private fish hatchery but when we started the hatchery we had a catastrophe. In the winter frogs clogged hatchery lines cutting off the oxygen supply to the breeders. The second catastrophe occurred in the spring when we had a lot of rain and the screening in the raceways collapsed and all the fingerlings went down into the lake. So our hatchery plans were curtailed.

"In 1965 we sold part of the farm to the Moriah Central School, which built a K-12 school building. Later my daughter Stacy and her husband Mark Robinson bought the other part of the farm."

Stacy Robinson

On February 12, 2010 I had a telephone interview with Stacy Robinson and asked about her property and if her home was on the aerial photo of the CCC camp that her mother shared with me.

"In 1992 my husband Mark and I purchased the land with the old Witherbee farmhouse from my parents. Our house is not in the photo but two of the original barns are shown in the lower right hand corner of this photo Both those barns are now gone. One we always called 'the shop' and the larger was 'the diary barn.' The two sheds that were built in the 30s and used by the New York State Field and Stream Improvement Board are still standing today on our property. They had not yet been erected at the time of this photo because they were next to the shop.

"The first winter we bought our place the shop was the only original outbuilding still standing but it caved under the very heavy snowfall we received that winter. The Witherbee Hunting Lodge, our home, is just a short distance further down the driveway (lower right hand corner of photo). My family lived in this before my parents moved to Ironville. Growing up here I recall that there was a creamery, a laundry, and an icehouse as well as the shop and dairy barn. All are sadly gone now. Following our first winter here in the Witherbee house, Mark dismantled what was left of the old shop and found a board inside the walls with the date August 1882 with the name of the wood butcher and a note saying no rain for two months."

An aerial view of Port Henry CCC camp in the mid-1930s. The lower right buildings are five barracks and an Army officers' headquarters. To the left are four buildings: showers, latrines, infirmary, and kitchen/mess hall. There are three garages near the tree line. County Route 4 is on the right and travels to the left near Mill Pond seen in the top left. Peggy Porter

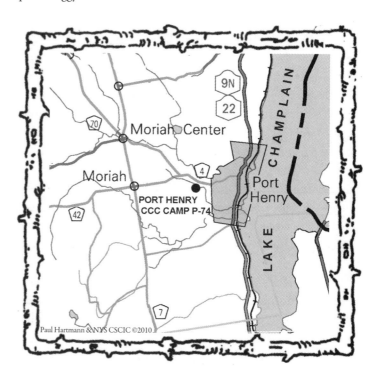

CHAPTER 24
SCHROON RIVER

The Army set up approximately 30 tents along a dirt road where 200 young men spent the summer and fall of 1933 working in the nearby forests. The enrollees had a circus-style tent for recreation. Three LEM are to the right enjoying themselves with the younger guys. Both courtesy Lorraine Dudley

HISTORY

The Schroon River CCC Camp S-65 (#5) Company 203 was established on June 15, 1933 on the Johnson Pond Road/County Rt. 2 A in North Hudson in Essex County. The site was on state land. This camp's primary work was blister rust control and reforestation.

The camp was named after the hamlet of Schroon River where it was located. Local resident Dot Liberty said Schroon River was a busy place with stores, post office, and a cemetery. Later it became part of North Hudson."

Company 203 was formed on April 10, 1933 at Fort Slocum (two islands on the western end of Long Island Sound). On June 2 an advance Army cadre came to North Hudson to establish the camp. The December 1935 issue of the Port Henry camp newspaper, The Adirondack Range, described the early days of the camp.

"Its members were largely city bred and the camp was on a lonely hillside called 'Bear Run.'" The enrollees had quite a few stories of bears visiting the camp at night and pulling down the tents and feasting in the mess hall. Captain Cooley remembers a midnight hunt and scary shadows and whistling sounds."

Captain R. F. Turrentine of the 18th Infantry commanded the camp aided by 1st Lt. K. Pierce and 2d Lt. E. J. Messinger, both 28th Infantry. Messinger was the finance officer for the camp.

The June 1, 1944 issue of The Ticonderoga Sen-tinel reported that Herbert J. McCasland of Redford was the superintendent of the camp. He had broad experience in forestry. In 1924 he graduated from the New York State College of Forestry and worked for the US Forest Service in Plumas National Forest in California. After that he was a forest ranger in Washington State. He came back East and was a teacher in the Willsboro and Westport schools in 1928 and 1929. In 1930 he was a foreman for the Conservation Department supervising blister rust control. Then in 1931 he became assistant pathologist for the US Department of Agriculture in the Albany and Catskill area. McCastland's experience with blister rust control and forestry were great

This tent at the 'Bear Run' Schroon River CCC camp was the headquarters for the Army and camp superintendent who planned the work projects. Each camp had a wooden platform and a stove was added as the weather got colder. Lorraine Dudley

qualifications for his job at Schroon River.

The Essex County Republican in its June 8, 1933 issue entitled "The Health and Morale of C. C. C. Men at Camp No. 5" described the reaction of local residents to the influx of 200 city boys in their town. "Two hundred boisterous city boys suddenly precipitated in a quiet rural region are sure to implant in the minds of the local folks the question of desirability in a healthy community...Everyone in the neighboring towns was questioning the health and morale of these young men. It is only natural at first for these people to consider such a group of young men a menace." Locals were worried about getting infectious diseases from them.

The article reported the Army worked to maintain sanitary conditions. Camp surgeon, Dr. Sidney B. Edelberg, conducted examinations and tests for diseases and gave the men instructions in personal hygiene. Every Saturday the men aired their tents, scrubbed the wooden tent platforms, and washed their clothes. The doctor also conducted inspections of the kitchen and staff.

Captain Roy T. Turrentine supervised the construction of a dam that created a supply water for the camp. He also made sure that sanitary conditions were maintained.

The reporter stated the residents said the boys' physical appearance has shown an improvement as compared to when they first arrived. "Flabby muscles have hardened, color has come to many pale faces, stooped shoulders are now straight, and the men have gained an average of ten pounds per man. The exercise that the men now enjoy makes itself very evident in their morale. Where once there was gloom, there is now joy and a spirit of well-being. Sad faces are now smiling and the neighboring towns are enjoying the buoyant spirit of the men when they enter the town dance, to attend shows or stroll along the streets." The churches welcomed the boys to services, too.

The article concludes: "The few months camp has been here have given the local people a better understanding of the character of the young men. The desirability of the camp in their midst was in now indisputable. The relations between the community and the camp have become most cordial."

The Conservation Report of 1933 stated the Schroon River camps' major project was blister rust eradication. Blister rust lived on a host, currant and gooseberry bushes (ribes), before the fungi was wafted up to the white pine trees. They searched for ribes, ripped them up, and let

CCC enrollees are gathered outside of the Army officers tent. One of the young men is holding the camp dog. Lorraine Dudley

them dry.

Another camp project was reforestation. The October 12, 1933 Ausable Forks Record Post reported Camp S-65 planted 343,000 trees during the month of September. The men continued planting trees in October. The October 13, 1933 issue of The Essex County Republican printed a notice to hunters to watch out for enrollees planting trees on lot 162 on the Johnson Pond Road and in the vicinity of nearby Hammond Pond and lot 56 on the Charlie Hill section in Schroon Lake.

Retired Forest Ranger Grant "Dick" Thatcher who worked in the North Hudson area told me, " I saw evidence of the enrollees' stabilization projects of small steams into Berry Mill Swamp and on the trail to Bass Lake. They used small cedar logs as water bars to stop erosion. Dan McKenzie was the Forest Ranger at that time. His daughter-in-law, Eleanor, taught in the one-room schoolhouse farther up the road on the left."

The December 1935 issue of The Adirondack Range newspaper described how the enrollees were affected by the weather. "The sun baked the tents during July, August, and early September.Then the well-remembered winter of 1933-34 set in. October brought serious snow storms and introduced near zero weather. Tents caved in under the weight of the snow and keeping warm became the major problem. Funnel-shaped field stoves, called Sibley stoves, was the solution offered by the government. October was bad and November was worse."

During these harsh times a group of local carpenters under the supervision of senior foreman Harvey Napier built the new camp in Port Henry that was the future home of Company 203.

Bernie DeZalia of Schenectady told me: "The big project of the camp was to build the new CCC camp in Port Henry. My father James was a foreman at that camp where I later worked. It's where the Moriah Junior Senior High School is located on County Highway 4/Plank Road approximately 17 miles away."

The Schroon River CCC camp closed on November 15, 1933 and moved into the new wooden buildings in Port Henry.

MEMORIES

Bernie DeZalia, a former resident of Schroon River, told me where the CCC camp was located: "I was about 16 and I remember the camp very well because I saw the camp in action. My grandfather, Joseph DeZalia, was a lumberman and he had a mill on a side road just past the camp on the left. The road went to Hatch Pond."

Then I told Bernie that I had driven on the Johnson Pond Road in 2007 but I wasn't sure where the camp was. He told me: "Drive up Rt. 9 north above the old Frontier Town Park and take the first right, Johnson Pond Road or County Rt. 2A. Then go a little more than a mile till you see the stream on the right. The camp was on both sides of the road just before the stream. The tents for the enrollees were on the right. These tents were on both sides of a dirt road that continued up the hill to the Fannon House. The road turned to the left and came back to the Johnson Pond Road. There were about 14 Army tents on each side of the road. There was a wooden building in back of the tents on the left. I think it housed a generator for electricity. Across Johnson Pond Road from these tents was the officer's tent and to the right of it was the mess and kitchen tents both by the stream. I remember they had a large canvas bag (lister bag holding treated water with chlorine) supported on tripod sticks that they used for drinking water. They probably used the water right from the nearby stream for cooking purposes. They had these barrels in the ground where they baked their own bread."

I told Bernie that I read a newspaper article about that oven entitled, "Novel Bake Ovens Draw Visitors to CCC Camp No.5" in the August 25, 1933 article in the Essex County Republican. It describes an Italian style oven on the side of a hill made of large oil drums. They built a fire inside the barrels that heated up the barrels and ground. When it was down to the coals they raked them out and filled the barrels with pans of dough. After an hour they had freshly baked bread. The reporter wrote, "Hardly a day passes that a few visitors do not

The mess sergeant sitting on the left supervises enrollees preparing food for the hungry enrollees lined up by the mess tent. Lorraine Dudley

arrive to see the wonders of the city boys baking bread in the hills. Although started as an experiment, the oven has cut in half the cost of supplying the camp with bread. The bakers are daily turning out 200 pounds of bread to satisfy the hungry lads who claim the bread is just like their mother makes."

Major General Dennis E. Nolan, Commander of the Second Corps Area was impressed with the Schroon River Camp when he visited in the afternoon on Sunday, August 20. In his inspection of the camp he said in the August 25, 1933 article in the Essex County Republican that it was a very fine camp. In fact it was the only camp he visited that baked their own bread.

If you would like to find the Schroon River CCC camp site, take the Northway I-87 to the North Hudson Exit 29. Take Rt. 2 east and drive past the old Frontier Town. Turn left and drive north on Rt. 9 for around one-half mile. Turn right on the Johnson Pond Road/County Rt. 2. Drive approx.1.3 miles up a hill that levels out. The area is heavily wooded. Watch for a stream that goes underneath the road. The camp was right before the stream. The barracks tents were on the right and the officers' headquarters, mess hall, and kitchen were on the left.

All that remains of the Schroon River CCC camp is a partial road. Trees have grown over the field that held tents where 200 enrollees lived over 75 years ago. Podskoch Collection

240

CHAPTER 25
SPECULATOR

Clockwise from Top - The entrance to Speculator CCC camp S-90 greeted the new recruits as they arrived. At the top of the two pillars were round gas pump topper signs that were painted with trees. The entrance gate is still standing almost 80 years later. Art Conduzio. An aerial view of Speculator CCC camp S-59 on August 15, 1933. The tents were pitched on both sides of the road to Moffitt Beach where

the enrollees began developing the state campsite. Sacandaga Lake is in the upper left. Minerva Historical Society. An aerial view of camp S-90 on Paige Street in Lake Pleasant. NYS Archives

HISTORY

Camp S-59 was established on June 12, 1933 on 4.4 acres of rented land owned by Harvey Behlen on Paige Street in the Town of Lake Pleasant in Hamilton County. It was located 1.5 mi. W of Speculator on Route 8.[1]

The men lived in tents and worked at the nearby Moffitt Beach State Park on Sacandaga Lake. The beach got its name from Josiah Moffitt who came to the area approximately in 1840. He mined high quality sand from the area and used it in his masonry business. Moffitt also had a woodworking mill.[2]

Another project was an extension and improvement of the Sacandaga (Wells) and Lewey Lake (Indian Lake) state campsites. They also improved the Northville-Placid Trail from Benson to Piseco.[3]

Camp S-59 also worked to eradicate blister rust by destroying the gooseberry and currant bushes. The young men did reforestation work on state land and did stream improvement projects.

Since it was too cold to live in the tents, the camp was closed after five months on November 11, 1933.[4]

To help the CCCs move men and material for a new camp, the Town of Lake Pleasant improved Page Street go-

An enrollee standing by an Army tent at the Speculator camp S-90. Adirondack Museum Archives. Camp S-90 enrollees removing rocks on the grounds of their camp. Adirondack Museum Archives

In 1934 the Speculator enrollees built a 79' 6" fire tower on Dairy Hill in the Town of Norway (near Newport). The following year it was staffed and the observer reported six fires. Paul Hartmann

ing to Moffitt Beach with, "a gravel base and crushed stone surface as of April 3, 1934 at a cost of $1,500."[5]

On May 11, 1934 the new camp was established at the same location and was named Camp S-90. The enrollees lived in tents while permanent barracks were built. S-90 continued for the next eight years working to improve the campsites that had been worked on the previous year. It also worked to eliminate blister rust, on forest stand improvement, thinning the forest in plantations, fighting fires, and construction of truck trails to aid in fire suppression.[6]

CCC Superintendent Scott Conry reviewed the Speculator camp projects in a March 31, 1936 article in The Evening Recorder. The new camp established on May 11, 1934 was composed of veterans who came from the Winooski Valley in Vermont. They remained until October 1935. Then junior enrollees took over the camp. From 1934-35 there was a side camp at Caroga Lake with 40 enrollees. They nearly doubled the number of campsites, erected a woven metal fence on the campsite, built and improved a diving float, and developed a new parking area.

Conry stated the Speculator camp maintained the two campsites on Piseco Lake: Point Comfort and Poplar Point. At Lewey Lake the enrollees nearly doubled the campsites capacity.

The Speculator veterans helped locate lost hunters and hikers. At the end of 1934 a severe snowstorm forced a 16-passenger American Airline plane down about ten miles from Moorehouseville. Camp S-90 enrollees plus Conservation Department employees helped rescue four men from the plane and transported the men to a Utica hospital.

Superintendent Conry concluded by describing the major projects at the nearby Moffitt Beach State Park. Work first began in 1933 with basic equipment of shovels,

rakes, picks, and wheelbarrows. They constructed 200 campsites, a 1,000-gallon concrete reservoir, 5,850' of water lines, and four bathhouses. They developed a half-mile beach and constructed a caretaker's cabin that had an office, two bedrooms, a kitchen, First-Aid room, bathroom and a large stone fireplace in the office. He also announced the campsite would open for the 1936 summer season.

The Evening Recorder dated June 7, 1935 describes the many educational programs for the enrollees. Each Wednesday evening a recreational program was provided. Various speakers talked to the men and showed movies. On one occasion Gardiner Kline of Amsterdam showed movies about his trips to Alaska and an island in the South Atlantic. Some of the evenings the men were treated to music. One evening Floyd Reesman played his violin along with Algernon Firth on the piano. Then Reverend Peter F. Cusick from the Shrine of North American Martyrs in Auriesville and Rev. Charles Neukirch of Wells spoke on religious topics.

In August 2006 Cynthia Dunham, the Sacandaga campsite supervisor told me that peddlers had used the location as a stopover on their trip between Gloversville and Speculator. Milk and bread trucks also stopped at the location on Route 30. Milk and bread trucks also stopped at the location on Route 30 during the early 1900s. In 1923 the state established the Sacandaga campsite in Wells that was known to locals as "The Forks," because it was located where

Above, Left - A state historical marker at the Sacandaga campsite near Wells states the camp was one of the first two established on Forest Preserve Land in 1920. CCC enrollees expanded the campsite during the 1930s. Podskoch Collection. Above, Right - Members of Speculator CCC camp S-90 clearing and leveling areas along Lewey Lake for the new state campsite in 1933.[8]

the East and West branches of the Sacandaga meet. Ten years later Camp S-90 worked at expanding the campsite.

Every six months enrollees could sign up for another term. Those that left were replaced. A new group of CCC volunteers came to Fort Dix, NJ for training in October 1935 and placed in Company 1208 under the command of 2nd Lt. W. W. Merrick. Capt. S. Gruneck then took command and brought the men to Speculator in the fall of 1935.[7]

During 1936 the camp did extensive work at Lewey Lake campsite near the southern end of Indian Lake. Campers who got there on a poor dirt road from Speculator had used the site since 1920. It was originally called Lewey Bridge after the local hermit Louis Seymour, "French Louie." The CCC boys enlarged the camping area, installed toilet facilities, and constructed a caretaker cabin and bathhouse. They also did maintenance and small development projects at the Sacandaga and Moffitt Beach campsites.[9]

On September 1, 1936 Capt. J. J. Ruddy Jr. took over command of the camp. The next month, 18 men from South Carolina were added.[10] Arnold Rhodes was the camp superintendent. His technical personnel were: Asa Barnes, Everett Call, Edward Carl, John C. Cronin, Orin Frasier, David Lemery, and Clifford Stoddard.[11]

During the winter of 1936-37 the camp searched 20 areas in Arietta, Benson, Wells and Lake Pleasant for balsam trees that were infected with the 'bark louse.' The CCC boys cut down 2,624 infested trees.[12]

In 1937 work began on the caretaker's headquarters at the Sacandaga campsite near Wells and the caretaker's headquarters at Lewey Lake.[13] The camp also built a bar-

rier dam to prevent pike from entering the trout waters of the West River near Speculator.[14]

In May 1937 they began constructing a 166' bridge. Cynthia Dunham said, "The CCCs established a sub-camp south of the camp entrance where there was a berry patch." They constructed concrete abutments on each side of the East Branch of the Sacandaga River. They connected the bridge abutments with 166' steel I-beam. Then they installed wooden planks to the beams for a road. The new bridge would carry campers to the piece of land separating the two branches of the Sacandaga River. They completed 75 per cent of the bridge by the end of 1938.[15] By the end of 1939 ninety-five per cent of the bridge was completed.[16]

In 1940 the camp continued to work on the campsites at Lewey Lake, Sacandaga, Moffitt Beach, and Caroga Lake.[17] The boys built a cement dam at the Wells campsite and repaired and installed new telephone lines to fire towers on Hamilton, Kane, T Lake, and Pillsbury mountains. The bridge across the Sacandaga River was finally completed.[18]

In 1941 the camp continued working at the Moffitt Beach and Sacandaga campsites. They also extended the water system to the new campsites across the East Branch of the Sacandaga River in Wells.[19]

The CCC enrollees built this caretaker's cabin at the Sacandaga public campground. Podskoch Collection

Clockwise from Top Left - The Army set up a side camp at the Sacandaga campsite. Army tents housed the enrollees and the mess tent was on the right. Adirondack Museum Archives. Workers are pumping water from the footings for the Sacandaga bridge abutments. Adirondack Museum Archives. Workers built a temporary walkway connecting the bridge abutments. A small metal crane on the bridge was used for moving materials and stones. Adirondack Museum Archives. Steel I-beams connected the concrete abutments and wooden planks formed a roadway. Adirondack Museum Archives Camp S-90 built wooden forms for the cement abutments for the bridge across the East Branch of the Sacandaga River. Adirondack Museum Archives.

WORK ACCOMPLISHED BY CAMP S-90[*]

PROJECT	1934	1935	1936	1937	1938	1939	1940	1941	TOTAL
Bathhouses - number		2					4		6
Beach improvement - mi.		19	23	24					28
Buildings, other - number		12		1	1		1		15
Campground facilities, other - number	50								50
Concrete masonry - yd³		20							20
Contact stations - number			1						1
Dams, recreational - number	1		2						3
Dwellings - number			1	1	2		2		6
Emergency work, search & rescue - man-days		50		25				495	598
Emergency work, other - man-days		754							754
Fences - rods		206							206
Fill, rock - yd³		100							100
Fine grading (road slopes) - yd²		5040	8350						13390
Fire fighting - man-days	1598	420	218	51		1480	40	47	3854
Fire hazard reduction (roadside) - ac.		5	5						10
Fire hazard reduction, other - ac.		175							175
Fire pre-supression - man-days						137	759	384	7280
Fire prevention - man-days		2							2
General clean-up - ac.	18	84	54	81	85	4		165	488
Guard rails - number						20			20
Insect pest control - ac.				220	350	710			1280
Impounding & large diversions - number		2							2
Lake & pond site clearing - ac.		12							12
Latrines & toilets - number		4		5	1		6		16
Lookout houses & towers - number		5		5	1		6		17
Parking areas - yd²			3900	10038	2648	1250	4800		22636
Pipe or tile line - linear ft.			5850	3950		200	3650	10024	23674
Planting/moving trees & shrubs - number					62				62
Preparation/transportation of materials - man-days		354	2119	4755		636	1071	2364	11299
Public campground clearing/development - ac.	7	10.6	17			7.5	21	50	113.1
Pump houses - number			1						1
Reservoirs, small - number				1					1
Seats, benches - number				8	52			2	62
Sewage & waste disposal systems - number			7	3	5	5	6	5	31
Shelters - number				4					4
Signs & markers - number			56	215	6	6			283
Stone walls - rods			30						30
Storage facilities - number				10					10
Stream & lake bank protection - yd²				487	545				1032
Structural improvements, other - number		160							160
Surveys - man-days			201			57	93		351
Table-bench combinations - number			201			57	93		351
Telephone line - mi.		0.5		1.5		1.1	34.3		37.4
Trails, foot - mi.		39.2							39.2
Trails, truck - mi.	1	0.6	0.1	0.5	0.2	1		1.1	4.5
Tree & plant disease control - ac.	1476	4029	2178	1319	1090	645			10737
Water storage facilities - gal.		1000			6000000			12000000	18000000
Water supply systems - number					2	1	2	1	6

[*]Numerical data from Conservation Reports

When the Speculator CCC camp closed in 1942 these five barracks were used by young 4-H campers when it became a summer camp in 1945. Adirondack Museum Archives

After eight years the Speculator camp closed in 1942. Judy Patrick in her article, "Campfire dies out at 4-H Camp Sacandaga" in the March 12, 2006 article in The Sunday Gazette wrote, "In 1945, the CC camp buildings and facilities were turned over to a coalition of 4-H groups representing Fulton, Herkimer, Montgomery, Oneida, and Warren counties. The 4.4 acres of land on which the original camp stood, however, were not part of the transfer. The land remained privately owned, leased to the 4-H camp in five-year increments through 1967, when it along with an adjoining five acres, was purchased."

Historian Don Williams said Fred Rulison purchased the land from Harvey Behlen estate. Rulison leased the land to the 4-H. Then in November1967 he sold the 4.4-acre parcel to the 4-H organization.[20]

The camp operated for almost 60 years. It did not open in 2005, because funding problems along with the expected cost of needed building repairs made it financially impossible to run the camp.

In 2006 the Cornell Cooperative Extension of Fulton and Montgomery counties began accepting bids on the camp. It is the only CCC camp in New York State that is still intact. A local historic group is seeking to have the camp placed on the National Historic Register.

In August 2010 Caroline and Don Naysmith from Charlotte, NC purchased the 4-H camp in August 2010. They hope to restore the camp and open it for children with special needs. The Naysmihs spend half of the year in the Speculator area where they have a home on Whitaker Lake.

MEMORIES

Joseph Frank Pugliese

In the spring of 2006 I got an email from Deb Hurteau of Little Falls:

"My grandfather, Joseph Frank Pugliese, was one of the first to work in a CCC camp in the Adirondacks in 1933-1934. He is still alive and has shared stories you may find interesting. Grandpa worked at the Speculator CCC campsite for six months and earned a dollar a day plus meals. The boys worked from 8 am to 5pm building the bridges, roads, and fireplaces. He said the food was a big bonus as they didn't have much at home. Grandpa specifically remembers the brown paper bag lunches and they would start a small fire and toast their peanut butter and jelly sandwiches for a real treat! My grandfather is 94 years old and is still very sharp with his memory but almost blind and ailing physically. We asked if he would like to speak with you, but he never uses the phone due to poor hearing. I think you would absolutely enjoy speaking with my grandfather as he is amazingly intelligent and it shows in his conversations. I am in awe of his remarkable memory. He has lived in this area all of his life. When we go to the campsites in the summer, he always asks us if the fireplaces are still intact. He remembers building them and never thought his great-grandchildren would be using them!"

On June 28, 2006 I was fortunate to visit the wonderful family of Joseph and Evelyn Pugliese at their home in Little Falls, NY. I was greeted at the front door with a big hug and a kiss from Evelyn and ushered to the dinning room. Her daughters and granddaughters were all seated and ready to meet the writer who was going to gather their

At the age of 21 Frank Pugliese joined the CCC in 1933. He worked at the Speculator camp for six months. Joanne Tucci. CCC alumni Joe Pugliese & wife Evelyn at their home in Little Falls. Podskoch Collection

father's CCC stories. They called Joe who was upstairs and a spry 94 year-old came into the room. He was about 5' 7" tall and slim. His daughters bragged about how great a shape he was in because he did his exercises every day and worked out on his stationary bike.

"I asked Joe to tell me about his family and why he joined the CCCs. "I was born in 1912 in Dolgeville. My dad, Frank, was a mason. He and my mother Mary had six children: Margaret, Joseph, Rose, Josephine, Stella, and my brother Nick who died when he was a baby.

"I joined the CCCs in 1933 because I had been laid off from the Daniel Green Factory in Dolgeville and I couldn't find another job. I went to Gloversville in October to sign up and was sent to the Speculator camp. There were Army barracks with 30 guys in each. They had a couple stoves that used coal. I was 21 years old.

"I built roads, cut down trees, built bridges, and shoveled snow. At first it was tough working in the snow. I never thought I'd make it, but after a couple of weeks I got used to it. It got really cold there. There was an old guy who was a foreman who taught us how to break rocks and build a bridge. I loved the work. You were hungry like a bear at the end of the day.

"The first day I was there some kid had an epilepsy fit and he fell to the ground. It was scary for me. He lay on the ground for about five minutes and then just got up as though nothing happened."

I asked Joe about the food in the camp. "The food we got in the mess hall was good. In those days you were happy to have any kind of food. For lunch we had peanut butter and jelly sandwiches. We had a fire and toasted them. It was the best thing I ever tasted.

"They gave us regular Army uniforms. I didn't like the long johns they gave us. I didn't like them around my legs.

"A couple times on the weekends they took us to the movies in Gloversville. One time they took us to Blue Mountain Lake where they had a horse-pulling contest.

"There was a canteen where they sold soft drinks, cigarettes, and coffee. They also had a small library at the camp and I read almost every book.

"I learned how to play cards and checkers from the New York City boys. We also played horseshoes. I beat a New York City guy for a nickel. Then I played him checkers and lost the nickel. Later I got wise and learned how to beat him.

"I only stayed for six months. They wanted me to go to Idaho. My friend, Mike Messina, was undecided and we both didn't know what to do. There were a couple of girls that were interested in me coming back and I missed my friends especially my good friend, Johnny De Nino. He was still working at the shoe factory so I decided to go home."

Evelyn added, "Joe had one picture of a girl friend in his wallet but when we got married I made him rip it up and put my picture in."

"When I came home I couldn't get a job. I went to Boston but everyone was laid off so I walked and bummed rides back home. It took me a week. I finally got a job at Eastern Footwear in Dolgeville."

I thanked Joe for his stories and Evelyn handed me a bottle of homemade Italian wine.

Captain Wolfert D. Conover

After I spoke at the Northville Library on August 1, 2006 Wolfert "Wolf" Conover told me that his father, Wolfert D. Conover, was a captain in the Army and supervised the nearby Speculator camp S-90. We agreed to meet the next morning for breakfast to get more details of his father's life.

Wolf and his wife Ginger were waiting for me when I arrived at the diner on Route 30 in Northhampton at eight o'clock. Wolf pulled out a large photo of his father on horseback holding a polo mallet. Behind him were tents on platforms.

"My dad was born right down the road in Amsterdam in 1898. He joined the Army as a private in 1918 with the 11th US Cavalry. He was 20 years old.

"After WW I he married Katherine Anibal Conover in 1925 and I was their only child. My parents were divorced in 1930.

"Dad worked his way up the ranks, took courses, and was commissioned a first lieutenant in September 1933. He was assigned to the CCC camp in Speculator.

In December 1933 Dad married Mary Eastwood and they had six

Captain Wolfert D. Conover on horseback with a polo mallet. He supervised the CCC camp S-90 in Speculator and Camp S-119 in Middleburg. Wolf Conover children: David (twin died at birth), Mary Ann, Donald, Peggy, Kurt, and Gerrit.

"My father was quite athletic. He won a ski championship in Speculator and received a silver platter. Unfortunately, Dad had an accident at this camp in March 1936. He had recently purchased a pistol and was showing it to the camp commander, Captain Gruneck. As he took the revolver out of his locker it accidentally discharged and shot him just above his right knee. He was taken to the Amsterdam City Hospital where X-rays showed the bullet was embedded in the bone. I'm not sure if they removed it. Dad always walked with a limp after that accident.

"Then Dad was sent to Middleburg to Camp S-119 where he was the commanding officer. One of the camp's projects was building the masonry wall along a creek. The camp did a lot of reforestation work, built truck trails, did fire hazard reduction, and blister rust control. They did stream improvement projects on Little Schoharie Creek. They also fought fires and built waterholes.

"In May 1936 he was placed on inactive status but was recalled to active duty in December 1940.

"Dad was then in WW II and was part of the occupation of Germany. From there he was assigned to the Korean War. He finished his Army career in Aberdeen Proving Ground Maryland in 1955 then moved to Florida. He died August 8, 1982."

Elwood Garrison

On July 13, 2007 I gave a talk on the CCC to the Hamilton County Historical Society and met a few people who had parents in the local Speculator camp. One of them was Letty Rudes. She said her dad was in the camp but she had very little information to give me. I suggested sending for her father's records at the National Personal records Center in St. Louis. That night Letty was also my hostess. She gave me a room at her motel. She was one of the many people who provided a place for me to stay as I traveled through the Adirondacks gathering stories for my books.

Two years later Letty sent me 15 pages of her dad's CCC records and this is what they revealed.

Letty's father, Elwood Garrison, was born in Quarryville, near Saugerties, on September 6, 1911. His father, Raymond, was a bus driver and his mother, Belva, was a housewife. He attended 2 years of high school and left in 1928. Garrison worked as a clerk at S. W. Teetsel's Grocery Store in Saugerties from 1930-32.

He first joined the CCC on July 14, 1933 and worked at the Boiceville camp near Woodstock in the Catskills. He was honorably discharged from this camp on October 1, 1934.

Elwood was unemployed from September 1935 but enlisted again on October 31, 1935 and sent again to Boiceville S-53. His jobs were scouting for gypsy moths, working as a clerk, and driving trucks. On January 6, 1936 Garrison was transferred to Tannersville and did general labor. His medical record indicated he came to the camp dispensary because his right calf was lacerated from a dog bite he received while walking in the Town of Tannersville near Hunter Mountain. He was treated with phenol and alcohol and given a sterile dressing. His bite was reported to the town health officer.

Elwood Garrison worked in a CCC camp in the Catskills and then came to the Speculator camp. In the baseball team photo Elwood is in the second row. Letty Rudes

On April 15, 1936 Garrison was transferred to the Adirondacks and sent to the Speculator camp. He constructed campsites and his work was rated excellent. He was promoted to assistant leader on November 11, 1936.

Garrison attended education classes in the evening and took English classes from October 1936 to September 1937. He also received on the job training while doing pest control work. His company commander rated his work "very good." Garrison was also active in all the camp sports and received Red Cross First Aid certification.

On July 26, 1937 he was discharged. Letty Rudes said: "Dad's experience working in the camp as a clerk paid off because he accepted employment at Bigelow-Sanford Co. where he worked as a clerk in the finishing room. His salary was $15 a week.

"Dad married Roselle Craft and had five children: Letty, Garrison, Betty, Raymond, and Randy. When Mom was expecting a new addition and my parents were moving to a new job in Amsterdam, Mr. And Mrs. Clyde Elliott kept me to help with the transition.

"My dad never really talked about the CCC period of his life. I think some members felt a stigma of being jobless and dependent on the government for work. Dad's participation did have a profound effect on my life because I grew up where the CCC camp was in Speculator and I still live here. I wish Dad had told me more about his CCC life but he died in 1979 and the only information I had were his discharge papers until I got all that information from the National Archives and Records Administration in St. Louis.

Al Mayers

On June 29, 2006 I visited a good friend in Speculator, Jack Leadly, and asked him if he knew anyone who was in the CCC camp in Speculator. He replied:

"I was just six years old when my family moved here in 1934 from Staten Island. I remember the CCC boys were young, healthy, vigorous fellows. They played a lot of baseball games where the firehouse is today. They built the concrete dam on Cedar Lakes just north of Pillsbury Mountain. There was a lumber camp there and the dam raised the lake.

"One of the enrollees was Alvin "Al" Mayers. He was a baseball player at the Speculator CCC camp and later worked at Charlie Johns Store. You should contact his son Dick who is a custodian at the school."

I visited Dickie Mayers on August 17, 2006 and asked him about his dad's life and his experiences in the CCC.

"My dad was born in Philadelphia on December 9, 1917. His parents, Edwin & Helen Barnes died from the influenza pandemic. Their good friends, the Mayers of Camden, NJ, adopted Alvin and his brother, Edwin, and sister, Mildred.

I asked Dickie why his dad joined the CCC.

"Dad was doing odd jobs such as carpentry and masonry in Philadelphia. Jobs were very hard to come by. He

Al Mayers (right) and friend at the Speculator CCC camp S-90. Dick Mayers. One of the many cartoons Al Mayers drew for the Speculator camp newspaper. Dick Mayers

kept looking for an opportunity to work. His life was in shambles till he joined the CCC.

"He was sent to Camp S-90 Company 1209 in Speculator. Dad worked as a supply clerk in the camp. He also was the cartoonist for the camp newspaper, 'Months and Days.'

"On the weekends he played baseball with the Speculator town team. The local teams were happy to recruit the athletic CCC boys. In the winter he went out on the lake on snowshoes and also went tobogganing on the hill behind the movie theater. There was a toboggan slide by Jack Leadly's land. Isaiah Perkins started the slide about 1928. Perkins used to cut blocks of ice from Lake Pleasant and stack it on the bottom and sides of the slide. I think the CCC helped cut the ice and transport it to the slide.

"Dad also went to the local dances where the guys met local girls and eventually some of them married and settled in the area. My father was one of those guys. He first married Ambernette Page. Her father was Walter Page a foreman at the CCC camp. My half-sister Helen Tyo was from that first marriage."

Dickie told me to contact his half-sister, Helen Tyo, who lived near Cold Brook in the town of Ohio. I contacted Helen and she told me a little more about her family.

"My grandfather, Walter Page, worked at the Speculator CCC camp, too, as a foreman. He was a mason and he did all the masonry work at the CCC camp. He built the entrance and the fireplace in the rec hall.

"Dad met my grandfather's daughter, Ambernette, in Speculator. They dated, fell in love, and got married in May 1939 after Dad got out of the CCC. I think Dad was also in the CCC in Washington State. They had two children Walter ("Butch") and me.

"During WWII he joined the Navy and was in the Aleutian Islands. After the war he came back to Speculator and worked in the Osborne Tap Room and was the bartender. They had a boxing ring and he used to box there, too. Some of the top boxers like Max Baer, Max Schmeling, and Gene Tunney came up to Speculator to train for their matches.

Helen said: "My mother died and Dad remarried Julie Anne Kinney Schidzick. They had two children Dickie and Roberta ('Birdie').

"Dad then worked at Charlie Johns Store until 1983 and he died the next year.

"If it wasn't for the CCC I wouldn't have been born.

Ralph Barton

I first met Ralph Barton when I was writing my book on Adirondack fire towers in 2001. He and his wife Mona told me great stories about her father, Joe Saverie, when he was an observer on Wakely Mountain. Ralph also had stories about his days as an observer on the Snowy Mountain fire tower. Whenever I was in Indian Lake I enjoyed visiting this warm couple. Mona would be busy doing laundry for a hotel in Blue Mountain or taking care of her blind brother who lived with them. Ralph also helped Mona with the folding of towels and sheets.

Then when I visited on August 30, 2007, Ralph surprised me with news that he had worked at the Speculator CCC camp. I asked Ralph to tell me about his early life and why he joined the CCCs.

"I was born in Glens Falls in 1919. My grandmother, Lisa Locke, lived in Sabael on Indian Lake. I came up to live with her in 1929 when I was 10 years old. My mom worked here and there around Lewey Lake to get money to raise her three children: Robert, Edith, and me. I went to Indian Lake School but I quit school when I was 16. I lived on and off with my uncle, Stewart King, who was a barber in Speculator. I got sick of working for nothing and went down to the CCC camp on Paige Street and signed up.

"I liked the work. We helped build the Lewey Lake campsite. Each day we drove by truck from the camp. I helped build the foundation for the ranger's cabin and camp fireplaces. Our foreman was a mason from Speculator. I busted stone with a sledgehammer and mixed cement by hand.

"We also worked at the Moffitt campsite. I cut trees and branches, graded campsites with shovels and rakes, and helped build fireplaces.

"Another job I had was working with Howard Vanderwhacker. Both of us were natives and knew the country. Our foreman was Oswald Thompson. We were sent out to scout trees that were infected by a disease. We marked the trees and the trail from the road to the trees. Then another detail of men came and cut the trees. We covered all the area from Indian Lake to Arietta and from Baker's Mills near Johnsburg to Northville."

I asked Ralph if the boys every played jokes on each other. He laughed. "Oh yes. One barracks would try to get even with another. We'd come in one door at night and flip the beds over then run out the other door in the back.

"We had one guy in our barracks called Barrett. He'd come in late at night and stumble around and wake us all up. So one night we got even. We put a bucket of water on the beam over his head and put a string from the bucket to his bedspring. When he came in late and sat on his bed the water spilled on him. He got the message and was quiet from then on.

"I was in the CCCs for three 6-month stints. Then I left around June 1936 and went to work with Charley Brown at his Camp Merryland on Lake Pleasant on Rt. 8. He had a store, livery and 14 cottages. I clerked at the store, cleaned cottages and moved furniture.

"The CCCs was a good experience for me. I had work and learned how to get along with others."

Charles W. Phillips

While doing a book signing at the Old Forge Hardware Store in the summer of 2007 Brooks Phillips of Oriskany, NY walked up to me and said: "My father, Charles Phillips was in the Speculator CCC camp and here is his CCC Yearbook." He showed me a picture of a group of guys and pointed to the second on the left in the front row and said:

"That's my dad. He told me one of his jobs was cooking at the camp. I read in the newspaper that you are writing a book on the CCC and I wanted to know if you could use his book in your research."

I thanked him for the offer and borrowed it for over a year. It was a great source of information because it had group pictures, listings of the supervisors, commanding officers, and names and towns of the enrollees. One of the best parts was a history of each of the camps from the Hudson Valley, Catskills, and Adirondacks."

After a year I was fortunate to buy my own copy and arranged to drop Brooks' book off at Canal Lock # 17 in Little Falls. He worked on many of the sections of the canal.

I misplaced his name and phone number but I fi-

Ralph Barton spent one and one-half years at the Speculator CCC camp building the nearby state campsites. He also liked playing his guitar in camp. Mona Barton

A group photo of the Speculator CCC camp in the 1937 Schenectady District Civilian Conservation Corps Area Yearbook. Podskoch Collection

nally tracked him down through fellow canal workers and got his phone number. I called him in September 2010 to get more information about his dad.

"My father came from a very poor family in Hampton, SC. He was born in 1910 and only went to seventh grade. His parents, Brooks and Elizabeth, had four children and Dad was the second oldest. My grandfather was a farmer during the Depression. Daddy's CCC discharge papers state his last job before joining the CCC was as a butcher. After being unemployed for three months he knew he had to get a job to help his family so he joined the CCC. I still call him Daddy because he died in 1963 when I was just 10 years old. I was young but I still remember the stories he told me.

"Daddy joined the CCC in Columbia, SC on October 17, 1936 and they sent him to Fort Bragg, NC for training. On October 25 Daddy left by train to New York State. He wasn't alone. There were around 20 other young boys from South Carolina with him. On the next day the enrollees arrived in Speculator. Here was this Southern boy who was used to warm weather and was now transported to the cold Adirondacks.

"Daddy didn't like the snow at all. In fact he always wanted to send me to a military school in South Carolina and when he retired Daddy was going to move back to SC but he never did.

"I know he met a lot of nice guys at the Speculator camp. In fact his records show he was promoted to assistant leader. There were guys that he stayed friends with like Al Mayers from Speculator and another was from Keesville. When we drove to visit family in SC, we always stopped at a CCC friend's motel in VA.

"His first job was a second cook. Besides cooking he also did a lot of work at Moffitt Beach State Park. He also told me he worked on Hamilton Mountain working on the telephone line and trail to the fire tower."

Then I asked Brooks what his father did for recreation.

"He might have played baseball because he loved that sport. Then at night or on weekends he'd walk or hitch-hike to town to drink beer. There was a bar called the Rat Trap (Sacandaga Hotel). He said that when they drank beer they'd give each other haircuts. Then they went outside and stood under the streetlight to see what they looked like.

"Daddy was honorably discharged from the CCC on September 30, 1937. He didn't rejoin because he got hired as a chauffeur for a Mr. Chalmers who owned a large knitting mill in Amsterdam. I have a picture of Daddy driving this big car. Chalmers also had a huge home on Lake Pleasant. Then Daddy worked at Hamilton Lake Lodge as a caretaker for John Starr who built steamboats on the Erie Canal. Starr had about 33,000 acres of land that he sold to International Paper (IP). It became a resort for the company big shots. Daddy worked there as a caretaker and built a nine-hole golf course for them.

"During WW II Daddy fought in Europe and lost one of his eyes fighting. He came back to the Adirondacks and resumed his job as caretaker for IP.

"In 1948 Dad married Doris M. Whitman from Lake Pleasant. Her father, Alan, owned the Lake Pleasant Garage. My parents had two children, myself and my sister Barbara.

"Daddy worked

After Charlie Phillips worked in the Speculator CCC camp, he served in the Army during WWII. Brooks Phillips for IP till he died in 1963. He was just 53. We didn't have anyplace to go to because we had always lived at the resort. Mom bought a camp on Lake Pleasant and that is where I grew up. Mom died in 1971 when I was 20 years.

"I'll never forget going for rides with Daddy. He enjoyed pointing out places where he worked in the CCC. He also took me to his old camp site that was used later by the 4-H for a summer camp. We went inside the old mess hall and he pointed to the big fireplace and said, 'Sonny, I sat many a night sitting by the warm fireplace because I hated the cold.'"

Abraham Lincoln Curtis

In the 1998 November/December issue of " Adirondack Life" magazine Donne Green described Abraham Lincoln Curtis' experiences in the Civilian Conservation Corps in Speculator.

Curtis said, "We had somebody standing over us all the time, and if you did something he didn't like, he could put your name down and you could work seven days that week, two days in the kitchen.

"In the morning the sergeant blew a whistle to wake us up. We made our beds, swept the barracks, and had a filling breakfast. We then put in an eight-hour workday. If we wanted weekends off we had to put in an hour after supper, digging or hauling coal or whatever they wanted."

Curtis laughed and said, "A bunch of guys would go out at night and when they came back they'd find their beds hung up in the rafters."

He often walked home to Wells on weekends. One time he had forty cents taken out of his pay for a movie that he said he didn't attend.

Curtis was involved in many projects. At the Lewey Lake campsite, they dug a ditch down from the nearby mountain to provide water for the campsite. They worked near Benson on the Northville-Lake Placid Trail, and fought a forest fire in 1938 on Speculator, Orey, and Dunham mountains.

Below zero temperatures did not always stop work. "When it would be way below zero, they'd wait until ten o'clock, but we still got out, One year, just as the cold weather was coming on, they shipped in a whole bunch of men from South Carolina and Georgia. They had to face that winter first thing.

"Oh, it was cold," remembers Curtis about the time when he was working in the woods near Indian Lake. "Logs were piled up on skidways and we had to go up there with crosscut saws and axes and cut that up and split it. And it had to be hauled out to the road to be put on trucks for summer use at the different campsites."

During the spring the workers were pestered by black flies. They didn't have the insect repellents we have today or head nets. "We just had to fight them off." The bugs, extreme weather, homesickness, hard work, and Army discipline caused many of the recruits to desert. "A lot of 'em just ran away."

Curtis wanted to honor his grandparents who were deeply religious and who had raised him. "I was trying to live my life according to what the Bible teaches; I made up my mind to endure." He was looked down by the city boys as a hillbilly. They even voted him "most religious' in a camp newspaper poll.

The boys were paid five dollars at the end of each month. Curtis remembered payday, "The captain would sit counting the silver dollars with a loaded revolver on the table." He said he didn't spend his money at the camp canteen on 3.2 beer or ten cents a pack cigarettes. He lent his extra money out at 10 per cent interest.

During the winter of 1937-38 a state supervisor liked his work habits and assigned him as a watchman and fireman. He stoked the potbellied stoves at night for five days and then went home for the weekend.

In the spring of 1938 Curtis worked with a crew at the Sacandaga campsite building a bridge across the East Branch of the Sacandaga River. Two crews worked in 6-hour shifts for two months. Curtis said they worked in, "water they couldn't keep out even with a pump." The young men struggled to dig six feet to build the cement piers. "Every bit had to be taken out by hand," said Curtis.

Then in March 1939 he was discharged from the CCCs and the following year he worked on a WPA project

CCC enrollee Lincoln Curtis on a wooden scaffold above a bridge abutment that the Speculator camp S-90 was building over the East Branch of the Sacandaga River near the Sacandaga state campsite. A CCC water pump was used to remove water from the abutment forms. Adirondack Museum Archives

where he loaded dynamite on a road project in Hope south of Wells. During WW II he was in the Air Force. After the war he worked throughout the west and returned to Wells around 1980. Curtis got a job at "The "Forks" state campground in Wells where he worked with the seniors' Green Thumb program. At 80 years old he helped maintain the campground. He enjoyed telling the visitors about his work in building the bridge in 1938 and considered it one of the best times in his life.

Art Conduzio

On June 15, 2006 I received an email from Art Conduzio Jr., of Lake George. He read about my search for CCC members in Mark Frost's article in the "Chronicle," a Glens Falls newspaper:

"My father worked at the Speculator CCC camp. His picture is on the wall at the Adirondack Museum in Blue Mountain Lake. He was in a group shot of the workers at the camp. He is now 87 and lives in Ballston Lake, NY. If you are ever in the area and wish to interview him, I can set it up for you.

"Good luck with your book."

By the time I tried to visit Art's father, he had passed away. I contacted Art to see if he had any information or photos. I asked him what work he did?

"He never spoke of any specific job. I got the impression he was just one of the CCC workers. I remember him telling me about fire detail so I assume they rotated in camp jobs while spending their days working outside the camp.

"He told me there were rumors about a gold mine in the Speculator area. But that's about all I remember."

I suggested getting his dad's discharge papers from the National Personnel Records Office in St. Louis.

About a year later Art sent me his discharge papers that revealed this information about his life before and during the CCC.

Arcangel "Art" Conduzio was born in Schenectady on March 19, 1919. His father's name was Luigi and he worked for GE. There were four children in the family: Vito, Sue, Anne, and Art. He dropped out of high school in his senior year and joined the CCC on October 11, 1937 at the age of 18.

The main type of work Art performed at the Speculator camp was campsite construction. Records don't specify what areas he worked at but during this time Camp

S-90 was working at the campsites at Sacandaga River, Lewey, and Moffitt Beach.

During the evenings Art attended the following classes during his two years at the Speculator camp: six classes in masonry, two on courtesy, and one each in auto mechanics and carpentry. He also received on-the-job training doing masonry, riprap construction, driving truck, and working as a stockroom clerk.

Conduzio (bottom right) and friends standing by the recreation hall. Art Conduzio

Art loved sports at camp such as swimming, skating, and skiing.

He received training in First Aid and water safety. In July 1938 he went for one week to Plattsburgh for lifeguard training. Then from February to April 1939 he completed an American Red Cross First Aid class at his camp. In June 1939 he completed a three-week Water Safety class in Boonville.

On April 19, 1939 Art became an assistant leader at the camp. Art worked at the Speculator camp for two years and left on September 31, 1939.

Art Jr., said that his father worked in the Navy on tankers in the Pacific during WWII. When he returned to the US he married Bridgett Amodeo and they had two children: Arthur and Joanne.

He worked at GE as a steamfitter and retired after 40 years. He passed away in 2006.

Bob Beirlein

Judy Wilcox met me at the Northville Library and told me her father, Bob Beirlein, had been in the CCCs. She invited me to her mother's home in Northville for an interview.

When I arrived Judy and her sister Jill introduced me to their mother, Vivien. She was seated at the kitchen table with a photo album and CCC memorabilia of her husband at the Speculator camp.

"My husband had just finished his first year at Cooper College when his father died. He had to do something to help his mother. He couldn't find a job and decided to join the CCCs. Bob was originally going to be sent out west but was sent to Speculator in the Adirondacks.

"Bob and I met when I went camping for two weeks at Moffitt Beach near Speculator with my friend Theresa Kadlic and her sister Bertha and her husband. We met some CCC guys working at the beach and they invited us to see their camp down the road.

"One night we walked up to the camp just to look around. A group of guys took us on a tour. We went into the office and as soon as I saw the typewriter I began typing. I had just gotten out of high school and enjoyed typing. All of a sudden in the doorway appeared a person who said, 'We need a secretary.' All I saw were his blue eyes and smile. He told me later that he had seen me on the beach and he knew I was the one for him.

"I was only camping for two weeks but Bob told me he was interested in visiting me at my home in Johnstown.

"I went back home but couldn't find a job. Bob would stop and visit about once a week when he came to town to pick up supplies. Then he started coming to town on Saturday nights when he brought the boys to go to the movie theater or dances. After he dropped them off he'd come over and visit me. We'd drive around town in the big Army truck and stop in front of my house and just talk.

"When my parents found out about him, they got nervous about me being with a guy from Brooklyn. But he was different from all the others. He was very intelligent. I never thought he would fall in love with me.

"After driving the truck for the camp he worked as First Aid person and drove the camp ambulance. He did

Vivien & Bob Beirlein met at the Speculator CCC camp, fell in love and got married. Here they are standing by a barracks in September 1938. In August of 2009 Vivien Beirlein is looking through an album pictures of her husband at the Speculator CCC camp. She reminisced about meeting her future husband at the Speculator CCC camp. Podskoch Collection

this for five months and then was honorably discharged on December 23, 1938.

"He went back to Brooklyn and got a job in a printing company. We wrote letters to each other, and he often mentioned marriage to me. He finally proposed and I went down to Brooklyn in May 1939. We got married and we lived with his mother for four years.

"Bob went off to war in 1943. After he returned he had many jobs. Later in the 1960s he had a Ford dealership in Speculator. We raised four children and our family often went camping at Moffitt Beach and passed his old CCC camp. He was proud of the work that they did in developing that state campground."

Ed Boice

Ed Boice of Wells called me during the summer of 2002. "In 1939 I was in the CCC camp near the outskirts of Speculator where the 4-H Camp is today. We had the job of putting new telephone lines up to the fire towers on Hamilton, Pillsbury, and T Lake Mountains. In the summer we put up telephone poles and in the winter we strung the telephone wire. I remember there was a lot of snow on Hamilton. Two guys and I used snowshoes to break the path. Then the other guys pulled the wire up the mountain. To keep warm we'd dig a hole by the pole and start a fire. We used stream water or melted snow to make coffee. At lunch we had sandwiches that the cooks made at camp. There were no plastic bags or wax paper. They wrapped the sandwiches in butcher paper."

I asked Ed how they coped with the cold? "We

Vivien Laning Beirlein and her girlfriends with Speculator CCC camp enrollees at the Moffitt Beach State campsite where Vivien and her friends were camping. Pictured standing are:(l-r) # E. Durante, Doris Laning, Max Sharpe, and Francis Cummings. Squatting (l-r) Viv Laning, and Tresa Kadric. Vivien Beirlein

In 1939 Ed Boice of Wells (right) and friend were in the CCC camp near the outskirts of Speculator where the 4-H Camp is today. Ed Boice

were young then. It didn't bother us much. We had a lot of fun working together. After work a truck picked us up and took us back to camp. Then in 1941 a lot of guys like myself left the CCC camp and were drafted. I served in the Navy in WW II."

John M. Kuczek

After interviewing Helen Tyo about her father, Al Mayers, and his experiences in the Speculator CCC camp, she told me to call her aunt, Vivian Page Kuczek, in Browns Mills, NJ because her husband, John, was also in Camp Speculator, Company 1208 in Speculator. I called her on October 2, 2010 and asked her to tell me about her husband's life and how they got together.

"John was born in 1919 in Amsterdam. His father, Joseph, lost his first wife and two children. He remarried and with his second wife, Agnes, had eight children. John was the eldest. His father was a farmer and then worked in a factory. His family was hard working but times were tough and when John graduated from high school he couldn't find a good job.

"It was around 1939 and he joined the CCC. He went to the Speculator camp. I think it was rough on John because he had a close family and I'm sure he hated to leave them but he had to help his family.

"As it turned out, John liked living and working at the camp. It was fun. He worked in the office as a clerk with other boys. The officers had a lot of respect for John.

"In his free time and on weekends John played sports at the camp. He was on the camp basketball team which played at our local school and at the hall at Camp Kunjamuk. They played against other CCC camps and town teams.

"I met John at my sister Ambernette Mayers' house. He was quiet guy. I liked sports along with hunting and fishing but he wasn't interested in outdoor sports so we didn't have that much in common. I had been dating a local boy but when I heard John was being used by another girl, I decided to break them up.

"One night I was getting dressed to go out and my boy friend came over to see me. He asked me where I was going and I said out but you're staying here.

"I went over to Ambernette's house because I heard John was going to be there. I talked to John about basketball because we both played on teams. I got to like him. I didn't leave that night until I had a date with him.

"We began dating in 1941. They had movies one night a week at the camp and the guys always reserved special seats in the rec hall for us.

"I worked during the week for the phone company as a switchboard operator. John and his buddy called me when I worked at night just before I left work at 10 pm. They'd sing, "You are my Sunshine."

"John used to walk to see me in the evenings. I lived on Route 8. We played a lot of cards with my parents. Then I'd borrow my dad's car and drive John back to camp.

"Shortly after I graduated from high school the phone company moved to another town so I worked at Charlie Johns Store. Charlie sold me his '37 Plymouth business coupe for $35. It was so fast I even outraced the police a couple times. Now that I had a car John and I drove to dances in town and to Avery's Dance Hall in Arietta.

"John was a very competent clerk and when the CCC needed an experienced clerk in another camp, they transferred him and he was made the subaltern, a subordinate officer under the captain. Then he was transferred to another camp but we kept in touch.

"When the camps closed and the US went to war John joined the Army in 1942 and went to Europe. When he came back from Europe in 1945, he worked with my father, Walter Page, doing masonry for a short time.

On May 11, 1946 John and I got married and we had six children: John, Barbara, Paul, Thomas, Mary, and Joan.

"John joined

John Kuczek dressed in his CCC uniform in front of the Speculator camp infirmary. Vivien Kuczek

Company 1208, at Speculator, N.Y.

Activity photos from the 1937 Schenectady District Civilian Conservation Corps Area Yearbook. Podskoch Collection

the Air Force in the late 40s. Because John had a lot of experience as a clerk in the CCC he continued in this field throughout his career in the Air Force. We traveled a lot: Port Slocum, Mitchell Field, Eniwetok, an atoll where they tested the first A bombs--1948-52 in the Pacific, and McGuire Air Force Base in NJ.

He retired in 1973. John passed away in 2006.

SPECULATOR CAMP NEWSPAPER STORIES

Here are a few interesting stories from an undated issue of a Speculator CCC Camp newspaper, "Months and Days," that Dick Mayers shared with me.

Night Fireman

There are 41 stoves in this camp to be kept going during the winter months. It is the duty of the night fireman to make his trip around the camp every hour, to check each stove. When the temperature is way below zero it is not an easy job to keep the pipes in the latrine, kitchen, and pump house from freezing. In case you don't know that when the pipes freeze, they sometimes burst and that would mean no water supply. When there is no water, there is no food, no washing facilities, and no means to fight a campfire.

Think of the importance of water to our well-being, and remember to give the fireman a break and LET HIM SLEEP. Make no unnecessary noises.

Pop Pop

Sam Fritz, our camp steward, was more than surprised when he opened the canteen one morning, to find fourteen bottles of soda had broken due to our low temperature of thirty degrees below zero. The recent weather that we had in the last two weeks would drive most people nuts. If you take off your winter undies you freeze. If you leave them on you roast. So what?!?!?!

Editorial: "An Open Letter to the Company-You Should Patronize the Camp Exchange"

Hello Buddy,

With the above greeting, we inaugurate this column which will be a regular feature of "Months & Days."

We will endeavor to impart as much "inside information" about the Camp Exchange, and it will be to the advantage of one and all to listen in closely.

The Camp Exchange is practically the sole source of revenue for making needed camp improvements, and for buying necessary incidentals in the routine of camp administration.

We wish to emphasize the fact that it is to the well being of us all, that every man trade at the Camp Exchange.

The articles for sale here have been purchased with our experience of knowing what you need and want. The prices have been altered to fit our buying capacity, and you must admit they are not more, and in many instances less, than articles of the same quality on sale at the local stores. Why not buy here what you need, and items which we do not carry by all means buy them in town.

The accumulating profits of our Exchange is turned into dividends of $125.00 a clip, and then absorbed by the Company Fund. The Company Fund is the responsibility of the Captain and he, in his better judgment, spent it 100% on camp improvements of all types. Improvements we all take for granted—look around us for just a moment. Only recently, brand new electric fixtures in the mess hall and latrine improved both buildings considerably. The shower has been brought up to date; three coats of paint and galvanized metal did the trick. The entire rec hall given a two-tone paint job, pictures have been ordered, and all new curtains are in the making at the present time. And I can enumerate a dozen smaller items of the same nature Spring is just around the corner, plans for a general overhaul of the camp have been mapped out. Grass and flower seeds will be purchased, gravel for new walks, any number of gallons of paint, and all these bills will be paid for by our Company Fund.

We are happy to add that the Camp Exchange will receive a complete remodeling. More floor space, a new counter, repainting, booths, chairs and tables, neon lights, atmosphere—it will have everything. How can we miss!! The Company Fund will also see this job through.

In conclusion fellows, I say that your purchases at the camp Exchange every now and then, help to put our Company Fund in a position to do things for us all. This is our Company, our home---let's make it as home-like and comfortable as possible. Let's be the leaders in our own endeavor! In the meantime, I think it is over, and, I'LL MEET YOU IN THE CANTEEN.

Sincerely yours,
Samuel Fritz

Poetry

Roses are red,
Violets are blue;

Dear old 1208,
We sure do love you.

You can tell a K. P.
By his vacant stare,
You can tell a rookie
By his "know-it-all" air;
You can tell an old fellow
By his polished touch.
You can tell him much.

He fell from the roof
And it happened by chance,
He tore a big hole in the seat of his pants.
In the dispensary he fainted with fright
When they told him that his end was in sight.

Beans, beans, beans—CHOW!!—And how!!
Calvin Morrison

Tom and Margie Perkins who helped me with my research on the Hamilton Mt. fire tower introduced me to their neighbor Calvin "Cal" Morrison of Speculator. Cal said he had lived near the Speculator CCC camp. "My mother, Nina, used to do laundry for the CCC camp.

"There was a path from my house through the woods that led to the camp. I was just a little boy. I was born in 1933 and that's when the camp began. It ended in 1942. I remember them playing baseball in the field next to our house. There was a backstop, too.

"The CCC used to play tennis on the two clay tennis courts that belonged to Camp Kunjamuk, which was on Lake Pleasant across from my house and the CCC camp. It was a boys' camp for kids from New York City. They had a large hall where they had group activities. I think the CCC boys may have used it, too.

Camp Kunjamuk closed and Chet Rudes moved the camp hall across the road into the field where the CCC used to play baseball. Chet converted the hall into a bowling alley downstairs and upstairs a place for dances and receptions. It was called 'The Pine Cone.' Eventually the Pine Cone closed and became Stevens Lumber Co.

"I also remember that the Perry boys from Hinckley were CCC members.

"The main project of the camp was building Moffitt Beach State Park. My dad told me that the area had been just an alder bed. There was just a lot brush along the shore. The CCC boys cleaned it up and made a beautiful park.

"I think there are only four original CCC buildings left: infirmary, medical center, kitchen, and rec hall. The CCC camp was built on land owned by the Bellen & Letson families. They were related to my mother."

Philip Cohen

While speaking at the Massena Library in 2007 I met Marilyn Clopman, who told me that her father, Philip Cohen, had been a truck driver in the Speculator CCC camp. She said he was still alive and that I should contact him.

I called Philip at his home in East Greenbush, NY in June 2008, and he told me about his life. "I was born in NYC in 1921. My father Frank was a tailor and my mother's name was Fannie. I had five brothers and sisters.

"When I was 17 I had a spinal operation and was in the hospital for five months. This caused me to miss almost a year of school. I had three and one-half years of high school but my friends had graduated and I decided to quit school, so I had to get a job.

"I heard about the CCCs from a friend who joined them and was in New Mexico. I was working six days a week and only making $12 a week pushing carts through the streets in the garment industry in New York City. The CCCs paid $30 a-month. That sounded good to me so I signed up in Brooklyn on January 3, 1941. It didn't bother me leaving home. Nobody knew if I was gone anyway. I was sent to Speculator in the Adirondacks.

"It was cold up there in January. They just had pot-bellied stoves. They would turn cherry red at first and then get cold and dark at night. Someone was supposed to be on duty to check on the stoves, but he didn't always do the job. A lot of times the water froze.

"The group I went to camp with was from NYC

Nina Morrison lived on Route 8 near the Speculator Camp S-90. Many of the Army officers and CCC boys brought their clothes to be laundered and ironed at her home. Cal Morrison

Speculator CCC enrollees: Anthony Zito, Durante, and Cummings are clowning around in front of other enrollees who enjoyed coming to nearby Moffitt Beach that their CCC camp developed and maintained during the 1930s. Vivien Beirlein

and half were from the local area like Gloversville & Johnstown. You couldn't get too friendly because most of the guys were of questionable character. We started with 200 and wound up with 90 in June. "One Saturday night one of the barracks caught on fire and we had to stay outside for fear that our barracks would start on fire, too, from the flying sparks. I grabbed a comforter and wrapped myself up and laid in the snow.

"I was fortunate to have a driver's license from NYC. A friend of mine had a 1931 Model A Ford that he paid $15 for, so I was able to learn on his car. I got a license for 50 cents. Since I had a license I got a job as a truck driver. We had five drivers and my job was to take the guys out to their job in a rack truck. We had three work sites: Moffitt Beach, Wells, and Piseco Lake.

"The crew put in roads, built fireplaces, and cut wood. After I took the guys to the worksite, I drove back to camp to get a dump truck because the guys needed rocks, sand, and gravel.

"It was no fun driving the truck because there was a governor on the engine that controlled the speed to not exceed 25 miles per hour. In fact when they needed a load of crushed stone in Gloversville I could only go 25 miles per hour. In some of the camps the Ford trucks had a lock with a key with a lock switch. One day someone was going down a hill and turned the key off to go faster. The steering wheel locked and the truck got wrecked. Next week they took out all the locks on the steering wheels.

"There was one job in camp that nobody wanted and that was cleaning out the latrine. It was a seven-seater raised outhouse. There were three steps to the toilet. Once a week there was a trap door that someone had to go down and clean out."

I asked Philip if he ever got injured at camp or if anything scary happened.

"No," he replied, "but I was lucky once when a doctor came to administer shots. The doctor gave the first shot to me and then handed it to his assistant, who was going to give the rest of the shots, and showed him how to do it. I'm glad I got the first shot because the assistant broke the needle off in the first guy's arm.

"I remember another incident at camp. A delivery truck came to camp one day with supplies. The truck driver said someone stole a bottle of liquor from the van. The lieutenant called everyone in separately to see who did it. A couple days later one fella who was eating in the mess hall said to me, 'You were the one who squealed.' For some reason he thought I had squealed but I hadn't. Retribution is quick. Word got around camp that I did it. Even though I was innocent the next day I had two sandwiches on the seat of my truck. When I came back the sandwiches were ground into the dirt.

"Driving a truck up north could be dangerous. There was a spring thaw and the mud was up to the rear axle. All the guys in one truck had to get out and push their truck out but my truck was able to get around it and the guys were happy that they didn't have to push.

"One time on our day off we had a scary incident in Lake Pleasant. It was a nice day and we were walking along the lake. We found a rowboat without oars. So we went back to camp and got a sheet and a broom and made a sail. We sailed across the lake and then the weather got choppy. We began taking on water and we couldn't swim. We went to the shore and tried to walk around the lake to get back to camp. We had to walk through the woods and then hit water that was over our heads. It was getting dark, and we were lost. We were thinking nobody knew where to look for us. So we kept walking for an hour. We thought we heard some cars but it was the sound of humming from some power lines. That's what saved us. We followed the sound to a road. We finally got back to camp at about 9 pm. Nobody knew we were gone. We went into the kitchen and the cook made us some sandwiches.

"The troopers had been looking for someone who stole a sailboat. We thought that it was us because we had a homemade sail. Later we found out that two other guys stole a sailboat. Troopers caught them and they wound up in the Hamilton County jail. That was a scary thing and we learned a lesson that day."

I asked Philip if they ever played jokes on one another? "There was a lot of hazing. Sometimes they'd stand your locker upside down. There was one guy from NYC who wasn't too bright. They'd put him up on the roof and tell him to wait for the sky mail."

Then I asked him what he did on the weekends.

During WW II Philip Cohen said it was easy to get used to being in the Army because of his experiences of working at the Speculator CCC camp because it was run by the Army. Marilyn Clopman

Philip replied, "We liked to do outdoor sports and played baseball in the baseball field in Speculator. The locals tolerated us but didn't like us. We played the locals in basketball games, too.

"In the winter we used the town toboggan run. People were paying for the rides down the run. We had to pull the toboggans up for the customers and when we pulled up a certain number then we got a free ride down.

"Every Saturday we went down to Amsterdam and just hung around. If we had 10 cents we went to the movies. "Some guys hitchhiked home on the weekend, but I never went home. While I was in camp my family moved back to Troy and that was too far to hitchhike."

Then I asked if he or any of the guys dated the local girls. "We didn't meet any girls. They wouldn't associate with us."

I questioned him on the food. Philip replied, "It was terrible! We mostly had mutton. One time the camp went on strike and refused to work. It lasted for a day. There was a rumor that the subaltern was pocketing money and that is why we were getting low quality food. Every lunch we got two liverwurst sandwiches. I made about two trips a day when I drove to Gloversville to pick up stone, and I'd throw the sandwiches into the reservoir to feed the fish.

"I left the CCCs on June 27, 1941 because it was not what I wanted to do and my family was now living in Troy where I'd have a better chance of getting a job. I got a job as a soda jerk but after three weeks they got rid of the soda fountain in the drug store. Then I worked for a valet service parking cars in a garage.

"After that I took a test at Watervliet Arsenal and took classes as a machinist at RPI. I worked at the arsenal till the next year when I was drafted in the Army in December 1942. There were 175 guys for the physical test and 175 passed. There were two drunks under the bench and they passed without a physical. I was used to the Army procedures so it wasn't entirely strange.

"I got married in 1944 to Eileen Dreisenenstock in Albany. We had three children: Robert, Marilyn and Susan.

"After WW II, I went into the oil and garage business.

"Then I went to work for the state as a truck weigher and got a job on the Thruway as a toll collector at Southern Blvd. in Albany. Later, I became the supervisor from Kingston to Canaan with eight toll stations. I retired in 1976 and have 75 acres to take care of. My experiences working out doors in the CCCs helped me when I bought my farm.

"While in the CCCs I liked being in the Adirondacks and getting away from the city, but the group at the camp was not of the best character. I didn't make any real friends because there were so many people going AWOL and not coming back. More than half of the 200 boys went AWOL during the six-month period. I never considered signing up again."

Five from Speculator CCC Camp Drown in 1934

The Morning Herald (Gloversville and Johnstown) reported on July 24, 1934 that four CCC enrollees and their foreman from the Speculator camp drowned when their 16' rowboat capsized on Round Pond in the Town of Providence in Saratoga County where they had been fighting a forest fire.

A fire was burning for a week or more in a very isolated area near Round Lake Reservoir. CCC enrollees, forest rangers, and volunteers were able to get the fire under control and 10 men spent the night watching so that it wouldn't spread. In the morning a crew of seven men and their foreman, Ernest Brooks were going to replace the 10-man fire crew.

Associated Press photographer, J. B. Gutler, was on the shore taking pictures of the departing crew. He felt Ernest Brooks had a premonition of what might happen as he prepared to board the boat. Gutler said:

"There were seven men in the boat already. When somebody said there was room for another. Forest Ranger McDonnell, of Saratoga Spa, expressed the belief that the boat already was fully loaded but a place was made and somebody called to Brooks.

"I'll never forget the look on his face. He (Brooks) glanced out over the water with a faraway look, said nothing, and hesitated as if he were about to refuse to go, but he stepped up, took his seat and the boat was shoved off."

Seven WW I veterans from the CCC camp in Speculator and their foreman, Ernest Brooks prepare to leave in a motor-driven rowboat to cross Round Pond to relieve fellow enrollee fire fighters.[21]

Speculator camp newspaper Months & Days Oct cover by Al Mayers

The craft was about halfway across the pond when it suddenly sank in nearly 60 feet of water for no apparent reason.

Persons interviewed at the scene of the drowning felt that possibly water went over the sides and into the boat due to a leak and caused it to sink. Another opinion is that some of the enrollees lost their head when the boat began to fill up and jumped out upsetting the boat.

The ten enrollees that were waiting on the other side of the pond saw the boat sinking and jumped in the water to save the men but only three were saved.

The July 22, 1933 Binghamton Press reported that the four CCC enrollees were WW I veterans: William H. Harris, Syracuse; Gerald Lynch, Harrison, NJ; Edgar J. Van Villard and Fred Rothfuss of Newark, NJ.

Foreman Ernest Brooks, an experienced woodsman and fire warden also drowned. He was the father-in-law of Robert Osborne, the proprietor of a camp where boxer Gene Tunney trained in Speculator.

At first it was theorized that the boat hit a stump but later it was noted that the boat had a leak and may have caused the disaster. An Army investigation found the men died "in the performance of duty."

Hunting cartoon by Al Mayers from Months & Days newspaper.

CHAPTER 26
TAHAWUS

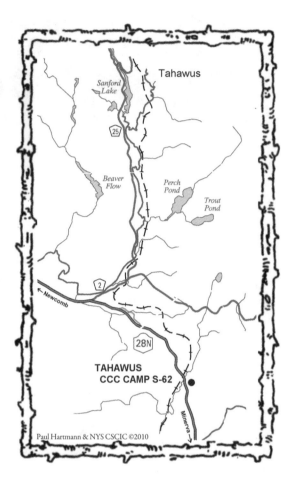

Above - The tent camp of a tree-planting crew in Tahawus. NYS Archives. Left - A Conservation Commission crew planting trees near Tahawus during the 1920s. Ten years later CCC camp S-62 was assigned to protecting this reforested area. NYS Archives

HISTORY

Camp S-62 Company No. 207 was established on June 27, 1933. and named after the Hamlet of Tahawus in the Town of Newcomb in Essex County which was the closest post office to its camp in the Town of Minerva.[1]

The primary purpose of the camp was fighting fires and doing fire prevention tasks such as removing slash along the roadsides, making trails, and maintaining fire roads. They also reconstructed telephone lines.[2]

On October 12, 1933 the Ausable Forks Record-Post reported that the camp planted 513,400 trees in southwestern Essex County.

When the fire season ended in November, the Tahawus fire control camp was no longer needed and it closed on November 11, 1933. After being in operation for a little over four months Company 207 was transferred from Minerva to Sherburne, NY.

After talking to local residents and historical societies in the area as to the exact location of the Tahawus camp, no one had any information. It was not until I searched old newspapers that I found these articles stating that the Tahawus camp S-62 was in Minerva.

In the December 22, 1933 The Essex County Republican one story's headline was, "Minerva CCC Camp Moved to Sherburne, NY." It stated: "Unprecedented speed in solving engineering and construction problems marked the transfer of Civilian Conservation Corps Company No. 207 from its old camp at Minerva, Essex County, to the new location at Sherburne, Chenango County, according to an enthusiastic report reaching CCC headquarters in Washington."

The second article, "For Re-location of CCC Camp in Town of Minerva," dated January 17, 1935 in the Record Post describes Minerva Town Supervisor Francis Donnelly's efforts to have another CCC camp in Minerva in 1935. He had a resolution passed by the Essex County board of supervisors which stated that a CCC camp had been located in Minerva in 1933 and that "much valuable work was performed in the forests during the construction of a highway in that locality which eliminates a considerable portion of the fire hazards surrounding the forests."

A third newspaper article that gave credence to the belief that the Tahawus camp was in Minerva appeared in the April 25, 1935 Au Sable Forks Record-Post. The article, "Four New CCC Camps Chosen in North Area" describes the selection of a site for Camp S-107 in Minerva "At a spot where the Vanderwhacker River crosses the state highway the fourth camp will be built. Located a mile and a half north of Aiden Lair the CCC camp will be at the foot of Kays Hill, the site of a summer camp last year."

On November 11, 1933 Camp S-62 left Tahawus one day after the completion of the Sherburne camp near Norwich, which had heated barracks. The young men were happy to leave their tents in the Adirondacks as winter approached.

MEMORIES

Anne Knox

On July 3, 2009 I visited Anne Knox at her home at the Tahawus Club (a private fish and game club founded in 1898). Anne said she spent her summers at the club.

"I was about eight years old and remember seeing a lot of young firefighters brought in and they went up Perch Pond Road to fight a big fire. That's the road that my home is on. The fire came from Newcomb and crossed the main road and came into Tahawus. The fire went part way up Mount Adams. Later that area became a lumber company. I think it was owned by Finch & Pryn."

CHAPTER 27
THENDARA

HISTORY

The Hamlet of Thendara, just south of Old Forge (Herkimer, Co.), was fortunate to have two CCC camps during the Great Depression. The first camp, Camp 32, was established to help the Town of Webb develop Thendara Lake by damming the Middle Branch of the Moose River for recreation. The camp was unique because it was supervised by the town board and under the National Parks Service and not by the NYS Conservation Department (CD). I gathered information from local newspapers at the Town of Webb Historical Association (TOWHA).

The April 27, 1933 issue of The Lowville Journal Republican reported a meeting in Albany with NYS CD Chairman Osborne and other officials to create a six-mile lake by damming the Middle Branch of the Moose River from Minnehaha in Thendara to the fish hatchery in Old Forge. They would be working with the US Temporary Relief Administration.

TOWHA newspaper files show that in June 1933 the CCC Project # S-14 was approved for the Town of Webb. The project called for the removal of dead timber and debris in the Moose River flow at Thendara and cleaning the shore lines of underbrush on land owned by the Town of Webb. Lyon deCamp, a large land holder, donated the 800-acre tract to the Town of Webb for $1. The land had accumulated many years of logs and stumps from past river drives and debris left from a former lumber mill.

Three days later, the Boonville Herald and Adirondack Tourist reported that the cost of the project was estimated at $247,000 using federal money and that a dam about 300' wide near the Thendara Bridge would require a section of railroad track to be raised five feet because of the elevated water level.

The Lowville Journal Republican reported in its June 15, 1933 issue that the Thendara Lake project was approved by the Federal Government and the CCC camp in Thendara and would employ some 400 men. The US National Parks Service would supervise the work.

Thendara CCC Camp 32 Company # 281 or "Joy Spring Camp" was established on June 16, 1933 a few miles south of Old Forge in Thendara during the summer of

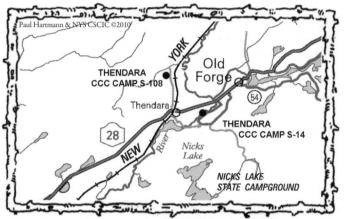

CCC enrollees lived in these army tents that were pitched along the Middle Branch of the Moose River in Thendara and Joy Spring. Town of Webb Historical Society Archives

1933. It was located near the Moose River on Moose River Trail Road by the Joy Spring, which got its name from a spring near a grove of hardwoods overlooking the Moose River near the Green Bridge.

The newspaper article titled "CCC Now at Thendara: 60 Men Reach Camp and Others Due Within One Week," describes the train arriving early on Thursday morning. Major T. D. Simkins from the Army Engineer Corps had come earlier to make certain all materials had arrived. Thirty men were to stay at the Joy Spring camp and the other 30 were going to work at Eighth Lake. These men were sent to establish Eighth Lake CCC camp S-58 near the old Uncas Road and on the carry between Eighth and Seventh lakes.

A 1933 The Lowville Journal Republican reported that 30 men, mostly from Manhattan and Brooklyn, were

Harold Evans (2nd left) of Utica with his friends in front of the Army tents that were pitched along the Middle Branch of the Moose River in Thendara. Janice Evans La Pointe

building and organizing the camp before the rest of the contingent of about 170 men arrived.

Another 1933 TWHA article "Last of CCC Quota Arrives at Joy Spring" states the full quota of men arrived by train on Thursday, June 29 at 11:15 am. Most of the men were also from Manhattan and Brooklyn. Their first meal was mashed potatoes, pork chops, string beans, bread and butter, and rice pudding.

The men who had already been there were busy getting equipment ready and pitching tents for the new arrivals.

Four Army officers ran the camp. Major R. S. Dodson commanded the camp along with First Lt. Margison and Second Lt Roy. An Army doctor was on duty in the hospital tent to help with emergencies.

Maj. Simkins stated the CCC camp was to clear the dead trees and debris in the Moose River flow in Thendara. They were also going to clear the brush on the shore that was owned by the town. The Town of Webb would direct the work and not the CD.

Some local boys who were recruited include: Charles "Buster" Wells, Richard Norton and Virgil Loomis of Old Forge, Arthur Madore of Thendara, and Robert McAllister of Big Moose.

The camp was originally planned to be on a field near the Joy Spring Bridge over the Moose River but the Joy Spring provided a better water supply for the camp and it was set up in a grove of young hardwoods overlooking the Moose River, a short distance from Old Forge. During the previous week men piped water from the Joy Spring to the camp.

P. J. Foley, the camp superintendent, said that the six-year project was to begin on July 5. Work began where the new bridge was built on the river between the Joy Tract and Thendara.

The Lowville Journal Republican reported on July 18, 1933 that the men did not have enough tools to work There were only a few axes, two picks, and four or five wheelbarrows in the camp.

Bob Crofut of Old Forge said, "They worked where the Green Bridge was. Originally there was a wooden bridge there and today there is a cement and steel bridge."

The CCC boys cleared the flow of dead wood, stumps, and logs left from river drives and a former lumber mill. They piled the debris on the riverbank and burned it. Most of the men worked well and hoped to reenlist for another six months. A few men didn't adapt and were sent home.

The Town of Webb board inspected the camp on August 10.

One 1933 newspaper clipping, "Pictures Made on Fungus by 2 at CCC Camp: View of Street of Tents on One Large Piece," describes two enrollees from Utica, Lewis Abrahams and Angelo Primarola, who collected tree fungi and drew pictures on them. One picture showed the main street in the camp with rows of tents on each side and forests in the distance.

A group of boys from Syracuse had two tents next to each other with the following members: Edward Long, Anthony Arillo, Frank Otto, Ray Murphy, Eugene Fournier, Joe Epalito, Albert Longo, E. Kehrill, Dominic Sici, Sam Guttsano, Anthony Cintrinti, and Jerry Bresso.

On Tuesdays or Thursdays the CCC boys improvised entertainment with music, wrestling, and boxing matches. CCC boys from Eighth Lake often came down for bouts and the Thendara boys went to the Eighth Lake camp to compete. Local residents and guests at hotels in the area also provided entertainment.

Another 1933 TWHA newspaper article, "Survey Is Made of Housing for Winter Quarters: If CCC Camp Continues, Town Faces Problem" described how Army officers and town officials tried to find housing for the CCC boys. They wanted to continue the work of developing "Thendara Lake." It was up to the town to find housing for 6-months. The town board estimated that 60 men could be housed in the town hall. It had a furnace and a kitchen could be set up but the Army decided to redeploy the camp to Port Byron, NY.

A winter storm came to Thendara in October. The October 29, 1933 issue of the Rochester Democrat and Republican had a picture of the Thendara CCC tent camp covered in snow. The 150 enrollees were getting ready to leave to spend the winter near Port Byron. W. Earl Smith, a NYC lawyer who came to visit his brother, Lt. Austin Smith, said the boys were huddled near stoves to keep warm. "Water

Above - Northwoods Snow Travelers purchased the old "Goose Patch" field that was the site of Camp S-108 and brought in this building for their snowmobile club. To the right shrouded in trees is a stone fireplace and chimney from the CCC camp. The CCC camp buildings were in the now empty field. Podskoch Collection. Right - This stone fireplace and chimney is the only remaining CCC Thendara camp structure. Podskoch Collection

pipes were frozen, electric lights and telephone wires were down, snow-laden branches were continually falling on the tents, and mild hardships were the lot of everyone. It's just a lot of fun for all of them. They have plenty of warm clothing and food and a few inconveniences are accepted as part of the game."

Although the camp closed late in the fall of 1933 the Town of Webb Board hoped to continue the project the next year but it did not have sufficient funds. On December 3, 1933 the board voted to apply for a grant from the Federal Public Works Administration, but this was denied and the Thendara Lake project ended.

A second camp, Camp S-108, began in Thendara on August 8, 1935.[1] It was located just north of the Thendara railroad station on Route 28 about a mile on Herreshoff Road in a field known as "The Goose Patch."

This camp was different from the first one because the CD planned and supervised the projects. Captain Henry Loveridge supervised the building of the camp, which eventually had 19 buildings.

In September 1935 a field day was held in Old Forge involving the Thendara and Boonville CCC camps. Thendara won the track & field competition: 21-20 and Boonville won the baseball game 6-3. The Madison Barracks Army Band played during the events and there was a dance in the evening in the new Thendara recreation hall.[2]

TOWHA has an invitation card sent to local girls in its collection:

"Miss Rita Gates is cordially invited to be a guest of the members of the Civilian Conservation Corps, Camp S-108 at an informal dance to be held at the camp from 9-1, Friday evening, October twenty-fifth, nineteen hundred and thirty-five. R.S.V.P. This card must be presented at the dance."

The Thendara camp had a basketball team that practiced in the Webb high school gym. The boys came from Ashville, NC, Newark, NJ, and Utica, Syracuse, Frankfort, and New York City. The team played other CCC camps and challenged local semi-pro teams.

In December 1935 the federal government announced a reduction of CCC enrollees to 300,000 in the US by July 1936. Local and state representatives tried to persuade Robert Fechner, the CCC Chairman in Washington, and CD commissioner, Lithgow Osborne, to keep the camp open. The state finally decided to close the Thendara camp on January 12, 1936 after only five months of operation.[3]

In April 1936 Charles McNally, a hired caretaker at the closed CCC camp, was knocked unconscious when lightning blew a transformer from its pole. Luckily he recovered after a few minutes. The paper also reported in June that a mysterious fire destroyed the camp infirmary and a nearby house owned by Moose River fire tower observer, Peter Walters.[4]

To visit the camp site drive down Herreshoff road for about a mile and you will find the large field and a two-story building on the left were the camp was located. Joy Loson, a member of the Northwoods Snow Travelers, said the snowmobile club purchased the nine-acre field from the daughters of George Yocum. When the CCC camp was

WORK ACCOMPLISHED BY CAMP S-108[*]

PROJECT	1935	1936	TOTAL
Excavation, channel - yd^2		3000	3000
Fire pre-suppression - man-days		112	112
General clean-up - ac.	10	10	20
Lake & pond site cleaning - ac.		24	24
Trails, Big Otter truck - mi.		1	1
Surveys - man-days		28	28

*Numerical data from Conservation Reports

closed he was hired as caretaker of the land and lived in the last CCC building. The club tore that building down and brought in another. Behind the snowmobile club building is a large stone fireplace. It is the only remaining CCC camp structure and might have been in the mess hall.

MEMORIES

Harold O. Evans

On October 20, 2009 I was surprised to get an email from Janice Evans La Pointe of Ann Arbor, Michigan. "Yesterday my 90 year-old aunt from Rome, NY sent me the picture and article about your quest to find CCC information.

"My father, Harold Owen "Ozzie" Evans, was a member of the CCC, although I never knew they had nice uniforms like in your picture. He lived on Gold Street right behind Utica Free Academy. He graduated from UFA in 1932 but because there were no jobs both he and my mother did one year of post-graduate work.

"I know he served in a CCC unit up in Thendara by Old Forge. He went there with a beautiful head of hair, a pompadour. They shaved his head and due to the extreme sun his scalp got burned and his hair never really grew back. I know I have some pictures. I just have to dig them out."

A few months later Janice sent me pictures, CCC discharge papers, and answers to a questionnaire I sent her.

"My father was born in October 1913 in Utica. His father, William G., had been a coal miner in Wales. After he came to the US he worked as a handyman. His mother, Elizabeth, had three children: Helena, Lewis, and my dad.

"I obtained his discharge papers and they state he joined on June 10, 1933 and was sent for training at the Madison Barracks west of Watertown. He arrived in Thendara on June 22, 1933. Some of his jobs there were clearing land and reforestation work. In the evenings I guess he sang and played his guitar.

"Dad worked at the Thendara camp till September 9, 1933. He was discharged because he got a job as soda jerk at Wittig's Ice Cream Parlor in Utica. He then got a job working at Savage Arms in Utica and finally spent over 20 years as a milkman/delivery man for Graffenburg Dairy in Utica.

"My dad married Edithe M. West in December 1938 and they had two children Westley and myself.

"The CCC was a big help for my dad because he was able

Above - Harold "Ozzie" Evans chopping wood at the Thendara CCC camp in the summer of 1933. He had his guitar nearby for when he took a break. Left - Harold Evans of Utica enjoying free time on a local lake and playing his guitar. Janice Evans La Pointe

to get a job when they were very scarce and he was able to help his parents."

Roland Brownell

After reading an article about my search for CCC information written by Dick Chase in the Syracuse newspaper, Joseph Brownell contacted me in 2007. He told me his father, Roland, had worked as a superintendent in CCC camps in the Adirondacks. Joe wrote an unpublished book about his life, "Almost Charlie, Growing up in the Twentieth Century," and he sent part of it to me for this article.

Joe said that his dad couldn't find a job and was living with his dad's family in Oswagatchie, NY.

"In mid-March (1935) my father suddenly came home from New York City and there was an air of excitement as he talked alone with Mother. He had a letter from Albany giving him a job with the NYS Conservation Dept. (CD). His friend, Al Davis, had spoken for him and in the late spring and summer of 1935 the two of them cruised the eastern Adirondacks looking for projects that could be started or updated with manpower from the new CCC camps. They planned dams, bridges, campgrounds, and truck trails in colorful places like Berrymill Pond, Cross Clearing, Cherry Patch, Dead Waters, and Pharaoh Lake.

The projects would be completed under the direction of the CD but because federal money was involved, the plans had to meet the US Forest Service specifications.

"Dad roomed in various places on the east side of the mountains and worked from dawn to dusk. He was in his element and came home to Oswagatchie each weekend tired but pleased. Most important of all, he was now a salaried professional again and the paychecks came regularly.

"He frequently went to the CD headquarters in Albany for meetings and on August 9 just after borrowing ten dollars from a friend, he received orders to report to Thendara to be superintendent of camp S-108. For him it was the most important event of the decade and one that would affect the lives of all of us for years to come."

Joe's family drove the three-hour trip to Old Forge to live with his parents who rented a home in the village. The CCC camp was less than two miles from their Old Forge home.

"The camp was close to the rail station and Rt. 28 highway. It was here that I learned about the curious make-up of these camps that were run by a combination of federal and state bureaucracies. My father worked for the CD, which supervised the work done by the young men. But the area of housing, mess, and general management was the responsibility of the US Army.

"At one end of the camp was the Army headquarters. The camp population was of company strength with a commanding officer, typically a captain or first lieutenant. Until a public uproar stopped it, the Army attempted to institute military training but eventually they contented themselves with keeping the men clothed, counted, and fed.

"One building housed the CD office. Here my father had a desk behind a wooden railing. One or two of the young men who could type served as clerks and there were several foremen who, like father, were salaried. They lived in a small foremen's cottage, which in most camps had a stone fireplace in its common room. My father's appointment letter specified that he must live in camp, but most married superintendents and foremen brought their families and lived 'off' camp.

"That year I was in the third grade. Getting there was easy; the school building was only two blocks away! The teacher was young and her boyfriend was a state trooper—a very tall trooper. We waited for him to come down the corridor each afternoon and peek in the transom. One day he even waved his revolver over the transom to the delight of all the small boys.

"It was on Saturday that I became acquainted with the CCC camp itself. My father worked until Saturday noon and I frequently walked the mile or two to the camp. Little work was done on the weekends and often Dad was the only person in the office, but sometimes a clerk was on duty and I would follow him around the camp.

Roland Brownell, the Conservation Department (CD) Superintendent of the Thendara S-108 camp, is working on developing a project in the CD office. Joe Brownell

"One man always served as camp barber and once a month my father took me in for a haircut. As the only child around I enjoyed a good deal of attention and banter. My young hair stood on end; it always had. The youthful barber solemnly assured me that I needed bear grease but that he was out of stock. He obviously expected me to recognize the joke but I took him at his word and each month asked if he had gotten any bear grease. Now he was too deeply into the story to back out and was saved only by Dad's moving to another camp.

"The elation over the new job was somewhat tempered by the fact that a visiting inspector frequently came to the camp and my father seemed to spend several sleepless nights until the man had come and gone. One, in particular, Bill Pendorf, caused Dad no end of grief. The mere mention of the man's name made the evening meal an uncomfortable affair. As a boy I thought that Bill Pendorf was a threat to our family. Actually this was my father's first managerial job and for the first time he had to contend with all the inspections and paperwork that come with the job. Pendorf was liked by most men who knew him.

"One Saturday I was at camp when Pendorf arrived without warning. I was sent outside to wander to the garage, the carpenter shop or the foremen's cabin—anywhere but the office where he was closeted with my father. Unfortunately Pendorf had brought a huge Alsatian dog which he turned loose in the camp. The inevitable happened; the dog and I came face to face around the corner of a building, and I screamed bloody murder. Pendorf came running with my father, ever protective of his only son. They must have had words because from that day forward his name never again seemed to cause dread in the Brownell household.

"The Army transported the young CCC men to town on Saturday nights and as an eight-year old in Old Forge I remember going to the movies and hearing the bustle in the rear rows. I also remember a peculiar odor and found that it stemmed from beer. Whether beer on the way down or back up I didn't know at the time.

"In those days the superintendent and his foreman wore green CD uniforms with 'Mountie' hats, breeches, high shoes, and leather puttees. One of the perks of the job was a green pickup truck assigned to the superintendent. At the end of Saturday morning Dad would pile me into the little truck and together we would rattle home to Old Forge.

"The superintendents had problems with bureaucracy and were swamped at times with paperwork like requisition forms. They often worked out shortages by telephone and drove back and forth balancing supply levels. Food was not a problem for dad because it was the Army's responsibility.

"Unfortunately, the Christmas holidays brought news of a different sort. With almost no warning Albany decided to close S-108. The men were sent to the camp at Fisher's landing while Dad was to be the new superintendent at Howland Island, an hour west of Syracuse."

NOTE - His father was later transferred to Paul Smiths CCC camp and the story will continue in that chapter.

CHAPTER 28
TUPPER LAKE

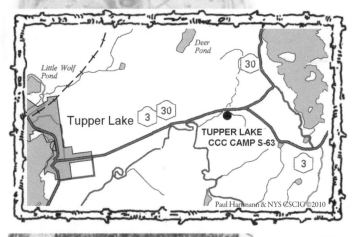

Clockwise - Camp S-63 constructed this fire line near Cross Clearing. Enrollees cleared a line of combustible material to prevent the spread of fire. NYS Archives. CCC Camp S-63 was established east of Tupper Lake on Rts. 30/3 at "Cross Clearing." The enrollees lived in army tents from May 26, 1933 till the wooden buildings were built that fall. NYS Archives. Clarence Petty (hand in pocket on right), is at the Axton Plantation with his College of Forestry Class of 1930. Three years later he worked as a forester supervising enrollees working at the Tupper Lake CCC camp. Chris Angus

HISTORY

On May 26, 1933 Company 257 established Camp S-63, also called No. 15th, at "Cross Clearing" about five miles east of Tupper Lake in Franklin Co. The camp was on the right side of Rts. 30/3 approximately one-half mile before the separation of Rts. 3 and 30 called "Call's (or Wawbeek) Corner." The area was near the Tromley Lean-to Trail.[1]

A little over 30 years before Bernhard E. Fernow (1851-1923), who was considered the "Father of American Forestry," established an innovative demonstration forest at Cross Clearing. The Prussian forester came to the US in 1876 and introduced European management techniques such as selective cutting. He was head of the US Division of Forestry (1886-1898). Fernow helped establish the first college of forestry in the US at Cornell University in 1898, and became its first director. He set up a demonstration forest on 30,000 acres in Axton near Upper Saranac Lake to show that a hardwood forest could be changed to more profitable

spruce and pine. The school established field headquarters in some of the old lumber settlement buildings at Axton, originally called Ax-town. Students began clear-cutting a 68-acre plot, burned the debris, and planted conifer seedlings.[2]

Cornell had a contract to sell the hardwood logs to the Brooklyn Cooperage Co. in Tupper Lake. They hoped that the money earned from the sale of logs would help fund their forestry program. Problems arose because affluent neighbors feared fires and loss of hunting grounds. They urged the state to stop funding the Cornell forestry program. The state voted to stop funding the forestry program in 1903 forcing the school and demonstration forest to close.[3]

The college continued to clear-cut the forest because they had a contract with The Brooklyn Cooperage Co. This company built a log railway to bring the timber to their factory in Tupper Lake. This necessitated clearing a 75-foot wide tract of forest four miles long. The college

Clockwise - These four Tupper Lake enrollees are taking care of their personal needs. One of them is washing something in a tub. They lived in tents during the summer and fall of 1933. Goff-Nelson Memorial Library. Tupper Lake Camp S-63 enrollees built this bridge on the Cold River truck trail. NYS Archives. Tupper Lake enrollees working on a truck trail to Cold River. Enrollees did not have heavy equipment for construction work in 1933 only hand tools. Joanne Petty Manning

eventually clear-cut 3,100 acres but only 440 acres were re-planted.[4]

Tupper Lake Historian Bill Frenette said: "Cross Clearing tract was totally denuded ... and was visually horrifying even if you believed in (Fernow's) experiment, which most observers did not."[5]

Thus the Conservation Department chose Cross Clearing for a CCC camp. Its major tasks were to reforest the area, improve fire protection by constructing fire lines along the highways, build trails, recondition fire roads, remove slash and flammable material along the highways, rebuild telephone lines, and suppress forest fires.[6]

A 1933 Saratogian newspaper reported that Captain Ernest Johns commanded Camp S-63. Officers of the 26th Infantry, Lts. D. P. Mc Gowan and W. J. Glasgow, Jr., assisted in camp supervision. The men lived in tents before wooden barracks were completed. Many of the enrollees were from New York City. A June 23, 1933 newspaper clipping from the Lake Placid Library file reported the young men "...have found that the mosquitoes are more dangerous than the bears. However, Captain Johns and his 'Romans' are conquering the mosquitoes with the assistance of the Army Medical corps."

Camp S-63 began doing fire line work to protect the pine plantations on Wawbeek Road and from the Saranac Inn Golf course to the Wawbeek.[7]

Workers also began constructing a road into the Cold River region. Forester E. A. Sterling planned the road and foreman Isaac Bourdage directed a group of 30 enrollees who lived in a side camp.[8] Conservation Commissioner Lithgow Osborne said that the new road was to be used only by Conservation Department trucks to fight fires. He ordered the construction of a gate with a padlock to prevent private individuals from using the road.[9]

After four months of work Camp S-63 accomplished the following: seven miles of fire lines, nine and one-half miles of truck roads, 15 vehicle bridges, and 20 foot bridges.[10]

Another camp project was clearing an eight-mile channel for boats on the Raquette River from Moody to Raquette Falls. The Tupper Lake Chamber of Commerce and town officials had asked Conservation Commissioner Osborne for this project to improve navigation and were happy when Osborne approved. E. A Sterling supervised a crew of 40 CCC workers who blasted out rocks and removed stumps.[11]

On Thursday October 12, 1933 the town of Tupper Lake celebrated Columbus Day with a parade and an estimated 3,000 marched. The town also celebrated the creation of the National Recovery Act (NRA). People hoped its programs would improve the economy. Camp-63 marched along with decorated floats, firemen and their equipment, three marching bands, children, and public officials.[12]

During the 1933 fall hunting season, District Forest Ranger James H. Hopkins urged hunters to use extreme caution in areas where CCC enrollees were at work. Camp S-63 was working on the Calkins Creek Road and another CCC group was on the slope of Mt. Morris.

As winter approached enrollees received a winter uniform approved by President Roosevelt. The uniform "comprises red, green, blue, or gray lumbermen's jackets, logger's cap with fur-lined ear muffs, leather windbreak-

Clockwise - The Army hired local carpenters and plumbers to build these wooden buildings for the 200 enrollees. This aerial view shows five barracks on the right that each housed 40 enrollees between the ages of 18-25. Each building had 2-3 wood stoves. In the upper right corner is the water tower and to the upper left is the garage area and Rt. 30. Bea Derouchie. A closer view of the five barracks on the left, and the mess hall on the upper right. Joy Long. Joy Prue Long sent me this tree-level view of the Tupper Lake CCC camp. Her father, Gay Prue, labeled the buildings. Joy Long.

ers, and sleeveless jerkins. Every part of the equipment is riotous colors, even to the heavy underwear, presumably red woolens and heavy scarlet socks."[13]

During the fall the Army quickly brought lumber to the tent camp and hired local carpenters and plumbers to build the various buildings for the men before winter set in. The boys continued living in tents that were heated by stoves and banked with snow for warmth. Workers also took steps to prevent the freezing of the water pipes.[14]

Workers finished 14 camp buildings before severe weather arrived. The recreation hall was 80' long. The main room in the middle was 48' x 80' and there were two 16' wings. The western wing was the canteen and library. The eastern wing was a classroom. It had a removable partition that converted the room to a stage for entertainment programs. The large center room had a boxing ring, game tables, and recreation equipment.

There were five barracks heated by stoves that each housed up to 50 enrollees. They added vestibules to help keep out the cold.

A 150' building housed the mess hall, kitchen, refrigerator, storeroom, and an officer/forester's mess hall.

Three buildings paralleled the road: officers' quarters, administration building, and forester's quarters. There were three garages: Conservation Department (10 trucks), Army (5 trucks), and repair garage.

The boys had difficulty excavating a rise at the rear of the camp for a sewage system, the latrine, and showers

but eventually succeeded.

The Tupper Lake Town Hall was the headquarters of District No. 1 of the Northern New York Zone under Col. Howard H. Smalley. They supervised these six camps: Tupper Lake, Goldsmith's, Fish Creek Pond, Paul Smiths, Eighth Lake, and Benson Mines. In November 1933 the staff and officers were transferred to the Plattsburgh Barracks.[15]

In the spring of 1934 Camp S-63 established two side camps housing 20 and 40 men who continued constructing the truck trail in the Cold River region.

Enrollees participated in the sporting events at the "CCC Field Days" in Saranac Lake on May 30, 1934. Other CCC boys from surrounding camps participated in the local parade and competed in track & field events, boxing and wrestling matches, and baseball games.

During the summer the Conservation Department called on Camp S-63 to fight a forest fire on Thompson Mountain near Pealseeville (near Saranac). When they were called out, the fire had already destroyed 700-800 acres. Eventually the CCC boys, rangers, and fire wardens brought it under control.[16]

In July 1934 a crew of 25 enrollees supervised by foreman Frank Dupree began building a new trail to the Mt. Morris fire tower. The project eliminated traveling on private land owned by the Strong family. The boys also installed new telephone poles and line from the town of Moody to the fire tower.[17]

Camp S-63 completed a similar project up Ampersand Mountain to the fire tower. They constructed a mile and a half of steps that numbered over 1,300. They also lengthened and improved the old road to Duck Hole Pond.[18]

In the fall Captain Allan G. Spitz announced that his men were widening the trail to the fire tower on Mount Morris that was built in the summer. A crew of approximately 46 enrollees cleared brush and widened the 2.5-mile trail from Waukesha Grill in Moody to halfway up the mountain. Local residents observed the plumes of smoke on the mountain as the young men burned the brush. Forestry superintendent E. H. Powell halted work when temperatures in December fell to more than 20 below zero on the 3,163-foot mountain. Workers were to continue the project in the spring.[19]

In September 1934, William McConvey, the camp's education advisor, planned a course in auto mechanics for 15 enrollees at the Central Garage in Tupper Lake. The boys attended two-hour class on Thursday evenings at 8:30 for six weeks. Mechanic Charles Whittemore taught the class.[20]

In November 1934 the community of Tupper Lake helped make the enrollees' stay interesting and educational. The Women of the Moose conducted a book drive for the CCC camp. By November 1 they collected over 200 magazines.[21]

Mr. McConvey also recruited people to talk to the enrollees. The Tupper Lake school principal L. P. Quinn gave a motivational speech. He urged the young recruits to take advantage of opportunities in the fields of chemistry, radio, and television.[22]

In July 1935 Raymond B. Tolbert, associate conservationist from the Department of Agriculture in Washington D. C., spoke to the men about forestry and conservation work. He showed over 60 pictures of the devastation to plants and animals caused by forest fires.[23]

When Thanksgiving arrived the boys ate well. For appetizers they ate clam chowder, lettuce,

tomatoes, stuffed olives, sweet pickles, and celery. The main course was: roast turkey, giblet gravy, mashed and sweet potatoes, sweet corn, buttered peas, cranberry sauce, scalloped cauliflower, American cheese, fruit salad, rolls, and raisin bread. For dessert: mince and pumpkin pies, ice cream, assorted fruits, mixed nuts, and candy. Then the boys relaxed with coffee, beer, cigars and cigarettes.[24] It's no wonder that most enrollees gained 10 or more pounds at the camp.

In the spring 1935 men enjoyed two shows in their camp. On March 28 a vaudeville group entertained. Then on April 11, a cast of nine men and three women presented the comedy, "Skinner's Dress Suit."[25] The entertainers were unemployed actors hired by the government.

The camp celebrated its second anniversary with an "Open House" for local officials, Army officers, and Conservation Department leaders who toured the camp. The camp held a program in the assembly hall and a dinner in the mess hall. The guests also enjoyed wrestling & boxing matches and a concert by the Tupper Lake Drum and Bugle Corps and Firemen's Band.[26]

Sporting activities were organized for the enrollees. In the summer the boys' baseball team competed against local and neighboring CCC camps. One game in June 1935 pitted the enrollees against the Fish Creek Pond camp. Camp S-63 won 4-1 on the Fish Creek field. Tupper Lake camp played their home games at the Sunmount diamond.[27]

When a young CCC boy drowned swimming at a side camp in

Above - Enrollees watch their friend take a picture from a tree at Shattuck Clearing near Cold River. Joy Long. Right - CCC enrollees built one and one-half miles of wooden stairs on the trail to the Ampersand Mt. fire tower. DEC Archives

Newcomb in 1934, the Northern CCC District decided to have a six-day lifesaving class conducted by the Red Cross. On July 10, 1935, two CCC enrollees from each camp came to Tupper Lake for training. These men then went back to their camps and served as lifeguards.[28]

A June 25-July 25 Conservation Department "Foreman Report" listed these foremen: T. Boudrage, E. Duprea, P. DeLaire, C. Haischer, R. Hayes, F. Delaire, C. Merrill, H. Plummer, B. Cameron, J. Dougherty, and V. Martel. T. Boudrage had a crew that worked 21 days cleaning the flow at Duck Hole dam site. Three foremen had crews working 17 days on weevil control. Three other foremen led groups who worked on the Ampersand-Preston Pond Road while another three foremen did maintenance work on the Calkins Creek truck trail. E. H. Powell was the camp superintendent.

Approximately a third of the CCC recruits were from Tupper Lake in 1935.[29]

In December Commissioner Osborne announced the closing of the Tupper Lake camp due to a federal reduction in the state's quota of CCC camps. Local officials argued the need to keep the camp but their efforts failed. The closing had an economic effect on the town because 60 men and enrollees had worked at the CCC camp.[30] After two and one-half years of operation Camp S-63 closed on January 3, 1936. Captain Spitz and his personnel were transferred to the Plattsburgh Barracks Camp A-4. Camp equipment and supplies were also transported to the Plattsburgh Barracks. The buildings were left intact.[31]

The Tupper Lake Free Press reported on February 10, 1938 that William McConvey visited old friends in Tupper Lake where he had been the chief educational advisor of CCC Sub-district 1. He was transferred in October 1937 to Bolton Landing CCC camp. He worked in the surrounding camps establishing camp newspapers, and training programs in carpentry, baking, and mechanics. He brought local businessmen to give vocational talks. McConvey also initiated the annual sub-district field days and boxing matches.

The camp accomplished many projects in its final year. They built fire lanes along the road from Saranac Lake to the Saranac Inn, truck trails in the dense forest of the Wawbeek and Axton areas, a new trail from Tupper Lake up Mount Morris, and cleared hundreds of acres of underbrush along highways and state forest plantations.[32]

An editorial in the March 17, 1938 issue of the Tupper Lake Free Press criticized the closing of S-63. "Just why

is it that huge sums continue to be spent in erecting buildings and developing costly programs only to abandon them a few years later as in these two CCC camp closings (Fish Creek Pond and Tupper Lake) is more than we can see. The taxpayers who ride past Cross Clearing and see nothing but rows of idle and empty buildings where so much activity centered three or four years ago can't help but wonder how many millions of dollars are 'gone in the wind' on similar projects in these United States every year."

Later in 1938 the Paul Smiths camp removed the building from Cross Clearing. If you drive by the camp site today the site is covered with white pine trees, There are a few water pipes protruding from the earth where the bathroom was.

Right - William McConvey was the chief education advisor who initiated vocational training classes in the Tupper Lake and surrounding CCC camps. Bill McConvey. Below. Tupper Lake enrollees loading a dump truck at a gravel pit. The material was used in road construction. DEC Archives

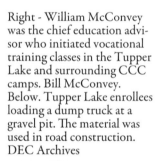

274

WORK ACCOMPLISHED BY CAMP S-53[*]

PROJECT	1934	1935	1936	TOTAL
Bridges, horse - number	7			7
Bridges, vehicle - number	25	8		33
Buildings, public campground - number	1			1
Buildings, other - number	1	1		2
Calkins Creek - mi.			5	5
Cold River - mi.		9		9
Deer Pond - mi.			2	2
Eradication of poisonous plants - linear mi.	17.6			17.6
Excavation, ditches/earth - yd^3		100		100
Fire breaks - mi.	3.3			3.3
Fire fighting - man-days	1636	476		2112
Fire hazard reduction (roadside) - mi.	2.2	1		3.2
Fire hazard reduction (trailside) - mi.		4.8		4.8
Fire hazard reduction, other - ac.	182.7	497.2		679.9
Fire pre-suppression - man-days			715	715
Forest stand improvement - ac.	356.7	15		371.7
General clean-up - ac.			15	15
Insect pest control - ac.	1985	112	112	2209
Lake & pond development - man-days		2286	552	2838
Lookout houses- number			2	2
Nurseries - man-days			2340	2340
Planting, forestation - ac.	44			44
Ponds for fish & birds - number	2			2
Power lines - mi.			2	2
Seed collection - bushels	10		22	32
Stream development - mi.	0.4	3.1		3.5
Structures, other - number	1			1
Surveys - mi.		43.9		43.9
Telephone line - mi.	4	2.6		6.6
Trails, foot - mi.	10.4	6.7		17.1
Trails, truck - mi.	9.1	3.5	0.9	13.5
Trombley Road - mi.			1.5	1.5

[*]Numerical data from Conservation Reports

C. C. C. CAMP *Cured* MY SICK NERVES

Oscar Langlois (left) was featured in the April 1936 issue of "Physical Culture" magazine. It described how his health improved after the hard physical work at the CCC camp in Tupper Lake. Bea Derouchie

MEMORIES

Oscar Langlois

On October 4, 2007 I gave a CCC talk at the Winthrop Legion Hall near Brasher Falls. I met Beatrice Langlois Derouchie of Brushton. She handed me a copy of the April 1936 issue of "Physical Culture," a health magazine that had a four-page story titled "C. C. C. Camp Cured My Sick Nerves" by David Arnold Balch.

In the article Beatrice's father, Oscar Langlois, stated that by joining the CCC his health was restored by working in the rugged Adirondack Mountains. At first Oscar said he couldn't believe the CCC accepted him because he was so sickly and a nervous wreck.

This is what he told the reporter, "No, I don't come from the city like the other recruits. I come from a farm up in the northerly corner of the state. My people are farmers and have been from way back. You'd think that would have guaranteed good health, now wouldn't you?" he grinned.

"Well, it didn't. When I signed up last spring and came here, I felt as though I was about on my last legs, and I don't mean maybe. I was surely a mess.

"I began to get sick at home when I was eighteen. A doctor called it neurasthenia gastric neurasthenia (chronic fatigue syndrome and fibromyalgia). I knew I was getting worse all the time, and that is what bothered me. At the start of it all may have been an unusually heavy summer's work that year when I was eighteen. The doctor asked me afterward if I'd received any injury to my spine, but I told him I hadn't. I used to think the backache was from all the heavy farm work I did, and I think it was this same heavy farm work that finally broke me down and made me sick. Something happened, at any rate, that weakened my whole general system, and when this occurred my nerves commenced going bad. Anybody who's had neurasthenia will know what I went through."

Oscar described how he had a bloated stomach and constipation. He also had trouble sleeping at night and woke up in the morning feeling worn out. Depression set in and he thought he'd never get better.

"Physically, I was a wreck. I suffered from a strange and constant sense of weakness and nerve exhaustion. I tired quickly of anything I started to do and you know a farm is a poor place for a fellow who hasn't got the strength. If you've ever milked cows or hoed corn and potatoes and cabbages, or plowed or pitched hay, you know it all takes strength and stamina. Once, I hadn't known what it was to be tired. Now I was tired all the time." So he went to a doctor.

"The doctor looked me over carefully and sounded my lungs. 'Well, Oscar, I'm afraid you've got a rich man's disease, neurasthenia gastric neurasthenia. I don't know what caused it, but you've got to get busy and cure it, or you'll go to pieces. Now, ordinarily we prescribe rest for neurasthenia—complete rest in bed or sometimes a change of scene. I don't think going to bed would do you as much good as a complete change of scene, a change in living habits, surroundings, everything.'

"For a minute I couldn't figure out what he meant. Then he explained.

"'You've heard of these CCC camps, haven't you, my boy?' the doctor asked me. 'Well, I believe one of those that are located in the Adirondacks might

After Oscar Langlois left the CCC in 1935 he married Barbara French. Bea Derouchie

be just the ticket for you. I think the altitude might do you good.'

"I went home and talked to the folks about it but as usual I couldn't decide what I wanted to do. I couldn't plan."

Finally Oscar made a decision. He signed up and was assigned to "Cross Clearing" Camp No. 15 near Tupper Lake. He was 20 years old when he arrived on April 4, 1934 and the temperature was 53 degrees below zero. He got his warm army clothes and went to the mess hall. He said he wasn't hungry and felt slightly sick. "My head ached and I was intolerably weary." He dragged his feet instead of walking. He went into the mess hall and saw about 200 boys about his age sitting at long wooden tables. There were eight boys to a table. Oscar sat down by a set of aluminum dishes and utensils and watched the others eat.

"I remember what we had for supper that night. It was roast beef hash, stewed tomatoes, applesauce, and a glass of milk. I drank a little of the milk and then took a spoonful of the applesauce. The doctor back home told me I must eat, whether I felt like it or not, so after a time I commenced to eat a little of the hash. It tasted better than I thought it would so I ate a little more of it…. Then afterward, I dragged myself over to the sleeping barracks and crawled into bed, so weak that it was all I could do to keep from blubbering."

Oscar had trouble sleeping and was homesick. The barracks was as cold as an icebox. When he finally got to sleep it was time to get up and go to breakfast. His first job was working in the kitchen.

"I felt miserable the first seven weeks of camp. My nervous condition was still bad and I still suffered from headaches and depression…It seemed no better than home. But my nights began to show improvement. I fell asleep now soon after I went to bed around ten and I slept till daybreak and sometimes later than that."

He began to feel better and was also able to plan ahead. He even regained his appetite.

"When the first warm days of May arrived, I was assigned to my first job out of doors, that of clearing a fire lane, on both sides of the Wawbeek Road to prevent fire hazard. Here with fifty other fellows, I began working, stripped to the waist, cleaning away fallen timber and underbrush and then burning it. It wasn't long before I was brown as an Indian from the waist up. But we all had to put on shirts again when June came with its black flies. They'd have eaten us alive if we hadn't."

Oscar said with this work outside he had energy and didn't have headaches. He also wasn't dizzy with chills running up his back.

The author of the story concluded stating the CCC program had three goals: conserve the forests, make youths stronger, and help the enrollees' families economically.

He wrote that Oscar said he "owes everything " to the CCC. He had once been so sick that he despaired of being well again. The author ended stating, "for today he is a pretty rugged specimen of young American manhood."

Beatrice "Bea" was very proud of the article written about her father. The ironic part of the story is that she never met him because he died before she was born. He was discharged on March 31, 1935 after serving a year at Tupper Lake. Five months later Oscar married Barbara French A few months later she became pregnant with Bea.

Bea said, "My father went to the hospital and was operated on for appendicitis. He was in the hospital for 15 days and died on April 25, 1936 from complications from pneumonia. He was just 22 years old. My mother was devastated along with his mother, father, and 10 brothers and sisters. They were all shocked at his death. I'm sure if it happened today he'd be still living because of all the new medicines."

Francis Leonard

In the spring 2007 I met Theresa Cleveland at the Raquette Lake Supply Store. She told me her stepfather, Francis Leonard, was in the Tupper Lake CCC camp and gave me his phone number. I did a telephone interview on May 18, 2007 at his home in Tupper Lake.

"Would you tell me about your life and family before you joined the CCC?"

"I was born on November 30, 1915 in Norfolk, north of Potsdam. My father was Michael "Pearley" Leonard and my mother was Charlotte. They had eight children: George, myself,

Francis Leonard at his home in Tupper Lake in 2007. Podskoch Collection

Margaret, Cecelia, Ruth, John, Eddy and Edgar who were twins. She also had twin daughters that died at birth. Mom also had another set of twins that died at birth.

"When I was seven years old I came to Tupper Lake in Oct. 1923. My father was ill. They sent him to rest homes in Saranac Lake because they thought he had TB but he had lead poisoning from his job as a painter and a wallpaper hanger. His lungs were filled with lead poisoning. He also used white lead for mixing paint. They made it themselves. They mixed white lead, linseed oil, turpentine, a dryer, and little can of paste color. He also worked in a pulp mill where he breathed sulfate.

"Dad then worked maintaining camps at Upper Saranac Lake. He also worked around town doing odd jobs like painting. We were on welfare. It was hard to get jobs then. When I was eight years old, I worked on a farm for five dollars a week. I had to get up at 4 am. to milk 10 cows, clean the barn, and throw down hay for the cows to eat. Also in the morning I worked as the janitor of my school. I started the fire in the stove, swept the floor and cleaned the chalkboard, then I had to go to school. After school I went back to the barn to milk the cows again.

"When I was 15 I quit school and worked at Oval Dish Co. I peeled bark off trees. Then I'd get laid off and looked for other work such as cutting trees in the woods. "In the spring of 1934 I joined the CCC and went to Cross Clearing. The Camp was across from the State Garage just down from the intersection everyone used to call "The Y." There was a State campsite behind the garage, but not many people used it. There were fireplaces and no one took care of the place. It had been closed. That is where some guys hid their cars because you weren't supposed to have a car at camp.

"When I got to camp the barracks were made of rough lumber with tarpaper on them. They had three stoves inside and about 24 guys were in each.

"Captain Spitz was a good guy. There were two lieutenants and a doctor.

What did you do in your free time?

"We had some shows in the canteen. One of the shows was a musical. Some of the guys played on the camp baseball team. They played other camps. There was an outdoor stage in town where they had golden glove boxing matches. Anyone could compete.

"A lot of the guys were from New York City. They were a wild bunch. When they came to town at night, they raised hell. Some didn't like it here and didn't come back.

"Lots of my friends from Tupper Lake were in camp along with other guys from farming towns and Malone. Most of the boys were Adirondack guys.

What jobs did you do?

"In the winter we cleared the highways from Tupper Lake and half way to Saranac Lake. We cleaned up the dead trees and brush that was within 500' of the road. We burned the brush because there was snow on the ground and no threat of forest fires. The guys cut up the good wood for stove wood and we piled it up along roadside. Some was taken to Fish Creek Pond campsite and people took the other wood for their homes. People needed wood to keep themselves warm. It was very tough in the Depression.

"In the spring we fought fires and one big fire was at Bay Pond. We stayed there for about ten days working with guys from the Fish Creek and Paul Smiths camps.

"We also built trails during the spring and summer. Our trucks drove up past Coreys, Axton, and the Rockefeller Preserve. Then we went through Rockefeller's gate and on the other side of the preserve where we built truck roads that would be used to fight forest fires. The road went towards the Saw Tooth Range. The guys put up tents for 24 men, a squadron, and camped there all summer. Our first camp was at # 4 logging camp. We dug sand pits on the right side of the mountain and used it for building roads because we didn't have gravel.

"They brought us back to camp on the weekends so some of us could go home. Sometimes I even came home at night as long as we were back to work for roll call at 7 am.

"The bugler woke us up every morning. We got dressed and stood in formation in front of your barracks for roll call.

"Then we ate our breakfast and lined up at 8 to go to work. We worked till 4 pm.

"We stayed in the side camp till the weather got bad. It was about the last week of September when the rains came. We didn't have four-wheel drive trucks so the roads got pretty muddy.

"The next year we moved up about four to five miles near Cold River. It was at the junction of Moose Creek and Cold River (only nine miles from Lake Placid). We built road trails through there.

"Another crew went from Coreys all the way to Long Lake. We cut all the cedar trees, built peers for bridges over all the creeks, and built railings on the bridges. After the CCC left, they didn't maintain them.

"I helped build a cabin for the observer on Mt.

Mt. Morris fire tower observer Adelard Fromaget sitting on the steps to the observer cabin in 1944. Francis Leonard and enrollees from the Tupper Lake CCC camp built the cabin in the 1930s. Shirley Hosler

Morris. We had to carry up the lumber and cement on our shoulders. There were no four-wheel trucks then.

"They closed the camp in Tupper Lake in 1936 and sent us to the Army Base in Plattsburgh. The 26th Infantry was based there. They also had a camp for Civilian Military Training Camp. They were only set up for the summer in tent camps. Another section was used for ROTC training.

"I bought a junk car, a 1927 Dodge, when I was in Plattsburgh. I drove back home on weekends and I drove guys back and forth. They paid $1.25 round trip. Some guys paid but others promised they would and never did. But I made money.

"For our first job we took all the lumber from the Fish Creek Pond Camp, took out all the nails in the boards so we could re use it for the Army platform tents. We had torn down that camp at Fish Creek Pond.

"Our jobs were mostly doing maintenance work on the base.

"The barracks were set up higher than at Tupper Lake, about 4' on posts. The buildings were warmer there than the buildings at our Tupper Lake camp.

"We built a big dock using logs. They used a pile driver for the piers. The dock was about 25 feet long on Lake Champlain.

"Then we went out to Crab Island near the Army Base and cleaned up the landscape. Crab Island was covered in poison ivy and we all got it bad. The Army had a picnic area and clubhouse. They rented a big passenger boat to take us over and back each day.

"The Army had a rifle range. We cut 12' cedar posts and used them to build woven wire fence around the range. We also put barbed wire on top.

"Another job we did was build cribbing form the lake up to the railroad track that went through the Army base. They brought stone in on railroad and dumped over it the side. We picked up stones along the road and used it for cribbing. We also built a dock on the lake.

"I got out of the CCC in June 1937 and good a job as a glassware washer in Cliff Haven Summer School in Plattsburgh. I worked only one month. They had Catholic kids and parents came up with them. I was so busy working from 4 am to the evening. I set tables, washed and polished all the glassware, and cracked ice. I got sick and quit. I lost 15 pounds from the steam in the kitchen and working so hard. The cook wanted me to stay but I told him I couldn't do it any longer. I was too sick from the work.

"Then I got a job in Lyon Mountain remodeling all the iron company homes in July. I was laid off in December because of an automobile accident.

"I came back to Tupper Lake and got a job with the Swenson Camp. I worked on their golf course. They gave me a hand scythe to cut the brush. In the winter I cut wood.

"In 1942 the Army drafted me. My job was taking care of land vehicles (heavy equipment, fuel trucks and such) at an Air Base in England.

On December 8, 1945 I got out and came back to Tupper. I worked in the woods till 1951 when I got a job as a painter at Sunmount VA Hospital. When it closed in 1965 they transferred me to Montrose, NY. I worked there till 1976.

"I didn't get married till I was 57. I took care of my parents. A lady named Edith De-Shaw was taking care of my mother. Her husband had died. Then in 1972 my mom was bed ridden and Edith took care of her. I married Edith in 1973. I took care of Edith when she became ill with breast and bone cancer. She

Francis Leonard at Seymour Johnson Army Air Force Base, NC. Janice Washburn

279

died at home in 2001. I have three stepdaughters; a stepson died in 1998.

"When I look back at my years in the CCC, I think we did a good job of cleaning the brush and dead trees along the roads. Now when you drive along the roads you see all these dead trees. They should have the CCC again. I think it was good for us. It taught us skills and how to work together."

Gay Prue

In January 2008 I received an email from Joy Long of Jordon, NY: "I read an article by Dick Case in this morning's Syracuse Post Standard about you gathering information on the CCC. My dad, Gay Prue was in the CCC at Camp S-63, Tupper Lake, NY from January 2, 1935 to August 24, 1936.

"He spent a lot of time at the Adirondack Museum at Blue Lake talking to the people there. He had given them a lot of information and photos he had taken of the hermit Noah John Rondeau. Dad visited Rondeau's camp and talked with him while he was in the CCC at Tupper Lake. The museum fashioned their display of Rondeau from a lot of what he had given them.

"I am very interested in helping you in any way I can to preserve this important part of our history and to carry on my dad's dream of telling his story. Thank you for writing this book."

Then Joy sent me 15 pictures of the Tupper Lake camp with her father and other enrollees building the truck trail into the Cold River region. These were the first pictures I saw of the camp and its buildings.

She also sent me a copy of her dad's discharge paper and a certificate from the American Red Cross dated December 10, 1935. It states he completed the "Standard Course of Instruction in First Aid to the Injured."

I asked Joy about her dad's family and what he did at the camp.

"My dad's parents were Arthur & Ella Mae (Mueller) Prue. Dad was born in 1915 in Moira, a town west of Malone. There were three other boys in the family: Edgar, Arthur, and a stepbrother Leon. I know his parents did split up but don't know if they actually got divorced or not. Dad's mom got sick and ended up in a hospital when Dad was five. Dad's grandparents took care of him after that. My grandfather was a farmer.

"When dad was 19 he joined the CCC on January 2, 1935. His job at camp was as a laborer. Dad was a very responsible guy. He was made an assistant leader at the Tupper Lake camp.

"Dad's favorite story was when he and a couple other men were told to bring a few bricks in knapsacks up the mountain to the fire tower observer. Every time they stopped to rest, they would each put one of their bricks into the knapsack of one poor fellow. By the time they reached the top of the mountain, the poor guy was carrying all the bricks. He kept commenting on how heavy the bricks were. They didn't tell him what they had done until they reached the fire tower.

"Dad worked at a side camp building roads into the Cold River region where the hermit, Noah Rondeau, lived. One time my dad got permission to look for the hermit.

In each camp enrollees were chosen to take Red Cross First Aid and Life Saving classes. Here is Gay Prue's First Aid certificate. Prue also received this Certificate of Leadership from Captain Spitz making him an assistant leader at the Plattsburgh Barracks camp. Joy Long

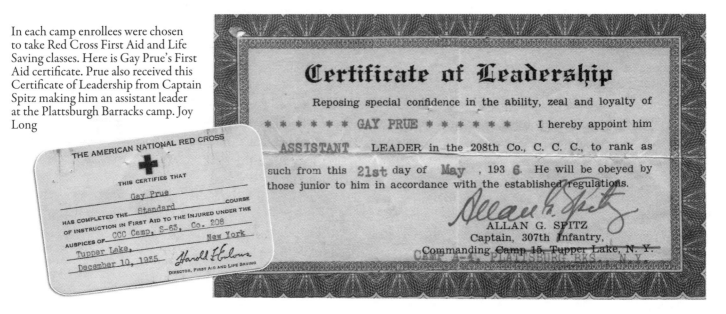

Above, Left - Gay Prue (right) and his friend Dufresne sitting on a compressor they used in breaking boulders while building the Cold River fire road. Above, Middle - Gay Prue and his fellow enrollees visited the famous hermit Noah Rondeau at his cabin near Cold River where they were building a truck trail. Noah (front row center) is showing the guys the bow and arrow he used for hunting. Above, Right - Joy Prue said: "I thought dad's nickname was 'Curly' because of his hair, but it was 'Shorty.' He was the biggest guy at the camp at 6' 1". Here he is holding two guys on his shoulders. All Courtesy Joy Long

Noah invited him into his camp and even let dad take pictures. They had quite a visit.

"When they closed the Tupper Lake camp in January 1936, Dad was transferred to Camp A-4 at the Plattsburgh Army Barracks. His job was truck driver. Project superintendent Frank P. Fitzpatrick wrote this comment on his discharge paper: 'As far as I have been able to observe Assistant Leader Gay Prue, he has always performed his work in the field and as a company driver satisfactorily.' Dad worked there till August 24, 1936 when he was discharged.

"Dad moved to Syracuse, NY and got a job delivering coal. He married Edna Latray on April 18, 1938. They had three children: Janice, Gary, and Joyanne. Then he worked for Ternstedt Manufacturing, a Division of General Motors, which eventually became Fisher Body. He also worked a second job for a number of years at Will & Baumer Candle Co.

"After 30 years Dad retired from General Motors in 1980. Dad spent all his free time remodeling an abandoned octagon one-room schoolhouse he bought in 1948 on six acres of land in Marcellus, NY. It became quite a showplace and is mentioned in several books on octagon houses. Dad died in 2006 at the age of 92.

"My father spent the better part of his life telling anyone who would listen to him about his time in the CCC. He took us to the Adirondacks on numerous occasions and showed us the area where he lived and worked. We enjoyed helping him find certain places he had visited. He treasured his days in the CCC."

"The Giant Dentist"

The headline of the June 13, 1934 Plattsburgh Daily Press, "Dr. Frank Gorham, Stationed at Tupper Lake Weighs 270, is 6 ft. 6 in." caught my eye while doing my research. The article described the three village dentists: Dr. N. F. Foote, Dr. Henry H. Facteau, and Dr, Rogers. The story jokingly states: "Although these men have the 'pull,' none can compare in stature to the CCC dentist who is a veritable giant."

The 32 year-old Brooklyn native graduated from Pennsylvania Dental College and works at the Tupper Lake camp. He said he thought the conditions at the camp were good but the rigors of winter were trying especially with the temperatures of the 1933-34 winter dropping from 35-50 degrees below normal.

One small enrollee who visited Dr. Gorham told the reporter, that 'the 'giant' picked him up from the dental chair with his forceps with one hand and held him at arm's length. Of course this was a joke but I'm sure he had no trouble pulling teeth when needed.

CHAPTER 29
WARRENSBURG

Huge white pines greet visitors at the entrance to the Pack Demonstration Forest just north of the intersection of Rts. 28 & 9 in Warrensburg. During 1934-35 it was the site of CCC Camp-S-101. Podskoch Collection

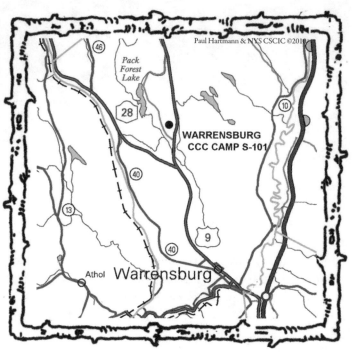

HISTORY

The site of CCC Camp S-101 Company 289 (1934-35) was in the Pack Demonstration Forest (PDF), five miles north of the hamlet of Warrensburg on Route 9 in Warren Co. The camp was established on May 17, 1934.

The PDF was established in 1927 after Charles Lathrop Pack (1857-1937), a wealthy landowner in the Midwest and other areas, donated 2,500 acres of woodland to the New York State College of Forestry in Syracuse to be used for research and training in environmental studies.

Steve Parisi invited me to speak to the Warrensburgh Historical Society in the fall of 2007. I met John T. Hastings, a retired state forester and historian, who said he had researched in the Warrensburg News for information about the local CCC camp and found that Company 289 had come from Front Royal, Virginia after spending six months in Cape Warren, Idaho.

Hastings stated, "Around ninety men, loaded to the limit in eight forestry trucks, traveled 600 miles from Virginia to Warrensburg. They arrived at Pack Forest on Wednesday, May 16, 1934. Most of the young men were from Manhattan, Brooklyn, and New Jersey. They pitched their tents under the supervision of Army Lieutenants Terrance J. Smith and Richard Raymond.

"Another group from Fort Dix, NJ traveled by train to Lake George and then by truck to the Pack Forest.

"The site of CCC Camp S-101 Company 289 (1934-35) was located near an old lime kiln behind the present Adirondack Resource Conservation and Development (RC & D) office building. The camp was not laid out in symmetrical streets as other camps in order to avoid cutting down large pine trees. Some eighteen tents made up the camp: cook tent, mess tent, infirmary, canteen, administration, and one large officers' club tent. The men were quartered in large hospital ward tents with 20 men assigned to each. They kept the food in a huge icebox. Around the camp were barrels and pans of water, as well as buckets and pumps, as precaution against fire.

"On Monday, May 21 over 100 young men from northern NY arrived from the Plattsburg Barracks. The camp was then at full strength with approximately 200 men.

"After four days of establishing the camp, the men began working on forestry projects under the supervision of Herbert Bullard, the Conservation Department Forestry Superintendent."

Warrensburg CCC Camp Co. 289 group photo was taken in October1934. An old lime kiln is in the upper right. Minerva Historical Society

Newcomb historian Ray Masters stated, "In the summer of 1934, there was a side camp of 50 men (at Huntington) from Camp S-101 at Pack Forest in Warrensburg. They continued doing: construction and maintenance work on roads and trails in the Huntington Wildlife Forest."

Hastings added, "The Front Royal boys boasted of having won the Virginia state basketball championship during the winter. They had many entertainers in the group. They had been on many radio programs in both Idaho and Virginia where they also presented programs in theaters, churches, schools, and civic centers. They organized a baseball team that played teams from the surrounding communities. The boys also set a record for forestry work in Virginia.

"During the winter the boys participated in outdoor sports. The February 28, 1935 issue of the Warrensburg News stated that at the Chestertown Outing Festival

Warren Kelley of Warrensburg and a member of camp S-101 won the cross-country snowshoe race of 1.5 miles in 13 minutes, 35 seconds. His first place prize was $10.

"On Friday, May 17, 1935 the Warrensburg News ran an article 'CCC Camp Has First Birthday.' It describes an "Open House" at the camp for townspeople to see the work accomplished over the past year.

"Many were invited to the anniversary luncheon but only three attended: Roy Randall, Supt. of NY Power and Light, M. J. Livingston, publisher of the Warrensburg News, and Postmaster Stewart A. Farrar. Prior to the luncheon, commanding officer Captain John I. Milligan, Lieutenants McElheny and Raymond, and education advisor, Gerald Gorman, escorted the visitors around the camp.

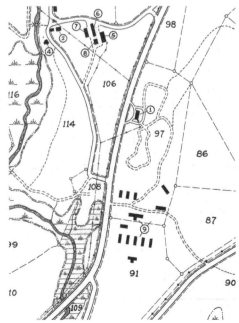

Above, Left - Aerial view of Camp S-101 in the Pack Forest. The road to the left of the buildings was old Route 9. The camp had 13 buildings. The five rectangular buildings in a row with trees on both sides were the barracks housing 40 men each. NYS Archives. Above, Middle - Warrensburg CCC enrollees filling up pails with water from to water newly planted trees. NYS Archives. Right - This Pack Forest Map shows five rectangular structures at the bottom which are the barracks. Below them is the bathroom and shower building. The numbered buildings in the upper left belong to the Pack Forest.

Ralph McSweeney, a former worker at the Warrensburg CCC camp, served in the Army in WWII and is pictured on November 1, 1943 in Bouconville, France. Ralph McSweeney

"The guests saw the men's well-ventilated barracks with comfortable cots. They then visited the recreation hall and reading room with facilities for holding plays and other entertainment. They viewed the well-stocked storeroom containing clothing and equipment. Then they went to the large mess hall with a seating capacity for 200 men. The guests and enrollees enjoyed their meal, which used: 60 loaves of bread, 125 pounds of potatoes, 25 gallons of coffee, 40 pounds of tomatoes, 12 heads of lettuce, 70 pounds of fish, 42 pies, and 12 cans of evaporated milk.

"After lunch Supt. Herbert Bullard took the visitors on a tour of the work projects. He reported that during the previous year, the boys cut approximately 1,700 cords of wood, improved 424 acres of forest land, built three miles of trail, treated 200 acres for blister rust (a disease of white pine), and built four bridges. In addition, they constructed one-half mile of fence and surveyed one-half mile of boundary line of land.

"It was noted that nearly all the boys were from farm areas extending from Warren County to the Capital District. This was quite a contrast to those who were there at the beginning of the camp."

In December 1935 the Federal government announced that it was going to reduce the number of CCC enrollees nationally to 300,000. New York State was forced to close 12 camps by January 1, 1936 and Warrensburg camp was one of them. Efforts were made to save the camp but after a year and a half in operation Camp S-101 was closed on January 9, 1936.

MEMORIES

William Danko

There were three deaths of Warrensburg camp enrollees. One of them was William Danko. His nephew, Dr. Bill D. Danko, sent me an email stating his uncle was in camp for only three weeks and died from meningitis. The nephew sent me his camp photo.

James Howard O'Donnell

I found an article in The Lake Placid News dated July 27, 1934 that reported the death of James Howard O'Donnell. There were approximately 50 CCC boys from Warrensburg were clearing the shore of Rich Lake in Newcomb. After Tuesday's dinner James Howard O'Donnell, 20, and eight others went swimming in the shallow lake water. Later, the young men found O'Donnell's clothes still on the shore. After a search they found his body but were unable to resuscitate him.

Ralph McSweeney

Richard Cipperly, a retired DEC Forester from Warrensburg, has given me some names of men who worked at the Bolton Landing CCC camp that resulted in almost a dozen interviews. Since he worked in the Warrensburg area I asked him to look at the story I was writing for the Warrensburg camp.

He returned my story and added a new contact, Ralph McSweeney from Carleton, Nova Scotia.

Richard said, "My wife and I were vacationing in Nova Scotia when a man came up to me and said, 'I see by your license plate that you're from Warrensburg, NY. That's where I was in a

William Danko (17 years old) (foreground) was just three weeks at Camp S-101 when he died from meningitis. Dr. Bill D. Danko

A September 16, 1935 group photo of the Warrensburg CCC camp. Minerva Historical Society

CCC camp back in 1934.' Ralph was a very friendly guy. He even said we could stay at his home if we needed a place to stay."

I called Ralph in November, 2009 and asked how a person from Nova Scotia wound up in a CCC camp in the Adirondacks?

"I was born in Worcester, Massachusetts on March 28, 1917. My father was a brick mason. My mother was sickly when I was young and my dad thought she was going to die. I was about 2 or 3 and Dad took me to live with my grandparents in Nova Scotia. I remained with them even though my mother got better.

"When I was 17 I came to visit my parents in Plattsburg where my dad owned a gas station. Later he owned a gas station in Dannemora and then Plattsburg. I remember the prison guards used to park their cars at his station in Dannemora. He sold liquor on the side to the guards. He said he made more money that way than selling gas.

"I tried to get a job around Plattsburg but there was nothing so in 1934 I joined the CCCs. They sent me to Camp S-101 in Pack Forest in Warrensburg. There were 200 guys in the camp. One day Superintendent Grant Beswick picked 50 guys to go to a side camp in Newcomb to work in Huntington Forest where there had been a CCC camp the previous year. We slept in large tents. Our jobs were cutting fire trails and building roads.

"In our free time we sometimes climbed Mount Goodnow. In 1942 I went back to Goodnow with a friend to climb that mountain again.

"One evening after working in the woods we were all swimming together in the lake. There was one big guy named O'Donnell who told us he couldn't swim. He stayed in the shallow water but later we noticed he was missing. We all dove in looking for him. Then someone found him lying face down and holding a tree stump. We pulled him out and gave him artificial respiration but it didn't help. I can still see the mosquitoes on his dead body. Someone came and took him to an undertaker.

"The drowned boy's brother was also swimming with us. That night we remember him snoring heavily in the barracks. He probably was so exhausted trying to find his brother and then seeing him dead."

I interrupted Ralph's story to tell him that the previous week I had came across the story of the CCC boy drowning in Rich Lake. It was a strange feeling to be talking to someone who had been there.

Ralph continued, "I stayed in the Warrensburg camp for about six months. Then in 1935 I joined the CCCs again in Vermont and was at the camp in Bellows Falls. I stayed there for about 10 months. I built roads and cut fire trails just like I did in New York.

"After the CCCs I worked at the Springfield Gun Company in Massachusetts. I got married in 1940 to Mable King. When I got a draft notice in 1942, I asked a distant uncle who was a recruiter for help and he got me in the Navy. I was in Rhode Island, California, and then in the Pacific. I was in the Navy Seabees and served on eight islands. After the war I did masonry in Worcester.

"It was good experience being in the CCCs. It helped me in the service with the regimentation and getting along with other guys."

Arthur Frasier

Arthur Frasier was the third enrollee that died while working at the Warrensburg camp. The Ticonderoga Sentinel reported on August 29, 1935 that Arthur and his brother Bernard were walking to Hague after attending a dance in Loon Lake. A car hit Arthur and sped away after the accident. Bernard was unable to get the license plate number from the fleeing car.

The injured young man died in an ambulance on his way to the hospital in Ticonderoga. Arthur' grew up in Hague. After his parents died he was living in Hague with Ralph Denno.

Andrew Aldrich

Andrew Aldrich lives in Centennial Colorado but he grew up at the Pack Forest during the 1930s and 40s where his father, Frank, was a forester. He said:

"My dad worked for Cliff Foster in implementing Syracuse Professor Svend Heiberg's research projects. The mess hall had a kitchen area at one end, a stone fireplace on one side of the large open area for dining, and a recreation area. To the east of the building was an open area for sleeping tents. It was a very short walk through the woods to the sawmill and nursery. The seed house and nursery beds were just east of the sawmill.

"When I visited Pack Forest in 1973 everything was basically the same as when we moved away in 1945."

Gradually the buildings decayed and were removed but the mess hall remained and was later used as a shooting range. It, too, was removed some time in the 1990s but the stone fireplace and chimney remain standing.

Tad Norton, Pack Forest caretaker, and his daughter in front of the CCC mess hall fireplace and chimney in 2007. It is the only remaining building structure from the CCC camp in the Pack Forest. Podskoch Collection

CHAPTER 30
NY BOYS IN OTHER STATE CAMPS

Jim Johnson
Stillwater, NY & Salt Lake City, Utah

On November 23, 2007 I visited Jim and Mary Johnson at their home in Gansevoort (south of Glens Falls). They proudly showed me their beautiful landscaped property and home that Jim built. Jim then showed me a cannonball displayed on a shelf.

"I found it while working at the Saratoga Battlefield when I was assigned to the Stillwater CCC camp."

I asked Jim why he joined the CCC: "I grew up in Cohoes and my family was very poor. There were six children in my family: Bill, Jim, Mildred, Leonard, Walter, and Dorothy. My father, Edward, worked at the Ford Motor Co. on Green Island but when he was working on the roof he fell off and couldn't work any more. There was no workman compensation in those days so everyone had to work to help our family survive.

"My mother, Mary, took in washing. My older bother Bill and I picked coal that had fallen along the railroad tracks and loaded it into burlap bags. Sometimes we hopped on railroad cars and kicked off coal and took it home to heat our home. We also walked two miles to a florist and picked up wooden crates they threw away. Sometimes Mom had to pull a wagon three miles to bring home fuel for our home.

"There were places we got free food. The APSO Bakery gave us old bread. It had a lot of green mold because they didn't use preservatives in those days. We were hungry and just cut off the green mold. There were apple trees along the canal in Cohoes where we picked old and scrubby apples. The welfare department gave us surplus commodities such as prunes, rice, powdered potatoes, etc.

"My brother Bill joined the CCC around 1938 when he was 16. He went to Cherry Plains, Newcomb, Lake Tahoe, and Stillwater camps. Each month he earned $25 for our family.

"In October 1936 I was 14 and decided to join the CCC. I quit school in eighth grade. I had to help my family. Since you had to be 17 years old I went to our church and got my birth certificate. I took a bottle of ink

eradicator and changed the year of my birth from 1924 to 1919. I went with to Troy with my certificate and gave it to the person registering the recruits.

"Two days later I was on a truck going to the Stillwater camp. It was behind the high school where the VFW is today. The Army officer assigned me to the same barracks with my brother. I felt bad about leaving home. For about the next 10 days I cried myself to sleep. I felt very bad. I was younger than everybody but I learned fast how to cope.

Jim Johnson of Gansevoort reminisces about his CCC experiences at the Saratoga Battlefield and out West near Salt Lake City, Utah. Podskoch Collection

"After about two weeks the guy next to me started to pick on me. My brother came over and thrashed him. "There were fights every day. The camp had 200 kids off the streets and they were tough. Jackie Martin, an amateur boxer from Troy, was in charge of the kitchen and his job was to keep peace in the mess hall. One time one big guy did something that Martin didn't like. He invited the guy outside and the both put on boxing gloves. Martin thrashed the hell out of him.

"My first job was working with a crew shoveling shale rock onto trucks that went up to the Saratoga Battlefield. Two guys were assigned to a truck and there were two trucks. The two man teams had bets to see who could load a truck the fastest. The winners got a cigarette.

"Another job I had was digging trenches on the battlefield. We were helping the archeologists look for artifacts. It was on this battlefield that my sixth grade class had a picnic. We found mini iron balls and buttons. Then I saw in the middle of a full skeleton a 4" cannon ball. I was only in sixth grade. I saw his teeth, too.

"I was there for three months and saw an announcement on the camp bulletin board. I couldn't read it. I'd say about 40 per cent of the guys couldn't read.

I couldn't even sign my own name. Schools weren't like they are today. There were so many poor people and education wasn't important. You had to go to work. There were children at home and it was my responsibility to help them out. I asked someone to read it to me. The announcement read, 'Anyone who would like to go out West should sign up here.'

"This adventure sounded great so I signed up. I went by train from Albany to Camp Kilmer in NJ. It was by the ocean and it was colder than hell. There was nothing but tents to live in. I was there for a week. Every day they were around 200-400 guys lined up and the officer read off the names of boys leaving the camp. When your name was called, the next day you were on a truck that took you to a train.

"When I got on the train I thought I didn't like sitting around so I volunteered to work in the kitchen. I'd sit by the open door way and peeled potatoes and washed trays. I enjoyed looking at the sky and beautiful scenery. There were hobo camps at every stop and I threw them some potatoes. At night they had bunks for us to sleep in.

"The trip took us four days and nights to get to Utah. Sometimes the train stopped to get provisions. "Our first stop for a CCC camp was in Green River, Utah. There were about a half-dozen houses. I was scared to death that my name would be called to get off. About 15-20 men got off but not me. Boy, was I glad.

"The next stop was Salt Lake City. They called another 15-20 guys and I was one of them. The Army loaded us up into a truck and drove us 15 miles to Cottonwood Canyon. It was on a plateau overlooking the valley. I could see refineries and Salt Lake in the distance. I was so home sick I cried myself to sleep for two weeks. Luckily I had a friend, Harvey Payette, from Cohoes. About half of the guys were from Puerto Rico The Army kept us segregated. There were a lot of fights.

"For my first job I was assigned to a logging crew. We cut wood with a buzz saw. The wood was later used for the first shelters for the ski center. Both the CCC and WPA worked together building the ski center and slopes. This is the same spot that the Winter Olympics were held.

"When lunch time came they brought the food in a box. We had PB&J sandwiches and an apple. There was also a big vat of coffee.

"At the end of the month we had $2 and we went to a roller skating rink in Salt Lake City.
"I'd say about three times we were pulled out of camp to dig out people who were caught in snow slides. We started by digging in from the bottom and made like stairs. Guys used poles and rods to probe for the bodies. Some of the people made it out alive.

"We also worked on the ski jump. It was the first in Utah. We brought in snow and passed it up in buckets. They packed it on the jump and hill. We prepared the jump for a competition. I'll never forget seeing Al Langon, a famous jumper, who was there.

"In the winter as we drove to work in Little Cotton Wood we always saw the National Guard shooting 75 mm cannons into the mountains to start snow slides.

"The camps out West were located away from people so the Army only took us to town once a month. They fed you and worked you. Out East the guys could go home on the weekends but out West they knew you'd never get away.

"One weekend my friend and I had some extra money. We decided to hitch hike to Murray, Utah. As we hitchhiked a car came out of the valley. It had water bugs hanging off the car. He stopped and gave us a ride. He said he was a miner and dropped us off in town that was about eight miles from our camp.

"I'll never forget that night. It was 11 pm and began snowing. The temperature was below zero. We went into the police station and asked if we could sleep in a cell. The officer said no. We left and went around to the back of the building and saw a coal chute. We crawled down the hole and tried to sleep on the coal. About a half hour later I felt a light shinning in my eyes. It was the cop and he kicked us out. He said, 'You found your way in now find your way out.'

"We started walking back to camp and we got about four miles out and I thought we were going to freeze to death. I felt warm and I was afraid of hypothermia. So we began running. We ran all the way back to camp. When we got to the canyon it was a little warmer. There were no lights and it was darker than hell. We wondered if we'd be attacked by wolves or mountain lions. When we got to camp we were really happy to get into our barracks with its warm stoves.

"I stayed in Utah till April 1940 and came back home. I worked at a brush company in Cohoes and got paid 18 cents an hour. Then I got a job at the Watervliet Arsenal. I worked seven days a week on the night shift. After eight months I was drafted in 1942 and was stationed at Camp Polk Louisiana.

"When I look back at my time in the CCC I think it wasn't easy or a joy ride. They worked the hell out of you. The Army stressed discipline and if you got in trouble you got KP duty or the leader of the barracks who was a big guy took you outside and knocked the crap out of you.

"On the other hand it was a good experience. It taught you about life and you grew up fast. It got you off the street. You were a lot better man.

"In 2002 Mary and I went out to Utah and visited my old camp site. Today it is a youth camp for juvenile delinquents.

Steve Thomas
Montana, California, & Catskills

Stanley "Steve Thomas" Tomaszewski came to the Schenectady Historical Society CCC Reunion in June 2010 and surprised everyone when he said he was 98 years old. The tall slim man looked more like 78 than a man approaching the 100-year mark. He told the audience that while in the CCC he had been to fabulous areas of the US like Death Valley, California, and Glacier National Park. He also bragged that he still drove in downtown Schenectady, didn't wear glasses, and he just gave up golf. He was accompanied by his niece Doreen May who later invited me to her home in Schenectady to interview "Uncle Steve" in August 2010.

When I arrived at Doreen's home there was a spit polished PT Cruiser parked in the driveway. When Doreen welcomed me in I asked Steve how he got there. He said he drove his car, the PT Cruiser. I was amazed that he was still driving and his car didn't have one scratch on it. "I only drive during the late morning and early afternoons when the traffic is low."

We sat at the kitchen table and Steve proudly showed me his large photo album chronicling the four CCC camps that he worked at from April 1934 to April 1937. I asked why he joined the CCC.

"When I was 16 years old I dropped out of high school at the beginning of tenth grade to help my parents Walter and Helen. They had four other children: Irene, Isabelle, Richard and Victor. I got a job as an office boy and worked there for four years till I was laid off. My parents separated. My mother and I invested in a gas station that went broke.

"Then I heard about the CCC in the newspaper. In April 1934 I signed up for the CCC here in Schenectady and they sent a group of enrollees down to Fort Dix, New Jersey. We stayed in tents and got some training. Then they shipped us by train to Virginia where we picked up a few more guys.

"After a few days on the train we arrived in Montana and they took us to Glacier National Park. It was raining and snowing. We were placed in four-man tents. Bus Cleary, Frank Thomas, Fred McCasland were my tentmates. The tents leaked a little so we moved the bunks closer together to stay dry. A couple guys got homesick and left. They hitchhiked back home.

"Our camp was at Lake Sherburne. About half of the guys were from our Schenectady group. One day a group of guys were crossing the lake and their boat tipped over. Three guys drowned.

"They brought between 30-40 Indians to our company but they only lasted about two weeks. They went back to their reservation.

"My first job was cutting up deadwood using an axe and crosscut saw. We piled the wood on huge stacks. The rangers were going to burn it in the winter.

"After work we had dinner. The food was good. In the evening we played cards and horseshoes. Some guys played instruments and we sang by the campfire. Sometimes we walked down to the campsite by the hotel on Swift Current Lake. The ranger gave talks about the

Steve Thomas (right) and tentmates: Fred McCasland, Frank Thomas, and B. Avery at their camp at Glacier Park, Montana. Notice the long pants cuffs. You wore what they gave you and if it didn't fit you traded or rolled them up. Steve Thomas. The CCC enrollees taking a break at one of the many small towns on their trip to the CCC camp at Glacier National Park. It was a great experience for the young men who were seeing the West for the first time. Steve Thomas

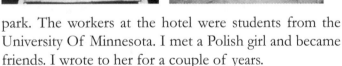

Clockwise from Top, Left - Steve Thomas played on the camp baseball team. They played against local CCC camps and town teams. One weekend Steve Thomas (left) and his friends, Dow Brunie and Browning, went to a rodeo in Montana. A postcard of Bad Waters in the Death Valley National Monument Park in California. One of Steve Thomas' friends holding two huge trout he caught in Lake Sherburne. Then he and his friends cooked them for dinner. Steve Thomas trying to beat the heat during the days in Death Valley, California, but in the evening his barracks had a wood stove because of the cold nights. All photos courtesy Steve Thomas.

park. The workers at the hotel were students from the University Of Minnesota. I met a Polish girl and became friends. I wrote to her for a couple of years.

"We tried swimming in the lake but it was ice cold and we got right out. One guy bet a girl to jump in the lake for a box of candy and she did.

"Sometimes we went hiking. One time we climbed up a mountain and I walked under a glacier. The elevation was over 4,000 feet.

"One time around 4:30 pm we hurried up and ate dinner and drove in a truck for 4-6 hours to fight a fire. By the time we got there it was pitch dark. They told us that the fire was under control and weren't needed. We slept the rest of the night on the ground. As we drove down the mountains we crowded to the left side of the truck because of the sheer drop off. There were no guardrails.

"The weather started to get cold and in October the Army shipped our company by train to Death Valley National Park in California. The train traveled through Seattle on its way to California.

"There were two companies and there were 40 guys to a barracks. I was made assistant leader and now I made $36 a month. During the day it was hot but cold at night. We burned wood at night in our stoves to keep warm.

"In August they had a heavy rain that washed out the roads. It took our two companies to rebuild the road and remove the large boulders. They had bulldozers to help.

"Three other guys and I were picked to keep the newly-built comfort stations clean. The buildings had concrete floors with flush toilets and showers. Besides maintaining the buildings we policed the roads. We drove around and took in all of the sights. There were 3-4 entrances into the park. Another job was putting up 4' x 10' signs. We had a racket of a job.

"In the evenings we played cards. They also had movies for us. My buddy Joe Parker who drove big machinery was a good friend with his foreman and wife. They had a cabin and we liked to visit them.

"When Christmas came we were divided into two

groups. The first group had a weeklong trip to Los Angeles. I was in the second group and we went to Pasadena for New Year's celebrations. They took us by truck and we almost froze to death traveling over those steep mountains. Luckily we had blankets and comforters. The first group that went for Christmas never made it back to camp till we got to Pasadena. We saw the Rose Bowl Parade and football game. Alabama beat Stamford. We found a guy from the first group who missed his ride back to camp and brought him with us. We also saw Grauman's Chinese Restaurant." Steve pulled out a menu he took from the restaurant.

"When spring time came our company left California in April 1935 and went back to a camp called Fish Creek on the west side of the lake in Glacier National Park. The towns of Babs and Bolton were the closest towns. They were mostly railroad stops. We did the same work we did on the east side of the lake, cut deadwood. We lived in tents.

"On the weekends I played on the baseball team and we had uniforms. I played in the outfield. We played some of the town teams. They had good players. Some of them retired from the big leagues and they clobbered us.

"Sometimes we just hung around camp. There weren't any girls around like our other camp. We liked to fish. There were beautiful rainbow trout that we caught. We cooked our fish on a campfire and the cook gave us salt and pepper. Almost every night you could smell fish being cooked on the fire.

"In October it was time to move again. This time they sent me to Middleburg in the Catskill Mountains. The camp was on Rt. 145, about one-half mile north of Preston Hollow and near Livingstonville. I was back living in wooden barracks and I spent one and a half years there.

"My first job was back in the hills where we burned dead trees and brush. We built truck trails to get up there. The weather wasn't bad that winter.

"In the spring we worked in back of our camp where there was a big open space. Here we did reforestation work. Guys lined up and spread out about 25-30 yards. One guy had an adz who dug a hole and his partner planted a tree. The trees were mostly white pine.

"Another project we did was digging water holes that provided water for fighting fires. The holes were 25' across and 4' deep. We lined them with rocks.

"Almost every weekend I went home because Schenectady was close by. Joe Parker's brother, Earl, joined the CCC and he had a car at our camp. He gave us rides. Sometimes we hitchhiked but when the weather was bad in the winter I stayed at camp.

"My grandfather made whiskey and I bartered it with the guys at camp to take my job on the weekends. The day before I left camp I got plastered on the leftover whiskey.

"For recreation they had boxing and I joined the basketball team. We played CCC camp teams from Gallupville and Breakabeen, and local town teams. On the weekends we went to movies and dances in Schoharie. One guy from Rochester, Tony Boss, met a girl and he took a liking to her. He married her and now lives in Cobleskill.

"I sent my extra money home to my parents.

"In October 1937 I left the CCC. I thought after three years I had a good chance of getting a job, but I only got odd jobs. It was not till the latter part of 1939 that I got a job as an inspector at Mica Insulator in Schenectady. I worked till April 1941.

"On April 25, 1941 I married Nellie Peter. Then I was drafted in the Army. I was a medic and stationed mostly in the US for four years. I got out in 1945 with the rank of staff sergeant. I went back to the Insulator Co. job. Later 3M Co. took over the company. In 1973 I retired.

"The CCC was good for me because I had a job. I met new fellows that were from many customs and religions. This taught me to be tolerant. I also learned how to live outdoors in all types of weather. If it wasn't for the CCC I wouldn't have traveled across the US and seen the beautiful national parks. I also learned disci-

The Middleburgh CCC camp during the winter. A large woodpile is stacked on both sides of the barracks door. The water tower is on the right. Steve Thomas

291

pline that helped out in the Army where they were stricter.

John S. Muscanell
California, Montana & Breakabeen, NY

On June 26, 2010 John Muscanell and his wife Fran of Gloversville came to the CCC Reunion at the Fulton County Historical Society in Gloversville. John shared his life story and experiences at three CCC camps:

"During the Depression life was tough for my family. My father Fiore worked for GE but was laid off. My mother Madeline had six other children: Veto (Red), Peter, Louis (Chick), Patsy (Put), Fred, and Bill. I quit school after eighth grade to help my family.

"I heard about the CCC in the newspapers. My close friend, Rint Lashansky, and I joined the CCC in summer of 1934. You had to be 18 but I lied about my age because I was only about fifteen-and-a-half. It was a challenge leaving home. I was worried about the money and helping my family. My brothers were too old to go or they didn't want to go.

"They took us by bus to Breakabeen. The camp was near Middleburgh in the Catskills. My first job was cleaning brush in the woods, planting a few trees, cleaning parks, and building fireplaces and picnic tables.

"In the fall I was only there for three months when our captain asked if anyone wanted to go to California. I volunteered and we picked up a train at the Schenectady Depot and went first to Fort Dix. We lived in tents. Then we boarded a train for California. It was a steam locomo-

John Muscanell and friend arriving at the station before being transported to the Breakabeen camp. Fran Muscanell

tive and, Boy! the dust and soot were terrible.

"After three days we arrived in Chico, California. An Army truck picked us up and took us to our camp in Soda Springs. Most of the guys in camp were from New York City or New Jersey.

"For my first job I drove a Chevy rack truck. In the morning I had breakfast, packed the crew's lunches in bags, and drove my crew (20-25) to work. The crew cleaned and burned brush, trimmed trees, and cut down dead trees. We planted thousands and thousands of pine trees. I made the coffee and took care of the trucks. I had to check tires and oil and keep it clean.

"Our foreman was a forest ranger and he rode with me. It was a mountainous area. We had a lot of treacherous roads. I had to keep it in first gear a lot of the times.

"There were a lot of wild animals. We moved rocks and had to watch out for timber rattlers. The first time I picked up a rock I saw one. It scared me to death. We all wore high boots for protection. There were a lot of bear, too. When I first saw one I ran right for the truck.

"We cut down a lot of mammoth trees. The Diamond Match Co. had land nearby and they were cutting trees, too. After driving the crew, I also cut trees and built wooden bridges.

"When we came back to camp, we showered, ate dinner, and watched movies or built a fire and shot the breeze. We played a lot of cards: rummy, pinochle, and poker and also craps games.

"Sometimes there were fights. Once the lieutenant heard about a possible fight. He got the guys to go outside and fight it out with boxing gloves.

"On weekends some guys went to town about 15-20 miles from camp. The town had a bank, bowling alley, pool hall, restaurant, and church.

"The camp food wasn't the best but wasn't that bad either. There was one time when the guys just hated the food. Before we got on the truck we told Captain Marcus that we weren't going to work unless we got better lunches. It worked and the food got better.

"For recreation we played softball and bocce ball. We didn't play other teams.

"I stayed in California for about a year. There wasn't much snow in the winter. We were about 90 miles from Sacramento. I had to drive there a couple times with another fellow to pick up food and supplies.

"When our camp closed we went by train to

John Muscanell (top) with friends at the CCC camp in Striker, Montana. Fran Muscanell

Striker, Montana. The scenery was beautiful. The camp was quite a distance from a town. It was a brand new camp in the valley.

"Our first job we worked planting trees and cleaning brush, and fixing roads and bridges. Then there was a big boulder at the end of the mess hall and we had to get it out of the way. A foreman had us drill several holes using a compressor. The foreman put powder in the holes. We covered the rock with branches and everyone had to get out of the way. The foreman pushed the plunger but he must have put too much powder in and he blew out part of the mess hall. The stuff really flew in the air. We cleaned up the mess and had to rebuild the mess hall.

"Then I was made assistant leader. I assigned work to the guys in the barracks and on the job. Then I was made leader and I got $45. I had three patches on my uniform. The guys were pretty good and I never had problems. I'd ask them but not demand them.

"After about nine months my two years were up and I left. I came home and I worked in Market Square where vendors and farmers sold vegetables and fruit. I worked for a man selling apples. I carried boxes to different vendors and customers.

"During WWII I tried to join the Army two or three times but failed because I had punctured ear drums. I married Marion Dupont in 1942 and we had ten children. We had it tough raising our family. I worked at GE's main plant. Then I got a job at Knolls Atomic Power Laboratory in Niskayuna, and retired in 1982.

"While in the CCC I learned mechanical skills like doing electrical and plumbing projects. I also learned to respect and get along with people. I got to meet a lot of people with other nationalities and religions."

Art Ploof

St. Mary's, Idaho & Twalame, California

In the summer of 2007 I stopped at the Newton Falls Post Office and asked the postmistress Vicky Davenport if she knew anyone who was in the CCC. She wasn't sure but then an elderly man walked in. "Hey Art," asked the postmaster: "Were you in the CCC?"

"Yes," replied Art Ploof. "When they asked me if I wanted to go to the nearby Benson Mines camp. I said: 'Hell no! I want to go far away from here.

"They took me to Plattsburgh and asked me where I wanted to go. I said. 'Idaho.'

"How did you like it out there?" I asked.

"It was great except for the time I had a toothache. They took me and a couple other guys into Boise to the dentist. The four of us sat in the waiting room and we were a little nervous. Then a door opened and out walked the nurse. Boy was she good looking and well built. Our eyeballs almost popped out of our eye sockets and our mouths dropped open. Wow, she was something.

"She said: 'Who would like to go first?' I stood up and raised my hand. 'I'd be happy to go first ma'am.'

"I followed her into the room and met the dentist. The dentist asked me what tooth was hurting and I showed him. He said it was really rotten and had to be taken out. This dentist didn't have any Novocain like we have today. He just reached in his pocket and pulled out pliers and began pulling and twist. The I heard a CRACK!

"The dentist said the tooth broke. He reached again into his pocket and pulled out his jackknife and started digging. The pain was so bad I began to groan and squirm.

"The nurse bent down and leaned toward my face with her large bosom right in my cheek and said: 'Try and stay calm it will be out soon.'

"After that I didn't feel any pain. I didn't care if he pulled all my teeth as long as she pressed her bosom forward."

The postmistress

Art Ploof holding "Buffy" in his living room in Newton Falls told humorous stories about his days in CCC camps in Idaho and California. Podskoch Collection

293

and I were rolling with laughter.

Then I asked if he had any more stories but he said he had to rush home.

It wasn't until September 2009 that I got back to Newton Falls and went to interview Art at his home. His daughter Donna greeted me and brought me into the kitchen where Art was sitting and holding his dog. Art told me the dentist story again and I asked him to tell me about his family and more of his experiences in the CCC.

"I was born in Tupper Lake in 1914. My father did whatever he could during the Great Depression. He did some painting and carpentry. I had to quit school to help my family. There were four kids in my family.

"I asked a guy in Tupper Lake how I could get into the CCC. He said you had to be on relief. I said, 'How do you get on relief?' He said, 'Just get in line over there.' I went in line and they gave me 30 pounds of meat.

"When I came home I said to my pa: 'We're on relief.' He wasn't too happy with that but he liked the meat.

"Now that we were on relief I could join the CCC.

"I asked my good friend from Tupper Lake, Big Sam Drew, why he was joining the CCC and he said: 'I'm going to Idaho.' The funny thing is he wound up in the Cross Clearing camp just a few miles from Tupper Lake.

"So in the fall of 1933 I signed up. It didn't bother me to go away from home because I was used to being by myself.

"They drove me to Albany and I was on a steam train. It took four days to get to St. Mary's, Idaho. When I got to camp I became an assistant leader of my tent. There were 32 men in it.

"After three months they made me a leader. I was just 19 years old. We did blister rust control work. There were flowers that grew in the spring on the currant bushes. A fungus on the bushes was carried by the wind onto the white pine trees. I had 15 tough Afro-Americans in my crew and they were all from New York City. I gave them 10-minute breaks but they said no. They wanted 15 minutes. I had a tough job.

"To mark where we had worked we put a heavy string boundary line on the surrounding trees. We had miles of string spread out in the woods. As the elk ran through the marked areas their legs got tangled in the string and they fell down. A few of the elk were injured or died.

"On weekends they took us by truck to the near-est town. One time I went to a whorehouse. Well I didn't start out looking for one but it just happened. It all started when I was eating in a restaurant. The waitress told me that when she was finished waitressing she worked upstairs. Then I knew what her other job was. I told her to put me at the head of the list. She had about 100 guys that night at $1 each. This woman made so much money she owned the whole town.

"After six months in Idaho they sent me to Twalame, California. We went there on a train and it was wintertime. They took us way up into the mountains and it was colder than a son of a b----. The road up the mountain had switchbacks all the way up. You looked up from the bottom and it looked like 20 roads. Everybody in the area was mining for gold.

"The CCC rented a big hotel. I slept on the porch and took my underwear and had them at the foot of my bed. A lady came by and took my underwear. I said to her: 'That's mine.' She said she was collecting clothes for the laundry.

"Our job was to make the road up the hill wider. We set off charges of dynamite with a battery. One of our guys said that it looked like fun and wanted to try it. So I let him try it. When the dynamite went off he was too close to the explosion and the dirt and stone went into the cheek of his ass. At dinnertime he couldn't sit down because of his sore rear end.

"I had to watch the boys because they were stealing dynamite. They didn't think it would go off. They hid the dynamite in the wall of the hotel. Well, it went off and blew out the plaster.

"We had another job further from our camp and we camped in tents where there were large sequoia trees.

"One night I was sleeping on a cot and a large snake crawled on my chest. He slept on me all night I guess for warmth. I didn't dare move. I took small breaths all night because I didn't want to move too much because I was worried that it might be a poisonous snake. Finally, in the morning he crawled off me and went into his pit in the ground. Then I could breath normally.

"I stayed there for two to three months. Then they shipped me back to Idaho.

"They sent me out on a wood detail. I had to take down a log cabin. I was unloading logs with a peavey. So I took a run and jumped in the air and grabbed a log with a peavey. The log fell to the ground and just missed me. The foreman swore at me and said: 'You could have been killed.' He sent me back to camp. I had to walk five miles to our camp. So I decided to take a shortcut through the woods. You can go for miles and miles and not know where you were. Finally I saw a cabin on the side of a mountain. There were two guys panning for gold. They told me to follow a trail that would take me back to camp. As I walked on the trail it got dark. I had to crawl on my hands and knees and feel for the trail. I finally made it back to camp.

"I stayed there for a month or so and came back home. I was in the CCC for about a year.

"They took me to the railroad station. As the train came in it went over a water trough and picked up water. As I stood by watching, water sprayed right into my face. It was so cold my face froze. The engineer jumped off the train and said: 'Boy, you are lucky you can move. The last guys who got sprayed were frozen to the platform. They had to chop them off because the feet were frozen to the platform.'

"When I came home from the CCC I worked at Sabattis Park right by the railroad tracks. The Daniels family owned it and I worked there for five to six years as a handyman.

"One day I was working near the railroad tracks I heard someone say: 'Hey Art!' It was Big Sam riding under the train on the brake rods. I used to do that myself. Well, that was the last time I saw him.

In 1937 I married Kate Patnode and we had five children: Artie, Lee, Harry, Carol, and Donna.

"Another job I had was driving truck. A guy told me to come with him to go to Newton Falls to get a job. The boss didn't hire him but hired me. I worked there at the Newton Falls Mill for 37 years and I was boss for 25 years.

"The CCC was good for me because it gave me a job and helped my parents."

George Spakoski
Ashton, Idaho

George Spakuski of Amsterdam, NY wrote to me in June 2010: "In June 1939 a group of my friends and I joined the CCC. We left school in our eleventh grade in Mineville. We rode a train from Schenectady to Fort Dix, NJ. We stayed there for two weeks and were told we were going to California but we ended up in Ashton, Idaho. The camp was called Camp Porcupine F-406 Co 3205. Army officer 2nd Lt. Orville Leddy was in charge.

"The camp was in the Taraghee National Forest. It was a beautiful place. There were long barracks for sleeping, a big mess hall, boxing ring, and baseball field. Our camp had 170 men plus the officers.
"We had a local doctor and dentist for medical care. When I went there I saw that the dentist used a foot powered drill and there was no Novocain but I never had to go to him.

George Spakuski of Mineville (2nd row, 6th from right) is in this group photo at a CCC camp in Ashton, Idaho. George Spakoski

"The first three months I worked in the kitchen and I liked it. We distributed the food and cleaned up the mess hall and kitchen before and after meals. We started in the morning for breakfast. The men left camp at 8 am and went to work in trucks and were back at 4 pm. The men that stayed in camp had lunch at noon. They had sandwiches and coffee. I had spare time till 3 pm. A friend of mine from Amsterdam, Gene Szpanik, and I went hunting for sage hens. The meat was nice like chicken. I was in good graces with the baker. He'd fix the chicken for a night snack.

"My next job was working on roads from Idaho to Jackson Hole, Wyoming. We started at Kelly's Canyon. There was another camp coming towards us from Jacksonhole. The men used bulldozers. I was picking up flat rocks for head walls along the side of the road. You had to be careful that you didn't pick up a timber rattlesnake when you moved a rock. I never saw one but the guys wore high top shoes for protection. We cut pine trees that were used for telephone poles. They soaked the logs in a big long tank filled with creosote and soaked them for a day or two in the tank. We also planted trees. We picked seedlings in the woods and replanted them.

"There was a side camp called Warm Springs where there was a fish hatchery. Seventeen men worked there. I just visited there on the weekend.

"When we came off from roadwork we washed up, had dinner, and went to one hour of classes. There were about four classes and we went to a different one each night. They were all lecture classes.

"Our camp had a good bunch of ball players. They played some local teams.

"The nearby town of Ashton had about 500 people. I remember going to the movies. They cost ten cents. There weren't too many buildings. We mostly went to Idaho Falls. There was much more to do there. They had pool halls and more stores. The girls gave us the bad eye and stayed away from us because the last group of guys caused trouble.

"I remember when three of us were walking back to camp after missing our 11 o'clock ride. We had to walk 12 miles in the summer time but it was cold. We tried sleeping in a haystack but there were too many mice so we kept walking.

"Finally, we got back just before daylight and we went straight to bed. It was Saturday and we were close to Yellowstone. There was a fire and we got called out to go.

I was in the truck and was told to get out. Only the men that had experience could go. I wanted to see Yellowstone but I never did.

"In the summer we swam in the Snake River. Yes, there were black snakes in the water. They were harmless. Guys made waves to scare them away. I still don't like any snakes.

"There was a dude ranch a couple miles away. Some of the guys rode the horses. I did not. There was also a pig farm close by. The farmer picked up our garbage every day for his pigs.

"For the six months we had great times. Some of the men signed up for another six months but my buddies decided to go home because winter was coming and didn't want to stay. So I left after serving six months.

"I learned a lot as a young 17-year-old boy in the CCC.

"When I got home they were hiring at GE because they knew the war was coming. I worked on radio transmitter sets for submarines. Then I was going to be drafted in September 1942 but I decided to join the Navy instead. I was in the Pacific on the USS Suwannee aircraft carrier.

"In December 1945 I got out and worked building houses for three years. Then I went back to GE and retired after 30 years.

"I married Jean Bylina in 1948. We had two children: Gregory and Jeanine.

"The CCC was very good to me. I gained experience and helped my family that had seven children."

Leland Casler
Gilbert Lake, NY & Priest Lake, Idaho

Leland Casler and his family of Watertown came to a CCC reunion at the Lewis County Historical Society in June 2010 and he told the audience about his life and experiences in the CCC:

"I was born in Depauville (near Clayton) on September 27, 1915. My father Burt worked on the town roads and my mother Bessie Reynolds had six children: Ruth, Kenneth, Dorothy, Mary, and me.

"I only went to eighth grade because I had to go to work and help the family. I worked on farms milking cows and was paid $12 a month plus room and board. It was a job where I worked seven days a week.

"In the fall of 1933 I saw guys in my town join-

Leland Casler looked great wearing his CCC uniform and his leader patch on his left arm at his CCC camp in Priest Lake, Idaho.

ing the CCC. I went to the town courthouse and said: 'I'd like to go, too.' The head of the courthouse drove me to Watertown and signed me up.

"There was a group of guys and we had to take a bus to Utica. From there we didn't know where we were going. On the bus they said we were going to Gilbert Lake.

"We got there and slept in tents because the barracks weren't built yet. It was the fall of the year. We woke up in the morning and there was snow on the tents.

"At first I kind of got home sick but I got over it fast.

"We did a lot of roadwork. Gilbert Lake was a big state park. We just had teams of horses and dump wagons to haul dirt and gravel. There were four guys who filled the wagons with shovels. We also did trail work.

"I looked forward to supper. The food was good but there were guys who were bitching. They were probably the ones who didn't have good food at home.

"They had a baseball team and played other camps. Once a year they had field days and all the camps came in and competed.

"Once I got sick, I had a bad cold. They had a doctor in camp all the time. I stayed right there in the infirmary till I got better.

"In the evening there wasn't too much to do. Later they built a rec hall. They had pool tables and we played cards. They showed movies once a week.

"On the weekends we went to Laurens. I had a friend, Roy Ostrander, in camp and we went to his home in Deposit.

"I stayed in Gilbert Lake for 15 months and then came home.

"I was out for about a year when my father told me that they were looking for guys to join again for the CCC. I said sure and I went to Munns Corner camp (near Watertown now part of Fort Drum).

"They had a big rec hall. It even had a basketball court. It caught on fire and burned down. One guy was sleeping in there and he died.

"I was there a couple of years and had a couple jobs. There was a foreman I knew and he asked if I wanted to run a roller. I said yes and did that for a while. Then I operated a bulldozer, steam shovels, grader, and whatever they wanted me to operate.

"Then they closed it up and sent us out west. I went to Priest Lake, Idaho. I ran equipment and built roads that they turned over to the towns. They made me a leader. The government paid extra to my friend and I. I got about paid $45 a month and sent it home. "I stayed there till 1940.

"Another camp we was plowing snow and we did that all winter. It was in Sand Point near Lewiston, Idaho.

"We went to town on the weekends for movies. There was even a bar in camp but we went to town because there were more girls.

"In June 1940 I left the CCC to find a job. I ended up working for anybody I could. I worked for a farmer who made plows. Then I got a job in his shop in the winter. The owner showed cattle all year. The name of his company was Frink's Snow Plows in Clayton.

"Then when WWII began I was called up for a physical but I got an exemption because I worked on a farm.

"I married Helen Balmat in December 1940. We have three girls Connie, Gerry, and Jill. My wife died in 1989 and Betty Bartlett is my companion.

I asked Leland, "When you look back at your time in the CCCs what did you learn and accomplish?"

"I learned how to operate equipment and I was able to work for Frink's Snow Plow Company for 18 years. Then I was a heavy equipment operator for the Conservation Department Dist. 6 and worked there for 20 years."

Leland passed away in June 2011.

Pat Frascatore
Salmon, Idaho

At the Schenectady Historical Society CCC Reunion in June 2010 I met Pat Frascatore. He was very proud of his experiences in the CCC in Idaho. A few months later I telephoned Pat and asked him to tell me about his family life and experiences in the CCC:

"Let's start out by saying everyone calls me 'Patsy.' I was born in Schenectady on July 19, 1919. I grew up in a large family. My parents Anthony and Jennie had eight children: Harry, Louis, Alexander, Joseph, Pat, Olivia, Anne, and Vina. It was hard for my father to feed and clothe us all during the Depression. He worked at GE six days a week for $15.

"After graduating from Schenectady High School, I had a hard time getting a job. I heard the government was hiring boys for the CCC so I went downtown and signed up in December 1939. I had no choice of where I was going. First they sent me to Fort Dix where the Army outfitted us. Then they put us on a troop train. The trip took two and a half days to get to Idaho. We slept on the coach seats. The Army passed out meals and we ate in our seats.

"When we arrived at the railroad station in Salmon, Idaho they drove us in Army trucks to camp. We were in Idaho near the Montana border. Even though I was the only one from Schenectady I wasn't homesick. The other guys were from Utica, Niagara Falls, and Albany. The camp was well established. It wasn't like some guys who had to live in tents. Our camp had a good bunch of guys. They never fought. We lived in three barracks.

"It was winter time and my first job was building a one-way road to get the sheep up the mountain in the summer. We did work by hand using picks and shovels. The winter wasn't bad. It was cold but there wasn't much snow. We were 125 miles from the nearest railroad station on the Montana/Canadian border. The Salmon River ran through the town. There was another camp about 50 miles below us. We were in no man's territory and 15 miles from Salmon, Idaho.

"My second job was keeping all the stoves in camp going for 24 hours. I'd get a three-hour break to take a nap and then get back to check and fill the stoves. There was a coal chute outside each building where I got the soft coal. I had this for three days and hated it so I asked to go back on the road.

"Then I became a truck driver. We had two trucks on the road job and a crew of about 20 guys. Our foreman lived in town. He made sure we were going in a straight line. Our job was making the narrow path wider.

"After work we had dinner but there was nothing to do like other camps. There were no pool tables, ping-pong, comma or canteen. We did have a camp newspaper that some guys worked on. Once in a while they showed us a movie. A couple guys boxed but without a boxing ring or gloves. We did a lot of running for exercise. We were in the sticks. There was a guy who had a ranch below our camp where we rented a horse. One time I rented a horse for a dollar and rode it up to our camp. It was fun riding up the roads.

"In the spring the sheep came up the roads by the hundreds. The kids went to school on horseback. "Once a week a truck took guys to town but the town only had one store, bar, and theater. I didn't smoke or drink. We'd go in the tavern and the owner let us warm up by a big potbelly stove.

"Our captain was a nice guy. We had our camp doctor who was from New York. He must have been broke to leave New York City. I couldn't figure out what the hell he was doing way out there.

"I only stayed in the CCC for six months and left Idaho in June 1940."

I asked Patsy why he didn't sign up for another six months in the CCC.

Patsy emphatically responded, "Are you crazy! I didn't want to come back and work on the roads for another winter.

"When I came home I didn't have a job. I tried to get in the Army but the recruiter said I had flat feet. Then I was afraid to join the Navy because I couldn't swim. In 1940 I was drafted and rejected. Then I went to a welding school in Cleveland and got a job in GE. I worked there for one and a half years and joined the Navy. They listed me as third rate because I was a welder and I still didn't know how to swim. I got on a ship in Newport, RI. I learned how to swim and was assigned to light cruiser Juno and went to Norfolk. Then the Navy shipped me to Trinidad to work at the repair base. Later The Juno got sunk with the five Sullivan brothers aboard. We were supposed to be on that Juno. Luckily, I didn't make it. I was shipped back to US. and went to a welding school in VA. They assigned me to a ship in Providence, RI.

"In Jan 1945 I came home but couldn't find a job for a year. Then I got a job working at GE.

"I got married in 1971 to Fanny and we had two kids. She died in 1981.

"I think the CCC was good for me. I never regretted it. It was a good experience and it showed me another way of life. It gave me a chance to travel and it was my first time on a train. I even took a correspondence course on radio repair in camp. The CCC also benefited my family because of the monthly checks that I and my two other brothers earned in the CCC. My brother Joe was in Cherry Plain and Louis was in a camp near Middletown."

Carl Camelo
Smokemont, NC; Sitkum, OR, & Johnsonville, NY

Carol Camelo of Utica wrote to me in February 2010:

"My dad Carl J. Camelo was a proud CCCer. My siblings and I grew up hearing stories and we always knew it was something special. As time passed I'm more amazed every day not just with Dad's time in the CCC, but all of his family's hardships and challenges along the way.

"Dad was born on February 10, 1917 in Utica. His father, Gaetano, worked as a day laborer and in the summer the whole family picked beans at local farms. His mother Angelina had nine children but died at childbirth at age 39. Gaetano had to raise the children aged 2-17: Charles, Cora, Mary, Josephine, Michael, Nicholas, Carl, Joseph, and Rita. Carl's one year-old twin sister, Margherita, died in 1918. Trying to earn money and raise his family was difficult and within a couple years Gaetano had to find alternate homes for them. The children stayed mostly in the Utica area.

"About a year after his mother's death, Carl and one of his brothers were placed in The House of Good Shepherd Orphanage. When he was 12 he could not stay any longer and was made a ward of the county. There was only one available place, The Detention Home that was run by Mr. & Mrs. Somers. He was placed there not because he was a wayward youth, but because there was no place else to go. The Somers gave Carl the choice of becoming an Evangelical minister after high school (which they would pay for) or drop out of school and do chores, etc. for them. My father wanted to be a pilot and not a minister so the Somers pulled him out of school. Dad did odd jobs and did mostly what was needed at the detention home for the Somers. His pay was room and board and nothing else.

"Eventually, there was a disagreement between my dad and Mr. Somers and Dad was told to leave. For a while he lived with the family of his best friend. Bob

Carl J. Camelo by Camp NP-14, Company 1214 in Smokemont, NC. Virginia Madore

Jess, but this didn't last forever. Dad couldn't find work. He sold his guitar and bicycle to get a little cash. Then he applied for Relief (Welfare). The social worker told him about the CCC. If he refused to join it would terminate his eligibility for Relief. In April 1935 he joined and the social worker gave him the choice of staying local or going to another state. He chose to leave NY. This gave him opportunities he could not get living in the Utica area. Dad and his siblings had been split up for so many years and had a lot of difficult times so leaving Utica was not a terrible hardship for him. He had to wait a couple weeks and during this time the county put him up in the Salvation Army.

"The Army shipped him and other enrollees by train to Fort Dix, NJ for conditioning. Dad and several boys from Utica were assigned to Company 1211 in Smokemont, NC. The boys arrived on April 24, 1935.

"Dad did landscape work, cleared debris along the roadsides, and helped build roads using bulldozers.

"In four months the daily routines, plentiful food, and physical labor turned my father from a scrawny 128 lbs. to a muscular 154 lbs. young man.

"In the evening dad played baseball, table games, cards, read, and made crafts in the recreation hall. On the weekends he visited nearby towns, went to movies, and watched the camp baseball team play other camps and local baseball teams. He also enjoyed taking walks and picking berries.

"My dad told me of a funny story that happened to him at Smokemont. He and three other boys heard that there was a church not too far from camp and that a few cute girls attended services. They decided to attend one of the services. They walked on a path to the wooden church that was deep in the woods. They went inside and sat down. Before the service began three cute girls left the building. The boys followed but when they got out the girls were nowhere to be seen. Then tree big guys came out of the church and asked the CCC boys why they left during prayers. These guys were also brandishing switchblades. Thinking fast the three CCC boys wove a story of needing to use a bathroom and thought there was an outhouse nearby. The big guys told the CCC boys not to come back into church until prayers were done. Dad and his buddies left in a hurry.

"They quickly walked though the dark woods. All the way back to camp they kept looking over their shoulders to make sure the big guys weren't following them. They never went back to that church again.

"On August 16 Dad's Company 1211 was transferred to Camp Sitkum, Oregon. After a long train ride his company arrived on August 22. The enrollees fought fires and worked in a rock quarry.

"At the Sitkum camp he helped establish a safety protocol at the stone crusher where he worked. Dad was working on the high catwalk and saw a fellow worker raking crushed stones in the hopper. Dad saw a dump truck pull under the trapdoor and saw the trap door open allowing the rocks and worker to fall into the truck. Dad yelled to shut the trap door and his words were finally heard. The enrollee was sunk up to his legs. Men rushed to dig the man out. He was badly bruised and shook up. From this episode a rule went into effect that whenever an enrollee was raking in the hopper, another enrollee would be on the catwalk as a lookout.

"Dad said the food was not fancy but good, plentiful, and nutritious. The camp had a canteen where enrollees purchased a 'Kanteen Gadget' (coupon book). They used the coupons to purchase goodies at a discount. "Dad was transferred from Oregon on January 8, 1936 to Fort Dix. He was reassigned to Camp P-114 in Johnsonville, NY. This camp planted trees and fought tree diseases such as gypsy moths and blister rust.

"At this camp Dad had a bad experience with the Army officials. Dad said his leader, Captain Carillio, was always looking for recruits for the Army. He made the mistake of telling him he was only interested in enlisting in the Artillery. He meant the Coast Artillery Corps but the captain thought he meant Field Artillery. The captain readily agreed to give Dad a weekend pass, so he could go home to Utica and enlist.

"The 1st Sergeant was furious when he heard what Dad was going to sign up for. He tried unsuccessfully to have the captain rescind his orders for the weekend pass, but Dad went to Utica.

"When he went to the Utica recruiting office on Saturday, the recruiter wasn't accepting enlistments till Monday. Dad said the captain at the enlistment center called Captain Carillio at his camp and explained that Dad would be late coming back to camp. He agreed to write a letter stating he would be charged with just 'Leave Without Pay' and not 'Absent Without Leave.'

"Dad signed up on Monday for the Infantry. Dad told me, 'I didn't want the infantry but it was a way of getting out from under the rule of the 1st Sergeant.'

"My father took a train to Albany and then a bus to Troy. He walked quite a distance through the city and then hoped to thumb a ride back to camp when he reached the outskirts of the city.

"When he reached the suburbs there were few cars going his way so he walked and walked and walked. It got dark and he was still walking. He looked at his watch and it was way past midnight. Dad told me this was the 'Longest Day in his life.'

"'Now, I couldn't miss roll call in the morning or even miss another day,' Dad told me. 'So I kept plodding. Finally, I came to another road that formed a T with the highway. I started thumbing and noticed a sign, 'Troy-7 miles'.

"He began walking but there was no traffic to get a ride. Then he saw the Hoosick River flowing down stream in his direction. He panicked and changed his course in search of a road going upstream. He walked and walked for a long time. Then the road ended at a highway with a T. He saw a road sign 'Troy-7 miles.'

"Dad said: 'I had gone in a BIG circle and wound up at the same sign. I was discouraged. I was either going to cry or walk on. I did the only thing I could do, and I walked on. The sky seemed to be lighting up as daybreak approached.

"'Finally, an old rattletrap of a milk truck came up the road. The old truck driver picked me up. I told him about my circular route. He told me I should have continued walking on that first road because it came to a bridge. If I had crossed it the road went upstream towards Johnsonville.'

"The truck took Dad to Johnsonville and then he got another break. He found another local truck that took him straight to his camp. He arrived just in time for roll call and work assignments. He said, 'Here!' when the 1st Sergeant called his name and the sergeant was very surprised that he was there. Dad missed out on breakfast and his 'Longest Day' continued.

"Dad's assignment was planting trees. When he and his crew arrived at their assignment Dad had to hike up a long hill. Luckily he had some lunch. Then it was the long, backbreaking task of planting all the way down the hill. Finally they reached the bottom. He couldn't wait to get back to camp and eat supper! Thus ended his 'Longest Day.'

"In 1995 my sister and I tried to retrace Dad's trek back to camp. When we followed his trail to Johnsonville the odometer read nearly 15 miles. Later we took our dad on the same trip. When we got to his camp site it was just a farm pasture with only the camp well remaining.

"On May 19, 1936 Dad left the Johnsonville camp. He came back to Utica and because he had enlisted up for the Army on his last visit to Utica He was stationed in Panama till 1938.

"He came back to Utica and painted interiors of houses, was a door-to-door Fuller Brush salesman, and did other odd jobs

"On February 24, 1941 he was drafted into the Army in February 24, 1941. While stationed at the Raritan Arsenal in NJ, Dad met Bianca Grace Scialla on a blind date. In 1943 they got married.

"When Dad came back from WWII Dad, my mother, and brother Carl, Jr. moved to New Jersey for a while and later moved back to Utica. Mom had two more children: myself (Carol) and Virginia.

"Dad passed away on July 18, 2001 at the age of 84.

"When Dad looked back at his CCC days he felt good that he helped restore and protect forests in North Carolina, Oregon, and New York. He learned a lot about nature, road construction, and fighting fires. The Army taught him discipline and neatness. Dad also learned how to get along with people in different situations."

Jim Nolan
Packwood, Washington

Jim Nolan of Plattsburgh sent me an email after reading

about my search for people in the Civilian Conservation Corps in the Adirondacks.

"Sorry I cannot help you out with info on the CCC in the Adirondacks. How about info about the CCC in Washington and Oregon...from a kid from 10th Avenue, NYC?

"After I quit school two close friends who had been in it told me about their experiences in the CCC and they impressed me with their enthusiasm. On October 1, 1940 I signed up for the CCC."

I decided I had to know more about Jim's life and add him to my book. I contacted him by email and phone and he said:

"I was born and raised in NYC (10th Ave). My parents, John and Mary, were from Dublin, Ireland. They had seven children: Edward, Charles, Cathryn, John, me, Kathleen, and Beatrice.

"In 1940 I completed my junior year of high school but dropped out at start of senior year. This was a special NYC vocational school dedicated to commercial art. Our education was not confined to dull classrooms and stodgy textbooks.

"This, however, was not enough to keep me in school. When I quit high school, I worked for a year ($6/ week) as an apprentice in a commercial art studio, NYC. Two of my close friends who had been in the CCC impressed me with their enthusiasm to join, too. You had to be a teenager to join. I was 17 and my mother signed for me. If you showed you were a conscientious worker, they signed you up at 16. I told an army guy I wanted to go to a forestry camp. Oct 1, 1940 I signed up and the army shipped me out West by train to Packwood, Washington. The thought of being so far from home made me homesick but I was looking for adventure.

While out West Jim Nolan took pictures with his Brownie box camera. Here is Jim in January 1941 working on a landscaping crew of Co. 252, Camp Woahink, near Florence, Oregon, on the Oregon Coast Highway. He was transplanting rhododendron bushes in the Jessie M. Honeyman State Park. Jim Nolan

"Packwood was in the NW section of Washington and was surrounded on the north by Mt. Rainier National Park and Snoquaime National Forest on the east. The camp had primitive facilities but the chow was excellent. I still have the original mimeographs of our Thanksgiving and Christmas dinners. I kid thee not. Those dinners were deluxe. I wrote home to my parents about them.

"It was very regimented. They wouldn't tolerate a goof-off. You wore an army uniform. A Regular Army captain ran each camp, and there was strict military discipline. The captain's uniform had bars and he had a .45 pistol. You stood at ease at your table dressed in uniform until the Captain came in. If you goofed up you were in trouble. I have a vivid memory of one such goof-off in Company 252, Packwood, Washington.

"There was rookie from NC who kept shirking the work our group was charged with. We had to kneel in the rain and saw off the very thick and wet stumps of the freshly felled Douglas Fir trees. It was, in fact, hard and dirty work.

"At evening mess, the custom was for us to stand at ease at our tables until the captain walked in and waved a brief, friendly Hello at which time we sat down and ate. On this particular evening, the captain did not wave, instead, with his Lieutenant and 1st Leader (Sgt) at his side, he walked down to the table where the goof-off was still standing with the rest of us.

"The scene is vivid because the captain had not done this before, and he wasn't smiling. He was dressed in his regulation captain's uniform, complete with a revolver. As he approached the table, he reached down, took out his pistol and pointed it STRAIGHT at the goof-off.

"Loudly, (so everyone could hear), he said something to the effect, 'Who the hell do you think you are!! You expect to get a free meal without working for it!! Get the hell out of here! Right NOW!!!!!!!!!' Marty, his words were a lot more coarse than my written words.

The kid was startled I'm sure, but the Lieutenant and sergeant wasted no time They grabbed him and booted him down the center of the mess hall and right out the door. With the captain and his leaders after him, the kid (I was later told) was marched to the edge of the company's camp and, again, kicked out onto the nearby two-lane highway. I do not recall any of us protesting this. My memory is that the captain did the right thing.

"The work was hard and dirty, but we were not only getting very well fed, more importantly, our parents were getting $22 every month out of our $30 month pay. Before the captain went into action, I know that the rest of us resented that goof-off, too.

"Whatever happened to that goof-off? I don't know. The nearest bus station was Morton, approximately 30 miles to the west of our camp. We never saw him again. I hope he wised up before the Army got him. In our company, he would not have lasted more than two days.

"As a 17 year-old, I was really scared. I may have come from 10th Ave. but had never seen anyone actually pull a gun on someone. Later I came to realize what a positive lesson this was for me and all of us young bucks. Back in civilian life, our age group was often resented, a threat to married guys whose jobs we could take at lower salaries.

"The incident in Co. 252 was a firm demonstration showing us that our jobs here were very important and we were each needed. My amateur psychology expertise tells me that this might be one reason why the CCC was such a success. We griped a lot but we also worked hard to do a damn good job whether cutting down a dirty stump or pounding in a set of creosoted planks. We took pride in driving more pipe this week than we did last week.

"During the week we did fire-trail work in Mt. Rainier National Park in Washington, landscape work in Jesse M. Honeyman State Park along the Oregon Coast, and irrigation pipe-laying in the Yakima valley, Washington.

"Then I went to Co. 252, Camp Woahink. It was about nine miles south of Florence, Oregon. It was actually very picturesque compared to my first camp. All the buildings, including barracks and the latrine, were shingled, not tar-paneled. There was on a wide grassy slope on the border of our camp and a lake on the other side.

"In the evenings we discussed politics, the Depression, the war in Europe, potential jobs, and sex. On the weekends we took walks, played casual baseball or basketball.

"There were some funny things we did and some tragedies occurred. One game we played was 'Johnny ride the horse' in the barracks. You had to do it sans shoes because of the frequent crashes.

"One sad thing happened on Christmas Eve in 1940. We were on a recreational trip to a local town along the Oregon Coast Highway. Our driver misjudged a curve and the truck plunged down a slope throwing out most if not all of the 25 enrollees. Most were minor injuries except for Emil Billings who was left paralyzed from the waist down for the rest of his life.

"I joined the CCC to work with live plants but the last camp I was sent to had me working with creosoted dead planks. I began reading the army rules more closely. Then I knew that the government could simply transfer me (and any other enrollee) to a full military obligation overnight. So after six months in the CCC I decided to go home.

"Out West, one boon we Eastern boys had were songs such as:

"Oh CC boy, your time is nearing
To board that eastbound train for home
You served your time, you won't regret it,
You might have been worse off at home.

"They fed you s----, you had to eat it,
And then they worked you to the bone,
But now you're cheerin'
Because you're nearin'
That eastbound train for home."

"I was discharged in April, 1941, because the camps were being closed down.

"Our gripes about the CCC were superficial. I have never met a CCC vet who is not proud of his time in the CCC. It is not just old age nostalgia. I felt this way from the beginning. When I got out in early '41, I was invited to a welcome home' party by my girlfriend. She told me not to mention to her friends that I had been in the 'icky' CCC. That made me mad. I deliberately showed up in my CCC uniform, and offered her college student friends Bull Durham tobacco for them to make a personal roll-your-own-cigarette. When they made a mess of trying to roll-a-butt I made fun of them.

"The Depression was still in full bloom. It took me two months to find a job as a dishwasher in a luncheonette across the street from Macy's. Then the Army took me on a three-year trip to North Africa, India, North Burma...all expenses paid.

"After the war I married Marta Bassoi on Feb 3, 1946, It was one month after returning to the States. We have three beautiful daughters: Patricia, Elizabeth, and Teresa.

"I worked briefly as a tree surgeon for Bartlett Tree Co. Then I spent the next years as a layout artist on Madison Avenue until around 1960. I got my high school Regents Diploma and then got a BS and PhD from Cornell University. I put in three years as a biology instructor at Antioch College, Ohio. Then I accepted the offer from SUNY, Plattsburgh, as a professor of biology, specializing in genetics and evolution. As a freebie (i.e., no extra pay), I threw in seven years teaching a course in the Evolution of the Roman alphabet. Hey, I've had a ball.

"Now, at age 88, I am a retired SUNY professor of botany. Still married to the loveliest girl west of the Suez Canal.

"I still say that the only fully honest day's pay I earned was in the CCC. Yes, the work was hard and rough. No nonsense. If you goldbricked on the job, the remedy was simple: You were booted the hell out of camp.

"I was proud of being in CCC then and there. I am still proud of the work I did. I helped to build something distinctive to improve the wellbeing of the natural wonders we have inherited. I helped to preserve the rich woodlands, the farms that sustain us, the facilities to replenish our spirits.

"I have never gone back to my CCC camps but spiritually I have never left the CCC. Downstairs in my home I still have my Army footlocker from the CCC, hand lettered with the two companies I was in: Co. 252, and Co. 208.

"The CCC gave me a greater appreciation and respect for all persons for what they are, not what titles or bank accounts they have. Secondly, I gained a deep appreciation for our country."

John Barnett
Lewiston, Idaho

Pat Barnett of Syracuse wrote to me in January 2008:

"My parents mentioned that my father was in the CCC but they never really made a fuss about it. After they died I began a genealogy research to find out more about my dad's family and his participation in the CCC. I want to share it with you for your book."

Pat sent me her dad's letters to his sister while he was in the CCC and her father's CCC discharge papers. This is what they reveal.

John Barnett at a CCC camp in Lewiston, Idaho. Pat Barnett

John Barnett grew up in a large family. He was born on October 7, 1912. His father, George, and mother, Minnie Collins, had six children: George, Hazel, Florence, Irene, Clarence, and John. Both of his parents died when he was just six years old. He went to live with his married sister Hazel.

Barnett quit school after his tenth grade in high school and worked as a mechanic but was unemployed since May 1932.

On May 20, 1933 Barnett went to the Department of Public Welfare on Clinton Street in Syracuse and signed up for the CCC. The next day he received a physical exam from an Army medical examiner and inoculations for typhoid, parathyroid, and small pox. The following days Barnett went by train to the Plattsburgh Barracks. He and other enrollees went through physical conditioning and companies of 200 men were organized. The CCC was brand new and this time gave the government time to organize camp sites and plan projects. Barnett was assigned to Company 1217.

Barnett wrote this letter to his sister Irene Sherpa on June 17, 1933:

Dear Irene,

Just a few lines to let you know everything is all right and hope you are all the same.

What was the trouble you didn't answer my card? I haven't got a cent to my name. I am putting the boys on the bum for cigarettes now.

We are delayed for a few days because the rations and supplies haven't arrived yet. When they do we are on our way.

I just as soon have you send me a carton of cigarettes instead of money. It's going to be a long trip to Lewiston, Idaho, almost 3,000 miles. When we get to Lewiston, we've got to go 96 miles up in the woods right near the Washington border. It will take ten to twelve days to get there. We may stop here in Syracuse for an hour or so. I hope so.

Did you get the paper I sent you, "Happy Days?" We get that every week.

Well, how is everything at home? How is Sunshine doing with the windows? How is the little runt... Junior and Leo?

Have you heard from Hazel yet? I got a letter from her. She said she was sore at you. Have you seen Clarence yet? I got his address for one of the boys...

Our commanding officer's name is Barnett. He is from the Naval Marine Corps. He is a white guy. I will be glad when we get out of here and on our way.

We had our picture taken yesterday. There are five of us. I will send one home as soon as they are developed. Well, that's about all I can think of right now. So Long.

Your loving bro,

John

P. S. Don't forget to send me some money or cigarettes and answer as soon as you can we might leave any day. If I'm not here when it comes, they will forward it to me on the train. Pullman sleepers.

After one month of conditioning Co. 1217 left Plattsburgh on June 22 and was shipped by train to Lewiston, Idaho. The trip took four days and they left the Lewiston railroad station and arrived at Camp F-8. Captain M. H. Flint supervised the camp.

Here is another letter John wrote to Irene, dated Aug. 21, 1933:

Dear Irene:

Received your letter and was glad to hear from you. Boy it's beginning to get cold out here. We wear the old overcoat from WWI.

We are pretty near through with the forest work out here. We are building forest fire trails. We expect to leave for San Diego, California for the rest of our time next month. It is a big naval base.

Well, that is the news. Joe's running for supervisor. Tell him I wish him all the luck in the world. Tell him the whole camp is behind him. Ha, Ha.

Tell him to not muscle in on the west end or he will get rubbed out. Ha! Ha! Ha! He is a politician now.

Well, how is little Junior. Yes, I'll have lots to tell Leo when I get home.

Well, I'm glad to hear you're having the home fix up. Now I won't have to do it when I come home. Ha! Ha!

So the Gallaghers got a new car. Always got to have a car. Never can do without one...

I appreciate you for wanting to send me something but I rather have you save what you can for me when I get home. You did not mention nothing about the watch I asked for. Some one swiped the one George gave me. I would like to get a box one.

Your loving bro,
John

Above - Jim Lloyd of Wilkes Barre, PA by the Camp S-263 sign in Coolin, Idaho. Linda Wilson. Right - Jim Lloyd holding the camp cat outside the mess hall where he just finished

Irene also received her brother's monthly CCC check of $25.

On October 2, 1933 John left Lewiston and arrived by train at Fort Dix on October 6. The next day Barnett was honorably discharged and went back to Syracuse.

Pat Barnett added, "In 1934 Dad married, Elizabeth Bianco. Dad got a job with Crucible Steel in Syracuse where he worked for 42 years and also worked part time for 10 years for the New York Central Rail Road.

James A. Lloyd
Coolin, Idaho

James "Jim" Lloyd of Saratoga Springs and his daughter, Linda Wilson, came to the Schenectady Historical Society CCC Reunion in June of 2010. He was one of 15 alumni who shared their stories about their time in the CCC.

A few weeks later I called Jim and asked him to tell me about his life. I was surprised when he told me he was from Edwardsville, PA because I grew up in Swoyersville about two miles away. Jim and his father worked in the coal mines just like my grandfathers.

Jim said: "I was born on August 7, 1922. My father James was a section boss who died in the Glen Alden mines in 1955. My mother, Lillian Reed, had three children: me, Mary, and Margaret.

"My family moved from Edwardsville to Wilkes Barre on the Heights. I started on my junior year in Newport Township High School, but I quit school in December 1940. I heard they were looking for recruits in the CCC. In January 1941 I signed up in Wilkes Barre. In

February a group of recruits and I were shipped out by train to Cumberland Army Base near Harrisburg. We got our shots and took a regular train to Idaho.

"A few days later we arrived at Coolin, Idaho on Priest Lake (60 miles from the Canadian border). There was a lot of snow in Idaho. A few trucks took us to our camp, S-263, Co. #2358. I was a little lonesome at first, but got acquainted with the fellows.

"My first job was cleaning snow from the trails. Then we cut pine trees along the road and deeper in the woods. Then we cut cedar trees to make telephone poles. I think the land was state owned. We shipped the trees out to places that needed poles.

"In the spring we started planting tamarack and jack pine trees.

"Later on when it was dry we fought fires. I only went to one in Spokane, Washington. We got relieved after so many hours. Some guys got small burns.

"When we cut trees we had two men for the saw. Other guys used two-bit axes. We brought wood back to camp for the cook stoves. In barracks they used coal for the stoves.

"The food was very good. After we worked in the woods we got hungry and we could eat anything. On the weekends we didn't get a cooked supper only two sandwiches (meat and P&J). Sometimes I had KP duty and washed the pots, pans, and dishes.

"I never got seriously sick. In the spring I got bit by a tick but they got it out quickly and I didn't get rocky mountain fever.

"In the evenings we played baseball in a big field in the center of the camp. Our camp team played other town or camp teams.

"We listened to a radio in the rec room and some guys had one in the barracks. Some guys played darts or horseshoes. We had movies about once a week in the rec hall.

"On the weekends we walked one-half mile down to the lake where there was a general store, boat livery, and clothing store. Then we walked to town for an ice cream or a hamburger. It was a lumber town. They rode the logs down the Priest River. I was at the camp till the middle of June and it was still too cool for swimming.

"When my six months was up in June 1941 I didn't sign up because I wanted to come home. They were also starting to close up camps and getting ready for a possible war. I was worried that I might get called into the Army.

"I came home and signed up at a trade school to be a welder. In Sept 19, 1942 I signed up for the Coast Guard. I served for four years. I was sent on a Coast Guard cutter to the Panama Canal and did convoy duty from the canal to Gauntanamo Bay, Cuba.

"I got married in 1946 to Edna Blackburn of Wanamie. We had a daughter, Linda.

"I got a job at the Glen Alden Coal Mine. I worked up at the top and not in the mine. In 1951 we moved up to Schenectady where my brother-in-law worked at GE. I worked at American Locomotive making tanks for Korean War. I then worked for the county as a custodian and I ran the boiler room in the Glendale Home.

"The CCC gave me army experience that helped me later on in life when I was in WWII."

Frank Morey
Rexford, Montana & Awendaw, SC

Carl Morey called me in January 2010 from New York City where he was a civil engineer on the new World Trade Center site. He told me his dad, Frank D. Morey, was in the CCC and thought it was out West somewhere. I told him how to secure his dad's records from the National Archives and Records Center and to fill out my questionnaire about his dad's life.

In September 2010 Carl called: "Marty, I got my dad's CCC records today and as I'm reading them tears are coming to my eyes. It is so good to read about my father's life in the CCC. I found out that he was in two states, Montana and South Carolina. I'm so thankful that you told me how to get this information. I will send you

Left - Frank Morey (right) and fellow workers hold a crosscut saw the used to cut trees. Workers are also holding an axe and shovel they used to clear the way for roads they were building in the Kootenai National Forest in Washington state. Frank Morey. Below - Frank Morey of Forestport (2nd on left back row) with other enrollees in Rexford, Montana in 1933. Carl Morey

all this information and pictures of him at his CCC camp. This is such an emotional experience. Thank you."

A few days later I received this information from Carl Morey.

"My father, Frank Morey, was born on September 28, 1911 in Utica, NY. Dad only went to the seventh grade. It was the Depression years and many didn't have work. He was out of work for two years between 1931-32. Dad's family had a farm on Paris Hill, SW of Utica. It must have gone sour and they moved to Forestport, five miles SE of Boonville, where my grandmother was a cook in the Adirondack logging camps. One of them was at Honnadaga Lake, approximately 16 miles NE of their home. These were hard times for my dad's family. Dad used to talk about eating woodchuck, raccoon, deer, bear, and rabbit. They were very poor and received government surplus food.

"Dad quit school after seventh grade and got odd jobs when he could. He heard of the CCC and his mother, Edna, encouraged him to join so that he'd be able to help the family.

"Dad joined the CCC on May 20, 1933. They

shipped him to the Madison Army Barracks near Watertown for three and one-half weeks and he was given a physical exam, shots for typhoid and smallpox, and physical training. He was 5' 9" tall and weighed 150 pounds This initial period gave the government not only time get the enrollees physically in shape but also time to prepare projects and gather materials for the camp sites for the brand new CCC program.

"On June 16, 1933 Frank went with Company 1207 by train to camp F-19, which had just begun on June 6, in Rexford, Montana. Rexford is located in the northwest corner, approximately nine miles from the Canadian border on Lake Koocanusa. The huge Kootenai National Forest is in this area. Frank worked there constructing roads until October 15, 1933.

"While he was in the CCC the government sent my grandmother a check for $22 to help the family.

"As winter began setting in Company 1207 was transported to warmer temperatures in South Carolina. After five days traveling by train and truck, he arrived at Camp F-4 in Awendaw, SC, approximately 20 miles NE of Charleston in the Francis Marion National Forest. He again did road construction work. My dad had this job for a little over five months and received a satisfactory grade from his supervisor.

"My mother told me Dad did not have much fun at night because he was tired from the hard work. He and his friends played some cards and then went to bed.

"On April 2, 1934 he was given a new job as the blacksmith's helper. In this shop he and the blacksmith made hardware such as latches and hinges. They also made and sharpened hand tools. Dad worked here till June 24, 1934 and received an excellent rating for his work.

"My mother said Dad loved the CCC and its good food. After a year in the CCC he did not want to leave but his year was up and he had to quit because of Roosevelt's idea of 'Spreading the Wealth.'

"After one year in the CCC he went by train to Fort Dix, NJ and was discharged on June 30, 1934. The Army provided him with train transportation to his home in Forestport, NY.

"Dad told me he had friends from around the US, and tried to communicate with them, but this was in the late 30s and 40s. I think he lost touch with them. I still have some of the letters and addresses but I presume they are all deceased.

"Dad got tuberculosis in Utica when he was working at Globe Woolen Mill. He was a patient in Broadacres in Utica. When released he lived in the Adirondacks because of its clean air.

"Dad had TB so he could not go into the military during WWII. He worked for Utica Structural Steel building steel pontoon bridges for the US Army during WW II prior to the invasion of Germany on D Day.

"My father married Eleanor Nelson of Alder Creek in 1944. They had five children, Bonnie, me, Wendy, Deborah, and Timothy. Dad worked as a lumberjack, Adirondack guide, track laborer for the NY Central RR Adirondack Division, tree cutter building the Rome Air Base in the1940s, elevator installer, union carpenter, and worker at Marcy State Hospital. My father was happiest in the outdoors. He also worked building the NYS Thruway Bridges (Thomas Dewey Thruway) near Albany, about 1950.

"One of the stories he told me is that when he was poor he claimed he went jacking deer near the famous author Walter D. Edmonds' home, and he and a friend accidentally shot Edmonds' prize horse.

"I was in Forestport yesterday and thinking of the CCC, and looking at all the trees planted by them. All of the white pine trees in the Forestport, White Lake, Boonville, and Port Leyden area, were planted by the CCC. The thousands of CCC boys and my father had a tremendous effect on our national and state forests. I'm proud of their work.

Sal Maggio
Nevada, Idaho & Oregon

Caroline Dobbins of Danbury, CT contacted me in August 2008 and invited me to her home to interview her father, Salvatore "Sal" Maggio, who had been in the CCC in Idaho, Nevada, and Oregon.

On August 28, 2008 I visited Sal. We sat in his apartment kitchen and had an afternoon glass of wine which he enjoys every day.

"You can probably tell that I'm not from Connecticut. I was born in Manhattan on September 26, 1922. During the Depression my father, Valentino, was out of work but eventually got a job knocking down buildings and working as a bricklayer's helper. Our family was on welfare and my mother, Maria, got free milk, butter, and cheese. It was hard for my parents to provide for their

Sal Maggio at his home in Danbury, CT telling about his western travels in the CCC. Podskoch Collection. Sal showed me a plaque with his Army picture and medals earned in WWII. Caroline Dobbins

five children. I was the second eldest in my family so the older children had to help by working. I had three sisters, Betty, Grace and Tina and one brother, Paul.

"When I was 17 I heard about the CCC. My good friend Fred and I signed up in Manhattan on July 2, 1940. We had just finished our junior year at Murray Hill High School."

(Caroline Dobbins sent for her father's discharge papers and these were helpful in piecing Sal's CCC life at the various camps he worked)

"On July 2, 1940 the Army sent me by train to Fort Dix, NJ for conditioning and training. Then on July ninth I went by train to Co. 1212 Camp F-1 in Lamoille, Nevada. We lived in tents that had wooden floors and we fought sage brushfires.

"After a week the army sent me on July 18 to Co. 291, Camp F-412 in Ketchum, Idaho. We did road construction work using picks and shovels. We also built wooden bridges.

"On October 14 our company moved to camp F-66 in Grimes Pass, Idaho. Here again we did road construction work. This was another short stay for me.

"The army transferred me to Co. 1231 in Canyon City, Oregon on October 23. I stayed there for eight months and did mechanics and telephone line maintenance work. We also cut trees. Our foreman went around and painted and marked the dead trees that needed cutting. Then we cut the trees down and cut the wood in pieces using a two-man saw. Then we split the wood and removed it.

"The food at camp was very good. At dinnertime they gave us two salt tablets because we sweated a lot.

"Each month the army sent my mother $22 and I got $8 for myself. I went to the camp canteen to buy treats.

"At this camp they had education classes. I took First Aid and mechanics classes. I enjoyed doing mechanics and I attended classes for two and one-half months. In my free time I liked reading non-fiction books and magazines.

"After dinner we sat around and threw the bull. Sometimes we went to the rec room and played ping-pong. Once a week we went into town. We walked around and talked with people. Some of us went to a farm and rode horses bear-back. The people were very friendly.

"I made a lot of nice friends in camp but I never kept in touch with them."

Sal handed me his camp yearbook and talked about some of his friends and camp pictures.

"After six months in the CCC I reenrolled on January 1, 1941.

"At the end of my six months I decided to go back to NYC and get a job. I received an honorable discharge and left Oregon on June 25, 1941. When I got home I applied for a civil service job with the V. A. I got a job and worked in Manhattan doing clerical work.

"In 1943 I was drafted. After basic training in Fort Dix I went by boat to Naples, then to Casablanca and back to Naples. While there I lost a toe due to frostbite.

"After the war I worked as a clerk for the VA Administration and then with the post office.

"I met Vienna Grimaldi at a Horn & Hardart Restaurant in 1947. We got married on June 13, 1948. We had four children: Richard, Robert, Lorraine, and Caroline.

"Then I worked for the Social Security Administration and retired in 1979.

"I think the CCC was good for me and the other guys. The working never killed anybody. It got us in good physical condition. I was also able to earn money to help my family. It was a good thing.

"When I was in the CCC's I learned a great deal, like how to take care of myself and to be a responsible person. I made a great many friends and I have all of their names and old addresses in my book. For a while we kept in touch, then gradually it stopped. My stay there still brings back great memories. On the train ride going from state to state to the west coast, I not only got to see a bit of the country, but we had so much fun. We sang songs and laughed and had lots to talk about. We continued to do this at the bonfires at camp. While I was at camp we met many friendly farmers, who would let us ride their horses bareback. One of those farmers gave me deer horns which were beautifully mounted. When it was time to leave I didn't have room in my trunk to take it home, so I gave it to a friend to take home and send it to me (he never did). Cutting down those massive trees, enjoying a totally different part of the country, and meeting people from other parts of the country are experiences that I have kept with me for a lifetime and I am so thankful for!"

Frank J. DiPerna
Bend, Oregon

Lucy Brodowski of Liverpool, NY read an article by Dick Case in the Syracuse newspaper about my search for CCC members. She contacted me and I asked her to interview her dad at his nursing home in Utica. In January 2008 she sent me this information that her father, Frank J. DiPerna, told her:

"I was raised in a large family. My parents were Asunta and Carmine DiPerna. My father worked in a manufacturing company in Utica called Joseph & Feiss Co. They had eight children: Rocco, Rose, Anthony, Elizabeth, Joseph, me, Enrico, and Susan. My mother lost four other children but I was too young to know why. I was born in 1920.

"I only went to fourth grade. I had difficulty learning but no one addressed these issues when I was young. I was also blind in my left eye. I never told my parents. I do not know if they were aware of this. When I joined the CCC I never told the authorities at the camp.

"My parents heard about the CCC from friends and I signed up. I felt sad leaving my parents. We were too poor to travel (no automobile) so the thought of 'being sent away' was frightening. I did receive letters from my mother telling me I was missed. Sometimes my sister Rose would write.

"The army shipped me by train to Bend, Oregon. It was about 180 miles east of Eugene and in the center of the state. The Deschutes National Park was nearby.

"I shared a room with another fellow. I cannot remember his name. We got up at 5 am, had roll call, and had breakfast. Then we worked from 6 am to 3:30 pm. We walked about four miles to our work carrying our axes and saws. They gave us a half an hour for lunch. There was plenty of water to drink but there was no milk or juices. We cut the trees that were marked. Each person had a partner and we cut about three trees a day. It was very hard work. I was not very muscular and not very strong. When our work was done we walked the four miles back to our barracks."

Lucy added: "My father said in the evening he listened to music on a radio. At 87 Dad still sings beautifully.

"On the weekends the guys went to town. The 16 year-old boys could get beer at certain places. Fights were common but Dad was never involved, He had an occasional beer but he mostly drank soda. Sometimes there were girls present. He did not elaborate on that point but some guys danced.

"When I asked Dad how they got to town, his reply was: 'We walked or hitched a ride.'

"He said the guys in charge of the camp were nice but that some kids were afraid of them.

"Dad said the food was good and they ate fried potatoes a lot. Sometimes they had apples or bananas. They rarely had milk to drink and never had desserts.

"They didn't do much recreation after dinner because they were too exhausted after working all day.

"At the end of Dad's six months he came home.

"He only remembered one guy's name, Joe Sequoia. He was from Utica. Once

Frank J. DiPerna told his daughter, Lucy Brodowski, about his experiences at his CCC camp in Bend, Oregon. Lucy Brodowski

Dad left camp he never communicated with anyone.

"Dad was always happy to talk with Mr. Sequoia whenever they met.

"After my father left the CCC he worked at two manufacturing companies: Scheidlmann's and Joseph & Feiss just as his father had done.

"Dad met my mother, Theresa at work. They had six children. My mother died in 2005.

"Dad said the only benefit the CCC held was money for his parents, and his mother had one less mouth to feed. He would have benefited more had they had schooling at camp and not just hard work. The CCC was forced labor and would probably benefit a troubled kid or a runaway from an abusive home but not for a good kid whose only problem was poverty."

"My father said: 'I learned I could survive away from my parents.'"

Russell Todd
Cades Cove, Tennessee

Robert Todd of Ballston Spa came to the Schenectady Historical Society's CCC Reunion during the summer of 2010. He brought pictures and information about his father, Russell, who was in the CCC in Tennessee. A few weeks later he sent these photos and stories of his dad.

"My father, Russell R. Todd was born in Downsville in the western Catskills. His parents were Rueben and Daisy. When they got a divorce my dad lived with his grandparents. Dad had one younger brother who died when he was two years old. His parents might have had a hard time dealing with this loss and probably led to the divorce.

"Dad never finished high school. He had a girlfriend who was 16. When she graduated high school she moved to Binghamton to attend a business school. When dad heard that there was a CCC camp in Deposit (close to Binghamton) he decided to join the CCC. He thought they would send him to the Deposit camp and he would be closer to her.

"When he did sign up on October 5, 1934 he got a big surprise. The Army sent him 739 miles south of Binghamton to Cades Cove, Tennessee. He first went to Fort Dix, NJ for conditioning and training. He left on October 23 and arrived on the 28th in Tennessee. This was in the Great Smoky Mountain National Park, about

Above - Russell Todd of Downsville by one of the camp trucks at the Cades Cove CCC camp. Robert Todd. Right - Some of the members of Russell Todd's barracks # 3 in Cades Cove, Tennessee during the winter of 1934-35. Robert Todd

an hour from Knoxville. He went by train and arrived by truck at Cades Cove camp NP-11, Company 1214.

"His camp did a lot of forestry work such as building roads and doing erosion control projects. Dad's job was driving dump trucks. He even got a letter of recommendation for his work, dated March 21, 1935:

"'Russell has come under my supervision as a dump truck driver in the quarry where I am in charge.

"He is particularly skillful in his ability to dump rock and in general he is a very competent operator, taking very good care of his truck and keeping it in the best conditions at all times.

"I heartily recommend him and know that he will be conscientious in whatever employ he might be.

Willey K. Cooper'"

On March 28, 1935 Dad was discharged and went home. He wanted to marry his childhood sweetheart, Edith Cicio, whom he had courted since the age of 12. Her father paid them $100 if they'd postpone their marriage for a year. He wanted them to save up money to furnish their first apartment. They agreed and got married. They had two sons Donald and myself and a daughter Joyce (Steflik).

"Dad worked on a farm for a while and on the Delaware and Northern Railroad. During WWII he worked in the defense plant in Scintilla in Sidney.
"After the war he had many truck driving jobs. He drove giant Eculids (off-road trucks) during the building of the Pepacton Dam in Downsville. Later he did long-distance

driving for Breakstone's Dairy in Walton, NY.

"During the early 1950s Dad drove us all down to Cades Cove to show us the work that he had been involved in.

"Dad was proud of his work in the CCC because he was a part of the growth of the Great Smokey Mt. National Park. The truck driving skills he learned in the CCC provided his livelihood for the rest of his life.

"The CCC is very important to me, too. After Dad's death I relocated his CCC silver ring and I will continue to pass it down in our family. My son currently has Dad's CCC camp trunk with his documents, photographs, and autograph book."

Marcus Gordon "Gordie" Vanderwarker
Clarkia, Idaho

On October 14, 2009 Sue Upham of Clearwater, Florida read a newspaper article in the Hamilton County Times about my search for CCC information and sent me photos of her father, Gordie Vanderwarker, when he was out West in the CCC. She said: "My dad told me that some daughters of an officer put this album together for him because they had a liking for him. Some of the photos are taken during their free time. They show him and his friends fishing, making mats (flat woven material), cooking, and even setting traps for foxes. Later he made a pet of a baby fox he caught."

I asked Sue to tell me more about her father's life.

"My father was born in Indian Lake on June 20, 1910. His father Marcus was a honest hard worker logger and guide. He floated logs down Indian Lake and then down the Hudson River. His dad's mother, Margaret (Hitchcock), was a very patient, kind, and beautiful person. She had eight children: Howard, Marcus, Clarence, Frank, Doris, Beatrice, Ethel, and Raymond.

"Dad only went to tenth grade and had to help his dad in the woods because he was the second oldest.

"He heard about the CCC from his friends, some of which joined with him. Dad joined to help bring money home to his parents and get a chance to get away from home.

"When Dad was chosen to leave Indian Lake I'll bet he was surprised to learn that he was going out West, The Army took him and others by train to Clarkia, Idaho (90 miles SE of Spokane, WA). It was near Saint Joe National Forest. He was in the 'Merry Creek,' Camp F-140,

Gordie Vanderwarker of Indian Lake felt right at home in the wilderness of Idaho when he was in the CCC. Here he is with his pet fox that he caught. Sue Upham

Co. 1239.

"Dad told me he climbed trees and cut trees in the forest. His camp also planted trees.

"In the evenings they washed their clothes and sharpened the saws for the next day.

"Dad loved the outdoors. He loved to hunt, trap, and fish. He and the guys loved to swim in the nearby river.

"I'm not sure how long Dad stayed in the CCC. When he came back East he worked on a dairy farm in Greenwich where he did milking, haying, and other farm work.

"In 1939 Dad and Eva Elsie Koch from Germany got married. They had 12 children: Marcus, Lucy, Carol Ann, Suzanne, Virginia, Bernard, Peter, Philip, twins Paul and Isaac, Gloria, and Samuel.

"Then dad went back to working as a logger with his father in Indian Lake. In 1951 he became the fire tower observer on Blue Mountain and worked there for four years. His last job he worked for the NYS Dept. of Transportation in Indian Lake.

"Dad passed away in 1991.

"My dad really enjoyed being in the CCC. He got to go out West, earned money to help his parents, and he met a lot of nice fellows.

Ernest Rack
Washington

On September 19, 2010 I received this email from Nancy Miner of Redmond:

Gordie Vanderwarker (back row 3rd from right) in this June 15, 1934 group photo at the Merry Creek camp in Clarkia, Idaho. Sue Upham

"I read the article this morning in the Plattsburgh Press Republican about the CCC of the Adirondacks. My father, Ernest Rack, was in the CCC in Washington state. Would you be interested in photos from his service out West?"

I said: "Sure!" and in a few days she sent me some pictures and his discharge papers. Here is his CCC story and life.

Ernest Rack was born in the Bronx on January 16, 1919. His father was Ernest and he worked as a sanitary engineer and his mother was Hilda.

After his sophomore year he quit Samuel Gompers High School in 1937. He worked for Western Union as a messenger at Radio City from February to October 1937, but after being unemployed for six months he heard about the CCC.

On April 19, 1939 he joined the CCC when he was 20 years old. The army sent him to Fort Dix, NJ for conditioning and training and placed him in Company 293. His company went by train to Washington and arrived on April 29 at Camp ONP-1 Port Angeles, in northwestern Washington near the Olympic National Park.

His records state he did pick and shovel work doing trail maintenance from April to September. In the fall he did equipment maintenance. From January to March 1940 Ernest did construction work.

Rack took many evening classes in camp. From April to June he took: Forestry, Arithmetic, and Truck Driving. From July to September he took Photography, First Aid, Aeronautics, Forestry, Arithmetic, and Truck Driving. During the fall he took Aeronautics class. In the winter he took Drafting and Aeronautics. One teacher wrote on January 10, 1940 that Ernest was "clean cut,

ambitious, and will finish high school in the future". His records also state he did outstanding work as a truck driver.

Each month Ernest's mother, Hilda, received a check for $22 for her son's work.

On October 1, 1939 Ernest re-enrolled in the Port Angeles camp. Nancy said, "My father built roads and worked on the visitor center in Port Angelos."

Ernest Rack's term ended in March and on March 3, 1940 he departed Port Angeles. After three days he arrived at Fort Dix and was discharged on March 29, 1940.

Nancy said, "My dad was in New Caledonia in WWII and afterwards worked for NY telephone. He married Elsie Schaefer on August 13, 1942.

"He may have visited his old CCC camp and in later years with my mother and brother definitely visited that visitor center that he helped build in later years with my mother and brother."

Ernest Rack of the Bronx worked at Camp Port Angeles in the Olympic National Forest. Nancy Miner

CHAPTER 31
NY BOYS IN NY CAMPS OUTSIDE THE ADIRONDACKS

John Czebiniak
Bockey Swamp, Harriman State Park

On November 10, 2009 I received an email from John Czebiniak Jr:

"My father, John Czebiniak, asked me to write to you regarding his serving in the CCC's in the Catskills. He is now 95 years old and doing well. He saw an article in the Syracuse Post Standard regarding the research you are doing on the CCC's. He is very proud of his involvement. He served in Camp 44 - Bockey Swamp. He has plenty of photos of the camp and his work. Let me know if you have any interest in hearing from him or seeing his photos."

I talked to John Jr. and arranged a telephone interview with his father in Liverpool on December 19, 2009. John said:

"I was at the Bockey Swamp Camp SP-27, Company 1231 at Iona Island in Harriman State Park. We were 9 miles SW of West Point. Our commanding officer was Col. Garback. The camp was established in the fall of 1933.

"I joined the CCC because I had a hard time finding a job. I had quit during my second year in high school. I think I was lazy. On October 4, 1934 I joined and was 19 years old. I went all by myself by train to camp. I didn't care that I left home. Times were hard and I had to do something.

"Each month my parents, Ladislaus and Anna, received $25 from my monthly check. This helped them raise my five brothers and sisters: Walter, Mary, Ann, Josephine, and Stanley. My father owned a saloon in Syracuse and that is where I was born in 1914.

"My job at camp was breaking big cobblestones with a sludge hammer. They used them for the concrete. We were building a dam up stream for a reservoir for NYC. Then I applied for a truck driver's job and I got it because I had a driver's license. I drove a three-quarter ton General Motors Master 6 truck.

"I had a funny experience as a driver. I was driving a load of chord wood in Bear Mt. State Park. Before I got to the lodge one of my rear wheels came off. It rolled right past me. Boy, was I surprised and I said I better stop. I went back up the road and found all of the lug nuts on the road.

Above - John Czebiniak was a truck driver at the Bockey Swamp CCC camp in the Harriman State Park where they were building a dam. John Czebiniak. Left - CCC Camp SP-27 at the early stages of building a concrete that formed Lake Nawahunta.

I couldn't believe they all came loose. I got the tire, put it back on, and continued driving the load to the lodge.

"We had a maintenance man who took care of the truck. I just did the driving hauling dirt, gravel, and sand. I never carried men.

"I never got hurt but I heard about one guy who died. He was digging in the gravel pit and the hill fell down on him. Guys had to dig him out. He was from NJ. I wasn't there but I heard about it.

"After supper we went to the barracks and had sing alongs. There were about eight barracks with about 35 guys in each.

"On weekends we went to a nearby town, took hikes, or stayed at camp. Once a month we went to Haverstraw and Newburg. We walked around, had a few beers, or went to the movies.

"One time we drove to another camp site (about five miles away). We decided to leave a driver and the truck and walk back to camp. We thought we'd be bold enough to make it back by our selves. We started walking but after a while we were lost. It took us all night to get back. The truck driver drove back to camp by himself. Luckily one of the guys climbed a tree and saw lights in the distance. It was our camp. We made it back about three o'clock in the morning.

"After six months I was discharged in April 1935. We were only allowed to stay for six months.

"After CCC I got a job through my dad in a steel mill as an apprentice machinist.

"On Oct. 8, 1935 I joined the Army, sent to Fort Slocum and then Fort Dix, NYC, and then to Hawaii. I got out in 1938 and I got my old job back at the steel mill.

"Then in 1941 Pear Harbor was attacked and I was recalled into service. They shipped me to Puerto Rico and worked on the coast artillery. I served there till 1945.

"After the war I came home and worked at Carrier Co. as a machine operator. I worked there for 34 years. After I retired I fished and traveled. We had a camper.

"I got married in 1947 to a pretty girl from Syracuse's west side named Josephine. We have three children: Jerome, John, and Joanne.

"The CCC helped me to co-mingle with men and abide by rules. It helped when I got in the Army. I knew what was expected of me. I also learned how to cut trees.

"I went back to my old camp site when I got married. There wasn't much to see, just a body of water. Lake Nawahunta was across from Rt. 6 where we built the dam."

Daniel DeForrest
Catskills

On June 13, 2006 I received this letter from Helen Sivack of Little Falls, NY:

"My brother (now deceased) Daniel DeForrest went to the CCC camp from Herkimer, NY. He used to wash the other fellows' clothes, and then sit under the clothesline until they dried, so they wouldn't be stolen. Then he brought his earnings home to my mother and told her it was for her groceries.

"My family lost their home during the Depression. There were six kids: Catherine, me, Jim, Mary, Bob, and Daniel. Dad had to support them by working for the W. P. A.

"If we had CCC camps today there would be less kids on drugs. It was a wonderful program."

I visited Helen at her home in Little Falls on June 27, 2006. Daniel DeForrest Jr. was also there. Helen told

me:

"My brother Daniel was born on April 13, 1922 in Herkimer. He joined the CCC about 1939 at the age of 17. Daniel joined to earn money. I think he was in a camp in the Catskills. He said he worked building firebreaks.

"They played cards for money. If you got ahead of the game you put the money in an envelope and sent it home. Then he played again but the money he won was safe and wouldn't be lost."

Daniel DeForrest of Little Falls near the Officers Quarters at an unknown CCC camp in the Catskill Mountains. Daniel DeForrest Jr.

Daniel Jr. added, "After my father left the CCC and worked in the Remington Arms Company in Ilion.

"He married Edna (McCoy) and had five children: Theresa, Edna, Albert, Patrick, and me.

"During WWII he was a cook in the Navy and served on destroyer escorts in the Atlantic. He volunteered for submarine duty when he was in the Pacific.

"After the war he went back to Remington Arms. He passed away in November 17, 1979.

"Dad's comments about the CCC were always positive. It gave him a chance to help his family. My father was a lifelong hard working man and believed in the importance of education. He worked two jobs so five of us could go to college."

Leo Murray
Cherry Plain

Josephine Murray of Pennellville, NY (18 miles NW of Syracuse) wrote to me on January 23, 2008 stating she read Dick Case's newspaper article, "Stories From the Woods," about my research on the Civilian Conservation Corps in upstate New York. She wrote:

"Though I had no relative who worked in the camps, my late husband did. His father, Leo Murray, worked in the CCC camp in Cherry Plain, NY. I am enclosing his discharge papers dated December 31, 1934.

Though my father-in-law died in 1960 at the age of 50, he often talked about the time he spent in the camp. By trade, he was a truck driver for the CCC, but often spoke of the tree planting, and other conservation efforts the CCC was involved in. Just as the other members did, he had $25 sent home to his mother Rose in Potsdam."

The discharge papers state Leo Murray was born in Colton (8 miles SE of Potsdam). He enrolled in the CCC on November 17, 1933 at the Plattsburgh Barracks. This was the first year of the CCC. Leo was 22 years old and his occupation was truck driver.

Murray stayed at the Plattsburgh Barracks from November 17 to December 8, 1933 for conditioning. On January 9 he was taken to Camp #34, S-78 in Cherry Plain, NY (20 miles SE of Troy near the Massachusetts border). Leo worked there for over a year as a truck driver. His work was rated "Excellent."

On December 31, 1934 Leo was discharged from the CCC in Cherry Plain.

The 1937 Schenectady Yearbook stated the Cherry Plain camp was established by Co. 219 that came from Shaker Place, Camp Arietta, in the Adirondacks on November 15, 1933. This meant Leo Murray was there at the beginning of the camp. The camp's main task was the construction of a 550' dam across the Black River Valley. Work on the concrete dam was restricted to 8 months due to the cold winters.

The area was a Game Refuge and work continued year-round building smaller dams, ponds, and feeding grounds.

During the winter of 1933-34 the snow was so severe that local town crews could not clear the roads. The CCC camp responded by sending enrollees to clear the roads with shovels. In some cases the men came out to help clear the road for a local doctor in an emergency.

The New York Herald on December 23, 1934 stated the Cherry Plain project was established for flood control. It also created a public fishing area and a wild waterfowl breeding area. The ponds and lake provided shelter for wild ducks and geese during their fall and spring migrations.

The camp had a very large contingent of 400 men compared with the average camp of 200. The enrollees cleared hundreds of acres of land and planted foods for game animals such as grouse and pheasants. They also cleared fire lines and trails around the refuge.

Leroy Simmons

Cherry Plain Camp #34 (later S-78) had two Companies: N0 205 and No. 209. These are the camp buildings that housed approximately 400 men who were building a large dam that would be used for flood control. Sharon Klein Berlin Historian

Fisher's Landing

Dick Case a writer for The Post Standard in Syracuse wrote about Leroy Simmons CCC days in a February 12, 2006 article, "Veteran Remembers His Days as 'Tree Soldier.'"

In 1937 Leroy, a Long Island native, joined the CCC at the age of 18. He traveled by train to camp S-54, Co. 1249 in Fisher's Landing (5 miles NE of Clayton) on the St. Lawrence River. It was located where Grass Point State Park is today. The trip was his first time outside of the metropolitan area.

The camp was composed of all African-Americans. Segregation didn't seem to be a big issue for Leroy. Most accepted it as a way of life. It was not till the end of WWII that the barriers of segregation slowly began to ease.

Leroy's parents, Alexander and Gladys, came from the British West Indies. They had Eric and Leroy.

Camp S-54 built a few parks along the St. Lawrence River between Clayton and Alexandria Bay. Leroy said, "We built roads, planted trees, everything."

"We stayed in camp most of the time. No one had a car. Once in a while they took us into Watertown for a movie. There were only a few Blacks around then."

Leroy and other CCC enrollees were at the dedication of the new bridge over the St. Lawrence for crowd control when President Roosevelt and Prime Minister Mackenzie King were there on August 18, 1938.

After working for two years in the CCC, Leroy went home to Jamaica, Long Island.

Two years later he was in the Army Quartermaster Corps during WWII providing supplies for the troops in the Philippines and Japan.

When he came home Leroy got a job at the NY Central Railroad. He then worked for 32 years for Carrier Corporation.

He married Dorothy and they had three children: Francine, Reggie, and Regina.

Leroy said his time in the CCC was, "a good life." It built him up and gave him ambition and discipline.

Leroy's younger brother, Eric, joined the CCC after Leroy left the camp. He, too, worked for two years at the Fisher Island camp site. "Look at my brother," said Leroy. "He was a leader in camp and a leader in life. I knew he always had it in him. The camp brought it out."

Michael "Mike" Zawada
Gallupville

Michael Zawada of Staten Island contacted me and said he was in the Gallupville CCC camp. He told me about his CCC camp experiences and his life.

"I joined the CCC in March 1938 when my brother Louis got a job with the WPA. I took his place and used his name. I went to the Gallupville Camp (4 miles E of Schoharie in N Catskills). We had nine kids in my family and I had to help my parents. My family was on relief. During the Depression we got a box of food each month from the agency at an abandoned glass factory building.

"My father worked only two or three days a week in a shipyard. Money was scarce. My father always said: 'If you have a trade you will go far.' I hoped by joining the CCC I'd not only make money but also learn a trade and skills.

"I was born on March 29, 1919. My parents Mark and Mary had seven boys and two girls. I graduated from high school but there weren't any jobs. A lot of guys only went to eighth grade.

"It was my first time being away from home at the CCC camp but I figured I wasn't alone. We had 5 bar-

Mike Zawada of Staten Island & his good friend Red Nolan on the hood of a REO truck Mike drove while at the Gallopville Camp in 1938. Mike Zawada

racks and a great bunch of guys. I wrote home about twice a week.

"During the first month of April we planted Douglas fir and pine trees. We were planting on abandoned farmland the state bought.

"Then I became a truck driver. I drove a REO truck and took guys out to the job site. I also helped guys work.

"My other job was to treat for snakebites. There were rattlesnakes in the area. When a guy got bit I'd cut near the bite and use a suction cup to remove the poisoned blood. Next I put an antiseptic and a bandage on the wound. Then I drove him back to the camp infirmary. One guy who got bit by a rattlesnake thought he was going to die. I had to keep calming him down.

"In May we had a big snowstorm that washed out the town bridge. We cleaned up the bridge. It was concrete and brick.

"In June I drove guys to fields where gooseberries were growing. They caused blister rust on white pine trees. We got in a line and when we found gooseberry bushes we used a mattock to pull the whole root out. We did this till the end of July.

"Then we put up barbed wire fences for farmers to keep their cows out of the fields where we had planted trees.

"We did a job at the Gilboa Dam. It was a big dam that made a reservoir for NYC water. We used cement to fill in the cracks in the rocks.

"On weekends we went to other camps and played baseball. I was the centerfielder. We played Margaretville a lot because it was close. Then we played for the NYS CCC championship in Schenectady but we lost.

"An Army truck took us to Schenectady for movies. Some fellows used to go up to Cohoes.

"The food was good. We had a good cook. He made the best SOS (Sh--On Shingle). Guys including me went up for seconds.

"In September 1938 I was discharged. I would have stayed longer but was limited to six months.

"I felt good that I had done something to help my family. When I left for camp my mother only had a washboard for washing clothes. Each month she got $25 of my pay. She saved most of it and when I came back she had a Sears and Roebuck washing machine that she bought with the CCC money. I will never forget it.

"When I came home from the CCC I got a job helping out in a linoleum and carpet store. I was a helper for the installer. In 1939 I got a job in the shipyard. I was a machinist helper.

"When the war began the shipyard workers were deferred. I went to Kearney, NJ and worked at Federal Shipyard. We built Liberty ships, the kind the five Sullivan brothers (Madison, Albert, Joseph, George, and Francis) died on Nov. 13, 1942 when their ship, the USS Juneau, was attacked by Japanese ships during the Battle of Guadalcanal. They served together because they refused to be separated.

"In November 1942 I married Margery Lisk. We had a son, Michael, Jr. and a daughter, Marieanne.

"1n 1957 I went to work as a machinist at Proctor and Gamble. I worked in the Duncan Hines cake mix factory fixing machines that mixed and filled bags. I worked there for 27 years. I retired in 1984. Now I work in my garden and do handy work and plumbing for people.

"On my honeymoon in 1942 I took my wife to Howe Caverns and we went by my camp. It looked abandoned and we went into one of the buildings. It was strange seeing these empty buildings. When I was there just three years before it was a busy place."

Burt Williams
Ithaca

Burt Williams called me from Benson, Arizona and told me about living near the Ithaca CCC camp:

"I was born in 1925 in N. Binghamton, NY. My dad had a dairy farm till I was two. Then Dad worked for Cornell as a teamster. He also assisted the professors in teaching students agriculture and trees. We were living in a Cornell house. They built a CCC camp in a field northeast of our house. It was on the Game Farm Road.

"My brother, James, and I played sports with the camp guys. They had a baseball field. I learned to pole vault.

"They took us under their wing. We also watched the mechanics working. I could hear them hit the big metal ring signaling a fire, a fire drill, or dinner. We always took home scraps from the kitchen for our dog.

"There were a few boys that had automobiles and parked them across the field by the Cornell barn. They went home on weekends.

"They did a lot of stone work in Treman State Park in Ithaca."

Walter T. Wojewodzic
Laurens

On June 18, 2006 Walter T. Wojewodzic of Port Henry sent me this letter:

"Reading the Valley News I came upon an article about the CCC. I was one of the last to join the CCC in 1941. I was stationed at Camp Laurens, SP-11, Co. 212, at Gilbert Lake (8 miles NW of Oneonta).

"We had quite a few from the Port Henry area. I had a brother, cousins, brother-in-law, and schoolmate in the CCC. We were well-represented from the Port Henry area.

"We all enjoyed serving in the CCC. As of now I can only remember three of us who are left.

"Some of the chaps served the New York area and some were shipped out west.

"One day my son was playing around the computer and found a book about President Roosevelt's CCC project. He bought it and surprised me for my birthday. What a nice present.

"I'm glad that somebody is thinking about this project that Mr. Roosevelt started. God bless him and the CCC."

Before my talk at the Sherman Library in Port Henry on July 10, 2006 I visited Walter at his home on Bridge Street. Walter's friend, Martin Bezon, was also there. We sat on the porch and enjoyed the beautiful view of Lake Champlain and the Green Mountains of Vermont in the distance. Walter gave me more information about his CCC days and life.

"I'll start at the beginning. I was born on June 1, 1923 in Port Henry. My parents were John and Mary. They had six children: Frances, John, Mary, Frank, Stanley, and me.

"My brother John was at the Paul Smiths camp. I saw a lot of local boys go to local camps and some even went out West.

"In January 1941 I decided to join the CCC and not finish my last year of high school. A bunch of my friends went with me to Ticonderoga. We got a bus to E'town (Elizabethtown 13 miles NW of Port Henry) and we signed up at the county court house. The Army sent us to Laurens near Oneonta.

"When we got to camp it was a mess. My friends said that they'd only stay for the night and then go home. We had to get the fires in the stove going because it was so

Walter T. Wojewodzic at his home grew up in Port Henry with views of Lake Champlain and the Vermont Green Mountains. He then joined the CCC in 1941 to get a job. Walter Wojewodzic & Joan Daby

cold.

"On the next day I told the guys: 'You guys can go but I'm staying.' If my father knew I signed up he'd chase after me because he wanted me to finish school. I think the guys felt sorry for me and they decided to stay, too.

"I did a few jobs. First we were busy clearing the brush around the fire tower.

In the spring we split rocks for building a new company garage. The old one was made of wood and had burned down. Another job I had was the latrine orderly. I cleaned the toilets and did laundry for the other guys. I made extra money this way. It was an enclosed building with running water.

"After six months I came home in May. My father had a job for me in June at Republic Steel. I was 17. My job was as a car unloader and I got 45 cents an hour.

"In 1943 the Army drafted me and sent me to Camp Upton. Then I went to the South Pacific and was an anti aircraft gunner. I fought in Guadalcanal and New Guinea.

"I came back to US in 1945. I went back to work at Republic Steel. I retired in 1975.

"In 1947 I married my next door neighbor, Florence Maple. We had three children: Jerry, Kathy, and Gerald.

"I have one funny story about the CCC. In Port Henry there are a lot a lot people named Wojewodzic and, believe it or not, many have John for their first name. I'm not sure what camp it was but one morning when the sergeant did roll call he called out 'John Wojewodzic.' Three guys stepped forward. The sergeant was surprised and got angry, 'Are you a bunch of wise guys?!' He then found out that they all had the same name and from then on they went by their middle name."

"The CCC was great for me. It gave me a job.

Marcus Kruger
McDonough

Marcus Kruger of Tribes Hill (4 miles west of Amsterdam) came to the Fulton County CCC Reunion in June 2010. He shared some of his stories of growing up during the Depression and his days in the CCC:

"I grew up in Amsterdam and it was mostly the poor kids who went into the CCC. In my high school there was the Contie family and their four boys were in the CCC.

"In 1940 I graduated from high school. There weren't any jobs so I tried to join the Army. The Army said I was supposed to go to Hawaii but I was rejected because I failed the eye test.

"There was no work and some jobs were paying 16 cents an hour. My father, Charles, only worked part time at Mohawk Mills. I finally got a job on the railroad during the summer but was laid off.

"So I joined the CCC in the fall. I went to Schenectady at the Army Depot and signed up. The Army put me and a bunch of other enrollees on a D & H train to Binghamton. Army trucks met us there and took us to camp. It was in the boondocks. Camp McDonough S-68, Co. #1282 was in an area with a lot of state forestland (12 miles W of Norwich).

"I was an adventurer and didn't mind leaving home. I used to go to the Adirondacks to camp and spent weekends with my grandfather on his farm.

"My first job at camp was the infirmary attendant because most of the guys didn't have a high school education. I didn't like the job. There were several other attendants and we alternated. I didn't have to sleep there but just stayed in my barracks. If someone needed me they came and got me.

"I applied for a truck driver position and got the job. I was lucky because I had a driver's license. My jobs

Marcus Kruger of Tribes Hill at the McDonough S-68 in 1940. Marcus Kruger

were taking crews into the woods to cut wood and hauling shale for the truck roads. My only maintenance job was checking the oil.

"In the evenings we had a nice library to relax and read. There were guys from NYC who were from Puerto Rico. I tried to learn some Spanish and helped them with their English. We also saw movies every week.

"There was a PX for soda. I learned about 200 proof ethyl alcohol in my infirmary job. We cut it down to 100 proof and put it in Coke soda. It made a good mixed drink.

"The guys liked to play jokes on each other. They took a lit cigarette and put it in a guy's new starched cuffed denim pants. Then they'd smell something burning and look at glowing coal embers in their pant cuffs. They did it with anybody, even while guys were working.

"We did a lot of hitchhiking. Some weeknights or on the weekends we went to Oxford or to Norwich for movies and gin mills.

"Sometimes it took my friends and I all night to get back home to Amsterdam. Then we met an enrollee who lived outside of Amsterdam. His brother used to drive to camp and pick him up. I asked for a ride and we gave him some gas money.

"Then I found out that one of our foresters was from Gloversville. He started giving us a ride home. On Monday mornings he picked us up at 4 am and brought us back to camp. He never charged us.

"After six months I decided to leave. The war was coming on and there were a lot more jobs. I also wanted to go to Alaska and seek adventure.

"When I came home I got a job as a delivery boy for a dry goods company. My second job was working for the New York Central railroad because my father's friend was a foreman. Then I became a seaman. I worked on a tanker traveling in the Caribbean and picking up oil in Aruba. Then the Germans began attacking us and I got tired of being shot at. I came home and went to work for American Locomotive.

"In 1943 I was drafted. I went to England and was at the Battle of the Bulge. I was wounded and got a Purple Heart.

"After the war I got married and we had two boys: Marcus and Dennis.

"I went back to American Locomotive. Then I did carpentry work for building the Thruway. My last two jobs were with Mohawk Carpets and GE where I was a material reclamation foreman.

"I learned a lot about people during my days in the CCC. I met all kinds of guys: city and country boys. You learned to get along with everyone.

"One day I decided to go back to my CCC camp but when I got there it was just a mud hole. The camp site was dammed and made into a lake,

Howard Cook
Newfield

I received this email from Frank Mosey on January 15, 2008:

"Read about you book project (Post Standard) and passed it on to a friend who was in the CCC. He is 93 yrs young and still quite sharp. He was in the camps near Ithaca, NY. He has some photos which he could share with you if you are interested. Thank you for your work in preserving a piece of history. PS - I think Howard met his wife through the CCC - his bunkmate's sister."

I asked Frank if he would interview Howard at his home. He went to Howard's home on January 31, 2008 and sent me this information.

"I was born in Rochester on August 14, 1916. My father Howard was an auto mechanic. My mother Alice (Quinby) was a cook. I was her only child.

"I lost my mother when I was 11. After two years of high school I dropped out of school because I didn't have any guidance. I was living with my dad.

"In the summertime I stayed with my grandparents in Holley, NY (west of Rochester). I worked for a farmer hoeing corn. I got paid $5 at the end of the summer.

"Then I'd come back home and go to school. Dad had a housekeeper and two roomers.

"My father

Howard Cook developed his driving skills at the Newfield CCC camp and later spent many years driving 18-wheeler trucks. He is now retired in Syracuse. Frank Mosey

319

CAMP VIEW

The Newfield Camp SP-6 buildings were built close together and surrounded on all sides by hills. Howard Cook.

found out about the CCC and he felt it would be a good idea for me to join.

"On August 31, 1935 I joined the CCC at the age of 18. I had mixed emotions about going away but I was glad to get the experience of being away and having a job.

"They sent me to Camp SP-6, Co. 1265 in Newfield (8 miles SW of Ithaca).

"A captain ran our camp and there was no fooling around. There were approximately 30 guys in a barracks. The camp had a central washroom. All the guys were around 18 years old. There were two coal stoves that heated our barracks and someone was in charge of filling the stoves.

"The food was good. After eating we played baseball or boxed. We competed against other camps. Our camp was all White but the nearby Fayetteville camp had Blacks.

"My job was a truck foreman. I loaded the trucks with men and kept track of where the trucks went. I came back to camp and did bookwork. Sometimes I'd drive the boys. As foreman I got paid $45 a month. I loved to drive as a kid. I got my license before I joined the CCC.

"The guys mined stone in the Taughannock Falls State Park and brought it back to the lower Robert H. Treman State Park just east of Ithaca. They built the stone bathhouse there. We had 1933 Dodge trucks that had weak springs. Then they got 1936 Dodge trucks that were stronger.

"All the trucks were kept under cover in a garage at camp. We had five Dodge stake bodies and four Chevy dump trucks. There were two mechanics at the Buttermilk State Park and they were busy all the time repairing our trucks.

"Steve Chelowski was my good friend. We remained good friends long after we left the camp.

"On the weekends I spent time visiting Loretta Veley who lived two miles up the road in Upper Enfield. I met her through her brother, John, who was in my barracks.

"Once a month on payday a truck took us to Ithaca. We went to watch movies.

"Some guys brought their car to camp and hid it off the camp site. You weren't supposed to do this but they did. Sometimes I'd borrow a car and pick up Loretta and go to the movies in Ithaca.

"One time gasoline was missing from the camp. The 'old man,' Captain Rafael Miranda, a Cuban, called the State Police but the crime was never solved.

"Once in a while I went home, probably five times in my four years. I usually hitchhiked home. One time I couldn't get a ride all the way home. I got about half way and a policeman stopped and felt sorry for me. He brought me back to camp. It got cold and spooky out there at night.

"For recreation we played baseball. In the summer there was a swimming hole behind the camp. We dammed the stream and had a nice place for swimming. Man, that water was cold!

"I married Loretta while at camp. She lived with her parents while I stayed at camp. We had one daughter, Linda.

"After four years in camp I felt it was time to find a job. I was discharged on May 11, 1939. The job situation on the outside began improving. I got a job driving truck with the Federal Interior Department and worked there for six months with $60 a-month. Then I went to work for a short time in a factory in Honeoye Falls. I left there and worked for Railway Express.

"In 1943 I was drafted into the Navy. I was a machinist mate for three years. I went to Africa and Italy and was on convoy duty.

"The CCC gave me experience driving trucks which proved to be my occupation. I met Loretta my future wife there. I learned to get along with people and how to live on my own.

"I ended up with Atlantic Refining Co. and drove 18-wheelers.

"I felt that being in the CCC was a good way to get a job. I was able to work till the job situation improved. The pay was good. I started at $30 a month. When I became an assistant leader I got two stripes and $36 a month. Then I got three stripes as a leader and was paid $45 a month. I got free food and medical care. Some guys wanted to stay longer. They even changed their name to stay and get another hitch. The CCC was a good thing for a lot of guys."

George Carr
Red House

In the spring of 2011 I was working on my last two chapters of this book on the Adirondacks and I visited my East Hampton, CT town library. I always ask people if they had a family member or friend in the CCC. Sometimes I strike out but on this day I was successful. As the older male clerk was checking my materials, I asked if he had any family in the CCC. He responded yes. I introduced myself and told him of my quest to find CCC alumni and family members for my book. His name was Philip Carr and he was from Rochester, NY. He said his father George Carr had been in a New York state camp. Philip told me to call his father in Melbourne, Florida.

On June 6, 2011 I interviewed George by phone.

"In 1936 I joined the CCC and was sent to Red House in Western NY, 60 miles south of Buffalo. Our camp was in the Allegany State Park. We did most of our work in the park. The CCC was for poor boys and my family was poor.

"I was born on June 29, 1918 in Rochester. My parents, Frank and May (Speceakheart) had three other children: Frances, Howard, and Matilda. I was the eldest. My mother died in childbirth and my sister June was later adopted.

"It was hard when my family lost our mother. My grandmother took care of me since I was five. My father lost all the children. I only saw him once when he came to visit my grandmother. So I not only lost my mother and father,

but my brothers and sisters were in foster homes.

"When I was older I was walking with my girlfriend. We stopped to talk to a friend and another girl I didn't know. Our friend asked me if I knew the other girl. I said no. She replied, 'Well, she is your younger sister June who was adopted after your mother died.'

"I went to high school for a couple of months and when my grandmother died I took off. I had different jobs. You name it and I had it. I worked as a dishwasher and

After working in the CCC camp near Red House, NY, George Carr worked in the NYA in Passamaquoddy Bay, Maine where he learned other work skills. Then he served in the Army Air Corps during WWII. Phil Carr

was able to get a hotel room for $3 a week. It was part of the Milner Hotel chain. They washed your clothes and cleaned your room. The hotel had wide hallways. There was a transom (window) above the door for air that helped to cool the room.

"I also sold magazines from town to town. Then I joined a gang of six guys. We took a pony to towns and gave the kids rides. At night the pony lived with us in the hotel and slept in our bedroom. If the manager found out he'd have thrown us out. We treated the pony like a baby because he was our moneymaker. During the day we walked up and down the streets looking for business. One of us had a camera and he took a picture of the kid on the horse wearing a cowboy hat.

"Then I heard by word of mouth about the CCC. I was about 18 years old. In 1936 I signed up in Buffalo. The Army shipped a group of us by bus to Red House. Our camp was SP-51, Company 249. We were building roads, cabins, benches, and moved stones in the Allegany State Park.

"I was basically a loner and didn't have too many friends but I did some things with others. The camp had sports teams like baseball and I went to watch.

"In the evenings or on weekends we went by Army truck to the Indian reservation in Salamanca to watch them dance. The Indians taught us leathercraft. The Seneca and a few other tribes lived there.

"During our free time we played baseball and went

on hikes.

"Pennsylvania was nearby. On some weekends an Army truck took us to Bradford where we just walked around. If we had some money we might have gone to a beer garden.

"After only four months in the CCC I went AWOL. I got sick of the routine work.

"Then I went into the NYA (National Youth Administration which gave unemployed youth training). They shipped me to Passamaquoddy Bay, Maine (NE Maine on the US Canadian border). The US engineers were working on the Passamaquoddy Tidal Power Project. They were trying to conquer the tides to make power. The tides are 40' high. We were going to build dams that locked the water in when the tides came in and when the tide went out they'd let the water out (Eastport, Maine). The water was to turn the generators and make electricity. President Roosevelt lived across from there on Campobello Island.

"NYA had us learn different trades. First I worked with the survey crew. Then they sent me to clerical school for typing. I also did carpentry and painting for a week. They did this to teach the guys skills so that when they left they'd be able to get a job. I did this for a year about 1938-39.

"The British came down from Canada and tried to recruit us to join the Royal Canadian Air Force for WWII. I almost joined but changed my mind. A couple friends did.

"After a year I got a ticket and went by train to Rochester. I got a job with E. W. Edwards Department Store. I worked on small and large appliances.

"In 1941 I got drafted. I was sent to basic training and then to the Army Signal Corps in Monmouth, NJ. I was a telegrapher.

"They transferred me to the Army Air Corps in Mitchel Air Force Base on Long Island. I went to Montgomery, Alabama and did basic flight training. Then I went to Orlando where I graduated in radar night fighter school.

"The war was coming to an end. I was a 2nd Lieutenant. The Battle of the Bulge was coming but I wasn't shipped out.

"After the war I worked for Eastman Kodak for 18 years. I was recalled for the Korean War and sent to Cape Canaveral. I was a guidance instructor. At that time there was only a lighthouse. We were testing ground to air defense missiles for distance and safety that would eventually go to Eastern Europe to stop the Russians.

"I married Lucille Weden from Rochester and we had one child, Philip.

"We were all mostly loners in the CCC. The camp taught us how to get along with one another."

Louis Iauco
Selkirk Camp

Louis Iauco of Cicero read a Dick Case story in the Syracuse newspaper and stated he was in the CCC in the Selkirk camp. I contacted him and this is his story:

"I was born on November 12, 1920 in Syracuse. My father was Salvatore. He had a grocery store. My mother ran it while my dad and older brother, Marty, drove all over the South picking up produce for the regional produce markets.

"During my junior year I quit high school. One day a friend of mine, Peratti, stopped by my house. He said he was going downtown to sign up for the CCCs.

"I asked, 'What is it?' And he said, 'They went all over the US and worked outside building parks and planting trees.' I said I'd walk down with him. When I got there I wound up joining with him.

"I came home and told my mom that I was joining the CCC and she said, 'OK. I'll at least know where you are.' She had nine children and one less to worry about was great.

"There were nine kids in my family: Marie, Lena, Marty, Louise, Antoinette, Freddy, me, Joseph, and Lucy.

"It honestly didn't bother me leaving home. I was active in sports, basketball, baseball, and football and I went to the boy's club continuously so I was used to being away from home.

"They sent me to Selkirk Shores State Park 4 miles west of Pulaski on Lake Ontario. The camp did tree planting and renovated the lakeshore so it would be accessible for boats.

"On the second or third day my friend got into trouble and for punishment he had to clean out the grease

Louis Iauco of Cicero worked as a dentist's assistant while at the Selkirk Camp near Pulaski. Marybeth Cerrone

trap. The next day he was 'gone over the hill.' He was never seen again.

"I liked living in the camp. I think I only went home once on a weekend.

"For the first three weeks I worked hauling rocks that were dumped off for road building.

"Then I saw a notice that there was a dentist in camp named Dr. Ben E. Pleshette and he asked for someone to be his assistant. I applied and got the job.

"He had patients come to the infirmary. My job was to keep records of what he did. Then he taught me how to mix the tooth fillings. I took mercury and amalgam filling. I used a mortar and pestle and mixed the ingredients. Then I handed it to him. The interesting thing was he had a pedal-operated drill that I pedaled. He had needles of Novocaine for his patients to ease the pain.

"One time a big husky farm boy came in and when the doctor took out the needle, the boy yelled. 'NO you don't! Just pull the tooth.' And the doctor did.

"We both stayed at the camp. I lived in the infirmary and he stayed in the officer's quarters.

"We also went to other camps in the state. He drove a coupe car (two-seater). He put all the equipment and the drill in the trunk and we went off to a camp. We put up a bulletin and set up for work. We'd stay two or more days in a camp. I slept in the infirmary and he slept in the officer's quarters.

"He told me if I wanted to work at night I could use his equipment to clean teeth. I was allowed to charge a $1 for each cleaning.

"One of the strangest things that happened to me while cleaning occurred with my first customer. The first guy who walked in sat down and I began working on his mouth. I took the instrument and began lifting the back gum and all of a sudden I yanked up a piece of black material that I thought was his tooth. I thought I pulled his tooth out. I ran to get the doctor to look at his mouth.

"The doctor came back and looked in the boy's mouth and said. 'Lou, it's OK. You did OK. It was just tartar. Keep working.'

"I'd get two or three patients a night. It was a great way to make money.

"The doctor was a really nice fellow and I enjoyed working with him. I even thought of being a dentist.

"I don't, however, remember any of the camps I visited.

"I stayed in the CCC for about six months and got discharged. I got a job working with my brother Marty who just opened a restaurant.

"My next job was at Day Brothers Department Store in Syracuse. I worked on the main floor as a check boy. The clerk could not accept a $20 bill so they yelled 'Check Boy.' I'd run it up to the office to get change. I was there for about a year then I left the store and went into Charlie D. Manning's Cigar Store and was a clerk. I stayed about eight months.

"Then I joined R. J. Reynolds Tobacco Co. till 1944 when I was drafted into the Army on Aug. 12, 1942.

"My CCC experiences benefited me because when I was in the Army I was already trained. I knew the proper way to make a bed because I worked in the infirmary where I knew how to make a hospital bed. Other guys were crying at night in the Army because they couldn't take it.

"I came out of the Army in 1945. I went back to R. J. Reynolds Co. I started out in sales, and then I moved up to assistant manager. In 1966 I became division manager in Indianapolis. Roma, my wife and I had five children. We lived there till 1980. Then my wife and I moved back to Syracuse when I retired.

"Looking back at my time in the CCC I realize the CCC made me grow up and realize the importance of education. I had quit high school in my junior year. When I got older I went back to school for my GED and then took some college courses."

Frank Nelson Tucker
Selkirk

Lisa Tucker of Port Leyden (7 miles north of Boonville) read one of my CCC articles in the Boonville Herald in 2009 and contacted me because her father-in-law, Frank Nelson Tucker Sr., was in the CCC. She gathered information from her husband, a camp group photo and his CCC discharge papers and sent them to me.

Frank Nelson Tucker was born on October 29, 1914 in Greig (10 miles SE of Lowville). He was the youngest child of Arthur, and Aphra Tucker. The other children were: Glenn, Bernard & Leo (half-brothers), Florence and Nina.

After completing 8th grade, Frank quit school and began doing farm and carpentry work. When Frank couldn't get a job in the fall of 1933 he went to Utica and signed up for the CCC on October 3rd, 1933. After a physical exam the Army transported him to Selkirk Shores on

Frank Tucker learned mechanic and building skills at the Selkirk CCC camp that helped him to be a successful land developer near Brantingham Lake,

Lake Ontario and west of Pulaski.

His first job was doing forestry construction work. On November 15th he began working as a mechanic and continued till December 31st

On April 1, 1934 the Army appointed Frank as an assistant leader.

Frank left the CCC in September 1934 and became a logger and a mechanic. Then he developed land for homes. He built a lake near Brantingham Lake and called it Lake of the Pines (13 miles SE of Lowville). Frank was severely burned on both legs refueling his bulldozer during his work. He was in a hospital for two months.

He married Bernette Bradish. His second wife was Shirley M. (Moody). Frank had six children: Frederick (with Bernette), Frank Jr., Jean, Tammy, Thomas, and John (with Shirley).

Lisa Tucker said: "My father-in-law learned a lot about construction and mechanics that helped him as a land developer and builder."

Gerald "Jerry" Griffith
Sempronius

Ginger Johnson of Pulaski (30 miles S of Watertown), contacted me by e-mail in the January 2008 and said she saw a story of my search for CCC alumni. She said she worked at a senior home and knew a gentleman, Gerald "Jerry" Griffith, who was in the CCC. She said he had interesting stories and I should contact him.

On February 29, 2008 I called Jerry at his apartment in Pulaski and he told me about his life and experiences in the CCC.

"I was born in Syracuse on March 29, 1917. When I was 17 years I couldn't afford to buy books or sneaks for school because Welfare wouldn't pay for them. So I quit school and tried to get a job but I couldn't find work.

"My parents Henry and Margaret (Allen), had eight children: Francis, Marty, Rusty, Edward, Mary, twins who died at birth, and me. My mother died when I was 9 years old. My father who was over 60 years old and unemployed during the Depression tried his best to raise me. The other children were all grown up.

"In the spring of 1934 my father took me to sign up for the CCC. There were all these other boys there because they were on welfare, too, and they needed a job. I was shocked that my father would do this to me. He probably needed me to get a job because he was out of work and our family was on welfare.

"The Army sent me to the Sempronius, 10 miles NW of Cortland, NY. It was camp S-96, Company 250. I was nervous about leaving home but once I got to camp I joined the baseball team and I liked it.

"I had a few jobs at the camp. On my fist day of work they handed me a sledgehammer to bust rocks for a road. I was ready to quit but I didn't. Then I worked in the woods, cutting trees and brush in Bear Swamp State Forest. Everything we cut down was piled by the road and taken to poor welfare families. In those days very few people had a car or truck. We also had dirty jobs cleaning toilets and keeping fires going in the barracks. We also had to carry coal to our barracks for the stove. We burned soft coal.

"The food was good and for breakfast and dinner we could eat all we wanted. For lunch they brought sandwiches water, milk, or coffee to our work site.

"We didn't mind it if it got really cold out because if it got to be 10 below zero we didn't have to work.

"In the evening we could sign for classes. I took up leather craft and made wallets, etc. They had a rec hall and I played ping-pong. I was pretty good at that. We also went to Rochester to put up a CCC exhibit.

"Our camp had teams that played other CCC camps and town teams. I played on the baseball team. I was a pitcher. We had a baseball field at our camp

"A couple of times I went home on weekends. Sometimes my brother Rusty came up and brought me home in Syracuse. One time when I got home I broke out with the measles. Rusty called my camp and they said to stay home till I got better.

"After a little over a year I was transferred to Camp SP-17, Co. 213 in Mt. Morris, near Letchworth State Park. It was a camp for unemployed WWI vets. This was a real nice finished camp that had nice floors.

"I worked in the woods in the state forest. We also had guard duty watching for fires.

"Another job we had was flood relief work down by Ithaca. The nearby creek flooded the town. We carted mud out of the cellars.

"In the summer of 1936 I left the CCC because I wanted to get a job. My brother Rusty got me a job sweeping floors at Porter Cable Machine Co. Then I got another job as shipping clerk in that company.

"Then I was drafted into the Army. The head boss of the factory, a retired Army Colonel, B. J. Riding, wrote a letter of recommendation that I took to the Army. When I was drafted I was shipped to Fort Niagara. I got an easy job taking care of the poolroom. I stayed there till there was an opening in Aberdeen Proving Ground.

"My job there was working in the machine shop where we made small arms. We were getting ready for the invasion for Europe. I went to England and worked for the Navy and was in the D-Day Invasion. Then I came back to the US.

"After WWII I went back to Porter Cable and worked there for 18 years. During that time I got married to Betty Weisenburger of Pulaski on April 26, 1946. We had two boys: Terry and Marty.

"I also worked part-time at Phoenix Gauge Company. My father-in-law taught me how to use tool-making equipment.

"Later I went to Crouse Hinds Co. as a machinist. "When I look back at my time in the CCC I think I benefited from the Army training because I learned discipline."

Jerry passed away October 31, 2008.

John Werbeck
Sempronius

Griffith-Sempronius of Pulaski worked in Camp S-96 in Sempronius near Cortland. Betty Griffith

On January 16, 2008 John Werbeck of Syracuse wrote me a seven-page letter outlining his CCC days at Sempronius, NY.

"I joined the CCC in 1934 and served one year. I quit school in the latter half of the eleventh grade and lost that half-year.

"I was sent to a camp in Sempronius (12 miles NW of Cortland). It was about a mile off of Rt. 41A from Homer to Skaneateles. We built the camp from scratch. Each barracks had a leader and an assistant for each barracks but they had their own living quarters.

"We fell out in the morning for roll call and reveille, the raising of the flag. In the evening we fell out for retreat and the lowering of the flag. Then we went to eat.

"In the summer we went out in trucks all over central NY planting trees, building fire roads, etc. In the winter the forester would mark trees to be cut down for thinning the forest.

"This is how we planted trees. We had teams of two men. One with a pail of water and small trees and the other with a wide angle pick who dug a hole. The one with the pail planted a seedling in the hole and both men stamped firmly on each side of the plant. Then each took another step forward and planted another tree.

"There were other teams that were spread 6' apart and they all walked forward for about a half-mile or the length of the field.

"As for the money, I sent $22 home and kept $8. We had a canteen where some of our money was spent. The men in the Army were furious that we got $30 a month and they were only getting $20.

"Every chance I got I went home on the weekend. I was 30 miles away from my home in Syracuse. We used to get out on the highway and thumb a ride. In those days people would pick you up because things were pretty peaceful then. Every time I went home my buddies would tell me to quit and go back to school and get an education. But the real reason was to play hockey.

"Many evenings the captain and forester sat down by their quarters and talked about the war, etc. in Europe. I can remember Captain Dillingham, an air commander, say that if we were in the war he would be glad to lead us. His words would eventually come true. That sent me thinking. The CCC was created to get the young men off the streets and put them to work. They also had in mind to get the men ready for the coming war. We lived the life of a soldier except there were no drills.

"The other value of the CCC was it created a lot of good things for our land such as planting trees, building fire trails, etc.

"After a year I got my discharge and went back to school. I had to make up the half-year I lost plus the 12th grade. I graduated from a vocational high school in Syracuse.

"I truly enjoyed my time in the CCC. We had discipline through our leaders in each barracks. Later I went in the Army in March 1942 and spent four years in the service.

Sherburne Camp S-73 where Nelson Avery lived in 1936. Nelson Avery

A year and a-half of that was spent overseas in France and Germany. I would say that living in the barracks and the life in the CCC prepared me for the Army life. I am 89 years old and I will be 90 in May.

"Many people joined the CCC by lying about their age and the people who were signing them up never questioned them or asked for proof. We had a lot of 16 and 17 year-old boys in my outfit.

Nelson Avery
Sherburne

In January 2008 Nelson Avery contacted me after reading about my search for CCC enrollees for my book. Here is what he said about his life and time in the CCC: "I was born in Arietta. My father, Edward, worked at Avery Hotel in Arietta. He married my mother, Ida Hatch who was a teacher in town. They had two children: Marian and I. Mother was from Clyde but she left Arietta when I was two or three years old. Dad liked to drink. My mother was a strict Catholic and hated drinking. I never heard from my dad again. We moved to South Sodus and stayed there for five years where Mom taught.

"When she lost that job we went to Cortland. Then we moved to Utica and I went back to Lyons High School. I graduated in 1933. I stayed with a cousin.

"After graduation I went to Solvay and hunted for jobs. I lived with my aunt and uncle. I felt like I should leave them because they had a big family. I did odd jobs for spending money. My mother was in ill health and living on a farm in Sandy Creek. My older sister was married and lived in Utica.

"In the spring 1934 I joined the CCC. I signed up in Syracuse. It was very populated. The CCC took a lot of the riffraff off the street.

"They sent me to the Sherburne, Camp S-73, Co. 207 (12 miles north of Norwich). The camp did a lot to develop game for hunting and fishing at the nearby State Game Farm (1909). The first three months I worked with a pick and shovel building a duck pond to raise ducks. There were state employees who were in charge of the work groups

"There was opening for the infirmary. I applied and I was made an assistant. One of my duties was to keep it clean. It had six cots. Sometimes they were full and sometimes empty. We had our own shower and bathroom. It had a stove that we had to keep going with soft coal. It gave out a cloud of smoke. We also had a separate room with two cots. One person had to be there 24 hours. The Army paid me an extra $6 a-month pay.

"Our camp doctor, a Lieutenant in Army, was in charge of two camps. He took care of us in morning. He lived in our camp. The doctor taught me a hell of a lot about first aid. He also taught boys in camp first aid.

"After sick call in the morning he drove over to another camp that was NE of Norwich. Sometimes he'd be back in evening or morning.

"The doctor treated a variety of illnesses. There were two cases of pneumonias and the doctor sent them to the hospital

"We also had a couple of broken arms. The doctor set them and put them in a cast. The guys were working on a duck pond so there were injuries every week such as a pick in the foot.

"Sometimes guys who came back to camp at night with bloody noses, black eyes, or a bruise from fighting in town with the local boys. They didn't like the CCC boys dating their girl friends.

"I had to bring food up from the mess hall for the sick. We had mess kits and had to make sure they were clean. The patients, if they could, cleaned up their mess kits.

"During two months (May and October) of the year, the camp was busy planting trees on abandoned farms in the towns of Otselic & South Otselic.

"The food was good. At dinnertime they called each barracks one at a time to eat. A guy blew a whistle. Sometimes there were fistfights in line.

"There were five barracks with 40 men in each. Two fellows in each barracks supervised the guys. They slept at either end of barracks.

"The camp had education classes in the evening. One of the classes I took was photography. The captain let me board up a room to make a dark room. I set up the room under one of the barracks where I developed pictures for myself and the other guys.

"They also had classes in a Sherburne school. I signed up for a Spanish class. The sessions were about once a week.

"In the evenings we went to the recreation hall. There were a couple of ping-pong tables, boxing gloves, and lots of card tables. We had to go back to our barracks at 9 pm. They blew taps and lights were out at 10. There was no talking after that. Some whispered.

"Guys could leave camp in the evening if they signed out. A lot of guys went to see their girl friends. It was about 2 miles to the town of Sherburne.

"On weekends I played pool a lot. During the day you had to take turns playing. I also went to Sherburne. There was a pool hall and bowling alleys there. We just hung out. Sometimes we walked back to camp. Once a week they had a truck to Norwich and you had to make dam sure you didn't miss the truck to get back. It was a long 12 miles back.

"I think I got a weekend pass once or twice to go home. I kept in touch with Mom by writing. She wrote me a letter every week.

"We had good times at camp. There were some fights but not fistfights. If some guys got into an argument and wanted to fight, they gave them boxing gloves. That was the way to settle problems.

In the spring of 1936 I left the CCC. I came back to Solvay and got a job with Remington Rand Typewriter in Syracuse. I was there for three years and worked as a tool and die maker. I got married in 1938 to Cora "Corky" Raymond and had a family.

"In 1949 I joined Carrier Corp. and stayed till I retired.

"A few years ago I went to Sherburne and visited the Game Farm that we developed. I took my journal that I kept at camp. I left it for their museum to copy but I never got it back.

"The CCC taught me how to get along with people. I learned a lot of first aid work, too."

Walter B. Krul
Sherburne

On May 2, 2007 I gave a CCC presentation at the New York Mills Library (near Utica) and had a large turnout. When I asked the audience if anyone was in the CCC and seven men raised their hands. One said that there would have been more if there wasn't a trip to the WWII Memorial in Washington that week.

At the end of my talk Walter Krul handed me a photos of his camp, barracks, and his discharge papers. He said he joined on April 4, 1939 and went to Camp S-131, Co. 3202 in Sherburne, NY (12 miles N of Norwich).

"On May 8, 2007 I telephoned Walter at his home in New York Mills to learn more about his CCC experiences.

"In summertime we pounded shale with sledgehammers for truck roads. It was hard work in the hot afternoon sun. We also planted trees. In the winter we cut old trees with two-man saws.

"I got another job in camp. I had to watch the numbers on the water tank as it filled up. When it was full I had to shut off the pump. Then I put chlorine in the booster pump to make the water safe to drink.

"The latrines had hot water and sinks. There were no partitions for privacy, just one long wood board bench with holes in it.

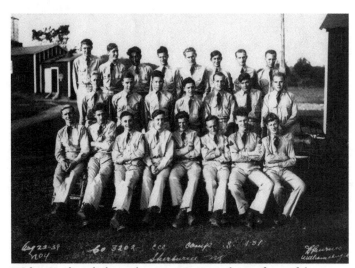

Walter Krul might be in this Aug. 22, 1939 photo of one of the five Sherburne barracks. The water tower he worked on is at the top left. Walter Krul

A 1936 group photo of the Van Etten Camp S-81. The members of the camp baseball team are seated on the left and three cooks dressed in white are on the right. Bob Donahue

"If guys came to camp and didn't want to be clean, we took them to the waterhole and dunked them in. Then we scrubbed them with good GI soap till they bled. After that they learned how to keep themselves clean. There was a bunch of guys from New York City that didn't want to keep clean. Some went over the hill because they wouldn't bathe. They got a dishonorable discharge."

After a year and a half at the camp Walter was honorably discharged on November 16, 1940. Walter said: "I was 18 years old when I left camp I had stayed for 19 months in the CCC and because my sister got me a job. When I came home I went to work in United Bleachery. I made boxes and took them upstairs where they put cloth in. Then they were shipped out. I worked there for three years.

"In 1942 I was drafted. They also drafted my four brothers.

"The CCC treated us good. We had good food and they supplied us with clothes."

Walter passed away on May 1, 2010.

Vernon "Vern" Belge
Van Etten & Schenectady

On January 7, 2008 I telephoned Vernon Belge of North Syracuse and asked him to tell me about his life and experiences in the CCC.

"I was born on December 18, 1917 in Syracuse. My parents Otto and Mary also had two daughters. Dad worked for H. H. Franklin Co. as a car painter.

"When I was 16 things were tough. It was my goal to join the CCC and get a job. I went to the town hall and told a lady that I wanted to join the CCC. She said you're not 17 but I kept pleading to her. She finally gave in. It was

about 1934. I had graduated from grammar school and maybe one year of high school. They didn't ask for a birth certificate or anything. I convinced her.

"It didn't bother me to leave home. I was working on farms for 10 cents an hour and I wanted a better job.

"The Army took me to the Van Etten Camp S-81 (15 miles south of Ithaca). I loved it. I worked in the woods cutting and planting. My buddy and I had a crosscut saw and an ax. He was from Elmira. In one year our camp planted 1 million or 1.5 million trees. The forest was connected with Cornell University. The foresters were from the college. It was tough going. We kept working. Instead of overtime pay they gave us time off or a week off. Some us went home.

"While cutting trees I had an accident. I dropped the ax on my knee and it gave me a pretty good gash. They took me to the infirmary and taped it together.

"After dinner we played cards. Sometimes the Army put on dances. They brought truckloads of girls from Elmira or vicinity to camp. The dances were held in the recreation hall.

"On weekends we went by truck to Elmira. They had an amusement park that had a merry-go-round. Sometimes we'd hitchhike home. If somebody had someone visit them they'd give you a ride.

"The food was good. Sometimes they served what we called 'sh-- on a shingle' that was anything left over the night before and put on toast. We took turns doing KP. I didn't like it. The dirtiest job was cleaning out the grease traps. I never did it. I kept away from it. In the Army SOS was always creamed beef in a sauce on toast.

"We played a lot of baseball, volleyball, and horseshoes.

"Then the Army transferred me to Oxford near Norwich. At this camp I was a truck driver. I took guys to

Vernon Belge worked in the Van Etten CCC camp S-81 and then transferred to the Oxford camp and worked as a truck driver. Dee Baker

work and picked them up. I polished and cleaned the truck. It was boring.

"I also worked on the roads digging ditches and building firebreaks, and waterholes. The holes were pretty deep, 10-20 feet. They filled up with water and were there in case there was a fire.

"In the creeks we built dams and rip rap. If a stream turned and you had erosion, we put huge rocks and logs against the sides.

"Nobody stood over you with a whip. They had foremen and assistant leaders. The foreman was an older guy. The assistant was a CCC boy who had leadership skills.

"My last camp was at Schenectady Army Depot in Rotterdam. I was there for six months. I helped the mechanics fix trucks. There were regular barracks where we lived. It was interesting. One time we went to a camp to bring back trucks.

"On weekends we were in the city of Schenectady. There was a lot to do there.

"I always wanted to go out West but I was sent to NYS camps. I left the CCC because I was homesick and wanted to get a job. I came home and my brother-in-law who was in the trucking business got me a job.

"During my time in the CCC I became independent and gained self-confidence. It was a great adventure. I'd do it again in a heartbeat."

Robert L. Donahue
Van Etten & Margaretville

Paul Dodd of Baldwinsville sent me this e-mail: "I saw Dick Case's article about your interest in writing about the Civilian Conservation Corps camps in New York. The person who probably knows more about the CCC camps here than anyone else ever did is Bob Donahue who lives in Syracuse. Bob worked in a number of the camps and eventually became the Administrative Officer for the Soil Conservation Service in New York."

I contacted Bob by email and he sent me this story of his life:

"My parents were Robert B. Donahue and Lillian Card Donahue. I lived on Franklin St. in Horseheads, NY. My birth date was February 14, 1916. My father was a telegrapher with the Pennsylvania RR in Horseheads. My father died in 1923 of Type 1 diabetes. He was one of the first insulin patients. After a year, my mother remarried. I was an only child. I learned about the CCC from my uncle, who was a Chemung County employee. I had been living with him during my post grad year at Horseheads High where I learned typing and shorthand. It was during the Depression and there was no money to send me to college. That was in the days before all the assistance programs that we have today. The CCC seemed like a good answer.

"On July 2, 1934 I enrolled in the nearby camp at Van Etten, NY. The camp was numbered 59 but soon changed to S-81. The CCC Company was 1277. I was 18. The camp site was in Arnot Forest, a good-sized woodland of much virgin timber, owned by Cornell University. I worked in the woods with an axe on forest-stand improvement and truck trail construction. In December I understudied for the company clerk position because the incumbent was due for discharge. At that time the limit for CCC service was 18 months. That was changed later.

"On January 1, I was made company clerk. The pay was that of an assistant leader at $36 a month of which I was paid $11. $25 was sent home to my mother. I was company clerk until Sept. 30, 1936, and was promoted to Supply Sgt. at $45 per month on October 1. While in the clerk's job I worked under the supervision of several different company commanders, all reserve captains, some were WWI vets. I had a good work experience learning to adapt to their different personalities. They ranged from good supervisors to one or two who were difficult to work for.

"I was not homesick that I can remember. After a short time, we were allowed weekend passes, which I used to go to Elmira and Horseheads on Saturday evenings. I would return to camp on Sunday night.

"My first weeks at camp were not altogether pleasant as I was harassed by some of the men who called themselves 'veterans.' I was forced to do KP when it was not my turn and suffered other indignities. After a few weeks this disappeared and I came to like the life fairly well, especially after I was made company clerk and had my own little room just off the orderly room where I worked. I became very efficient at both typing and shorthand, which served me well later. As company clerk I did payrolls, purchase orders, and handled the mail, duty rosters, and similar work. I learned

Army-style correspondence.

"I was informed by the camp educational adviser that I could take a Civil Service exam for Junior Assistant to Technician. I took the exam and scored in the high nineties. Another education adviser, P.J. Coyle, told me about Civil Service exams for typist and stenographer. I borrowed the company typewriter and went to the Elmira Post Office and took the exam. I learned later that I scored 89 or thereabouts. Meanwhile, I took the Supply Sgt. Job and had it for six months.

"In the spring of 1937, I was notified that I was to report at the home camp. On April 1, 1937 as Jr. Asst. to Technician, grade SP-1 I received $1020 per year. I was assigned to work crews in the forest planting trees until May 30. I was informed by the camp superintendent, Abe George (he was preceded by William E. Petty in that job), that the camp would be closing and I would be transferred effective June 1, to the camp at Margaretville in Delaware County.

"In 1937 I was a junior technician in the Margaretville, CCC. I went up to the Depot in Schenectady to pick up trucks.

"I enjoyed the work in Margaretville. I was assigned to a crew building a telephone line to a nearby fire tower on a mountain. We were dynamiting holes in the underlying rock for telephone poles. They were small, not the conventional poles on main lines.

"Later I was assigned to supervise a crew of seven CCC boys pulling ribes (gooseberry) plants from surrounding white pine plantations, as they were a host for the white pine blister rust. I stayed on that work most of the summer.

"In October 1937, I received a letter from the Civil Service Commission asking if I was interested in a clerk-typist position at the U.S. Soil Conservation Service (SCS) tree nursery in Tully, NY, just south of Syracuse. I agreed, as it paid more and was more in line of what I wanted in my

Above - Bob Donahue (rear row 3rd from right) with the guys who worked with the blacksmith. One enrollee is holding an axe by the grinding stone wheel that was used to sharpen tools. Bob Donahue. Left - Bob Donahue at the VanEtten CCC camp near Ithaca where he was the company clerk. Bob Donahue

career. It paid $1,260 per year, $105 per month.

"I reported for duty in Tully on Oct. 27 and I was driving my new car, a 1937 Plymouth two-door standard model that cost $686. I had learned the scientific names and their spelling of most of the northeast hardwoods and conifers. This was of immense help to me in my job at the nursery.

"John Doerr, the camp forester at Margaretville, was a most wonderful young man. He was a 1935 grad of NYS College of Forestry at Syracuse University. He was a star member of the swimming team. After I knew him, he was married and had two children. During WWII, he joined the US Army Air Corps, became a pilot and Lieutenant. He was killed in a plane crash in the U.S. in 1942. I read it in the paper and was so sad. What a waste! It is another one of many reasons why we should never have gone to war.

"While in Tully, in 1938, I met my future wife, Denise Palin, who was a teacher there. We were married in 1940 and had two daughters. She died in 1995, after 55 years of marriage.

"In 1943, I was drafted in the Army. At that time I was a GS-7 administrative officer with the SCS. After one year in the US went to the Pacific. I was in the Solomon Islands, the Philippines, and Japan. I had served as company clerk, supply sgt., and finally as a battalion sgt. major (Master Sgt.) I owe much of this to my career and training in the CCC.

"After the war I continued working for the SCS. I retired as a GS13 State Administrative Officer in 1976. I was given credit for my CCC service toward my retirement, a total of 42 years."

Herbert C. Thorpe
Van Etten

I first met Herb Thorpe of Rome when he came to a CCC reunion at the Oneida Historical Society in Utica in June 2010. He was the only Afro-American who I interviewed over my five years of doing research on the CCC. Herb fascinated the audience when he said he had been a "Tuskegee Airman" during WWII. Here is what he told me in an e-mail interview:

"I grew up in New York City. I graduated from high school in 1940 and joined the CCC on October 10, 1940. My parents Denzil and Dorine had six children: Victor, me, Richard, Evelyn, Joseph, and Grace.

"There were stories in the newspaper about the CCC and that is where I got the idea of joining. When I signed up I was a little apprehensive but eager to try a new experience. The Army sent me to Camp S-81, Co. 3263-C in Van Etten, NY (15 miles south of Ithaca)."

Camp-S-81, Co. 3263-C was a segregated camp with all Afro-Americans. The letter C stood for Colored. There was still a lot of prejudice then so it was accepted by many to separate blacks from whites. There were nine C camps and three C-V (veterans) camps in New York State.

Herb added: As an African-American all of the camps in which I was stationed were segregated and populated by young men like myself who came primarily from places like New York City and Buffalo. Needless to say, all of our camp administrators were White men.

"The camp was a very interesting place. It taught me how to interact with new people and how to learn new skills. I met a lot of nice guys and one friend was S. Mervyn Charles who I continued to communicate with after we left the camp.

"Some of the work I did at the camp was: cleared brush, built weirs and culverts, took surveyor's notes, did general typing & record keeping, and office work. I did auto repair work and fought forest fires. I also became a barracks leader.

"The food was plentiful, but not especially tasty. After dinner I enjoyed reading, playing pool, cards, checkers, and chess.

"Sometimes I'd go for long walks through the woods and along country roads. I would visit old farms, swim in streams or ponds. There were camp sports teams

but I did not join them.

"On the weekends we went on trips to movies in nearby towns. Sometimes I went home. Once I almost got in trouble because I missed the ride back to camp after returning from a home visit. I had to walk all night in the dark so I could make roll call in the morning.

"In December 1941 I was sent to my second camp in Empeville, NY. It was 15 miles NW of Rome. I was there for a short time and left in January of February.

"My last camp was In Beltsville, Maryland. When it was going to close the Army sent everyone home. On July 27, 1942 I was discharged from the CCC.

"When I came home I did factory work for a few months. The war was going on and I decided to enlist in the US Army in 1942. I went to Signal Corps School in Troy, NY. Then I went on active duty and took basic training at Kearns Field, UT.

"In June 1943 I applied for Aviation Cadet School and was accepted to go to Tuskegee Army Air Field for cadet training in early 1944. I passed orientation tests at Keesler Field, Biloxi, MI. The Army then sent me to Tuskegee in February 1944. I completed Bombardier, Navigator, and Twin-Engine Pilot Training and was commissioned as 2nd Lieutenant. I did not serve overseas.

"After the war I returned home and attended college under the GI Bill. I graduated from New York University in 1953. I came to Rome in 1959 and worked as a radar research engineer with the Rome Air Development Center at Griffiss Air Force Base.

"On January 27, 1951 I married Jessie M. Shorts. We have two children, Jessica and R. Clifton.

"I visited my old CCC camp sites but could only find traces of the Van Etten and Empeyville camps.

"After my time in the CCC I realized that whatever progress I made had to be done on my own initiative. I worked my way from the lowest to the highest rank. I learned how to take

Herb Thorpe of Rome worked at three CCC camps and then went on to be a "Tuskegee Airman" during WWII. They were America's first Black military airmen. Herb Thorpe

and give orders, acquire new skills, such as driving cars and trucks, taking surveying notes, and map reading."

Herb retired in 1982, and later served as part-time counselor at Mohawk Valley Community College. He's a member and past president of the Rome Branch NAACP, and also is a member of Prince Hall Military Lodge No. 112, Afro-American Heritage Association, and Mohawk Valley Frontiers Club. Herb is also on the advisory board of the Oneida County Office for the Aging.

Art Semione
Speculator

I met Art Semione of Gloversville at the CCC Reunion at the Fulton County Historical Society in June 2010. The following month I interviewed him by phone and asked him about his life and the CCC.

"I joined the CCC early in February 1940 and went to the Speculator camp. I did not like leaving home because I had never been away and I was homesick. My family was really poor and by working in the CCC my dad got $22 each month for my work.

"I grew up in a large hard-working Italian family. My father Joseph did everything from landscaping and masonry to wallpapering and painting. My mother Angelina had ten children: Louis, Rose, Pasquale, Americus, Anne, Virginia, Gloria, Joseph, Elizabeth, and me. I was the fifth oldest.

"On December 26 1939, my 16th birthday, I quit school. I just didn't like it. I tried to get a job but couldn't find any. I always knew about the CCC. A neighbor, Will Dorman, was in the CCC. I can remember when I was 12 years old seeing Will wearing the CCC uniform from WWI. When I got in they had forest green uniforms. When I left the CCC, I had to hand in the dress uniform.

"One day in February 1940 my friends Ray Bohanna and Steve Hill decided to sign up for the CCC. We went down to the city hall in Gloversville and told the clerk we wanted to sign up. The clerk said we had to be 17. I lied to her and said I was 17. She never asked for identification. Then she said we should come back in a few days. We did and a pickup truck took us to the Speculator camp.

"At camp I did a variety of jobs. My first job I was assigned to a crew doing miscellaneous work. We shoveled snow from the two state parks on Piseco Lake. We were getting them ready for the spring season. There were 15-20 guys in a row shoveling snow. We didn't have a plow.

"Then I got to work with foreman Bell's crew. He was a carpenter and he knew his stuff. He also knew masonry. The senior leader was Sleezer who was also an excellent carpenter. We went to Wells campsite. Our crew finished the ranger cabin, the bridge across the river, and did some stonework on the approaches to the bridge.

"There was a lot of camaraderie even though there were quite a few rough guys from the cities. We always stuck together.

"We went on strike because we didn't like our lunches. They just gave us a piece of fruit and P & J sandwich. On the morning of the strike the sergeant blew the whistle but nobody came out to work. He called the captain and he went into the barracks and asked what the problem was. We told him our complaints and he listened. After that the food got better.

"Each crew had a truck driver. One small guy made the coffee for our morning break. We rounded up dry wood for a fire. He had a pail that he brewed the coffee in. We drank coffee from cans that we got from the kitchen. We had it for lunch, too. That's what we had for lunch. After work we came back to camp each day.

"We had a side camp when we worked at the Caroga State Park. There were six to eight guys in a tent and we had a mess tent for cooking. Our jobs were cleaning up the site, repairing the roads, and building a bathhouse. I also remember putting up the flagpole and building the gatehouse.

"Then our crew worked at Moffitt Beach State Park that was near our camp. We did a lot of raking and cleaning up the campsite.

"There were guys always busting on the new guys. They had fun getting me to wait on the top of the barracks roof and wait for a snipe to come by. Then guys came up and said get down. It's only a joke.

"Another joke they played on rookies was to say: 'Go down to the garage and ask someone to give you a rock stretcher.

"The idea was to get a stretcher to carry big rocks. That guy was in on the joke and they'd send you to another place, and then another. "I did get sick and stayed a few days in the infirmary. If someone got seriously ill they called the doctor from Speculator. One guy name Eddie Bush took care of the infirmary and stayed there all the time.

"One time I got in a truck accident. The truck flipped over and hit a bridge. One guy was stuck under the truck. The other guys lifted the truck up and got him out.

He was taken to the hospital for just a few days.

"In the evenings we went to the rec hall and played ping pong and shot pool. The guys put on shows such as plays or music. We weren't welcome in town unless we behaved. As long as we were decent they welcomed us. Some of the town the girls came over to our camp on weekends for dances.

"I just remember going to Bleeker Stadium in Albany for competition with other CCC camps. I liked to pitch hose shoes. Another boy and I practiced at camp and then we went to Albany and represented our camp. There were others who competed in a tug of war, baseball, etc. We lost in our event. We were against some tough competition but it was fun.

"On the weekends some guys went to Gloversville on an Army truck and went to the movies. Just about every weekend I came home. I either hitchhiked or a friend had a car and I came home with him. One time while hitchhiking I couldn't get a ride and had to walk a good seven or eight miles till I got a ride. If I couldn't get a ride home I'd call my dad to bring me home. But then I became a nuisance and he didn't like that.

"In September I didn't sign up for another six months. I felt good that I made it through for a half a year. They induced me to try and stay and become a leader but I wanted to go home.

"When I came home my first job was working in a leather factory. Later my brother-in-law was in the union and he got me a union card. I got a permanent job in Johnstown.

"The CCC was a good experience. I learned to take people the way they are and not everyone is going to be what you expect. It also prepared me for Army life where I had to have discipline and take orders. I also made sergeant quickly because of my experience.

"I was drafted into the Army on my nineteenth birthday in 1942. They placed me in antiaircraft artillery and I fought in Europe.

"After the war I went back to my old factory job. Then a girl told me to go to school and get an education. I took her advice and went to Albany Business College and got a degree in accounting. I then worked for the state taxation department.

"In 1950 I married Anne Grieco and we had a son, Joseph."

Left to Right - John Musconell (Gloversville), Marcus Kruger (Tribes Hill), and Art Semione (Gloversville) met at the Fulton County Historical Society Museum in Gloversville for a CCC Reunion in June 2010. Podskoch Collection

333

NOTES

Chapter 1 - History

1 Diane Galusha, "Another Day Another Dollar The Civilian Conservation Corps in the Catskills, Black Dome Press Corp., Hensonville, NY, 2009, 7.
2 Ibid.
3 Ibid., 7.
4 Ibid., 8-9.
5 http://www.nps.gov/archive/elro/glossary/roosevelt-franklin.htm.
6 Edgar Nixon, "Franklin D. Roosevelt and Conservation, 1911-1945," Franklin D. Roosevelt Library; 1957, 3-4.
7 Galusha, 15.
8 http://www.nps.gov/archive/elro/glossary/great-depression.htm
9 Arthur M. Schlesinger, Jr., The Age of Roosevelt, III, The Politics of Upheaval, Boston: Houghton Mifflin Company, 1960, 251.
10 George P. Rawick, "The New Deal and Youth: The Civilian Conservation Corps, the National Youth Administration, the American Youth Congress," unpublished Ph.D. dissertation, University of Wisconsin, 1957, 18-29.
11 "Message to Congress on Unemployment Relief. March 21," The Presidential Papers of Franklin D. Roosevelt, 1933.
12 Salmond, 14.
13 Cohen, 6-7.
14 Ibid., 2.
15 NYS Conservation Department Annual Report, 1934, 141
16 Mark Neuzil, "Roosevelt's Tree Army," The History Channel Magazine, November/December 2010, 57.
17 Salmond, 90-91.
18 Ibid., 33.
19 NYS Conservation Department Annual Report, 1934, 141.
20 Salmond, 34.
21 Franklin Folsom, Impatient Armies of the Poor, Niwot, Colorado: University Press of Colorado, 1991, 310-322.
22 Galusha, 41.
23 NYS Conservation Department, Annual Report. 1936, 140.
24 NYS Conservation Department Annual Report, 1942, 108.
25 Harper, 104, Salmond, 111.
26 NYS Conservation Department Annual Report, 1935, 170-171.
27 Galusha, 64.
28 "Youths, 17 May Enter the CCC," Plattsburgh Daily Press, September 27, 1935.
29 Salmond, 58-59.
30 Charles Price Harper, The Administration of the Civilian Conservation Corps, Clarksburg Publishing Co., Clarksburg, W. Va., 1939, 39-41.
31 Salmond, 59-61.
32 NYS Conservation Department Annual Report, 1936, 140.
33 Salmond, 68.
34 NYS Conservation Department Annual Report, 1937, 19, 134.
35 Ibid., 133.
36 NYS Conservation Department Annual Report, 1938, 126-127.
37 Salmond, 137-138.
38 Ibid., 176
39 NYS Conservation Department Annual Report, 1939, 118.
40 Salmond, 200.
41 Ibid., 200.
42 NYS Conservation Department Annual Report, 1941, 113.
43 Salmond, 208-210.
44 Ibid., 211-212.
45 Franklin D. Roosevelt, letter to James McEntee, March 25, 1942.
46 NYS Conservation Department Annual Report, 1942, 109.
47 (http://www.ccclegacy.org/CCC_brief_history.htm)
48 NYS Conservation Department Annual Report, 1942, 109.
49 http://www.thesca.org/.
50 Galusha, 181.
51 http://www.americorps.gov/about/ac/index.asp.

Chapter 2 - Camp Organization

1 Charles Price Harper, The Administration of the Civilian Conservation Corps, Clarksburg Publishing Co., Clarksburg, WV, 1939, 39-41.
2 Schenectady District Civilian Conservation Corps Area Yearbook, 1937, 23.
3 "Re-District Plans Made for the CCC," Plattsburgh Daily Press, June 5, 1936.
4 NYS Conservation Department Annual Report, 1935, 170.
5 Salmond, 135-136.
6 Stan Cohen, The Tree Army, A Pictorial History of the Civilian Conservation Corps 1933-1942. Missoula MT: Pictorial Histories Publishing Co., 1980, 46.

Chapter 3 - Enrollee's Life in Camp

1 "The Conservation Corps, What It Is and What It Does, " Civilian Conservation Corps Office of Director, Washington, D. C., June, 1939, 10.
2 Stan Cohen, The Tree Army, A Pictorial History of the Civilian Conservation Corps 1933-1942, Missoula, MT: Pictorial Histories Publishing Co., 1980, 47.
3 "The Conservation Corps, What It Is. . . , 8.
4 Salmond, 51.
5 Ibid., 53.
6 NYS Conservation Department Annual Report, 1935, 170.

Chapter 4 - Work Projects

1 Galusha, 102.
2 Van Valkenburgh, Adirondack Forest Preserve, A Narrative of the Evolution of the Adirondack Forest Preserve of New York, Blue Mountain Lake: The Adirondack Museum, 1979, 172.
3 Ibid., 172-173.
4 NYS Conservation Department Annual Report, 1935, 173.
5 Ibid., 171-72.
6 Harper, 65.
7 NYS Conservation Department Annual Report, 1934, 143-144.
8 Ibid., 145.

Chapter 5 - Arietta

1 Schenectady District Civilian Conservation Corps Area Yearbook, 1937, 79.
2 (Ibid.)
3 (Ibid.)
4 Audrey Preston, Sesquicentennial of the Town of Arietta, (n. p. , 1986), 86.
5 Ibid.
6 Ibid.
7 Ibid.
8 Schenectady District CCC, 79.

Chapter 6 - Benson Mines and Wanakena
1 Schenectady District Civilian Conservation Corps Area Yearbook, 1937, 33.
2 Ibid.
3 Ibid.
4 Schenectady District CCC, 33.
5 NYS Conservation Department Annual Report, 1933, 115.
6 Commercial Advertiser, December 26, 1933.
7 Schenectady District CCC, 33.
8 NYS Conservation Department Annual Report, 1935, 136.
9 NYS Conservation Department Annual Report, 1936, 147.
10 Ibid.
11 Ibid.
12 NYS Conservation Department Annual Report, 1938, 132.
13 Conservation Report, 1936. 147.
14 Ibid.
15 untitled, Lowville Journal Republican, undated.
16 NYS Conservation Department Annual Report, 1937, 135.
17 Ibid., 137.
18 untitled, Gouverneur Press, 1963.

Chapter 7 - Bolton Landing, Alma Farm, & Burgess Farm
1 NYS Conservation Department Annual Report, 1936, 140.
2 Schenectady District Civilian Conservation Corps Area Yearbook, 1937, 79.
3 Ibid.,61.
4 Ibid.
5 NYS Conservation Department Annual Report, 1938, 128.
6 NYS Conservation Department Annual Report, 1939, 128-129.
7 NYS Conservation Department Annual Report, 1940, 101.
8 NYS Conservation Department Annual Report, 1933, 115.
9 Ibid., 116.
10 Conservation Report, 1940, 108.
11 Conservation Report, 1933, 40.
12 Conservation Report, 1936, 141.
13 Conservation Report, 1937, 62.
14 Ibid., 135.
15 Conservation Report, 1938, 128.
16 Conservation Report, 1940, 119.
17 NYS Conservation Department Annual Report, 1941, 115.
18 Conservation Report, 1940, 121.
19 "CCC Workers Make New Ski Trails," Ticonderoga Sentinel, January 2, 1936.
20 Schenectady District CCC, 57.
21 Conservation Report, 1940, 120
22 Civilian Conservation Corps Schenectady District Yearbook 1937, 57.
23 untitled, The Essex County Republican, August 24, 1934.
24. Schenectady District CCC, 57.
25 Ibid.

Chapter 8 - Boonville
1 NYS Conservation Department Annual Report, 1941, 106.
2 NYS Conservation Department Annual Report, 1939, 88.
3 (Ibid., 118)
4 NYS Conservation Department Annual Report, 1940, 112.
5 Conservation Report 1941, 129.
6 Ibid., 129.
7 Ibid., 129.
8 Conservation Report 1940, 124.

9 Conservation Report 1941, 120.
10 n. t., Citizen(Cato New York), November 14, 1940.
11 Conservation Report 1940, 120.
12 "A Stern but Humble Captor, During World War II, Prisoners Found a Peaceful Existence in NY," Tracy Valentine, Watertown Daily Times, September 23, 2001.

Chapter 9 - Brasher Falls
1 "Large CCC Camp Is Established Near Brasher," May 15, 1934, St. Lawrence County Historical Association Archives.
2 "Empire State Notes Northern N. Y. News," Essex County Republican, Nov. 30, 1934.
3 Schenectady District Civilian Conservation Corps Area Yearbook, 1937, 57.
4 The North Woodsman, March 1938.
5 NYS Conservation Department Annual Report, 1937, 139.
6 Ibid.,136.
7 "Brasher Camp Changes Force," Massena Observer, April 4, 1937.
8 "Lions Club Guest of CCC Camp," Potsdam Courier Freeman, January 26, 1938.
9 "CCC Engineers To Build Pond to Hold Trout" Ogdensburg Journal August 2, 1937.
10 NYS Conservation Department Annual Report, 1940, 66-67.
11 Ibid., 112.
12 NYS Conservation Department Annual Report, 1941, 106.
13 Ibid., 147.
14 The Sixty-Niner, July 31, 1935.
15 The Sixty-Niner, September 7, 1935.
16 The Sixty-Niner, March 21, 1936.
17 The North Woodsman, November, 1938.
18 The North Woodsman, November, 1938.
19 Schenectady District CCC, 57.
20 "Dismantling of CCC Camp at Brasher Falls to Start Soon," Courier and Freeman, January, 1945.
21 North Woodsman, June. 1936.

Chapter 10 - Brushton
1 Schenectady District Civilian Conservation Corps Area Yearbook, 1937, 43.
2 Ibid.
3 Ibid.
4 "Fort to Put Fast Action Quint Into Court Play, " Fort Covington Sun, 1938.
5 Schenectady District CCC, 43.
6 Ibid.
7 Schenectady District Civilian Conservation Corps Area Yearbook, 1937, 41.
8 Ibid.
9 Ibid.
10 Ibid.
11 NYS Conservation Department Annual Report, 1937, 141.
12 NYS Conservation Department Annual Report, 1938, 135.
13 NYS Conservation Department Annual Report, 1939, 107, 122.
14 NYS Conservation Department Annual Report, 1940, 109, 122.
15 NYS Conservation Department Annual Report, 1941, 103, 106.
16 Conservation Report 1940, 119.
17 "CCC Sub-District Baseball Championship to Be Played at Tupper Lake," Tupper Lake Free Press, May 20, 1937.
18 Conservation Report 1941, 114.
19 "Work Commenced on a New Church in North Bangor Par-

ish, Chateaugay Record, July 21, 1944.

Chapter 11 - Canton
1 "C. C. C. Camp Site to Be in Pierrepont," St. Lawrence Plaindealer, May 7, 1935.
2 "Work Starts on CCC Camp Pierrepont," St. Lawrence Plaindealer, June 25, 1935.
3 Schenectady District Civilian Conservation Corps Area Yearbook, 1937, 49.
4 Ibid.
5 "Write-Up on the Pierrepont C. C. C.," St. Lawrence Plaindealer, undated.
6 Schenectady District CCC, 49.
7 "Write-Up on the Pierrepont."
8 Schenectady District CCC, 49.
9 "Says Canton Can Help C. C. C. Camp," St. Lawrence Plaindealer, August 27, 1935.
10 "Fourth CCC Anniversary," Herald Recorder, April 2, 1937.
11 NYS Conservation Department Annual Report, 1936, 113.
12 Schenectady District CCC, 49.
13 "Write-Up on the Pierrepont."
14 Schenectady District CCC, 49.
15 Schenectady District Civilian Conservation Corps Area Yearbook, 1937, 47.
16 Ibid.
17 Ibid.
18 "Pierrepont C. C. C. Camp to Be Closed," St. Lawrence Plaindealer, March 24, 1936.
19 "Fourth CCC Anniversary."
20 NYS Conservation Department Annual Report, 1937, 201.
21 DEC Potsdam Archives.
22 "Co. K Infantrymen to Set Up Tent City," Norwood News, May 29, 1940.
23 NYS Conservation Department Annual Report, 1941, 114.
24 Conservation Report 1941, 114.
25 Ibid.

Chapter 12 - Eighth Lake
1 NYS Conservation Department Annual Report, 1941, 114.
2 NYS Conservation Department Annual Report, 1933, 40-41.
3 Conservation Report 1933, 40.
4 Conservation Report 1941, 114.
5 Untitled, Lowville Journal Republican, June 1, 1939.

Chapter 13 - Fish Creek
1 Andy Flynn, "Adirondack Attic," Adirondack Daily Enterprise, July 29, 2005.
2 NYS Conservation Department Annual Report, 1933, 40.
3 "Sugarbush Native Died at Saranac Lake," Plattsburgh Daily Press, July 30, 1941.
4 "CCC Boys Will Take Course in Auto Mechanics," Tupper Lake Free Press, September 20, 1934.
5 "H. K. DeWitt Speaker on CCC Vocational Program at Camp 8," Tupper Lake Free Press, November 29, 1934.
6 "Thanksgiving No Time to Go on a Diet at CCC Camp 8 and 15 Menue Show," Tupper Lake Free Press, November 29, 1934.
7 "Basketball and Bowling Teams at CCC Camp 8 Ready to Take on All Comers—Line-Up Strong," Tupper Lake Free Press, November 29, 1934.
8 "CCC Camp S-56 Will Be Moved to Camden, N. Y.," Tupper Lake

Free Press, October 17, 1935.
9 Tupper Lake Free Press, December 26, 1935.
10 Tupper Lake Free Press, January 16, 1936.

Chapter 14 - Fort Ann
1 Schenectady District Civilian Conservation Corps Area Yearbook, 1937, 63.
2 Ibid.
3 NYS Conservation Department Annual Report, 1936, 101.
4 Schenectady District CCC, 63.
5 Ibid.
6 Conservation Report 1937, 124.
7 Schenectady District CCC, 63.

Chapter 15 - Goldsmith
1 Amelia S. Baumann, "Goldsmith, Mill Town Long Ago," Volume 7, Franklin County Historical NS Review, 1970, 47-49.
2 Teresa R. Eshelman, "Town of Franklin 1836-1987, They Told Me so... Goldsmith's Continued," August 1, 1987.
3 Schenectady District Civilian Conservation Corps Area Yearbook, 1937, 37.
4 Ibid.
5 NYS Conservation Department Annual Report, 1933, 92.
6 "Forester Transferred to Plattsburgh Post," Au Sable Forks Record-Post, September 28, 1933.
7 "More Than a Million Trees Planted by Local Foresters," Adirondack Daily Enterprise, October 5, 1933.
8 Schenectady District CCC, 37.

Chapter 16 - Harrisville
1 "County CCC Camp Is Established," Black River Democrat, May 31, 1934).
2 Ibid.
3 Ibid.
4 Ibid.
5 NYS Conservation Department Annual Report, 1936, 147.
6 NYS Conservation Department Annual Report, 1939, 118.
7 Ibid. 89.
8 Conservation Report, 1939, 119.
9 Ibid.,106.
10 Ibid., 124.
11 Ibid., 119
12 NYS Conservation Department Annual Report, 1940, 132.
13 Ibid., 106.

Chapter 17 - Indian Lake
1 Schenectady District Civilian Conservation Corps Area Yearbook, 1937, 55.
2 Ibid.
3 NYS Conservation Department Annual Report, 1934, 43.
4 Ibid., 145.
5 NYS Conservation Department Annual Report, 1937, 135.
6 NYS Conservation Department Annual Report, 1936, 142.
7 Schenectady District CCC, 55.
8 Ibid.
9 NYS Conservation Department Annual Report, 1941, 114.
10 Ibid.
11 NYS Conservation Department Annual Report, 1940, 119.
12 Conservation Report 1941, 114.
13 Ibid.,117.

Chapter 18 - Lake Placid
1 (NYS Conservation Department Annual Report, 1937, 134.
2 "CCC Recruits Go to Barnum Pond," Post Standard, April, 1934.
3 "C. C. C.'s Improve 90 Acres by Pruning Trees," undated article in Lake Placid Library Archives.
4 Schenectady District Civilian Conservation Corps Area Yearbook, 1937, 37.
5 untitled and undated newspaper article in Lake Placid Library Archives.
6 Schenectady District CCC, 37.
7 "Telephone on Whiteface Is Nearly Ready," Au Sable Record Post, September 27, 1934.
8 Ibid.
9 "To Build Lake at Wilmington Notch," Essex County Republican, April 5, 1935.
10 "Local CCC Company Fights Fire This Week," Lake Placid News, August 31, 1934.
11 "Turkey for the Boys in Local CCC Camp," Lake Placid News, November 23, 1934.
12 Schenectady District CCC, 37.
13 "CCC Workers Make New Ski Trails," Ticonderoga Sentinel, January 2, 1936.
14 "Warn Hunter to Watch for CCC Groups in Woods," Lake Placid News, October 18, 1935.
15 NYS Conservation Department Annual Report, 1936, 141-142.
16 Schenectady District CCC, 37.
17 "Brown Memorial to Be Unveiled at North Elba," Ausable Forks Record-Post, May 9, 1935.
18 Schenectady District CCC, 37.
19 NYS Conservation Department Annual Report, 1937, 43.
20 "Katharin Dewey Wins All Honors in Bob Sled Races," Lake Placid News, January 17, 1936
21 "Kalinsack and Sterns Novice Winners," Lake Placid News, February 23, 1936.
22 Schenectady District Civilian Conservation Corps Area Yearbook, 1937, 35.
23 "To Stage Ad'k Golden Gloves Championship," Lake Placid News, June 22, 1934.
24 "50 Years of Conservation in New York State, Official Program," Minerva Historical Society Achieves.
25 Schenectady District CCC, 37.
26 Conservation Report 1937, 137.
27 Ibid., 139.
28 "Just Fishing by Jorge," Lake Placid News, June 11, 1937.
29 NYS Conservation Department Annual Report, 1940, 117.
30 Plattsburgh Daily Press, Oct. 12, 1940.
31 Conservation Report 1940, 120.
32 NYS Conservation Department Annual Report, 1941, 114.
33 Conservation Report 1940, 124.
34 NYS Conservation Department Annual Report, 1942, 108.

Chapter 19 - Minerva
1 NYS Conservation Department Annual Report, 1936, 140.
2 Ibid., 156-157.
3 Ibid., 140.

Chapter 20 - Newcomb
1 NYS Conservation Department Annual Report, 1941, 114.
2 Schenectady District Civilian Conservation Corps Area Yearbook,

1937, 45.
3 Ibid.
4 Raymond D. Masters, A Social History of the Huntington Wildlife Forest, (Utica: North Country Books, 1993), 68.
5 Schenectady District CCC, 45.
6 Ibid.
7 Ibid.
8 n. t., The Essex County Republican, October 11, 1935.
9 Conservation Report 1937, 45.
10 Ibid., 137.
11 NYS Conservation Department Annual Report, 1938, 130.
12 NYS Conservation Department Annual Report, 1940, 124.
13 NYS Conservation Department Annual Report, 1941, 1117.
14 Masters, 75-76.

Chapter 21 - Paul Smiths
1 Schenectady District Civilian Conservation Corps Area Yearbook, 1937, 31.
2 "State Officer Views Camps in Mountains," Syracuse Post Standard, June 10, 1933.
3 Schenectady District CCC, 31.
4 "State Officer Views Camps in Mountains," Syracuse Post Standard, June 10, 1933.
5 "Pharmacist, Aviator Among Conservation Corps for the Summer," Plattsburgh Daily Press, July 14, 1933.
6 "Pharmacist, Aviator Among Conservation Corps for the Summer," Plattsburgh Daily Press, July 14, 1933.
7 "Forest Camps in Double Task," New York Sun, July 11, 1933.
8 "Six Fires Break During Day," Adirondack Enterprise, June 10, 1933.
9 "Form Committee to Arrange C.C.C. Entertainment," Lake Placid News, July 28, 1933.
10 "C. C. C. Men Get Experience As Adirondack Lumberjacks," Syracuse Post Standard, August 13, 1933.
11 "More than Million Trees Are Planted by Local Foresters," Adirondack Daily Enterprise, October 5, 1933.
12 "C. C. C. Director Praises Work," Syracuse Post Standard, October 16, 1933.
13 "Accomplishments and Record of Barnum Pond CCC Camp S-60," Tupper Lake Free Press, April 2, 1936.
14 "Early Snow Hits Forest Camp", Syracuse Post Standard, October 27, 1933.
15 "State Converts Lake Resort Into Camp Site for Tourists," Syracuse Herald, April 28, 1934.
16 "C. C. C. Camp 63 Have Two Sub Stations," unidentified newspaper, April 27, 1934.
17 Schenectady District CCC, 31.
18 "Forest Fire Rages in Bay Pond Tract," Syracuse Post Standard, May 30, 1934.
19 "Thomas Showers, CCC Worker, Found Guilty of Murder, 2nd Degree," Ticonderoga Sentinel, November 29, 1934.
20 "Man Injured at CCC Camp Dies Friday," Lake Placid News, November 30, 1934.
21 NYS Conservation Department Annual Report, 1934, 153.
22 "Governor's Annual CCC Award Will be Made here in February to Camps 60 and 84 by Commissioner Osborne," Tupper Lake Free Press, January 17, 1935.
23 "8 Vocational Classes Set For CCC Camps," Au Sable Forks Record Post, January 3, 1935.
24 Schenectady District CCC, 31.
25 "Origin and Progress of New York's New Stream Improvement

Program," Lake Placid News, March 22, 1935."
26 "Accomplishments and Record of Barnum Pond CCC Camp S-60," Tupper Lake Free Press, April 2, 1936.
27 "Guide House at Paul Smith's is Burned," Lake Placid News, May 24, 1935.
28 "Accomplishments and Record of Barnum Pond CCC Camp S-60," Tupper Lake Free Press, April 2, 1936.
29 "Accomplishments and Record of Barnum Pond CCC Camp S-60," Tupper Lake Free Press, April 2, 1936.
30 "Accomplishments and Record of Barnum Pond CCC Camp S-60," Tupper Lake Free Press, April 2, 1936.
31 NYS Conservation Department Annual Report, 1936, 140.
32 Ibid., 147.
33 "Accomplishments and Record of Barnum Pond CCC Camp S-60," Tupper Lake Free Press, April 2, 1936.
34 "Find Missing Man in Woods Near Tupper," Plattsburg Daily Press, May 1, 1936.
35 "Women Drowned at Saranac Lake," Plattsburgh Daily Press, September 10, 1936.
36 NYS Conservation Department Annual Report, 1937, 182.
37 Ibid., 136.
38 Conservation Corps Deserves Another Look," Adirondack Daily Enterprise, September 20, 1983.
39 Conservation Report 1937. 139.
40 Schenectady District CCC, 31.
41 Ibid.
42 "Crowds Expected at Camp Sites," Au Sable Forks Record-Post, June 2, 1938.
43 NYS Conservation Department Annual Report, 1938, 136.
44 "Shock Kills Sergeant at CCC Camp," Chateaugay Record, July 29, 1938.
45 NYS Conservation Department Annual Report, 1939, 118-119.
46 Ibid., 122.
47 NYS Conservation Department Annual Report, 1940, 93 & 121.
48 Ibid., 124.
49 Ibid., 119.
50 Ibid.,117.
51 NYS Conservation Department Annual Report, 1941, 84-85.
52 Ibid., 115.
53 "Historical Society Meets," Malone Telegram, August 30, 1995.

Chapter 22 - Plattsburgh
1 Au Sable Forks Record-Post, January 10, 1935.
2 The Plattsburgh Daily Press November 13, 1937.
3 Schenectady District Civilian Conservation Corps Area Yearbook, 1937, 51.
4 Plattsburgh Daily Press, February 23, 1936.
5 Plattsburgh Daily Press, July 21, 1936.
6 The Ausable Forks Record-Post, September 28, 1933.
7 Schenectady District CCC, 51.
8 NYS Conservation Department Annual Report, 1937, 135.
9 NYS Conservation Department Annual Report, 1938, 114.
10 The Fore Ranker, December 1939, 5.
11 NYS Conservation Department Annual Report, 1935, 176.
12 Ibid., 134-135.
13 The Plattsburgh Daily Press, March 31, 1938.
14 The Ausable Forks Record-Post, March 23, 1939.
15 Schenectady District CCC, 51.
16 Ibid.
17 Plattsburgh Daily Press November 13, 1937.

18 Essex County Republican September 30, 1938.
19 NYS Conservation Department Annual Report, 1940, 117.
20 The Fore Ranker, June, 1940, 2.
21 Ibid. 10.
22 Ibid. 2.
23 The Plattsburgh Daily Press, October 10, 1940.
24 The Plattsburgh Daily Press, October 19, 1940.
25 Ibid., 117.
26 The Plattsburgh Daily Express, April 4, 1941.
27 The Plattsburgh Daily Express June 18, 1941.
28 NYS Conservation Department Annual Report, 1941, 103, 105.
29 The Plattsburgh Daily Press, October 18, 1941.
30 NYS Conservation Department Annual Report, 1942, 108.
31 The Plattsburgh Daily Press, June 30, 1945.
32 The Plattsburgh Daily Press, November 14, 1946.
33 The Plattsburgh Daily Press, May 18, 1935.
34 The Plattsburgh Daily Press, November 2, 1935.
35 The Plattsburgh Daily Press, December 23, 1935.
36 The Plattsburgh Daily Press, July 7, 1937.
37 The Plattsburgh Daily Press, January 11, 1936.
38 The Plattsburgh Daily Press, July 22, 1937.
39 The Plattsburgh Daily Press, September 29, 1937.

Chapter 23 - Port Henry
1 NYS Conservation Department Annual Report, 1934, 153.
2 Ibid., 39.

Chapter 25 - Speculator
1 Don Williams, "Bring Back the Civilian Conservation Corps," Adirondack Daily Enterprise, July 30, 1994.
2 Moffitt Beach - Camping in New York State - Department of Environmental Conservation facilities, http://www.dec.ny.gov/outdoor/24483.html.
3 NYS Conservation Department Annual Report, 1933, 41.
4 Louis C. Curth, The Forest Rangers, (Albany: N. Y. S. Department of Environmental Conservation, 1987), 182.
5 Ted Aber, & Stella King, The History of Hamilton County, (Great Wilderness Books, Lake Pleasant, NY, 1965), 737.
6 NYS Conservation Department Annual Report, 1934. 43.
7 Schenectady District Civilian Conservation Corps Area Yearbook, 1937, 39.
8 NYS Conservation Department Annual Report, 1933, 40.
9 NYS Conservation Department Annual Report, 1936, 142.
10 Schenectady District CCC, 39.
11 Ibid., 38.
12 Conservation Report 1937, 133.
13 Ibid., 135.
14 Ibid., 141.
15 NYS Conservation Department Annual Report, 1938, 132.
16 NYS Conservation Department Annual Report, 1939, 119.
17 NYS Conservation Department Annual Report, 1940, 122.
18 Ibid., 124.
19 NYS Conservation Department Annual Report, 1941, 115.
20 Williams, "Bring Back the Civilian Conservation Corps."
21 "Probe Into Drowning of CCC Men in Round Pond Fails to Explain Why Boat Capsized," The Morning Herald, July 24, 1934.

Chapter 26 - Tahawus
1 NYS Conservation Department Annual Report, 1936, 140.
2 NYS Conservation Department Annual Report, 1939, 92.

Chapter 27 - Thendara
1 NYS Conservation Department Annual Report, 1941, 114.
2 "Thendara CCC Athletes Win Field Honors," Observer Dispatch, September 23, 1935.
3 NYS Conservation Department Annual Report, 1941, 114.
4 "Mohawk Man Knocked Unconscious at CCC Camp by Lightning," Observer Dispatch, April 3, 1936.

Chapter 28 - Tupper Lake
1 NYS Conservation Department Annual Report, 1936, 140.
2 Marty Podskoch, Adirondack Stories II, (Colchester, CT: Podskoch Press, 2009), 81.
3 William Donaldson, A History of the Adirondacks: Vol. II, (Fleischmanns, NY: Purple Mountain Press, 1996), 202-203.
4 Ibid. 204-205.
5 Bill Frenette, "Transitions No. 74," Tupper Lake Free Press, June 20, 2001.
6 NYS Conservation Department Annual Report, 1933, 92.
7 "No Tree Planting by C.C.C. in Mountains," Lake Placid Library Archives, June 9, 1933.
8 "To Construct Highway into Cold River," Essex County Republican, July 28, 1933.
9 "Build Road for Fire Trucks near Ampersand," Tupper Lake Free Press, July 25. 1933.
10 "More Than Million Trees Are Planted by Local Foresters," Adirondack Daily Enterprise, October 5, 1933.
11 "Racket Upper Reaches Cleared of Debris," Essex County Republican, October 13, 1933.
12 "Workers Build Camp Replacing Tents," Tupper Lake Free Press, October 12, 1933.
13 "New Uniforms Are to Be Given C. C. C. Men," Watertown Daily Times, September 28, 1933.
14 "Workers Build Camp Replacing Tents," Tupper Lake Free Press, October 12, 1933.
15 "Headquarters of C. C. C. at Tupper Lake Are Moved," Au Sable Forks Record-Post, November 2, 1933.
16 "Local CCC Company Fight Fire This Week," Lake Placid News, August 31, 1934.
17 Crew of 25 CCC's from Camp 15 Already at Work Opening the New Trail up Mount Morris," Tupper Lake Free Press, July 26, 1934.
18 Ibid.
19 "Abandon Work on Mt. Morris until Spring," Tupper Lake Free Press, December 24, 1934.
20 "CCC Boys Will Take Course in Auto Mechanics," Tupper Lake Free Press, September 20, 1934.
21 "W. O. T. M. Notes," Tupper Lake Free Press, November 1, 1934.
22 "A Definite Goal and Hard Work Essential, Speaker Tells CCC's," Tupper Lake Free Press, November 29, 1934.
23 "Federal Forestry Expert Lauds Work of CCC's in Flood Area at Lecture in Cross Clearing Camp Tuesday," Tupper Lake Free Press, July 25, 1935.
24 "Thanksgiving No Time to Go on a Diet at CCC Camps, Camp 8 and 15 Menus Show," Tupper Lake Free Press, November 29, 1934.
25 "More Vaudeville Coming to CCC Camp," Lake Placid News, March 22, 1935.
26 "Flashbacks April 18-25, 1935," Tupper Lake Press, April 23, 1980.
27 "Cross Clearing Nine Wins at Fish Creek," Tupper Lake Press, July 4, 1935.
28 "78 Men To Be Trained At Camp S-63," Tupper Lake Free Press, July 4, 1935.
29 "Flash Backs April 18-25, 1935," Tupper Lake Press, April 23, 1980.
30 "CCC Camp Near Tupper Lake to Be Abandoned," Tupper Lake Press, December 26, 1935.
31 "Shifting CCC Activities Are Observed Here," Tupper Lake Press, January 16, 1936.
32 "CCC Camp Closes," Lake Placid News, January 10, 1936.

BIBLIOGRAPHY

Books
Boas, Norman Francis and Meyer, Barbara Linton. Alma Farm An Adirondack Meeting Place, Mystic, CT: Boas & Myers Publishers, 1999.

Cohen, Stan. The Tree Army, A Pictorial History of the Civilian Conservation Corps 1933-1942. Missoula MT: Pictorial Histories Publishing Co., 1980.

Folsom, Franklin. Impatient Armies of the Poor, Niwot, Colorado: University Press of Colorado, 1991.

Galusha, Diane. Another Day Another Dollar The Civilian Conservation Corps in the Catskills, Black Dome Press Corp., Hensonville, NY, 2009.

Harper, Charles Price. The Administration of the Civilian Conservation Corps, Clarksburg Publishing Co., Clarksburg, WV, 1939.

Hochschild Harold K., Township 34: A History with Digressions of an Adirondack Township in Hamilton County in the State of New York,
Preston, Audrey. Sesquicentennial of the Town of Arietta. n. p., 1986.

Nixon, Edgar. "Franklin D. Roosevelt and Conservation, 1911-1945," Franklin D. Roosevelt Library; 1957.

Official Annual, Schenectady District Civilian Conservation Corps, Second Corps Area. Schenectady, NY: CCC District Headquarters, 1937.

Podskoch, Marty. Adirondack Stories: Historical Sketches, Colchester, CT: Podskoch Press, 2007.

Salmond, John. The Civilian Conservation Corps, 1933-1942, A New Deal Case Study, Durham, NC: Duke University Press, 1967.

Seaver, Frederick J. Historical Sketches of Franklin County. Malone, NY: Franklin County Historical and Museum Society Collections 1918.

Schlesinger, Jr., Arthur M. The Age of Roosevelt, III, The Politics of Upheaval, Boston: Houghton Mifflin Co., 1960.

State of New York, Conservation Department. Annual Reports, 1933-42.

Van Valkenburgh, Norman J. Adirondack Forest Preserve, A Narrative of the Evolution of the Adirondack Forest Preserve of New York, Blue Mountain Lake: The Adirondack Museum, 1979.

Journals, Pamphlets, etc.
Baumann, Amelia S., Goldsmith, Mill Town Long Ago, Volume 7 Franklin County Historical NS Review, 1970, 47-49.

Eshelman, Teresa R., Town of Franklin 1836-1987, "They Told Me so... Goldsmith's Continued," August 1, 1987.

"The Conservation Corps, What It Is and What It Does" Civilian Conservation Corps Office of Director, Washington, D. C. June 1939.

Letters
Franklin D. Roosevelt, letter to James McEntee, March 25, 1942.

Other
Rawick, George P. The New Deal and Youth: The Civilian Conservation Corps, the National Youth Administration, the American Youth Congress, unpublished Ph.D. dissertation, University of Wisconsin, 1957.

Newspapers

Magazines
Adirondack Daily Enterprise
Au Sable Forks Record-Post
Boonville Herald
Chateaugay Record
Essex County Republican
Gouverneur Press
Herald Recorder
Leader Herald
Lowville Journal Republican
Malone Telegram
Massena Observer
New York Sun
Norwood News
Observer Dispatch
Ogdensburg Journal
Plattsburgh Daily Express
Plattsburgh Daily Press
Potsdam Courier Freeman
St. Lawrence Plaindealer
Syracuse Post Standard
Ticonderoga Sentinel
Tupper Lake Free Press
Watertown Daily Times

Neuzil, Mark. "Roosevelt's Tree Army, " The History Channel Magazine, November/December 2010.

Camp Newspapers
The Fore Ranker
The North Woodsman

Online Sources
Americorp Corporation for National & Community Service, http://www.americorps.gov/about/ac/index.asp

Civilian Conservation Corps Legacy, CCC Brief History, http://www.ccclegacy.org/CCC_brief_history.htm

Civilian Conservation Corps Legacy, CCC Facts, http://www.ccclegacy.org/ccc_facts.htm

Eleanor Roosevelt National Historic Site Hyde Park, NY, http://www.nps.gov/archive/elro/glossary/great-depression.htm

Eleanor Roosevelt National Historic Site Hyde Park, NY, Franklin D. Roosevelt (1882-1945), http://www.nps.gov/archive/elro/glossary/roosevelt-franklin.htm

Student Conservation Association, http://www.thesca.org/

ACKNOWLEDGMENTS

I would like to thank my wife, Lynn for her support and patience over the past five years of research and writing. My children, Matthew, Kristy, and Ryan for encouraging and accompanying me on trips and hikes; my parents, Martin M. and Joan, who instilled in me the importance of hard work and provided me with a college education that enabled me to achieve my goals my son-in-law Matthew Roloff who helped me with computer problems and Kira and Lydia Roloff for going on research trips with me.

To the following people I'd like to also give a special thanks:

My dedicated editor, David Hayden, who was always there to correct and guide me through the writing of newspaper articles and this book. I never would have completed this book without his insightful questions and suggestions.

My old publisher, Wray Rominger, gave me encouragement and support in self-publishing.

Retired District Ranger Paul Hartmann who drew all of the maps for this book. He also checked the chapters for their historical accuracy.

To David Van Patten for improving old photos.

Thanks to my son, Tony Sansevero in Austin, Texas, who did a magnificent cover for this book and my two Adirondack fire tower books.

A special thanks Amanda Beauchemin who spent many hours and weeks doing an excellent job in the layout of this book. And thanks to the rest of the staff of Ford Folios: Barry Ford and Carrie Hubbard.

Many weekly newspapers published my articles about the Adirondack CCC camps and resulted in locating many CCC alumni and their families. Thanks to these publishers and editors: Mark Frost, Glens Falls Chronicle; Joe Kelly, The Boonville Herald; Peter Crowley & Brittany Proulx , Saranac Lake Daily Enterprise; Tim Fonda, Gloversville/Johnstown Leader Herald, Meixner, Hamilton County Express; Adam Atkinson, Lowville The Journal Republican; Dan McClelland and Sue Mitchell, Tupper Lake Free Press, and John Gereau of Denton Publishing in Elizabethtown,.

Thanks to these two invaluable web sites: Northern New York Library Network, Northern New York Historical Newspapers (http://news.nnyln.net) and Old Fulton New York Post Cards (www.fultonhistory.com/Fulton.html). They provided easy access old Adirondack newspaper articles.

The following families and organizations took me into their homes or let me camp on their property: Carolyn and Gene Kaczka, Hannawa Falls; Frances and Dale Reandeau, Tupper Lake; Joe Gaetano, Dolgeville; Sandy Hildreth, Saranac Lake; Arnold, Rita & Valerie Muncy, Watson; Keith McKeever, Keene Valley; Paul and Alice Hartmann, Little Falls; Greg, Sallie, Billy & Sarah Way, Galway; Gretna and Stub Longware, Elizabethtown; Karen & Bob Peters, Wilmington; Gail Simmons, The Ranger School, Wanakena; Patty & Bill Nurney; David, Mike, Dave & Merri Rama, Delhi; Sylvia & Chris Morgan, Walton; Hope & Arthur Marston, Black River; Kay & Art Belles, Schroon Lake; Fran & Kathy Gramlich, Speculator; Kathy & Jonathan Dorr, Rome; Sam & Sue Glanzman, Maryland, NY; Cynthia Ford Johnston, Keene Valley; Paul Hai, Stacy McNulty, Bruce Breitmeyer, Kathy Poulton, & Ray Masters, College of Environmental Science and

Forestry, Newcomb; Bruce, Holly, Barb, and Dick Catlin, Timberlock Lodge, Indian Lake; John and Jackie Mallery, Long Lake; Beverly & Vernis Knickerbocker, Pottersville; Chuck Boylen, The Darrin Fresh Water Institute, Bolton Landing; Old Forge Library; Betty and John Osolin, Schroon Lake; Janet and Lynn Chapman, Tupper Lake; Nina & Gordon Taylor, Cranberry Lake; John Simons, Piseco; Dan & Laura Singer, Northville; Doug Wolf, Atmospheric Research Center, Wilmington; Elaine and Bob Archer, Edwards; Lake George Historical Society; Hague Historical Society; Jen Kretser, Thea & Matt Maloney ADK LOJ, Lake Placid; Bill Zullo, Indian Lake; Jerry Pepper, Adirondack Museum; John Huther, Woodgate; Dan & Marie Tefoe; Peter Hallock, Piseco; Karen Glass, Keene Valley; Wally Low, Boonville; James & Mary Ann Stevens, Hudson Falls; Bob & Brenda Foley, Minerva; Judy Jerome, Whitesboro Library; Clinton County Historical Association; Linda Stivala, Little Falls, and Jeri Wright, Wilmington.

To the many CCC alumni and families who shared their wonderful old pictures and stories.

I would like to thank Austin Shea and his mother Cathy who helped me with my research at the UCONN Library.

Thanks to Charles Vandrei, DEC Historic Preservation Officer, for making available the state documents and photos.

To District Rangers: Captain John Streif, Ray Brook; Dick Van Lear (Herkimer), and Pat Kilpeck (Schenectady), who made available CCC records and documents. Also to District Forester Tom Martin, and forester Sean Reynolds for proofreading chapters.

These present and retired forest rangers provided valuable information, pictures and stories: Bob Bailey, Richard van Laer, Dan Singer, Greg George, Randy Kerr, Morgan Roderick, Gary Lee, Don Perryman, Marty Hanna, Bruce Coon, Jim Lord, Gib Manley, John Gillen, Robert Weitz, Frank Dorchack, Grant "Dick" Thatcher, Joe Rupp, Bob Marone, and Clarence Petty.

I especially appreciate the many wonderful pictures from Bill Petty's collection generously provided by his daughter Joanne Petty Manning.

I am grateful for the research material and photographs gathered for me by these local historians: MaryEllen Salls, Brighton; Bill Frenette, Tupper Lake; and Wayne Allen, Bill Gleason, and Allen Ditch, Wanakena.

Thanks to the following libraries and librarians: Patti Prindle and Dick Tucker, The Adirondack Research Library of. Protect the Adirondacks, Niskayuna; Jerry Pepper, Adirondack Museum Library; Bruce Cole, Crandall Public Library; Emily Farr, Long Lake Library; Dr. Jim Folts, New York State Archives; Megan Baker, Bolton Library; David Minnich, Malone Wead Library; Michael Burnett, Northville Public Library; Michelle Tucker, Saranac Lake Library; Kathy Dorr, Westernville Library; Neil Suprenant and Susan Mitchell, Joan Weill Adirondack Library, Paul Smith's College; Jackie Viestenz, Sherman Free Library, Port Henry; Elaine Archer, Hepburn Library, Edwards; Dennis Eickhoff, Hepburn Library, Colton; Carol Lewis & Angela Strong, Schenectady County Museum Library; Joy Eliezer, Lake Pleasant Library; Patty Perez, Lake Placid Library; Andrea Arquette, Cranbury Lake Library; Isabelle Worthen and Karen Lee, Old Forge Library; Jane Bouchard, Schroon Lake; Donna Ripp, Erwin Library, Boonville; Carol

McDowell, Wells Memorial Library; Upper Jay; Karen Glass, Keene Valley Library; Rebecca Fasulo & Michael Hadfield, Corinth Library; Susan Doolittle and Margaret Gibbs, Essex County Historical Society Library, Elizabethtown; John Isley, Woodgate Library; Joan Kampnich , Croghan; Regina Doi, Galway Library; Barry Hampton, Mayfield Library; Pat Musante, Potsdam Library; Nancy Carry, New York Mills Library; Cindy McVoy, Holland Patent Library; Paul Schaffer, Massena Library; Marie Gando, Hudson Falls Library; Susan Schmidt, Johnsburg Library; Linda Auclair, Goff-Nelson Memorial Library, Tupper Lake; Steve Batt, UCONN Library; Sally Cranston, Walton Ogden Library; Judy Gray, Sidney Library; Cathy Johnson, Cannon Library, Delhi; Alma Alvarez, Chestertown Library, and Lyn Swafford, Canton.

To these historians and historical societies, thank you for opening your files and pictures to me: Ted Caldwell, Town of Bolton; John Hastings, Richard Cipperly, & Steve Parisi, Warrensburgh Historical Society; Peg Masters, Town of Webb; Jim Kammer, Raquette Lake; Carl B. Goodrich, Brasher Falls; Jim Bailey, Plattsburgh; Gail Murray, Town of Webb; Anne Werley Smallman, Franklin County Historical Museum, Malone; Bill Zullo Hamilton County Historian; Brian Howard, Oneida Historical Society, Utica; Colleen Murtaugh, Horicon Historical Society; Mimi VanDeusen, Potsdam Public Museum; Sue Rawson, Shirley McNally, Bob Saverie, Martha Galusha, & Bob Foley, Minerva Historical Society; Joe Provoncha, North Hudson; Margaret Gibbs, Essex County Historical Society; Karen Peters and Merry Peck, Wilmington Historical Society; Jeanne F. Plumley , Long Lake; Betty Osolin, Schroon Lake and North Hudson Historical Society; George Cataldo, Glenfield; Jack & Mary Sweeney, Croghan; Jim Pitcher, Boonville; Barbara Daniels, Pierrepont, and Ross Young, Diana.

INDEX

Index compiled by Mary
Pelletier-Hunyadi